Hispanic Surnames

and

FAMILY HISTORY

Lyman D. Platt

Published by Genealogical Publishing Co., Inc.
1001 N. Calvert St., Baltimore, MD 21202
Library of Congress Catalogue Card Number 95-81292
International Standard Book Number 0-8063-1480-X
Made in the United States of America

CONTENTS

INTRODUCTION

T his is the first comprehensive analytical work on Hispanic surnames and the most extensive bibliography of family histories ever compiled. In saying this, there are some limitations that must be recognized. This is not a study of surnames or family history in Spain per se. Rather, it is a review of the development of Spanish surnames in Latin America and the Hispanic United States — where there are obvious links between the Latin American and Spanish families — with references to the availability of surname studies in Spain found in the appendices and, in a few cases, in the bibliography.

Several terms need to be defined at the beginning of this reference work. The word *Spanish* must be understood in context where it does not refer to individuals but to the language itself, or to the culture in general. There has been a deliberate attempt to avoid referring to individuals in Latin America as *Spanish* and to use the word *Hispanic* instead. Therefore, the word *Spanish* refers to individuals born in Spain, or whose parents were born in Spain. The word *Hispanic* refers to individuals born in Latin America or the United States, whose parents spoke Spanish and whose principal cultural background was Spanish. The phrase *Latin America* refers to those countries south of the U.S. border, including Puerto Rico and Cuba in the Caribbean, where Spanish is the dominant language. This excludes Brazil in South America and all islands of the Caribbean except Puerto Rico and Cuba. The phrase *Hispanic United States* refers historically to California, Arizona, Utah, Colorado, New Mexico, Texas, Louisiana, Alabama, and Florida. However, in its modern context it must also include New York, New Jersey, Illinois, and to a limited extent, every other state of the United States of America. The word *Latino* tends to be a more modern word, used at times to include Brazilians and Italians; therefore, it is rarely used in this work.

This book contains the introductory material to a multi-volume work entitled *The Hispanic Book of Generations*. It stands alone, however, in its content and completeness with regard to the subject material discussed. A review of the historical development of Hispanic surnames in Latin America and the Hispanic United States is the principal goal of this volume. This is accomplished in two ways. The principal Hispanic surnames that exist throughout the Americas are studied as to their dispersion and commonality, with two principal studies showing the popularity of the top 1,000 surnames in the U.S. and in Latin America. In addition, an extensive review of library and archival card catalogs, genealogical magazines, and other literature over a period of twenty-five years has brought together all known references to family histories and historical sketches of Hispanic families. These have been indexed by principal surnames, then referenced by author and country of origin. Thus, in these two ways, any researcher can determine the commonality and accessibility of information pertaining to any given surname.

The Institute of Genealogy and History for Latin America (IGHL), 316 West 500 North, St. George, Utah 84770, is the organization responsible for the materials contained herein. The Institute, in its twenty-five years of existence, has dedicated its resources to identifying all information available on Hispanic families. It has compiled a series of research guides to assist the novice and the expert in locating these materials, and in understanding how they can be used in furthering genealogical and family history research. Now, for the first time, through a cooperative effort with Genealogical Publishing Co., these materials will be more widely distributed and used within the genealogical and library community. Other volumes in this series will include the family historical sketches of more than 1,500 Hispanic surnames, showing their origins in Spain, their arrival and dispersion in Latin America, and their history in the United States. These volumes, which will be entitled *Hispanic American Family Histories,* are being compiled from 103 sources, containing over 600 volumes. Subsequent volumes will comprise a *Hispanic American Genealogical Gazetteer*, which will contain an alphabetical review of the best out-of-print genealogical references to individuals in the Americas; they will give the full genealogical and biographical data contained in these earlier references and note not only the original published sources but also the original records from which the references were taken, thereby providing valuable research information for compiling pedigrees and family group records on one's ancestry. When finished, this series will become an encyclopedic reference for Hispanic genealogical research. All materials needed to compile the series are already in the hands of IGHL, and many of the volumes are currently being written.

Hispanic Surnames
and Family History

HISPANIC SURNAMES

Demographics: Twentieth-Century Development of Hispanic Surnames

T he history of surnames is one of constant change. Over the centuries many surnames have developed and then disappeared. Today, there are approximately 60,000 Hispanic surnames in use throughout Latin America, down from a total of about 250,000 in 1750. In Latin America there were approximately 250,000,000 people in 1990: Argentina had 32,000,000; Bolivia, 7,000,000; Chile, 13,000,000; Colombia, 30,000,000; Costa Rica, 2,800,000; Cuba, 10,500,000; Dominican Republic, 6,000,000; Ecuador, 9,000,000; El Salvador, 5,200,000; Guatemala, 6,500,000; Honduras, 4,000,000; México, 75,000,000; Nicaragua, 3,000,000; Panamá, 2,000,000; Paraguay, 4,000,000; Perú, 18,000,000; Puerto Rico, 4,000,000; Uruguay, 3,200,000; and Venezuela, 14,500,000. In the same year in the United States there were 22,354,059 people with Hispanic surnames, making the U.S. the fourth largest Hispanic country in the Americas, behind Mexico, Argentina, and Colombia.

The Hispanic surname database used to create statistics for the 1980 census was compiled by a group of experts called to Washington, D.C. in 1979. The resulting report, "1980 Census List of Spanish Surnames," showed a total of 12,567 surnames, all of which are listed later in this book. The Bureau of the Census decided not to create a similar study in 1990. The only study done for the 1990 census on Spanish surnames has yet to be published, being in its 12th draft at the time of this publication. It is called "The Population Estimates Working Papers" and is based on a 3% sample of the 1990 population. The study shows that 640 names occurred more than twenty times in the 3% sample, while 4,000 occurred at least once; there were 8,614 surnames considered "highly Spanish." Only the list of 640 surnames will be released at some future date. After comparing this list of 640 surnames with the studies already available and finding no significant differences, except for Abeyta (ranked 476th), it has been decided to forego the use of this 1990 list. The premises used to create it do not fit the genealogical standards used to create the other lists, anyway; it is strictly a statistical analysis and makes assumptions that are not necessarily true in the

11

genealogical world. There are statements such as, "Of the top 715 surnames 93% are more than 75% Spanish." Surnames such as Machado and Franco, for example, are considered to be borderline Spanish. This is a statistical decision. In fact, these surnames have been in the Spanish community for hundreds of years. In summary, these unpublished working papers show that 715 surnames cover 70% of the Hispanic population, 1,300 surnames deal with 91%, and 2,100 handle 94%.

By contrast, the studies done by The Institute of Genealogy and History for Latin America in 1987 and 1991 show that eleven surnames accounted for 25% of the population throughout the Americas. As few as sixty-four surnames were needed to cover 50% of the population, and 238 to cover 75%. Five hundred and six surnames represented a total of 90% and 1,000 a total of 95% of the living persons using Hispanic surnames. It is estimated that at the beginning of 1987 the countries of Latin America were represented with the following numbers of individuals in the United States: Argentina 54,810; Bolivia 50,250; Chile 70,350; Colombia 333,650; Costa Rica 69,300; Cuba 1,000,000 (1,043,932 in 1990); Dominican Republic 800,000; Ecuador 100,000; El Salvador 108,900; Guatemala 99,000; Honduras 79,200; México 10,140,000 (13,495,938 in 1990); Nicaragua 64,350; Panamá 74,250; Paraguay 10,050; Perú 100,500; Puerto Rico 2,300,000 (2,727,754 in 1990); Uruguay 40,200; Venezuela 60,300; other Hispanics, such as second, third, or fourth generation Hispanics born in the United States, 3,361,000 — for a total of 18,916,110. In 1990 the Hispanic origins other than Mexico, Puerto Rico, and Cuba were tabulated at 5,086,435.

With the continually changing ethnic makeup of the United States since 1987, it is important to understand some of what has been taking place. An article in *U.S. News & World Report,* dated January 30, 1989, noted that in the late 1980s certain nationalities came into the United States in greater numbers than others. In some cases these numbers were dramatic. For example, in 1987 there were 2,800,000 people in Nicaragua. In that year alone, 200,000 of them were granted asylum in this country, this number representing about 7% of the entire population of that country. During 1989 about 1,000 Nicaraguans per week were crossing the Texas border, as well as entering southern Florida. Officials at that time were predicting that 100,000 refugees from Nicaragua would arrive in the United States during 1989. These numbers, which were, in fact, realized, almost equaled those of the Mariel boat people, 125,000 of whom came to the United States from Cuba in 1980.

In 1990, with the cessation of most hostilities in Nicaragua, this steady influx from Central America diminished, but in the meantime close to 1,000,000 Nicaraguans became residents of the United States, equaling, if not surpassing, Cubans as the third most populous group in this country. This is not reflected in the 1990 census statistics noted above, but Nicaragua was not separated in the study, so the exact situation remains unknown. Some of these refugees have returned to their homeland, but most have stayed in the United States. Additionally, despite the official U.S. quota restrictions, many refugees from El Salvador and high numbers of immigrants from Colombia and Ecuador continued to change the Hispanic face of the United States, where for centuries Mexican nationals had been, and still are, the largest group, albeit their percentage of the total Hispanic population is diminishing. As can be seen from these statistics, Mexican, Puerto Rican, Nicaraguan, Cuban, and Dominican nationals constitute the majority, or about 70%, of the entire Hispanic population, each representing a major percentage of that country's population now in the United States.

In *USA Today*, July 5, 1995, the first comprehensive poll of immigrants ever conducted sheds more information and gives updated statistics on this continuing migration from Latin America to the United States. About three million formerly illegal immigrants were legalized after the 1986 law gave them amnesty. In 1992 alone there were 240,252 people naturalized nationwide. In 1995 the backlog of naturalization requests is nearly that number in Los Angeles alone. The increases are unprecedented and backlogs are growing nationwide. There were 880,014 immigrants who gained legal admission to the United States in 1993. The Immigration and Naturalization Service reports that applications for residency have nearly doubled since 1994. Between October 1994 and January 1995 applications rose to 232,850, about 80% above those from the same period the previous year. Because immediate relatives of those who have become citizens are eligible to naturalize more quickly, the surge is likely to increase even more. The INS projects about 760,000 applications in 1995 and 920,000 for fiscal year 1996. Illegal immigration, mostly from Latin America, is placed at about 300,000 people per year in 1995. Only Cuba and Haiti are currently on the list of Latin American countries from which refugees are allowed admission to the United States. Many immigrants and refugees believe that the U.S. is a racist country; that their homelands are better places to raise children; and that at home they were safer from crime in societies that espouse better moral values. However, 67%

of them say that they would stay in the United States even if it were possible for them to do as well financially at home. Immigrants want the opportunities and freedoms our society presents.

All of this is a preface to earlier studies of Hispanic surnames in the United States and Latin America. Going back to the earliest-known statistics available in this country somewhat pertinent to our subject, there were 5,000 foreign-born individuals considered "Spanish" in the United States in 1880. By 1910 this number had increased to 22,000. These numbers do not reflect the "Mexican" and other "Latino" populations, but appear to refer particularly to Spain.

For specific Latin American populations some limited statistics have been identified. In 1930, for example, there were 53,000 Puerto Ricans living in the United States. By 1950 there were 250,000 Puerto Ricans in New York City alone. Other large centers also existed in South Boston, South and North Chicago, Northwest Cleveland, Newark, Camden, Bridgeport, Philadelphia, and Miami. In that same year, 1950, the national census only coded 700 Spanish surnames in the United States.

One study of Hispanic population centers in the United States from 1950 shows the following counties with over 20,000 white inhabitants of Spanish (Mexican) origin.[1] This study has obviously omitted the Puerto Rican and Cuban populations. Mr. Dobyns was not interested in those populations in any of his writings, dealing strictly with the American Southwest. His definition of "Spanish" appears to mean Mexican only. Of course, in his defense, as noted above, the Puerto Rican influence was minimal until after 1930 and really not significant until about the time of his study, and the Cuban mass migrations did not begin until 1980, which follows his study by thirty years.

COUNTY	STATE	POPULATION
Los Angeles	California	287,614
Béxar	Texas	176,877
Hidalgo	Texas	112,422
El Paso	Texas	089,555
Cameron	Texas	081,080
Nueces	Texas	058,939
Webb	Texas	047,425

---

[1] Henry F. Dobyns, *Spanish Colonial Tucson: A Demographic History* (Tucson, Ariz.: The University of Arizona Press, 1976), p. 152.

COUNTY	STATE	POPULATION
Bernalillo	New Mexico	043,723
Maricopa	Arizona	042,560
Harris	Texas	039,171
Alameda	California	035,578
San Bernardino	California	035,330
Santa Clara	California	035,306
Fresno	California	032,678
Marin (San Francisco)	California	031,433
San Diego	California	028,926
Pima	Arizona	027,224
Arapahoe (Denver)	Colorado	024,950
Orange	California	023,680
Santa Fé	New Mexico	023,034
Ventura	California	021,697
Doña Ana	New Mexico	020,883
San Miguel	New Mexico	020,524
Río Arriba	New Mexico	020,056

From 1951 to 1973 immigrants to the United States from all nationalities totaled about 7½ million. Of these, 300,000 came from South America, 400,000 came from Cuba, over a million came from Mexico (and perhaps as many as 3,000,000 came illegally). From 1976 to 1986 there were 258,000 immigrants from Cuba and 211,000 from the Dominican Republic.

Between 1820 and 1975 there were 1,900,000 Mexican immigrants to the U.S. Immigrants from Mexico totaled 31,200 from 1900 to 1909; 185,300 from 1910 to 1919; 498,900 from 1920 to 1929; 32,700 from 1930 to 1939; 56,200 from 1940 to 1949; 273,800 from 1950 to 1959; 441,800 from 1960 to 1969; and 364,100 from 1970 to 1975. Between 1976 and 1986 there were 720,000 legal Mexican immigrants to the U.S. In 1978 it was estimated that 7,200,000 people of Mexican descent were living in the United States.

"In 1964, the United States Department of Health, Education, and Welfare, Social Security Administration made a report of the 'Distribution of Surnames in the Social Security Account Number File.' The file contained 152,757,455 account numbers."[2] This 1964 information

[2] Elsdon C. Smith, *American Surnames* (Baltimore: Genealogical Publishing Company, 1994), p. 299. Originally published by Chilton Book Company, 1969.

was further analyzed by the SSA and the 2,000 most common surnames in the United States and approximate numbers of individuals for each were recorded. Those of Hispanic origin are as follows:

U.S. RANK	HISPANIC RANK	SURNAME	ESTIMATED # OF PERSONS
44	1	Rodríguez	292,600
58	2	García	242,000
85	3	González	189,600
93	4	López	178,500
94	5	Rivera	176,500
108	6	Martínez	164,600
112	7	Hernández	159,100
124	8	Pérez	148,350
176	9	Sánchez	121,100
183	10	Torres	120,100
241	11	Ortiz	093,700
255	12	Ramírez	087,800
303	13	Flores	076,500
318	14	Ramos	074,410
328	15	Morales	072,300
335	16	Díaz	071,570
353	17	Cruz	068,590
367	18	Gómez	065,240
377	19	Santiago	064,190
394	20	Gonzáles	063,200
418	21	Fernández	060,275
434	22	Reyes	057,130
491	23	Camero	051,670
492	24	Silva	051,590
515	25	Colón	049,760
536	26	Gutiérrez	048,030
542	27	Ruiz	047,665
564	28	Romero	045,940
574	29	Garza	045,480
585	30	Alvarez	044,980
605	31	Chávez	044,110
614	32	Medina	043,200
633	33	Castro	042,120

U.S. RANK	HISPANIC RANK	SURNAME	ESTIMATED # OF PERSONS
648	34	Vázquez	041,260
664	35	Figueroa	040,110
700	36	Moreno	038,015
704	37	Castillo	037,800
719	38	Maldonado	036,990
727	39	Santos	036,535
744	40	Román	035,700
749	41	Jimínez	035,400
755	42	Vásquez	034,880
767	43	Delgado	034,555
775	44	Soto	034,300
823	45	Herrera	032,375
832	46	Vargas	032,110
864	47	Méndez	031,275
893	48	Mendoza	030,485
900	49	Ríos	030,340
902	50	Vega	030,305
904	51	Padilla	030,260
908	52	Vélez	030,185
915	53	Marino	030,036
933	54	Valdez	029,450
988	55	Múñoz	027,890
993	56	Salazar	027,775
996	57	Molina	027,685
1004	58	Espinosa	027,550
1009	59	Guzmán	027,190
1025	60	Costa	026,700
1032	61	Domingo	026,625
1053	62	Meléndez	025,960
1067	63	Peña	025,605
1115	64	Miranda	024,385
1131	65	Ortega	024,160
1165	66	Mercado	023,635
1167	67	Navarro	023,590
1184	68	Rosario	023,390
1185	69	Nieves	023,340
1186	70	Aguilar	023,335
1190	71	Acosta	023,305

U.S. RANK	HISPANIC RANK	SURNAME	ESTIMATED # OF PERSONS
1233	72	Pacheco	022,770
1239	73	Guerrera	022,700
1249	74	Trujillo	022,575
1253	75	Alvarado	022,470
1279	76	Sandoval	022,080
1281	77	Gabriel	022,065
1291	78	Villarreal	021,855
1304	79	Espósito	021,695
1308	80	Durán	021,675
1315	81	Quiñones	021,530
1329	82	Ayala	021,305
1338	83	Serrano	021,125
1356	84	Estrada	020,845
1362	85	Gallegos	020,665
1397	86	de Jesús	020,290
1401	87	Luna	020,220
1404	88	Rosado	020,180
1412	89	Montoya	020,105
1437	90	Robles	019,705
1455	91	Márquez	019,405
1457	92	Guerra	019,395
1467	93	Núñez	019,260
1503	94	Rosa	018,757
1505	95	Contreas	018,755
1519	96	Treviño	018,567
1558	97	Corcorán	018,200
1562	98	Manuel	018,115
1563	99	Acevedo	018,110
1596	100	Cortez	017,780
1620	101	Dorán	017,577
1656	102	Súarez	017,180
1674	103	Salinas	016,946
1690	104	Velázquez	016,776
1692	105	Souza	016,762
1732	106	Cárdenas	016,320
1744	107	Arroyo	016,202
1749	108	Camacho	016,178
1776	109	Feliciano	015,946

U.S. RANK	HISPANIC RANK	SURNAME	ESTIMATED # OF PERSONS
1780	110	Salmón	015,918
1795	111	Lucero	015,772
1804	112	Carrillo	015,707
1835	113	Dávila	015,425
1841	114	Barón	015,405
1911	115	Negrón	014,857
1914	116	Rodríquez	014,838
1942	117	Beauchamp	014,642
1952	118	Cantú	014,566
1959	119	Avila	014,513
1972	120	Campos	014,445
1975	121	Fuentes	014,416

The surname Martin was left out of this list as recorded here, it being number thirteen with 603,400, because it is the number one surname in France, has English derivations, and has not been distinguished from Martín. Other surnames have been included which are not strictly Spanish in origin, but which have significant Spanish populations in Latin America. These include Barón, Beauchamp, Camero, Castro, Corcorán, Costa, Durán, Feliciano, Gabriel, Gonzáles, Manuel, Marino, Rodríquez, Román, Rosa, Rosario, Salmón, Santiago, Santos, and Souza. Most of these are also Italian or Portuguese and have not been distinguished in the Social Security study from their Spanish cousins. Given this limitation, the list is the most comprehensive list compiled up to 1964 in the United States on Hispanic surnames. The entire list of 121 surnames represents 5,228,976 individuals out of a total population of 152,757,455 account numbers, or .0342% of the population. Mr. Smith, in his book *American Surnames,* estimated that this was from a population of 1,500,000 surnames, but as will be shown below, in 1974 there were only 1,286,556 surnames listed by the Social Security Administration; therefore, his estimate is undoubtedly too high for 1964. Of the 121 surnames and the 5,228,976 individuals listed in those surnames, the top five surnames represent 20.638% of the total; ten surnames represent 34.277%; eleven surnames represent 36.069%; and sixteen surnames equal 43.386%.

In 1974 the Social Security Administration listed a total of 1,286,556 surnames from all races, of which 448,663 appeared only once on their rolls. In that same year other Spanish surnames besides Rodríguez began to appear in the top fifty surnames in the country: Rodríguez (31st place — it alone was ranked in the top fifty in 1964), González (42nd place), and García (44th place). García began losing ground shortly thereafter as the total Hispanic population became less Spanish and more Latino.

The following chart[3] shows the top eleven Hispanic surnames in the United States in 1964 and 1974 and their ranking in the overall population. Unfortunately, Mr. Hook left Martínez out of his 1964 data. The population number and rank for Martínez are, therefore, estimates.

SURNAME	NUMBER IN 64	NUMBER IN 74	RANK 64	RANK 74
Rodríguez	292,600	416,178	44	31
García	242,000	346,175	58	44
González	189,600	360,994	85	42
López	178,000	254,535	93	65
Rivera	176,500	238,457	94	73
Martínez	164,600	c. 237,000	108	74
Hernández	159,100	235,498	112	75
Pérez	148,350	217,801	124	86
Sánchez	121,100	175,104	176	114
Torres	120,100	170,507	183	120
Ortiz	93,700	130,631	241	184

Throughout the hemisphere there are new Hispanic surnames being continually created, and there continue to be those that die out. As an example of how surnames develop, in 1992 the following variations existed on the Social Security Administration rolls for the surnames Rodríguez and González:

Rodrig, Rodrigs, Rodríguez, Rodríquez, Rodríquiz, Rodrígues, Rodríques, Rodríges, Rodrígres, Rodrígquez, Rodrgquez, Rodrgíuez,

---

[3] Julius Nicholas Hook, *Family Names: How Our Surnames Came to America, the Origins, Meanings, Mutations, and History of More Than 2,800 American Names* (New York: Macmillan Publishing Co., 1982), p. 165. Mr. Hook used Elsdon C. Smith's *American Surnames* 1964 study for the 1964 information, but overlooked Martínez, ranked 108 in his comparison. He does not state where he got the 1974 data, but that has been noted above.

Rodríauez, Rodrígnez, Rodríqueq, Rodgrígues, Rodrguez, Rodrúguez, Rodríquenz, Rodúguez, Rodríquzes, Rodrígoez.

Gonzal, Gonzálas, Gonsáles, Gonsález, Gonzáles, González, Gonzáliz, Gonzlaes, Gonzélos, Gonzóles, Gonález, Gongáles, Gongález, Goncáles, Gonzeález, Gonzhlez, Gonzálzles, Gonzállez.

Besides the information noted previously, there was no body of information that was easily accessible at the beginning of this study from which to draw data. One of the first sub-projects that had to be completed was to identify the Hispanic family histories that existed in Latin America and the United States. Some 1,883 titles, consisting of nearly 3,000 volumes, were found and are included at the end of this book. This compilation is the only one of its kind to date on Hispanic families. It is not complete by any means but is fairly comprehensive and representative of the period prior to 1986. Since that period there has been a proliferation of publications, which have not been cataloged. Also, there are more and more family histories being published by means of computers, with limited circulation and copies, which are impossible for the bibliographer to catalog.

Secondly, a number of sources were consulted, including: 1) telephone directories of the eleven largest Hispanic centers in the country: New York City, Jersey City, Miami, Chicago, Dallas, Houston, San Antonio, Denver, San Diego, Los Angeles, and San Francisco; 2) population returns and statistics for the 1970, 1980, and 1990 censuses, compiled by the United States Department of Commerce, Bureau of the Census, and 3) projections of the Bureau of the Census for 1972, 1976, 1985, and 1987. Neither the 1987 nor the 1990 projections identified the component parts of Central America, South America, or the Dominican Republic; therefore, those figures were interpolated from earlier data.

In 1987 staff from The Institute of Genealogy and History for Latin America (IGHL) hand-counted 2.3% of the living U.S. Hispanic population to determine surname prevalence. In 1992 IGHL updated the earlier study, the counting being done by computer and expanded to include both the deceased and living Hispanic populations. The deceased population was studied using the massive files of the Social Security Administration and their Social Security Death Benefit Index, with June 1992 being the cutoff date. The living population was studied using the compact discs produced by PhoneDisc USA and ProPhone, which have identified over 50,000,000 individuals in the United States, 1991 and 1992 being the editions used to compile statistics on Hispanic families. These databases have identified over twice the number of Hispanic individuals as the 1987 study did. The Death Benefit Index represents nearly the entire deceased population that received benefits. In the case of the telephone studies, at least 6% of the population has been identified directly by surname. It should be remembered, however, that only one surname per household is being studied in most families from the telephone databases. The actual population represented may be as high 20 – 25%, as the head-of-household surname may be the same surname as that of other members of the family. Duplicate entries exist in the PhoneDisc USA directory, which is good in some cases when these represent more than one individual per household.

The following statistics from the study show the continually changing nature of surname development.

SURNAME	PHONE-DISC	RANK	PRO-PHONE	RANK	S.S.	RANK	1987 STUDY	RANK
Rodríguez	92,174	3	35,535	4	26,153	2	737,461	1
González	94,727	2	43,550	2	26,590	1	666,722	2
García	98,463	1	48,688	1	19,295	4	660,481	3
Martínez	89,659	4	38,373	3	24,586	3	592,201	4
Hernández	69,614	6	32,446	5	15,215	6	493,658	5
López	72,513	5	29,521	6	16,877	5	420,839	6
Pérez	57,217	7	22,153	7	12,963	7	411,760	7
Sánchez	50,856	8	20,589	8	12,008	8	305,085	8
Ramírez	39,811	10	16,951	10	8,864	10	241,533	9
Díaz	33,647	14	14,328	13	7,736	14	232,454	10
Fernández	25,356	17	11,468	17	7,314	15	225,834	11
Torres	39,926	9	14,434	12	8,068	12	210,514	12
Gómez	35,333	13	16,604	11	11,375	9	199,355	13
Rivera	36,514	11	11,320	18	8,258	11	175,523	14
Alvarez	20,159	24	9,215	26	4,402	16	159,635	15
Flores	35,898	12	17,628	9	8,045	13	153,015	16

The Social Security studies shown earlier and here indicate some very interesting demographic data. Historically — that is, for the older Hispanic population — the most prevalent surnames in 1964 were Rodríguez, García, González, López, Rivera, Martínez, Hernández, Pérez, Sánchez, Torres, and Ortiz. In 1974 González and García changed positions, with all others in the top ten remaining the same. In 1992 González gained first place, followed by Rodríguez, Martínez, García, López, Hernández, Pérez, Sánchez, Gómez, Ramírez, and Rivera. This is not significantly different from either the 1987 IGHL study or the modern ProPhone study. However, the statistics show a dynamically changing population over time.

One important note with regard to the statistics is that the heavy Portuguese population in Connecticut, Massachusetts, Rhode Island, New York, New Jersey, and Hawaii has been picked up in the "es" endings of these top names, because of their eventual common origins.

State by state, and in a few regions, there are some interesting points to note. In Alabama the most common Hispanic surname historically was González; in Alaska, García; in Arizona, García; in Arkansas, González; in California, García; in Colorado, Martínez; in Connecticut, Rodríguez because of the Portuguese influence, followed by Lópes and Gómes also of Portuguese extraction; in Delaware, Rodríguez; in Washington, D.C., Rodríguez; in Florida, Rodríguez; in Georgia, González; in Hawaii, Rodríguez because of the Portuguese influence, followed by López, then Torres; in Idaho, González; in Illinois, García; in Indiana, González; in Iowa, García; in Kansas, García; in Kentucky, Martínez; in Louisiana, Rodríguez; in Maine, García and López tied; in Maryland, Rodríguez and Martínez tied; in Massachusetts, Rodríguez because of the Portuguese influence, followed by Lópes and Gómes also of Portuguese extraction; in Michigan, González; in Minnesota, García; in Mississippi, García; in Missouri, García; in Montana, Martínez; in Nebraska, Hernández; in Nevada, Rodríguez; in New Hampshire, Rodríguez; in New Jersey, Rodríguez because of the Portuguese influence, followed by González; in New Mexico, Martínez; in New York, Rodríguez; in North Carolina, Martínez; in North Dakota, García; in Ohio, González; in Oklahoma, Martínez; in Oregon, Martínez; in Pennsylvania, Rodríguez; in Rhode Island, López; in South Carolina, López; in South Dakota, Martínez; in Tennessee, García; in Texas, García; in Utah, Martínez; in Vermont, where virtually no Hispanics have resided historically, the numbers are irrelevant but Rodríguez, Martínez, and López tied; in Virginia, García; in Washington, García; in West Virginia, García; in Wisconsin, González; and in Wyoming, Martínez.

This study shows an increase in the Martínez surname and a definite dispersion pattern of the Martínez family out of New Mexico into Utah, Colorado, Wyoming, Montana, and possibly Oklahoma. This study also shows one surname declining dramatically. Rivera is ranked 5th in 1964 and 1974, but drops to 11th, then 14th, and finally 18th in the other studies. Rodríguez and Fernández have lost ground over time while García has picked up ground. The PhoneDisc USA and the ProPhone statistics show that the ranking of the surname Alvarez in the 1987 IGHL study is probably too high. Even the historical data from the Social Security Administration, based on the numbers, appear to correlate closer to the compact disc studies as pertains to Alvarez than to the 1987 IGHL study. In this book the 1987 IGHL study's findings have been kept intact for purposes of comparison. Overall, there are no definite trends showing major differences, except the probable rising of the surname García to first place by the year 2,000 to coincide with the ranking in Spain, the dramatic slide of the surname Rivera, and the popularity of Martínez. The most impressive statistic shown between the Social Security study and the 1987 IGHL study is the population increase within the Hispanic United States. The demographic movement out of Latin America is truly significant.

In the 1987 IGHL hand-counted analysis 451,189 individuals out of the projected 18,914,110 were identified. From this, it was determined that the percentages in the United States were slightly different for the top surnames than those in the Latin American and Spanish studies noted below. For example, based on those studies, 3.6% of the population (16,243) should have been surnamed Rodríguez. It was found that there were actually 3.9% (17,593) in the sample. This would project out over the entire U.S. population to a total of 737,461 persons with that surname. Comparing the top sixteen surnames in the IGHL study, the first eight were slightly higher and the last eight slightly lower than in the Latin American and Spanish studies. The Maduell study of Spain lists García as the most popular surname and Rodríguez as the seventh most popular.[4] The Gorden study showing the popularity of surnames in Latin America ranks Rodríguez, González, Fernández, Martínez, López, Pérez, Sánchez, Gómez, Díaz, and Alvarez as the top ten surnames.[5] The top sixteen Hispanic surnames identified in IGHL's U.S. study were as follows. The information included here is the same as given previously, with the addition of the "Percentage" column, which is the basis for estimating the "Total Population" column.

---

[4] Charles R. Maduell, Jr., *The Romance of Spanish Surnames* (New Orleans, Louisiana: priv. pub., 1967), p. x.

[5] Raymond L. Gorden, *Spanish Personal Names as Barriers to Communication between Latin Americans and North Americans* (Yellow Springs, Oh.: Antioch College, 1968), p. 15.

SURNAME	PRIORITY	TOTAL POPULATION	PERCENTAGE
RODRÍGUEZ	1	737,461	3.899
GONZÁLEZ	2	666,722	3.525
GARCÍA	3	660,481	3.492
MARTÍNEZ	4	592,201	3.131
HERNÁNDEZ	5	493,658	2.610
LÓPEZ	6	420,839	2.225
PÉREZ	7	411,760	2.177
SÁNCHEZ	8	305,085	1.613
RAMÍREZ	9	241,533	1.277
DÍAZ	10	232,454	1.229
FERNÁNDEZ	11	225,834	1.194
TORRES	12	210,514	1.113
GÓMEZ	13	199,355	1.054
RIVERA	14	175,523	.928
ALVAREZ	15	163,015	.844
FLORES	16	159,635	.809

In conclusion, then, Hispanics are coming to the United States in record numbers. They are coming for economic and political reasons. They are making the United States one of the largest Hispanic countries in the world; it is likely to pass both Colombia and Argentina in total Hispanic population by the end of the century or shortly thereafter, becoming the second largest Hispanic country (behind Mexico only, which it is unlikely to ever surpass). Long-standing Hispanic population centers are becoming even larger, while places like Atlanta are becoming the newest hubs for immigrants, particularly Mexicans. Most immigrants, according to the *USA Today* article cited previously, say they are not isolated from ordinary Americans. They are assimilating much faster than they did several generations ago. With this assimilation, many of their surnames will be lost, while others will continue their dramatic increases. Some new surnames will be added to the pool, in part because of the Americanization of surnames, in part because of the variations as noted in the Social Security lists, and in part because there are surnames in Latin America that have never been in the United States and will become established and flourish over time as has been shown in a few cases above.

THE HISTORY OF SURNAMES

Surnames were unnecessary when the population of the earth was small. Individuals were recognized as "Seth son of Adam," "David ben Jesse," "Jesus of Nazareth," and so forth. Each was recognized sufficiently in his time and throughout history without a surname. For our purposes here, we will discuss the history of surname development on the Iberian Peninsula (Spain and Portugal) and the spread of the growing list of identifications from there to the Americas.

Prior to the advent of the Roman Empire, the Iberian Peninsula followed the general custom decribed above, each person being identified by a name and possibly a relationship to another person or a place. As the Roman naming customs began to pervade the peninsula the old naming traditions gave way. "In the beginning only one [surname] was used, later two, three and four, as was the custom with the Romans, who frequently took their surnames from family deeds, other times from lands which they had conquered, etc. Their custom entered the peninsula with the Roman Empire and that usage was adopted until the entrance of the Goths, who conquering and driving out the Romans, also prohibited the system of acquiring apellidos [surnames], so that again only the singular proper names were known, without any surnames. This lasted until the invasion of the Arabs, after which was introduced the usage of patronymics, . . . which surnames or patronymics, passing the fourth generation, finished by being *apellidos* [surnames]. To the more common patronymic surnames was added the names of cities, towns, places, and estates in which men lived, or of which they were native."[6]

In fact, the meaning of a surname was the meaning ascribed to it at the time it was adopted. Sometimes, when alternate derivations are given, there are two separate sources to the origin of that surname.[7] Throughout history many names originated in more than one way, and for any particular person's surname it is impossible to be sure which one is the correct origin, although when the country and the part of a

---

[6] Charles F. Gosnell, *Spanish Personal Names: Principles Governing Their Formation and Use Which May Be Presented as a Help for Catalogers and Bibliographers* (New York: H.W. Wilson Co., 1938), pp. 85 – 86.

[7] Smith, *op. cit.,* p. x.

country where the person's ancestors lived are known, a more nearly accurate derivation can be determined.[8]

Spanish surnames have originated from three basic classifications: 1) family names (patronymics), 2) place names, and 3) descriptive names. Nearly every surname has various spellings, and it can be a very difficult task to identify all of them. This is further complicated in the United States where Spanish surnames may become altered to give them an English sound. There is also the possibility that a Spanish surname may have derived from English, German, Dutch, Italian, French, or Portuguese surnames.

"Patronymic" refers to the phenomenon common in the post-Gothic (after 710 A.D.) history of the Iberian Peninsula as surnames were developing, when the **az, as, ez, es, iz, is, oz, os, uz,** and **us** endings were placed on given names to indicate that a certain person was the son of another.[9] Smith says that in Spain "the majority of the names are patronymic"[10] but this is not true. Even though, as was noted above, the Arabs' surname base was patronymic, the majority of surnames originated from place names and descriptive names and are not patronymic. As a general rule, the **as, es, is, os**, and **us** endings are more commonly Portuguese endings, whereas the **az, ez, iz, oz**, and **uz** endings tend to be attached to Spanish surnames. For example, Martín, son of Rodrigo, might have been known as Martín Rodríguez. Surnames in the beginning of their development were not static. For example, Diego, son of this same Martín Rodríguez, might have been called Diego Martínez, Diego Rodríguez, or even another surname totally unrelated to this patronymic system, but rather based on the illustriousness of the mother's or the grandmother's lineages.

Listings of Spanish patronymics are found, along with their derivations, in the *Diccionario Etimológico Comparado de Nombres Propios de Personas* by Gutierre Tibón. In this work Tibón analyzes a considerable number of Spanish proper, or given, names, discussing not only their derivations but also their etymology, variations in spelling, equivalents in English, German, French, Italian, etc., and often a variety of additional, enlightening information.

---

[8] Smith, *op. cit.,* p. xvi.
[9] Rodolfo M. Ragucci, *El Habla de mi Tierra.* 24th ed. (Buenos Aires, Argentina: Instituto Salesiano de Artes Gráficas, 1960), pp. 126, 135.
[10] Smith, *op. cit.,* p. 7.

Surnames naturally derived from place names because of patronymics, discussed above, and because of the antiquity of towns and villages in Spain (many of them antedate 600 A.D.). Consequently, a man named Lope living at Avila would become Lope de Avila, particularly if he were given property there by a royal grant, concession, or from fighting in the wars.

The ancient and very strange language of the Basques, who live in the Pyrenees of northern Spain and southern France, has produced many surnames within the Spanish culture. Basque surnames are basically derived from place names associated almost entirely with height or the lack of it, with other geography, new and old things, trees and other simple aspects of nature. It is possible to determine the meaning of many Basque surnames by knowing a few facts: *aga* and *equi* (place of), *barri* or *berri* (new), *be* (below), *garay* (on high), and *buro* (boundary). Several Basque place names and surnames are *Bilbao* (house of the beautiful peak), *Unamuno* (hill of asphodels), *Guevara* (flat area), *Gutiérrez* (little burned), *Echegaray* (house on a hill), and *Goya* (higher up).[11] One of the best studies of Basque surnames is *Linajes Vascos y Montañeses en Chile* by Pedro Xavier Fernández-Pradel (Santiago, Chile: Talleres Gráficos "San Rafael," 1930). The majority of the book is devoted to the discussion of Basque surnames, but the book also includes a Basque vocabulary and a treatment of the provinces of Guipúzcoa, Vizcaya, Alava, and Navarra in Spain; the ancient Montañas de Burgos and Montañas de Santander; and Benabarre, Laburdi, and Zuberoa in France.

As is to be expected, the more popular surnames, because of their patronymic origins, cannot be traced back to a common ancestor. It is impossible, for example, to identify all the Rodrigos in Spanish history who left descendants surnamed Rodríguez. Even if these could be identified, there are many named Rodríguez today who actually got their surnames from one of the other traditional methods discussed in this section. Consequently, the more common the surname, the more general the information on that surname. There are several exceptions within the ranks of the more popular surnames. In the United States the surnames Garza, Treviño, and Cantú have, for the most part, descended from common ancestors, either directly for Spanish descendants, or by association insofar as Indian and Negro families are concerned.

---

[11] Leonard R.N. Ashley, *What's in a Name? Everything You Wanted to Know* (Baltimore: Genealogical Publishing Co., 1989), p. 143.

Even in the late colonial period in Latin America, surnames were not always fixed within families. There are many instances where children continued to take their mother's surname, one of the surnames of other ancestors, or compounds of these. Among the native Americans, the church had established what was called the "privilege of neophytes," which lasted more than 200 years, in some cases up into the early 1800s in New Mexico and other border areas. Not even when the northern missions were annexed by the Bishop of Durango from 1730 on did this practice change. This practice concerned the strict native rules governing clan and family admixtures. These rules are extensive, and several volumes could be written on the practices. Because of these rules many Indians did not adopt Spanish surnames until the early 1800s, and quite often the researcher will be lucky enough to find records giving the Indian surnames or their equivalents. One of the best studies to be published to date on a variety of subjects within this general area is *Familias Novohispanas, Siglos XVI al XIX* by Pilar Gonzalbo Aizpuru (Mexico City: Centro de Estudios Históricos, El Colegio de México, 1991).

The descriptive category of surnames can be broken down into additional groupings. There are surnames that derive from occupations, nicknames, titles, physiognomy, descriptions as to some deed or action, and a multitude of other variations. These surnames are the hardest to trace historically because their origins have usually been lost in antiquity, or in some cases have been taken in lieu of the birth surnames. Some examples of these are the surname Alfonso (*athel + fons,* noble + ready) and the usually proclaimed patronymic surname Hernández (*fardi + nantha,* journey + risk). These surnames, along with others, were inherited from the Gothic invaders.[12]

It is also important to note that individuals did over their lifetimes take various surnames, change surnames, and generally do as they pleased within certain basic guidelines. It was important, as a matter of law, that a male heir to a family property or title retain the surname attached to that property (*mayorazgo* or entailed estate) or title. It was also important that if a child were called by one surname and became the heir apparent of the property or title of a grandmother or other distant relative, he would assume as part of his surname thereafter that surname by which the property or title was designated, or in some cases

---

[12] George F. Jones, *German-American Names.* 2nd ed. (Baltimore: Genealogical Publishing Co., 1995), p. 19.

totally change his surname. There are a myriad of examples of these naming changes throughout the records used in genealogy.

There are many spelling variations other than those noted earlier between Spanish and Portuguese surnames. There are also abbreviations found even in modern records such as the Social Security Death Benefits Index, census records, or telephone directories, such as those given on pages 20–21 for Rodríguez and González, and others such as Hernandz, Herndez, Sanchz, and Martnez. Abbreviations such as CdeBaca for Cabeza de Baca or DCruz for De Cruz will appear in the records. Even more obscure abbreviations may exist, such as A° or Al° for Alonso, R° for Rodrigo, P° for Pedro, Brme for Bartolomé, and so forth. An exhaustive list of these types of abbreviations is found in the author's study *Genealogical Historical Guide to Latin America* (Detroit: Gale Research Company, 1978).

Misspellings — such as Fracisco [Francisco], Greigo [Griego], DeLoen [De León], and Deluao [de la O] — will be found. Spanish names that do not fit the rules of Spanish spelling (also within the misspelling criteria) — such as Garciav, Goycoolea, Maritnez, Mattillo, Monnar, Paddilla, Sifventes, Soegaard, and Swazo — will be noted. Compounds — such as Zayasbazan and Poncedeleon, which are never spelled together but are spelled Zayas Bazan or Ponce de León, respectively — may cause confusion, especially in records that have no upper-case first letters. There are many **de, de la, del**, and **de los** prefixes which should be separated in the records but sometimes are not. Titles such as *virrey* (viceroy) or *teniente* (lieutenant) will be confusing at times.

Finally, a note about naming customs as they apply to saints' days and holy days. Some saints and holy days are recognized throughout the Catholic world. Many others, however, are important only to one country or to just a part of that country, or even to just a parish.

Patron saints, saints of the various professions and employments, saints who were in charge of curing specific diseases or granting special favors, saints belonging to certain of the religious or monastic orders, and saints who attracted the devotion of individuals were all given special consideration on their feast day. Children were given names based on the name of the saint whose day was closest to the day they were born or baptized, or for whom their parents, priest, or parish had particular devotion or association. In some cases it is very helpful to know this kind of information in searching through the records of a certain area, or in looking for the records of a person for whom the full name is known. For example, if an ancestor was named José Luciano Torres, it is possible that he was born or baptized on January 7th, that being the day of Saint Luciano. A complete study of these saints' days is found in the author's *Genealogical Historical Guide to Latin America*, cited above.

SURNAMES AND HERALDRY

Heraldry, as we know it, originated around the time of the Crusades. It developed into a complicated and valuable genealogical tool during the following centuries. By the end of the sixteenth century, however, heavy armor and heraldic pageantry were at a point of decline and play almost no role in the genealogies of Latin American families. Up to that point heraldry had a functional purpose, but since that era it has become a self-defeating, vain science. Families striving for impressiveness in their armorial bearings over-adorned or complicated their shields so as to destroy their distinctiveness and initial character and value.

The greatest value these shields provide to the modern researcher is when a given surname in one province carries the same armorial bearings as that surname in another province. This shows the common ancestry of the two branches. Also, many shields are subdivided, usually into two and four parts, these parts maintaining in some cases enough of the symbolism of the former shields from which they derived to show the two or four surnames represented in the new configuration. Many of the family histories and general references noted below contain descriptions of these coats of arms. Researchers should preserve these descriptions and compare them to earlier coats of arms for clues of the common origins of given surnames.

ONE THOUSAND MOST COMMON SURNAMES

The following Spanish surnames study was compiled in 1987 by The Institute of Genealogy and History for Latin America from census, telephone, demographic, and other historical studies. It consists of the top 1,000 surnames as to the percentage of times they appear among the living population. These 1,000 surnames are found as the surnames of 95% of the living population. An additional 11,567 surnames cover the other 5%. In perspective, these 12,567 active surnames comprise 5.27%

of the known (historical) Spanish surnames. This seems like a small number, but in fact these are the surnames that have been the exceptions to the rule. As with families, so with surnames: most die out over time. It is a rarity to have a surname continue for hundreds of years. It is thus with some degree of pride when a family can trace its paternal line, or any of the collateral lines, for ten, fifteen, or at times twenty generations.

TOP 25%

1 Rodríguez, 2 González, 3 García, 4 Martínez, 5 Hernández, 6 López, 7 Pérez, 8 Sánchez, 9 Ramírez, 10 Díaz, 11 Fernández, 12 Torres, 13 Gómez.

TOP 26–50%

14 Rivera, 15 Alvarez, 16 Flores, 17 Cruz, 18 Gutiérrez, 19 Vásquez, 20 Morales, 21 Garza, 22 Reyes, 23 Ortiz, 24 Ramos, 25 Ruiz, 26 Castillo, 27 Valdez, 28 Herrera, 29 Romero, 30 Jiménez, 31 Moreno, 32 Medina, 33 Castro, 34 Delgado, 35 Chávez, 36 Mendoza, 37 Peña, 38 León, 39 Múñoz, 40 Vargas, 41 Súarez, 42 Espinoza, 43 Domínguez, 44 Guzman, 45 Aguilar, 46 Guerrero, 47 Silva, 48 Núñez, 49 Treviño, 50 Guerra, 51 Villareal, 52 Cortez, 53 Ortega, 54 Soto, 55 Vega, 56 Salazar, 57 Ríos, 58 Méndez, 59 Santos, 60 Alvarado, 61 Estrada, 62 Santiago, 63 Navarro, 64 Cabrera.

TOP 51–75%

65 Contreras, 66 Miranda, 67 Campos, 68 Velásquez, 69 Maldonado, 70 Molina, 71 Padilla, 72 Fuentes, 73 Rojas, 74 Sandoval, 75 Luna, 76 Acosta, 77 Salinas, 78 Márquez, 79 Solis, 80 Cantu, 81 Alonso, 82 Figueroa, 83 Cardenas, 84 Ibarra, 85 Aguirre, 86 Lozano, 87 Blanco, 88 Avila, 89 Ayala, 90 Carrillo, 91 Cervantes, 92 Martín, 93 Barrera, 94 Riva, 95 Robles, 96 Mejia, 97 Calderón, 98 Juárez, 99 Lara, 100 Valle, 101 Sosa, 102 Mesa, 103 Salas, 104 Franco, 105 Durán, 106 Santana, 107 Dávila, 108 Serrano, 109 Colón, 110 Villanueva, 111 Rosales, 112 Escobar, 113 Pacheco, 114 Ochoa, 115 Castañeda, 116 Gallegos, 117 Velez, 118 Macias, 119 Arias, 120 Mercado, 121 Leal, 122 Castellanos, 123 Meléndez, 124 Orozco, 125 Camacho, 126 Mon-

tes, 127 Trujillo, 128 Zamora, 129 Palacios, 130 de la Cruz, 131 Riveros, 132 Benítes, 133 Menéndez, 134 Cisneros, 135 Reyna, 136 Quiñones, 137 Román, 138 Mata, 139 Rubio, 140 Mora, 141 Villa, 142 Barrón, 143 Acevedo, 144 Piñeda, 145 Quintero, 146 Bernal, 147 Marín, 148 Cepeda, 149 Valencia, 150 Rocha, 151 Gallardo, 152 Montoya, 153 Córdoba, 154 Zúñiga, 155 Enríquez, 156 Esparza, 157 Ponce, 158 Huerta, 159 Benavides, 160 Rangel, 161 Arroyo, 162 Correa, 163 Guevara, 164 Galván, 165 Caballero, 166 Andrade, 167 de la Rosa, 168 Sierra, 169 Alfonso, 170 Cuevas, 171 Marrero, 172 Quintana, 173 Valenzuela, 174 Bautista, 175 Medrano, 176 Abreu, 177 Morán, 178 Beltrán, 179 Esquivel, 180 Cano, 181 Barrios, 182 Rosario, 183 Duarte, 184 Villegas, 185 Olivas, 186 Galindo, 187 Olivares, 188 Bravo, 189 Montalvo, 190 Arredondo, 191 Múñiz, 192 Sáenz, 193 Salgado, 194 Ferrer, 195 Prieto, 196 Murillo, 197 Vela, 198 Machado, 199 Zabala, 200 Canales.

TOP 76–95%

201–300

201 Gil, 202 Hidalgo, 203 Vidal, 204 Bonilla, 205 Alfaro, 206 Tapia, 207 Betancourt, 208 Bruno, 209 de la Torre, 210 Rosas, 211 Cáceres, 212 Iglesias, 213 Nieves, 214 Tobar, 215 Romo, 216 Cordero, 217 Barajas, 218 Padrón, 219 Cardona, 220 Costa, 221 de Jesús, 222 Hinojosa, 223 Lugo, 224 Parra, 225 Puentes, 226 Velasco, 227 Otero, 228 Amador, 229 Longoria, 230 Villalobos, 231 Ventura, 232 Cuéllar, 233 Elías, 234 Alemán, 235 Arellano, 236 Bermúdez, 237 Paredes, 238 Báez, 239 Carrasco, 240 Vera, 241 Cavazos, 242 Zapata, 243 Rosado, 244 Rosa, 245 Cerda, 246 Elizondo, 247 Marroquín, 248 Corona, 249 Felix, 250 Lorenzo, 251 Fonseca, 252 Avilés, 253 Coronado, 254 Corrales, 255 Rendón, 256 Gallo, 257 Becerra, 258 Aguilera, 259 Chapa, 260 Amaya, 261 Falcón, 262 Toledo, 263 Pagan, 264 Salaña, 265 Chacón, 266 Varela, 267 Serna, 268 Matos, 269 Yáñez, 270 Saucedo, 271 Quezada, 272 Crespo, 273 Arce, 274 Gabriel, 275 Hurtado, 276 Manuel, 277 Peralta, 278 Casillas, 279 Trejo, 280 Nava, 281 Alaniz, 282 Prado, 283 Ledesma, 284 Uribe, 285 Carmona, 286 Gámes, 287 Portillo, 288 Bustamante, 289 Espósito, 290 Mena, 291 Escamilla, 292 Piña, 293 Argüellos, 294 Granados, 295 Ojeda, 296 Pereira, 297 Perales, 298 Escobedo, 299 Avalos, 300 Vallejos.

301–400

301 Leiva, 302 Roque, 303 Paz, 304 Casas, 305 Collazo, 306 Guajardo, 307 Casanova, 308 Valadez, 309 Mireles, 310 Guillén, 311 Baca, 312 Angel, 313 Montaño, 314 Tobías, 315 Arreola, 316 Rico, 317 Rentería, 318 Aquino, 319 Brito, 320 Soriano, 321 Carranza, 322 Jaramillo, 323 Zaragoza, 324 Concepción, 325 Segura, 326 Pardo, 327 Lima, 328 Pinto, 329 Carrera, 330 Linares, 331 Quirós, 332 Rey, 333 Aragón, 334 Nieto, 335 Alba, 336 Telles, 337 Montero, 338 Burgos, 339 Gálvez, 340 Horta, 341 Madrigal, 342 Moya, 343 Cadena, 344 Llamas, 345 Marino, 346 Naranjo, 347 Ceballos, 348 Gamboa, 349 Tamayo, 350 Tirado, 351 Olvera, 352 Lemus, 353 Irizary, 354 Reynosa, 355 Bello, 356 Escalante, 357 Arevalo, 358 Quintanilla, 359 Izquierdo, 360 Osorio, 361 Aranda, 362 Bustos, 363 Gaytan, 364 Porras, 365 Ramón, 366 Jaime, 367 Lucero, 368 Esteves, 369 Francisco, 370 Vigil, 371 Chavarría, 372 Covarrubias, 373 Lazo, 374 Pino, 375 Dumas, 376 Patiño, 377 Perdomo, 378 Venegas, 379 Saldivar, 380 Arriaga, 381 Ocampo, 382 Aponte, 383 Magaña, 384 Montemayor, 385 Noriega, 386 Olivera, 387 Dorán, 388 Páes, 389 Tijerina, 390 Acuña, 391 del Río, 392 Sepúlveda, 393 Pulido, 394 Delgadillo, 395 Madrid, 396 Negrón, 397 Orellana, 398 Tenorio, 399 Fajardo, 400 Valdivia.

401–500

401 Palma, 402 Riojas, 403 Carvajal, 404 Mendiola, 405 Saavedra, 406 Dueñas, 407 Ferro, 408 Solano, 409 Tejada, 410 Henríquez, 411 Menchaca, 412 Garay, 413 Polanco, 414 Rincón, 415 Cintrón, 416 Támez, 417 Barrientos, 418 Ferreiro, 419 Garrido, 420 Viera, 421 Narvaez, 422 Conde, 423 Angulo, 424 Briones, 425 Godínez, 426 Segovia, 427 Borges, 428 Luján, 429 Sarmiento, 430 Soler, 431 Armas, 432 Berríos, 433 Ornelas, 434 Regalado, 435 Resendez, 436 Carrizales, 437 Navarrete, 438 Arteaga, 439 Nájera, 440 Nevares, 441 Solórzano, 442 Ontiveros, 443 Calvo, 444 Lira, 445 Llanes, 446 Roldán, 447 Almeida, 448 Limón, 449 Carballo, 450 Frías, 451 Ordóñez, 452 Ulloa, 453 Zambrana, 454 Barragán, 455 Bertrán, 456 Bueno, 457 Montenegro, 458 Sarabia, 459 Banda, 460 Forte, 461 Robledo, 462 Cifuentes, 463 Toro, 464 Briceño, 465 Farías, 466 Zayas, 467 Barraza, 468 Borrego, 469 Salcedo, 470 Zárate, 471 Araujo, 472 Carbajal, 473 Ibáñez, 474 Cabral, 475 Martino, 476 Villaseñor, 477 Alarcón, 478 Infante, 479 Rubalcaba, 480 Holguín, 481 Losada, 482 Santa María, 483 Balderas, 484 Pantoja, 485 Arena, 486 Barreto, 487 Caro, 488 Carreón, 489 Espino, 490 Milián, 491 Ferrera, 492 Jáuregui, 493

Anguiano, 494 Sotelo, 495 Jorge, 496 Mares, 497 Galán, 498 Montañes, 499 Caraballo, 500 Fierro.

501–600

501 Carrión, 502 Cortina, 503 de Hoyos, 504 Fraga, 505 Alcalá, 506 Béjar, 507 Mójica, 508 Olmos, 509 Medellín, 510 Tejeda, 511 Villar, 512 Amaro, 513 Centeno, 514 Zaragoza, 515 Loera, 516 Pimentel, 517 Fariña, 518 Almanza, 519 Valladares, 520 Pedraza, 521 Salmón, 522 Arango, 523 Barba, 524 Duque, 525 Pedrosa, 526 Salomon, 527 Pascual, 528 Sanabria, 529 Urbina, 530 Bañuelos, 531 Quiroga, 532 Vergara, 533 Arispe, 534 Bolaños, 535 Dávalos, 536 Godoy, 537 San Miguel, 538 Soria, 539 Echeverría, 540 Luis, 541 Morejón, 542 Preciado, 543 Carlos, 544 del Rosario, 545 Girón, 546 Mederos, 547 de la Fuente, 548 Echevarría, 549 Millán, 550 Negrete, 551 Pastor, 552 Heredia, 553 Agüeros, 554 Palomo, 555 Pelayo, 556 de la Vega, 557 Meneses, 558 Calvillo, 559 Olivos, 560 Peraza, 561 Posadas, 562 Tavares, 563 Terrazas, 564 Botello, 565 Capote, 566 Bazán, 567 Haro, 568 Adame, 569 Diez, 570 Sevilla, 571 Almagüer, 572 Barbosa, 573 Lerma, 574 Zelaya, 575 Arana, 576 Candelario, 577 Garcés, 578 Manríquez, 579 Puig, 580 Quijano, 581 Mayorga, 582 Placencia, 583 Salvador, 584 Lucío, 585 Monzón, 586 Quevedo, 587 Mancilla, 588 Camarillo, 589 Cardos, 590 Collada, 591 Cornejo, 592 Figueredo, 593 Trinidad, 594 Vila, 595 Chavis, 596 Jasso, 597 Leos, 598 Osuna, 599 Peláez, 600 Manzano.

601–700

601 Talamantes, 602 Zamudio, 603 Aguayo, 604 Curiel, 605 Estrella, 606 Llano, 607 Moreira, 608 Sotolongo, 609 Urrutia, 610 Cuervo, 611 Paniagua, 612 Araiza, 613 Barroso, 614 Triana, 615 Cota, 616 Aceves, 617 Argüelles, 618 Jimínez, 619 Lagos, 620 Alcántara, 621 Cázares, 622 Mota, 623 Agueta, 624 Castellón, 625 Cedillo, 626 Gracia, 627 Aparicio, 628 Alejandro, 629 Asencio, 630 Cuesta, 631 Massa, 632 Munguia, 633 Oquendo, 634 Partida, 635 Roca, 636 Rodarte, 637 Tello, 638 Mateo, 639 Santillán, 640 Aldana, 641 Badillo, 642 Guardado, 643 Lacayo, 644 Magallenes, 645 Ovalle, 646 Terán, 647 Marcos, 648 Monroy, 649 Montiel, 650 Pabón, 651 Restrepo, 652 Cardozo, 653 Ceja, 654 de la Paz, 655 Real, 656 Durand, 657 Garibay, 658 Landa, 659 Serra, 660 Valverde, 661 Merino, 662 Palomino, 663 Pons, 664 Ruelas, 665 Aguila, 666 Carbonell, 667 Maya, 668 Abrego, 669 Carreno, 670 Villagómez, 671 Borjas, 672 Oropeza, 673 Andrés, 674

Armendariz, 675 Oviedo, 676 Travieso, 677 Altamirano, 678 Llerena, 679 Obregón, 680 Parada, 681 Plaza, 682 Recio, 683 Almendarez, 684 Bustillos, 685 Cedeño, 686 Cueto, 687 Granda, 688 Grande, 689 Iñíguez, 690 Pichardo, 691 Ravelo, 692 Zaldivar, 693 Campa, 694 Lagunas, 695 Monge, 696 Samaniego, 697 Agosto, 698 Castaño, 699 Chao, 700 Grau.

701–800

701 Piedra, 702 Piñeiro, 703 Cabezas, 704 Sales, 705 Abad, 706 Apodaca, 707 Domingo, 708 Feliciano, 709 Luciano, 710 Menjívar, 711 Almaraz, 712 de la O, 713 Lanza, 714 Olguín, 715 Ruaño, 716 Ballesteros, 717 Miramontes, 718 Perera, 719 Mosqueda, 720 Novoa, 721 Rueda, 722 Sauceda, 723 Sotomayor, 724 Alcaraz, 725 Angeles, 726 Arencibia, 727 Arocha, 728 Camargo, 729 Rizo, 730 Colunga, 731 Montelongo, 732 Rodas, 733 Talavera, 734 Chaidez, 735 Laríos, 736 Lobos, 737 Loza, 738 Olmeda, 739 Piñera, 740 Valero, 741 Favela, 742 Cobos, 743 Maciel, 744 Melgar, 745 Nápoles, 746 País, 747 Perea, 748 Quiles, 749 Alicea, 750 Alves, 751 del Campo, 752 Frausto, 753 Galarza, 754 Góngora, 755 Jara, 756 Lamas, 757 Mariano, 758 Roa, 759 Vanegas, 760 Armenta, 761 de Anda, 762 Guariño, 763 Mas, 764 Monterosa, 765 Santa Cruz, 766 Baltazar, 767 Moncada, 768 Tolentino, 769 Zamarripa, 770 Antonio, 771 Escareno, 772 Gaona, 773 Lucas, 774 Segarra, 775 Varona, 776 Alderete, 777 Meraz, 778 Almonte, 779 Buenrostro, 780 Camarena, 781 Céspedes, 782 Lomelí, 783 Loya, 784 Melchor, 785 Pizarro, 786 Salcido, 787 Javier, 788 Mariscal, 789 Mondragón, 790 Pita, 791 Sanz, 792 Velarde, 793 Alejos, 794 Cuadra, 795 Jurado, 796 Portela, 797 Tapanes, 798 Barela, 799 Caldera, 800 Evangelista.

801–900

801 Huizar, 802 Lazaro, 803 Loredo, 804 Navas, 805 Castañón, 806 Curbelo, 807 Espinal, 808 Viramontes, 809 Mestre, 810 Barros, 811 Mirabel, 812 Olivero, 813 Ordaz, 814 Pozo, 815 Rojo, 816 Socarras, 817 Verdugo, 818 Corpus, 819 Grillo, 820 Vicente, 821 Cosentino, 822 Pujol, 823 Ugarte, 824 Carpio, 825 Cepero, 826 Cervera, 827 Elizalde, 828 Grijalva, 829 Herrero, 830 Nazario, 831 Ricardo, 832 Armenteros, 833 Cabello, 834 Camejo, 835 Celis, 836 Dieguez, 837 Doria, 838 Escoto, 839 Hevia, 840 Jacobo, 841 Pereda, 842 Valderrama, 843 Artigas, 844 Coronel, 845 de la Peña, 846 Fundadora, 847 Montijo, 848 Serrato, 849 Zendejas, 850 Palomares, 851 Piñón, 852 Roig, 853

Vidaurri, 854 Abarca, 855 Alcantar, 856 Bocanegra, 857 Cabanas, 858 Guardiola, 859 Lizarraga, 860 Mier, 861 Noguera, 862 Nuño, 863 Recinos, 864 Barahona, 865 Barceló, 866 Callejas, 867 Chirinos, 868 Cid, 869 Cubas, 870 del Pino, 871 Dorado, 872 Fabela, 873 Machin, 874 Mijares, 875 Pastrana, 876 Plata, 877 Revilla, 878 Serpa, 879 Araos, 880 Barcena, 881 Cañas, 882 Escalera, 883 Felipe, 884 Landeros, 885 Leija, 886 Muro, 887 Polo, 888 Robaina, 889 Sáez, 890 Buentello, 891 Puga, 892 Riverón, 893 Umaña, 894 Valiente, 895 Alegría, 896 Chavira, 897 Corea, 898 Giraldo, 899 Hoyo, 900 Villalba.

901–1000

901 Zertuche, 902 Fragosa, 903 Morera, 904 Urena, 905 Valera, 906 Varas, 907 Veliz, 908 Calles, 909 Castillas, 910 Castillejas, 911 Delfino, 912 Febles, 913 Luevanos, 914 Montesinos, 915 Reza, 916 Viñas, 917 Alberto, 918 Amescua, 919 Cosio, 920 Encarnación, 921 Escudero, 922 Espíritu, 923 Melo, 924 Piloto, 925 Bojórquez, 926 Mendieta, 927 Villavicencio, 928 Yepes, 929 Bejarano, 930 Calero, 931 Esqueda, 932 Junco, 933 Ortegón, 934 Pinedo, 935 Arreguin, 936 Arrieta, 937 Ignacio, 938 Salguero, 939 Santiestéban, 940 Solares, 941 Armand, 942 Bacallao, 943 Comas, 944 Cuenca, 945 Freire, 946 Mosquera, 947 Noda, 948 Peñate, 949 Pupo, 950 Ambriz, 951 Burciaga, 952 Nodarse, 953 Redondo, 954 Tafoya, 955 Andino, 956 Gurrola, 957 Lora, 958 Madruga, 959 Merida, 960 Planas, 961 Turcios, 962 Urias, 963 Anzaldúa, 964 Galicia, 965 Lastra, 966 Merlos, 967 Alvarenga, 968 Barreiros, 969 Berlanga, 970 Carrazana, 971 Chamorro, 972 Londoño, 973 Negrin, 974 Castells, 975 Obando, 976 Pazos, 977 Villagran, 978 Arcos, 979 Caicedo, 980 Encinas, 981 Giménez, 982 Jérez, 983 San Martín, 984 Uresti, 985 Abascal, 986 Andreu, 987 Diego, 988 Portuondo, 989 Adorno, 990 Almodovar, 991 Antunez, 992 Archuleta, 993 España, 994 Feria, 995 Izaguirre, 996 Marmolejo, 997 Portal, 998 Tinoco, 999 Vizcaino, 1000 Aguinaga.

IGHL'S HISPANIC SURNAME STUDY— 1500 SURNAMES: ALPHABETICAL LISTING

The following list of surnames, in alphabetical order, is for those surnames that have been studied to date in detail by IGHL. The alphabetizing follows the English alphabet rather than the Spanish for ease of access for the majority of readers. The exception is ñ, which comes after n. A history of each of these surnames has been compiled from several hundred sources in Spain, Latin America, and the Hispanic United States. The 1,000 surnames just listed are included in the following list, together with an additional 500 surnames that have been of interest to clients of IGHL, or have received attention in one way or another by IGHL staff. Copies of these histories are available for a minimal fee by contacting IGHL at 316 West 500 North, St. George, Utah 84770.

Aanda, Aba, Abad, Abadia, Abadiano, Abadín, Abaitua, Abajo, Abalar, Abalo, Abanades, Abarca-Avarca, Abascal, Abasta(o), Abaunza, Abba, Abeyta, Abrego, Abreu, Acedo, Acevedo, Aceves(z), Acosta, Acuña, Adame, Adauto, Adorno, Agosto, Aguasvivas, Aguayo, Agüero, Aguila, Aguilar, Aguilera, Aguirre, Aja, Alaniz, Alarcón, Alba, Alberto, Alcalá, Alcalde, Alcantar, Alcántara, Alcaras, Alcorta, Aldana, Alderete, Alegría, Alejandro, Alejo, Alemán, Alfaro, Alfonso, Alicea, Almaguer, Almanza, Almaraz, Almeida, Almendarez, Almodóvar, Almonte, Alonso, Altamirano, Alvarado, Alvarenga, Alvarez, Alvear, Alves, Amador, Amaro, Amaya, Ambriz, Amézaga, Amescua, Anaya, Andazola, Andino, Andrade, Andrés, Andreu, Angel, Angeles, Anguiano, Angulo, Antonio, Antúnez, Anzaldua, Aparicio, Apodaca, Aponte, Aquino, Aragón, Araiza, Arana, Aranda, Arango, Araujo, Arauz, Arce, Archibeque, Archuleta, Arcos, Arellano, Arena, Arencibia, Arevalo, Argüelles, Argüello, Argueta, Arias, Arizmendi, Arispe, Armand, Armas, Armendariz, Armenta, Armenteros, Arocha, Arredondo, Arreguin, Arreola, Arriaga, Arrieta, Arroyo, Arteaga, Artiga, Arvizu, Asencio, Avalos, Avaristo, Avellano, Avelleyra, Avila, Avilés, Avisto, Ayala, Baca, Bacallao, Badillo, Baez, Baijo, Balderas, Baldés, Ballesteros, Balli, Baltazar, Banda, Bañuelos, Barahona, Barajas, Barba, Barbosa, Barceló, Barcenas, Barela, Barragán, Barrazas, Barreiro, Barrera, Barreto, Barrientos, Barriga, Barrios, Barrón, Barros, Barroso, Basurto, Batista, Baula, Bautista, Bayanito, Bazán, Becerra, Béjar, Bello, Beltrán, Benavides, Benitez, Berlanga, Bermúdez, Bernal, Bernaus, Berríos, Bertrand, Betancourt, Blanco, Bocanegra, Bojorquez, Bolaños, Bonilla, Borges, Borjas, Borrego, Botello, Bracamontes, Bravo, Briceño, Briones, Brito, Brun, Bruno, Bueno, Buenrostro, Buentello, Burciaga, Burgos, Burrola, Bustamante, Bustillos, Busto, Caballero, Cabanillas, Cabañas, Cabello, Cabezas, Cabral, Cabrera, Cáceres, Cadena, Caicedo, Caldera, Calderón, Calero, Calle, Calleja, Calvillo, Calvo, Camacho, Camarena, Camargo, Camarillo, Camejo,

Camiña, Campa, Campesano, Campos, Candelaria, Cano, Cantoya, Cantu, Cañas, Capote, Caraballo, Carbajal, Carballo, Carbonell, Cárdenas, Cardona, Cardosa, Cardozo, Carlos, Carmona, Caro, Carpio, Carranza, Carrasco, Carrazana, Carreño, Carreón, Carrera, Carrillo, Carrión, Carrizal, Carvajal, Casanova, Casas, Casillas, Castañeda, Castañón, Castaños, Castellán, Castellanos, Castells, Castilla, Castilleja, Castillo, Castro, Caudillo, Cavazos, Cázares, Ceballos, Cedeño, Cedillo, Cejas, Celis, Ceniceros, Centeno, Cepeda, Cepero, Cerda, Cervantes, Cervera, Céspedes, Chabolla, Chacón, Chaidez, Chamorro, Chao, Chapa, Chasco, Chavana, Chavarría, Chavera, Chávez, Chavira, Chavis, Chirino, Cid, Cifuentes, Cintrón, Cisneros, Citrón, Claudio, Cobo, Coello, Collada, Collazo, Colón, Colunga, Comas, Concepción, Conde, Constanza, Contreras, Corbalán, Cordero, Córdova, Corea, Cornejo, Coronado, Coronel, Corpus, Corral, Correa, Cortez, Cortina, Corzo, Cosentino, Cosío, Costa, Cota, Covarrubias, Crespo, Cruz, Cuadra, Cuba, Cuéllar, Cuenca, Cuervo, Cuesta, Cueto, Cuevas, Curbelo, Cuza, D'Abate, Davalos, Dávila, De Anda, De Hoyos, De Jesús, De la Cruz, De la Fuente, De la O, De la Paz, De la Peña, De la Rosa, De la Torre, De la Vega, Del Campo, Del Pino, Del Río, Del Rosario, Delfino, Delgadillo, Delgado, Díaz, Diego, Dieguez, Diez, Dobles, Domenzain, Domingo, Domínguez, Dondero, Dorado, Dorán, Doria, Duarte, Dueñas, Dumas, Duque, Durán, Durand, Echevarría, Echeverría, Elías, Elizalde, Elizondo, Ellín, Encarnación, Encinas, Enríquez, Escalante, Escalera, Escamilla, Escárcega, Escareno, Escobar, Escobedo, Escoto, Escudero, España, Esparza, Espinol, Espino, Espinoza, Espíritu, Espun, Esqueda, Esquivel, Esteves, Estrada, Estrella, Evangelista, Expósito, Fabela-Favela, Fajardo, Falcón, Farias, Fariña, Febles, Feliciano, Felipe, Felix, Feria, Fernández, Ferreiro, Ferrera, Ferro, Fierro, Figueredo, Figueroa, Flanega, Flores, Fonseca, Fontes, Forte, Fraga, Fragoza, Francisco, Franco, Frausto, Freiro, Frias, Fuentes, Fundadora, Gabriel, Gaitán, Galán, Galarza, Galicia, Galindo, Gallardo, Gallegos, Gallo, Galván, Galvez, Gamboa, Games, Gaona, Garay, Garced, Garces, García, Garibay, Garrido, Garza, Gatica, Gavira, Gil, Gimenez, Giraldo, Girón, Godinez, Godoy, Gómez, Góngora, González, Gordoa, Gracia, Granado, Granda, Grande, Grau, Grijalva, Grillo, Guajardo, Guardado, Guardiola, Guariño, Guerra, Guerrero, Guevara, Guillén, Gurrola, Gutiérrez, Guzmán, Hara, Haro, Hernández, Henríquez, Heredia, Herrera, Herrero, Hevia, Hidalgo, Hinojosa, Holguín, Horta, Hoyos, Huerta, Huizar, Hurón, Hurtado, Ibáñez, Ibarra, Iglesias, Ignacio, Infante, Iñiguez, Ipatzi, Iriarte, Irizarry, Isaguirre,

Izquierdo, Jacobo, Jaime, Janero, Jara, Jaramillo, Jasso, Jáuregui, Javier, Jérez, Jiménez, Jorge, Juárez, Junco, Jurado, Lacayo, Lagos, Lagunas, Lamas, Landa, Landeros, Lanza, Lara, Larios, Lastra, Lazaro, Lazo, Leal, Ledesma, Legorreth, Leija, Leiva, Lemos, León, Leos, Lerma, Licea, Liendo, Lima, Limón, Linares, Lira, Lizárraga, Llamas, Llanes, Llanos, Llerena, Llorente, Lobos, Loera, Lomelí, Londoño, Longoria, López, Lora, Loredo, Lorenzo, Losada, Losoya, Lotero, Loya, Loza, Lozano, Lucas, Lucero, Luciano, Lucío, Luevano, Lugo, Luis, Luján, Luna, Machado, Machín, Macías, Maciel, Madrid, Madrigal, Madril, Madruga, Madueño, Maes, Magallanes, Magaña, Malaspina, Maldonado, Manchego, Mancillas, Manríquez, Manuel, Manzano, Marcano, Marcel, Marcial, Marcos, Marella, Mares, Mariano, Marín, Marino, Mariñez, Mariscal, Marmolejo, Marquecho, Márquez, Marrero, Marroquín, Marti, Martín, Martínez, Martino, Más, Massa, Mata, Mateo, Matos, Maya, Mayorga, Mayortena, Medellín, Mederos, Medina, Medrano, Mejía, Melchor, Melendez, Melgar, Melo, Mena, Menchaca, Mendez, Mendieta, Mendiola, Mendoza, Menéndez, Meneses, Menjívar, Meraz, Mercado, Mérida, Merino, Merlo, Mesa, Mestre, Mier, Mijares, Milian, Millán, Mirabel, Miramontes, Miranda, Mireles, Mójica, Molina, Moncada, Mondragón, Monge, Monroy, Monsolo, Montalvo, Montáñez, Montaño, Montelongo, Montemayor, Montenegro, Montero, Monterosa, Montes, Montes de Oca, Montesinos, Montiel, Montijo, Montoya, Monzón, Mora, Morales, Morán, Moreira, Morejón, Moreno, Morera, Moscoso, Mosqueda, Mosquera, Mota, Moya, Munguía, Múñiz, Múñoz, Murillo, Muro, Múzquiz, Nájera, Nápoles, Naranjo, Narvaez, Nava, Navarre, Navarrete, Navarro, Nazario, Negrete, Negrin, Negrón, Nevares, Nieto, Nieves, Noda, Nodarse, Noguera, Noriega, Novoa, Núñez, Nuño, Obando, Obregón, Ocampo, Ochoa, Ojeda, Olguín, Oliva, Olivares, Olivera, Olivero, Olivo, Olmeda, Olmo(s), Olvera, Ontiveros, Oquendo, Orantes, Orci, Ordaz, Ordoñez, Ordorica, Orellana, Ornelas, Oropesa, Orozco, Ortega, Ortegón, Ortiz, Osorio, Osuna, Otero, Ovalle, Oviedo, Pabón, Pacheco, Pacheo, Padilla, Padrón, Paes, Pagán, Pais, Palacios, Palma, Palomares, Palomino, Palomo, Paniagua, Pantoja, Parada, Pardo, Paredes, Parra, Partida, Pascual, Pastor, Pastrana, Patiño, Paz, Pazos, Pedraza, Pedrosa, Peinado, Pelaez, Pelayo, Pelegrina, Pendril, Peña, Peñate, Perales, Peralta, Peraza, Perdomo, Perea, Pereda, Pereira, Perera, Pérez, Perojo, Picazo, Pichardo, Piedra, Piloto, Pimentel, Pina, Pino, Pinto, Piña, Piñeda, Piñedo, Piñeiro, Piñera, Piñón, Pita, Pizarro, Placencia, Planas, Plata, Plaza, Polanco, Polo, Ponce, Pons, Porras, Portal, Portela, Portillo, Portuondo, Posada, Pozo, Prado, Preciado,

Puente, Puga, Puig, Pujol, Pulido, Pupo, Quevedo, Quezada, Quijano, Quiles, Quintana, Quintanilla, Quintero, Quiñones, Quiroga, Quirós, Ramírez, Ramos, Rangel, Razo, Rendón, Rentería, Reyes, Reyna, Rincón, Ríos, Rivas, Rivera, Rivero, Robles, Roca, Rocha, Rodríguez, Roig, Rojas, Román, Romero, Rosado, Rosales, Rosario, Rossi, Rubilar, Rubio, Ruibal, Ruiz, Saavedra, Sada, Saez, Salas, Salazar, Salcedo, Salcido, Saldaña, Saldívar, Sales, Salguero, Salinas, Salmón, Salvador, Samaniego, Samudio, San Martín, San Miguel, Sanabria, Sánchez, Sandoval, Sanjurjo, Santa Cruz, Santa María, Santana, Santiago, Santiestéban, Santillán, Santos, Santovena, Sanz, Sarabia, Saragoza, Sariego, Sarmiento, Sauceda, Saucedo, Segarra, Segovia, Segura, Sellas, Sepúlveda, Sermeño, Serna, Serpa, Serra, Serrano, Serrato, Sevilla, Sías, Sierra, Sigala, Silva, Socarrás, Solano, Solares, Soler, Solis, Solórzano, Soria, Soriano, Sosa, Sotelo, Soto, Sotolongo, Sotomayor, Súarez, Sulsona, Tafoya, Talamantes, Talavera, Tamayo, Tamez, Tapanes, Tapia, Tarín, Tautímez, Tavares, Tejada, Tejeda, Telles, Tello, Tenorio, Tepezano, Terán, Terrazas, Tijerina, Tinoco, Tirado, Tobia, Toledo, Tolentino, Toro, Torres, Tovar, Travieso, Trejo, Treviño, Triana, Trinidad, Trujillo, Tur, Turagano, Turcios, Turrieta, Ubieta, Ugarte, Ulibarri, Ulloa, Umaña, Uranga, Urbina, Ureña, Uresti, Urias, Uribe, Urrutia, Uzcategui, Valadez, Valderrama, Valdes, Valdivia, Valencia, Valentín, Valenzuela, Valera, Valero, Valiente, Valladares, Valle, Vallejo, Valpais, Valverde, Vanegas, Vara, Varela, Vargas, Varona, Vásquez, Vega, Vela, Velarde, Velasco, Velásquez, Velez, Veliz, Venegas, Ventura, Vera, Verdugo, Vergara, Vicente, Vidal, Vidaurri, Vidiuera, Viegas, Viera, Vigil, Vila, Villa, Villagómez, Villagran, Villalba, Villalobos, Villanueva, Villar, Villareal, Villaseñor, Villavicencio, Villegas, Viña, Viramontes, Virgin, Vivero, Vizcaino, Yáñez, Yepes, Yznaga, Zaldívar, Zamarripa, Zambrana, Zamora, Zamorano, Zamudio, Zapata, Zaragoza, Zárate, Zayas, Zelaya, Zendejas, Zertuche, Zúñiga.

MAJOR RESEARCH SOURCES FOR HISPANIC RESEARCH

A cronyms have been used in writing the 1,500 plus family history sketches noted in alphabetical order on pages 37–41 and will appear in subsequent volumes of this series. At this point, only a list of the 103 sources, containing over 600 volumes, is given, together with the areas of principal interest for each source. For example, the acronym **ACP** given below under California can be found under "List of Sources with their Acronyms" beginning on page 44. The **ACP** reference is as follows: ACP Mutnick Dorothy G. *Some Alta California Pioneers and Descendants*. It is further identified in the Bibliography as: Mutnick, Dorothy G. *Some Alta California Pioneers and Descendants. Parts 1 and 2,* Lafayette, California, 1982. This list of acronyms, by state or region, will allow the researcher to quickly find the principal published sources available for that area. Other references may also be found in the index to the family histories (see page 51). These are more specific to given families, rather than being statewide or regionwide.

THE UNITED STATES OF AMERICA IN GENERAL — BOC, CEN, IGI, VIS.

ARIZONA — CEN, CSB, IGI, PA.

CALIFORNIA — ACP, CEN, CMV, CPR, IGI, ITP, MAR, PSC, SMF.

COLORADO — CEN, CG, IGI, NR, PEV, TSC.

FLORIDA — CEN, CGS, CIM, DBC1, DBC2, DNC, HFC, IGI, ISC, RCA, SCP, TDC.

LOUISIANA — ALS, CEN, CGS, CIM, DBC1, DBC2, DNC, HFC, IGI, ISC, LCM, RCA, ROT, SCP, TDC.

NEW MEXICO — CEN, IGI, NMR, ONM, ROT.

UTAH — CEN, IGI, NMR, NR, ONM.

TEXAS — BGR, CEN, HGJ, IGI, LPS, MIL, MSA, ROT, WAA.

LATIN AMERICA IN GENERAL — ANE, CIG, CPI, DME, EHG, FH, GDF, GPC, HDS, IEI, IGH, IGI, INQ, LAO, NHA, RGB, RGL, RSS, SPN, VIS.

ARGENTINA — BCA, CEN, CRP, CEG, EGC, FHJ, IAC, IGI, LGT, IAC.

BOLIVIA — BCA, CEG, CEN, CRP, CEG, EGC, FEP, FHJ, IAC, IGI, IGP, IPI, LGT, LMA.

CHILE — ACH, CEN, IGI, LCT, NCG, RCH, REH.

COLOMBIA — none specifically; see Latin America in General.

COSTA RICA — ACC, CEN, IGI, GC.

CUBA — CEN, CGS, CIM, DBC1, DBC2, DNC, HFC, IGI, ISC, RCA, SCP.

ECUADOR — CAG, CEN, IGI, SNT.

EL SALVADOR — none specifically; see Latin America in General.

GUATEMALA — CEN, IGI, RAG.

HONDURAS — none specifically; see Latin America in General.

MEXICO — ACP, AGH, AMG, AMH, APE, BGR, BYA, CEN, CMV, COM, CPR, CSB, CVV, DAC, DBT, GYT, HGJ, IGI, ITP, LPS, MAR, MIL, MNE, MSA, NMR, ONM, PA, PSC, RCA, RNG, ROT, SMF, TMN, WAA.

NICARAGUA — none specifically; see Latin America in General.

PANAMA — none specifically; see Latin America in General.

PARAGUAY — APV, BCA, CEG, CEN, CRP, EGC, FHJ, IAC, IEG, IGI, LGT.

PERU — CEN, FEP, IGI, IGP, IPI, LMA.

PUERTO RICO — BP, CEN, FPP, IGI, IPR.

REPUBLICA DOMINICANA — CEN, FD, IGI, RBD.

URUGUAY — APV, CEN, IEG, IGI.

VENEZUELA — CEN, IGI, IVG, POE.

LIST OF SOURCES WITH THEIR ACRONYMS

The following references are not complete in their bibliographic detail. For purposes of showing the major references used in compiling family histories and sketches, the information given is sufficient.

AAI	Automated Archives, Inc., followed by a disc number.
ACC	*Revista*, Academia Costarricense de Ciencias Genealógicas.
ACH	*Boletín*, Academia Chilena de Historia.
ACP	Mutnick, Dorothy G. *Some Alta California Pioneers and Descendants.*
AGH	*Anuario*, Academia de Genealogía y Heráldica, "Mota Padilla."
ALS	West, Robert C. *An Atlas of Louisiana Surnames of French and Spanish Origin.*

AMG	*Memorias*, Academia Mexicana de Genealogía e Historia.
AMH	*Memorias*, Academia Mexicana de la Historia.
ANE	Vilar y Pascual, Luis. *Anuario de la Nobleza Española.*
APE	González de la Garza, Rodolfo. *Apellidos de Tamaulipas, Nuevo León, Coahuila, y Texas.*
APV	Azarola Gil, Luis Enrique. *Apellidos de la Patria Vieja.*
BCA	Levillier, Roberto. *Biografías de Conquistadores de la Argentina en el Siglo XVI.*
BGR	*Los Bexareños Genealogical Register*, Los Bexareños Genealogical Society.
BOC	United States Department of Commerce, Bureau of the Census. *1980 Census List of Spanish Surnames.*
BP	Rosa-Nieves, Cesáreo. *Biografías Puertorriqueñas: Perfil Histórico de un Pueblo.*
BYA	Múñoz Altea, Fernando. *Blasones y Apellidos.*
CAD	Archivo Histórico Nacional. *Catálogo Alfabético de los Documentos referentes a Hidalguías Conservadas en la Sección de Consejos Suprimidos.*
CAG	Colección Amigos de la Genealogía.
CEG	*Revista*, Centro de Estudios Genealógicos de Buenos Aires.
CEN	Census, followed by the specific reference.
CG	Colorado Genealogical Society. *The Colorado Genealogist.*
CGS	*Revista*, Cuban Genealogical Society.
CIG	Archivo Histórico Nacional. *Catálogo de las Informaciones Genealógicas de los Pretendientes a cargos del Santo Oficio.*
CIM	Villeré, Sidney Louis. *The Canary Islands Migration to Louisiana, 1778–1783.*
CMV	Workman, Thomas. *An Alphabetized Listing of the California Mission Vital Records.*
COM	Martínez, Leopoldo. *Los Caballeros de las Ordenes Militares de México.*
CPI	Bermúdez Plata, Cristóbal. *Catálogo de Pasajeros a Indias.*
CPR	Bancroft, Hubert Howe. *California Pioneer Register and Index, 1542–1848.*

CRP	De Lafuente Machain, Ricardo. *Conquistadores del Río de la Plata.*
CSB	Arizona State Genealogical Society. *Copper State Bulletin.*
CVV	Ibarrola, Gabriel. *Familias y Casas de la Vieja Valladolid.*
DAC	Icaza, Francisco. *Diccionario Autobiográfico de Conquistadores y Pobladores de Nueva España.*
DBC1	Peraza, Fermín. *Diccionario biográfico cubano.*
DBC2	Calcagno, Francisco. *Diccionario biográfico cubano.*
DBT	Zorrilla, Juan F. *Diccionario Biográfico de Tamaulipas.*
DHA	Atienza, Julio de. *Nobiliario Español: Diccionario Heráldico de Apellidos.*
DME	Vilar y Pascual, Luis. *Diccionario Histórico, Genealógico y Heráldico de las familias Ilustres de la Monarquía Española.* 8 volumes.
DMG	Santiago Rodríguez, Miguel de. *Documentos y manuscritos genealógicos.*
DNC	Nieto, Rafael. *Dignidades Nobiliarias en Cuba.*
EGC	*Boletín*, Centro de Estudios Genealógicos de Córdoba.
EHG	García Carraffa, Arturo. *Enciclopedia Heráldica y Genealógica.*
FD	Larrazábal, Carlos. *Familias Dominicanas.*
FEP	Lasarte Ferreyros, Luis. *Familias Establecidas en el Perú durante la Conquista y el Virreinato.*
FH	Rodríguez, Emilio. *Familias Hispanoamericanas.*
FHJ	Castellano Sáenz Cavia, Rafael M. *Familias de Traslasierra, Jurisdicción de Córdoba.*
FOF	Rottenberg, Dan. *Finding our Fathers: A Guidebook to Jewish Genealogy.*
FPP	Cifre de Loubriel, Estela. *La formación del pueblo puertorriqueño.*
GC	Sanabria Martínez, Víctor. *Genealogía de Cartago hasta 1850.*
GDF	Dirección General de Archivos. *Guía de Fuentes para la Historia de Ibero-américa conservadas en España.*
GPC	Almelá, Juan. *Guía de Personas que cultivan la Historia de América.*

GYT Mendirichaga Cueva, Tomás. *Origen de los apellidos Garza y Treviño en Nuevo León.*

HDS Patronato Nacional de Archivos Históricos. *Secretaría de Guerra (Siglo XVIII): Hojas de Servicios de América.*

HFC Santa Cruz, Francisco Xavier. *Historia de Familias Cubanas.*

HGJ *Houston Genealogical Journal.*

IAC *Genealogía,* Revista del Instituto Argentino de Ciencias Genealógicas.

IEG *Revista,* Instituto de Estudios Genealógicos Uruguayos.

IEI *Revista,* Instituto de Estudios Iberoamericanos.

IGH *Revista,* Instituto Genealógico e Histórico Latinoamericano.

IGI International Genealogical Index, Family History Library, Salt Lake City, Utah.

IGP Lohmann, Guillermo. *Informaciones Genealógicas de Peruanos seguidos ante el Santo Oficio.*

INQ Any number of Inquisition archives.

IPI *Revista,* Instituto Peruano de Investigaciones Genealógicas.

IPR Cifre de Loubriel, Estela. *La Inmigración a Puerto Rico durante el Siglo XIX.*

ISC Maduell, Charles R., Jr. *Index of Spanish Citizens entering the port of New Orleans between January 1840 and December 1865.*

ITP Eldredge, Zoeth S. *Index to the Padrones of California.*

IVG *Revista,* Instituto Venezolano de Genealogía.

LAO Lohmann, Guillermo. *Los Americanos en las Ordenes Nobiliarias.*

LCM Robichaux, Albert J., Jr. *Louisiana Census and Militia Lists, Volume 1: 1770–1789.*

LCT Amesti, Luis. *Las Casas Troncales.*

LGT G. de Lazcano Colodrero, Arturo. *Linajes de la Gobernación del Tucumán.*

LMA Lohmann, Guillermo. *Los Ministros de la Audiencia de Lima en el reinado de los Borbones.*

LPS Journal, Las Porciones Genealogical Society.

MAR Martínez, Pablo L. *Guía Familiar de Baja California.*

MIL González, Rodolfo. *Mil Familias de Tamaulipas, Nuevo León, Coahuila y Texas.*

MNE	Fernández de Recas, Guillermo S. *Mayorazgos de la Nueva España.*
MSA	Chabot, Frederick C. *With the Makers of San Antonio.*
NCG	Espejo, Juan Luis. *Nobiliario de la Capitanía General.*
NHA	Montoto, Santiago. *Nobiliario Hispano-Americano del Siglo XVI.*
NMR	Chávez, Angélico. *New Mexico Roots.* 11 volumes.
NR	*Nuestras Raíces,* The Genealogical Society of Hispanic America.
ONM	Chávez, Angélico. *Origins of New Mexican Families.*
PA	Sierras, Eugene L. *Mexican Census—Pre-Territorial: Pimería Alta, 1801.*
PEV	López T., Olibama. *The People of "El Valle."*
POE	Arcaya, Pedro M. *Población de Origen Europeo de Coro en la Epoca Colonial.*
PSC	Nakayama, Antonio. *Pioneros Sinaloenses en California.*
RAG	*Revista,* Academia Guatemalteca de Estudios Genealógicos, Heráldicos e Históricos.
RBD	García, José Gabriel. *Rasgos Biográficos de Dominicos Célebres.*
RCA	Archivo del Ilustre y Real Colegio de Abogados de la Ciudad de México. (Microfilm 691305-691348; 694717-694722)
RCH	*Revista Chilena de Historia y Geografía.*
REH	*Revista de Estudios Históricos.*
RGB	*Revista Genealogica Brasileira.*
RGL	*Revista Genealogica Latinoamericana.*
RNG	González-Leal, Mariano. *Retoños de España en la Nueva Galicia.* 2 volumes.
ROT	University of Texas. *Residents of Texas, 1782–1836.* 3 volumes.
RSS	Maduell, Charles R. Jr., *The Romance of Spanish Surnames.*
SCP	Coker, William S. *The Spanish Censuses of Pensacola, 1784–1820.*
SMF	Northrop, Marie. *Spanish-American Families of Early California.* 2 volumes.
SNT	Costales, Piedad y Alfredo. *Los Señores Naturales de la Tierra.*

SPN   Gorden, Raymond L. *Spanish Personal Names.*

TDC   Mahy, José Antonio. *Testamentos de Camagüey.*

TMN   Ladd, Doris M. *The Mexican Nobility at Independence, 1780–1826.*

TSC   Territorial Daughters of Colorado. *Territory of Southern Colorado.* 4 volumes.

VIS   Family histories published by VISTA, and prepared by Dr. Lyman De Platt.

WAA   Duaine, Carl L. *With All Arms.*

SPANISH SURNAMES FOR
WHICH THERE EXIST HISTORIES
OR HISTORICAL SKETCHES

IN THE UNITED STATES AND LATIN AMERICA

T he following index of surnames has been gathered from the historical sketches compiled by the author from the 1,500 plus surnames noted on page 37 and from some of the histories found in the bibliography. It is limited to those sources and, for that reason, is not complete insofar as what actually exists. However, it is a good beginning. Following the index is a bibliography of histories and historical sketches. The surnames found in the titles and subtitles, and at times in the tables of contents of these works, have been indexed. This bibliography contains 1,883 titles consisting of approximately 3,000 volumes. A full index to this collection will take years to complete.

The structure of the current index notes the surname of the author, followed by a number if there exists more than one work by authors of that surname or by that particular author, followed by a list of states and/or countries for which information exists in that particular work. In the bibliography, the various books or publications have a number following the name of the author except where there is only one work by a given surname or author. As an example, under the surname **ABARCA** there exists a reference: **FUENTES 1**. This annotation refers to the first book listed in the bibliography under the author Fuentes, as follows: Fuentes, Hernán 1 "La Hidalguía en Costa Rica: Los Descendientes de Don Lucas González de Abarca," *Comunicaciones al XV Congreso Internacional de las Ciencias Genealógicas y Heráldicas 2* (1983): 91–112.

As noted above, most of the references in the index have a state or states, and/or a country or countries, listed in parentheses following the author or the author number. In some cases it could not be determined what country was the country of origin of the surname. In most cases, however, it is apparent from the author or the title. Thus, the first entry **ABANDO** refers to the surname Abando contained in the twelfth title of the author Allendesalazar and references the development of that surname in Chile.

The abbreviations used for states or countries are standard abbreviations: L.A. = Latin America; COL = Colombia; COLO = Colorado; C.R. = Costa Rica; N.M. = New Mexico; U.S. = United States. All others should be self-explanatory.

ABANDO	ALLENDESALAZAR 12 (CHILE)
ABARCA	FUENTES 1 (C.R.); GONZALEZ 13 (C.R.)
ABASCAL	NIETO 18 (PERU)
ABEYTA	MILLIGAN (N.M., COLO)
ABREU	MELGAR (L.A.)
ACEVEDO	ACEVEDO (ARG); AZAROLA 6 (CHILE); LUQUE 4 (ARG)
ACOSTA	CASTRO 18 (C.R.); FERNANDEZ 47 (ARG); GONZALEZ 9,14 (C.R.); PRADO 5 (C.R.); REVOLLO 3 (C.R.)
ACUÑA	ALLENDE 7 (CHILE); BROMLEY 2 (PERU); LUJAN 6 (C.R.); MARTINEZ 28 (CHILE); NUÑEZ (PERU)
ACHAVAL	GONZALEZ 7 (ARG)
ACHUCARRO	AZAROLA 9 (URU); CARRANDI 2 (ARG)
AGRAZ	AGRAZ 5 (MEX)
AGREDA	ROBLES 14 (ECU)
AGUADO	FERNANDEZ 76 (C.R.)
AGUERO(S)	AMEZAGA (PERU); TEJERINA 2 (ARG)
AGUILA	ZAÑARTU (CHILE)
AGUILAR	CASTRO 18 (C.R.); FERNANDEZ 47 (ARG); FERNANDEZ 1 (C.R.); MARTINEZ 30 (CHILE); MILLIGAN (N.M., COLO); QUIROS 2 (C.R.)
AGUILERA	CAMPOS 1 (CHILE); FERNANDEZ 15 (ARG); MALDONADO 1 (ARG); ROA 1 (ARG)
AGUIÑAGA	CABRERA 8 (MEX); LANCASTER 7 (MEX)
AGUIRRE	BARRIOS 2 (CHILE); CASTAÑOS 1 (MEX); LAFUENTE 7 (ARG); LARRAIN 2 (CHILE); LIRA (CHILE); SILVA 2 (CHILE); THAYER 17 (CHILE)
ALAMO(S)	ALAMOS (CHILE); STAGG (ARIZONA)
ALANIS	MARTINEZ 2 (CALIF)
ALBA	ALBA 2 (MEX); PUEYRREDON (ARG)
ALBIN	GOMENSORO (ARG)

ALBORNOZ	NIETO 42 (CUBA, GUA, MEX)
ALCALDE	CUADRA 6 (CHILE); PEREZ 5,9 (MEX); VERGARA 2 (CHILE); VILLAR 2 (CHILE)
ALCANTARA	BARRANTES 1 (C.R.)
ALEM	FERNANDEZ 43 (ARG)
ALEMPARTE	CERVERO (CHILE)
ALFARO	ALFARO 1 (C.R.)
ALFONSO	CASTRO 3A (CUBA); MENDEZ 2 (MEX)
ALIAGA	DIAZ 8 (ARG); FEP,18
ALLENDE	ALLENDE 3,5,7 (CHILE); DAVILA 6 (MEX); RUBIO 5 (MEX); TEJERINA 4 (ARG)
ALLENDE-SALAZAR	ALLENDE 4,5,7 (ARG, CHILE); ALLENDE-SALAZAR 3,14,15,24 (CHILE); DAVILA 6 (MEX)
ALLO	CASTRO 3A (CUBA)
ALMADA	STAGG (ARIZONA)
ALMAZAN	MILLIGAN (N.M., COLO)
ALMESTO	VILLASEÑOR 5 (MEX)
ALMONACID	GONZALEZ 4 (CHILE)
ALSINA	ALSINA (ARG)
ALTHAUS	BARREDA 2 (PERU)
ALTOAGUIRRE	ESTRADA (ARG)
ALURRALDE	ALURRALDE (ARG); DOMINGUEZ (ARG)
ALVA	ALBA (MEX)
ALVARADO	BARRANTES 2 (C.R.); FERNANDEZ 10,11,67 (C.R.); GUARDA (PERU); GONZALEZ 12 (C.R.); KEITH (C.R.); LUJAN 7 (C.R.); PARDO (MEX); PRADO 2,6 (C.R.); RUJULA 3 (L.A.); SANCHEZ 10 (ARG)
ALVAREDA	CABALLERO (ARG)
ALVAREZ	ACEVEDO (ARG); AZAROLA 6 (CHILE); BINAYAN 2 (ARG); GARCIA 6 (TEXAS); GONZALEZ 7 (ARG); NIETO 1,2,69 (CUBA); ROBLES 9 (ECU); SALAS (VEN); THAYER 24 (CHILE); VIDELA 2 (PERU)
ALVAREZ ABREU	MELGAR (L.A.)
ALVISO	PONSFORD 1 (CALIF)
ALZAGA	GANDIA 6 (ARG); URQUIZA (ARG)
ALZAYBAR	AZAROLA 9 (URU)

AMADO	AMADO (MEX)
AMADOR	WAID (CALIF)
AMARAL	MARTINEZ 39 (CHILE)
AMERLINCK	AMERLINCK 1 (MEX)
AMIGO	AMIGO (C.R.)
AMPUERO	HART (PERU)
AMUNATEGUI	CUADRA 5 (CHILE); SELVA (ARG)
ANCHORENA	SEBRELI (ARG)
ANAYA	ANAYA (MEX); DAVILA 2 (MEX); MILLIGAN (N.M., COLO)
ANDONAEGUI	ESPINOSA 2 (CHILE, ARG)
ANDRADE(S)	ANDRADE 1 (ECU)
ANGULO	ACUÑA (CHILE); YSABEL (PERU)
ANTUÑA	SILVA 4 (URU)
AÑORGA	LANCASTER 4 (MEX)
APARICIO	APARICIO 18 (GUA); MARTINEZ 11 (GUA); MONTUFAR 1 (GUA); NIETO 31 (CUBA, GUAT)
APESTEGUI	FERNANDEZ 60 (C.R.)
ARA	CUNEO 3 (PERU)
ARAGON(A)	ALLENDESALAZAR 22 (CHILE); CUEVAS (MEX) FERNANDEZ 37 (ARG); GOMEZ 1 (CHILE); MOLINA 4,7 (ARG); NIETO 10 (CUBA); OTAROLA 5 (ARG)
ARANDA	CHAUNY (PERU)
ARANGO	PUENTE (PERU)
ARAUZ	MORENO 2,3 (ARG)
ARBAROLA	FERNANDEZ 78 (C.R.)
ARBOLEDA	ARBOLEDA (COL)
ARBURDA	CASTRO 7 (C.R.)
ARCAYA	LARRAIN 7 (CHILE, PERU)
ARCHER	NIETO 42 (CUBA, GUA, MEX)
ARCHULETA	MILLIGAN (N.M., COLO)
ARDUZ	COSTA 4 (BOL)
ARELLANO	GOLDBERG (MEX); MILLIGAN (N.M., COLO); MORENO 4 (ARG); ROBLES 10 (ECU); RUBIO 1 (MEX); VISO (ARG)
ARENA(S)	MORALES 5 (ARG); MUJICA 3 (PERU)

AREVALO(S)	CASTRO 18 (C.R.); PRADO 5 (C.R.); REVOLLO 3 (C.R.)
ARGERICH	MASSINI (ARG)
ARGUELLES	TORIJA (MEX)
ARGUELLO(S)	VISO (ARG)
ARGUIBEL	MOYANO 4 (ARG)
ARISTEGUI	SUCRE 3 (VEN)
ARISTIGUIETA	SUCRE 3 (VEN)
ARIZA	APARICIO 8 (GUA)
ARIZAGA	APARICIO 8 (GUA); ARIZAGA (ECU); ROMEO (ECU)
ARIZPE	DURON (MEX, TEXAS)
ARIZTIA	IBARRA (CHILE)
ARMENTEROS	SANTA CRUZ 3 (CUBA)
ARRIAGADA	AMESTI 3 (CHILE)
ARTIGA(S)	AZAROLA 9 (URU); CASTRO 1 (ARG); FERNANDEZ 20 (URU); FERREIRA 2 (URU); LLAMBIAS (URU); THEVE-NET (URU)
ARTOLA	DELAUNET 3 (CHILE)
ARZU	APARICIO 13 (GUA)
ARREDONDO	BACA (PERU)
ARRIAGADA	AMESTI 3 (CHILE)
ASPILLAGA	GILBERT (PERU)
ASTABURUAGA	IBARRA (CHILE); ZAÑARTU (CHILE)
ASTOUL	VILLANUEVA 1 (U.S.)
ATENCIO	MILLIGAN (N.M., COLO)
AUBAIN	SADOUS (ARG)
AUBONE	MARTINEZ 15 (ARG)
AULESTIA	ALLENDESALADAR 1 (CHILE)
AUTRAN	NIETO 30 (CUBA, ESPAÑA)
AVELLANEDA	SANCHEZ 2 (ARG); URRUTIA 2 (CHILE, ESPAÑA)
AVILA	MILLIGAN (N.M., COLO); GONZALEZ 7 (ARG); PALOMINO 5 (MEX)
AVILES	ROBLES 9 (ECU); VEGAS (PERU); VIGIL (FLORIDA)
AYALA	AYALA (PANAMA)
AYERZA	FRIAS (ARG)
AZAROLA	AZAROLA 2 (URU)

AZCUENAGA	MAKINTACH (ARG)
AZCUENGA	VITON (ARG)
AZOCA	FERNANDEZ 39 (CHILE)
AZUA	GOMEZ 1 (CHILE)
AZUOLA	FERNANDEZ 57 (C.R.)
BACA	MILLIGAN (N.M., COLO); SOLANO (CALIF)
BACHILLER	CASTRO 3A (CUBA)
BAEZ	BAEZ 1 (VEN)
BALCARCE	BERNARD (ARG)
BALDARES	FERNANDEZ 74 (C.R.)
BALLI	GARCIA 9 (MEX, TEXAS)
BANDA	MOLINA 5 (ARG)
BAÑUELOS	PALOMINO 1 (MEX)
BAQUEDANO	DIAZ 22 (CHILE)
BARAGAN	CABRERA 1 (MEX)
BARAHONA	EYZAGUIRRE 3 (CHILE); OPAZO 1 (CHILE)
BARAJA(S)	BLINN (ARG)
BARANDA	PALOMINO 1 (MEX)
BARCELO	DURAÑONA 4 (ARG)
BARKER	VALLADARES (CHILE)
BARNOYA	BARNOYA 1 (GUA)
BARRA	GONZALEZ 4 (CHILE); LEON 3,4 (MEX)
BARRAGAN	CABRERA 1 (MEX)
BARRANTES	BARRANTES 1,5 (C.R.)
BARREDA	APARICIO 16 (GUA); SWAYNE (PERU)
BARRENECHEA	BARRENECHEA (PERU)
BARRERA(S)	GARZA (TEXAS); ROA 2 (CHILE)
BARROETA	GONZALEZ 12 (C.R.); KEITH (C.R.)
BARROS	ALLENDESALAZAR 4 (CHILE); BARROS (CHILE)
BAS	VISO (ARG)
BASAH	VALGOMA 2 (ESPAÑA)
BASTIDAS	CAMPOS 1 (CHILE); UTRERA 1 (R.D.); WAID (CALIF)
BASUALDO	FERNANDEZ 16 (ARG)
BAZAN	ALLENDESALAZAR 6 (PERU); MARTINEZ 9 (ARG); ZAVALIA (ARG)
BECK	BARNARD (ARG)

BECQUER	NIETO 17 (CUBA)
BEECHE	DIAZ 2 (C.R.)
BEITIA	CASTRO 3A (CUBA)
BELGRANO	TROSTINE 3 (ARG)
BELTRAN	MARIN 1 (MEX); SANTANA (MEX)
BENAGIAR	VALGOMA 3 (CHILE)
BENAVIDES(Z)	ANDRADE 1 (ECU); MILLIGAN (N.M., COLO); MOLINA 9 (ARG); PRADO 2 (C.R.); GARZA (TEXAS)
BENET	FERNANDEZ 58 (C.R.)
BENITEZ	BENITEZ 3 (MEX)
BEQUER	NIETO 17 (CUBA)
BERASTEGUI	CABRERA 3 (MEX)
BERECEDO	EYZAGUIRRE 6 (CHILE)
BERMUDES	CASTRO 3A (CUBA)
BERNABE	GUARDA 1 (CHILE)
BERNAL	MILLIGAN (N.M., COLO); PONSFORD 2 (CALIF); SOBERANES 1 (CALIF); WAID (CALIF)
BERNARD	BARNARD (ARG)
BERNEDO	BERNEDO (PERU)
BERRIO(S)	MENDIVE (PERU); TERRY 2 (PERU)
BERRO	BERRO (URU)
BERROETA	THAYER 23 (CHILE)
BERROTARAN	MAYOL (ARG)
BERTENDOÑA	THAYER 11 (CHILE)
BESANILLA	COO 3 (CHILE)
BESELAMANO	VELEZ (PERU)
BESSE DE MORIAN	ROBLES 14 (ECU)
BETANCOURT	MARTINEZ 13,20 (ARG)
BILBAO	REYES 1 (CHILE)
BLANCO	FERNANDEZ 79 (CHILE); LUJAN 8 (C.R.); QUIROS 6 (C.R.); WALKER (CHILE)
BLAS	MARTINEZ 2 (CALIF)
BOADO	VON DER HEYDE 4 (ARG)
BOBADILLA	VILLANUEVA 2 (PERU)
BOCANEGRA	BLOOM (N.M.); NIETO 32 (MEX)
BOHORQUEZ	MARTINEZ 2 (CALIF); NIETO 9 (CUBA, MEX)

BOLAÑO(S)	FERNANDEZ 56 (C.R.)
BOLIO	CASTRO 19 (MEX)
BOLIVAR	CRESPO 1 (COL); FUENTES 4 (VEN); SUCRE 2 (VEN); TALLERI (VEN)
BONACHEA	CARBONELL (CUBA)
BONAPARTE	NIETO 33 (CUBA)
BONILLA	FERNANDEZ 74 (C.R.); SERRANO 1 (C.R.)
BORJA(S)	GANGOTENA 2 (ECU)
BORREGO	CASTRO 3A (CUBA)
BOTELLO	MENDIRICHAGA 1,2 (MEX)
BOTEROS	BERNAL 2 (BOL)
BOTSADILLA	VILLANUEVA 2 (PERU)
BOUTHILLIER	WAID (CALIF)
BOZA	JENSEN 3 (PERU)
BRACAMONTES	AMAYA 3 (MEX); CASTAÑOS 4 (MEX)
BRAGANZA	FREITAS (ARG); NIETO 25 (MEX)
BRAVO	ALLENDE 1 (ARG, CHILE, BOL, PERU)
BRICEÑO	DAVILA 30,34,35 (VEN)
BRIONES	APARICIO 15 (GUA); SANTANDER (ARG)
BRIZUELA	APARICIO 15 (GUA); COGHLAN (ARG)
BROWN	BROWN (MEX, TEXAS); OTAROLA 6 (ARG)
BRUM	DELGADO 1 (URU)
BUENDIA	BROMLEY 1 (PERU)
BUENTELLO	MENDIRICHAGA 1,2 (MEX)
BULNES	BULNES (ARG); ESPEJO 9 (CHILE); VALGOMA 3 (CHILE); VISO (ARG)
BUONAFEDE	ORDOÑEZ 2 (ELS, GUA, NIC)
BURGOS	BUSCA 1 (CHILE); FERNANDEZ 41 (ARG)
BUSTAMANTE	AGUIAR 1 (URU); APARICIO 6 (GUA); MUJICA 1 (PERU); SANCHEZ 10 (ARG); ZENARRUZA 4 (ARG)
BUSTILLO(S)	ROBLES 6 (MEX)
BUSTOS	MILLIGAN (N.M., COLO)
CABALLON	CASTRO 9 (C.R.)
CABARRUS	APARICIO 9 (GUA)
CABELLO	NIETO 34 (CUBA)
CABEZAS	FERNANDEZ 47 (ARG)

CABRERA	ALLENDE 3 (CHILE); APARICIO 11 (GUA); ARENAS 2 (ARG); ARENAS 3 (ARG); ARENAS 4 (ARG); ARENAS 6 (ARG); CABRERA 5 (MEX); MARTINEZ 10 (ARG); MASSINI (ARG); MILLIGAN (N.M., COLO); ROMAN 2 (ARG); TERRY 3 (PERU); VIDELA 2 (ARG); VILLANUEVA (PERU)
CACERES	FREUNDT 3 (PERU); MARQUEZ 4 (ARG)
CADIMO	MILLIGAN (N.M., COLO)
CAICEDO	URICOECHEA (COL)
CAJAL	MARTINEZ 36 (CHILE)
CAJIGAL	GONZALEZ 5 (CHILE)
CALAR	NIETO 3 (MEX)
CAMACHO	DAVILA 8 (MEX)
CAMEJO	AZAROLA 9 (URU)
CAMERA	IBARGUREN 1 (ARG)
CAMET	OTAROLA 6 (ARG)
CAMINO	FONTECILLA (CHILE)
CAMPA	FALLA 4 (GUA)
CAMPABADAL	FERNANDEZ 56 (C.R.)
CAMPECHE	GEIGEL (P.R.)
CAMPILLO	BUSTOS (ARG)
CAMPO	BARREIRO 1 (ARG)
CAMPOFRIO	ESPEJO 11 (CHILE)
CAMPOY	ACOSTA 1 (MEX)
CAMUS	CAMUS (CHILE)
CAÑAS	CAÑAS (C.R.)
CAÑEDO(S)	PALOMINO 4 (MEX); SANTOSCOY (MEX)
CAPDEVILA	CEBALLOS (ARG)
CARBAJO	PAZOS (PERU)
CARBONELL	CASANOVA 3 (P.R.)
CARDENAS	CASTRO 3A (CUBA)
CARDONA	FERNANDEZ 56 (C.R.)
CARAZO	CABRERA 9 (MEX); FERNANDEZ 63 (C.R.)
CARO	HOLGUIN (COL)
CARRANZA	NIETO 8 (MEX)
CARRASCO	MOLINA 11 (CHILE)
CARRENO	VEGAS (PERU)

CARRER	CASTELLON (CHILE)
CARRERA	DIAZ 14 (CHILE); ONDARZA 2 (CHILE); TEJERINA 3 (ARG)
CARRILLO	DAVILA 17 (MEX); GALLAGHER (CALIF); GONZALEZ 15 (C.R.); MCGINTY (COL); MARTINEZ 2 (COL); NIETO 42 (CUBA); PRADO 3 (C.R.)
CARRIO	MOREYRA 3 (PERU)
CARRION	GANGOTENA (ECU)
CARRIZOSA	NIETO 67 (CUBA)
CARVAJAL	ESPEJO 11 (CHILE); FIGUEROA 2 (L.A.); MILLIGAN (N.M., COLO); TORO 1 (MEX)
CARVALLO	GUARDA 1 (CHILE); LARRAIN 3 (CHILE)
CASCO	MOLINA 7 (ARG)
CASTAÑEDA	FERNANDEZ 8 (C.R.)
CASTAÑO DE SOSA	DURON (MEX, TEXAS)
CASTAÑOS	CASTAÑOS 1 (MEX)
CASTELLI	OLMEDO (ARG)
CASTELLON	BROMLEY 1 (PERU)
CASTELLS	CASTELLS (URU)
CASTELO	NIETO 37 (MEX)
CASTEX	RICHIERI 2 (ARG)
CASTILLA	DAVILA 4 (MEX)
CASTILLO	APARICIO 2 (MEX); FERNANDEZ 32 (MEX); JIMENEZ 3 (C.R.); MILLIGAN (N.M., COLO)
CASTRILLON	PUENTE (PERU)
CASTRO	BAEZ 3 (VEN, ESPAÑA); CASTRO 3A (CUBA); CASTRO 4 (CALIF); CASTRO 5 (CALIF); CASTRO 16 (C.R.); CUADRA 2 (CHILE); DIAZ 8,9 (ARG); MALO 2 (MEX); MARTINEZ 2 (CALIF); MILLIGAN (N.M., COLO); SOBERANES 2 (CALIF); TORRE 2,4 (ARG, ESPAÑA); TROSTINE 1 (ARG); URICOECHEA (COL); WAID (CALIF)
CAVAZOS	BALLI (MEX, TEXAS)
CAVIA	CASTELLANO 2 (ARG)
CELIS	BUSCA 1 (CHILE); CELIS (CHILE); DAVILA 9 (MEX)

CENTURION	FERNANDEZ 17 (ARG); LABOUGLE 1 (ARG); PERAZZO (ARG)
CEPEDA	PEÑA 4 (CHILE)
CERDA	LARRAIN 1 (CHILE); MANNS 2 (CHILE)
CERRO	FALLA 3 (ELS)
CERVANTES	ALGARA (MEX); DAVILA 8,10,23 (MEX); NIETO 56 (MEX)
CESPEDES	FERNANDEZ 56 (C.R.); PEREZ 7 (L.A.)
CEYES	IUSEM (ARG)
CHACON	NIETO 36 (CUBA)
CHAMIER	FERNANDEZ 61,62 (C.R.)
CHAMORRO	ALVAREZ 1 (NIC)
CHAPA	BROWN (MEX, TEXAS)
CHAVEZ	CHAVEZ 3 (PERU); MILLIGAN (N.M., COLO); MORALES 3 (BOL)
CHOPITEA	LIRA 2 (CHILE)
CHOQUEHUANCA	PUERTOS (PERU)
CHUQUIHUANCA	TORRES 2 (PERU)
CIENFUEGOS	ORTIZ 3 (COL)
CLAVIJERO	CASTRO 3 (MEX)
CLEVES	CLEVES (COL)
COELHO	OTAROLA 6 (ARG)
COELLO	ROBLES 19 (ECU)
COLCHADO	NIETO 66 (MEX)
COLIO	DAVILA 15 (MEX), 28 (CUBA)
COLON	FIGUEROA 2 (L.A.); NIETO 12 (GUA), 40 (CUBA)
COLONNA	BINAYAN 1 (ARG)
COLLADO	FERNANDEZ 58 (C.R.)
CONGET	FERNANDEZ 45 (ARG)
CONSUEGRA	SERRANO 1 (C.R.)
CONTRERAS	GUTIERREZ (MEX)
CORBALAN	COMADURAN (ARG, CHILE)
CORDERO	DARIO 3 (VEN); ROBLES 14 (ECU); SUAREZ 6 (VEN)
CORDOBA	NIETO 39 (CUBA); ZAVALA 1 (PERU)
CORDOVA	MILLIGAN (N.M., COLO)
CORDOVES	MOLINA 8 (ARG)

CORNEJO	CORNEJO 1,4 (ARG), 2,3 (PERU)
CORONADO	BLOOM (N.M.); CASTRO 21 (C.R.); ESPINOSA 1 (MEX); FERNANDEZ 13,70,76 (C.R.,MEX); FUENTES 2 (C.R.); ESPINOSA 1 (MEX); LUJAN 1 (C.R.); REVOLLO 2 (C.R.)
CORRAL	FERNANDEZ 78 (C.R.)
CORRALES	BARRANTES 3 (C.R.)
CORREA	CARBO 1 (ARG); COMADURAN (ARG); DIAZ 13 (URU); LORENZO (URU)
CORSO	BACA (PERU); CASTRO 8 (C.R.)
CORTES	CUEVAS 1 (MEX); ESCUDERO (MEX); FERNANDEZ 26 (MEX); GOLDBERG (MEX); RIOLO (ARG); ROMERO 3 (MEX); VALGOMA 1 (MEX)
CORTINA	CORTINA (MEX)
COSBAN	LIS (ARG)
COSIO	ESPINO (MEX); NIETO 41 (CUBA)
COSTILLA	DAVILA 16,26 (MEX); DE LA FUENTE (MEX)
COTA	CANTERA (C.A.); MARTINEZ 2 (CALIF); WAID (CALIF)
COX	MIERS (CHILE)
CRUZ	MILLIGAN (N.M., COLO); ZAÑARTU (CHILE)
CUADRA	CUADRA 7 (PERU)
CUCALON	CUCALON (ECU)
CUCULLA	CUCULLA (ARG)
CUELLAR	CASTAÑOS 5 (MEX); CUELLAR (MEX)
CUETO	QUIROS 2 (C.R.)
CUEVAS	PEREIRA 2 (ARG); THAYER 18 (CHILE); ZAÑARTU (CHILE)
DANIEL	ALLENDE 6 (FRANCIA)
DARACT	SOSA 1 (ARG)
DAROCH	MUJICA 8 (CHILE)
DAVALOS	CASTAÑOS 4 (MEX); ROSAS 1 (PERU)
DAVILA	CANTERA (C.A.); DAVILA 8,26 (MEX)
DE LA BANDA	MOLINA 5 (ARG)
DE LA BANDERA	MOREYRA 3 (PERU); ROA 2 (CHILE)
DE LA BARRA	LEON 3,4 (MEX)
DE LA CAMARA	IBARGUREN 1 (ARG)
DE LA CAMPA	FALLA 4 (GUA)

DE LA CANAL	MALO 5 (MEX)
DE LA CEJA	PALACIOS (COL)
DE LA CERDA	LARRAIN 1 (CHILE); MANNS 2 (CHILE); VALGOMA 3 (ARG)
DE LA CRUZ	RAMIREZ 3 (MEX)
DE LA CUEVA	AGRIZ 4 (MEX); APARICIO 7 (GUA); MOLINA 10 (CHILE); PEREIRA 2 (ARG)
DE LA ESQUINA	FERNANDEZ 64 (C.R.)
DE LA FLOR	CASTRO 14 (C.R.); ROBLES 12 (ECU); VILLAVICENCIO (C.R.)
DE LA FUENTE	LA FUENTE 3 (ARG)
DE LA GANDARA	NIETO 47 (CUBA)
DE LA GARZA	BALLI (MEX, TEXAS); GARZA (MEX, TEXAS)
DE LA GUARDIA	FERNANDEZ 5 (C.R.)
DE LA HAYA	ALBA 1 (C.R.)
DE LA HUERTA	SANCHEZ 5,6 (CHILE)
DE LA LANZA	MONTAÑO 1 (L.A.)
DE LA LLAVE	TORIJA (MEX, U.S.)
DE LA MADRID	MORENO 3 (ARG)
DE LA MOTA	JAUREGUI 1 (ARG)
DE LA PEÑA	CABRERA 2 (MEX); PEÑA 2,3 (ARG, CHILE); VILLASEÑOR 3 (MEX)
DE LA PEZA	MALO 4 (MEX)
DE LA PLAZA	EZCURRA (ARG)
DE LA RENTA	LLUCH (P.R.)
DE LA ROCHA	DE LA ROCHA (NIC)
DE LA SIERRA	JURADO 2 (ECU)
DE LA TORRE	COSTA 1 (BOL); MUJICA 5 (PERU); TORRES 6 (ARG)
DE LA VARA	CABRERA 3 (MEX)
DE LA VEGA	JURADO 1 (S.A.); LASO 1 (CHILE); LOHMANN 3 (PERU); RUBIO 8 (MEX); VEGA (CHILE)
DE LAS HEVAS	MARTINEZ 35 (CHILE)
DELGADO	APARICIO 12 (GUA)
DE LOS OLIVOS	MARTINEZ 30 (CHILE)
DE LOS RIOS	NIETO 50 (CUBA); VICUÑA 2 (CHILE)
DEL PINO	VALGOMA 3 (CHILE)
DEL RIO	RIO 1,2 (L.A.)

DEL VALLE	FERNANDEZ 73 (MEX)
DE SOTO	SOLAR (FLORIDA)
DIAZ	APARICIO 2 (MEX); BAEZ 2 (VEN); MARTINEZ 14 (ARG); ONDARZA 2 (CHILE); OTAROLA 3 (ARG); RODRIGUEZ 13 (BOL); TORRES 6 (ARG)
DIAZ DEL CASTILLO	FERNANDEZ 32 (MEX)
DIAZ GRANADOS	FERNANDEZ 56 (C.R.)
DIAZ HERRERA	MOLINA 1 (ARG); NIETO 59 (CUBA)
DIEZ	COSTA 5 (BOL)
DOLORES	CARDOZO (MEX)
DOMINGUEZ	DOMINGUEZ (CHILE); MILLIGAN (N.M., COLO)
DONOSO	GANGOTENA 1 (ECU)
DORANTES	NIETO 8 (MEX)
DORIA	COGHLAN (ARG)
DUBLE	DUBLE 2 (CHILE)
DULZAIDES	CASTRO 3A (CUBA)
DUQUE	URICOECHEA (L.A.)
DURAN	GUIRDALEAL (GUA); MILLIGAN (N.M., COLO)
ECHANDI	QUIROS 5 (C.R.)
ECHARTE	CASTRO 3A (CUBA)
ECHAURREN	(Unk.) 1 (ARG)
ECHAVARRIA	LUJAN 3 (C.R.)
ECHEBARNE	BERRO (URU)
ECHENIQUE	GUARDA 2 (CHILE)
ECHEVERZ	FOZ (L.A.)
EGUIGURA	ARRAYA 2 (CHILE)
EGUINO	COSTA 3,5 (BOL)
EGURBIDE	FERNANDEZ 57 (C.R.)
EIJO	MARTINEZ 17 (ARG)
ELESPURU	BARREDA 1 (PERU)
ELIZONDO	GARZA (TEXAS)
EMPARAN	B (CHILE)
ENCALADA	VALGOMA 3 (CHILE)
ENCINA	VALLADARES (CHILE)

ENCIO	ENCIO (ARG)
ERCILLA	ALLENDESALAZAR 10 (CHILE)
ERRAZU	GUARDA 2 (CHILE)
ERRAZURIZ	AMUNATEGUI 2 (CHILE); DIAZ 24 (CHILE); ZAÑARTU (CHILE)
ESCALADA	FERNANDEZ 41 (ARG); MARTINEZ 16 (ARG); MORENO 4 (ARG)
ESCALANTE	LUJAN 4 (C.R.)
ESCOBA	THAYER 12 (CHILE)
ESCOBAR	CASTRO 3A (CUBA); ESCOBAR (L.A.)
ESPARZA	MILLIGAN (N.M., COLO)
ESPEJO	ESPEJO 7,8 (CHILE)
ESPINACH	ESPINACH (C.R.); FERNANDEZ 56 (C.R.)
ESPINOSA	LOHMANN 4,5 (PERU); MARTINEZ 2 (CALIF), 28,31 (CHILE); MILLIGAN (N.M., COLO); PEREDA (L.A.)
ESQUIVEL	CASTRO 6 (C.R.); PRADO 1 (C.R.)
ESTELLA	JAUREGUI 1 (ARG)
ESTRADA	CASTRO 24 (C.R.); BERNARD (ARG); FERNANDEZ 24 (MEX); URICOECHEA (L.A.)
EVANS	OPAZO 3 (CHILE)
EYZAGUIRRE	EYZAGUIRRE 2,4 (CHILE)
FABRE	RICHIERI 1 (ARG)
FACIO	FERNANDEZ 56 (C.R.)
FACUNDO	DEVOTO (ARG)
FALCON	GARCIA 7 (MEX, TEXAS)
FALLA	FALLA 1 (CUBA)
FARNESE	SALAZAR 3 (L.A.)
FAURA	NIETO 46 (CUBA)
FEBRES-CORDERO	DARIO 3 (VEN); ROBLES 14 (ECU); SUAREZ 6 (VEN)
FEIJOO	PEREZ 5 (ARG)
FELIU	FIGUEROA 10 (CHILE); MATURANA 1 (CHILE)
FERNANDEZ	ALBA 1 (C.R.); BACA (PERU); BAUDEAN 1 (URU); CARBO 2 (ARG); CORNEJO 1,2,3 (ARG); DAVILA 12 (MEX); DOERSAM (ARG); FERNANDEZ 9,70 (C.R.), 23 (URU);

GOMEZ 1 (CHILE); GONZALEZ 10 (C.R.);
JIMENEZ 2 (COL); LABOUGLE 2 (ARG);
LUJAN 6 (C.R.); MARTINEZ 2 (CALIF), 7
(ARG); MILLIGAN (N.M., COLO);
MONTUFAR 3 (C.R.); NIETO 41 (CUBA);
PEÑA 2 (ARG, CHILE); QUIROS 1,4 (C.R.);
SALAZAR 1 (C.R.); URRUTIA 4 (CHILE);
UTRERA 1 (R.D.); VILLANUEVA 2 (PERU);
ZAVALA 1 (PERU)

FERNANDEZ DAVILA FERNANDEZ 29 (PERU), 78 (MEX)

FERNANDEZ DE HIJAR AMAYA 3 (MEX)

FERNANDEZ DE LIMA CABERA 1 (MEX)

FERNANDEZ DE SOTOMAYOR JIMENEZ 2 (COL)

FERNANDEZ DE TEJADA FERNANDEZ 79 (CHILE)

FERNANDEZ VAL FERNANDEZ 6,12,52 (C.R.), 78 (MEX)

FERRAZ SALAZAR 1 (C.R.)

FERREIRA FERREIRA 2 (URU); LUQUE 4 (ARG)

FIERRO FIERRO (ARG); MORENO 5 (ARG)

FIGUEROA ARBOLEDA (COL); CASTAÑOS 5 (MEX);
CAMUS (CHILE); FIGUEROA 6 (C.R.);
FRIAS (ARG); VIDELA 2 (ARG);
VILLASEÑOR 5 (MEX)

FILIANO IBARGUREN 2 (ARG)

FLORES ARMELLA (MEX); AZAROLA 5 (CHILE);
FLOREZ 2 (L.A.); VICUÑA 2 (CH)

FLOREZ FLOREZ 1 (CHILE); URICOECHEA (L.A.)

FONROUGE SAGUIER 1 (ARG)

FONTALBA DE ANGULO ACUÑA (CHILE)

FONTECILLA SANCHEZ 4 (CHILE)

FONSECA QUIROS 12 (C.R.)

FOSTER REYES 5 (CHILE, U.S.)

FRANCO DAVILA 11 (MEX); NIETO 65 (MEX)

FREIRE MUJICA 11 (CHILE)

FREITES SALAS (VEN)

FREUNDT	FREUNDT 1 (PERU)
FREYRE	
DE ANDRADE	CASTRO 3A (CUBA)
FRIAS	FRIAS (ARG)
FUENMAYOR	UTRERA 1 (R.D.)
FUENTE	LAFUENTE 3 (ARG)
FUENZALIDA	FUENZALIDA 3 (CHILE); THAYER 11 (CHILE)
FUNES	LUQUE 2 (ARG); MORALES 5 (ARG); PEÑA 3 (ARG)
GAETE	JAUREGUI 2 (ARG)
GAINZA	FIGUEROA 1 (GUA)
GALINDO	SOBERANES 3 (CALIF)
GALVEZ	ESTEVEZ (CUBA); MARTINEZ 18 (ARG)
GALLARDO	GALLARDO (CHILE); ZAYAS 1 (MEX)
GALLEGO(S)	CRESPO 5 (ARG); MILLIGAN (N.M., COLO); PANESSO (COL)
GALLEGUILLO	BARRIOS 1 (CHILE)
GAMBIA	FERNANDEZ 28 (MEX)
GAMBOA	ALLENDESALAZAR 2 (CHILE); THAYER 11 (CHILE)
GAMEZ	PEREIRA 2 (ARG)
GANDARA	NIETO 47 (CUBA)
GANDIA	GANDIA 1 (ARG)
GANOZA	RAMON 3 (CHILE)
GARAY	CALVO 6 (ARG); CRUZ (ARG); VAZQUEZ 1 (CHILE)
GARAYCOA	ROBLES 11 (ECU)
GARCES	GARCES (CHILE)
GARCIA	(Unk.) 1 (ARG); AMUNATEGUI 4 (CHILE), 5 (CHILE); CAMPOS 4 (URU), 5 (URU); COO 1 (ARG, CHILE, URU); GONZALEZ 9 (C.R.); LOBUGLIO (CALIF); MILLIGAN (N.M., COLO); MONTANO 1 (L.A.); NIETO 13 (MEX); ROBLES 18 (GUA); RUJULA 4 (CHILE); SANCHEZ 5,6 (CHILE); TRAZEGNIES 2,3 (PERU); URICOECHEA (L.A.)
GARIBAY	DAVILA 9 (MEX)
GARIBI	DAVILA 1,7,8,18,26 (MEX)

GARLAND	BARREDA 4 (PERU)
GARRETON	THAYER 3 (CHILE)
GARRIGOS	VON 1,2 (ARG)
GARRO	CASTRO 3A (CUBA)
GARZA	BROWN (MEX, TEXAS); GARCIA 7 (MEX, TEXAS); GARZA (MEX, TEXAS); MENDIRICHAGA 4,5 (MEX, TEXAS)
GARZON	VISO (ARG)
GAZCON	OTAROLA 6 (ARG)
GAZTELU	ROBLES 18 (GUA)
GEISSE	GUERIN (PERU)
GIL	PRADO 2 (C.R.)
GILES	CRESPO 8 (ARG)
GIOL	ALSINA (ARG)
GIRADO	RIOLO (ARG)
GODOY	MILLIGAN (N.M., COLO)
GOLFIN	BARRANTES 2 (C.R.); CASTRO 22 (C.R.)
GOMAR	PEREZ 5 (ARG)
GOMENSORO	GOMENSORO 4 (ARG, URU)
GOMEZ	ALLENDESALAZAR 19 (CHILE); APARICIO 16 (GUA); CASTRO 3A (CUBA); ELLIS 1 (URU); FERNANDEZ 18,19 (ARG); GOMEZ 1 (CHILE); MILLIGAN (N.M., COLO); SUAREZ 2 (ARG); THAYER 11 (CHILE); TORRES 8 (MEX); URICOECHEA 1 (L.A.); VAAMANDO (L.A.); VIDELA 5 (ARG)
GONZALEZ	ALFARO 2 (C.R.); AMESTI 1 (CHILE); DAVILA 12 (MEX); FUENTES 1 (C.R.); GONZALEZ 7 (ARG), 13 (C.R.); IBARGUREN 2 (ARG); LANCASTER 1 (GUA); MILLIGAN (N.M., COLO); PACHECO 2 (VEN); PALOMINO 3 (MEX); PRADO 7 (C.R.); SUAREZ 2 (ARG); URICOECHEA (L.A.)
GONZALEZ DE ACOSTA	FERNANDEZ 47 (ARG)
GORDILLO	SERRANO 2 (ARG)
GOVIN	CASTRO 3A (CUBA)
GOYA	GOYA (MEX)
GOYENA	ROBLES 18 (GUA)
GOYENECHE	GUARDA 5 (CHILE)

GRANADOS	FERNANDEZ 56 (C.R.)
GRANDA	TRAZEGNIES 4 (PERU)
GRANJA	VALGOMA 3 (CHILE)
GRAW	ALAMO (MEX)
GRIEGO	MILLIGAN (N.M., COLO); THAYER 11 (CHILE)
GUADALCAZAR	ALIAGA 1 (PERU)
GUAJARDO	GUAJARDO (C.R.)
GUAL	GARAY 1 (ECU)
GUARCO	QUIROS 11 (C.R.)
GUERRA	GONZALEZ 20 (MEX); MENDIRICHAGA 1 (MEX, TEXAS)
GUERRERO	MILLIGAN (N.M., COLO)
GUEVARA	ERRENDERI (CHILE); MOYANO 3 (ARG)
GUILIZASTI	NIETO 9 (CUBA)
GUIÑAZU	DIAZ 3 (ARG)
GUTIERREZ	ANAYA (MEX); APARICIO 17 (GUA); BERNARD (ARG); DAVILA 2,17 (MEX); DOERSAM (ARG); ESPEJO 8 (CHILE); FALLA 1 (CUBA); GUTIERREZ 2 (MEX); MARTINEZ 2 (CALIF); MILLIGAN (N.M., COLO); PRADO 11 (C.R.); ROBLES 6 (MEX); VICUÑA 2 (CHILE)
GUTIKE	AMESTI 3 (CHILE)
GUZMAN	LANCASTER 8 (MEX); MARIN 1 (MEX); MARTIN 3 (ARG); OLMOS 1 (ARG); OTAROLA 3 (ARG); PARDO (L.A.); QUIROS 8 (C.R.); ROBLES 4 (ECU); ROJAS 2 (ARG); SANTANA (MEX); SERRANO 3 (ARG)
HACK	MORA (C.R.)
HAEDO	ARENAS 1 (ARG); AZAROLA 9 (URU)
HELGUERO	MURGA (ARG)
HENRIQUEZ	GUARDA 4 (CHILE)
HERAS	DOMINGUEZ 1 (CHILE); ESCOBOSA (MEX)
HEREDIA	CRISOSTOMO (CHILE); LOBUGLIO (CALIF); URICOECHEA (L.A.)
HEREÑU	CARRANZA (ARG)
HERGO	VITON (ARG)
HERNANDEZ	MORENO 5 (ARG); RAMON 2 (CHILE)
HERNANDEZ SOTO	CABRERA 5 (MEX)

HERRERA	AZAROLA 9 (URU); HACK 1,2 (CALIF); MARTIN 1,2 (ARG); MILLIGAN (N.M., COLO); MOLINA 1 (ARG); NIETO 59 (CUBA); ORDONEZ 4 (GUA); RAMON 2 (CHILE); THAYER 11 (CHILE)
HERRERO DE LARA	FERNANDEZ 56 (C.R.)
HERRERO DEL PERAL	FERNANDEZ 56 (C.R.)
HERRERO RODRIGUEZ	FERNANDEZ 56 (C.R.)
HERRERO VITORIA	FERNANDEZ 56 (C.R.)
HEVAS	MARTINEZ 35 (MEX)
HIDALGO	AMAYA 1 (MEX); 2 (MEX); DAVILA 4,16,26 (MEX); DE LA FUENTE (MEX); THAYER 11 (CHILE)
HIERRO	ALLENDESALAZAR 17 (CHILE)
HIGUERA	MOLINA 3 (ARG); SOBERANES 4 (CALIF)
HIJAR	AMAYA 3 (MEX); HUTCHINSON (CALIF)
HINE	CASTRO 12 (C.R.)
HINOJOSA	ARPEE (MEX, TEXAS); BALLI (MEX, TEXAS); GARCIA 9 (MEX, TEXAS); MENDIRICHAGA 1 (MEX, TEXAS)
HOLGUIN	BINAYAN 2 (ARG); MILLIGAN (N.M., COLO)
HOMEN	FERNANDEZ 42 (CHILE)
HONORATO	MARTINEZ 33 (CHILE)
HORCASITAS	QUINTANA 1 (MEX)
HORTUN	ALLENDESALAZAR 14 (CHILE)
HOYOS	IBARGUREN 3 (ARG)
HOZ	OTAROLA 6 (ARG)
HUAYNA CAPAC	TEMPLE 1 (ECU, PERU)
HUIDOBRO	(Unk.) 1 (ARG); RUJULA 4 (CHILE)
HUMERES	DIAZ 16,21 (CHILE)
HURTADO	MILLIGAN (N.M., COLO)
HURTADO DE MENDOZA	BRICEÑO 2 (VEN); MARTINEZ 3 (VEN); SERRANO 4 (ARG)
IBAÑEZ	FERNANDEZ 65 (C.R.)
IBARGUREN	IBARGUREN 4 (ARG)

IGLESIAS	ESPINACH (PERU); FERNANDEZ 69 (C.R.)
IGUINIZ	IGUINIZ 3 (MEX)
INCAS	MUJICA 3 (PERU)
INFANTE	MANSANO (L.A.)
IPIÑA	CABRERA 7 (MEX)
IRALA	OTAROLA 1,2,3,6 (ARG); ZENARRUZA 2 (ARG)
IRARRAZABAL	LIRA 9 (CHILE); SILVA 5 (ARG); THAYER 19 (CHILE)
IRIARTE	BERRO (URU)
IRIBARREN	BARRIOS 1 (CHILE)
IRIONDO	ARENAS 6 (ARG)
IRISARRI	APARICIO 14 (GUA); VALGOMA 3 (CHILE)
IROLO	NIETO 3 (MEX)
ITURBIDE	AMERLINCK 2 (MEX); DAVILA 15 (MEX)
IZAGUIRRE	DELAUNET 2 (L.A.)
IZARRA	CALVO 5 (ARG)
IZQUIERDO	IZQUIERDO 1 (MEX)
JACOT	NIETO 43 (CUBA)
JAEN	TORRES 9 (MEX)
JARAMILLO	MILLIGAN (N.M., COLO)
JAURISTI	COSTA 5 (BOL)
JEREZ	SUCRE 3 (VEN)
JIMENEZ	CASTRO 17 (C.R.); FERNANDEZ 13 (C.R.); LUJAN 5 (C.R.); MATA 1 (C.R.); MILLIGAN (N.M., COLO); MOREYRA 2 (PERU); QUIROS 5 (C.R.); THAYER 11 (CHILE); TRISTAN 1,2 (CUBA)
JINESTA	OROZCO 1 (C.R.)
JONAMA	ORDONEZ 3,5 (GUA)
JORGE	MILLIGAN (N.M., COLO)
JOVA	JOVA (CUBA, U.S.)
JUAREZ	VILLASEÑOR 5 (MEX)
JUFRE	MANNS 3 (CHILE)
JUGO	DAVILA 7 (MEX)
JURADO	MILLIGAN (N.M., COLO)
KAREL	MILLIGAN (N.M., COLO)
LACALLE	AGUIAR 2 (URU)

LACAYO	APARICIO 15 (GUA)
LACOIZQUETA	CALVO 7 (ARG)
LACUNZA	DOUGNAC (CHILE)
LADRON DE GUEVARA	MOYANO 3 (ARG)
LAFUENTE	LAFUENTE 3 (ARG)
LAGUNAS	ALLENDE 1 (ARG, BOL, CHILE, PERU)
LAHMANN	FERNANDEZ 56 (C.R.)
LAHITTE	ARENES 7 (ARG); PEREIRA 1 (ARG)
LAMARCA	FERNANDEZ 49 (ARG, CHILE)
LARA	DIAZ 4 (ARG); FERNANDEZ 56 (C.R.); SALAZAR 2 (L.A.); TORRE 4 (L.A.)
LARRAIN	AMUNATEGUI 2 (CHILE); CUADRA 5 (CHILE); ESPEJO 6 (CHILE); FLEURY (CHILE); IRRARAZAVAL (CHILE); LARRAIN 6 (CHILE); MARIN 2 (CHILE); THAYER 23 (CHILE)
LARRALDE	MENDIRICHAGA 1,2 (MEX, TEXAS)
LARREA	COMADURAN (ARG)
LARREATEGUI	NIETO 12 (GUA)
LAS HEVAS	MARTINEZ 35 (CHILE)
LASTRA	MARTINEZ 19 (ARG)
LASSO DE LA VEGA	JURADO 1 (S.A.); LASO 1 (CHILE)
LAUDIVAR	APARICIO 6 (GUA)
LAVALLE	FRIAS (ARG); REYES 2 (CHILE)
LAVELLI	SEGOVIA (ARG)
LAVOYEN	ROBLES 20 (ECU)
LAZCANO	VALDES 7 (CHILE)
LECAROS	ZAÑARTU (CHILE)
LECLERC	VALGOMA 8 (CHILE)
LEDESMA	CRESPO 6 (ARG)
LEIVA	FERNANDEZ 47 (ARG); GOMEZ 1 (CHILE)
LELOIR	RICHIERI 4 (ARG)
LEON	AZAROLA 5 (CHILE); FERNANDEZ 24 (VEN), 70 (C.R.); LARROUZ (ARG); LEON 1 (CHILE), 3 (MEX); MARTINEZ 2 (CALIF); SALAZAR 1 (C.R.); URICOECHEA (COL)
LEROY	ESTEVEZ (CUBA)

LESSAPS	SAGUIER 1 (ARG)
LETELIER	OPAZO 4 (CHILE)
LEYVA	MILLIGAN (N.M., COLO)
LEZICA	MARQUEZ 4 (ARG)
LILLO	PEÑA 5 (CHILE)
LIMA	CABRERA 1 (MEX)
LIRA	DIAZ 23 (CHILE); LIRA 1,7 (CHILE)
LISPERGUR	VICUÑA 2 (CHILE); ZEVALLOS 2 (PERU)
LIVAUDIAS	NIETO 44 (LUISIANA)
LIZARRARAS	CUELLAR (MEX)
LLAGUNO	ROBLES 11 (ECU)
LLORENTE	PRADO 9 (C.R.); YGLESIAS 1 (C.R.)
LOERA	MILLIGAN (N.M., COLO)
LOPEZ	BAUDEAN 2 (URU); BLIN (ARG); CASTRO 14 (C.R.); DAVILA 13 (MEX); DOMINGUEZ 2 (ARG); FANDIÑO (ARG); FERNANDEZ 28 (MEX), 77 (C.R.); LOPEZ 1 (MEX); LOPEZ MORTON (MEX); LUX (ARG); MILLIGAN (N.M., COLO); NIETO 10 (CUBA, MEX), 67 (MEX); NORTHROP 1 (CALIF); ROBLES 12 (ECU); VILLAVICENCIO (C.R.)
LOPEZ PORTILLO	GARCIA (MEX); PEREZ 10 (MEX)
LORENZO	FERNANDEZ 56 (C.R.); VIDELA 2 (ARG)
LORIGA	NIETO 45 (CUBA)
LOSADA	ALLENDE 1 (ARG, BOL, CHILE, PERU); MARTINEZ 2 (CALIF); SALAS (VEN)
LOYOLA	CAMUS (CHILE)
LUCERO	MILLIGAN (N.M., COLO)
LUCO	GOMEZ 1 (CHILE)
LUGO	BARROWS 1 (CALIF); WAID (CALIF)
LUGONES	ALVA (ARG)
LUJAN	MILLIGAN (N.M., COLO); PRADO 7 (C.R.)
LUNA	LUNA 1 (ARG)
LUQUE	ARENAS 5 (ARG)
LURO	OTAROLA 6 (ARG)
LYNCH	BARRA (CHILE); LEON 2 (CHILE)
MACAYA	FERNANDEZ 64,65 (C.R.)
MACCLURE	DIAZ 12 (ARG)

MACEO	FRANCO (CUBA); FRANCO (CUBA)
MACHADO	MARIE (CALIF)
MACHAIN	LAFUENTE 4 (ARG)
MACIEL	AZAROLA 8 (ARG), 9 (URU)
MACKENNA	FLOREZ 1 (CHILE)
MADAN	CASTRO 3A (CHILE)
MADARIAGA	THAYER 23 (CHILE)
MAES	MILLIGAN (N.M., COLO)
MALAGA	BERNEDO (PERU)
MALDONADO	CASTRO 17 (C.R.); MALDONADO 2 (VEN); ROBLES (ECU, PERU); RODRIGUEZ (COL); DAVILA 13 (MEX); FERNANDEZ 13 (C.R.); ROBLES 1 (PERU); RODRIGUEZ 4 (COL)
MALO	MALO 3 (MEX)
MANDARTE	DE LA FUENTE (MEX)
MANERO	MANERO (MEX)
MANNS	MANNS (CHILE)
MANRIQUE(Z)	TORRE 4 (L.A.)
MANTILLA	JARAMILLO (CHILE)
MANZANO	URRUTIA 4,7 (CHILE); ZAÑARTU (CHILE)
MARCAYDA	FERNANDEZ 26 (MEX)
MARCILLA	GARCES (CHILE)
MARCO DEL PONT	OLIVARES 1 (PERU)
MARIATEGUI	SWAYNE (PERU)
MARIN	GOMEZ 1 (CHILE)
MARIÑAS	VAAMANDO (L.A.)
MARQUEZ	MALDONADO 4 (VEN); MILLIGAN (N.M., COLO); MARTIN FALLA 3 (ELS); FERNANDEZ 28 (MEX); GANDIA 6 (ARG); MARTIN 2 (ARG); MARTINEZ 20 (ARG); MORENO 5 (ARG); NIETO 49 (CUBA)
MARTINEZ	COMADURAN (ARG); FERNANDEZ 2,9 (C.R.); FRIAS (ARG); GARCIA 12 (TEXAS); GARZA (MEX, TEXAS); GUARDA 1 (CHILE); LOBUGLIO (CALIF); MARTINEZ 11 (GUA), 13 (ARG), 37 (CHILE), 40 (ARG); MILLIGAN (N.M., COLO); RODRIGUEZ 13 (BOL); VIDELA 3 (ARG)

MATA	FERNANDEZ 56 (C.R.); LUJAN 9 (C.R.)
MATIENZO	DOMINGUEZ 2 (ARG)
MATURANA	MATURANA 2 (CHILE)
MATUZ	RODRIGUEZ 10 (NIC)
MAURA	SALVADOR (L.A.)
MAURY	LUNA 2 (GUA)
MAYAS	PINAL (MEX)
MAZA	MAZA (ARG)
MAZARIEGO	NIETO 11 (CUBA)
MEDINA	AMESTI 1 (CHILE); COSTA 5 (BOL); FERNANDEZ 23 (URU); LUQUE 3 (ARG); MEDINA 3 (ARG, CHILE); MILLIGAN (N.M., COLO); RODRIGUEZ 13 (BOL); VIDELA 3 (ARG)
MEDRANO	EZCURRA (ARG); ROBLES 7 (ECU)
MELGAR	MELGAR (L.A.)
MELLON	VON 1 (ARG)
MENA	CASTRO 3A (CUBA)
MENDEZ	FERNANDEZ 46 (ARG); MENDEZ 1 (URU)
MENDIGUTIA	BOUCHET (ECU)
MENDOZA	CARRIL (ARG); CUEVAS 2 (ARG); DARIO 2 (VEN); ESPINOSA 1 (MEX); MARTINEZ 3 (VEN); RODRIGUEZ 4 (COL); SERRANO 4 (ARG); SUAREZ 5 (VEN); SWAYNE 1 (PERU)
MENENDEZ	VIGIL (FLORIDA)
MERINO	CRISOSTOMO (CHILE)
MERLO	TORRE 3 (ARG)
MESSIA	MANNS 2 (CHILE)
MESTRE	HURTADO (CUBA)
MEYRELES	OTAROLA 6 (ARG)
MIER	MIER (MEX)
MIJARES	LANCASTER 5 (MEX)
MILLAN	FERNANDEZ 28 (MEX); NIETO 9 (CUBA)
MINA	RIVERA 1 (MEX)
MINAYA	THAYER 12 (CHILE)
MIRANDA	CELIS (CHILE); FERNANDEZ 21,22 (VEN); MARTINEZ 2 (CALIF); THAYER 11 (CHILE)
MIRO	GILBERT (PERU)

MITRE   AZAROLA 9 (URU); DURAÑONA 1 (ARG);
                         MARTINEZ 22 (ARG)
MIYARES   ZAZO (L.A.)
MOCTEZUMA   DAVILA 3 (MEX); ESCUDERO (MEX);
                         LOHMANN 8 (MEX); RODRIGUEZ 2 (MEX)
MOLINA   BAUDEAN 1 (URU); DIAZ 4 (ARG); FRIAS
                         (ARG); MOLINA 12,14 (CHILE); THAYER 21
                         (CHILE); VICUÑA 2 (CHILE)
MONCADA   TRAZEGNIES 6 (PERU); VAZQUEZ 5 (CALIF)
MONJE   BARRANTES 4 (C.R.); DAVILA 22 (MEX)
MONROY   CASTAÑOS 5 (MEX); DAVILA 20 (MEX)
MONTALVO   CASTRO 3A (CUBA); MOREYRA 2 (PERU)
MONTAÑAR   SALVADOR (L.A.)
MONTAÑO   MILLIGAN (N.M., COLO)
MONTEALEGRE   FERNANDEZ 72 (C.R.); MARTINEZ 24 (C.R.)
MONTEJANO   CABRERA 8 (MEX); LANCASTER 7 (MEX)
MONTEJO   RUBIO 1,4 (MEX); RUJULA 1 (MEX)
MONTELLANO   RUJULA 1 (MEX)
MONTEMAYOR   DUAINE (MEX, TEXAS); GARZA (MEX,
                         TEXAS); SOMONTE (MEX, TEXAS);
                         SWAINE (PERU)
MONTENEGRO   CUNEO 1 (ARG)
MONTEPIO   LARRAIN 2 (L.A.)
MONTERO   ALLENDE 1 (ARG, BOL, CHILE, PERU);
                         PEREDA (L.A.)
MONTERREY   PEREZ 3,4 (MEX)
MONTIEL   LABOUGLE 2 (ARG)
MONTOYA   MILLIGAN (N.M., COLO); URICOECHEA
                         (L.A.)
MONT-ROIG   NIETO 48 (CUBA)
MONTT   LIRA 4,9 (CHILE); MONTT (CHILE)
MONTUFAR   FERNANDEZ 50 (C.R.); MONTUFAR 1,4 (GUA)
MONZON   FIGUROA 1 (GUA)
MORA   QUIROS 2 (C.R.)
MORAGA   MCANDREWS (L.A.)
MORALES   CASTRO 3A (CUBA); NIETO 50 (CUBA);
                         ROBLES 14 (ECU)
MORAZAN   FERNANDEZ 72 (C.R.); TURCIOS (C.R.);
                         ZUÑIGA (VEN)

MORELOS	GONZALEZ 17 (MEX)
MORENO	BAEZ 2 (VEN); MARTINEZ 15 (ARG); MILLIGAN (N.M., COLO); RIVERA 1 (MEX); SERRANO 2 (ARG); URICOECHEA (L.A.)
MOSCOSO	MOSCOSO (PAN)
MOSQUERA	ARBOLEDA (COL)
MOTA	CASTAÑOS 2 (MEX)
MOYA	ALLENDESALAZAR 21 (CHILE); CASTRO 15 (C.R.); NIETO 51 (CUBA)
MOYANO	CORNEJO 4 (ARG)
MUJICA	SANCHEZ 8 (CHILE)
MUNERA	URICOECHEA (L.A.)
MUÑIZ	MILLIGAN (N.M., COLO)
MUÑOZ	COO (CHILE); GARAY 2 (ECU); GIL (URU); HOGLE (U.S.); NIETO 58 (CUBA)
MUZQUIZ	CONDE 1 (L.A.)
NAJERA	APARICIO 12 (GUA)
NAVARRETE	DIAZ 4 (ARG)
NAVARRO	ALLENDE 2 (CHILE); DURON (MEX, TEXAS); HARRIS (MEX); LUJAN 3 (C.R.)
NEGRO	WALKER (CHILE)
NIETO	NIETO 22 (CUBA, MEX)
NIÑO	PEÑA 4 (CHILE)
NORES	VISO (ARG)
NORIEGA	MILLIGAN (N.M., COLO)
NOVALICHES	NIETO 34 (CUBA)
NOVOA	GONZALEZ 5 (CHILE); JURADO 2 (ECU)
NUÑEZ	COSTA 3 (BOL); VICUÑA 2 (CHILE)
NUÑEZ DE CASTRO	CASTRO 3A (CUBA)
ÑUFLO	MORALES 3 (BOL)
O'DONNELL	ARBOLEDA (COL)
O'HIGGINS	VALDES 9 (CHILE); VICUÑA 4 (CHILE)
O'PHELAN	MARQUEZ 2 (PERU)
OBARRIO	MARQUEZ 4 (ARG)
OCAMPO	ALLENDE 2 (CHILE); BARRANTES 2 (C.R.); CASTRO 22 (C.R.); PARESSO (COL) THAYER 11 (CHILE)

OCAÑA	DAVILA 9 (MEX)
OCHOA	GARAY 2 (ECU)
ODIO	HACK 1,2 (C.R.)
ODUBER	FERNANDEZ 53 (C.R.)
OGAZON	LANCASTER 6 (MEX)
OJEDA	THAYER 4 (CHILE)
OLASCOAGA	CASTRO 2 (ARG)
OLGUIN	BINAYAN 2 (ARG)
OLIDEN	PICO (ARG)
OLIVAR	THAYER 13 (CHILE)
OLIVAS	MARTINEZ 2 (CALIF); MILLIGAN (N.M., COLO)
OLIVERA	PEÑA 1 (ARG)
OLIVOS	MARTINEZ 30 (CHILE)
OLMEDO	NOBOA (ECU)
OLMOS	MALDONADO 1 (ARG); OLMOS 2 (CHILE)
ONDEGARDO	ESPEJO 15 (CHILE)
ORDAZ	NIETO 14 (CUBA, MEX)
ORDOÑEZ	MALDONADO 2 (VEN); ORDOÑEZ 6 (C.R.)
OREAMUNO	OREAMUNO (C.R.)
ORIAMUNOS	CASTRO 20 (PAN)
ORIBE	AZAROLA 9 (URU)
OROZCO	ANAYA (MEX); DAVILA 2,25 (MEX); GOMEZ 2 (MEX); MALO 1 (MEX)
ORSINIS	BINAYAN 1 (ARG)
ORTA	CONDE 1 (L.A.)
ORTEGA	GALLAGHER 1 (CALIF); FERNANDEZ 33 (MEX); MILLIGAN (N.M., COLO); NORTHROP 1 (CALIF)
OTERO	PRADO 11 (C.R.)
ORTIZ	BARREIRO 3 (ARG); GANDIA 3 (ARG); LLUCH (P.R.); MILLIGAN (N.M., COLO); OLMSTED 1 (N.M.); SOAJE 3 (ARG)
OSSANDON	OSSANDON (L.A.)
OVALLE	ESPEJO 1,2 (CHILE); ORTIZ 1 (CHILE); OVALLE (CHILE, ITALY); ZAÑARTU (CHILE)
OVANDO	OVANDO 1 (MEX)

OVIEDO	NIETO 62 (MEX); UTRERA 1 (R.D.)
OYAGUE	JENSEN 2 (PERU)
OYARZUN	THAYR 15 (CHILE)
PACHECO	DAVILA 34 (VEN); MILLIGAN (N.M., COLO); PONSFORD 3 (CALIF); SOBERANES 5 (CALIF)
PADILLA	LAMBI 1 (COLO); LOBUGLIO (CALIF); MILLIGAN (N.M., COLO); PALOMINO 5 (MEX)
PADRES	HUTCHINSON (CALIF)
PAGOLA	ROBLES 14 (ECU)
PALACIO	PALACIO 2,3 (MEX)
PALAFOX	GONZALEZ 5 (CHILE)
PALAZUELOS	LARRAIN 5´(CHILE)
PALOMAR	PALOMAR (MEX)
PALOMARES	BARROWS 2 (CALIF)
PALOMO	APARICIO 19 (GUA)
PARADA	(Unk.) 4 (MEX)
PARDO	BARREDA 5 (PERU); VALGOMA 2 (L.A.); VIDELA 5 (ARG)
PAREDES	FUGUET (VEN)
PARRAGUEZ	VICUÑA 2 (CHILE); VIDELA 5 (ARG)
PARRAVICINI	STAUDT 2 (ARG)
PASTENE	ESPEJO 1,2 (CHILE); ORTIZ 1 (CHILE); OVALLE (CHILE, ITALY); THAYER 14 (CHILE)
PAUL	EYZAGUIRRE (VEN)
PAZ	ARENAS 1 (ARG); FRIAS (ARG); PAZ SOLDAN (PERU)
PAZ SOLDAN	PAZ SOLDAN (PERU)
PEDASI	MOSCOSO (PAN)
PEDRARIAS	CANTERA (C.A.)
PEÑA	PEÑA 5 (CHILE); SOLANO (CALIF)
PEÑALOZA	TEJERINA 5 (ARG)
PERAGALLO	MARTINEZ 28 (CHILE)
PERAL	FERNANDEZ 56 (C.R.)
PERALES	GUARDA 4 (PERU)

PERALTA	AMIGO (C.R.); ATIENZA 3 (SPAIN); BUSTO (PERU); CABRERA 9 (MEX); FERNANDEZ 3 (L.A.), 4,7,10,11,14, 67, 71,74 (C.R.); MANNS 1 (CHILE); MATA 2 (C.R.); MONTU-FAR 3 (C.R.); NIETO 49 (CUBA); OTAROLA 6 (ARG); ROJAS 1 (MEX)
PEREDA	SAGUIER 2 (ARG)
PERDRIEL	VITON (ARG)
PEREIRA	DOERSAM (C.R.)
PEREZ	ALVAREZ 2 (PERU); DAVILA 11 (MEX); DE LA VEGA (PERU); FONTECILLA (CHILE); GARCILASO (PERU); LABOUGLE 1 (ARG); MILLIGAN (N.M., COLO); PEREZ 5 (ARG); PONCE DE LEON (L.A.); ROBLES 21 (ECU); VAAMANDO (L.A.)
PERICHON	PERICHON (ARG)
PESADO	TORIJA (MEX, U.S.)
PESSOA	FERNANDEZ 42 (CHILE)
PIAR	LANDAETA (VEN)
PICO	MARTINEZ 2 (CALIF); WAID (CALIF)
PIERES	BARREIRO 2 (ARG)
PINEDA	GARCIA 12 (TEXAS)
PINEDO	LARROUZ (ARG)
PIGNATELLI	CUEVAS 1 (MEX)
PIMENTEL	MARTINEZ 8 (ARG); PIMENTEL (VEN); PUEYRREDON (ARG)
PINO	PINO (L.A.)
PINOCHET	LEON 1 (CHILE)
PINTADO	LASO 1 (CHILE)
PINTO	FRIAS (ARG); FERNANDEZ 51 (C.R.); SANCHEZ 10 (ARG)
PIÑERES	FERNANDEZ 56 (C.R.)
PIRIZ	DIAZ 13 (URU)
PISQUERA	CID (GUA)
PITA	CASTRO 3A (CUBA)
PIZA	FERNANDEZ 59 (C.R.)
PIZARRO	DAVILA 20 (MEX); RUJULA 2 (PERU)
PLANCARTE	RAMIREZ 4 (MEX)
PLATA	RODRIGUEZ 12 (COL)

PLAZAERT	ROBLES 22 (ECU)
POLO	ESPEJO 15 (CHILE)
POMAR	POMAR (CHILE)
PONCE DE LEON	GARCIA 11 (L.A.); ROJAS 2 (ARG)
PONTE	PERERA 2 (VEN)
PONTON	NIETO 20,29 (CUBA)
PORLIER	CADENAS 1 (L.A.)
PORRAS	PALOMINO 1 (MEX); QUIROS 2 (C.R.)
PORTALES	LARRAIN 5 (CHILE)
PORTILLO	GARCIA 1 (MEX); PEREZ 10 (MEX)
PORTUGAL	APARICIO 1 (GUA)
PORTUGALETE	CALVO 2 (ARG)
POSADAS	VON 3 (ARG)
POSTIGO	VALGOMA 3 (CHILE)
POVEDA	GOMEZ 1 (CHILE)
POZOS-DULCES	NIETO 5 (L.A.), 43 (CUBA)
PRADO	COSTA 3 (BOL); FIGUEROA 2 (ARG); GILBERT (PERU); MALDONADO 4 (VEN)
PRIETO	CHARLIN (CHILE)
PRIMO	LAFUENTE 2 (ARG)
PUIG	SOAJE 1 (ARG)
PULIDO	NIETO 13 (MEX)
POZUELO	FERNANDEZ 60 (C.R.)
PRESTINARY	MORA (C.R.)
PUELLO	GARRIDO (R.D.)
PUEYRREDON	FRIAS (ARG); MARTINEZ 21 (ARG); OTAROLA 6 (ARG)
PUGA	GONZALEZ 5 (CHILE)
PUNILLA	MALDONADO 1 (ARG)
QUEPO	QUIROS 11 (C.R.)
QUESADA	GILBERT (PERU); TURCIOS (C.R.)
QUIJANO	MUJICA 1 (PERU)
QUIJAS	ZENARRUZA 4 (L.A.)
QUINTANA	MARTINEZ 16 (ARG); MILLIGAN (N.M., COLO); QUINTANA 1,2 (MEX); SANCHEZ 10 (ARG)
QUINTANILLA	SAENZ (C.R.); VICUÑA 1 (CHILE)
QUINTERO	MARTINEZ 2 (CALIF)

QUINTRALA	VICUÑA 2 (CHILE)
QUIÑONES	ORTIZ 3 (COL)
QUIROGA	BUSCA 1 (CHILE); DEVOTO (ARG); GARIBALDI (ARG); THAYER 11 (CHILE)
QUIROS	FERNANDEZ 1,2 (C.R.); QUIROS 3,6,10,11 (C.R.); REVOLLO 1 (C.R.); VAZQUEZ 3 (PERU)
RABELL	NIETO 16 (CUBA)
RADA	JIMENEZ 3 (COL)
RADILLO	CASTRO 3A (CUBA)
RAEL	MILLIGAN (N.M., COLO)
RAMIREZ	BUSCA 2 (CHILE); CASTRO 3A (CUBA); MARTINEZ 1 (MEX, TEXAS); ROBLES 9 (ECU); VISO (ARG)
RAMOS	MARTINEZ 34 (CHILE); OTAROLA 6 (ARG)
RAUDON	IZQUIERDO 2,3 (MEX)
RAVELO	FERNANDEZ 22 (VEN); UTRERA 2 (L.A.)
RECABARREN	NIETO 52 (CUBA)
RECIO	FERNANDEZ 18,19 (ARG)
REGLA	ROMERO 2,4 (MEX)
REINA	MARQUEZ 4 (ARG)
REYES	AMUNATEGUI 4 (CHILE); MARTINEZ 2 (CALIF); REYES 4 (CHILE); ZAÑARTU (CHILE)
REYNAFEE	FERREIRA 1 (ARG)
REZOLA	DELAUNET (L.A.)
RIBERA	RIVA 1 (PERU)
RIESCO	VALDES 10 (CHILE)
RINCON	ZAYAS 1 (MEX)
RIO	RIO 1,2 (L.A.)
RIQUELME	OLMOS 1 (ARG); ROA 2 (CHILE); ROJAS 2 (ARG)
RITTSCHER	RITTSCHER (GUA)
RIVADENEIRA	BARREDA 5 (PERU)
RIVAROLA	FERNANDEZ 35 (ARG)
RIVAS	HERNANDEZ 2 (COL); MONTUFAR 4 (GUA); RESTREPO 2,3,4 (COL); RUZ (MEX)
RIVERA	ABAD (URU); ALLENDESALAZAR 9 (CHILE); APARICIO 19 (GUA); DAVILA 18 (MEX);

	LAFUENTE 2 (ARG); MARTINEZ 2 (CALIF); ROSAS 1 (PERU); VAZQUEZ 5 (CALIF)
RIVEROS	CAMUS (CHILE)
RIZZO	ARELLANO (ECU)
ROBLEDO	MILLIGAN (N.M., COLO)
ROBREDO	MATA 1 (C.R.)
ROCA	ARENAS 2 (ARG); NIETO 63,64 (CUBA)
ROCAFUERTE	ROBLES 16,17 (ECU)
ROCAMORA	FINESTRAT 1 (L.A.)
ROCO	ESPEJO 11 (CHILE)
RODAS	AMADO (MEX)
RODRIGUEZ	CASTRO 3A (CUBA); DURON (MEX, TEXAS); ESPEJO 1,2 (CHILE); GONZALEZ 13 (C.R.); MILLIGAN (N.M., COLO); MOLINA 5 (ARG); MONTUFAR 4 (GUA); QUIROS 3 (C.R.); RODRIGUEZ 10 (NIC)
RODRIGUEZ DE CASTRO	CASTRO 16 (C.R.)
RODRIGUEZ DEL MANZANO	ESPEJO 1,2 (CHILE); ORTIZ 1 (CHILE); OVALLE (CHILE, ITALY); ZAÑARTU (CHILE)
ROHRMOSER	FERNANDEZ 61 (C.R.)
ROIG	NIETO 48 (CUBA)
ROJAS	BARRIOS 1 (PERU); VALGOMA 3 (CHILE)
ROMAN	BUSCA 3 (ARG)
ROMERO	MARTINEZ 2 (CALIF); MILLIGAN (N.M., COLO); VALLADARES (CHILE); WAID (CALIF); ZAYAS 1 (MEX)
ROMO	DAVILA 9,11 (MEX)
ROMO DE VIVAR	DAVILA 11 (MEX); TOPETE (MEX)
ROQUE	ARENAS 7 (ARG)
ROSELL	FREUNDT 1,2 (PERU)
ROSS	FERNANDEZ 56 (C.R.)
ROVIROSA	ROSADO (MEX)
ROZAS	AZAROLA 9 (URU)
RUCABADO	VALVERDE 2 (C.R.)
RUEDA	VISO (ARG)

RUIZ	ALLENDESALAZAR 2 (CHILE); DIAZ 3 (ARG); EYZAGUIRRE 6 (CHILE); GOMEZ 1 (CHILE); MANNS 1 (CHILE); MILLIGAN (N.M., COLO); MORENO 3 (ARG); THAYER 11,12 (CHILE); VILLASEÑOR 3 (MEX)
RUZ	RUZ (MEX)
SAA	FERNANDEZ 43 (CHILE); MOLINA 9 (ARG)
SAAVEDRA	ALGARA (MEX); LAFUENTE 6 (CHILE); NIETO 27 (COL, MEX, PERU)
SADA	SADA (MEX)
SAENZ	CASTELLANO 2 (ARG); FRIAS (ARG); GONZALEZ 11 (C.R.); LA FUENTE (ARG); MIRANDA 1 (MEX); SAENZ (C.R.)
SAENZ-PEÑA	ARENAS 7 (ARG); VICUÑA 5 (CHILE)
SAGRERA	QUIROS 9 (C.R.)
SALAS	COMADURAN (ARG); DIAZ 24 (CHILE); MILLIGAN (N.M., COLO)
SALAZAR	ALLENDESALAZAR 14 (CHILE); FERNANDEZ 75 (C.R.); HACK 3 (C.R.); MILLIGAN (N.M., COLO); SALAZAR 1 (C.R.)
SALCEDO	FERNANDEZ 79 (CHILE)
SALGADO	MARTINEZ 2 (CALIF)
SALINAS	ANDA (ECU)
SAN JORGE	NIETO 15 (MEX)
SAN MARTIN	AZAROLA 7 (URU); BERNARD (ARG); CALVO 2 (ARG); DIAZ 6 (ARG, FILIPINAS); GANDIA 5 (PAR); FERNANDEZ 41 (ARG); LEON 5 (ARG); OTAROLA 6 (ARG); VIDELA 4 (ARG)
SAN MIGUEL	THAYER 11 (CHILE)
SAN ROMAN	NIETO 15 (MEX)
SAN VICENTE	ENCIO (ARG)
SANABRIA	MARTINEZ 13 (ARG); SANABRIA 1 (BOL)
SANCHEZ	GURRIA (MEX); HARRIS (MEX); HEBEL (FLA); MILLIGAN (N.M., COLO); PEREZ 9 (MEX); SANCHEZ 10 (ARG); WAID (CALIF)
SANCHEZ NAVARRO	DURON (MEX, TEXAS)
SANCHO	FERNANDEZ 8 (C.R.)

SANDOVAL	ESCUDERO (MEX); FINESTRAT 2 (L.A.); LACHNER (C.R.); MILLIGAN (N.M., COLO); ORDOÑEZ 1 (GUA); SUAREZ 2 (ARG)
SANHUEZA	GONZALEZ 5 (CHILE)
SANTA ANA	AGRAZ 1 (MEX); MOLINA 3 (ARG)
SANTA CRUZ	ALIAGA 2 (PERU); DIAZ 1 (ARG); FIERRO (ARG)
SANTA MARIA	MIRANDA 1 (MEX); ZAÑARTU (CHILE)
SANTANDER	NIETO 20,29 (L.A.); PACHECO 1 (COL)
SANTELICES	DIAZ 15 (CHILE)
SANTISTEBAN	MILLIGAN (N.M., COLO)
SANTOÑA	NIETO 4 (L.A.)
SANTOS	NIETO 53 (CUBA); RODRIGUEZ 12 (COL); RUBIRA (ECU)
SARACHAGA	CASTRO 23 (MEX); SOAJE 2 (ARG)
SARMIENTO	GARIBALDI (ARG); MARTINEZ 12 (ARG)
SASO	AMADO (MEX)
SEDANO	NIETO 45 (CUBA)
SEGUI	SAGUIER 3 (ARG)
SEGURA	REVOLLO 1 (C.R.); TORIJA (MEX, U.S.)
SEGUROLA	PICO (ARG)
SEPULVEDA	MENDIRICHAGA 1 (MEX, TEXAS)
SERDAN	FLORES (MEX)
SERRANO	ALLENDESALAZAR 16 (CHILE); MILLIGAN (N.M., COLO); SERRANO 1 (C.R.)
SEVILLA	VEGAS (PERU)
SILVA	ALLENDESALAZAR 19 (CHILE); ARANEDA (CHILE); SILVA 1 (CHILE)
SILVEIRA	MARTINEZ 34 (CHILE)
SINOVA	MARTINEZ 2 (CALIF)
SISNEROS	MILLIGAN (N.M., COLO)
SOBERANES	SOBERANES 6 (CALIF)
SOLAR	CUADRA 5 (CHILE); GANDIA 3 (ARG); GONZALEZ 5 (CHILE); TROSTINE 2 (ARG)
SOLDAN	PAZ SOLDAN (PERU)
SOLER	OTAROLA 3 (ARG)
SOLERA	FERNANDEZ 56 (C.R.); FUENTES 2 (C.R.)
SORIA	AZAROLA 9 (URU)

SORUCO	RIPAONTI (BOL)
SOSTOA	AZAROLA 9 (URU)
SOTO	AZAROLA 9 (URU); ESCOBOSA (MEX); OROZCO 2 (CHILE); PRADO 4 (C.R.); RODRIGUEZ 13 (BOL); SOLAR (FLA)
SOTOMAYOR	COMADURAN (ARG); GONZALEZ 5 (CHILE); JIMENEZ 2 (COL); MARTIN 1 (ARG); THAYER 11 (CHILE)
SOUSA	MUJICA 10 (CHILE)
STEFFENS	ALFARO 3 (C.R.)
SUAREZ	CAMUS (CHILE); FERNANDEZ 51 (C.R.); NIETO 53 (CUBA); PEREZ 6 (ARG); SUAREZ 1 (L.A.); TORRE 3 (ARG)
SUBERCASEAUX	ZAÑARTU (CHILE)
SUCRE	CASTRO 3A (CUBA)
SUNSIN	ORDOÑEZ (GUA)
SWAYNE	SWAYNE (PERU)
TABALOSOS	GUARDA 3 (CHILE)
TAFOYA	MILLIGAN (N.M., COLO)
TALAMANTES	MARIE (CALIF)
TAPIA	CASTAÑOS 3 (MEX); FERNANDEZ 28 (MEX); GURRIA (MEX); RUBIO 2 (MEX)
TARAZONA	PAZOS (PERU)
TARIJA	BAUDEAN 2 (URU)
TEBES	DEL BUSTO (PERU)
TEJADA	FERNANDEZ 79 (CHILE); NIETO 38 (CUBA)
TELLES	PALOMINO 2 (MEX)
TELLO	BUSCA 2 (CHILE)
TENA	ALLENDESALAZAR 20 (CHILE); NIETO 54 (MEX); RODRIGUEZ 3 (MEX)
TENERIO	MILLIGAN (N.M., COLO)
TERMIÑO	PALOMINO 1 (MEX)
TERREÑO	VILLAR 1 (MEX)
TERRERO(S)	ALLENDESALAZAR 21 (CHILE); PLATT 6 (NIC, VEN); ZAYAS 1 (MEX)
TEZANOS	SANCHEZ 10 (ARG)
THAMES	LUQUE 1 (ARG)
THAYER	THAYER 2,7,20 (CHILE, U.S.)
TIBON	TIBON (MEX)

TINOCO	ROBLES 14 (ECU)
TIXERA	SANCHEZ 4 (CHILE)
TISNES	TISNES (COL)
TOCCO	MARINO (ARG)
TOCORNAL	MUJICA 10 (CHILE)
TOGORES	NIETO 63,64 (CUBA)
TOJO	ZENARRUZA 1 (ARG)
TOLEDO	ALLENDE 3 (CHILE); MARTINEZ 8 (ARG); NIETO 1,2 (CUBA), 65 (MEX); PUEYRREDON (ARG); THAYER 24 (CHILE); VIDELA 2 (ARG)
TOLOSA	ESCUDERO (MEX)
TORANZO	CABRERA 6 (MEX)
TORCONAL	MUJICA 9 (CHILE)
TORDOYA	TERRY 1 (PERU)
TORO	TORO 2 (VEN)
TORRE	ALLENDE 3 (CHILE); ALLENDESALAZAR 10,14 (CHILE)
TORRES	ALLENDESALAZAR 3,10,14 (CHILE); JAUREGUI 2 (ARG); MARTINEZ 29 (CHILE); TORRES 9 (MEX); VALDES 3 (CHILE)
TOVAR	BAEZ 6 (VEN)
TOVILLA	FALLA 2 (GUA)
TREJO	DOERSAM (ARG); QUIROS 4 (C.R.)
TREVIÑO	MENDIRICHAGA 4,5 (MEX, TEXAS)
TRONCOSO	LIRA 7 (CHILE)
TRUJILLO	MILLIGAN (N.M., COLO); VALGOMA 3 (CHILE)
TRUQUE	FERNANDEZ 56 (C.R.)
TUDELA	ALVAREZ 2 (PERU)
TUPAC AMARU	VALCARCEL (PERU)
TUPPER	ZAÑARTU (CHILE)
UGARTE	CASTRO 3A (CUBA); ROSAS 2 (PERU)
UGARTECHE	PRADO 10,11 (C.R.); VON 3 (ARG)
UHAGON	UHAGON (L.A.)
ULLOA	FREUNDT 3 (PERU); SANZ (L.A.)
UNAMUNO	ROBLES 3 (ECU)
UNDA	APARICIO 20 (GUA)

UNZAGA	ALLENDE 5 (CHILE); 7 (CHILE); RUBIO 7 (MEX)
URDANETA	DAVILA 31 (VEN)
URDANIVIA	CHAVEZ 4 (PERU)
URETA	MARTINEZ 36,37 (CHILE)
URIBURU	ARENAS 8 (ARG)
URICOECHEA	URICOECHEA (L.A.)
URIONES	ALLENDESALAZAR 1 (CHILE)
URQUIZA	AZAROLA 9 (URU); URQUIZA (ARG)
URREJOLA	ARAYA (CHILE); ARRAYA 1 (CHILE)
URRESTILLA	DELAUNET (L.A.)
URRUELA	ECHEVERRIA 2 (GUA)
URRUTIA	D.D.H. (CHILE); DUBLE 1 (CHILE), MANSANO (L.A.); URRUTIA 1,6 (CHILE)
URSUA	RUIZ 1 (GUA)
UZTARIZ	MARTINEZ 28 (CHILE)
VACA	SOLANO (CALIF)
VALCARCEL	NIETO 55 (CUBA)
VALDERRAMA	CRESPO 6 (ARG)
VALDEZ	CASTRO 3A (CUBA); ESPEJO 4,5 (CHILE); MILLIGAN (N.M., COLO); MOLINA 5 (ARG); ONDARZA 2 (CHILE); VALDES 11 (CHILE)
VALDIVIA	ALLENDESALAZAR 13 (CHILE); DIAZ 19 (CHILE); HANISCH (CHILE)
VALDOSERA	MALDONADO 3 (VEN); NIETO 38 (CUBA)
VALDOVINOS	VALENZUELA 1 (CHILE)
VALENCIA	ARBOLEDA (COL); PANESSO (COL)
VALENZUELA	VALENZUELA 2 (CHILE)
VALIENTE	FRIAS (ARG); GONZALEZ 4 (CHILE)
VALLARTA	LANCASTER 3 (MEX)
VALLEJOS	MILLIGAN (N.M., COLO)
VALLELLANO	NIETO 35 (CUBA)
VALLERIESTRA	OLIVARES 2 (PERU); QUIROS 7 (C.R.)
VALVERDE	TRAZEGNIES 1 (PERU)
VAN DE WALLE	FIERRO (ARG)
VAN PATTEN	VAN PATTEN (C.R.); YGLESIAS 2 (C.R.)
VARAS	ROBLES 6 (MEX)

VARGAS	AZAROLA 9 (URU); DE LA VEGA (PERU); GARCILAZO (PERU); ROBLES 4,21 (ECU)
VASCONCELOS	VICUÑA 2 (CHILE)
VASCONEZ	JURADO 3 (ECU)
VASQUEZ	MILLIGAN (N.M., COLO)
VASTIDA	MARTINEZ 2 (CALIF)
VAZQUEZ	D.D.H. (CHILE); FUENTES 2 (C.R.); PEREZ 5 (ARG); RAMON 3 (CHILE); SAENZ (C.R); SCHULKIN (ARG, URU); TRAZEGNIES 5 (PERU); URRUTIA 1,2 (CHILE); VAZQUEZ 3 (PERU)
VAZQUEZ DE ACUÑA	BROMLEY 2 (PERU)
VAZQUEZ DE CORONADO	CASTRO 8,21 (C.R.); ESPINOSA 1 (MEX); FERNANDEZ 13,70,76 (C.R.); LUJAN 1 (C.R.); REVOLLO 2 (C.R.)
VEDIA	DURAÑONA 1,3 (ARG)
VEEDOR	NIETO 62 (MEX)
VEGA	DIAZ 9 (ARG); FERNANDEZ 74 (C.R.); LASO 1 (CHILE); JURADO 1 (S.A.); LOHMANN 3 (PERU)
VELA	GARZA (MEX, TEXAS); OTAROLA 5 (ARG); RAMIREZ 1 (TEXAS); ROBLES 15 (ECU)
VELARDE	LOPEZ 1 (MEX)
VELASCO	MARQUES 1 (L.A.); TRAZEGNIES 5 (PERU)
VELAZQUEZ	CASTRO 3A (CUBA); LANCASTER 6 (MEX)
VERA	ALLENDESALAZAR 9,22 (CHILE); LASO 1 (CHILE); MOLINA 4,8 (ARG); OTAROLA 5 (ARG); ROBLES 18 (GUA); ROJAS 2 (ARG)
VERAGUA	DIAZ 5 (ARG); NIETO 28 (CUBA, P.R.)
VERDES	NIETO 39 (COL, CUBA)
VERDIA	PEREZ 9 (MEX)
VERDUGO	BARNOYA 2 (GUA); MARTINEZ 2 (CALIF); NAKAYAMA 1 (MEX)
VERGARA	ALLENDESALAZAR 8 (CHILE); CASTELLON (CHILE)
VIAL	DIAZ 15,17,20,25 (CHILE); VALGOMA 3 (ARG)
VIALPANDO	MILLIGAN (N.M., COLO)
VIANA	AZAROLA 9 (URU)

VICUÑA	FLOREZ 1 (CHILE); MARIN 2 (CHILE); THAYER 23 (CHILE); VICUÑA 1 (CHILE)
VIDELA	COMADURAN (ARG); MANSILLA 1 (ARG, CHILE); VIDELA 1 (ARG)
VIGIL	MILLIGAN (N.M., COLO)
VILCHES	APARICIO 11 (GUA)
VILLADA	ARENAS 4 (ARG)
VILLAFAÑE	SERRANO 3 (ARG)
VILLALOBOS	LUX (ARG)
VILLANUEVA	VILLANUEVA 1 (U.S.)
VILLAR	CRESPO 5 (ARG)
VILLAROCHA	SANCHEZ 7 (CHILE)
VILLAQUIRAN	MALDONADO 2 (VEN); ORDOÑEZ 6 (C.R.)
VILLARREAL	SHOEMAKER (MEX, TEXAS)
VILLASEÑOR	ALLENDE 7 (CHILE); DAVILA 21,25 (MEX); GOMEZ 2 (MEX); MALO 1 (MEX); NIETO 56 (MEX); ROMO 2 (MEX); VILLASEÑOR 6 (MEX)
VILLA URRUTIA	NIETO 57 (CUBA, MEX)
VILLAVICENCIO	TERRY 2 (PERU)
VILLEGAS	COMADURAN (ARG); ORIBE (URU)
VILLELA	ALLENDESALAZAR 12 (CHILE)
VILLOTA	LIRA 2 (CHILE)
VILLUENDAS	NIETO 19 (CUBA)
VINCES	ROBLES 24 (ECU)
VISO	VISO (ARG)
VITON	VITON (ARG)
VIVAR	TOPETE (MEX)
VIZCAINO	VIZCAINO (MEX)
VIZCAYA	MUJICA 6 (L.A.)
VOLIO	LUJAN 5 (C.R.)
VON GREGGART	ALFARO 3 (C.R.)
WARNES	CAMPOS 5 (URU); COO 1 (ARG, CHILE, URU); GANDIA 4 (ARG)
XIMENEZ	ELLIS 1,2 (URU); SUAREZ 2 (ARG)
YANZI	BARREIRO 4 (ARG)
YAÑEZ	CUNEO 1 (ARG)
YAVAR	ALLENDESALAZAR 17 (CHILE)

YCAZA	GANGOTENA 5 (ECU); PINO (L.A.)
YRAETA	INSTITUTO (MEX)
YURRITA	LUNA 2 (GUA)
ZABALA	AZAROLA 9 (URU)
ZALDARRIAGA	OLMEDO (ARG)
ZALDIVAR	DOERSAM (ARG)
ZAMBRANA	RODRIGUEZ 11 (CUBA); ZAMBRANO (CUBA)
ZAMBRANO	MENDIRICHAGA 1 (MEX, TEXAS)
ZAMORA	MILLIGAN (N.M., COLO); RAMIREZ 1 (TEXAS)
ZAMUDIO	DIAZ 10 (ARG)
ZAÑARTU	(Unk.) 1 (ARG)
ZAPATA	ORDOÑEZ 1 (GUA)
ZARATE	GANDIA 3 (ARG)
ZAVALA	GOMENSORO 2 (URU)
ZAYAS	ZAYAS 2 (L.A.)
ZEGERS	FERNANDEZ 80 (CHILE)
ZELA	GALVEZ 1 (PERU); PLATT 7 (PERU)
ZELAYETA	AGUIAR 2 (URU)
ZELEDON	FUENTES 3 (C.R.)
ZEPEDA	PEÑA 4 (CHILE)
ZEVALLOS	SOTOMAYOR (L.A.)
ZIRION	AMERLINCK 1,3 (MEX)
ZUÑIGA	CAMPOS 4 (URU); 5 (URU); COO 1 (ARG, CHILE, URU)

BIBLIOGRAPHY OF FAMILY HISTORIES IN THE UNITED STATES AND LATIN AMERICA

For twenty-five years the author has been collecting titles to family histories and noting the whereabouts of historical sketches on families as they are found in newspapers, magazines, historical compilations, and larger family studies. The following are the results of this work. It is by no means complete, but is the first extensive attempt to catalog this massive amount of material.

Not all works have been personally seen by the author; consequently, some bibliographic references are not complete. Whenever possible, attempts have been made to locate and review each work so that any peculiarities it contains could be annotated.

(Unk.) 1. *Descendencia de Federico Errázuriz Zañartu y Eulogía Echaurren García Huidobro*. Fuerza Aerea de Chile, 1949.

(Unk.) 2. "Descendencia de las Familias Costarricenses que Emigraron a California en el año 1872," *ACC 23* (1976): 253–273.

(Unk.) 3. *Relación y Genealogía de los Señores de la Nueva España y Origen de los Mexicanos*. n.p., 1532.

(Unk.) 4. *Revista de Historia y Genealogía Española: La Casa de Parada en México*. Madrid, 1917.

Abad, Plácido. *General Fructuosa Rivera*. Montevideo, 1939.

Acevedo, Eduardo. "El Carácter Hereditario en la vocación de Don Tomás Alvarez de Acevedo," *IAC 11* (1955): 41–68.

Acosta, Roberto 1. "Apuntes Históricos Sonorenses: Guadalupe de Thobaca y sus Fundadores: la Familia Campoy," *AMH 14* (1955): 5–17.

Acosta, Soledad 2. *Biografías de Hombres Ilustres . . . de Colombia*. Bogotá, 1883.

Acosta, Ursula 3. *Familias de Cabo Rojo.* Santurce, Puerto Rico, 1983. Genealogies of the following families: Acosta, Brau, Wiscovich, Cofresí, Colberg, Cuesta, del Toro, Doitteau, Graniela, Jorge, Ortiz de Peña, Ortiz de la Renta, Pabón-Dávila, Quiñones, Ramírez de Arellano, Ronda, and Zapata. In addition, there are 164 genealogical charts in the work.

Acuña, Daniel. "Fontalba de Angulo," *REH 10* (1960–1961): 129–134.

Agraz, Gabriel 1. "Desenvolvimiento de la Familia Santa Ana," *AGH 1* (1953–1954): 61–146.

Agraz, Gabriel 2. *Esbozos históricos de Tecolotlan, Jalisco.* Guadalajara, 1950.

Agraz, Gabriel 3. *Jalisco y sus hombres: Compendio de geografía, historia y biografía jaliscienses.* Guadalajara, 1958.

Agraz, Gabriel 4. "Origen y desenvolvimiento de la familia de la Cueva en Tecolotlan, Jalisco," *AMG 7*, 1ª Series (1952–1953): 53–108.

Agraz, Gabriel 5. "Un linaje de San Agustín de Tecolotlan: los Agraz," *AGH 2* (1957): 214–285; reprinted in Guadalajara, 1957.

Aguado, Pedro de. *Historia de Santa Marta y el Nuevo Reino de Granada.* 2 vols. Madrid, 1916.

Aguiar, Elsa 1. "Aporte para el estudio de la familia de los Bustamante," *IEG 1* (1980): 33–36.

Aguiar, Elsa 2. "Linaje de Rocha: Los LaCalle y Zelayeta," *IEG 2* (1981): 53–54.

Aguirre, Celso 1. *Compendio Histórico-Biográfico de Mexicali, 1539–1966.* 2nd edition. Tijuana, 1968.

Aguirre, Celso 2. *Tijuana: su historia—sus hombres.* Tijuana, 1975.

Alamo, Joaquín del. *La sucesión legítima a la Corona de México.* 2nd edition. Paris, 1952. Genealogy of Don Guillermo Graw de Moctezuma, 11th great-grandson of the emperor Moctezuma.

Alamos, Vicente. *Linajes de los Alamos y sus Alianzas en Chile.* Santiago, 1979.

Alanis Tarnez, Juan. *Diccionario Biográfico de Santiago, Nuevo León.* Monterrey, Mexico, 1992.

Alba Chacón, Luz 1. *Don Diego de la Haya Fernández*. San José, Costa Rica, 1967.

Alba, Miguel 2. *Una Sección de los Alba de los Altos de Jalisco*. México, D.F., 1981.

Alfaro, Anastacio 1. "Apuntes Genealógicos: Los Alfaro," *Repertorio Americano 15* (1943).

Alfaro, Anastacio 2. "Apuntes Genealógicos: Los González," *Repertorio Americano 15* (1943).

Alfaro, María Eugenia 3. "Familia Steffens Von Greggart: La Descendencia de Don Joseph Friedrich Steffens," *ACC 27–28* (1981): 223–270.

Algara, José. *Los descendientes de Miguel de Cervantes y Saavedra*. México, D.F., 1891. Collection of genealogical articles that appeared in "El Nacional" in 1891.

Aliaga, Jerónimo 1. "La Casa de Guadalcázar en el Perú," IPI 6 (1953): 31–57.

Aliaga, Jerónimo 2. "Los Santa Cruz," *IPI 3* (1948): 213–234.

Allende, Fernando 1. "Antecedentes de la Familia Losada Bravo," *IAC 8* (1948–1949): 275–287. Genealogy that begins with Francisco de Losa Bravo de Lagunas, from Jérez de la Frontera, Spain, and his wife María de Montero. They immigrated to Potosí, Bolivia. Descendants are found today in Perú, Argentina, and Chile, as well as throughout Bolivia.

Allende, Fernando 2. *Apuntes genealógicos de las Familias Navarro y Ocampo*. Santiago, 1959.

Allende, Fernando 3. "Doña María de Toledo y los Cabrera Americanos," *ACH 64* (1961): 107–128.

Allende, Fernando 4. *La Casa-Torre de Allende del Valle de Gordejuela: Origen y Descendencia*. Santiago, 1964.

Allende, Fernando 5. "Los Antepasados Paternos y Maternos del General Insurgente Don Ignacio de Allende y Unzaga," *AMG 5*, 1ª Series (1947): 21–35.

Allende, Fernando 6. "Los Corsarios Franceses en las Costas del Brasil y en los Mares del Sur," *REH 10* (1960–1961): 5–36. Genealogy of the Daniel family of France.

Allende, Fernando 7. "Los Villaseñor y Acuña en Chile: Los Antepasados del General Don Ignacio de Allende y Unzaga," *AMG 5*, 1ª Series (1947): 17–19.

Allendesalazar, Jorge 1. "Aulestias y Uriones," *REH 4–5* (1954–1955): 17–23. Also published separately.

Allendesalazar, Jorge 2. "El Mariscal Don Martín Ruiz de Gamboa, Gobernador de Chile," *Revista Criterio 7–8* (1940).

Allendesalazar, Jorge 3. "Casas Torres de Allende Salazar en Irazagorria." *Hidalguía 13* (1955): 937–942; reprinted *REH 8–9* (1958–1959): 9–13. An analysis of the family seats of the founding fathers of this lineage in Gordejuela.

Allendesalazar, Jorge 4. "Cuatro siglos de la familia Barros," *El Diario Ilustrado*. Santiago, 24 June 1957.

Allendesalazar, Jorge 5. "Del Catastro del Marqués de la Ensenada: Familias Chilenas de Origen Montañés," *Hidalguía 50* (1962): 65–100.

Allendesalazar, Jorge 6. "Doña Mariana de Bazán, Princesa Coya del Cuzco," *IPI 2* (1947): 13–16.

Allendesalazar, Jorge 7. "Ejército y Milicias del Reino de Chile, 1737–1815," *ACH 66* (1962): 102–178; *67* (1962): 197–271; *68* (1963): 200–281; the index to the three references is found in the last one, pages 282–305.

Allendesalazar, Jorge 8. "El Capitán Gaspar de Vergara, Compañero de Almagro: Noticias Genealógicas," *REH 6–7* (1956–1957): 59–71.

Allendesalazar, Jorge 9. "El General Don Francisco de Rivera y Vera y su Descendencia," *REH 2* (1950–1951): 77–101.

Allendesalazar, Jorge 10. "El Señorío de la Torre de Ercilla: El Linaje de Ercilla," *RCG 126* (1958): 336–354.

Allendesalazar, Jorge 11. *Etimología Vasco–Navarra de 200 Apellidos Chilenos*. Madrid, 1959.

Allendesalazar, Jorge 12. "La Casa de Villela y su rama de Abando," *Hidalguía 6* (1954): 533–555. Descendancy of General Don Juan Ortiz de Allende Salazar y Villela, and his wife Doña Contanza de Uriona y Escobar Villarroel, who arrived in Chile at the beginning of the XVII century.

Allendesalazar, Jorge 13. "La Estirpe de Don Pedro de Valdivia en Nueva Extremadura." An unpublished paper given before the Instituto Chileno de Cultura Hispánica in 1950.

Allendesalazar, Jorge 14. *Linaje de Hortún de Salazar, Señor de la Torre de Allende, 1400–1943*. Santiago, 1944.

Allendesalazar, Jorge 15. "Los Allendesalazar de San Juan de la Frontera," *REH 10* (1960–1961): 123–126.

Allendesalazar, Jorge 16. "Los Serrano de Melipilla," *REH 17* (1972): 69–72; *18* (1973): 158. Also published as *Serrano de Melipilla: un linaje Castrense*. Santiago, n.d.

Allendesalazar, Jorge 17. "Los Yavar, Señores de la Casa de Hierro," *REH 12* (1964): 47–66; expanded *13* (1965): 64. The publication by Liliana Ruiz Carrasco, entitled *Bibliografía Heráldica, Genealógica y Nobiliaria, Reseñada en la Revista Hidalguía, 1953–1977*, noted this article as *"Los Yavar, Señores de la Casa de Herrero."* It was published in volume 71 of *Hidalguía*.

Allendesalazar, Jorge 18. *Marginaciones a una filiación*. Santiago, 1964.

Allendesalazar, Jorge 19. "Origen Cidiano de los Gómez de Silva," *REH 3* (1952–1953).

Allendesalazar, Jorge 20. *Sangre de Tena en la Colonia*. Santiago, 1941.

Allendesalazar, Jorge 21. "Una Línea Chilena de Moya: Descendencia del Gaditano, Don Antonio de Moya y Terreros, " *RGB 17* (1948): 231–235.

Allendesalazar, Jorge 22. "Una Línea Chilena de Vera y Aragón," *REH 1* (1949): 67–78.

Allendesalazar, Jorge 23. "Una Relación de Militares Nobles del Real Ejército de Chile, con Apellidos Vascos y Navarros," *Hidalguía 38* (1960): 77–96.

Allendesalazar, Jorge 24. *Varonía de los Allendesalazar en el Reino de Chile*. Madrid, 1957. Revised and published as #14.

Almada, Francisco R. 1. *Diccionario de Historia, Geo grafía y Biografía Chihua huenses*. 2nd edition.. n.p., n.d.; 1st edition was printed in 1928.

Almada, Francisco R. 2. "Los Primeros Pobladores de Santa Eulalia y San Francisco de Cuéllar," *AMH 2* (1943).

Almelá, Juan. *Guía de Personas que Cultivan la Historia de América.* México, D.F., 1951.

Alsina, Pablo. "Información del Origen y Distinguido Nacimiento de Don Pablo Alsina y Giol, Librada Ante la Justicia de Cardedeu, Corregimiento de Malaio, Barcelona el 21 de junio de 1768," *IAC 3* (1944): 173–189.

Alurralde, Nicanor. "Genealogía de la Familia Alurralde," *IAC 4–5* (1945): 207–277.

Alva, Tomás. *El Linaje de los Lugones.* Buenos Aires, 1963.

Alvarez L., Emilio 1. *Familia Chamorro.* Donation made to the ACC in 1953. Mr. Alvarez was a Nicaraguan genealogist.

Alvarez, Juan 2. "Los Pérez de Tudela del Perú," *IPI 14* (1965): 41–78.

Alvarez, Senón 3. *Apuntamientos Genealógicos para la Inteligencia de las Casas Nobles de Asturias.* 3 vols. Santiago, Chile, 1924–1925. Also called *Biblioteca Histórico–Genealógica Asturiana.*

Amado, Robert J. *Descendientes de Indalecio Amado Sazo y Tomasa Rodas de Amado.* Manuscript, 1984, of 11 pages, found in the Family History Center, Oakland, California.

Amador, Florencio. *Catalógo de Genealogías.* Bilbao, 1958.

Amaya, Jesús 1. *El Padre Hidalgo, Sus Antepasados y Parientes.* México, D.F., 1952.

Amaya, Jesús 2. "La Estirpe de Don Lorenzo," *AMG 1*, 2ª Series (1957): 111–117.

Amaya, Jesús 3. *Los Conquistadores Fernández de Híjar y Bracamonte: Ensayo Bio-geneográfico.* Guadalajara, 1952.

Amaya, Jesús 4. "Nuevos Datos Acerca de la Ascendencia Paterna de Hidalgo," *AMG 8*, 1ª Series (1953): 59–72.

Amerlinck, Teodoro 1. "Genealogía y Heráldica del Primer Emperador de México, Don Agustín I.," *AMG 4*, 2ª Series (1968): 349–358; reprinted in *RAG 5–6* (1971–1972): 437–450; reprinted as *Genealogía de SS.MM. los Emperadores de México: Maximiliano y Carlota.* Madrid, 1971. It also appeared in volume 115 of *Hidalguía.*

Amerlinck, Teodoro 2. *La Familia de Zirión.* México, D.F., 1951. Descendants of Antonio de Zirión, Urruela, Urruela y Valle, native of Retas de Tudela. Ancestors back to 1693 and Domingo de Zirión, resident of Santa María de Llano in the Valley Tudela.

Amerlinck, Teodoro 3. "Genealogía de Teodoro Amerlinck y Zirión," *AMG 6*, 1ª Series (1950–1951): 85–102.

Amesti, Luis 1. "Notas Genealógicas y Biográficas: Doña Carmen Arriagada de Gutike," *ACH 51* (1954): 87–90.

Amesti, Luis 2. "Casas Troncales de Colchagua: Los González de Medina," *RCH 51* (1923): 324–332.

Amesti, Luis 3. *Las Casas Troncales de Colchagua.* Volume 1. Santiago, 1926.

Amézaga, Jorge. "El Conquistador Don Diego de Agüero y Los Mayorazgos de su Casa," *IPI 15* (1970): 165–176.

Amigó, Carlos. "Extracto del Dictamen del Abogado Español Don Carlos Amigó, del Colegio de Abogados de Barcelona, Sobre el Mayorazgo de Don Manuel María de Peralta," *ACC 2* (1955): 32–36.

Amunátegui, D. 1. *La Sociedad Chilena en el Siglo XVIII: Mayorazgos y Títulos de Castilla.* 3 vols. Santiago, 1901–1904.

Amunátegui, D. 2. *Hijos Ilustres de Chillán.* Santiago, 1935.

Amunátegui, D. 3. "Larraines y Errazuriz en la Revolución de 1810," *ACH 35* (1946): 43–60.

Amunátegui, Miguel 4. *Don Antonio García Reyes i algunos de sus Antepasados, a la luz de Documentos Inéditos.* 6 vols. Santiago, 1929–1936.

Amunátegui, Miguel 5. "Don Antonio García Reyes a la luz de Documentos Inéditos," *RCH 62* (1928): 41–80.

Anaya Chávez, Aurora and José Ignacio Paulino Dávila Garibi. *Arbol Genealógico de la Señora Doña Isabel Gutiérrez Orozco, Vda. de Anaya, con motivo del Nonagésimo Aniversario de su Natalicio.* México, D.F., 1953.

Anda, Alfonso. *Datos más Detallados sobre el Linaje de Don Juan de Salinas y Loyola.* Loja, Ecuador, 1982.

Andrade, César 1. *Vigencia de un Corregidor. Cédula de Identidad del Sargento Mayor Don Joseph Andrade y Benavides, Caballero de la Orden de Santiago y Señor de la Villa de Salas y Ribera, Corregidor de Cuenca de América; noticias sobre sus Ascendientes Filiación de sus Descendientes y Recuento Documentado y Escriturario de sus Servicios.* Cuenca, Ecuador, 1955.

Andrade, Manuel 2. *Próceres de la Independencia: Indice Alfabético de sus Nombres con Algunos Bocetos Biográficos.* Quito, 1909.

Aparicio, Edgar 1. "Arbol Genealógico de los Castilla y Portugal," *RAG 1* (1967): 53–61.

Aparicio, Edgar 2. *Bernal Díaz del Castillo y sus Descendientes.* 1st edition. México, D.F., 1959.

Aparicio, Edgar 3. "Conquistadores de Guatemala a quienes le fue concedido escudo de armas y que dejaron descendencia," *Hidalguía 172–173* (1982): 433–454.

Aparicio, Edgar 4. *Conquistadores de Guatemala y Fundadores de Familias Guatemaltecas.* 2nd edition., revised. México, D.F., 1961. It also appeared in *Hidalguía*, volume 48.

Aparicio, Edgar 5. "Datos Genealógicos de los trece Próceres que firmaron el Acta de la Independencia de Centroamérica en 1821," *RAG 5–6* (1971–1972): 11–38.

Aparicio, Edgar 6. "Don Juan Antonio Ruiz de Bustamante, Caballero Santiaguista, y su Nieto Rafael Laudivar, Ilustre Poeta Guatemalteco," *Estudios a la Convención del Instituto Internacional de Genealogía y Heráldica con Motivo de su XXV Aniversario,* págs. 55–62. Madrid, 1979.

Aparicio, Edgar 7. "Doña Isabel Clara de Quiñones y de la Cueva y su Entronque con la Casa Real de la Francia," *RAG 8* (1983): 411–434.

Aparicio, Edgar 8. "Familia Ariza o Arizaga," *RAG 8* (1983): 119–180.

Aparicio, Edgar 9. "Familias Cabarrús," *RAG 3–4* (1969–1970): 321–346.

Aparicio, Edgar 10. "Familias de Guatemala con Ascendencia Real," *Estudios Genealógicos, Heráldicos y Nobiliarios.* Tomo 1: 47–62. Madrid, 1978.

Aparicio, Edgar 11. "Genealogía de la Familia Vilches de Cabrera: Ascendencia y Familia del Ilustrísimo Señor Don Juan Carlos de Vilches y Cabrera, Obispo de Nicaragua," *ACC 11–12* (1963–1964): 62–65.

Aparicio, Edgar 12. *Historia de la Familia Delgado de Najera.* Guatemala, 1965.

Aparicio, Edgar 13. "La Familia de Arzú," *RAG 3–4* (1969–1970): 69–114.

Aparicio, Edgar 14. "La Familia de Irisarri," *RAG 1* (1967): 17–25.

Aparicio, Edgar 15. "La Familia Lacayo de Briones," *RAG 5–6* (1972–1973): 463–476.

Aparicio, Edgar 16. "La Familia Maestre (Marqueses de Gómez de Barreda)," *RAG 5–6* (1971–1972): 335–382.

Aparicio, Edgar 17. *Los Caballeros de las Ordenes Militares en Guatemala.* México, D.F., n.d. It also appeared in *Hidalguía*, volume 124.

Aparicio, Edgar 18. *Los Gutiérrez Marroquin y sus Descendientes.* Guatemala, 1956.

Aparicio, Edgar 19. *Manuel Martínez Aparicio, Primera Autoridad de Quezaltenango Después de la Independencia y Hermano Mayor de la Primera Junta de Gobierno del Hospital de San Juan de Dios.* Guatemala, 1949.

Aparicio, Edgar 20. "Palomo de Rivera," *AMG 5–6*, 1ª Series (1947): 37–41.

Aparicio, Edgar 21. *Recopilación Histórica, Genealógica y Heráldica de la Familia de Unda.* Guatemala, 1963.

Apolant, Juan A. 1. *Genealogía de los Treinta y Tres.* Montevideo, 1975.

Apolant, Juan A. 2. *Genesis de la Familia Uruguaya: Los habitantes de Montevideo en sus primeros 40 años, filiaciones, ascendencias, entronques, descendencias.* Montevideo, 1966. The 2nd edition was expanded and published in 1975 in four volumes.

Apolant, Juan A. 3. *Operativo Patagonia: Historia de la Mayor Aportación Demográfica Masiva a la Banda Oriental: con Nómina Completa, Filiaciones y Distino de las Familias Pobladores.* Montevideo, 1970.

Aragón, Juan. *Biografías en Síntesis.* Mérida del Yucatán, 1963.

Aramburu, Andrés. "Linajes del Perú," *IPI 7* (1954): 119–151.

Araneda Bravo, Fidel. *Linaje Sacerdotal: Sobre la Familia Silva.* Unpublished manuscript, Chile.

Arango, Gabriel 1. *Genealogías de las Familias de Antioquia.* Medellín, 1911.

Arango, Gabriel 2. *Genealogías de Antioquia y Caldas.* 2nd edition. 2 vols. Medellín, 1942.

Arango, Gabriel 3. *Monografías de Antioquia.* Medellín, 1941.

Arango, Gabriel 4. *Las Familias de La Ceja, Colombia.* Medellín, 1959.

Araujo, Horacio 1. *Los Italianos en el Uruguay.* Barcelona, 1920. Contains more than 1,000 biographies of Italian Uruguayans.

Araujo, Orestes 2. *Gobernantes del Uruguay.* Montevideo, 1903.

Aravena, Hector. "Relación de familias Curiccanas," *ACH 24* (1943).

Araya, Ramón 1. "La Familia Urrejola," *RCH 21* (1916): 112–125.

Araya, Ramón 2. "Los Eguigura," *RCH 21* (1916).

Arboleda, Gustavo 1. *Diccionario Biográfico y Genealógico del Antiguo Departamento de Cauca.* Bogotá, 1962. The 2nd edition was revised and published in Cali in 1962.

Arboleda, Hernán 2. *Descendencia Española de Algunas Familias Colombianas: Datos Biográfico-Genealógicos.* Popayán, 1984. Families Arboleda, Valencia, O'Donnell and Mosquera Figueroa.

Arcaya, Pedro M. *Población de Origen Europeo de Coro en la Epoca Colonial.* Caracas, 1972.

Archivo Histórico Nacional, Madrid. *Catálogo de las Informaciones Genealógicas de los Pretendientes al Santo Oficio de la Inquisición de Toledo.* Madrid, 1903.

Archivo Histórico Nacional, Madrid. *Indice de los Pleitos sobre Mayorazgos, Estados, y Señoríos.* Madrid, 1927.

Archivo Militar General, Segovia. *Indice de Expedientes Personales.* 9 vols. Madrid, 1959.

Arco, Fernando del. *Hidalguías Madrileñas.* Madrid, 1977.

Arellano, Victor Hugo. "Los Rizzo en Guayaquil," *CAG 15* (1985): 61–77.

Arenas Luque, Fermín V. 1. "Apuntes para la Genealogía del General Don José María Paz y Haedo," *IAG 6–7* (1946–1947): 187–195.

Arenas Luque, Fermín V. 2. *Cabrera y los Roca: Genealogía.* Buenos Aires, 1942.

Arenas Luque, Fermín V. 3. *El Fundador de Córdoba, Don Jerónimo Luis de Cabrera y sus Descendientes.* Buenos Aires, 1939. Reprinted under the title: *Don Gerónimo Luis de Cabrera y sus Descendientes.* Buenos Aires, 1980. See *EGH 15* (1982): 111–120 for an analysis of this book.

Arenas Luque, Fermín V. 4. "Genealogía de Don Clemente José Villada y Cabrera," *IAC 2* (1943): 71–85.

Arenas Luque, Fermín V. 5. "Los Luque: Un Linaje que Honra a la Iglesia Católica, Apostólica y Romana," *IAC 4–5* (1945): 126–134.

Arenas Luque, Fermín V. 6. *Noticias Genealógicas e Históricas de los Cabrera y los Iriondo.* Buenos Aires, 1944.

Arenas Luque, Fermín V. 7. "Roque, Saénz Peña y Lahitte," *IAC 7* (1950–1951): 328–339.

Arenas Luque, Fermín V. 8. *Uriburu: Genealogía.* Buenos Aires, 1944.

Argamasilla, J. *Nobiliario y Armería General de Navarra.* 3 vols. Madrid, 1899.

Arízaga, Max. "El Sacerdocio en la Casa de Arízaga," *CAG 15* (1985): 79–86.

Armella, Virginia. *Memoria de una Familia: Flores Alatorre.* México, D.F., 1984.

Arpée, Marion B. *The Hinojosa Family of Northeastern Mexico and the Lower Río Grande Valley: Its Background and History.* Harlingen, Texas, 1985.

Arrigunaga, Joaquín. *Estirpe de Conquistadores: Familias de Yucatán.* Mérida, 1967.

Atienza, Julio 1. *Diccionario Nobiliario.* Madrid, 1954.

Atienza, Julio 2. *Grandezas y Títulos del Reino Concedido por S.M. el Rey Don Alfonso XIII.* Madrid, 1963; reprinted 1965.

Atienza, Julio 3. "Linajes de la Villa de Deva (Guipúzcoa)," *Hidalguía 20* (1957): 113–128. "Extract of the genealogy of the Peralta family" according to *Mundo Hispánico* 145 (1960): 5.

Atienza, Julio 4. *Títulos Nobiliarios Avecinados en Sevilla en el Año 1770*. Madrid, 1970.

Atienza, Julio 5. *Títulos Nobiliarios Hispanoamericanos*. Madrid, 1947.

Avella, Francisco. *Diccionario Biográfico del Clero Secular de Buenos Aires, 1580–1900*. Buenos Aires, 1983.

Avilez, Alexander. *Population Increase into Alto California in the Spanish Period, 1769–1821*. Unpublished Master's Thesis, University of Southern California, 1955. Beginning on page 74 there are lists of soldiers, settlers, artisans, prisoners, mariners, governors, priests, and where applicable, the spouses and children of each.

Ayala, Manuel Josef. "Pruebas de Lexitimadad, Nobleza, Vida y Costumbres de Don Manuel Josef de Ayala, Natural de Panamá, 1785," *Revista de los Archivos Nacionales, San José, Costa Rica 1* (1936–1937): 427–429.

Azarola, Luis E. 1. *Apellidos de la Patria Vieja*. Buenos Aires, 1942.

Azarola, Luis E. 2. *Azarola: Crónica del Linaje*. Madrid, 1929.

Azarola, Luis E. 3. *Contribución a la Historia de Montevideo: Veinte Linajes del Siglo XVIII*. Paris, 1926. Families Zabala, Alzaybar, Archucarro, Viana, Camejo Soto, Sostoa, Maciel, Soria, Vargas, Herrera, Artigas, Haedo, Oribe, Mitre, Urquiza Rozas, etc.

Azarola, Luis E. 4. *Crónicas y Linajes de la Gobernación del Plata: Documentos Inéditos de los Siglos XVII y XVIII*. Buenos Aires, 1927.

Azarola, Luis E. 5. "Don Diego Flórez de León," *RCH 74* (1931): 254–259. Between pages 242–246 is information on his children and grandchildren.

Azarola, Luis E. 6. "Linaje de Alvarez de Acevedo," *RCG 74* (1931): 254–259. Genealogy of Tomás Alvarez de Acevedo, born in 1735, with six generations of ancestors and various generations of descendants.

Azarola, Luis E. 7. *Los San Martín en la Banda Oriental*. Buenos Aires, 1936.

Azarola, Luis E. 8. *Los Maciel en la Historia del Plata, 1604–1814.* Buenos Aires, 1940.

B., S.M. "Emparán," *REH 10* (1960–1961): 126–127.

Baca, Gustavo. "Las Familias Fernández de Arredondo y Corzo," *IPI* 4 (1949): 166–191.

Báez, Jesús 1. *Notas sobre los Báez de Simancas que se Establecieron en Caracas en el Siglo XVII.* Caracas, 1966.

Báez, Julio 2. *Apuntes sobre la Descendencia del Capitán Alonso Díaz Moreno, Fundador de la Nueva Valencia del Rey.* Caracas, n.d.

Báez, Luis 3. *Antecesores y Descendientes de los Hermanos Mariano y Luisa de Castro, quienes proceden de Menorca y fundaron familia en el Oriente de la República.* Caracas, 1969.

Báez, Luis 4. Familias Venezolanas con Antecedentes en el Algarve," *Hidalguía 172–173* (1982): 419–432.

Báez, Luis 5. "Grandeza del Alma del Libertador: Un Hidalgo de la Comunidad Hispánica," *Hidalguía 29* (1981): 369–381. Genealogy of Don Fernando Miyares y Pérez Bernal, born in 1749 in Santiago de Cuba; resident of Caracas. His ancestors were from Parres, Asturias. Genealogy of the Bolivar family of Venezuela.

Báez, Luis 6. "Información de Nobleza, Méritos y Servicios de Don Francisco y Don José Rafael de Tovar, Arcediano de la Catedral de Caracas y Regidor Perpétuo de la Misma Ciudad, Respectivamente," *Estudios a la Convención del Instituto Internacional de Genealogía y Heráldica con Motivo de su XXV Aniversario,* pp. 73–91. Madrid, 1979.

Báez, Luis 7. "Militares con Calidad de Nobles en las Antiguas Hojas de Servicio Existentes en el Archivo General de la Nacion," *Estudios Genealógicos, Heráldicos y Nobiliarios 1* (1978): 83–98.

Balli de Chavana, Herminia. *The History of the Prestigious Balli Family: Story of the First Pioneer Settlers of the Río Grande Valley.* Austin, Texas: n.p. Story of Pedro Balli, third printer of New Spain; genealogies of Balli, Hinojosa, Cavazos, and de la Garza.

Baraya, José M. *Biografías Militares.* Bogotá, 1874.

Barbadillo, Pedro. *Historia del Ilustre Colegio de Abogados de Madrid: Relaciones de Abogados que hicieron Pruebas de Limpieza de Sangre.* 3 vols. Madrid, 1956–1960.

Barcón, J. *Monografía completa de la región del Colla o sea Rosario de Colla, Colonia Suiza, Nueva Helvecia, Colonia Valdense o Piamontesa, La Paz, Colonia Cosmopolitana, Puerto del Sauce, Departamento de Colonia, República Oriental del Uruguay.* Rosario, Uruguay, 1902. Lists of its founders and settlers.

Barnard, Charles B. *Familias Colonizadoras: Los Apuntes de Carlos Beck Barnard, 1859–1861.* Edited by Gastón Gori. Santa Fé, Argentina, 1954. The Swiss in Santa Fé.

Barnoya, Francisco 1. *Genealogía de las Familias Barnoya, de España y de Guatemala, 1614–1966.* Guatemala, 1967.

Barnoya, Francisco 2. *Genealogía de la Familia Verdugo, 1663–1969.* Guatemala, 1969.

Barozzi, Baldissini. *Dizionario Biográfico degli Italiani al Plata.* 1st edition. Buenos Aires, 1899.

Barra, Luis León. "Alrededor de la Familia Lynch," *RCH 96* (1940): 323–336.

Barrantes, Mario 1. "Barrantes: Orígenes Remotos, Barrantes de Alcántara, Barantes de Costa Rica," *ACC 18–20* (1973): 40–59.

Barrantes, Mario 2. "La Familia Corrales de Costa Rica (Bonifaz)," *ACC 16–18* (1970): 97–102.

Barrantes, Mario 3. "Hay Parentescos entre las Familias de Pedro de Alvarado y Francisco de Ocampo Golfín," *ACC 18–20* (1973): 73–77.

Barrantes, Mario 4. "La Familia Monge de Costa Rica," *ACC 18–20* (1973): 62–72.

Barrantes, Mario 5. *Orígenes de los Costarricenses: Los Barrantes de Costa Rica.* San José, 1967.

Barreda, Felipe A. 1. *Al Servicio del Perú: Genealogía del General Clemente de Althaus.* Lima, 1958.

Barreda, Felipe A. 2. *Dos Linajes.* 1st edition. Lima, 1955; 2nd edition. Lima, 1960. Genealogy of the families Soria and Bolivar with information also on the families Carranza, Rocha, Vivar, Garcés, de Marcilla, Jufré de Loayza, and others in Perú and Chile.

Barreda, Felipe A. 3. "Los Garland," *IPI 6* (1953): 63, 78.

Barreda, Felipe A. 4. *Elespuru.* Lima, 1957.

Barreda, Felipe A. 5. *Manuel Pardo Ribadeneira: Regente de la Real Audiencia del Cuzco*. Lima, 1954. Ancestry and posterity of Don Manuel Pardo Ribadeneira, including various Chilean lineages; the complete descendancy of Don José Manuel de la Trinidad Pardo y Aliaga and Doña Josefa Correa y Toro; the descendancy of Don Antonio de Ulloa, conquistador of Chile.

Barreda, Felipe A. 6. "Mis Antepasados," *RGL 11* (1951): 315.

Barreiro, Carlos 1. "Bicentenario de la Creación del Virreinato de las Provincias del Río de La Plata," *IAC 16* (1976): 12–24. Biographies of Pedro de Cevallos, Juan José de Vertiz, Nicolás del Campo, Nicolás Antonio de Arredondo, Pedro Melo de Portugal, Antonio de Olaguer y Feliu, Gabriel de Avilés, Joaquín del Pino, Rafael de Sobremonte, Santiago de Liniers, and Baltasar Hidalgo de Cisneros.

Barreiro, Carlos 2. "Linajes Hispanoamericanos: Los Pieres," *IEI 1* (1980): 9–28.

Barreiro, Carlos 3. *Los Ortiz de San Luís y Otras Genealogías*. Buenos Aires, 1967; reprinted, 1977.

Barreiro, Carlos 4. "Yanzi," *IAC 14* (1961): 136–144.

Barrenechea, José. *José Antonio Barrenechea, 1829–1889: Su Vida y Su Obra*. Lima, 1929.

Barreto V., et al. *Diccionario Biográfico de Figuras Contemporáneas*. Lima, 1926.

Barrios, Juan 1. "El Conquistador Diego de Rojas y su Descendencia," *REH 3* (1952). The author also studies the families Galleguillos and Iribarren.

Barrios, Juan 2. "El Conquistador Francisco de Aguirre y su Descendencia," *REH 1* (1949): 6–54.

Barros, Julio. *La Familia Barros en Chile, 1525–1926*. Santiago, 1928.

Barrows, H.D. 1. "The Lugo Family of California," *Historical Society of Southern California 9* (1914): 34–39.

Barrows, H.D. 2. "The Palomares Family of California," *Historical Society of Southern California 5* (1902): 254–255.

Basanta, Alfredo 1. *Catálogo Genealógico de Vizcainos*. Madrid, 1934.

Basanta, Alfredo 2. *Nobleza Alavesa*. Valladolid, 1930.

Basanta, Alfredo 3. *Nobleza Guipuzcoana*. Madrid, 1932.

Basanta, Alfredo 4. *Sala de Hijosdalgo de la Real Chancillería de Valladolid*. Madrid, 1955.

Basas, Manuel. *La Sección de Genealogías del Archivo Municipal de Bilbao*. Madrid, 1958.

Baudean, Julio C. 1. "Juan Fernández de Molina: Su Vida, Su Descendencia," *IEG* 2 (1981): 47–52; *3* (1982): 29–39; *4* (1982): 41–62.

Baudean, Julio C. 2. "La Descendencia de Pedro López de Tarija," *IEG 1* (1980): 21–22.

Beltroy, Manuel, editor. *Peruanos Notables de Hoy*. 1st edition. Lima, 1957.

Bello, Ruth T. "The Descendants of Feliciana Goceascochea and Juan José Tijerina," *Los Tejanos, Journal of Hispanic Genealogy and History 1* (1990): 2–4.

Benítez, José R. 1. "Conquistadores de la Nueva Galicia," *Boletín de la Junta Auxiliar Jalisciense 7* (1942): 277–287.

Benítez, José R. 2. "Fundadores de la Ciudad de Guadalajara," *Boletín de la Junta Auxiliar Jalisciense 7* (1942): 277–287.

Benítez, José R. 3. "Noticias Genealógico–Biográficas del Sr. Coronel Prisciliano M. Benítez," *AGH 1* (1943): 161. Also printed in Guadalajara in 1943.

Benítez, José R. 4. "Primeros Vecinos Pobladores," *Boletín de la Junta Auxiliar Jalisciense 7* (1942): 313–322.

Benvenutto, Neptalí. *Parlamentarios del Perú Contemporáneo, 1904–1921*. Lima, 1921.

Bermejo, Vladimiro. *Arequipa: Bio-bibliográfico de Arequipeños Contemporáneos*. Arequipa, 1954.

Bernal, Jesús 1. *Apuntes Históricos, Geográficos y Estadísticos del Estado de Aguascalientes*. 1st edition. Aguascalientes, 1928.

Bernal, Nazario 2. "Divagaciones Genealógicas sobre los Boteros," *Revista Universidad Pontificia Bolivariana 69*. Condensado en *RGL 7* (1947): 99–104.

Bernard, Tomás D. "Sobre la Genealogía de la Familia San Martín: Doña Josefa Dominga Balcarce y San Martín de Gutiérrez de Estrada," *IAC 12* (1957): 161–178.

Bernedo, José Carlos. *Poesía y Genealogía de los Bernedo, y Málaga, de la Villa de Yarabamba.* Arequipa, 1973.

Berro, Arturo. "La Familia Berro: Decendencia de Bernardo Berro Iriarte y de Catalina Echebarne," *IEG 2* (1981): 35–40; *3* (1982): 13–28.

Binayán, Narciso 1. "Colonnas y Orsinis en Córdoba del Tucumán," *Hidalguía 30* (1982): 747–758.

Binayán, Narciso 2. "En Torno a Pedro Alvarez Holguín," *IAC 17* (1977): 11–18.

Blin, Adolfo José. "Los Lopez Barajas," *IAC 2* (1943): 27–37.

Bloom, Leonard B. "The Coronado-Bocanegra Family Alliance," *New Mexico Historical Review 16* (1940): 401–431.

Borrero, Maximiliano. *Orígenes Cuencanos.* 2 vols. Cuenca, 1962.

Bouchet, Jorge du. "Apuntes para la Genealogía de las Familias Espirituanas; Dedicados a la Ciudad de Sancti-Spiritus: Los Mendigutia," *Correo del Instituto Cubano de Genealogía y Heráldica 2* (1958): 7–11.

Boyd-Bowman, Peter. *Indice Geográfico de Cuarenta Mil Pobladores Españoles de América en el Siglo XVI.* Volume 1: 1493–1519. Bogotá, 1964; volume 2: 1520–1539. México, D.F., 1985; volume 3: *Indice Geográfico de Cincuenta y Cinco Mil Pobladores Españoles de América: 1493–1519.*

Brading, D.A. *Mineros y Comerciantes en el México Borbónico, 1763–1810.* México, 1975.

Briceño, Américo 1. *La Ciudad Portátil: Historia de la Provincia de Trujillo.* Caracas, 1939.

Briceño, Mario 2. *Los Fundadores de Trujillo de Nuestra Señora de la Paz.* n.p., n.d.

Briceño, Mario 3. *Genealogía del Dr. Cristóbal Hurtado de Mendoza.* Caracas, 1967.

Bromley, Juan 1. "La Casa Marquesal de Castellón: Los Buendía," *IPI* 7 (1954): 31–38.

Bromley, Juan 2. "Los Vásquez de Acuña, Condes de la Vega del Rén," *IPI 8* (1955): 275–287.

Brown, Edna Garza 1. *Origin of the Surnames Garza and Treviño in Nuevo León.* Translation of the work by Tomás Mendirichaga Cueva (q.v.). Corpus Christi, 1989.

Brown, Edna Garza 2. *The Genealogy of Edna Garza Brown.* Houston, 1980.

Buck, Samuel M. *Yanaguana's Successors: The Story of the Canary Islanders' Immigration into Texas in the Eighteenth Century.* Reimpreso por Robert M. Benavides, San Antonio, 1980. Describes the life and times of colonial Spanish Texas, 1731–1793. A new appendix lists the *alcaldes* of San Antonio, 1731–1836; mayors, 1837–1981; and judges of Béxar County, 1839–1981.

Bulnes, Alfonso. *Bulnes, 1799–1866.* Buenos Aires, 1946.

Bunker, Oscar L. *Historia de Caguas.* 2 vols. Caguas, Puerto Rico, 1975.

Bunster, Enríque. *Chilenos en California.* Santiago, 1954.

Burke, Oscar D. "Descendencia de los Delgado de Caguas, Puerto Rico," *IGH 2* 1st Series (1983): 46–56. Re-edited in *IGH 1* 2nd Series (1989): 117–127.

Burkholder, M.A. & D.S. Chandler. *Biographical Dictionary of Audiencia Ministers in the Americas, 1687–1821.* Westport, Conn., 1982.

Busca-Sust, Jorge 1. "Los Burgos (o Celis de Burgos) y los Celis de Quiroga," *EGC 15* (1982): 7ff.

Busca-Sust, Jorge 2. "Ramírez Tello," *EGC 15* (1982): 25–32.

Busca-Sust, Jorge 3. "Román," *IAC 18* (1979): 15–22.

Bustamante, Luis 1. *Diccionario Biográfico Cienfueguero.* n.p., n.d.

Bustamante, Manuel 2. *Mis Ascendientes.* Lima, 1955.

Bustamante, Tránsito 3. *Simientes del Pionero Suizo en la Frontera.* Victoria, Chile, 1984.

Busto, José Antonio. "La Casa de Peralta en el Perú," *IPI 15* (1970): 99–140; *16* (1975): 15–84.

Bustos, Carlos P. "Los del Campillo," *CEG 6*, 24–30.

Buxton, Margaret L. *The Family of Lucero de Godoi: Early Records.* Albuquerque, n.d.

Caballero, Fernán. *La Familia de Alvareda.* 4th edition. Buenos Aires, 1945.

Cabrera, Cayetano 1. *Escudo de Armas de México.* México, D.F. 1981. Facsimile edition of 1743.

Cabrera, Matilde 2. "Cuatro Grandes Dinastías Mexicanas en los Descendientes de los Hermanos Fernández de Lima y Barragán," *AGH 2* (1957): 5–181. Also published as a book, México, D.F., 1950; San Luis Potosí, 1956. Genealogical charts of various Indian nations in Mexico from 900 A.D. until the Conquest.

Cabrera, Matilde 3. *De la Peña.* México, D.F., 1985.

Cabrera, Matilde 4. "Don Paulo de Berastegui y de la Vara," *AMG 4*, 2ª Series (1968): 218–315. Also published under the title of *Berastegui.* México, D.F., 1969.

Cabrera, Matilde 5. *La Casa de Cabrera en San Luis Potosí.* n.p., 1975.

Cabrera, Matilde 6. *La Familia Hernández Soto de San Luis Potosí.* México, 1966; reprinted, 1975.

Cabrera, Matilde 7. *La familia Toranzo de San Luis Potosí.* México, D.F., n.d.

Cabrera, Matilde 8. *María Ipiña: Una Familia de Hacendados Potosinos.* Tlaxcala, 1984.

Cabrera, Matilde 9. *Refutación Genealógica del Libro* El Valle del Maíz, San Luis Potosí *del Lic. Rafael Montejano y Aguiñaga.* México, D.F., 1970.

Cadenas, Ampelio 1. "Genealogía de la Familia Noble de Porlier," *Hidalguía 28* (1980): 683–690. Descendants of Don Antonio Aniceto de Porlier, resident of Mojo, Perú in 1760, Charcas, Bolivia in 1765. Family has dispersed throughout South America, Mexico, Spain, and Cuba.

Cadenas, Francisco 2. *Nobiliaria Extranjera.* Madrid, 1963.

Cadenas, Vicente 3. *Caballeros de la Orden de Santiago en el Siglo XVIII, 1761–1762.* 5 vols. Madrid, 1977–1979. Genealogical extracts.

Cadenas, Vicente 4. *Extracto Genealógico de los Expedientes de la Orden de Carlos III., 1777–1847.* 6 vols. Madrid, 1979.

Cadenas, Vicente 5. *Pleitos de Hidalguía de la Real Chancillería de Valladolid: sus extractos Genealógicos, Siglo XVIII.* 6 vols., letters A–C. Madrid, 1981–1984.

Cadenas, Vicente 6. *Pleitos de Hidalguía de la Real Chancillería de Valladolid Seguidos Durante el Siglo XIX: Extractos de las Genealógicos.* 8 vols. Madrid, 1975–1980.

Calcagno, Francisco. *Diccionario Biográfico Cubano.* New York, 1878. Biographies through 1878 of distinguished Cubans in and out of Cuba.

Calvo, Carlos 1. "Indice de Genealogías Argentinas," *IAC 4–5* (1945): 135–171. Alphabetical list of surnames whose genealogies were published before 1945 in Argentina, giving the origin of the surname and the publication reference.

Calvo, Carlos 2. "Los San Martín de Portugalete," *IAC 2* (1943): 39–41.

Calvo, Carlos 3. *Nobiliario del Antiguo Virreinato del Río de la Plata.* Buenos Aires, 1936–1943. The first volume originally came out in 1924.

Calvo, Joaquín B. 4. *Notas para un Libro de Familia.* Washington, D.C., 1899. Reprinted in 1945 with Enríque Fonseca, no place.

Calvo, Luis María 5. "Descendencia Santafesina del Capitán Pedro de Izarra, Vecino Fundador de Buenos Aires," *IEI 1* (1980): 35–55.

Calvo, Luis María 6. "Dos Ramas de Linaje de Garay en Santa Fé," *IAC 19* (1981): 12–22.

Calvo, Luis María 7. "Lacoizqueta," *IAC 18* (1979): 23–26.

Camp, Roderic A. *Mexican Political Biographies, 1935–1981.* Tucson, 1982.

Campos, Fernando 1. "Los Aguilera y los Bastidas en la Conquista," *REH 12* (1964): 77–94.

Campos, Fernando 2. "Los Defensores del Rey," *REH 7* (1958).

Campos, Fernando 3. "Veleros Franceses en el Mar del Sur," *REH 12* (1964).

Campos, Ricardo D. 4. "Brigadier General Doctor Thomas García de Zúñiga," *Grandes Hombres en la Provincia Oriental, 1781–1843*. Montevideo, 1946. Contains the lineage of the García de Zúñiga and their descendants.

Campos, Ricardo D. 5. *Las Grandes Familias Patricias Rioplatenses: Los García de Zúñiga y los Warnes*. Montevideo, 1948.

Camus, José María. *Apuntes Genealógicos de las Familias de Camus Loyola y de Riveros Suárez de Figueroa*. Santiago, 1930.

Cantera, Francisco. *Pedrarias Dávila y Cota, Capitán General y Gobernador de Castilla de Oro y Nicaragua: Sus Antecedentes Judíos*. Madrid, 1971.

Cañas, Rafael. "Genealogía del General Don José María Cañas," *Revista de los Archivos Nacionales, San José 5–6* (1940): 301.

Capriles, Alejandro M. *Coronas de Castilla en Venezuela*. Madrid, 1967.

Caraffa, Pedro I. *Hombre Notables de Cuyo*. 2nd edition. La Plata, 1912.

Carbo, Jorge 1. "Correa," *IAC 14* (1961): 8–10.

Carbo, Jorge 2. "Fernández," *IAC 14* (1961): 11–14.

Carbonell, N. *El General Ramón Leocadio Bonachea de La Habana*. La Habana, 1947.

Cárdenas, Emilio. *Catálogo de Títulos Nobiliarios Sacados de los Legajos de Estado en el Archivo Histórico Nacional*. Madrid, 1982.

Cardozo, Eduardo. *Dolores en su 150 Aniversario*. Dolores, México, 1951.

Carillo, Anastacio. "Pruebas de Nobleza," *Hidalguía 166–167* (1981): 522–523.

Carrandi, Florencio 1. *Descendiente de Guipúzcoa: Presidente del Perú*. Valencia, 1953.

Carrandi, F. Amador 2. "Vizcainos en las Genealogías Argentinas: Achucarro," *IAC 9–10* (1950–1951): 514–517.

Carranza, Arturo. "Un Linaje Fundador de Entre Ríos: Los Hereñú," *IAC 14* (1961): 15–18.

Carril, Bonifacio del. *Los Mendoza en España y en América en el Siglo 15 y en la Primera Mitad del Siglo 16: Comprobaciones Sobre la Genealogía de Don Pedro de Mendoza, Fundador de Buenos Aires.* Buenos Aires, 1954.

Carrizosa, Enríque. *Linajes y Bibliografías de Nuestros Gobernantes, 1830–1982.* Bogotá, 1983.

Casanova, Gustavo 1. *Cuatro Genealogías y Dos Biografías.* Hato Rey, Puerto Rico, 1983. Genealogy of Dr. José de Diego Martínez, born in 1866 in Aguadilla, P.R.; genealogical studies of the Cofresí family, beginning with Ignacio Cofresí, born in 1789; genealogical connections of nine great-great-grandsons of Roberto Cofresí; Corsos Family; Ocasio Family, of Naguabo, P.R.; "Gela," granddaughter of Joaquina, slave of the Ramírez de Arellano family.

Casanova, Gustavo 2. *Esbozos Genealógicos: Familias de Cabo Rojo y Mayagüez, Puerto Rico.* Carolina, Puerto Rico, 1982. Genealogies of the families Chardón, Arredondo, Laforet, Cuebas, Carbonell, Tió, Colberg, Cuesta, Valines, Asencio, Cofresí, Boscio, Souffront, Bischoff, Brau, Ubarri, and Betances.

Casanova, Gustavo 3. *Genealogía de la Familia Carbonell de Cabo Rojo, Puerto Rico, 1800–1979.* Santa Rita, Río Piedras, Puerto Rico, 1980.

Castellano, Rafael 1. *Familias de Traslasierra, Jurisdicción de Córdoba.* Buenos Aires, 1970.

Castellano, Rafael 2. "Pedro Feliciano Saínz de Cavia," *IAC 16* (1976): 25–50.

Castellón, Alvaro. *Familia del Libertador: Don José Miguel de Carrer Verdugo.* Santiago, 1984.

Castells, Carlos A. *Familia Castells: Apuntes para su Historia.* Montevideo, 1978.

Castillo, Abel Romero. *Ecuatorianos Ilustres en Costa Rica durante el Siglo XIX.* San José, 1978.

Castro, Antonio P. 1. "Artigas y sus Descendientes en Concordia," *IAC 9–10* (1950–1951): 363–369.

Castro, Antonio P. 2. "El Jesuita Domingo de Olascoaga: Una Vida al servicio de Dios. Sus Vinculaciones en América," *IAC 11* (1955): 123–144.

Castro, Efraín 3. *Documentos Relativos al Historiador Francisco Javier Clavijero y su Familia*. Puebla, 1970.

Castro, Fernando R. de. 3a. *Genealogía, Heráldica e Historia de Nuestras Familias*. n.p., 1990. This book interrelates genealogy, heraldry, noble titles, genealogical trees, and positions which families related to the author contributed to the development of Cuba.

Castro, Kenneth M. 4. *Castro of California: Genealogy of a Colonial Spanish California Family*. Murphys, 1975.

Castro, Kenneth M. 5. "The Castro Family and Other Families of Alta California," *Comunicaciones al XV Congreso Internacional de las Ciencias Genealógicas y Heráldicas 1* (1983): 385–390.

Castro, Norberto 6. "Aclaración de la Genealogía y Armas del Linaje de Esquivel," *Revista de los Archivos Nacionales, San José 7–8* (1942): 401–407.

Castro, Norberto 7. "Antecedentes Genealógicos de los Arburda," *RAC 13–14* (1965–1966): 73–82.

Castro, Norberto 8. "Ascendencia Genealógica de Vázquez de Coronado," *Revista de los Archivos Nacionales, San José 1–2* (1948): 26–32.

Castro, Norberto 9. "Cuarto Centenario de Costa Rica: Con Datos Genealógicos Inéditos Sobre Juan Caballón," *La Prensa Libre*, San José, 3 de febrero 1962.

Castro, Norberto 10. "Familias Patricias de Costa Rica," *RAC 22* (1975): 11–190. Genealogies of the families Peralta, Guardia, Tenorio y Azofaifo, Laya y Bolivar, Mora Salado, Chinchilla y Garavatea, Tlatoques, Solano de Grado, Ramiro Corajo y Zúñiga, Farfán de los Godos, Zamora-Romero, Moya Colmenero, Jiménez-Maldonado, Chávez y Alfaro, Arburola-Iribarren, Alvarado de Estrada, Fernández-Val, Oses-Navarro, Lacayo de Briones, Sarmiento de Sotomayor, García de Argueta, Mendiola, and Gutiérrez de Lizaurzabal.

Castro, Norberto 11. "Fundadores de Casas Hidalgas en Costa Rica: Proemio y Nomenclatura en Orden Alfabético," *Revista de los Archivos Nacionales, San José 9–10* (1942–1943): 518–529.

Castro, Norberto 12. "Genealogía de la Casa de Hine," *RAC 16–17* (1970): 107–114.

Castro, Norberto 13. *Genealogía Mesoamericana: Datos Genealógicos y Biográficos Contenidos en los Expedientes de Pruebas de Limpieza de Sangre y Otros Papeles del Secreto de la Inquisición de la Nueva España, Referentes al Reino de Guatemala, Siglos XVI y XVII, Extractados de los Documentos Originales, Que Reposan en el Archivo General de la Nación, Ciudad de México, D.F.* México, D.F., 1944.

Castro, Norberto 14. "Genealogía de la Noble Casa de López de la Flor," *Revista de los Archivos Nacionales,* San José 11–12 (1945): 609–624.

Castro, Norberto 15. "Genealogía de la Noble Casa de de Moya de Costa Rica," *Historia Genealógica Latina 7* (1950): 724–773. Reimpresa *ACC 27–28* (1981): 161–178.

Castro, Norberto 16. "Genealogía de la Noble Casa de Rodríguez de Castro," *Revista de los Archivos Nacionales, San José 11–12* (1943): 635–640.

Castro, Norberto 17. "Genealogía de la Noble Familia Jiménez Maldonado," *Revista Costarricense de Historia y Genealogía 1* (1942): 17–24.

Castro, Norberto 18. "La Cognación de Doña Josefa de Aguilar, Consorte de Antonio de Acosta Arévalo, Griego," *ACC 2* (1955): 80–83.

Castro, Norberto 19. "La Noble Casa de los Bello de Yucatán," *Revista de los Archivos Nacionales, San José 7–8* (1943): 431–433.

Castro, Norberto 20. "Los Oriamunos en Panamá," *ACC 11–12* (1963–1964): 66–71.

Castro, Norberto 21. "Los Vázquez de Coronado," *ACC 11–12* (1963–1964): 40–61. House and family seat in Salamanca.

Castro, Norberto 22. "Pruebas de Genealogía y Limpieza de Francisco de Ocampo Golfín, Vecino de Cartago, Pretendiente de Familiar," *Revista de los Archivos Nacionales, San José 3–4* (1945): 178–181.

Castro, Norberto 23. "Una Rama de la Casa de Sarachaga en México," *AMG 1*, 1ª Series (1945): 131–143.

Castro, Norberto 24. "Verdadera Paternidad del Tesorero Alonso de Estrada," *ACC 25* (1978): 259–276. Printed originally in Madrid, 1948.

Cavada, Francisco J. *Apuntes Biográficos de Personas y Familias de Chiloé Insular.* Santiago, 1934.

Cavazos, Israel 1. *Catálogo y Síntesis de los Protocolos del Archivo Municipal de Monterrey.* 3 vols. 1966–1989.

Cavazos, Israel 2. *Cedulario Autobiográfico de Pobladores y Conquistadores de Nuevo León.* México, D.F., 1964. A biographical dictionary of conquistadores and settlers of Nuevo León by way of government permit requests for grants, encomiendas, etc.

Ceballos, Aldo Angel. "Cepdevila," *EGC 15* (1982): 33–46.

Celis, Carlos 1. *La Familia Celis en Chile.* Santiago, 1970.

Celis, Carlos 2. "Salas Varonía de Miranda en Chile desde 1555," *REH 24* (1980): 95–122. Published separately, Santiago, 1980.

Centro de Estudios Históricos Militares. "Santuarias Patrióticos: Cripta de los Héroes de la Guerra de 1879," *Guía Histórica y Biogrfica.* Lima, 1968.

Cervantes, Enríque. *Documentos Relativos a la Villa de los Cinco Señores, Capital del Nuevo Santander, hoy Jiménez, Tamaulipas.* México, D.F., 1947.

Cerveró, Jorge. "Genealogía del Linaje de Alemparte," ACH 15 (1940): 89–129.

Chabot, Frederick C. *With the Makers of San Antonio.* San Antonio, Texas, 1937.

Charlin, Raimundo. "Casa Prieto," *REH 1* (1949): 55–66.

Chauny, Gilbert. *Sánchez de Aranda en Trujillo del Perú.* Lima, 1966.

Chávez, Angélico 1. *Origins of New Mexico Families in the Spanish Colonial Period.* Santa Fe, 1973. Reimpreso, Albuquerque, 1973.

Chávez, Angélico 2. *Roots of New Mexico Families.* 12 vols. Manuscripts.

Chávez, Modesto 3. *Biografías Olvidadas.* Guayaquil, 1940.

Chávez, Juan M. 4. "Francisco de Chávez," *IPI 8* (1955): 259–273.

Chávez, Juan M. 5. "Los Urdanivia de Arequipa," *IPI 6* (1953): 101–105.

Ciadoncha, Marqués de. *Nobiliario de Badajoz*. Badajoz, 1944.

Cid, Enríque del 1. "Genealogía Incompleta del Señor Capitán Don Manuel de Pisquera," *RAG 1* (1967): 75–82.

Cid, Enríque del 2. *Presencia de Guatemala en México*. Guatemala, 1961.

Cifré, Estela 1. *Catálogo de Extranjeros Residentes en Puerto Rico en el Siglo XIX*. Palencia de Castilla, Spain, 1962.

Cifré, Estela 2. *La Formación del Pueblo Puertorriqueño: La Contribución de los Catalanes, Balaericos y Valencianos*. Barcelona, 1975.

Cifré, Estela 3. *La Inmigración a Puerto Rico Durante el Siglo XIX*. Palencia de Castilla, Spain, 1964.

Cleves, Jorge. *Los Cleves*. Bogotá, 1964.

Coello, Manuel. *Casa Solariega y Ancestral de Linajes Galaico-Americanos de Rancia Nobleza que Conquistaron Trofeos y Blasaron Escudos*. 2nd edition. n.p., n.d.

Coghlan, Eduardo A. "Los Brizuela y Doria," *IAC 14* (1961): 19–23.

Coll, Cayetano. *Puertorriqueños Ilustres*. 2nd edition. Bilbao, 1956.

Comadrán, Jorge. "Las Tres Casas Reinantes de Cuyo," *RCH 126* (1958): 77–127. Genealogies of José Perfecto de Salas, born 1714 en Buenos Aires; María Josefa Corvalán, his wife, born in Santiago, Chile; José Sebastián Sotomayor, born in La Rioja, Argentina, married in 1744 to Isabel Videla y Zalazar; Juan Martínez de Rozas, born in Regules, Montañas de Burgos, Spain, married in 1746 at Mendoza to María Prudencia Correas de Larrea y Villegas. Biographical information regarding these families along with demographic information for Cuyo.

Conde, José Ignacio 1. *Ascendencia, Vida, y Descendencia de Don Juan Casimiro de Orta y Múzquiz, tercer Marquéz de Rivascacho*. Madrid, México, D.F., 1979.

Conde, Vallellano 2. *Nobiliario Cubano: Las Grandes Familias Isleñas*. 2 vols. Madrid, 1928.

Conrad, Glenn R. *The First Families of Louisiana*. 2 vols. Batón Rouge, 1970.

Coo, José Luis 1. "Don Martín Warnes y García Zúñiga (1786–1842): Su Descendencia en Argentina, Chile, y Uruguay," *IEG 2* (1981): 41–46.

Coo, José Luis 2. "Familias Extranjeras en Valparaiso en el Siglo XIX," *REH 15* (1968–1968): 37–84.

Coo, José Luis 3. "La Familia Muñoz de Bezanilla," *REH 13* (1965): 35–48.

Cornejo, Atilio 1. *Genealogías de Salta: Los Fernández Cornejo*. 1st edition. 1940; 2nd edition, revised, Salta, 1972.

Cornejo, Atilio 2. "Los Fernández Cornejo del Perú," *IPI 4* (1949): 105–135.

Cornejo, Atilio 3. "Los Fernández Cornejo del Perú: Antecedentes Genealógicos," *Boletín del Instituto de San Felipe y Santiago de Estudios Históricos de Salta 21–22* (1948).

Cornejo, Atilio 4. "Los Moyano Cornejo (Ramificación en Salta)," *IAC 1* (1942): 93–120.

Cortés, Ernesto 1. *Las Generaciones Colombianas*. Tunja, 1968.

Cortés, José D. 2. *Diccionario Biográfico Americano*. 2nd edition. Paris, 1876.

Cortina, Manuel. *La Familia Cortina*. México, D.F., 1968.

Costa, Arturo 1. *Ensayo Genealógico de la Familia de la Torre: Sucesión y Descendencia en Bolivia*. La Paz, 1971.

Costa, Arturo 2. *Genealogías de la Ciudad de Nuestra Señora de la Paz*. n.p., n.d.

Costa, Arturo 3. *Genealogías de las Familias Arduz, Núñez del Prado Arduz, Eguino Arduz, y Núñez del Prado: Sucesión y Descendencia en Bolivia*. La Paz, 1977.

Costa, Arturo 4. *Romance y Descendencia del Gran Mariscal de Ayacucho en la Ciudad de La Paz*. La Paz, 1961.

Costa, Arturo 5. *Vida de la Heroina Doña María Visencia de Jauristi Eguino Diez de Medina (Históricamente llamada Vicenta Eguino)*. n.p., n.d.

Costales, Piedad. *Los Señores Naturales de la Tierra*. Quito, 1982.

Covarrubias, Ricardo. *Nuevoleonese Ilustres*. Monterrey, Mexico, 1990. Contains biographical information on professors, lawyers, doctors, governors, priests, militarists, writers, poets, impresarios, educators, historians, engineers, revolutionaries, etc.

Cox, Isaac J. "The Early Settlers of San Fernando," *Quarterly of the Texas State Historical Association 5* (1901), No. 2.

Crespo, José Santiago 1. *Ascendencia Gallega de Bolivar*. Bogotá, n.d.

Crespo, José Santiago 2. *Blasones y Linajes de Galicia*. Santiago de Compostela, 1957. 2nd edition, revised and expanded. 5 vols. Pontevedra, Galicia, 1982.

Crespo, José Santiago 3. "Casas Gallegas en el Perú," *IPI 6* (1953): 123, 168.

Crespo, José Santiago 4. *Linajes de Galicia en el Perú*. Bogotá, 1953.

Crespo, Juan Carlos 5. "El Mayorazgo de Villar Gallegos," *IAC 19* (1981): 23–33.

Crespo, Juan Carlos 6. "El Ultimo Conquistador: Martín de Ledesma Valderrama," *IEI 1* (1980): 57–74.

Crespo, Juan Carlos 7. "Familias del Virreinato Entroncadas," *IAC 18* (1979): 27–36.

Crespo, Juan Carlos 8. "Giles," *IAC 17* (1977): 19–28.

Crespo, Juan Carlos 9. "Los Vecinos de Santa Fé en 1622," *IAC 16* (1976): 51–66.

Crisóstomo, Juan P. *Descendencia de Don Juan Nicolás Merino de Heredia en Chile, 1650–1971*. Santiago, 1971.

Cruz, Josefina. "Juan de Garay el Conquistador, Conquistado," *IEI 1* (1980): 75–84.

C Signo Editorial Argentino. *Diccionario Biográfico, Provincia de Buenos Aires*. Volume 1, Buenos Aires, 1954.

Cuadra, Guillermo 1. *Abogados Antiguos, 1776–1876*. Santiago, 1948.

Cuadra, Guillermo 2. "El Apellido Castro Durante la Colonia," *RCH 41* (1921): 302–320.

Cuadra, Guillermo 3. *Familias Chilenas*. Santiago, 1948. Also published in *RCH 64, 68, 71, 73, 75*.

Cuadra, Guillermo 4. "Fundadores de Capellanías en Chile," *ACH 36–37*.

Cuadra, Guillermo 5. "Genealogía Chilena," *Homenaje a Don Domingo Amunátegui Solar* (1935): 309–330.

Cuadra, Guillermo 6. "La Familia de Alcalde en Chile," *RCH 22* (1916): 217–226.

Cuadra, Guillermo 7. "Los de la Cuadra," *IPI 2* (1947): 21–40.

Cuadra, Guillermo 8. "Los de Larraín en Chile," *RCH 27* (1917): 112–127.

Cuadra, Guillermo 9. *Origen y Desarrollo de las Familias Chilenas*. Volume 1, Santiago, 1948.

Cuadra, Guillermo 10. *Origen de 200 Familias Coloniales de Santiago*. Santiago, 1914. Also published in *RCH 15–18, 29–34, 53–55*. Also combined with "Familias Coloniales de Santiago," in *Familias Chilenas*. Santiago, 1949.

Cuadra, Guillermo 11. "Pruebas de Nobleza de la Real Compañía de Guardias Marinas," *REH 2* (1950–1951).

Cucalón, José María. "Los Cucalón en América," *CAG 15* (1985): 25–33.

Cuculla, Luis María. *Familia Cuculla Argentina*. Buenos Aires, 1970.

Cuéllar, B. *Pedigree and Family History of Lizarrarás y Cuéllar Family, Founders of Saltillo, Coahuila, Mexico in 1621*. Revised edition. n.p., 1949. Contains genealogical charts, transcripts of documents, and maps.

Cuesta, David E. *Familias de Cabo Rojo*. Santurce, Puerto Rico, 1983.

Cuevas, Javier 1. "Hernán Cortés y los Pignatelli: Aragón Cortés," *Excélsior 7* (30 de abril de 1947).

Cuevas, Javier 2. "La Ilustre Casa de Mendoza," *Excélsior 7* (21 de mayo y 17 de junio de 1947).

Cúneo, Luis 1. "El Linaje de los Yáñez de Montenegro," *IPI 12* (1961): 7–26.

Cúneo, Rómulo 2. *Historia de las Insurrecciones de Tacna por la Independencia del Perú.* Lima, 1921.

Cúneo, Rómulo 3. "Los Ara," *IPI 11* (1958): 5–16.

Cutolo, Vicente O. *Nuevo Diccionario Biográfico Argentino, 1750–1930.* 6 vols. Buenos Aires, 1968–1980.

Dahl, Torsten. *Linajes de México.* Volume 1, México, 1967.

Dario, Luis 1. *Genealogía del Libertador.* 2nd edition, revised. Mérida, Venezuela, 1972.

Dario, Ramón 2. *Historial Genealógico del Doctor Cristóbal Mendoza, 1772–1829.* Caracas, 1972.

Dario, Ramón 3. *Historial Genealógico de los Febres-Cordero y Algunas de sus Alianzas.* Mérida, Venezuela.

Daró, Delmo. *Apuntes Históricos de la Colonia y el Pueblo de Armstrong.* Santa Fé, New Mexico, 1978.

Dávila, J. Ignacio 1. *Algo acerca de la Familia Garibi.* Guadalajara, 1937.

Dávila, J. Ignacio 2. "Arbol Genealógico de Doña Isabel Gutiérrez Orozco," *AMG 8,* 1ª Series (1953): 159–167. Also published as *Arbol Genealógico de la Señora Doña Isabel Gutiérrez Orozco, Viuda de Anaya, con motivo del Nonagésimo Aniversario de su Natalicio.* México, D.F., 1953.

Dávila, J. Ignacio 3. *Arbol Genealógico de los Emperadores Aztecas.* México, D.F., 1926.

Dávila, J. Ignacio 4. "Ascendencia Materna de Don Miguel Hidalgo y Castilla, a la luz de Nuevo Documentos," *AMG 8,* 1ª Series (1953): 15–58.

Dávila, J. Ignacio 5. *Cuadro Genealógico.* México, D.F. 1926.

Dávila, J. Ignacio 6. "Datos Genealógicos Pocos Conocidos Referentes al General Insurgente Don Ignacio Allende," *AMG 2–3,* 1ª Series (1946): 93–97.

Dávila, J. Ignacio 7. *Don Mateo y Don Francisco Antonio de Garibi y Jugo.* México, D.F. 1954.

Dávila, J. Ignacio 8. "Del Comendador Don Leonel de Cervantes, Conquistador de Nueva España a Ignacio Luis Manuel Dávila Garibi y Camacho," *AMG 5,* 1ª Series (1949): 47–78.

Dávila, J. Ignacio 9. "El Capitán Don Diego de Ochoa Garibay, Conquistador de Nueva Galicia y Poblador muy Antiguo en la Provincia de Michoacán Avencindado en Zamora, y Relación Genealógica entre éste y el Lic. Don Guillermo Romo Celis," *AMG 1,* 2ª Series (1957): 139–150.

Dávila, J. Ignacio 10. "El Comendador Don Leonel de Cervantes y Conquistador de Nueva España: Noticias Genealógicas y Biográficas Extractadas de Varios Documentos Existentes en el Archivo General de Indias," *AMG 5,* 1ª Series (1949): 25–36.

Dávila, J. Ignacio 11. *El Ilmo, y Rvmo. Monseñor Don Luis Gonzaga Romo de Vivar y Pérez Franco: Sus Progenitores y Antepasados.* Tomo 1, México, 1943.

Dávila, J. Ignacio 12. *Estudio Histórico, Genealógico, Biográfico y Estadístico Referente al Lic. Cesáreo L. Gonzáles y Fernándes.* Guadalajara, 1926.

Dávila, J. Ignacio 13. *Escala Genealógica Ascendente del Doctor Don Enríque López Maldonado.* Guadalajara, 1924.

Dávila, J. Ignacio 14. *Estudio Genealógico-Biográfico del Capitán Don Diego de Colio, Conquistador de la Nueva España.* México, D.F., 1927. There are also references to this book under the title: *Estudio Genealógico del Capitán A. Diego de Colio.* Guadalajara, 1927.

Dávila, J. Ignacio 15. *Genealogía de Don Agustín de Iturbide, Emperador de México.* México, D.F., 1952.

Dávila, J. Ignacio 16. *Genealogía de Don Miguel Hidalgo y Costilla, Iniciador de la Independencia de México.* México, D.F., 1951.

Dávila, J. Ignacio 17. *Genealogía del Conquistador Don Alvaro Carrillo y Francisco Gutiérrez.* Guadalajara, 1926.

Dávila, J. Ignacio 18. *Genealogía del Nuevo Canónigo Doctoral de la Metropolitana de Guadalajara: Dr. Don José Garibi Rivera.* Guadalajara, 1924.

Dávila, J. Ignacio 19. *La Sociedad de Zacatecas en los Albores del Regimen Colonial.* México, D.F., 1939.

Dávila, J. Ignacio 20. *Los Monroy Pizarro de Nueva Galicia*. México, D.F., 1947–1948.

Dávila, J. Ignacio 21. *Los Nietos de Don Juan*. México, D.F., 1949. Also published in *AMG 6–7*, 1ª Series (1948): 21–100. Also published as *Los Nietos de Juan de Villaseñor Orozco, Fundador de Valladolid*. Michoacán, México, 1948.

Dávila, J. Ignacio 22. *Martín Monje, Conquistador de Nueva España*. México, D.F., 1951.

Dávila, J. Ignacio 23. *Noticias Genealógicas y Biográficas Referentes al Comendador Don Leonel de Cervantes*. México, D.F., 1950.

Dávila, J. Ignacio 24. *Reliquias Históricas de Familias*. 3 vols. n.p., n.d.

Dávila, J. Ignacio 25. *Selección Genealógica: Ramas Seleccionadas del Arbol Genealógico del Capitán Don Juan de Villaseñor y Orozco*. México, D.F., 1952.

Dávila, J. Ignacio 26. *Revelación del Parentezco Entre Don Miguel Hidalgo y Costilla y Don José Ignacio Dávila Garibi, Descendientes del Conquistador de la Nueva España, Capitán Don Juan de Villaseñor*. México, D.F., n.d.

Dávila, Marqués de 27. *Nobiliario de Soria*. Madrid, 1967.

Dávila, Valentín 28. *Nobiliario de la Ciudad de Burgos: los Caballeros de las Ordenes de Calatrava, Alcántara, Montesa, y San Juan de Jerusalén (Malta)*. Madrid, 1955.

Dávila, Vicente 29. *Diccionario Biográfico de Ilustres Próceres de la Independencia Suramericana*. Volume 1, Caracas, 1924.

Dávila, Vicente 30. *Don Sancho Briceño y su Descendencia*. n.p., n.d.

Dávila, Vicente 31. *Historial Genealógica de la Familia del General Rafael Urdaneta y su Descendencia*. Caracas, 1945.

Dávila, Vicente 32. *Investigaciones Históricas*. Volume 2, Quito, 1955.

Dávila, Vicente 33. *Próceres Merideños: Biografías de Algunos Ilustres Próceres de la Antigua Provincia de Mérida*. n.p., 1918.

Dávila, Vicente 34. *Próceres Trujillanos: Geografías de casi todos los Ilustres Próceres de la Antigua Provincia de Trujillo, con un Extenso Arbol Genealógico de los Briceños y otro de los Pacheco*. n.p., 1921.

Dávila, Vicente 35. *Sancho Briceño: su Monumento en Trujillo; el Arbol de los Briceños*. Caracas, n.d.

D.D.U. *Hojas de Servicios y Antecedentes Familiares del General de División Don Basilio Urrutia Vásquez: Los Urrutia en Chile*. Santiago, 1949.

De la Fuente, José. "Apuntes documentos sobre las Familias Hidalgo y Costilla, Gallega Mandarte, y Villaseñor," *Anales del Museo Nacional de Arqueología, Historia, y Etimología 12* (1910): 531–552.

De la Rocha, Guillermo. "Genealogía Historia de la Familia de la Rocha," *Boletín Nicaragüense de Bibliografía y Documentación 22* (1978): 31–54.

De la Torre, José. "Apuntes Documentales sobre Cordobeses en el Perú," *IPI 6* (1953): 12, 30.

Delaunet, Amadeo 1. *Catálogo de una Biblioteca de Genealogía y Heráldica*. San Sebastián, 1960.

Delaunet, Amadeo 2. *Historia Genealógica de la Casa Solar de Izaguirre en Urrestilla, 1500–1950*. San Sebastián, 1948.

Delaunet, Amadeo 3. *Historia Genealógica de la Casa Solar de Rezola, 1480–1948*. San Sebastián, 1948.

Delaunet, Amadeo 4. *Noticias Históricas y Genealógicas de la Casa Solar de Artola, 1450–1955*. San Sebastián, 1955.

De la Vega, Garcilaso. "Relación de la Descendencia de Garci Pérez de Vargas," *Revista del Archivo Histórico 10* (1959): 378–405.

Del Busto, J.Antonio. "Los Tebes Limeños," *IPI 13* (1963): 59–69.

Delgado, Lily 1. "Historia y Genealogía de la Familia Brum y sus Entronques," *IEG 3* (1892): 40–70.

Delgado, José 2. "Donativo Mexicano Convertido en Mayorazgo," *Hidalguía 166–167* (1981): 431–448.

Delpar, Helen. *Encyclopedia of Latin America*. New York, 1974.

De María, Isidoro. *Rasgos biográficos de hombres notables de la República Oriental del Uruguay*. 4 volumes in 2 volumes. Reprint of the 1870–1876 edition. Volume 4 contains some Argentine biographies.

Derkum, Adam C. "Spanish Families of California." Manuscript in the Family History Center at Los Angeles.

Devoto, Lucrecia. "Quiroga: Rama Facundo Quiroga," *IAC 17* (1977): 29–34.

Díaz, Alfonso 1. "Genealogías de San Juan," *IAC 17* (1977): 35–43.

Díaz, Alfredo 2. "Genealogía de la Familia Beeche," *Revista de los Archivos Nacionales, San José 11–12* (1943): 641.

Díaz, Alfredo 3. "Historial del Linaje Ruiz Guiñazu," *IAC 6–7* (1946–1947): 28–47.

Díaz, Alfredo 4. "La Casa de Lara en la Argentina: Los Molina Navarrete," *IAC 14* (1961): 24–31.

Díaz, Alfredo 5. "La Casa de Veragua en la Argentina," *IAC 1* (1942): 17–19.

Díaz, Alfredo 6. "La Descendencia en Filipinas del Teniente Coronel Juan de San Martín, Hermano del Libertador," *IAC 9–10* (1950–1951): 244–247.

Díaz, Alfredo 7. "La Sociedad Argentina y sus Orígenes Hispánicos, Siglos XVI y XVII," *IAC 8* (1948–1949): 58–79. Published separately in Buenos Aires, 1949.

Díaz, Alfredo 8. "Linaje de Aliaga," *IAC 12* (1957): 53–89.

Díaz, Alfredo 9. "Los de la Vega y Castro," *IEI 1* (1980): 85–89.

Díaz, Alfredo 10. "Los Zamudio," *IAC 18* (1974): 37–42.

Díaz, Alfredo 11. "Orígenes Insignes de la Argentina: La Casa del Marqués de Santa Cruz," *IAC 3* (1944): 43–47.

Díaz, Hernán 12. "La Ascendencia Vasca y Castellana de Don Agustín Edwards MacClure," *IAC 4–5* (1945): 336–341.

Díaz, Manuel A. 12A. *Catálogo de Genealogías 1565–1810*. Bogotá: Archivo Nacional, 1981.

Díaz, María A. 13. "Primitivas Familias de San Carlos: Los Correa; Los Piriz," *IEG 3* (1982): 71–78; *4* (1981): 73–80.

Díaz, Raul 14. "Descendencia de los Hermanos Carrera," *El Diario Ilustrado 8* (1952).

Díaz, Raul 15. "Don Juan de Dios Vial Santelices y su Sucesión," *RCH 117–120*.

Díaz, Raul 16. *El Linaje de Humeres, Crónica de Cuatro Siglos, 1550–1950*. Santiago, 1951.

Díaz, Raul 17. *El Linaje de Vial: Sucesión y Vinculaciones*. Madrid, 1960.

Díaz, Raul 18. "Familias de Ascendencia no Hispana," *El Diario Ilustrado 14* (1951).

Díaz, Raul 19. "Familia Valdivia de La Serena," *REH 8–9* (1960): n.d.

Díaz, Raul 20. "Fichas del Archivo de Don Raul Díaz Vial," *REH 14* (1966–1967): 145–159; *18* (1973): 154–157.

Díaz, Raul 21. "Humeres," *REH 13* (1965): 59–64.

Díaz, Raul 22. "La Ascendencia del General Baquedano," *REH 11* (1963).

Díaz, Raul 23. "La Casa de Lira," *El Diario Ilustrado 28* (1952).

Díaz, Raul 24. "Sucesión de Don Antonia Salas de Errázuriz *RCH 76* (1932).

Díaz, Raul 25. *Una Línea Vial en Concepción*. Santiago, 1952.

Diekamper, Barnabas. "Mexican-Americans: A Jewish Background for Some?" *LBN 1* (1984): 26–28.

Dodds, James. *Records of Scottish Settlers in the River Plate and Their Churches*. Buenos Aires, 1897.

Doersam, Eugenio G. "Genealogía de la Familia Trejo," *ACC 5* (1958): 11–15; *13–14* (1965–1966): 11–19. Pages 12–19 also include information about the families Trejos-Gutíerrez, Fernández, Pereira, and Zaldívar.

Domínguez, Arturo 1. *Don Francisco Domínguez Heras, llegado a Chile en la Expedición de la Fragata Reina María Isabel, el 17 de noviembre de 1818*.

Domínguez, Santos 2. "Genealogía del Precursor y Benemérito de la Aeronáutica Argentina, el Teniente Aviador Militar Don Benjamín Matienzo López Alurralde," *IAC 17* (1977): 45–69.

Dorantes, Baltasar. *Sumaria Relación de las Cosas de Nueva España con Noticia Individual de los Descendientes Legítimos de los Conquistadores y Primeros Pobladores Españoles*. México, D.F., 1902.

Dougnac, Antonio. "Parientes del Padre Lacunza por Línea Femenina," *REH 17* (1972): 17–26.

Doussinague, José María 1. "Genealogía de la Ciudad de Cañete," *REH 6–7* (1956–1957): 11–52.

Doussinague, José María 2. *Genealogía de la Ciudad de Osorno.* San Francisco, 1954.

Duaine, Carl Laurence. *With All Arms.* Edinburg, Texas: New Santander Press, 1987.

Dublé, Diego 1. *El General Don Basilio Urrutia y su Familia.* n.p., 1949.

Dublé, Diego 2. *Memoria Genealógica de la Familia Dublé.* Santiago, 1942.

Durañona, Jorge 1. "Doña Delfina de Vedia de Mitre," *IAC 11* (1955): 69–79.

Durañona, Jorge 2. "La Casa de Borbón en la Argentina," *IAC 8* (1948–1949): 47–57.

Durañona, Jorge 3. "La Casa de Vedia," *IAC 18* (1979): 55–118.

Durañona, Jorge 4. "Linaje de la Familia Barceló," *IAC 1* (1942).

Durón Jiménez, Martha. *Orígenes de una fundación: Genealogía de Don José García Rodríguez, 1530–1992.* Saltillo, 1992. Of particular interest to Hispanic American families are the genealogies of Baltazar Castaño de Sosa and Inés Rodríguez; Juan Navarro and María Rodríguez; the Arizpe and Sánchez Navarro families.

Echeverría, Juan 1. "Blasones de Familias Guatemaltecas," *RAG 1* (1967): 62–68. Also found in *RAG 3–4* (1969–1970): 367–374.

Echeverría, Juan 2. *Historia Genealógica de la Familia Urruela.* Madrid, 1962; Guatemala, 1963.

Editorial Revesa. *Diccionario Biográfico de México.* Tomo 1, Monterrey, 1968; Tomo 2, Monterrey, 1970.

Ellis, Roberto J.G. 1. "Descendencia de Manuel Ximénez y Gómez," *IEG 4* (1982): 27–40.

Ellis, Roberto J.G. 2. "Los Ximénez de Montevideo y sus Raíces en el Linaje del Cid," *IEG 2* (1981): 7–8. Empresa Periodística Chile *Diccionario Biográfico de Chile.* 6th edition. Santiago, 1946.

Encío, José María de. "El Maestre de Caballería Coragas Españolas, Don José de Encío y San Vicente," *IAC 1* (1942): 140–149.

Erenchun, Juan de. *Apellidos Blasonados*. San Sebastián, 1965.

Ericson, Carolyn R. *Nacogdoches—Gateway to Texas: A Biographical Directory, 1773–1849*. Forth Worth, 1974.

Errenderi, Zócimo. *Los Guevara de Chile*. Santiago, 1956.

Escayedo, Mateo 1. *Indice de Montañeses Ilustres: Los Montañeses en las Ordenes Militares de Santiago, Calatrava, y Montesa*. Cádiz, 1925.

Escayedo, Mateo 2. *Solares Montañeses*. 8 vols. Santoña, 1925.

Escobar, Ramón. "Familia Escobar," *RGL 7* (1955): 120–121.

Escobedo, Raquel. *Galeria de Mujeres Ilustres*. México, D.F., 1967.

Escobosa, Magdalena. *El Palacio de los Condes de Heras Soto: Estudio Histórico y Genealógico*. México, D.F. 1984.

Escudero, J.Antonio. *Tolosa, Cortés, Moctezuma, y Sandoval*. México, D.F., 1980. Escuela de Estudios Hispano-Americanos de Sevilla. *Virreyes de Nueva España*. 4 vols. Seville, 1967. Biographical details for the period 1759–1808.

Espejo, Juan Luis 1. *Arboles de las Descendencias de las muy Nobles Casas y Apellidos de los Rodríguez del Manzano, Pastenes y Ovalles*. Cervantes, 1923. See also Ortiz, Alonzo, and Ovalle, Alonso.

Espejo, Juan Luis 2. *Biblioteca Chilena de Genealogía: Familia Ovalle, Pastene, Rodríguez del Manzano*. n.p., 1922. Reproduction of the work by Alonso Ortiz de Ovalle, published in Rome in 1646. Commentary regarding the 1646 edition found in *RCH 46* (1922): 47–68.

Espejo, Juan Luis 3. *Biblioteca Chilena de Historia, Genealogía y Heráldica*. Cervantes, 1922.

Espejo, Juan Luis 4. "Biblioteca Chilena de Genealogía," *Familia Valdés 1* (1920).

Espejo, Juan Luis 5. *Documentos Genealógicos de la Familias Valdés*. Santiago, 1920.

Espejo, Juan Luis 6. "Discordias Coloniales Familia Larraín," *RCH 27* (1919).

Espejo, Juan Luis 7. "Don Alonso de Espejo, Corregidor, Minero y Azoguero," *ACH 71* (1964): 19–75.

Espejo, Juan Luis 8. "Don Francisco Gutiérrez de Espejo, Gobernador de las Islas de Chiloé y de Juan Fernández," *ACH 69* (1963): 30–84.

Espejo, Juan Luis 9. "El Linaje de Bulnes," *ACH 74* (1966): 33–36.

Espejo, Juan Luis 10. "Familias Coloniales de San Marcos de Arica," *IPI 3* (1945).

Espejo, Juan Luis 11. "Genealogía de la Familia Roco Campofrío de Carvajal," *ACH 2* (1933).

Espejo, Juan Luis 12. "Genealogías de Ministros del Santo Oficio de la Inquisición de Lima," *RCH 57* (1928): 297ff.

Espejo, Juan Luis 13. "Genealogía de Ministros del Santo Oficio de la Inquisición de Lima," *IPI 10* (1957): 53–77.

Espejo, Juan Luis 14. *Genealogías de Ministros del Santo Oficio de la Inquisición de Lima.* Madrid, 1927. Reproduced in the *Boletín de la Academia de la Historia* y en *Revista del Instituto Peruano de Investigaciones Genealógicas.*

Espejo, Juan Luis 15. "La Familia del Licenciado Polo de Ondegardo, Conquistador del Perú," *REH 6–7* (1956–1957): 53–58.

Espejo, Juan Luis 16. *Linajes Troncales de los Corregimientos de Chile.* n.p., n.d.

Espejo, Juan Luis 17. *Los Encomenderos de Chiloé.* n.p., n.d.

Espejo, Juan Luis 18. *Nobiliario de la Antigua Capitanía General de Chile.* 2 vols. Santiago, 1967.

Espejo, Juan Luis 19. "Relaciones de Méritos y Servicios de Funcionarios del Reino de Chile," *RCH, 50, 52, 53* (1926).

Espinach, Ulises. *Historia Familiar: El Ex-Presidente del Perú, Don Miguel Iglesias, Visita a sus Familiares, los Espinach, de Costa Rica.* San José, 1948.

Espino, Rafael. *Linajes Mexicanos: El Condado de la Torre de Cossío.* México, D.F., 1944.

Espinosa, Gustavo 1. "Los Personajes Relacionados con la Ilustre Casa de Mendoza en la Gran Expedición de Francisco Vázquez de Coronado," *AMG 3*, 2ª Series (1965): 95–114.

Espinosa, Oscar 2. *Andonaegui de Vizcaya, de Chile y de Argentina.* Santiago, 1984.

Estévez, José. *Trabajos Científicos: Apuntes Biográficos y Recopilación de Luis F. LeRoy y Gálvez.* La Habana, 1951.

Estrada, Marcos. "La Casa de Alto Aguirre," *IAC 12* (1957): 139–151.

Eyzaguirre, Jaime 1. *El Conde de la Conquista.* n.p., 1951.

Eyzaguirre, Jaime 2. *Archivo Epistolar de la Familia Eyzaguirre, 1747–1854.* Buenos Aires, 1960.

Eyzaguirre, Jaime 3. "El Conquistador Andrés de Barahona y sus Descendientes," *RCH 71* (1932): 118–134.

Eyzaguirre, Jaime 4. *Eyzaguirre: Generaciones y Semblanzas.* Volume 1, Santiago, 1937.

Eyzaguirre, Jaime 5. "Los Antepasados del Prócer Felipe Fermín de Paul," *Boletín de la Academia Nacional de la Historia de Caracas Venezuela* (1959).

Eyzaguirre, Jaime 6. "Los Ruiz de Berecedo," *REH 4–5* (1954–1955): 25–31.

Ezcurra, Alberto. "Don Pedro Medrano y de la Plaza: Antecedentes Biográficos y Genealógicos," *IAC 11* (1955): 175–178.

Falla, Eutimio 1. *Genealogía de la Familia Falla Gutiérrez.* La Habana, 1953.

Falla, Juan José 2. "La Familia de la Tovilla," *RAG 8* (1983): 207–312.

Falla, Juan José 3. "La Familia Martín del Cerro, Fundadora de la Villa de San Vicente de Austria," *RAG 3–4* (1969–1970): 157–260.

Falla, Juan José 4. "Origen de la Familia de la Campa en Indias," *RAG 34* (1969–1970: 261–272.

Fandiño, Carlos E. "Juan López, el Vizcaino, y su Familia," *IAC 19* (1981): 34–46.

Feliu, Sebastián. *Notas Genealógicas sobre algunas Familias Mallorquinas Extinguidas: con Espicificaciones de su Representación en la Actualidad.* Mallorca, 1951.

Fernández, Alvaro 1. "Ascendencia de Don Ernesto Quirós Aguilar," *ACC 5* (1958): 32–43.

Fernández, Alvaro 2. "Ascendencia de Juan Fernández Martínez," *ACC 3* (1956): 32–43.

Fernández, Alvaro 3. "Datos sobre algunos Prelados y otras Distinguidas Personas de la Antigua Familia Peralta en España y América," *ACC 7* (1959): 16–19.

Fernández, Alvaro 4. "Don José María Peralta y de la Vega," *ACC 2* (1955): 39–40.

Fernández, Alvaro 5. "Familia de la Guardia (Principios del Siglo XVII)," *ACC 6* (1958): 19–31; *7* (1959): 8–15.

Fernández, Alvaro 6. "Familia Fernández-Val (Principios del Siglo XVII)," *ACC 9* (1961): 35–86.

Fernández, Alvaro 7. "Familia Peralta (Mediados del Siglo XIV): Ramas de Navarra y Andalucía, hasta Don José María de Peralta, Fundador de la Familia en Costa Rica," *ACC 2* (1955): 37–38.

Fernández, Alvaro 8. "Familia Sancho Castañeda," *ACC 8* (1960): 33–45.

Fernández, Alvaro 9. "Jefes de Estado y Presidentes de la República, Descendientes de Don Juan Fernández Martínez," *ACC 10* (1962): 6–8.

Fernández, Alvaro 10. "La Familia de Alvarado (Fines del Siglo XIV): Descendencia de Don Jorge de Alvarado hasta su Entronque con la Familia de Peralta," *ACC 5* (1958): 2–6.

Fernández, Alvaro 11. "Los Alvarado (Fines del Siglo XIV): Descendencia de Don Jorge, hasta su Enlace con los Peralta," *ACC 2* (1955): 42–43.

Fernández, Alvaro 12. "Los Fernández-Val: Miembros de la Familia que han Figurado en el Poder Ejecutivo de la Nación," *ACC 2* (1955): 26–28.

Fernández, Alvaro 13. "Los Vázquez de Coronado (Principios del Siglo XIV): Hasta su Enlace con los Jiménez-Maldonado," *ACC 2* (1955): 22–25.

Fernández, Alvaro 14. "Títulos Nobiliarios de la Familia Peralta," *ACC 3* (1956): 19–20.

Fernández, Augusto 15. "Aguilera," *IAC 14* (1961): 35–37.

Fernández, Augusto 16. "Basualdo: El Origen de este Linaje Comineza en un Vecino Fundador de dos Ciudades," *IAC 14* (1961): 32–34.

Fernández, Augusto 17. "Centurión," *IAC 14* (1961): 35–37.

Fernández, Augusto 18. "Juan Gómez Recio el Viejo y su Linaje," *IAC 6–7* (1946–1947): 118–132.

Fernández, Augusto 19. "Los Gómez Recio," *IAC 9–10* (1950–1951): 320–327.

Fernández, David W. 20. "Antepasados de Artigas en las Islas Canarias," *Boletín Histórico 80–83* (1959): 215–217.

Fernández, David W. 21. *Familia de Miranda: Historial Genealógico de la Familia del Precursor Miranda en Canarias y en América.* Caracas, 1972.

Fernández, David W. 22. "Galería de Canarios Notables en Venezuela: Sebastián de Miranda Ravelo (1721–1791)," *Canarias Gráfica 8* (1972): 4–6.

Fernández, David W. 23. "José Fernández Medina," *IEG 4* (1982): 3–4.

Fernández, David W. 24. *Juan Francisco de León y su Descendencia.* Caracas, 1979.

Fernández, Francisco 25. "Alonso de Estrada: su Familia," *AMH 1* (1942).

Fernández, Francisco 26. *Doña Catalina Juárez Marcayda, Primera Esposa de Hernán Cortés y su Familia.* México, D.F. 1980.

Fernández, Francisco 27. *Historia Genealógica y Heráldica de la Monarquía Española, Casa Real y Grandes de España.* Vols. 1–2, Madrid, 1897–1920.

Fernández, Francisco 28. *Tres Conquistadores y Pobladores de la Nueva España.* México, D.F., 1927. Andrés de Tapia, Cristóbal Martín Millán de Gambia, and Gerónimo López.

Fernández, Guillermo 29. *El Solar de los Fernández-Dávila: Historia y Genealogía de una Familia Española Durante Cerca de Cuatro Siglos en América, 1580–1960.* Lima, 1960.

Fernández, Guillermo S. 30. *Aspirantes Americanos a Cargos del Santo Oficio: Sus Genealogías Ascendentes*. México, D.F., 1956.

Fernández, Guillermo S. 31. *Cacicazgos y Nobiliario Indígena de la Nueva España*. México, D.F., 1961.

Fernández, Guillermo S. 32. "Descendencia de Bernal Díaz del Castillo en Nueva España," *AMG 2–3*, 1ª Series (1946): 145–152.

Fernández, Guillermo S. 33. "Enmendaturas a la Genealogía de Ortega," *AGH 2* (1957): 187–194.

Fernández, Guillermo S. 34. *Mayorazgos de la Nueva España*. México, D.F., 1965.

Fernández, Hugo 35. "Algunos Antecedentes Acerca del Antiguo Linaje de Rivarola y sus Ramas en el Río de la Plata," *Hidalguía 175* (1982): 881–920.

Fernández, Hugo 36. *Aportes Bio-genealógicos para un Padrón de Habitantes del Río de la Plata*. Volume 1: A–B, Buenos Aires, 1986.

Fernández, Hugo 37. "Aragón en Buenos Aires," *Hidalguía 160–161* (1980): 337–358.

Fernández, Hugo 38. "Dos Linajes Chileno-Argentinos," *REH 13* (1965): 69–72.

Fernández, Hugo 39. *El Linaje de Azoca*. Santiago, 1963.

Fernández, Hugo 40. "Fundadores de Linajes en El Plata," *IAC 11* (1955): 154–164.

Fernández, Hugo 41. "La Casa de Escalada de Burgos y la Epopeya Sanmartinina," *IAC 9–10* (1950–1951): 177–220.

Fernández, Hugo 41a. "Libro Primero de Matrimonios y Confirmaciones de la Parroquia de Barader," *IAC 19* (1981): 136–160.

Fernández, Hugo 42. "Linaje Troncal de los Homen de Pessoa de Sáa en Chile y Argentina," *IAC 8* (1948–1949): 217–234.

Fernández, Hugo 43. *Los Antepasados de Alem Fueron Gallegos*. Buenos Aires, 1955.

Fernández, Hugo 44. *Los Cabo San Martín no son Parientes del Gran Capitán*. Buenos Aires, 1957.

Fernández, Hugo 45. "Los Conget en Buenos Aires (Siglos XVII y XVIII)," *Hidalguía 180* (1983): 805–814.

Fernández, Hugo 46. "Méndez," *IAC 18* (1979): 119–170.

Fernández, Hugo 47. "Noticias sobre los Antiguos Linajes Porteños de González de Acosta, Cabezas, y Leiva," *IAC 17* (1977): 71–89.

Fernández, Hugo 48. "Sangre de Conquistadores," *Hidalguía 166–167* (1981): 481–517.

Fernández, Hugo 49. "Un Linaje Argentino — Chileno: Los LaMarca (Lamarque)," *REH 12* (1964): 94–104.

Fernández, Joaquín 50. "Ascendencia del Doctor Don Lorenzo de Montúfar," *ACC 16–17* (1970): 18–67.

Fernández, Joaquín 51. "La Descendencia de Don Antonio Pinto Soares," *ACC 27–28* (1981): 179–297.

Fernández, Joaquín 52. "Los Fernández del Val en la Política Costarricense," *Comunicaciones al XV Congreso Internacional de las Ciencias Genealógicas y Heráldicas 2* (1983): 5–28.

Fernández, Joaquín 53. "Oduber," *ACC 24* (1977): 54–106.

Fernández, José M. 54. *Fichas para un Diccionario Uruguayo de Biografías*. 2 vols. Montevideo, 1945.

Fernández, Luis T. 55. *A Eirexa de Santa María de Viveiro*. Santiago, 1933.

Fernández, Mario 56. "Armorial General de Costa Rica," *ACC 25* (1978): 28–256. Families Bolaños, Campabadel, Cardona, Céspedes, Díaz-Granados, Espinach, Facio, Piñeres, Herrero del Peral, Herrero Vitoria, Herrero de Lara, Herrero Rodríguez, Lahmann, Mata, Lorenzo, Ross, Solera, and Truque.

Fernández, Mario 57. "Azuola de Egubide," *ACC 24* (1977): 7–22.

Fernández, Mario 58. "Collado de Benet," *ACC 24* (1977): 23–34.

Fernández, Mario 59. "Genealogía de la Noble Casa de Piza," *ACC 21* (1974): 59–74.

Fernández, Mario 60. "Genealogía de la Noble Casa de Pozuelo de Apéstegui," *ACC 21* (1974): 75–82.

Fernández, Mario 61. "Genealogía de la Noble Casa Rohrmoser Von Chamier," *ACC 21* (1974): 83–96.

Fernández, Mario 62. "Genealogía de la Noble Casa Von Chamier," *ACC 21* (1974): 97–102.

Fernández, Mario 63. "Informaciones de Nobleza Cristiandad Vieja y Limpieza de Sangre de Don Pedro Carazo," *ACC 27–28* (1981): 13–69.

Fernández, Mario 64. "Macaya de la Esquina," *ACC 24* (1977): 35–46.

Fernández, Mario 65. "Macaya de Ibáñez," *ACC 24* (1977): 47–53.

Fernández, Mario 66. "Pruebas de Genealogía y Nobleza Efectuadas Ante la Asociación de Hidalgos a Fuero de España," *ACC 25* (1978): 16–27.

Fernández, Olga 67. "Don Francisco Manuel Peralta de Alvarado (Breve Biografía)," *ACC 26* (1980): 5–8.

Fernández, Pedro X. 68. *Linajes Vascos y Montañeses en Chile.* Santiago, 1930.

Fernández, Ricardo 69. "Ascendencia de Don Joaquín de Iglesias," *ACC 16–17* (1970): 125ff.

Fernández, Ricardo 70. "Breve Noticia de la Descendencia de Juan Vázquez de Coronado," *Fernández, León, Historia de Costa Rica Durante la Dominación Española, 1502–1821* (1889): 589–590.

Fernández, Ricardo 71. "El Capitán Antonio de Peralta," *ACC 11–12* (1963–1964): 33–39.

Fernández, Ricardo 72. "Familia Montealegre de Costa Rica," *ACC 10* (1962): 16–20.

Fernández, Ricardo 73. "General Francisco Morazán: Datos Genealógicos," *ACC 16–17* (1970): 117–123.

Fernández, Ricardo 74. "Línea de Enlace del Benemérito de la Patria, Profesor Don Abelardo Bonilla Baldares, con la Familia de Don José María de Peralta y la Vega," *ACC 16–17* (1970): 129–130.

Fernández, Ricardo 75. "Los Salazar Aguado," *ACC 16–17* (1970): 75–88.

Fernández, Ricardo 76. "Los Vázquez de Coronado eran Descendientes Legítimos de los Reyes de Francia," *Revista de los Archivos Nacionales, San José 7–8* (1948): 325–328.

Fernández, Ricardo 77. "Tomasa Joaquina López del Corral y Arbarola," *ACC 16–17* (1970): 69–72.

Fernández, Roberto 78. *Fernández del Valle: Un Linaje Asturiano.* México, D.F., 1972.

Fernández, Sergio 79. "Ruta Hispano-Americana de los Linajes de Blanco de Salcedo y Fernández de Tejada," *REH 17* (1972): 109–174.

Fernández, Silvia 80. *La Familia Zegers de Chile.* Santiago, 1981.

Ferreira, José V. 1. "Los Reynafée," *CEG 6,* 4–12.

Ferreira, Mariano 2. *Apuntes Biográficos de la Familia Artigas y Ferreira.* Montevideo, 1919.

Fierro, María del C. "El Linaje Van de Walle y su Entronque con los Fierro Santa Cruz," *CEG 6,* 34–39.

Figueroa, Alfonso 1. "Los Monzón: Antepasados y Parientes del General Don Gabino Gainza," *RAG 8* (1983): 338–396.

Figueroa, Alfonso 2. "Una Familia al Servicio de la Hispanidad: La de Prado y Colón de Carvajal," *IEI 1* (1980): 91–133.

Figueroa, Andrés A. 3. *La Autonomía de Santiago del Estero y sus Fundadores, 1820–1920.* Santiago, 1920.

Figueroa, Andrés A. 4. *Linajes Santiagueños.* Córdoba, 1927.

Figueroa, Fernando 5. *Diccionario Biográfico de Salteños.* Salta, 1980.

Figueroa, José María 6. *Albumes de Figueroa.* San José, 1873–1895.

Figueroa, Pedro P. 7. *Diccionario Biográfico de Extranjeros en Chile.* Santiago, 1900.

Figueroa, Pedro P. 8. *Diccionario Biográfico General de Chile, 1550–1887.* 2nd edition, revised. Santiago, 1888.

Figueroa, Virgilio 9. *Diccionario Histórico y Biográfico de Chile, 1800–1925.* Santiago, 1925.

Figueroa, Virgilio 10. *Historia de la Familia Feliú en Chile.* Balcells, 1929.

Finestrat, Barón de 1. *Los Rocamora*. n.p., n.d.

Finestrat, Barón de 2. *Los Sandoval y sus Alianzas*. n.p., n.d.

Fleury, José E. *La Ilustre Casa de Larraín*. Santiago, 1917.

Flores, Jesús. *La Familia Serdán*. México, D.F., 1976.

Florez, Carlos 1. "La Ascendencia Hispánica de Vicuñá Mackenna," *RCH 74* (1931): 198–201.

Florez, Carlos 2. "Los Florez de León," *RCH 74* (1931).

Florez, Juan 3. *Libro Primero de las Genealogías del Nuevo Reyno de Granada: Recopilolo Don Ivan Florez de Ocariz*. Madrid, 1674. Reprinted in 1724. Volume 2 was reprinted in Madrid in 1776. Volumes 1–3 were published by the Archivo Nacional de Colombia, directed by Enríque Ortega Ricaurte, Bogotá, 1943, 1944, y 1945.

Fontecilla, Mariano. "Familia Pérez Camino," *REH 12* (1964).

Foz y Foz, Pilar. *Genealogía del Apellido Echeverz y Otros*. Madrid, 1981.

Francia, Felipe. *Genealogías Venezolanas*. n.p., n.d.

Franco, José L. *La Verdad Histórica sobre la Descendencia de Antonio Maceo*. La Habana, 1954.

Freitas, Newton. *Los Braganza*. Buenos Aires, 1943.

Freundt, Alejandro 1. *Freundt, Rosell: Dos Apellidos Centenarios en el Perú*. Lima, 1962.

Freundt, Alejandro 2. "La Primitiva Casa de los Rosell en la Ciudad de Arequipa," *IPI 4* (1949): 5–9.

Freundt, Alejandro 3. "Linajes del Reino de Suecia Entroncados con Antiguas Familias del Peru," *IPI 9* (1950): 35–37.

Freundt, Alejandro 4. "Los Cáceres y Ulloa," *IPI 2* (1947): 5–12.

Freundt, Alejandro 5. *Recopilación de Datos Cronológicos de Familia*. Arequipa, 1945.

Frías, Jorge H. *De Donde Venimos y con Quien nos Vinculamos*. Buenos Aires, 1956. Genealogies on the surnames Frías, Paz, Figueroa, Molina, Pinto, Ayerza, Martínez, Lavalle, Sáenz, Valiente, Pueyrredón, etc.

Fuente, José María de la. *Hidalgo Intimo: Estudio Histórico y Genealógico.* Toluca, México, facsimile edition of 1910.

Fuentes, Hernán 1. "La Hidalguía en Costa Rica: Los Descendientes de Don Lucas González de Abarca," *Comunicaciones al XV Congreso Internacional de las Ciencias Genealógicas y Heráldicas 2* (1983): 91–112.

Fuentes, Hernán 2. "Los Vázquez de Solera: Descendientes del Adelantado Don Juan Vázquez de Coronado," *ACC 27–28* (1981): 371–378.

Fuentes, Hernán 3. "Sobre el Origen de la Familia Zeledón y su Apellido," *ACC 23* (1976): 245–251.

Fuentes, Jordi 4. *Diccionario Político de Chile, 1800–1966.* Santiago, 1967.

Fuentes, Rafael L. 5. *Estudio sobre la Genealogía del Libertador.* Madrid, 1974.

Fuenzalida, Enríque 1. *Hombres Notables de Chile, 1850–1901.* Volume 1, Valparaiso, 1901.

Fuenzalida, Osvaldo 2. In the newspaper "El Mercurio," of Santiago, from August 1959 to 1961, Fuenzalida published various articles under the pseudonym "Juan de Naveda," which he entitled: "Esposas Españolas de Conquistadores," with their more illustrious ancestry and descendants.

Fuenzalida, Osvaldo 3. *Fuenzalida: Un Linaje de Cuatro Siglos.* Santiago, 1962.

Fuguet, Euclides. *Linajes Paredes en Venezuela.* Caracas, 1979.

Galante, Obdulia E. *Biografías Sintéticas de Autores Argentinos.* 2nd edition. Buenos Aires, 1945.

Gallagher, J.V. 1. *The Carrillo Family Research.* n.p., n.d.

Gallagher, J.V. 2. *Ortega Family Research.* n.p., n.d.

Gallardo, Pedro N. *Arbol Genealógico de la Familia Gallardo de Chiloé.* Wainstein, 1933.

Gálvez, Anibal 1. *Zela.* Lima, 1911. Francisco Antonio Zela was one of the first Peruvian creoles to rebel against Spanish domination. As history *Zela* is a good book; as a genealogy it is poor, but should be used as a reference to the Zela and Siles families. Descendants of this family (children of the author of this bibliography) live throughout the United States.

Gálvez, José 2. "Algunos Datos Sobre Familias Peruanas de Origen Argentino y de Familias del Plata Oriundas del Peru," *IPI 7* (1954): 83–97.

Gamiz, Everardo. *Leyendas Durangeñas y Biografías de Personas Célebres de Durango*. Durango, 1930.

Gammalsson, Hialmar. *Los Pobladores de Buenos Aires y su Descendencia*. Buenos Aires, 1930.

Gandía, Enríque de 1. *Crónica Genealógica de los Gandía*. Buenos Aires, 1930.

Gandía, Enríque de 2. *Del Origen de los Nombres y Apellidos y de la Ciencia Genealógica*. Buenos Aires, n.d.

Gandía, Enríque de 3. "Información Genealógica de Juan Ortiz de Zárate," *Homenaje a Don Domingo Amunátegui Solar 1* (1935): 331–340.

Gandía, Enríque de 4. "Genealogía de Ignacio Warnes, El Héroe de Santa Cruz de la Sierra," *IAC 2* (1943): 173–181.

Gandía, Enríque de 5. "Los Parientes del General San Martín en el Paraguay," *IAC 1* (1942): 20–35.

Gandía, Enríque de 6. "Martín de Alzaga, Precursor de la Independencia Argentina," *IAC 4–5* (1945): 288–325.

Gangotena, Cristóbal 1. "Donoso: Genealogía," *ANH 81* (1953).

Gangotena, Cristóbal 2. *Genealogía de la Casa de Borja*. Quito, 1932.

Gangotena, Cristóbal 3. *Genealogía de la Familia Carrión*. Quito, 1924.

Gangotena, Cristóbal 4. *La Familia de Ycaza*. Quito, 1932.

Garay, Ezio 1. "Origen de Don Pedro Gual," *CAG 15* (1985): 51–59.

Garay, Ezio 2. "Una Familia Cuencana que se Establece en Guayaquil: Los Muñoz-Ochoa," *CAG 15* (1985): 35–50.

Garcés, Hernán. *Familia Garcés de Marcilla*. Santiago, 1981.

García, A. y A. 1. *El Solar Catalán, Valenciano y Balear.* 4 vols. San Sebastián, 1968.

García, A. y A. 2. *Enciclopedia Heráldica y Genealógica.* Madrid, 1950s–1960s.

García, Adrián 3. *López Portillo: Raíces en Sinaloa.* n.p., n.d.

García, Antonio 4. *Diccionario Geográfico, Histórico y Biográfico de los Estados Unidos Mexicanos.* 5 vols. México, D.F., 1888–1891.

García, César 5. *El Libro de los Escribanos Cubanos de los Siglos XVI, XVII y XVIII.* La Habana, 1982.

García, Clotilde P. 6. *Captain Alonso Alvarez de Pineda and the Exploration of The Texas Coast and The Gulf of Mexico.* Austin, 1982.

García, Clotilde P. 7. *Captain Blas María de la Garza Falcón: Colonizer of South Texas.* Austin, 1984.

García, Clotilde P. 8. *Captain Enríque Villarreal and Rincón del Oso Land Grant.* Corpus Christi, 1986.

García, Clotilde P. 9. *Padre José Nicolás Ballí and Padre Island.* Corpus Christi, 1979.

García, Clotilde P. 10. *Siege of Camargo.* Austin, 1975.

García, Emilio 11. *El Nobiliario: Los Ponce de León hasta el Siglo XVII.* Toledo, 1947.

García, Félix 12. *The Children of Bartolomé Martínez: A Brief Genealogical Sketch.* Laredo, 1983.

García, Gabriel 13. *Ebozos Históricos de Tecolotlán.* Jalisco, 1950.

García, Joaquín 14. *Opusculos y Biografías.* México, D.F., n.d.

García, José 15. *Chaco Crisol de Razas: Homenaje a los Inmigrantes y sus Descendientes.* Resistencia, 1981.

García, José G. 16. *Rasgos Biográficos de Dominicanos Célebres.* Santo Domingo, 1971.

García, Julián 17. *Hidalguías de las Merindades de Castilla la Vieja.* Burgos, 1969.

García, Rafael 18. *Diccionario Biográfico de Historia Antigua de México.* 3 vols. México, D.F., 1952–1953.

Garcilaso, Inca. *Relación de la Descendencia de Garci Pérez de Vargas, 1596.* Lima, 1951.

Garibaldi, María M. "Entronque de Quirogas y Sarmientos," *IAC 9–10* (1950–1951): 340–362.

Garibay, Angel María. *Diccionario Porrua de Historia, Biografía y Geografía de México.* 2nd edition. México, D.F., 1965.

Garmendia, José I. *Un Libro de Familia.* Buenos Aires, 1892.

Garrido, Víctor. *Los Puello.* 2nd edition. Santo Domingo, 1974.

Garza, Lionel. *Our Family, Garza-Vela, Barrera-Martínez: From the Roots to the Fruits.* Kingsville, TX 1986.

Gaudier, Martín 1. *Genealogías, Biografías e Historia del Mayagüez de Ayer y Hoy.* San Germán, Puerto Rico, 1959.

Gaudier, Martín 2. *Genealogías Puertorriqueñas.* Volume 1, Burgos, Spain, 1963.

Gaudier, Martín 3. *Genealogías Puertorriqueñas.* Volume 2, n.p., n.d.

Gaudier, Martín 4. *Genealogías Puertorriqueñas.* Volume 3, Barcelona, 1973.

Gaudier, Martín 5. *Partidas de Nacimiento.* Barcelona, 1974.

Geigel, Luisa. *La Genealogía y el Apellido de Campeche.* Barcelona, 1972.

Geiger, Maynard 1. *Biographical Dictionary of the Franciscans in Spanish Florida and Cuba: 1528–1841.* Paterson, N.J., 1940.

Geiger, Maynard 2. *Franciscan Missionaries in Hispanic California, 1769–1848: A Biographical Dictionary.* San Marino, 1969.

Gil, Germán T. "Biografía y Linaje del General Agustín Muñoz (1797–1897)," *IEG 4* (1982): 15–26.

Gilbert, Dennis L. *La Oligarquia Peruana: Historia de Tres Familias.* Lima, 1982. Genealogy of the families Aspíllaga, Prado, and Miro Quesada.

Goldaracena, Ricardo 1. "Algo más Sobre la Progenie de San Fernando en la Genealogía Uruguaya," *IEG 2* (1981).

Goldaracena, Ricardo 2. *El Libro de los Linajes: Familias Históricas Uruguayas del Siglo XIX.* 3 vols. Montevideo, 1976–1981.

Goldberg, Rita. "Don Jerónimo Cortés y Arellano, Nieto de Hernán Cortés," *Boletín X, AGN* (1969): 371–494.

Gomensoro, Hubert 1. *Apuntes Genealógicos.* Buenos Aires, 1937.

Gomensoro, Hubert 2. "Descendencia del Fundador de Montevideo, Don Bruno Mauricio de Zavala," *IAC 12* (1957): 179–184.

Gomensoro, Hubert 3. "Linajes Vascos," *IAC 8* (1948–1949): 288–295.

Gomensoro, Hubert 4. *Los Albín y Gomensoro.* n.p., n.d.

Gómez, Ernesto 1. "Historia de Una Familia Chilena," *RCH 45* (1922): 56–106. Genealogy of the Luco family of Aragón. The pueblo of Luco. The Lucos and Lugos. The Lucos and the conquest of the Canary Islands. Luco y Ruiz de Azúa. The Marquis of Cañada Honda. The Ruiz de Azúa y Marín de Poveda. The Luco y Fernández de Leiva. No documentation. Lacking some generations.

Gómez, Federico 2. *Apuntes Genealógicos Referentes a Don Juan de Villaseñor Orozco.* México, D.F., 1920.

Gómez, Federico 3. *Doña Marina, La Dama de la Conquista.* México, D.F., 1942.

Gómez, Federico 4 *¿Quién es Cada Quién en Monterrey?* n.p., n.d.

Gómez, Lino 5. *Primeras Exploraciones y Poblamientos de Texas (1686–1694).* Monterrey, 1968.

Gómez, Rafael L. 6. "Triptico Sanmartiniano," *IAC 9–10* (1950–1951): 68–132.

Gonzalbo Aaizpuru, Pilar. *Familias Novohispanas, Siglos XVI al XIX.* México, D.F., 1991.

González, Amada 1. *Diccionario Geográfico, Histórico, Biográfico y Estadístico del Estado de Sinaloa.* México, D.F., 1959.

González, Angel 2. *Biblioteca Histórica y Genealógica.* Madrid, 1930.

González, Alfredo 3. "Breves Acotaciones a Familias del Antiguo Obispado de Concepción," *REH 8–9* (1958–1959): 59–72.

González, Alfredo 4. "Naturaleza y Calidad del Maestre de Campo Pedro Valiente de la Barra," *REH 11* (1962–1963): 27–54.

González, Alfredo 5. "Semblanzas de Penguistas de Antaño," *REH 12* (1964): 1–46. Biographies of Alonso de Puga y Novoa, Simón de

Sotomayor y Almonacid, Juan de Sanhueza Palafox, and Mateo de Cajigal y Solar.

González, Alfredo 6. "Un Meritorio Ciudadano de la Antigua Penco," *REH 15* (1968–1969): 5–21.

González, Carlos 7. *Información Genealógica Sobre las Familias González, Alvarez, Achaval y Avila*. Rosario, 1948.

González, César 8. *Vieja Gente del Tachira: Crónica Genealógica.* Caracas, 1975.

González, Cleto 9. "Ascendencia de Doña Jesús García de Acosta," *ACC 9* (1961): 29–34.

González, Cleto 10. "Familia de Doña María Fernández," *Dobles Segreda* (1922): 75–82.

González, Cleto 11. "Fundadores de las Familias Costarricenses: Sáenz," *Revista de los Archivos Nacionales, San José 3–4* (1937): 199–204; *5–6* (1938): 312–317.

González, Cleto 12. *Historia de la Familia Alvarado Barroeta: Genealogía de Manuel Alvarado y Alvarado*. San José, 1972.

González, Cleto 13. "La Ilustre Descendencia de Don Lucas González de Abarca y Rodríguez," *ACC 27–28* (1981): 87–120.

González, Cleto 14. "Los Acosta," *Revista de Costa Rica, San José 2* (1919): 28–32.

González, Cleto 15. "Sobre la Genealogía de Don Braulio Carrillo," *Revista de los Archivos Nacionales, San José 9–10* (1940): 542–544.

González, Ignacio 16. *El Palacio de los Condes de Santiago de Calimaya: Estudio Histórico y Genealógico*. México, D.F., 1983.

González, Ignacio 17. *La Estirpe y el Linaje de José María Morelos*. México, D.F., 1981.

González, Ma. del C. 18. *De Santander a San Luis Potosí: Montañeses en este Estado Mexicano*. Santander, 1981.

González, Mariano 19. *Pueblo de Hidalgos: Unión de San Antonio, Jalisco*. Guanajuato, 1980. Historical, demographic and genealogical studies.

González, Mariano 20. *Estudio Histórico-Genealógico Sobre la Familia Guerra.* Guanajuato, 1982.

González, Mariano 21. *Retoños de España en la Nueva Galicia: Estudios Históricos, Antropológicos, Genealógicos, y Biográficos sobre la Población Española de la Zona Oriental de la Nueva Galicia, desde su Establecimiento en la Región hasta nuestros Días.* Volume 1, Guanajuato, 1982–1983. Volume 2, León de Guanajuato, 1985.

González, Rodolfo 22. *Apellidos de Tamaulipas, Nuevo León, Coahuila y Téxas.* 1st edition. Nuevo Laredo, 1980.

González, Rodolfo 23. *Mil Familias de Tamaulipas, Nuevo León, Coahuila y Téxas.* 2 vols. Nuevo Laredo, 1980–1981.

Gordillo, Octavio. *Diccionario Biográfico de Chiapas.* México, D.F., 1977.

Gori, Gastón. *Familias Fundadoras de la Colonia Esperanza.* Santa Fé, 1974.

Goya, Angel de. "Certificación de Genealogías y Armas de Apellido Goya," *AMG 5*, 1ª Series (1949): 79–92.

Guajardo, Alonso. "Documentos Presentados en una Información Genealógica en Cartago en Mayo de 1612, A Pedimento de Alonso Guajardo de Hoces," *León Fernández: Colección de Documentos para la Historia de Costa Rica* (1882): 288–306.

Guarda, Fernando 1. "Don Pedro de Usauro Martínez de Bernabé, Cronista y Poeta de Valdivia," *ACH 54* (1956): 61–100.

Guarda, Fernando 2. "El Palacio de Echenique en Errazuy su Descendencia en Chile," *REH 4–5* (1954–1955): 87–103.

Guarda, Fernando 3. "La Casa de los Condes de Cartago y Marqueses de Tabalosos," *Hidalguía 17* (1956): 481–596.

Guarda, Fernando 4. "La Familia de Fray Camilo Henríquez," *REH 3* (1952–1953).

Guarda, Gabriel 5. "Carvallo Goyeneche o Goyonete: El Cronista y su Familia," *REH 11* (1962–1963): 5–26.

Guarda, Gabriel 6. "Formación de la Sociedad Valdiviana," *ACH 47.*

Guarda, Gabriel 7. "Los Caciques Gobernadores de Toltén," *ACH 78* (1968): 43–69.

Guérin, Teresa. "Descendencia de la Casa de Geisse en el Perú," *IPI* 15 (1970): 177–188.

Guerra, Eduardo. *Historia de la Laguna: Torreón, su Origen y sus Fundadores*. Saltillo, 1932.

Guerrero, César 1. *Sanjuaninos del Ochenta*. Buenos Aires, 1965.

Guerrero, Julián 2. *100 Biografías Centroamericanas*. Managua, 1973.

Guiñazú, Fernando. *Genealogía de los Conquistadores de Cuyo y Fundadores de Mendoza*. Buenos Aires, 1932.

Guirolaleal, Mercedes. "La Familia Durán," *RAG* 5–6 (1971–1972): 199–334.

Gurria, Jorge. *Relación y Méritos y Servicios del Conquistador Bernardino Sánchez de Tapia*. México, D.F. 1953.

Gutiérrez, Miguel 1. *Tepatitlán: Primeros Pobladores y Colonizadores*. México, D.F., 1977.

Gutiérrez, Salvador 2. *La Familia Gutiérrez Contreras: Breve Información Genealógica y Otras Noticias*. México, D.F., 1978.

Guzmán, José A. *Títulos Nobiliarios en el Ecuador*. Madrid, 1957.

Hack, Franz 1. "Ascendencia Cubana del Tercer Arzobispo de Costa Rica, Monseñor Don Rubén Odio y Herrera," *ACC 1* (1953): 8–12.

Hack, Franz 2. "Ascendencia del Excmo. y Revmo. Sr. Arzobispo de Costa Rica, Dr. Don Rubén Odio y Herrera," *ACC 1* (1953): 5–7.

Hack, Franz 3. "Genealogía de la Casa de Salazar," *ACC 3* (1956): 30–34.

Hadley, Philip L. *Minería y Sociedad en el Centro Minero de Santa Eulalia, Chihuahua, 1709–1750*. México, D.F., 1979.

Hanisch, Walter. "La Familia del P. Luis de Valdivia en Granada," *ACH* 77 (1967): 129–146.

Harris, Charles H. *A Mexican Family Empire: The Latifundio of the Sánchez Navarros, 1765–1867*. Austin, 1975.

Hart, Berry Turner. *Conquistador, Luca Princess, and City Fathers: The Ampuero Family of Lima, Peru in the 16th Century*. Miami, n.d.

Hebel, Ianthe Bond. *The Sánchez Family of St. Augustine, Florida*. n.p., n.d.

Hernández, Alfonso 1. *Estudios Genealógicos.* Bogotá, 1928.

Hernández, Guillermo 2. "Linajes Bogotanos: La Familia Rivas," *Boletín de Historia y Antigüedades 18* (1941): 323–324.

Herrera, Diego. "Don Domingo de Acassuso y el Verdadero Origen de su Devoción a San Isidro Labrador," *IAC 17* (1977): 91–97.

Heyde, Alejandro. "Breve Historia de dos Siglos o de Cuatro Generaciones de Garrigos en el Río de la Plata," *IAC 19* (1981): 47–69.

Hogg, Ricardo. *Yerba Vieja.* Buenos Aires, 1945.

Hogle, DeWitt, Jr. *La Familia Muñoz: A Condensed History of the Family of Frank Muñoz and Lydia Smith Muñoz.* n.p., n.d.

Holguín, Margarita. *Los Caros en Colombia: su Fé, su Patriotismo, su Amor; Papeles de Familia.* Bogotá, 1942.

Hoyo, Eugenio del. *Historia del Nuevo Reino de León, 1577–1723.* México, D.F., n.d.

Hurtado, Enríque. "Con Motivo del Compromiso del Heredero del gran Ducado de Luxemburgo: Apuntes sobre la Familia Mestre en Cuba," *Hidalguía 164* (1981): 17–44.

Hutchinson, Cecil A. *Frontier Settlement in Mexican California: Híjar-Padrés Colony and its Origins, 1769–1835.* New Haven, 1969.

Ibarguren, Carlos 1. "De la Cámara," *IAC 18* (1979): 171–192.

Ibarguren, Carlos 2. "González Filiano," *IAC 17* (1977): 113–120.

Ibarguren, Carlos 3. "Hoyos," *IAC 17* (1977): 121–136.

Ibarguren, Carlos 4. "Los Ibarguren," *IAC 14* (1961): 41–68.

Ibarguren, Carlos 5. *Familias Guanajuatenses.* México, D.F., 1975.

Ibarrola, Gabriel. *Familias y Casas de la Vieja Valladolid.* Morelia, 1967.

Icaza, Francisco A. *Diccionario Autobiográfico de Conquistadores y Pobladores de Nueva España.* 2 vols. Guadalajara, 1969.

Iguíniz, Juan B. 1. *Bibliografía Biográfica Mexicana.* México, D.F., 1969.

Iguíniz, Juan B. 2. "Los Gobernantes de Nueva Galicia: Datos y Documentos para sus Biografías," *AMH 7* (1948).

Iguíniz, Juan B. 3. *Los Iguíniz de México.* México, D.F., 1967.

Iguíniz, Juan B. 4. *Los Marqueses de Uluapa: Monografía Genealógica.* México, D.F., 1969.

Independencia, La. *Apuntes Tomados de la Revista De Nuestra Historia Dirigida por el Presbítero José Ignacio Yani.* Buenos Aires, 1916.

IAC 1. "Hombre de Mayo," *IAC 13* (1961): 1–383.

IAC 2. "Hombres del Nueve de Julio," *IAC 15* (1966): 7–216.

IGG . *Hidalguías Guayaquileñas.* Guayaquil, 1958.

Instituto Hispano-Cubano de Historia de América. *Documentos Americanos del Archivo de Protocolos de Sevilla, Siglo XVI.* Madrid, 1935.

Instituto Mexicano de Comercio Exterior. *La Compañía de Comercio de Francisco Ignacio de Yraeta, 1767–1797.* 2 vols. México, D.F., 1985. Social, economic, and genealogical studies of this family.

Irrarázaval, José M. *El Marqués de Larraín y su Descendencia.* Santiago, 1940.

Iturriza, Carlos 1. *Algunas Familias Caraqueñas.* Caracas, 1967.

Iturriza, Carlos 2. *Algunas Familias de Cumaná.* Caracas, 1973.

Iturriza, Carlos 3. *Algunas Familias Valencianas.* Caracas, 1955.

Iusem, Miguel. *Diccionario de los Celles de Buenos Aires.* Buenos Aires, 1971.

IVG. *Matrimonios y Velaciones de Españoles y Criollos Blancos Celebrados en la Catedral de Caracas desde 1615 hasta 1831.* Caracas, 1974.

Izquierdo, José J. 1. *Breve Reseña Genealógica de la Familia Izquierdo.* México, D.F., 1922.

Izquierdo, José J. 2. *Orígenes del Linaje Inglés de Raudón y su Continuación en la Nueva España.* México, D.F., 1952.

Izquierdo, José J. 3. "Sobre los Orígenes del Linaje Inglés de Raudón y su Continuación en la Nueva España, hoy México," *AMG 6*, 1ª Series (1950–1951): 29–70.

Jalabert, Ricardo. *Album Biográfico Ilustrado.* Buenos Aires, 1903.

Jaramillo, J. *La Familia Mantilla de los Ríos.* Santiago, 1946.

Jáuregui, Carlos 1. *Genealogía Rioplatense de los Marqueses de Estella, Duques de Primo de Rivera, y Condes del Castillo de la Mota, El Alcazar.* Madrid, 1973.

Jáuregui, Carlos 2. "Introducción al Estudio de los Torres Gaete," *IAC 16* (1976): 77–155.

Jáuregui, Carlos 3. *Matrimonios de la Catedral de Buenos Aires, 1656–1702.* Buenos Aires, 1985.

Jensen, James 1. *Apuntes para el Estudio Genealógico de Familias Limeñas de los Siglos XVII y XVIII.* 2 vols. Lima, 1969, 1971.

Jensen, James 2. "La Descendencia de Don Mateo de Oyagüe en el Perú," *IPI 15* (1970): 189–251.

Jensen, James 3. *Los Boza de Lima.* Lima, 1966.

Jiménez, Claudio 1. *Indice del Archivo del Juzgado de Bienes de Difuntos de la Nueva Galicia: Siglos XVI y XVIII.* México, D.F. 1978.

Jiménez, Gabriel 2. *Linajes Cartageneros: Los Fernández de Sotomayor.* Cartagena, 1950.

Jiménez, Gabriel 3. *Linajes Cartageneros: Los Castillo y Rada.* Cartagena, 1950.

Jiménez, Gabriel 4. *Linajes Cartageneros.* 2 vols. Cartagena, 1958.

Jova, Joseph John. *The Jova Family of Sitges, Cuba and the United States.* n.p., 1977.

Jurado, Fernando 1. "Los Lasso de la Vega y los Grupos de Poder en la Conquista de los Países Andinos," *CAG 15* (1985): 87–142.

Jurado, Fernando 2. *Los Noboa de la Sierra.* Quito, 1985.

Jurado, Fernando 3. *Los Vasconez en el Ecuador, 1635–1986.* Quito, 1986.

Keith, Henry M. *Historia de la Familia Alvarado—Barroeta.* San José, 1972.

Labougle, Raul de 1. "El Capitán Diego Pérez de Centurión," *IAC 14* (1961): 81–84.

Labougle, Raul de 2. "Fernández Montiel," *IAC 14* (1961): 69–80.

Ladd, Doris M. 1. *The Mexican Nobility at Independence, 1780–1826.* Austin, 1976.

Ladd, Doris M. 2. *La Nobleza Mexicana en la Epoca de la Independencia, 1780–1826.* México, D.F., 1984.

Lafuente, Ricardo de 1. *Conquistadores del Río de la Plata.* Buenos Aires, 1937.

Lafuente, Ricardo de 2. *Familias Coloniales: Ascendientes Americanos de la Casa Primo de Rivera.* Buenos Aires, 1927.

Lafuente, Ricardo de 3. *Los de Lafuente.* Buenos Aires, 1941.

Lafuente, Ricardo de 4. *Los Machaín.* Buenos Aires, 1926.

Lafuente, Ricardo de 5. *Los Portugueses en Buenos Aires.* Buenos Aires, 1927.

Lafuente, Ricardo de 6. "Los Saavedras en Buenos Aires," *RCH 65* (1929): 335–350.

Lafuente, Ricardo de 7. *Los Sáenz Valiente y Aguirre.* Buenos Aires, 1931.

Lancaster, Ricardo 1. "Don Nicolás Carlos Gómez de Cervantes, XV Obispo de Guatemala," *RAG 8* (1983): 397–410.

Lancaster, Ricardo 2. "El Primer Mayorazgo Tapatío," *AGH 2* (1957): 286–295.

Lancaster, Ricardo 3. *Estudio Genealógico sobre la Familia Vallarta de México.* Guadalajara, 1950.

Lancaster, Ricardo 4. "Genealogía de la Familia de Añorga y sus Ramas de México," *AMG 5*, 1ª Series (1949): 93–102.

Lancaster, Ricardo 5. "La Familia Mijares de Jalisco," *AMG 3* (1965): 115–129.

Lancaster, Ricardo 6. *Noticia Genealógica sobre las Familias Ogazón y Velázquez de la Nueva Galicia.* Guadalajara, 1951.

Lancaster, Ricardo 7. *Refutación Genealógica del Libro **El Valle de Maíz, San Luis Potosí**, del Lic. Rafael Montejano y Aguiñaga.* México, D.F., 1970.

Lancaster, Ricardo 8. "Un Hijo de Don Nuño de Guzmán," *AMG 6*, 1ª Series (1950–1951): 170.

Lachner, Vicente. *Los Sandoval en Costa Rica y sus Des cendencias: Siglos* XVI–1824. n.p., n.d.

Landaeta, Manuel. *Procedencia del General Manuel Piar.* Caracas, 1963.

Lanuze, Miguel de. *Publicaciones Genealógicas y Literarias de Don Luis Thayer Ojeda.* Santiago, 1909.

Larraín, Carlos J. 1. "Antecedentes del Linaje Chileno de Cerda," *ACH 71* (1964): 101–109.

Larraín, Carlos J. 2. *El Mayorazgo de Aguirre y el Marqués de Montepío.* n.p., 1952.

Larraín, Carlos J. 3. "Carvallo: Un Linaje Colonial de la Provincia de Valdivia," *REH 1* (1949): 79–132; *2* (1950–1951): 112–176; *4–5* (1954–1955): 105–111.

Larraín, Carlos J. 4. "Documentos Inéditos para la Historia de los Linajes Chilenos," *ACH 8* (1937).

Larraín, Carlos J. 5. "Los Antepasados de Don Diego Portales Palazuelos," *ACH 8* (1937).

Larraín, Carlos J. 6. *La Familia Larraín: Sus Orígenes en España e Historial de la Rama Mayor en Chile.* Santiago, 1982.

Larraín, Carlos J. 7. "'Lo Arcaya' y Tierras de Colina," *ACH 26* (1959): 52–90.

Larrazábal, Carlos 1. *Familias Dominicanas.* 9 vols. Santo Domingo, 1967–1980.

Larrazábal, Carlos 2. "Origen Hispano-Americano de Algunas Familias Caraqueñas," *IVG 2* (1971): 11–56.

Larrouz, Antonio. *La Familia de Antonio León Pinedo en el Río de la Plata.* Buenos Aires, 1912.

Lasarte, Luis. *Familias Establecidas en el Perú Durante la Conquista y el Virreinato.* Lima, 1938.

Laso, Felipe 1. "Descendencia de Don Bernardo Vera y Pintado," *REH 11* (1963): 236–238.

Laso, Felipe 2. "Los Lasso de la Vega," *REH 8–9* (1958–1959): 27–33.

Lazcano, Arturo G. 1. *Linajes de la Gobernación de Córdoba del Tucumán: Los de Córdoba.* Córdoba, 1936.

Lazcano, Arturo G. 2. *Linajes de la Gobernación del Tucumán.* Córdoba, 1968.

Ledue, Alberto. *Diccionario de Geografía, Historia y Biografía.* México, D.F., 1910.

León, Justo R. 1. *Genealogía de la Familia León-Pinochet de la Provincia de Maule.* Mejía, Talca, 1935.

León, Luis 2. "Alrededor de la Familia Lynch," *RCH 96* (1940): 323–336.

León, Luis 3. "Apuntes Genealógicos sobre los León de la Barra," *AMG 1*, 1ª Series (1945): 87–119.

León, Luis 4. "Historia de un Linaje: Los León de la Barra y sus Alianzas," *AMG 2*, 2ª Series (1961): 181–182. Also published in México, D.F., 1958.

León, Luis 5. "La Familia en México del Libertador San Martín," *IAC 9–10* (1950–1951): 223–230.

Levillier, Roberto. *Biografías de Conquistadores de la Argentina en el Siglo XVI: Tucumán.* Madrid, 1928, 1933.

Liebman, Seymour B. *A Guide to Jewish References in the Mexican Colonial Era, 1521–1821.* Philadelphia, 1964.

Lira Montt, Luis 1. "Algunos Apuntes Sobre el Apellido Lira," *REH 6–7* (1956–1957): 73–83.

Lira Montt, Luis 2. "Genealogía de la Venerable Sierva de Dios, Chilena Doña Dorotea de Chopitea y Villota," *Hidalguía 180* (1983): 917–928.

Lira Montt, Luis 3. "Hábito de Santiago del Conquistador," *REH 13* (1965): 89.

Lira Montt, Luis 4. "Hojas de Servicios Militares de Don Filiberto y Don Lorenzo Montt," *REH 17* (1972): 75–76.

Lira Montt, Luis 5. "Las Relaciones de Méritos y Servicios de los Americanos y su Valor Probatorio de Nobleza," *Estudios Genealógicos, Heráldicos, y Nobiliarios 1* (1978): 465–478.

Lira Montt, Luis 6. "Las Ordenes y Corporaciones Nobiliarias en Chile," *REH 11* (1962–1963): 139–216.

Lira Montt, Luis 7. "Notas Genealógicas sobre los Linajes de Lira y Troncoso," *REH 13* (1965): 73–84.

Lira Montt, Luis 8. *Recuerdos de Familia.* n.p., 1943.

Lira Montt, Luis 9. "Reseña Biográfica de Don José Santiago Montt Irarrazával," *REH 17* (1972): 77–80.

Lis, Estanislao. "Vladimir Bem de Cosbán: Un Genealogista Polaco en Buenos Aires," *IAC 12* (1957): 185–188.

Llambias, R. *Ensayo Sobre el Linaje de los Artigas en el Uruguay.* Montevideo, 1925.

Lluch, Francisco. *Catálogo de Inscripciones Demográfico y de Otro Indole del Linaje Puertorriqueño Ortiz de la Renta.* Buenos Aires, 1976.

Lobato, Arturo R. *Nombres Propios que se Ostentan como Apellidos y se les Concedieron Armas.* México, D.F., 1978.

LoBuglio, Rudecinda A. *Las Familias de García, Heredia, Martínez, Padilla y otras del Pueblo de San José.* Alta, California, n.d.

Lockhart, James M. *The Men of Cajamarca: A Social and Biographical Study of the First Conquerors of Perú.* Austin, 1972.

Lohmann V., Guillermo 1. "Informaciones Genealógicos de Peruanos Seguidos ante el Santo Oficio," *IPI 8* (1955): 7–10.

Lohmann V., Guillermo 2. *Informaciones Genealógicos de Peruanos Seguidos ante el Santo Oficio.* Lima, 1957.

Lohmann V., Guillermo 3. "La Ascendencia Española del Inca, Garcilaso de la Vega," *Hidalguía 28* (1958): 369–384; *29* (1959): 681–700.

Lohmann V., Guillermo 4. "La Descendencia del Licenciado Gaspar de Espinoza," *IPI 13* (1963): 9–15.

Lohmann V., Guillermo 5. *Les Espinosa: Une famille d'hommes d'affaires en Espagne et aux Indes á l'epoque de la Colonisation.* Paris, 1968.

Lohmann V., Guillermo 6. *Los Americanos en las Ordenes Nobiliarios, 1529–1900*. Madrid, 1947.

Lohmann V., Guillermo 7. *Los Ministros de la Audiencia de Lima en el Reinado de los Borbones, 1700–1821*. Sevilla, 1974.

Lohmann V., Guillermo 8. "Notas y Documentos acerca de la Descendencia de Moctezuma II," *Hidalguía 10* (1955): 381–400.

Lohmann V., Guillermo 9. "Tres Catalanes, Virreyes en el Perú," *Hidalguía 50* (1962): 101–127.

López, Benito 1. *Genealogía López Velarde*. Aguascalientes, 1972.

López, Delfina E. 2. *La Nobleza Indígena de Pátzcuaro en la Epoca Virreinal*. México, D.F., 1965.

López, Juan 3. *Diccionario Biográfico y de Historia de México*. México, D.F., 1964.

López Morton, Myrna. "Genealogía de Juana Días López," *IGH 1* 1ª Series (1984): 42–44.

Losada, Cristina L. "El Comendador Correa y su Linaje," *IEG 1* (1980): 23–32; 2 (1981): 23–30.

Luján, Enríque R. 1. "Algunos Datos Sobre la Descendencia de Doña Andrea Vázquez de Coronado," *ACC 2* (1955): 4–21.

Luján, Enríque R. 2. *Biografía de Costa Rica del Siglo XVI*. Unpublished manuscript in the Archivo de la Academia Costarricense de Ciencias Genealógicas.

Luján, Enríque R. 3. "Estudio de la Familia Echavarría-Navarro," *ACC 11–12* (1963–1964): 7–32.

Luján, Enríque R. 4. "Familia Escalante: La Ascendencia de la Señorita Doña Manuela Escalante," *ACC 27–28* (1981): 121–129.

Luján, Enríque R. 5. "Genealogía de Don Jorge Volio Jiménez," *ACC 27–28* (1981): 379–420.

Luján, Enríque R. 6. "Genealogía del Sr. Lic. Don Mauro Fernández Acuña," *ACC 2* (1955): 97–103.

Luján, Enríque R. 7. *Genealogía de Pablo de Alvarado: Precursor y Prócer de la Independencia de Costa Rica*. San José, 1976.

Luján, Enríque R. 8. "La Familia Blanco de Costa Rica," *ACC 18–20* (1973): 18–39.

Luján, Enríque R. 9. "La Numerosa Familia Mata, de Cartago," *ACC 21* (1974): 7–58.

Luna, Félix C. 1. "El Doctor Pelagio B. Luna: Relación Genealógica de su Ascendencia," *IAC 4–5* (1945): 191–206.

Luna, Francisco 2. "Necrología de Don Pedro de Yurrita y Maury," *RAG 5–6* (1971–1972): 505–510.

Luque, Carlos A. 1. "Ascendencia del Dr. Don José Ignacio Thames," *IAC 1* (1942): 38–41.

Luque, Carlos A. 2. *El Deán Doctor Don Gregorio Funes: Arraigo de su Familia en América.* n.p., n.d.

Luque, Carlos A. 3. *Gaspar de Medina: Conquistador y Genearca.* Córdoba, 1948.

Luque, Carlos A. 4. *Itinerario Histórico-Genealógico de los Ferreira de Avevedo.* Córdoba, 1940.

Lux, Hernán Carlos. "La Sangre de Doña Sevilla López de Villalobos en la Genealogía Argentina," *IAC 17* (1977): 137–143.

Macomber, James Dale. *Six Families.* Tucson, 1983.

Madrid, Alfonso de la. *Colima Colonial a Través de sus Testamentos y Archivos.* México, D.F., 1978.

Magdaleno, D. Ricardo. *Títulos de Indias: Catálogo XX el Archivo General de Simancas.* Valladolid, 1954.

Makintach, Tomás. "Memorial Genealógico, Histórico y Heráldico de la Casa de Azcuenaga," *IAC 17* (1977): 145–159.

Maldonado, Jorge A. 1. *Los de Olmos y Aguilera de Punilla.* Córdoba, 1981.

Maldonado, Ramón J. 2. *Crónica de la Familia y Linaje del Capitán Don Juan Maldonado y Ordoñez de Villaquirán, Fundador de la Ciudad de San Cristóbal de Venezuela.* Almargo, Venezuela, 1959.

Maldonado, Ramón J. 3. *Hidalguías Riojanas: El Solar de Valdeosera.* Zurita, Venezuela, 1949.

Maldonado, Ramón J. 4. *La Casa de Márquez de Prado y sus Entronques*. Madrid, 1956.

Maló, Miguel J. 1. "Algo más acerca de los Villaseñor y Orozco en la Nueva España," *AMG 5–6*, 1ª Series (1947): 43–57.

Maló, Miguel J. 2. "Doña María Gertrudis de Castro y su Familia," *AGH 1* (1953–1954): 157–160.

Maló, Miguel J. 3. *Genealogía, Nobleza y Armas de la Familia Maló*. San Miguel de Allende, 1971.

Maló, Miguel J. 4. "Genealogía y Heráldica de la Familias de la Peza: Siglos XVII, XVIII, y XIX," *AMG 4*, 2ª Series (1968): 433–450.

Maló, Miguel J. 5. *La Casa y Mayorazgo de la Canal de la Villa de San Miguel el Grande, Nueva España*. México, D.F., 1963.

Manero, Enríque. "Doce Generaciones de **Manero** y sus Ramas Troncales, 1360–1960," *AMG 4*, 2ª Series (1968): 381–420. Published previously as *Análisis Genealógico de una Familia Mexicana, 1560–1960*. México, D.F., 1963.

Mangudo, Ernesto. "En Archivos Correntinos," *IAC 11* (1955): 165ff.

Manns, Ricardo 1. "El Condestable Mosén Pierres de Peralta y los Ruiz de Peralta de Chile," *REH 13* (1965): 96.

Manns, Ricardo 2. "Familia Messia de la Cerda," *REH 12* (1964).

Manns, Ricardo 3. "Genealogía y Descendencia del General Juan Jufré," *REH 10* (1960–1961): 67–108.

Manríque, Francisco. "Información Genealógica de Peruanos Seguidas ante el Santo Oficio," *IPI 9* (1956): 115, 252.

Mansano, Sr. "Genealogía de Zenón Urrutia Infante," *RGL 11* (1959): 302–303.

Mansilla, Mariano 1. *Historia de la Casa de Videla desde 1526: Ramas Americanas de Cuyo en el Reyno de Chile*. 2 vols. Buenos Aires, 1941.

Mansilla, Luis 2. *Relación Genealógica de Varias Familias Chilenas*. Santiago, 1927.

Mansilla, Luis 3. *Relación Genealógica de Varias Familias de Chiloé*. El Colono, Angol, 1914.

Marie, Clementia. "The First Families of LaBallona Valley," *Historical Society of Southern California Quarterly 37* (1955): 48–55.

Marín, Fausto 1. "Esbozo Genealógico de Nuño Beltrán de Guzmán," *AMG 4*, 2ª Series (1968): 367–376.

Marín, Santiago 2. "Don Joaquín Vicuña y Larraín: Sus Ascendientes y Descendientes," *RCH 41* (1921): 126–134.

Marino, Juan Carlos. *Genealogía de los Tocco*. Buenos Aires, 1965.

Márques, Sr. 1. "Los Velasco, Linaje Palentino," *Hidalguía 180* (1983): 853–864.

Márquez, Felipe 2. "Los O'Phelan en Lima," *RGL 2* (1950): 190–192.

Márquez, Fernando 3. *Arqueología Nobiliaria del Reyno de Chile*. 7 vols. n.p., n.d.

Márquez, Fernando 4. *Vida de Don Francisco Javier de Reyna: Primera Parte, Río de la Plata*. Buenos Aires, 1940. Surnames Obarrio, Lezica, Reyna y Cáceres.

Márquez, Fernando 5. *Vida de un Consejero de Indias*. Santiago, 1937.

Márquez, Joaquín 6. *Hombres Célebres de Chihuahua: por Nacimiento y por Adopción*. México, D.F., 1953.

Márquez, Joaquín 7. *Hombres Célebres de Puebla, por Adopción*. 2 vols. México, D.F., 1952, 1955.

Marrazzo, Javier. *Nuevo Diccionario Geográfico, Histórico de la República Argentina*. Buenos Aires, 1921.

Martín, Félix F. 1. "Linaje del Gobernador Joseph Antonio de Herrera Sotomayor y Rivadeneyra," *IAC 14* (1961): 88–95.

Martín, Félix F. 2. "Los Martín y Herrera," *IAC 12* (1957): 115–131.

Martín, Félix F. 3. "Reseña Histórica de los Guzmán: sus Caballeros de Santiago y de Malta," *IAC 19* (1981): 83–87.

Martín, Luis 4. *Daughters of the Conquistadores: Women of the Viceroyalty of Peru*. Albuquerque, 1983.

Martínez, Eliseo L. 1. *Ramireño en la Historia*. San Antonio, 1984.

Martínez, Evelyn 2. *My Family Back Bone: A Genealogy of the Romero, Olivas, Cota, Picó, Story and Eddy Families*. n.p., 1984. Includes histories on the families Alanis, Blas, Bojórques, Carrillo, Castro, Espinoza, Fernández, Gutiérrez, León, López, Lugo, Miranda, Quintero, Reyes, Rivera, Salgado, Sinova, Vastida, and Verdugo.

Martínez, Jerónimo 3. "Familia Hurtado de Mendoza," *IVG 2* (1971): 57–61.

Martínez, Jerónimo 4. *Linaje de Diego de Losada.* n.p., n.d.

Martínez, José A. 5. *Catálogo de Informaciones Genealógicas de la Inquisición de Córdoba Conservadas en el Archivo Histórico Nacional.* 2 vols. Madrid, 1970.

Martínez, Julían 6. *Los Mayorazgos del Conde Fundador.* San Sebastián, 1969.

Martínez, Leopoldo 7. *Los Caballeros de las Ordenes Militares en México: Catálogo Biográfico y Genealógico.* México, D.F., 1946.

Martínez, Luis G. 8. "La Familia Toledo Pimentel en la República Argentina," *La Memoria del Primer Congreso de Genealogía y Heráldica.* Barcelona, 1929.

Martínez, Luis G. 9. "Los Bazán," *Revista de la Universidad Nacional 7–8* (1939): 1257–1287; *9–10* (1939): 1657–1679; *11* (1940): 12–45.

Martínez, Luis G. 10. *Los Cabrera.* Córdoba, 1938.

Martínez, Manuel 11. "Martínez Aparicio: Marqueses de Vista Bella," *RGL 7* (1955): 111–118.

Martínez, Miguel A. 12. "Antepasados Americanos de Domingo Faustino Sarmiento," *Historia 23*, 11ff.

Martínez, Miguel A. 13. "Béthencourt (Rama de Sanabria): Martínez de Béthencourt," *IAC 9–10* (1950–1951): 371–398.

Martínez, Miguel A. 14. "Díaz," *IAC 8* (1948–1949): 21–48.

Martínez, Miguel A. 15. "Genearquía de la Familia de Moreno," *Historia 19*, 12ff.

Martínez, Miguel A. 16. "Los Escalada y Quintana," *IAC 9–10* (1950–1951): 135–146.

Martínez, Miguel A. 17. "Los Fernández de Eijo (del Rincón de Noario)," *IAC 12* (1957): 95–108.

Martínez, Miguel A. 18. "Los Gálvez: Genealogía," *IAC 11* (1955): 80–105.

Martínez, Miguel A. 19. "Los Lastra," *IAC 6–7* (1946–1947): 12–22.

Martínez, Miguel A. 20. "Los Martín de Betancur," *IAC 14* (1961): 96–105.

Martínez, Miguel A. 21. Los Pueyrredón," *IAC 3* (1944): 16–41.

Martínez, Miguel A. 22. "Origen y Linaje de los Mitre," *IAC 2* (1943): 15–19.

Martínez, Miguel A. 23. *Orígenes y Linajes Argentinos.* n.p., 1944.

Martínez, Modesto 24. "La Casa Solariega de los Montealegre," *Revista de los Archivos Nacionales, San José 9–10* (1943): 482–487.

Martínez, Pablo L. 25. *Guía Familiar de Baja California 1700–1900.* México, 1965.

Martínez, Rufino 26. *Diccionario Biográfico-Histórico Dominicano, 1821–1930.* Santo Domingo, 1971.

Martínez, Santiago 27. *Fundadores de Arequipa.* Arequipa, 1936.

Martínez, Sergio 28. "Cuatro Linajes de Copiapó, *REH 10* (1960–1961): 127–129. Genealogies of the families Acuña, Espinoza, Peragallo, and Ustariz.

Martínez, Sergio 29. "El Coronel Don Domingo de Torres," *REH 17* (1972): 93–101.

Martínez, Sergio 30. "El Doctor Don Francisco Aguilar de los Olivos, Fundador de Familia en Chile," *REH 11* (1962–1963): 127–138.

Martínez, Sergio 31. "Espinoza," *REH 13* (1965): 95.

Martínez, Sergio 32. "Familia Emparan," *REH 10* (1962).

Martínez, Sergio 33. "Honorato," *REH 17* (1972): 107–108.

Martínez, Sergio 34. *La Descendencia del Portugués Don Antonio Ramos y Silveira.* n.p., n.d.

Martínez, Sergio 35. "La Familia del General Las Hevas," *REH 8–9* (1958–1959): 41–58; *10* (1960–1961): 57–66.

Martínez, Sergio 36. "Los Ureta y Cajal y sus Ascendientes," *REH 12* (1964): 65–76.

Martínez, Sergio 37. "Segundo Centenario de la Familia Martínez Ureta de Santiago," *REH 17* (1972): 103–106.

Martínez, Sergio 38. "Tribulaciones de un Funcionario del Siglo XVIII," *RCG 129.*

Martínez, Sergio 39. "Familia Amaral," *REH 11* (1963).

Martínez, Vicente 40. "La Casa Solariega de los Martínez en Corrientes," *IAC 8* (1948–1949): 120–140.

Massini, J.M. *Los Cabrera.* Córdoba, 1938.

Mata, Jesús 1. "Genealogía de la Familia Jiménez, desde Don Ramón Jiménez Robredo para Acá," *Monografía de Cartago* (1930): 453–464.

Mata, Jesús 2. "La Familia Peralta," *Monografía de Cartago* (1930): 481–489.

Mata, Jesús 3. *Monografía de Cartago.* Cartago, 1930.

Mateu, Josefina. "La Enseñanza de Genealogía y Heráldica en la Universidad Española," *Comunicaciones al XV Congreso Internacional de las Ciencias Genealógicas y Heráldicas 3* (1983): 83–90.

Maturana, Humberto 1. "Origen y Entroncamiento de la Familia Feliú," *RCH 29*, 218.

Maturana, Pedro H. 2. "Los Maturanas," *RCH ?* (1931).

Mayochi, Enríque M. *Los Congresistas de Tucumán: Rasgos Biográficos.* Buenos Aires, 1966.

Mayol, Carlos "Linaje del Vale de Tegua," *CEG 6*, 31–33.

Maza, Agustina. "Cronología y Semblanza Genealógica del Coronel Argentino Don Mariano Maza," *IEG 4* (1982): 63–72.

McAndrews, Robert J. *Moraga History.* n.p., n.d.

McGinty, Brian. "The Carrillos of San Diego: A Historic Spanish Family of California," *Historical Society of Southern California Quarterly 39* (1957): 3–13.

Meade, Adalberto W. *Origen de Mexicali.* Mexicali, 1980.

Medellín, Melquisidec. *Biografía y Genealogía de Familia, 1700–1947.* Bogotá, 1947.

Medina, José T. 1. *Historia del Tribunal de la Inquisición de Lima, 1569–1820.* Santiago, 1956.

Medina, José T. 2. *La Inquisición en el Río de la Plata.* Buenos Aires, 1945.

Medina, José T. 3. *Notas Biográficas y Documentos para la Historia de esta Familia en Chile.* Santiago, 1898.

Melgar, Manuel de. *Indice Genealógico de Varias Familias.* Madrid, 1935.

Méndez, Olga 1. "Apuntes Biográficos y Genealógicos de la Familia Méndez Caldeira," *IEG 1* (1980): 37–44.

Méndez, Rodrigo 2. *Ascendencia Ilustre: Gloriosos Hechos y Posteridad Noble del Famoso Nuño Alfonso.* Facsimile edition. México, D.F., 1975.

Mendiburu, Manuel de. *Diccinario Histórico-Biográfico del Perú.* 2nd edition. 15 vols. Lima, 1931–1938.

Mendirichaga, Tomás 1. *Apellidos de Nuevo León.* México, D.F., 1958–1968. Includes articles about the surnames Guerra, Botello y Buentello, Hinojosa, Zambrano, Cavazos, Sepúlveda, and Larralde.

Mendirichaga, Tomás 2. *Apellidos de Nuevo León: Botello y Buentello.* México, D.F., 1961.

Mendirichaga, Tomás 3. "Apellidos de Nuevo León: Larralde," *Revista de Cultura Mexicana 32* (1968): 299ff.

Mendirichaga, Tomás 4. *Origen de los Apellidos Garza y Treviño en Nuevo León.* Monterrey, 1982.

Mendirichaga, Tomás 5. *Origen of the Surname Garza and Treviño in Nuevo León.* México, D.F., 1982. Translated by Edna G. Brown, and published in Corpus Christi, 1989.

Mendive, Antonio. "Familias de Cuzco: Filiación y Genealogía de la Familia de los Berrios," *Revista del Archivo Histórico 8* (1957): 115–129.

Mendoza, Víctor. *La Heráldica en Chihuahua.* Chihuahua, 1983.

Mestre, Manuel. *Efemérides Biográficas (Defunciones —Nacimientos).* México, D.F., 1945.

Mexia, Pedro. "La Ovandina, 1621," *Hidalguía, 166–167* (1981): 657–676.

Mier, Joaquín. *Los Mier: 200 Años en Morelia.* Morelia, 1978.

Miers, Nathaniel. *Los Cox en Chile.* n.p., 1903.

Miguel, José María. *Diccionario de Insurgentes.* México, D.F., 1969.

Millares Carlo, A. *Indice y Extracto de los Protocolos del Archivo de Notarías de México, D.F.* 2 vols. México, D.F., 1946.

Milligan, Donald. *Genealogy of Selected Hispanic Families of New Mexico and Southern Colorado.* Commerce City, Colorado: private publication, 1990.

Miranda, Ignacio 1. "El Dr. Don Andrés Sáenz de Santa María: Datos Biográficos y Genealógicos," *AMG 2–3* (1946): 99–115.

Miranda, Marta Elba 2. *Mujeres Chilenas.* Santiago, 1940.

Molina, Angel José 1. *Los Herrera y Díaz Herrera de la Ciudad de la Santísima Trinidad y Puerto de Santa María del Buen Aire.* Buenos Aires, 1970.

Molina, Apolinario 2. *Diccionario Biográfico Nacional.* Buenos Aires, 1877.

Molina, Raul A. 3. "Antón Higueras de Santana: El Andaluz de las Cuatro Estancias, Vecino Fundador de Buenos Aires," *IAC 12* (1957): 21–46.

Molina, Raul A. 4. *Casco de Mendoza y los Vera de Aragón.* Buenos Aires, 1949.

Molina, Raul A. 5. *Don Diego Rodríguez Valdez y de la Banda: El Tercer Gobernador del Paraguay y Río de la Plata por S.M., Después de la Repoblación de Buenos Aires, 1599–1600.* Buenos Aires, 1949.

Molina, Raul A. 6. "Don Jerónimo Luis de Cabrera y la Caballería de Santiago," *IAC 11* (1955): 21–40.

Molina, Raul A. 7. "Los Casco de Mendoza y los Vera de Aragón," *IAC 8* (1948–1949): 163–216.

Molina, Raul A. 8. "Los Cordovés," *IAC 14* (1961): 106–121.

Molina, Raul A. 9. "Salvador Correa de Sáa y Benavidez: un Héroe Americano Ligado al Brasil y a la Argentina," *IAC 9–10* (1950–1951): 263–309.

Molina, Luis 10. "Descendencia del General Bartolomé de las Cuevas," *ACH 16.*

Molina, Luis 11. "Familia Carrasco," *REH 8–9* (1958–1959): 15–25.

Molina, Luis 12. "Los Ascendientes del Abate Don Juan Ignacio Molina," *REH 14* (1966–1967): 121–126.

Molina, María 13. *Bibliografía de Estudios Genealógicos y Heráldicos (y Temas Afines) de Costa Rica.* San José, 1967.

Molina, María 14. *La Familia Molina en Costa Rica.* n.p., 1960.

Montaño, Alberto 1. *Biografías de los Hermanos García de la Lanza.* 2 vols. n.p., 1950, 1959.

Montaño, Alberto 2. *Diccionario Biográfico de Bolivia.* n.p., n.d.

Montoto, Santiago 1. *Nobiliario Hispano-Americano del Siglo XVI.* Madrid, n.d.

Montoto, Santiago 2. *Nobiliario de Reinos, Ciudades y Villas de la América Española.* Madrid, 1928. Volume 3 of the *Colección de Documentos Inéditos para la Historia de Hispanoamérica.*

Montt, Manuel. "La Prosapia Intelectual de Don Manuel Montt," *REH 17* (1972): 73–74.

Montúfar, José M. 1. "Los Pintores Montúfar en la Ciudad de Santiago de Guatemala, en el Siglo XVII," *RAG 5–6* (1971–1972): 383–429.

Montúfar, José M. 2. *Manuel Martínez Aparicio, Primera Autoridad de Quezaltenango Después de la Independencia y Hermano Mayor de la Primera Junta de Gobierno del Hospital de San Juan de Dios.* Guatemala, 1949.

Montúfar, José M. 3. "Somerás Adicionales al Estudio de Don Alvaro Fernández Peralta Titulada," *ACC 6* (1958): 63–64.

Montúfar, José M. 4. "Tercer Abuelo del Porta José Batres Montúfar fue el Capitán General de Guatemala, Don Francisco Rodríguez de Rivas," *RAG 1* (1967): 11–16.

Mora, Fernando. "La Familia Hack Prestinary," *ACC 2* (1955): 69–77.

Morales, Adolfo 1. "El Tronco Hispano de la Raza en el Alto Perú," *IAC 2* (1943): 87–89.

Morales, Adolfo 2. *Nobiliario de la Antigua Real Audiencia de Charcas.* n.p., n.d.

Morales, Adolfo 3. "Parentesco entre los Conquistadores Españoles: La Familia de Ñuflo de Chávez," *Revista de la Universidad Gabriel René Moreno* (1958): 35–42.

Morales, F. 4. "El General Aldao: sus Ascendientes y Descendientes," *Revista de la Junta de Estudios Históricos de Santa Fé 14* (1939): 73–84.

Morales, Fernando 5. "Los Arenas y los Funés," *IAC 3* (1944): 48–61.

Morales, Fernando 6. *Genealogía de los Conquistadores de Cuyo y Fundadores de Mendoza.* Buenos Aires, 1932.

Morales, Manuel 7. *Los Altamirano.* México, D.F., 1966.

Moratorio, Arsinoe. *Mujeres del Uruguay.* Montevideo, 1946.

Moreno, Isidoro J.R. 1. *Crónica de Familia, 1742–1982.* Buenos Aires, 1983.

Moreno, Ivan Carlos 2. "Linaje del General Gregorio Aráoz de la Madrid, Ayudante de Campo del Libertador," *IAC 9–10* (1950–1951): 248–260.

Moreno, Ivan Carlos 3. *Linaje Troncal de los Ruiz de Arellano en el Río de la Plata.* Buenos Aires, 1937.

Moreno, Ivan Carlos 4. "La Escalada y sus Descendientes en Buenos Aires," *IAC 6–7* (1946–1947): 179–186.

Moreno, Ivan Carlos 5. "Los Hernández del Martín Fierro," *IAC 8* (1948–1949): 140–153.

Moreno, María A. 6. *Heráldica y Genealogía Granadina.* Granada, 1976.

Moreno, Pablo C. 7. *Galería de Coahuilenses Distinguidos.* Torreón, 1966. 2nd edition. Torreón, 1967.

Moreyra, Manuel 1. *Biografías de Oidores del Siglo XVII.* Lima, 1957.

Moreyra, Manuel 2. "Juan Jiménez de Montalvo," *IPI 9* (1956): 5, 25.

Moreyra, Manuel 3. "La Genealogía de Alonso Carrio de la Vandera," *IPI 16* (1971): 91–98.

Moscoso, Antonio. *Los Moscoso de Pedasi hasta la Generación Quinta.* Panamá, 1969.

Moyano, Alejandro 1. *Hijos y Nietos de Fundadores de Córdoba.* Córdoba, 1973.

Moyano, Alejandro 2. "Notas Genealógicas sobre Gobernadores del Tucumán, 1600–1650," *IAC 17* (1977): 161–174.

Moyano, Alejandro 3. "Rama Cordobesa de los Ladrón de Guevara," *EGC 15* (1982).

Moyano, Miguel 4. "La Familia Arguibel," *IAC 17* (1982): 175–179.

Mújica, Alberto 1. "El Sargento Mayor Don Juan Antonio de Bustamante y Quijano, y su Descendencia," *IPI 9* (1956): 39, 64.

Mújica, Juan de 2. *Antigüedades Curicanas.* Santiago, n.d.

Mújica, Juan de 3. "Descendencia de los Incas," *IAC 3* (1944): 140–143.

Mújica, Juan de 4. "El Conquistador Bartolomé de Arenas," *REH 10* (1960–1961): 37–42.

Mújica, Juan de 5. "El Conquistador Juan de la Torre," *IPI 13* (1963): 95–98.

Mújica, Juan de 6. *La Casa de Vizcaya y sus Linajes.* Madrid, 1960.

Mújica, Juan de 7. "La Familia Corbalán," *ACH 5*.

Mújica, Juan de 8. "La Familia de Don Juan José Daroch," *REH 2* (1950–1951): 102–111.

Mújica, Juan de 9. *Linajes Españoles: Nobleza Colonial de Chile (1927): Los Tocornal.* n.p., 1959.

Mújica, Juan de 10. "Notas a la Casa de Souza," *Hidalguía 28* (1958).

Mújica, Juan de 11. "Notas y Documentos: La Familia Paterna del General Freire," *ACH 47* (1952): 157–159.

Muñoz, Ignacio 1. "Títulos de Nobleza y Condecoraciones," *El Verdadero México: Guía Completa de la Ciudad y Valle de México Formada con Datos Tomados con la Revisión de Don Luis González Obregón* (1927): 369–376.

Muñoz, Sr. 2. "Dos Linajes Extremeños," *IPI 15* (1970): 141–163.

Murga, Ventura. "Helguero," *IAC 18* (1979): 223–228.

Muría, José María. *Historia de Jalisco.* 4 vols. Guadalajara, 1980–1982.

Mutnick, Dorothy. *Some Alta California Pioneers and Descendants.* Parts 1 and 2, Lafayette, California, 1982.

Muzzio, Julio A. *Diccionario Histórico y Biográfico de la República Argentina.* Buenos Aires, 1920.

Nagel, Kurt. *Algunas Familias Maracaiberas.* Maracaibo, 1969.

Nakayama, Antonio 1. "Familias de Culiacán: El Apellido Verdugo," *AMG 3* 1ª Series (1965): 85–94.

Nakayama, Antonio 2. *Pioneros Sinaloenses en California.* Culiacán, 1970.

Navarro, Jorge 1. *El Club de Residentes Extranjeros.* Buenos Aires, 1941.

Navarro, Luis 2. *Sonora y Sinaloa en el Siglo XVII.* Sevilla, 1967.

Negrón, Angela. *Mujeres de Puerto Rico, Desde el Período de Colonización hasta el Primer Tercio del Siglo XX.* n.p., 1935.

Nieto, Rafael 1. "Apuntes Genealógicos sobre Don José Alvarez de Toledo: su vida, su familia," *Revista de la Biblioteca Nacional 2* (1954).

Nieto, Rafael 2. *Apuntes Genealógicos sobre el Habanero Don José Alvarez de Toledo: su vida, su familia.* La Habana, 1954.

Nieto, Rafael 3. "Apuntes Genealógicos sobre los Calar de Irolo," *AMG 14* 1ª Series (1953): 139–146.

Nieto, Rafael 4. "Ascendencia Cubana de los Duques de Santoña," *Revista, Habana Yacht Club 255* (1950).

Nieto, Rafael 5. "Ascendencia Habanera del IV Conde de Pozos Dulces (Ensayo Genealógico)," *Revista de la Biblioteca Nacional 3* (1952).

Nieto, Rafael 6. *Dignidades Nobiliarias en Cuba.* Madrid, 1954.

Nieto, Rafael 7. *Documentos Sacramentales de Algunos Cubanos Ilustres.* La Habana, 1954.

Nieto, Rafael 8. "Don Baltasar Dorantes de Carranza: sus Ascendientes, Descendientes y Parientes," *AMG 5* 1ª Series (1947): 59–73.

Nieto, Rafael 9. "Dos Apellidos Cubanos del Siglo XVI: Guilizasti y Millán de Bohorques," *AMG 6–7* 1ª Series (1948).

Nieto, Rafael 10. "El Apellido López de Aragón en México y La Habana," *AMG 10–13* 1ª Series (1951): 119–130.

Nieto, Rafael 11. "El Gobernador Mazariegos no fue Conquistador de Chiapas," *Boletín del Archivo Nacional de Cuba 55* (1956).

Nieto, Rafael 12. "El Ilustrísimo Señor Don Fray Mauro de Larreategui y Cólon, Decimotercer Obispo de Guatemala, Quinto Nieto del Almirante Cristóbal Colón," *RAG 5–6* (1971–1972): 47–58.

Nieto, Rafael 13. "El Linaje García Pulido," *AMG 2* 2ª Series (1968): 359–366.

Nieto, Rafael 14. "El Linaje Ordaz en México y Cuba," *AMG 8–9* 1ª Series (1949): 103–140.

Nieto, Rafael 15. "El Marquesado de San Jorge, hoy de San Román de Ayala," *AMG 6–7* 1ª Series (1948).

Nieto, Rafael 16. "El Marqués de Rabell y su Familia," *Revista, Habana Yacht Club 248* (1953).

Nieto, Rafael 17. "El Poeta Béquer, su Ascendencia Flamenca y sus Parientes Cubanos," *Revista de la Biblioteca Nacional de Cuba 3* (1955): 107–158. Also published as *Bécquer, el Poeta, su Ascendencia Flamenca y sus Parientes Cubanos.* La Habana, 1955.

Nieto, Rafael 18. "El Virrey Abascal: su Familia," *Revista de la Biblioteca Nacional 4* (1953).

Nieto, Rafael 19. "Enríque Villuendas: su Familia," *Revista de la Biblioteca Nacional 4* (1953).

Nieto, Rafael 20. *General Santander y sus Parientes Habaneros, Los Pontón.* La Habana, 1957. See also #29 for additional information.

Nieto, Rafael 21. *Genealogías Habaneras.* 2 vols. Madrid, 1979–1980.

Nieto, Rafael 22. "Historia de mi Familia (obra inédita)," *AMG 6* 1ª Series (1950–1951): 119–130.

Nieto, Rafael 23. "Ilustraciones Genealógicas," *Correo del Instituto Cubano de Genealogía y Heráldica* (1957–1958).

Nieto, Rafael 24. "Indice de Varios Linajes Portugueses Establecidos en Cuba," *RGL 2* (1950): 177–182.

Nieto, Rafael 25. "La Casa de Braganza," *AMG 2* 1ª Series (1946): 49–56.

Nieto, Rafael 26. "La Casa de Francia," *Revista, Habana Yacht Club 57* (1930).

Nieto, Rafael 27. "La Casa de los Saavedra en Nueva Granada, Perú y Nueva España," *IPI 4* (1949): 29–57.

Nieto, Rafael 28. "La Casa Ducal de Veragua en 1957 y Cuadro Sinóptico de la Ascendencia del Actual y XVII Duque de Veragua y su Consorte como Descendientes de Cristóbal Colón," *Boletin de la Academia Cubana de Ciencias Genealógicas 5* (1957).

Nieto, Rafael 29. *La Generala Santander y sus Parientes Habaneros: Los Pontón.* Bogotá, 1957. See also #20 for additional information.

Nieto, Rafael 30. "Los Autrán y sus Ramas Cubanas," *AMG 5–8* 1ª Series (1953).

Nieto, Rafael 31. "Los Aparicio de La Habana, Cuba, con línea en Guatemala," *RAG 2* (1968).

Nieto, Rafael 32. *Los Boca Negra en la Nueva España.* México, D.F., 1949.

Nieto, Rafael 33. "Los Bonaparte," *Revista, Habana Yacht Club 70* (1931).

Nieto, Rafael 34. "Los Cabello Habaneros, Ascendientes de los Marqueses de Novaliches," *Revista, Habana Yacht Club 240* (1951).

Nieto, Rafael 35. "Los Cabello Habaneros, Ascendientes de los Vallellano," *Revista, Habana Yacht Club 240* (1951).

Nieto, Rafael 36. "Los Chacón: su Rama de Marinos," *Revista, Habana Yacht Club 243* (1953).

Nieto, Rafael 37. "Los Condes de Casteló," *AMG 2* 1ª Series (1957): 151–168.

Nieto, Rafael 38. "Los Condes de Tejada de Valdosera," *Revista, Habana Yacht Club 236* (1950).

Nieto, Rafael 39. "Los Córdoba-Verdes: Estudio Genealógico de una Familia Habanera," *Boletín del Archivo Nacional 57* (1959): 215–241.

Nieto, Rafael 40. *Los Descendientes de Cristóbal Colón.* La Habana, 1952.

Nieto, Rafael 41. *Los Fernández de Cossio.* La Habana, 1955.

Nieto, Rafael 42. "Los Hermanos Carrillo de Albornoz y Archer, Oaxaquenses Distinguidos: sus Parientes Cercanos y sus Descendientes en Guatemala y La Habana," *Revista de Historia de América 65–66* (1968).

Nieto, Rafael 43. "Los Linajes de Jacott y el Condado de Pozos Dulces," *IPI 2* (1958).

Nieto, Rafael 44. "Los Livaudais de la Nueva Orleans," *Correo del Instituto Cubano de Genealogía y Heráldica 1* (1957).

Nieto, Rafael 45. "Los Lóriga y su Enlace con los Condes de Casa Sedano," *Revista, Habana Yacht Club 249* (1953).

Nieto, Rafael 46. "Los Marqueses de Faura," *Revista, Habana Yacht Club 238* (1951).

Nieto, Rafael 47. "Los Marqueses de la Gándara," *Hidalguía 4* (1954).

Nieto, Rafael 48. "Los Marqueses de Mont Roig," *Revista, Habana Yacht Club 247* (1953).

Nieto, Rafael 49. "Los Martín y los Peralta," *Revista, Habana Yacht Club 246* (1953).

Nieto, Rafael 50. "Los Morales de los Ríos," *Revista de la Biblioteca Nacional 3* (1957). Also published separately at La Habana, 1957.

Nieto, Rafael 51. "Los Moya en Cuba," *Revista Latina 3* (1951): 137–146.

Nieto, Rafael 52. "Los Recabarren Habaneros y sus Descendientes Chilenos," *Revista de la Biblioteca Nacional 3* (1953).

Nieto, Rafael 53. "Los Santos Suárez y su Ascendencia Cubana," *Revista, Habana Yacht Club 242* (1952).

Nieto, Rafael 54. "Los Tena, de Celaya," *AGM 2* 1ª Series (1957): 208–213.

Nieto, Rafael 55. "Los Valcárcel," *Revista, Habana Yacht Club 239* (1951).

Nieto, Rafael 56. "Los Villaseñor — Cervantes en Celaya," *AMG 4* 1ª Series (1947): 49.

Nieto, Rafael 57. *Los Villa-Urrutia: un Linaje Vasco en México y en La Habana.* La Habana, 1952.

Nieto, Rafael 58. "Muñoz, Guardia de Corps y Duque," *Revista, Habana Yacht Club 85* (1932).

Nieto, Rafael 59. "Otro Linaje de Marinos: los Díaz de Herrera," *Revista, Habana Yacht Club, 244* (1952).

Nieto, Rafael 60. "Presencia Habanera en los Ascendientes de la Reina de los Belgas," *IPI 15* (1970): 69–97.

Nieto, Rafael 61. "Terratenientes de la Hacienda 'San Diego de Corralejo' Donde Naciera el Cura Hidalgo," *Boletín del Comité de Archivo, La Habana* (1958): 23. Also published separately, La Habana, 1958.

Nieto, Rafael 62. "Una Familia Burguesa: Los Veedor de Oviedo," *AMG 5* 1ª Series (1947).

Nieto, Rafael 63. *Una Rama Cubana de los Roca de Togores.* La Habana, 1955.

Nieto, Rafael 64. "Una Rama Habanera de los Roca de Togores," *Revista de la Biblioteca Nacional 1* (1955).

Nieto, Rafael 65. "Un Linaje de Abogados: Franco de Toledo," *AMG 5* 1ª Series (1947): 75–91.

Nieto, Rafael 66. "Un Linaje de Querétaro: Los Colchado," *AMG 14–17* 1ª Series (1953): 109–112.

Nieto, Rafael 67. "Un Linaje Jerezano en La Habana: Los López de Carrizosa," *Revista, Habana Yacht Club 237* (1951).

Nieto, Rafael 68. "Un Linaje Montañés en Santiago de Cuba," *Revista, Habana Yacht Club 245* (1953).

Nieto, Rafael 69. "Un magnate Tabacalero y su Descendencia Habanera: Los Alvarez," *Revista, Habana Yacht Club* (1953).

Nieto, Rafael 70. "Un Personaje no Estudiado de Nuestra Historia: de Clouet," *Revista de la Biblioteca Nacional 4* (1952).

Noboa, Luis. *Genealogía de Olmedo.* Guayaquil, 1980.

Northrop, Marie E. 1. "Genealogical Notes on the Family of José María Ortega and Francisco López, 1760–1874," *The Historical Society of Southern California Quarterly 1* (1961): 106–107.

Northrop, Marie E. 2. "Las Familias de California," *The Historical Society of Southern California Quarterly 1* (1960): 89–90.

Northrop, Marie E. 3. *Spanish-Mexican Families of Early California, 1769–1850.* 2 vols. Burbank, 1984.

Northrop, Marie E. 4. "The Founding Families of Los Angeles," *Communicaciones al XV Congreso Internacional de las Ciencias Genealógicas y Heráldicas 3* (1983): 241–250.

Núñez, José. *Un Virrey Limeño en México.* México, D.F., 1927.

O'Gorman, Edmundo 1. *Catálogo de Pobladores de Nueva España.* México, D.F., 1941.

O'Gorman, Edmundo 2. "Vecinos y Pueblos de Colima en 1532," *Boletín del Archivo General de la Nación 1* (1939): 5–20.

Olivares, Emilio 1. "Los Marco del Pont," *IPI 12* (1961): 41–66.

Olivares, Emilio 2. "Los Valle-Riestra en el Perú," *IPI 10* (1957): 32–48.

Oliveres, Francisco. "Los Pleitos Sobre el Ejido de Treinta y Tres," *Apuntes.* Treinta y Tres, 1929.

Olmedo, José I. "Libro de Familia de Don Luis Josef de Zaldarriaga y sus Esposa Doña Mónica Castelli," *IAC 6–7* (1946–1947): 157–178.

Olmos, Alejandro 1. "Alonso Riquelme de Guzmán," *IAC 17* (1977): 181–210.

Olmos, Amalio 2. *Arbol Genealógico de la Familia Olmos.* Santiago, 1938.

Olmsted, Virginia L. 1. *The Ortiz Family of New Mexico: The First Six Generations.* Albuquerque, 1978.

Olmsted, Virginia L. 2. *Spanish and Mexican Censuses of New Mexico, 1750–1830.* Albuquerque, 1981.

Olmsted, Virginia L. 3. *Spanish and Mexican Colonial Censuses of New Mexico, 1790, 1823, 1845.* Albuquerque, 1981.

Ondarza, Antonio S. 1. *Ascendientes y Descendientes del Prócer Don José Miguel Carrera V. en Chile.* Santiago, 1959.

Ondarza, Antonio S. 2. *Descendencia Familiar del Asesor de la Capitanía General de Chile, Pedro Díaz de Valdés y Javier Carrera.* Neupert, 1963.

Opazo, Gustavo 1. "El Conquistador Andrés de Barahona y su Descendencia," *RCH 75.*

Opazo, Gustavo 2. *Familias del Antiguo Obispado de Concepción, 1551–1900.* Santiago, 1957. Also published in *RCH 81, 82, 83, 85, 86, 91, 92, 94, 95, 96, and 98.*

Opazo, Gustavo 3. "Juan Evans y su Descendencia, Actual Familia Ibáñez," *La Nación,* 1928.

Opazo, Gustavo 4. "La Familia Letelir," *La Nación,* 1927.

Opazo, Gustavo 5. *Origen de las Antiguas Familias de Chillán, 1589–1800.* Santiago, 1935.

Opazo, Gustavo 6. "Origen de las Familias de Maule," *RCG* (1924–1928).

Ordoñez, Ramiro 1. "Fray Juan de Zapata y Sandoval, VI Obispo de Guatemala y sus Parientes," *RAG 8* (1983): 23–64.

Ordoñez, Ramiro 2. "La Familia Buonafede de Zacapa y sus Descendientes en Guatemala, El Salvador y Nicaragua," *RAG 5–6* (1971): 85–198.

Ordoñez, Ramiro 3. "La Familia de Jonama," *RAG 1* (1967): 35–52.

Ordoñéz, Ramiro 4. "La Familia Sunsín de Herrera," *RAG 8* (1983): 313–342.

Ordoñez, Ramiro 5. "Noticias Antiguas de Jonama," *RAG 5–6* (1971–1972): 67–84.

Ordoñez, Ramiro 6. "Probanza Hecha en la Real Audiencia de Guatemala a Pedimento de Pedro Ordoñez de Villaquirán de la Calidad de su Persona y Méritos y Servicios que ha Hecho a su Majestad," *León Fernández: Colección de Documentos para la Historia de Costa Rica, San José 1* (1881): 137–158.

Oreamuno, Nicolás. "La Familia Oreamuno," *Monografía de Cartago* (1930): 499–503.

Oribe, Emilio N. *Los Villegas: Una Antigua Familia de Montevideo, 1777–1951.* Montevideo, 1966.

Orozco, Raul 1. "Genealogía de la Familia Jinesta," *Revista de los Archivos Nacionales, San José 9–10* (1944): 525–528.

Orozco, Raul 2. "Genealogía de la Familia Soto," *Revista de los Archivos Nacionales, San José 3–4* (1943): 135–143.

Ortega, Enríque 1. *Colombian Heraldry.* Bogotá, 1952.

Ortega, Ricardo 2. *Estudios Genealógicos.* México, D.F., 1902.

Ortega, Ricardo 3. *Historia Genealógica de las Familias más Antiguas de México.* 3rd edition. 3 vols. México, D.F., 1908. Vol. 1: Dukes and Marquises; Vol. 2: Marquises and Counts; Vol. 3: Families.

Ortiz, Alonso 1. *Arboles de la Descendencias de las Muy Nobles Casas, y Apellidos de los Rodríguez del Manzano, Pastenes, y Ovalles.* Santiago, 1922.

Ortiz, Sergio Elías 2. "El Pleito de la Nobleza," *Boletín de Estudios Históricos 5* (1932): 213–220.

Ortiz, Sergio Elías 3. "Notas Sobre las Familias Quiñones y Cienfuegos," *Nariño Turístico 1* (1963): 12–13.

Ospina, Joaquín. *Diccionario Biográfico y Bibliográfico de Colombia Desde la Conquista Hasta Nuestros Días.* 3 vols. Bogotá, 1927–1939.

Ossnadón, Carlos. *Junto a mi Padre.* n.p., 1951.

Otárola, Alfredo J. 1. *Antecedentes Históricos y Genealógicos: El Conquistador Don Domingo Martínez de Irala; su Numerosa y Distinguida Descendencia.* Buenos Aires, 1967.

Otárola, Alfredo J. 2. *Cunas de Ilustres Linajes.* Buenos Aires, 1970. Descendancy of Domingo Martínez de Irala y Otras de la Epoca de la Conquista.

Otárola, Alfredo J. 3. *Datos y Linajes: Nuevos Estudios Históricos Genealógicos Milenarios: Domingo Martínez de Irala; Ruy Díaz de Guzmán; El General Miguel Estanislao Soler.* Buenos Aires, 1970.

Otárola, Alfredo J. 4. *Estudios Genealógicos Sobre Antiguos Apellidos del Río de la Plata y Remotos Orígenes del Patriarcado Argentino.* Buenos Aires, 1969.

Otárola, Alfredo J. 5. *Los Vela Vera de Aragón y Vera, y otros Linajes, Semblanzas y Recuerdos.* n.p., 1968.

Otárola, Alfredo J. 6. *Mar de Plata y Genearquía de sus Fundadores.* Buenos Aires, 1972. Genealogies of Peralta, Ramos, Martínez de Hoz, Luro, Camet, Coelho de Meyrelles, Pueyrredón, El Almirante Brown, Don Julio César Gazcón, and El Maestre de Campo Juan de San Martín.

Ovalle, Alonso. *Arboles de las Descendencias de las Muy Nobles Casas y Apellidos de los Rodríguez del Manzano, Pastenes, y Ovalles.* Roma, 1646.

Ovando, Carlos 1. "La Casa de Ovando de la Puebla de los Angeles," *AMG 4* 2ª Series (1968): 451–514.

Ovando, Carlos 2. *Los Obispos de Chile, 1561–1978.* Santiago, 1979.

Pacheco, Luis E. 1. *Familia de Santander.* 3rd edition. Cucutá, Colombia, 1940.

Pacheco, Luis E. 2. *Orígenes del Pdte. Gómez.* Caracas, 1968.

Páez, Luis E. 1. "Los Fundadores de Pamplona," *Boletín de Historia y Antigüedades 321* (1941): 617–656.

Palacio, Lucas de 1. *De Genealogía y Heráldica.* México, D.F., 1946.

Palacio, Lucas de 2. *La Casa de Palacio.* México, D.F., n.d.

Palacio, Lucas de 3. "La Casa de Palacio, Rama de México," *AMG 1* 1ª Series (1945): 11–60.

Palacios, T. de J. *Familias de la Ceja.* Medellín, 1959.

Palomar, Miguel. *A la Memoria del Señor Don José Palomar.* Guadalajara, 1944.

Palomino, Jorge 1. "Baltasar Termiño de Bañuelos y Diego de Porras Baranda, Genearcas en Nueva Galicia: Datos inéditos Aclaratorios de sus Sendos Orígenes y Ascendientes Inmediatos," *AMG 3* 1ª Series (1965): 205–218.

Palomino, Jorge 2. *Cuatro Memoriales Mendocinos e Información de Francisco Telles, 1541.* Guadalajara, 1986.

Palomino, Jorge 3. "El Coronel Don Santiago González, Insurgente; y el General Don Refugio González, Liberal, su Hijo," *AMG 2–3* 1ª Series (1946): 117–144.

Palomino, Jorge 4. *La Casa y Mayorazgo de Cañedo en Nueva Galicia.* 2 vols. México, D.F., 1947.

Palomino, Jorge 5. *Los Padilla de Avila.* Guadalajara, 1986.

Panesso, Fernando. "Familias de Antioquia," *La Revista Universitaria Pontificia Boliviana 22.* Also published as *Familias de Antioquia: Ocampo, Valencia, y Gallego.* Medellín, n.d.

Pardo, J. Joaquín. "Real Cédula de 7 de mayo de 1776, sobre que se informa del Entronque de los Cuatro Hijos de Don Manuel de Alvarado y Guzmán, Descendiente del Adelantado Don Pedro de Alvarado," *Boletín del Archivo General de Gobierno 2* (1936): 79–121.

Pasqual, Leonardo 1. *Títulos de Villa y Escudos de Armas de Xalapa.* México, D.F., 1969.

Pasqual, Leonardo 2. *Xalapeños Distinguidos.* México, D.F., 1975.

Pazos, J.F. *Genealogía de Don Nicolás Carbajo y Tarazona.* Lima, 1939.

Paz Soldán U., Manuel. "Genealogía Paz Soldán," *IGH 2* 1ª Series (1983): 39–45. Re-edited in *IGH 1* 2ª Series (1989): 110–116.

Peña, Arturo 1. "Linaje de los Olivera de Buenos Aires," *IAC 11* (1955): 181–197.

Peña, Francisco 2. *Antecedentes Biográficos de Don Francisco de la Peña Fernández: su Descendencia en la Argentina y en Chile.* Buenos Aires, 1951.

Peña, Horacio J. 3. "Una Dama Patricia Cordobesa del Siglo XIX, Doña Eugenia Funes de la Peña," *IEI 1* (1980): 161–178.

Peña, Pedro 4. "El Conquistador Don Gabriel de Cepeda y los Niño de Zepeda en Chile," *REH 13* (1965): 49–58.

Peña, Pedro 5. "Los Peña y Lillo," *REH 14* (1966–1967): 79–92.

Peraza, Fermín. Diccionario Biográfico Cubano. 14 vols. n.p., 1951–1968.

Perazzo, Carlos E. "Sobre los Centurión de Santa Fé," *IAC 17* (1977): 211–220.

Pereda, Rufino. *Los Monteros de Espinoza.* Madrid, 1923.

Pereira, Carlos T. 1. "Los Ascendientes Paternos del Doctor Carlos de LaHitte," *IAC 12* (1957): 153–159.

Pereira, Carlos T. 2. "Los Games de las Cuevas: Nuevos Aportes Genealógicos," *IAC 14* (1961): 122–128.

Perera, Ambrosio 1. *Historial Genealógico de Familias Caroreñas.* 2 vols. Carora, 1933.

Perera, Ambrosio 2. "Los Ponte," *Boletín del Centro de Investigaciones Históricas 12–17* (1947).

Pérez, Braulio 1. *Diccionario Biográfico del Ecuador.* Guayaquil, 1928.

Pérez, Carlos 2. *La Ciudad Metropolitana de Nuestra Señora de Monterrey.* Monterrey, 1946.

Pérez, Carlos 3. "Los Condes de Monterrey, *AMG 4* 2ª Series (1968): 335–348.

Pérez, Carlos 4. *Monterrey: Cosas Poco Conocidas Acerca de este Nombre y de su Heráldica.* Monterrey, 1944.

Pérez, Celia S. 5. *Biografías y Genealogías de las Familias Vázquez Feijoo, Pérez y Gomar.* Buenos Aires, 1942.

Pérez, Celia S. 6. *Biografía de Don Joaquín Suárez: su Descendencia en el Uruguay, Brasil y Argentina.* Buenos Aires, 1941.

Pérez, J.M. 7. *Los Primeros Esbozos Biográficos de Céspedes.* n.p., n.d.

Pérez, José María 8. *Diccionario Geográfico, Estadístico, Histórico, Biográfico, de Industria y Comercio de la República Mexicana.* 4 vols. México, D.F., 1874–1875.

Pérez, Luis 9. *Biografías.* Guadalajara, 1952. Genealogical data on José Luis Verdía, Jesús López Portillo, Antonio Alcalde, and Prisciliano Sánchez.

Pérez, Luis 10. *Estudio Biográfico Sobre el Sr. Lic. Don Jesús López-Portillo.* México, D.F., 1908.

Pérez, Merchant 11. Diccionario Biográfico del Ecuador. n.p., n.d.

Pérez, Tomás 12. *Estudio Genealógico.* Caracas, 1980.

Perichón, Máxima. *Máxima Perichón.* Buenos Aires, 1935.

Petriella, Sara. *Diccionario Biográfico Italo-Argentino.* Buenos Aires, 1976.

Picardi, Ernesto. *Estudios Genealógicos sobre Algunas Familias Venezolanas.* Volume 1. Caracas, 1960.

Piccirilli, Ricardo. *Diccionario Histórico Argentino.* 6 vols. Buenos Aires, 1953–1954.

Picó, José María. "El Brigadier General Don Sebastián de Segurola y Oliden," *IAC 11* (1955): 201–206.

Pimentel, Carlos. *Evocaciones Familiares: Rasgos Biográficos.* Caracas, n.d.

Pinal, Salvador. "Forma Socio-Jurídica del Parentesco entre Los Mayas y Los Aztecas," *Comunicaciones al XV Congreso Internacional de las Ciencias Genealógicas y Heráldicas 3* (1983): 311–326.

Pino, Clemente. *Apuntes Genealógicos sobre los Apellidos Pino e Ycaza.* Madrid, 1960.

Pizano, Fernando. *Varones Ilustres del Nuevo Mundo, y Observaciones Políticas de sus Sucesos.* Madrid, 1634.

Platt, Lyman De 1. "A Selective Bibliography of Hispanic-American Family History and Related Sources," *IGH 1* 1ª Series (1982): 7–15.

Platt, Lyman De 2. "Cuban Family History Collection of Francisco Xavier de Santa Cruz y Mallén," *IGH 2* 1ª Series (1983): 3–12.

Platt, Lyman De 3. "Hidalguías," *IGH 1* 1ª Series (1982): 78–79.

Platt, Lyman De 4. "Hispanic American Records and Research," *World Conference on Records 9* (1980): Number 708.

Platt, Lyman De 5. "Hispanic-American Records and Research," *Ethnic Genealogy, A Research Guide.* Westport, Connecticut and London, 1983.

Platt, Lyman De 6. "The Terrero Family of Spain, Venezuela and Nicaragua," *IGH 1* 1ª Series (1982): 16–28.

Platt, Lyman De 7. "The Zela Family History," *IGH 1* 1ª Series (1984): 81–85. See also Anibal Gálvez, *Zela*, for additional information on this family.

Platt, Lyman De 8. *Una Guía Genealógico-Histórica de Latinoamérica.* Ramona, California, 1978. Also published in English under the title of *Genealogical-Historical Guide to Latin America.* Detroit, 1978.

Plazas, Francisco. *Genealogías de la Provincia de Neiva.* Neiva, 1967.

Pomar, Carlos. *Linaje de Pomar.* Santiago, 1971.

Ponce de Léon, Brígido. *Historia y Grandeza del Apellido Pérez.* Madrid, 1948.

Ponsford, Keith 1. *The Alviso Family.* n.p., n.d.

Ponsford, Keith 2. *Bernal Family History, 1776–1953.* n.p., n.d.

Ponsford, Keith 3. *Pacheco Family History, 1776–1950.* n.p., n.d.

Posada, Joaquín de. *Anuario de Familias Cubanas.* Puerta de Tierra, Puerto Rico, 1974.

Prado, Eladio 1. "De Mis Apuntes Genealógicos-Esquivel," *Revista de los Archivos Nacionales, San José 1–2* (1941): 51–67.

Prado, Eladio 2. "De Mis Apuntes Genealógicos: Descendencia Sacerdotal de Don Gil de Alvarado y Benavides," *Revista de los Archivos Nacionales, San José 3–4* (1941): 207–216; *5–6* (1942): 322–330.

Prado, Eladio 3. "De Mis Apuntes Genealógicos: Genealogía de la Familia Carrillo," *Revista de los Archivos Nacionales, San José 7–8* (1943): 425–435; *9–10* (1943): 532–542.

Prado, Eladio 4. "De Mis Apuntes Genealógicos: Soto," *Revista de los Archivos Nacionales, San José 3–4* (1941): 164–174; *5–6* (1942): 304–317.

Prado, Eladio 5. "El Griego Antonio de Acosta Arévalo y su Descendencia," *Dominical, San José 123* (1935): 7, 34; *124* (1936): 8,32.

Prado, Eladio 6. "Genealogía Costarricense: Alvarado y Líneas Conlaterales," *Revista de Costa Rica, San José 1* (1929): 39–40; *3* (1931): 58–64; *4* (1932): 75–84; *5–6* (1933): 103–106.

Prado, Eladio 7. "Genealogía del Doctor Don Alejandro González Luján." Manuscript in the possession of Alejandro González Luján, n.p., n.d.

Prado, Eladio 8. "Los Fundadores Españoles de Costa Rica," *ACC 13–14* (1965–1966): 31–70.

Prado, Eladio 9. "Los Llorente," *Revista de Costa Rica, San José 3* (1923): 33–39; *4* (1932): 49–55.

Prado, Rosita 10. "Ascendientes de Juan Antonio de Ugarteche." Unpublished manuscript.

Prado, Rosita 11. "Ascendientes de María Josefa Ugarteche y Gutiérrez de Otero." Unpublished manuscript.

Puente, José A. "Los Bienes de Francisco Castrillón y Arango," *IPI 10* (1957): 7–18.

Puertos, Castro N. "Genealogía de José Domingo Choquehuanca," *IPI 10* (1957): 26–29.

Pueyrredon, Carlos A. "Don Fernando de Toledo Pimentel, Descendiente de los Primeros Duques de Alba," *IAC 11* (1955): 145–153.

Pyzik, Estanislas P. *Los Polacos en la República Argentina y América del Sur desde el Año 1812*. Buenos Aires, 1966.

Quintana, Andrés 1. *Las Casas de Horcasitas y de Quintana: Originales del Valle de Arcentales*. México, D.F., 1960.

Quintana, José M. 2. "La Familia Quintana y Algunas de sus Alianzas," *AMG 4* 2ª Series (1968): 553–610.

Quirós, Ernesto 1. "Apuntes Genealógicos: Rama de los Fernández," *Academia de Geografía e Historia de Costa Rica, San José 6* (1950): 28–30.

Quirós, Ernesto 2. "Ascendencia del Benemérito de la Patria, Don Juan Rafael Mora Porras y de su Esposa, Doña Inés Aguilar Cueto de Mora," *ACC 3* (1956): 4–16.

Quirós, Ernesto 3. "Ascendencia el Excelentísimo Monseñor y Doctor Don Carlos Humberto Rodríguez y Quirós, Cuarto Arzobispo de San José de Costa Rica," *ACC 8* (1960). Also published separately in San José, 1960.

Quirós, Ernesto 4. "Ascendencia del Profesor Don José Joaquín Trejos Fernández," *ACC 13–14* (1965–1966): 19–30.

Quirós, Ernesto 5. "Ascendencia del Sr. Presidente de la República, Lic. Don Mario Erhandi Jiménez," *ACC 6* (1958): 418.

Quirós, Ernesto 6. "Ascendencia y Descendencia de El Teniente Don Florencio Quirós Blanco," *ACC 4* (1957): 63.

Quirós, Ernesto 7. "El Capitán Don Antonio ValleRiestra y sus Descendientes," *ACC 3* (1956): 17–18.

Quirós, Ernesto 8. "Genealogía, Descendencia del Licenciado Don Juan José Guzmán," *Revista de los Archivos Nacionales, San José 1–2* (1943): 91–99.

Quirós, Ernesto 9. "La Familia Sagrera," *Revista de los Archivos Nacionales, San José 1–3* (1952): 73–75.

Quirós, Ernesto 10. *Los Quirós en Costa Rica.* San José, 1948.

Quirós, Ernesto 11. *Mi Ascendencia Real Indígena.* San José, 1947. Descendancy of the *caciques* Guarco and Quepo.

Quirós, Floris 12. "Familia Fonseca: La Descendencia de Don Gabriel Fonseca," *ACC 27–28* (1981): 141–150.

Quirozz, Alberto. *Biografías de Educadores Mexicanos.* 1º Part, México, D.F., 1970.

Ramírez, Alfonso 1. *Four Generations of Velas.* Edinburg, Texas, 1986.

Ramírez, Enríque 2. *Orígenes Puertorriqueños, 1553–1853.* San Juan, 1942.

Ramírez, Guillermo 3. *La Familia de Sor Juana Inés de la Cruz.* México, D.F., 1947.

Ramírez, R.P.F. 4. *Memorial de la Santa Vida y Glorioso Tránsito de el Buen Beneficiado Pedro Plancarte.* México, D.F., 1950.

Ramón, J. Armando 1. *La Sociedad Española de Santiago de Chile Entre 1581 y 1596.* n.p., 1965.

Ramón, J. Armando 2. "Linaje del Conquistador Francisco Hernández de Herrera, 1575–1850," *REH 6–7* (1956–1957): 85–134.

Ramón, J. Armando 3. "Vásquez de Ganoza," *REH 8–9* (1960).

Ravelo, Temistocles. *Diccionario Biográfico Dominicano.* 2 vols. Unpublished manuscript in the AGN, Santo Domingo.

Recalde, Sergio. *Crónica de Una Estirpe Prócer.* Asunción, 1976.

Restrepo, José M. 1. *Genealogía Episcopal de la Jerarquía Eclesiástica en los Países que Formaron la Gran Colombia, 1513–1966.* Bogotá, 1968.

Restrepo, José M. 2. *Documentos Relativos al Doctor Don Miguel de Rivas, 1729–1804, Tronco de la Familia en Santa Fé de Bogotá.* Bogotá, 1930.

Restrepo, José M. 3. *Documentos Relativos al Maestre de Campo Don Juan de Rivas, 1677–1755, Fundador de la Familia en el Nuevo Reinos de Granada.* Bogotá, 1930.

Restrepo, José M. 4. *Familia Rivas: Datos tomados de las Genealogías de Santa Fé de Bogotá.* Bogotá, 1930.

Revollo, Julio E. 1. "Descendencia del General Don Juan Bautista Quirós Segura," *ACC 10* (1962): 11–15.

Revollo, Julio E. 2. "La Descendencia del Adelantado de Costa Rica, Don Juan Vázquez de Coronado," *ACC 9* (1961): 13–28.

Revollo, Julio E. 3. "La Ilustre Descendencia de Don Antonio de Acosta Arévalo," *ACC 8* (1960): 17–32.

Reyes, Rafael 1. "Antepasados de Don Francisco Bilbao en Chile," *REH 13* (1965): 21–34.

Reyes, Rafael 2. "El General Juan LaValle y su Familia," *REH 17* (1972): 1–16.

Reyes, Rafael 3. "La Familia del Primer Arzobispo de Guatemala," *RAG 3–4* (1968–1969): 22–35.

Reyes, Rafael 4. "La Familia Reyes de Santiago," *REH 13* (1965): 96.

Reyes, Rafael 5. "Una Antigua Familia Norteamericana en Chile: Foster," *REH 15* (1968–1969): 22–35.

Rezende, A. "Genealogía Minera," *AMG.*

Richieri, Arturo 1. "El Doctor Agustín Eusebio Fabré y su Descendencia," *IAC 19* (1981): 94–113.

Richieri, Arturo 2. "Los Cásares en el Río de la Plata," *IAC 18* (1979): 239–290.

Richieri, Arturo 3. "Los Castex," *IAC 16* (1976): 179–205.

Richieri, Arturo 4. "Los Leloir," *IAC 17* (1977): 235–251.

Río, Abraham del 1. *Libro Verde de la Familia del Río.* n.p., 1919.

Río, Abraham del 2. *Los del Río.* n.p., 1919.

Riolo, Sr. *Don Francisco Girado y Doña Francisca Cortés: Descendencia y Alianzas.* Buenos Aires, 1941.

Ripamonti, Raul. "La Rama Chilena de los Soruco del Alto Perú," *REH 12* (1964).

Rittscher, Enríque. *Rittscher Family in Guatemala.* Guatemala City, 1976.

Riva, José de la 1. *El Primer Alcalde de Lima, Nicolás de Ribera, el Viejo, y su Posteridad.* Lima, 1935.

Riva, José de la 2. *Estudios de Genealogía Peruana.* Lima, 1983.

Rivas, Raimundo. *Los Fundadores de Bogotá: Diccionario Biográfico.* Bogotá, 1923.

Rivera, Antonio 1. *Francisco Xavier Mina y Pedro Moreno.* México, D.F., 1917.

Rivera, Josefina 2. *Diccionario de Literatura Puertorriqueña.* n.p., 1967.

Roa, Luis de 1. "Los Aguilera," *IAC 1* (1942): 135–139.

Roa, Luis de 2. "Casa Riquelme de la Barrera," *RCH 58* (1927): 389–404.

Robertson, Thomas A. *A Southwestern Utopia.* Los Angeles, 1964.

Robles, Pedro 1. "Apuntes para un Estudio Genealógico de la Familia Maldonado y sus Enlazados," *IPI 9* (1956): 25, 34.

Robles, Pedro 2. *Breves Apuntes Sobre los Deudos de Santa Teresa en Guayaquil.* Guayaquil, 1970.

Robles, Pedro 3. "Carta Genealógica de Don Miguel de Unamuno a una Dama de Este Linaje en Guayaquil," *Estudios Genealógicos, Heráldicos, y Nobiliarios 2* (1978): 239–246.

Robles, Pedro 4. "Conquistador Don Rodrigo de Vargas Guzmán," *Boletín del Centro de Investigaciones Históricas de Guayaquil 5* (1940).

Robles, Pedro 5. "Contribución para el Estudio de la Sociedad de la Antigua Gobernación de Guayaquil," *Boletín del Centro de Investigaciones Históricas de Guayaquil 5* (1940). Also printed under the same title at Guayaquil, 1938.

Robles, Pedro 6. "Don Fernando Bustillos Varas y Gutiérrez, Abogado que fue de las Reales Audiencias de Nueva España y Regidor Perpétuo de la Ciudad de Guadalajara, en la Provincia de la Nueva Galicia," *AMG 2–3* 1ª Series (1946): 153–165.

Robles, Pedro 7. "Don Gabino Gainza y Medrano: Datos Genealógicos," *Contribución para el Estudio de la Sociedad Colonial de Guayaquil 1–2* (1941): 109.

Robles, Pedro 8. *Estudio Histórico-Genealógico de la Familia Alvarez de Avilés.* Guayaquil, 1959.

Robles, Pedro 9. "Familias Coloniales: Los Ramírez de Arellano," *Boletín del Centro de Investigaciones Históricas de Guayaquil 5* (1940).

Robles, Pedro 10. "Familias de Guayaquil," *Estudios a la Convención del Instituto Internacional de Genealogía y Heráldica con Motivo de su XXV Aniversario* (1979): 421–437.

Robles, Pedro 11. *Francisco Xavier de Garaycoa y Llaguno, Primer Obispo de Guayaquil en el Centenario de su Fallecimiento, 1859–1959.* Guayaquil, 1959.

Robles, Pedro 12. "Genealogía de la Noble Case de López de la Flor I: Los López de la Flor, en Guayaquil," *Revista de los Archivos Nacionales, San José 11–12* (1945): 605–608.

Robles, Pedro 13. *Hidalguías Guayaquileñas.* Quito, 1958.

Robles, Pedro 14. *Isabelita Morales y sus Linajes.* Guayaquil, 1960. Contains the surnames Morales, Febres-Cordero, Tinoco, Agreda, Pagola, Besse de Morián.

Robles, Pedro 15. "La Casa de Vela," *Boletín del Centro de Investigaciones Históricas 12–17* (1947).

Robles, Pedro 16. *Los Antepasados de Rocafuerte.* Guayaquil, 1947.

Robles, Pedro 17. "La Familia de Rocafuerte," *Boletín del Centro de Investigaciones Históricas 4* (1936): 64–79.

Robles, Pedro 18. *Los Ascendientes del Doctor Don Rafael García Goyena y Vera-Gaztelu.* Guatemala, 1969.

Robles, Pedro 19. "Los Coello de Portugal," *Boletín del Centro de Investigaciones Históricas 6* (1941): 125–133.

Robles, Pedro 20. *Los Lavoyen.* Guayas, 1960.

Robles, Pedro 21. "Los Pérez de Vargas," *IAC 6–7* (1946–1947): 314–320.

Robles, Pedro 22. "Los Plazaert," *IPI 1* (1946): 35, 40.

Robles, Pedro 23. "Notas Genealógicas para el Estudio de la Sociedad Colonial de la Provincia de Manabí," *Boletín del Centro de Investigaciones Históricas 6* (1941): 107–114.

Robles, Pedro 24. *Un Linaje Vasco de Origen al Nombre del Actual Cantón de Vinces.* Guayaquil, 1954.

Rodríguez, Angel 1. *Catálogo de Documentos y Referencias a Filiaciones, Nobleza e Hidalguía, y Limpieza de Sangre que se Conservan en el Archivo Municipal de Santiago de Compostela.* Madrid, 1962. Consistory Book.

Rodríguez, Blas E. 2. *Una Fiesta de Moctezumas.* México, D.F., 1943.

Rodríguez, Carlos 3. *Hacienda de Tena.* Bogotá, 1943.

Rodríguez, Carlos 4. *Vida de Don Francisco Maldonado de Mendoza.* Bogotá, 1946.

Rodríguez, Emilio 5. "Familias Hispanoamericanas," *Boletín del Archivo General de la Nación 95* (1958): 6–133; *97–98* (1958): 269–374; *99–100* (1959): 9–85; *101–102* (1959): 139–178.

Rodríguez, Emilio 6. *Familias Hispanoamericanas.* Ciudad Trujillo, R.D., 1959.

Rodríguez, Emilio 7. *Hojas de Servicio del Ejército Dominicano, 1844–1865.* Santo Domingo, 1976.

Rodríguez, Emilio 8. *Próceres de la Restauración: Noticias Biográficas.* Santo Domingo, 1976.

Rodríguez, Esther M. 9. "Catálogo Heráldico," *IAC 17* (1977): 277–300.

Rodríguez, Felipe 10. *Estudio Genealógico de las Familias Matuz y Rodríguez.* Managua, 1963.

Rodríguez, Gerardo 11. *Los Zambrana.* La Habana, 1947.

Rodríguez, Horacio 12. *Antonia Santos Plata: Genealogía y Biografía.* Bogotá, 1969.

Rodríguez, Manuel 13. *Certificación Relacionada de la Filiación, Nobleza, y Genealogía del Coronel Don Clemente Díaz de Medina y la Soto.* La Paz, 1791.

Rodríguez, Pedro 14. "Sobre Parentescos de los Oidores con los Grupos Superiores de la Sociedad Limena," *IPI 14* (1965): 17–24.

Rodríguez, Salvador 15. *Monografía de la Villa de Pampacolca.* Arequipa, 1971. Genealogical trees of some families of Pampacolca are found on pages 247–307.

Roel, Santiago. *Nuevo León: Apuntes Históricos*. Monterrey, 1952.

Rojas, Ernesto 1. "Genealogía de Don Gastón de Peralta, III Marqués de Falces, Virrey de la Nueva España," *AMG 3* 1ª Series (1965): 77–83.

Rojas, María Irene 2. "Ascendencia del Conquistador Español Alonso Riquelme de Guzmán, Ponce de León Vera, al Rey Alfonso IX de León . . . :Parte de su Descendencia en Buenos Aires," *IAC 17* (1977): 253–276.

Rojas, Uliseo 3. *Escudos de Armas e Inscripciones Antiguas de la Ciudad de Tunja*. Tunja, 1939.

Román, José R. 1. "El Primer Genealogista de Nuestro Gran Capitán," *IAC 9–10* (1950–1951): 168–171.

Román, José R. 2. "La Descendencia de Don Jerónimo Luis de Cabrera," *IAC 4–5* (1945): 185–190.

Román, José R. 3. "Nobiliario del Antiguo Virreinato del Río de la Plata," *IAC 1* (1942): 57–65.

Romero, Carlos 1. "Disquisiciones Acerca del Escudo y de la Genealogía del Fundador de Salta," *IAC 8* (1948–1949): 155–162.

Romero, Manuel 2. *El Conde de Regla, Creso de la Nueva España*. México, D.F., 1943.

Romero, Manuel 3. *Hernán Cortés, sus Hijos y Nietos, Caballeros de las Ordenes Militares*. 2nd edition, revised. México, 1944.

Romero, Manuel 4. *Los Condes de Reglas: Apuntes Biográficos*. México, 1909.

Romeo, Max. *Los Arizaga en la Cultura Ecuatoriana*. Guayaquil, 1986.

Romo, Guillermo 1. "Descendencia de Hidalgo," *AMG 8* 1ª Series (1953): 73–86.

Romo, Guillermo 2. "Una Visita a Cedros, Solar de los Villaseñor," *AMG 1* 1ª Series (1945): 61–86.

Rosa, Esther M. *Biografías Puertorriqueñas: Perfil Histórico de un Pueblo*. Sharon, 1970.

Rosado, Manuel. *Origen Histórico de la Familia Rovirosa de Tabasco*. n.p., 1976.

Rosas, Alberto 1. "Información de la Filiación y Nobleza del Gobernador Don Nicolás Dávalos y Rivera," *IPI 16* (1975): 105–110.

Rosas, Alberto 2. "Los Ugarte," *IPI 8* (1955): 225–236.

Rosell, Alejandro. "La Primitiva Casa de los Rosell en la Ciudad de Arequipa," *IPI 4* (1949): 5, 9.

Roselli, Bruno. *The Italians in Colonial Florida, 1513–1821.* Miami, 1940.

Rouaix, Pastor. *Diccionario Geográfico, Histórico, y Biográfico del Estado de Durango.* México, D.F., 1946.

Rousseau, Pablo. *Memoria Descriptiva, Histórica y Biográfica de Cienfuegos.* n.p., n.d.

Rowland, Leon. *Los Fundadores de California . . . 1769–1785.* Fresno, 1951.

Rubicam, Milton. *The Spanish Ancestry of American Colonists.* Washington, D.C., 1963.

Rubio, Ignacio 1. "Don Carlos de Arellano, Yerno de Montejo el Mozo, Diario de Yucatán," *AMG 5* 1ª Series (1949): 202.

Rubio, Ignacio 2. "El Conquistador Andrés de Tapia y su Familia," *Boletín del AGN 2* 2ª Series (1964): 185–241.

Rubio, Ignacio 3. *Gente de España en la Ciudad de México, Año de 1689.* n.p., n.d.

Rubio, Ignacio 4. *La Casa de Montejo.* México, D.F., 1949.

Rubio, Ignacio 5. "Los Allende de San Miguel el Grande," *Boletín del AGN 4* 2ª Series (1961): 517–556.

Rubio, Ignacio 6. "Los Primeros Vecinos de la Ciudad de Mérida, Yucatán," *AMH 3* (1944).

Rubio, Ignacio 7. "Los Unzagas de San Miguel el Grande," *Boletín del AGN 4* 2ª Series (1961): 557–568.

Rubio, Ignacio 8. "Noticias de una Hermana del Inca Garcilaso de la Vega y de su Descendencia en Yucatán," *Boletín del AGN 4* 1ª Series (1944): 623–648.

Rubio, Luis 9. *Inventarios del Archivo General de Indias: Audiencia de Santa Fé.* Madrid, 1924.

Rubira, Guillermo. "Los Santos de Charapotó," *CAG 15* (1985): 143–260.

Ruiz, Alfonso 1. "Los Ursúa," *RAG 3–4* (1969–1970): 475–548.

Ruiz, Carlos 2. *Reseña Biográfica de los Sacerdotes que Formaron Parte en las Asambleas de los Años 1810–1813 y en el Congreso de Tucumán*. Buenos Aires, 1916.

Rújula, José 1. *Francisco de Montejo y los Adelantados del Yucatán: Genealogía de los Condes y Duques de Montellano*. n.p., 1932.

Rújula, José 2. "El Escudo de Armas de Francisco Pizarro, Conquistador del Peru," *Revista de Historia y de Genealogía Española 4* (1913): 136–143.

Rújula, José 3. "Los Alvarado en el Nuevo Mundo," *ACH 105:* (1934–1935): 257–294; *106*: 485–529; *107*: 133–170, 515–546; *108:* 183–226, 562–604; *109*: 263–356.

Rújula, José 4. *Los García de Huidobro de Chile, Marqueses de la Casa Real*. Madrid, 1922.

Ruz, Rodolfo. "La Familia Ruz Rivas de Yucatán: Don José María, Con Ildefonso y Fray Joaquín," *Boletín del AGN 3–4* 2ª Series (1969): 589–599.

Saavedra, Sr. *Biografía Escrita por Encargo de la Comisión Nacional de Homenaje al Prócer*. Buenos Aires, 1929.

Sada, Pablo. *Apuntes Genealógicos Acerca de los Sada*. Monterrey, 1945.

Sadous, Eduardo A. "El Doctor Teodoro Aubain y su Descendencia," *IAC 19* (1981): 114–121.

Sáenz, Jorge Francisco. "Don Juan Francisco Sáenz-Vázquez de Quintanilla, Gobernador y Capitán General de la Provincia de Costa Rica," *ACC 26* (1980): 17–105.

Salas, Manuel. *Biografía Genealógico del General José Gabriel Alvarez de Lugo y Freites*. Caracas, 1921.

Saguier, Alberto G. 1. "Apuntes para una Crónica Genealógica e Histórica del Linaje del Coronel Julio Fonrouge de Lessaps y sus Alianzas," *IAC 17* (1977): 301–318.

Saguier, Alberto G. 2. "Genealogía de los Pereda," *IAC 18* (1979): 321–346.

Saguier, Alberto G. 3. "Genealogía de los Segui," *IAC 18* (1979): 291–320.

Saguier, Alberto G. 4. "Los Testamentos Porteños de los Siglos XVII y XVIII," *IAC 17* (1977): 319–382.

Salazar, Caridad 1. "Genealogía de la Familia de Salazar de León y de Fernández y Ferraz," *Revista de los Archivos Nacionales, San José 5–6* (1946): 291–296.

Salazar, Luis de 2. *Historia Genealógica de la Casa de Lara, 1696.* n.p., 1696.

Salazar, Luis de 3. *Indice de las Glorias de la Casa Farnese, 1716.* n.p., n.d.

Salvador, Felipe de. *Biografía Genealógica del Excmo. Sr. Don Antonio Maura y Montaner.* Barcelona, 1953.

Sanabria, Hernando 1. "La Descendencia del Adelantado Juan de Sanabria en el Alto Perú," *RGL 13* (1961): 261–267.

Sanabria, Víctor 2. *Genealogías de Cartago hasta 1850.* San José, 1957.

Sánchez, Carlos 1. *Memorias de un Viejo Palacio.* México, D.F., 1950.

Sánchez, Cornelio 2. "Ascendencia Catamarqueña del Presidente Avellaneda," *IAC 2* (1943): 105–117.

Sánchez, Federico 3. "Dos Informaciones Genealógicas Impugnadas por el Santo Oficio," *REH 8–9* (1960).

Sánchez, Federico 4. "Los Fontecilla de la Tixera," *REH 4–5* (1954–1955): 34–85.

Sánchez, Federico 5. "Los García de la Huerta," *REH 3* (1952–1953).

Sánchez, Federico 6. *Los García de la Huerta.* San Francisco, 1954.

Sánchez, Federico 7. "Los Marqueses de Villa Rocha," *REH 2* (1950–1951): 46–76.

Sánchez, Federico 8. "Los Muxica," *REH 8–9* (1958–1959).

Sánchez, José R. 9. *Autores Españoles e Hispano-Americanos.* Madrid, 1911.

Sánchez, Juan 10. *Genealogía de las Familias Sánchez de Bustamante, Quintana, Tezanos Pinto, y Alvarado.* Jujuy, 1888.

Sánchez, Teófilo 11. *Biografías Históricas de Jujuy.* Tucumán, 1958.

Sangroniz, José A. *Familias Coloniales de Venezuela.* Caracas, 1943.

Santana, José E. *Nuño Beltrán de Guzmán y su Obra en la Nueva España.* México, D.F., 1946.

Santa Cruz, Francisco 1. "Cinco Señoríos de Vasallos," *IAC 6–7* (1946–1947): 321–325.

Santa Cruz, Francisco 2. *Historia de Familias Cubanas.* 7 vols. La Habana, 1940–1944. The 7th volume was ready to print at the time of the author's death but was not actually published until 1985. His son revised his father's notes and published volumes 8 and 9 before his own death in 1989. Vol. 7, Barcelona, 1985; Vol. 8, Barcelona, 1986; and Vol. 9, Barcelona, 1988.

Santa Cruz, Francisco 3. "La Ilustre Familia de Armenteros," *Diario de la Marina*, 1947.

Santaella, Eliseo. *Biografías de Hombres Ilustres.* México, D.F., 1930.

Santander, Alberto. *Isleños-Briones.* La Nación, 1942.

Santoscoy, Alberto. *Los Cañedos.* Guadalajara, 1902. Sanz, Francisco *Memorial de la Casa y Servicios de Don Alvaro Francisco de Ulloa, Caballero de la Orden de Alcántara, Señor del Castillejo.* Badajoz, 1982. Facsimile edition edited in Madrid in 1675.

Sarandeses, Francisco. *Heráldica de los Apellidos Asturianos.* Oviedo, 1966.

Sarmiento, Domingo F. *Recuerdos de Provincia.* Santiago, 1850.

Scarpetta, Sr. *Diccionario Biográfico.* Bogotá, 1879.

Schulkin, Augusto I. "La Posteridad Genealógica del Dr. Santiago Vázquez," *IEG 2* (1981): 31–34.

Schwarzenberg, Ingeborg. "Origen de Algunas Familias Alemanes Radicadas en Chile," *REH 14* (1966–1967): 31–78; *15* (1969): 94–102; *16* (1971); *17* (1973): 81–92; *18* (1974): 141–153.

Scott, Florence J. *Historical Heritage of the Lower Río Grande.* Río Grande City, 1972.

Scotto, José Arturo 1. *Notas Biográficas Publicadas en la Sección Efemérides Americanas de "La Nación" en los Años 1907–1909.* 4 vols. Buenos Aires, 1910.

Scotto, José Arturo 2. *Origen y Antigüedad de las Familias Argentinas.* Volume 1º. Buenos Aires, 1909.

Sebreli, Juan José. *Apogeo y Ocaso de los Anchorena.* Buenos Aires, 1972.

Segovia, Mariano. "Lavelli: Condes de Premio Real y de San Antonio de Vista Alegre," *IAC 3* (1944): 144–168.

Selva, Juan B. "Los Amunátegui," *Boletín de la Academia Argentina de Letras 14* (1936): 249–260.

Serrano, Carlos A. 1. "Familia Serrano Bonilla: La Descendencia de Don Manuel Antonio Serrano Consuegra," *ACC 27–28* (1981): 311–322.

Serrano, Jorge A. 2. "Genealogía de los Moreno Gordillo," *IAC 1* (1942): 42–67.

Serrano, Jorge A. 3. "Introducción al Estudio de la Casa de Villafañe y Guzmán (Siglos XVII y XVIII)," *IAC 2* (1943): 42–69.

Serrano, Jorge A. 4. "Posible Ascendencia del General Pedro Hurtado de Mendoza," *? 172–173* (1982): 529–549.

Serrano, Jorge A. 5. "Una Benefica Fundación y una Antigua Genealogía," *Estudios Genealógicos, Heráldicos, y Nobiliarios 2* (1978); 267–314.

Serrano, Jorge A. 6. "Un Olvidado Nieto del Fundador de Tucumán," *Centro de Estudios Genealógicos de Córdoba 10* (1976).

Sevilla, Felipe. *Breve Estudio de la Conquista y Fundación de Colima.* México, D.F., 1973.

Shoemaker, Cathleen. "Descendants of Juan José Cisneros and María Antonia Villarreal," *Los Tejanos, Journal of Hispanic Genealogy and History 1* (1990): 7–10.

Silva, M. Jaime 1. *Casa de Silva en Chile.* Santiago, 1981.

Silva, Luis 2. *El Conquistador Francisco de Aguirre.* Santiago, 1953.

Silva, Ismael 3. *Hombres y Mujeres del Siglo XVI Venezolano.* 4 vols. Caracas, n.d.

Silva, Julio C. 4. "La Familia Antuña en el Uruguay," *IEG 4* (1982): 5–14.

Silva, Raul 5. *Los Irrarázaval de Chile.* Buenos Aires, 1957.

Soaje, E. 1. "Apuntes Sobre los Puig: Sus Antepasados en España," *IAC 3* (1944): 106–107.

Soaje, E. 2. "Los Sarachaga," *IAC 1* (1942): 83–92.

Soaje, Manuel A. 3. "Linaje de los Ortiz de Rozas," *IAC 18* (1979): 347–386.

Soaje, Manuel A. 4. "San Luis Rey de Francia, Patronato de San Luis," *IEI 1* (1980): 195–212.

Sobarzo, Horacio. *Crónicas Biográficas.* Sonora, 1949.

Soberanes, Irene 1. *The Bernal Family in California, 1776–1957.* n.p., 1957.

Soberanes, Irene 2. *History of the Castro Family in California, 1776–1956.* n.p., 1956.

Soberanes, Irene 3. *History of the Galindo Family in California, 1775–1956.* n.p., 1956.

Soberanes, Irene 4. *History of the José Manuel Higuera Family, 1774–1957.* n.p., 1957.

Soberanes, Irene 5. *History of the Pacheco Family in California, 1776–1959.* n.p., 1959.

Soberanes, Irene 6. *Soberanes Family History, 1769–1957.* n.p., 1957.

Sociedad de Bibliofilos Españoles. *Nobiliario de Conquistadores de Indias.* Madrid, 1892.

Solá, Miguel. *Diccionario Histórico-Biográfico de Salta.* Salta, 1964.

Solano County Historical Society. *Peña and Vaca Families.* n.p., n.d.

Solar y T., Antonio. *El Adelantado de Soto: Breves Noticias, Nuevos Documentos para su Biografía y Relación de los que le Acompañaron a la Florida.* Badajoz, 1929.

Sosa, Carlos E. 1. "La Descendencia de Don José Daract," *IAC 16* (1976): 207–210.

Sosa, Lily 2. *Diccionario Biográfico de Mujeres Argentinas.* Buenos Aires, 1972.

Sotela, Rogelio. *Escritores y Poetas de Costa Rica.* San José, 1923.

Sotomayor, Justiniano. *Los Zevallo.* n.p., 1898.

Stagg, Albert. *The Almadas and Alamos, 1783–1867.* Tucson, 1978.

Staudt, Richard W. 1. *Consangineos Argentinos de Bernardo, Príncipe de los Países Bajos.* Buenos Aires, 1951.

Staudt, Richard W. 2. "Los Parravicini," *IAC 8* (1948–1949): 81–101.

Suárez, Celia 1. "La Familia Suárez," *RGL 3* (1951): 157–162.

Suárez, Celia 2. "Linaje de Don Manuel Ximénez de Sandoval y Gómez González," *IAC 9–10* (1950–1951): 311–319.

Suárez, Fernando 3. *Nobiliario Cubano* . . . . 2 vols. n.p., 1921.

Suárez, J. Bernardo 4. *Biografías de Hombres Notables.* Valparaiso, n.d.

Suárez, Ramón Dario 5. *Historial Genealógico del Doctor Cristóbal Mendoza, 1772–1829.* Caracas, 1972.

Suárez, Ramón Dario 6. *Historial Genealógico de los Febres-Cordero y Algunas de sus Alianzas.* Mérida, 1969.

Sucre, Luis Alberto 1. *Gobernadores y Capitanes Generales de Venezuela.* Caracas, 1964.

Sucre, Luis Alberto 2. *Historial Genealógico del Libertador.* Caracas, 1930.

Sucre, Luis Alberto 3. "Nuestras Grandes Familias Coloniales: Jerez de Aristiguieta," *Boletín de la Academia Nacional de la Historia 94* (1941): 249–255.

Swadesh, Frances Leon. *Los Primeros Pobladores: Hispanic Americans on the Ute Frontier.* Notre Dame, 1974.

Swayne, Guillermo. *Mis Antepasados: Genealogía de las Familias Swayne, Mariátegui, Mendoza y Barreda.* Lima, 1951.

Talleri, Guillermo. "Ascendencia del Libertador Simón Bolivar," *IPI 7* (1954): 5–22.

Taracena, Arturo. "Biografías Sintéleas de Guatemaltecos Distinguidos," *RAG 1* (1967): 69–74; *3–4* (1969–1970): 374–389; *5–6* (1971–1972): 451–462.

Tauro, Alberto. *Diccionario Enciclopédico del Perú.* 3 vols. Buenos Aires, 1966–1967.

Tejerina, Ignacio G. 1. *Apuntes Sobre Antiguos Linajes del Río Seco.* Córdoba, 1972.

Tejerina, Ignacio G. 2. "El Linaje Agüero y sus Ramas del Valle de Tulumba," *EGC 15* (1982): 47–59.

Tejerina, Ignacio G. 3. *Los Carreras.* Córdoba, 1983.

Tejerina, Ignacio G. 4. "Los Linajes Allende en Córdoba," *EGC 6*, 13–23.

Teletor, Celso Narciso. *Síntesis Biográfico del Clero de Guatemala.* Guatemala, 1966.

Temple, Ella Dunbar 1. "La Descendencia de Huayna Capac," *Revista Histórica 1* (1937): 284–323; *2* (1938): 204–245; *3* (1940): 31–77.

Temple, Thomas W. 2. "Soldiers and Settlers of the Expedition of 1781: Genealogical Record," *Historical Society of Southern California 15* (1931): 99–116.

Texas General Land Office *An Abstract of the Original Titles of Record in the General Land Office of Texas.* Austin, 1964.

Terry, Pedro 1. "Don Gómez de Tordoya, Conquistador del Perú," *IPI 11* (1958): 17–26.

Terry, Pedro 2. "El Conquistador Juan de Berrio," *IPI 1* (1946): 5–15.

Terry, Pedro 3. "La Familia Cabrera del Cuzco," *IPI 7* (1954): 23–30.

Thayer, Luis 1. *Apuntes Genealógicos Relativos a Familias Chilenas.* Santiago, 1911.

Thayer, Luis 2. *Catálogo Biográfico de la Casa de Thayer de Braintree.* n.p., 1904.

Thayer, Luis 3. *Familia Garretón: Apuntes para una Monografía Biográfico-Genealógica.* Valparaiso, 1933.

Thayer, Luis 4. *Familia Ojeda de Valparaiso.* Valparaiso, 1933.

Thayer, Luis 5. *Familias de Valparaiso.* n.p., n.d.

Thayer, Luis 6. *Familias Chilenas.* Santiago, 1905.

Thayer, Luis 7. *Genealogy of the Descendants of William Turpin Thayer of Bellingham.* Valparaiso, 1933.

Thayer, Luis 8. *Memoria Genealógica de la Familia Ojeda de Valparaiso.* Valparaiso, 1933.

Thayer, Luis 9. *Navarros y Vascongados en Chile.* Santiago, 1904.

Thayer, Luis 10. *Notas Genealógicas para la Historia Social de Valparaiso.* Valparaiso, 1934.

Thayer, Tomás 11. "Biografías de Conquistadores," *RCH 52* (1923): 201–209. Contains biographies of Fuensalida, Gómez Hidalgo, Griego, Herrera, Sotomayor, Jiménez de Bertandona, Miranda, Ocampo de San Miguel, Quiroga, and Ruiz de Gamboa.

Thayer, Tomás 12. "Biografías de Conquistadores: Andrés Escoba y Minaya," *RCH 46* (1922): 478–485.

Thayer, Tomás 13. "Diego Ruiz de Olivar," *RCH 49* (1923): 474–488.

Thayer, Tomás 14. "El Capitán Juan Bautista Pastene," *RCH 15* (1914): 372–419.

Thayer, Tomás 15. "Familia Oyarzún," *ACH 42* (1950): 61–64.

Thayer, Tomás 16. *Formación de la Sociedad Chilena.* 3 vols. Santiago, 1939–1943.

Thayer, Tomás 17. "Francisco de Aguirre," *RCH 64.*

Thayer, Tomás 18. "La Familia del Conquistador Juan de Cuevas," *ACH 15* (1940): 157–178.

Thayer, Tomás 19. *La Familia Irarázaval en Chile.* Santiago, 1931.

Thayer, Tomás 20. *La Familia Thayer.* Santiago, 1967.

Thayer, Tomás 21. *Las Biografías de los Cristobales de Molina.* Santiago, 1920.

Thayer, Tomás 22. *Los Conquistadores de Chile.* 3 vols. Santiago, 1908–1913.

Thayer, Tomás 23. "Los de Vicuña," *RCH 20* (1915): 72–113. A genealogical study of the families in Legazpia, Navarra, and Vera, Spain.

Extinguished lineages in Chile are identified; the descendancy of Tomás de Vicuña y Berroeta; Tomás Vicuña y Madariaga; and Rafael de Vicuña y Larraín.

Thayer, Tomás 24. *Memoria Histórica sobre la Familia Alvarez de Toledo en Chile*. Santiago, 1903.

Thayer, Tomás 25. "Reseña Histórico-Biográfica de los Eclesiásticos en el Descubrimiento y Conquista de Chile," *RCH 35* (1921).

Thayer, Tomás 26. "Santiago Durante el Siglo XVI: Constitución de la Propiedad Urbana y Noticias Biográficas de sus Primeros Pobladores," *Anales de la Universidad de Santiago 96* (1905).

Thevenet, Luis A. *De la Estirpe Artiguista*. Montevideo, 1925.

Tibón, Gutiérrez. *Origen, Vida y Milagros de su Apellido*. México, D.F., 1946.

Tisnés, Roberto María. *Apuntes Genealógicos: los Tisnés en Colombia y Argentina*. Medellín, 1971.

Tobar, Julio. *Los Miembros de Número de la Academia Ecuatoriana, 1875–1975*. Quito, 1975.

Tola, Marqués de. "Indice Alfabética de Familias Hidalgas de la Villa de Elorrío en Vizcaya. *IPI 6* (1953): 58–60.

Topete, Alejandro. "Familia Romo de Vivar: Una de las Ramas de Aguascalientes y Teocaltiche," *AMG 5* 1ª Series (1949): 141–167.

Tormer, Florentino M. *Creadores de la Imagen Histórica de México*. México, D.F., 1953.

Toro, Alfonso 1. *La Familia Carvajal*. México, D.F., 1944.

Toro, Miguel 2. *Genealogía de la Casa de los Marqueses del Toro*. Caracas, 1979.

Torre, Luis Guillermo 1. "Los Castro Porteños," *IAC 18* (1979): 403–428.

Torre, Luis Guillermo 2. "Los Ramos de Castro," *IAC 17* (1977): 383ff.

Torre, Luis Guillermo 3. "Los Suárez Merlo (Buenos Aires, Siglos XVIII a XX)," *IAC 19* (1981): 122–135.

Torre, Pedro de la 4. *Historia Genealógica de la Noble Familia de los Manríque de Lara*. Valencia, 1751.

Torrea, Juan Manuel 1. *Diccionario Geográfico, Históico, Biográfico y Estadístico de la República Mexicana.* México, D.F., 1940.

Torrea, Juan Manuel 2. *Funcionarios de la Secretaría de Relaciones Exteriores desde el Año de 1821 a 1940.* México, D.F., 1940.

Torres, Alberto M. 1. "Uno de los Fundadores de Guayaquil," *Boletín del Centro de Investigaciones Históricas de Guayaquil 5.*

Torres, Alfonso 2. "Los Chuquihuancas," *Puno Histórico* (1968): 183–203.

Torres, Enríque 3. *Biografías de los Rectores de San Marcos.* Lima, 1888.

Torres, Enríque 4. *Los Títulos de Castilla en las Familias de Chile.* Santiago, 1894. 2nd edition. Santiago, 1949.

Torres, Enríque 5. *Títulos de Castilla y Mayorazgos del Perú.* n.p., n.d.

Torres, Estéban 6. *Ahondando en la Historia: Los Díaz de la Torre.* Buenos Aires, 1938.

Torres, Estéban 7. "Hijos y Nietos de los Primeros Conquistadores que Llegaron por el Perú y Chile, Nacidos en Córdoba," *Revelaciones Históricas 1* (1939).

Torres, Gonzalo 8. "Descendencia de Don Pedro Gómez, Fundador y Primer Poblador de la Villa de San Sebastián de León de la Nueva España, Hoy Ciudad de León, Guanajuato," *AMG 2* 2ª Series (1961): 109–148.

Torres, Gonzalo 9. *Los Torres de Jaén en México: Raíces, Troncos, y Ramas de una Estirpe Milenaria.* México, D.F., 1975.

Torrija, Samuel. *La Familia Pesado.* Brooklyn, 1889. Family of José Joaquín Pesado and his two wives María de la Luz de la Llave y Segura, and Juana de Segura y Argüelles. He died in 1861.

Trazegnies, Ferdinand 1. "Descendencia Peruana del Conquistador Don Francisco de Valverde," *Estudios Genealógicos, Heráldicos y Nobiliarios 2* (1978): 347–364.

Trazegnies, Ferdinand 2. *García.* Lima, n.d.

Trazegnies, Ferdinand 3. "Los Garcías," *IPI 14* (1965): 135–156.

Trazegnies, Ferdinand 4. *Los Granda en el Perú.* Lima, 1948.

Trazegnies, Ferdinand 5. *Los Vázquez de Velasco: Historia Genealógica de una Noble e Ilustre Familia Española del Perú.* Lima, 1945.

Trazegnies, Ferdinand 6. "Moncada," *Hidalguía 159* (1980): 273–281.

Trelles, José Manuel. *Asturias Ilustrada: Origen de la Nobleza.* 2 vols. Madrid, 1734.

Tristan, Guillermo 1. "Ascendencia Paterna del Lic. Don Manuel de Jesús Jiménez O." *Monografía de Cartago* (1930): 156.

Tristan, Guillermo 2. "Doña Esmeralda de Jiménez," *Monografía de Cartago* (1930): 176.

Trostiné, Rodolfo 1. "Genealogía del Doctor Don Manuel Antonio de Castro, 1776–1832, Fundador de la Academia TeóricoPráctica de Jurisprudencia en 1815," *IAC 2* (1943): 21–123.

Trostiné, Rodolfo 2. "La Familia del General Solar," *IAC 2* (1943): 119–120.

Trostiné, Rodolfo 3. "Los Belgrano," *IAC 3* (1944): 123–130.

Turcios, Salvador. "Genealogía del General Francisco Morazán y Quesada," *Revista de los Archivos Nacionales, San José 9–10* (1942): 463–464.

Udaondo, Enríque 1. *Diccionario Biográfico.* Buenos Aires, 1939.

Udaondo, Enríque 2. *Diccionario Biográfico Argentino.* Buenos Aires, 1945.

Udaondo, Enríque 3. *Diccionario Biográfico Colonial Argentino.* Buenos Aires, 1938.

Ugarteche, Félix. *Hombres del Coloniaje.* Buenos Aires, 1932.

Uhagón, Valeriano. *Memorial Genealógico de la Casa de Uhagón.* Madrid, 1949.

Urdaneta, Ramón. *El Sentido de la Tradición.* Bogotá, 1966.

Urías, Margarita. *Formación y Desarrolo de la Burguesía en México, Siglo XIX.* México, D.F., 1978.

Uricoechea, José M. *Noticias Genealógicas.* n.p., 1972. Contains the genealogies of the families Uricoechea, Moreno, Caicedo, León, Duque de Estrada, Montoya, González de Castro, Florez, García de Heredia, and Gómez de Múnera.

Urquidi, José M. *Bolivianas Ilustres*. La Paz, 1918.

Urquiza, Eduardo. *Ensayo Genealógico de la Familia Urquiza: Rama de Don José Narciso de Urquiza y Alzaga*. Buenos Aires, 1951.

Urrutia. D.D. 1. *Hojas de Servicios y Antecedentes Familiares del General de División Don Basilio Urrutia Vázquez: Los Urrutia en Chile*. Santiago, 1949.

Urrutia, José María 2. *La Casa Urrutia de Avellaneda y Familias Enlazadas Españolas y Americanas*. Bilbao, 1968.

Urrutia, Zenón 3. "El Espaldarago de un Penguista en Lima," *REH 15* (1968–1969): 91–93.

Urrutia, Zenón 4. "El Linaje de los Fernández del Manzano," *REH 2* (1950–1951): 21–45.

Urrutia, Zenón 5. "El Obispado de Concepción, 1567–1957," *REH 6–7* (1956–1957): 135–195.

Urrutia, Zenón 6. "Familia Urrutia, de Chile," *RGL 12* (1960): 247–252.

Urrutia, Zenón 7. "Genealogía de la Familia Manzano, de Chile," *RGL 13* (1961): 269–271.

Utrera, Cipriano 1. "Genealogía de las Familias Solariegas de Bastidas, Fernández de Oviedo y Valdez, Fernández de Fuenmayor, Dávila y Entronques, 1468–1926," *Santo Domingo, Dilucidaciones Históricas 1*, 424–492.

Utrera, Cipriano 2. "Genealogía de Ravelo," *Boletín del Archivo General de la Nación, R.D. 75* (1952): 433–443.

Vaamando, Cesar. *Gómez Pérez das Mariñas y sus descendientes. Apuntes históricos y genealógicos*. La Coruña, 1917.

Valcárcel, Carlos D. "Genealogía y Persona de Tupac Amaru," *IPIG 15* (1970): 59–68.

Valdés, Ambrosio 1. *Carrera*. n.p., 1888.

Valdés, Ambrosio 2. *Genealogías de famílias*. Santiago, 1890.

Valdés, G. Antonio 3. *Los Torres*. Valparaiso, 1900.

Valdés, José María 4. *A Traves de las Centurias*. Mérida, 1931. Facsimile edition, México, D.F., 1978, with notations by Ignacio Rubio Mañé. Genealogy principally of Yucatán.

Valdés, Luis 5. *Memorias de Asturias: Historia y Genealogía*. Gijón, Asturias, 1978.

Valdés, Salvador 6. "Cincuenta Familias Chilenas Descendientes de Argentinos," Unpublished conference report.

Valdés, Salvador 7. "El Linaje de Lazcano," *REH 11* (1962–1963): 55–82.

Valdés, Salvador 8. "Familias Chilenas Descendientes de Peruanos," *IPI 6* (1953): 113–120.

Valdés, Salvador 9. "La Familia O'Higgins," *El Diario Ilustrado 9* (1942).

Valdés, Salvador 10. *La Familia Riesco*. Carabineros, Chile, 1962.

Valdés, Salvador 11. "La Familia Valdés," *Tradiciones y Recuerdos 2* (1963).

Valdés, Salvador 12. *Semblanzas de Chilenos Ilustres*. Santiago, 1954.

Valenzuela, Lizahno 1. "Los Valdevinos," *RCH 65* (1929).

Valenzuela, Régulo 2. "Valenzuela, Historia de un Linaje Chilena de Cuatro Siglos," *REH 16* (1971); *17* (1972): 27–56; *18* (1973): 21–48.

Válgoma, Dalmiro 1. *Ascendientes y Descendientes de Hernán Cortés: Línea de Medina Sidonia y Otras*. Madrid, 1951.

Válgoma, Dalmiro 2. *La Condesa de Pardo Basáh y sus Linajes*. Burgos, 1952.

Válgoma, Dalmiro 3. *Real Compañía de Guardiamarinas y Colegio Naval*. 7 vols. Madrid, 195?–1956. Genealogies of Latin America, and particularly of the families Acosta, Allendesalazar, Buelnes, Cañas Trujillo, Cerda, Del Pino, Encalada, García de Postigo, Herrera, Irizarri, Leclerc, Rojas, Vial, Warnes, etc.

Valladares, Jorge. "Hogares Linarenses: Romero (con sucesión Encina y Barker)," *REH 15* (1968–1969): 86–90.

Valle, Rafael H. *Santiago en América*. México, D.F., 1946.

Valles, Luis. *Españoles del Uruguay, 1918.* Montevideo, 1919.

Valverde, Emeterio 1. *Bio-Bibliográfica Eclesiástica del Estado de México.* México, D.F., 1976.

Valverde, Enríque 2. "Genealogía de la Familia Rucabado," *ACC 26* (1980): 107–179; *27–28* (1981): 298–310.

Van Patten, Charles. "El Origen de la Familia Van Patten," *ACC 16–17* (1970): 133–135.

Varela, Luis 1. *Apuntes para la Historia de la Sociedad Colonial.* 2 vols. Lima, 1905.

Varela, Luis 2. *Los Presidentes de la H. Cámara de Diputados del Perú: Apuntes Biográficos.* Lima, 1916.

Vázquez, Isidoro 1. *Garay: Un Linaje Portugués en el Archipiélago de Chiloé.* Madrid, 1959.

Vázquez, Isidoro 2. "Las Ciudades Espectrales y sus Fundadores," *Hidalguía 30* (1958): 873–904.

Vázquez, José 3. "Genealogía e Historia de una Familia Gallega Vázquez Quiróz," *IPI 7* (1954): 193–206.

Vázquez, Nadine M. 4. *Sinaloa Roots: An Account of the 1781 Expedition to Alta California and Ancestral Records of Early California Settlers, 1723–1808.* Carmichael, 1974.

Vázquez, Raul 5. *Quién es Quién en Durango.* Durango, 1966–1967.

Vega, Carlos. "De la Vega," *REH 14* (1966–1967): 93–114.

Vegas, Ricardo. "Los Carrión, de Avilés y Sevilla," *IPI 6* (1953): 5–11.

Velandia, Roberto. *Hombres y Letras y Grandes Hombres de Cundinamarca.* Bogotá, 1978.

Vélez, José M. "Un Curioso Beselamano," IPI 10 (1957): 19–23.

Vera, Juan de. *Catálogo de la VIII Exposición de Arte Antiguo: Heráldica y Genealogías Segovianas.* Segovia, 1955.

Vergara, Felipe 1. *Relación Genealógica.* Bogotá, 1962.

Vergara, José Luis 2. *Descendencia de la Familia Alcalde en Chile, 1729–1941.* Santiago, 1942.

Vicuña, Benjamin 1. *Del Origen de los Vicuña.* Española, 1902.

Vicuña, Benjamin 2. *Los Lisperguer y la Quintrala.* Valparaiso, 1877. Genealogies of the families Flores, Gutiérrez de los Ríos, Lisperguer, Molina Parraguez, Núñez, and Vasconcelos.

Vicuña, Benjamin 3. *Los Orígenes de las Familias Chilenas.* 3 parts. Santiago, 1903.

Vicuña, Carlos 4. "El Origen de Don Ambrosio O'Higgins y sus Primeros Años en América," *RCH 21* (1916): 126–172.

Vicuña, Julio 5. *Historia de la Familia Sáenz de la Peña.* Santiago, 1978.

Vidargas, Juan D. *Guía de Personas que Cultivan la Historia de América.* México, D.F., 1967.

Vidaurrazaga, José L. *Nobiliario Alavés de Fray Juan de Victoria, Siglo XVI.* Bilbao, 1975.

Videla, Gregorio 1. *Los Videla de Córdoba.* Córdoba, 1948.

Videla, Mario E. 2. "El Ilustrísimo Linaje de Don Lorenzo Suárez de Figueroa, Capitán, Alférez Real y Teniente de Gobernador de Córdoba la Llana de la Nueva Andalucía: Hononímos Ingresados Contemporáneos en el Río de la Plata, Córdoba del Tucumán y Cuyo: su Parentesco con el Virrey del Perú Don Francisco Alvarez de Toledo y con Don Jerónimo Luis de Cabrera," *IAC 16* (1976): 211–217.

Videla, Mario E. 3. "Los de Medina de Río Seco," *IAC 17* (1977): 388–409.

Videla, Mario E. 4. "San Martín y sus Vinculaciones Familiares," *IAC 18* (1979): 429–434.

Videla, Mario E. 5. "Una Antigua Familia Mendocina Olvidada: La de los 'Gómez Pardo' o 'Pardo Parragues.'" *IAC 14* (1961): 129–135.

Vigil, Ciriaco M. *Noticias Biográfico-Genealógicas de Pedro Menéndez de Avilés, Primer Adelantado y Conquistador de la Florida, Continuadas con las de Otros Asturianos que Figuraron en el Descubrimiento y Colonización de las Américas.* Avilés, 1892.

Vilanova, Alberto. *Los Gallegos en la Argentina.* 2 vols. Buenos Aires, 1966.

Villalpando, César. *El Panteón de San Francisco de la Ciudad de México*. México, D.F., 1981. There are are numerous individuals from the history of Mexico buried in this book.

Villanueva, Marcel 1. *Historia de la Familia Villanueva-Astoul.* Orange, N.J., 1957.

Villanueva, Rafael 2. "Don Francisco Fausto Fernández de Cabrera y Botsadilla: Primer Marqués de San Martín de la Vega," *IPI 8* (1955): 215–221.

Villanueva de Cavazos, Lilia E. *Testamentos Coloniales de Monterrey.* Monterrey, Mexico, 1991. Contains thirty-seven wills of famous Nuevo León figures.

Villar, Ignacio 1. *Cedulario Heráldico de Conquistadores de Nueva España.* México, D.F., 1933.

Villar, Luis 2. *Genealogía de la Familia de Alcalde.* Santiago, 1939.

Villaseñor, Alejandro 1. *Biografías de los Héroes y Caudillos de la Independencia.* 2 vols. México, 1962.

Villaseñór, Alejandro 2. *Los Condes de Santiago: Monografía Histórica y Genealógica.* México, D.F., 1901.

Villaseñor, Rubén 3. "Algunos Descendientes Cercanos de Hernando Ruiz de la Peña," *AGM 2* 1ª Series (1957): 195–207.

Villaseñor, Rubén 4. *Anotaciones Genealógicas.* Autlán, Jalisco, 1949.

Villaseñor, Rubén 5. *El Conquistador Juan de Almesto y su Esposa Leonor Juárez de Figueroa.* Autlán, 1951.

Villaseñor, Rubén 6. "Los Villaseñor con Cepa en la Neo-gallega Provincia de Autlán," *AMG 4* 2ª Series (1968): 515–552.

Villaseñor, Rubén 7. *Síntesis de una Investigación Genealógica.* Autlán, 1956.

Villavicencio, César. "Genealogía de la Noble Casa de López de la Flor. II: Los López de la Flor en Ibarra (Ecuador); y Addenda Genealógica," *Revista de los Archivos Nacionales, San José 3–4* (1945): 183–189.

Viquez, Juan Rafael. *Raza de Conquistadores y Primeros Pobladores: Casta de Hidalgos.* n.p., n.d.

Viso, Rosario Libia. *Origen y Entronque de Familias de Córdoba, República Argentina.* Córdoba, 1981. Genealogy of the families Argüello, Bas, Balnes del Viso, Garzón, González, Nores, Ramírez de Arellano, and Rueda.

Vitón, Alfredo. *Río de la Sangre: un Album de Familia: Los Azcuenga, Los Hergo, Los Perdriel, Los Vitón.* Buenos Aires, 1959.

Vizcaino, Ignacio. *Obras completas de Ignacio Vizcaino.* n.p., n.d.

Von der Heyde, Alejandro 1. "Agustín Garrigos Mellón," *IAC 18* (1979): 435–450.

Von der Heyde, Alejandro 2. "Breve Historia de dos Siglos o de Cuatro Generaciones de Garrigos en el Río de la Plata," *IAC 19* (1981): 47–69.

Von der Heyde, Alejandro 3. "Coronel Juan Antonio Ugarteche y Posadas," *IAC 17* (1977): 99–111.

Von der Heyde, Alejandro 4. "Cresencia Boado de Garrigos: Una de las Grandes Matronas Argentinas del Siglo XIX," *IAC 16* (1976): 67–76.

Waid, Beverly H. *My Inherited Destiny: The First Families of California.* Anaheim, 1986.

Walker, Alejandro. *Los Parlamentarios de Hoy y de Mañana.* Santiago, 1921.

Yaben, Jacinto R. *Biografías Argentinas y Sudamericanas.* 5 vols. Buenos Aires, 1938–1940.

Yglesias, Rubén 1. "Información de Nobleza de la Familia Llorente," *Revista de los Archivos Nacionales, San José 9–10* (1940): 520–527.

Yglesias, Rubén 2. "Notas Sobre la Familia Van Patten," *ACC 26* (1980): 9–12.

Ysalsel, Z. "El Linaje de Angulo y sus Armas en el Perú," *IPI 8* (1955): 167–206.

Zambrano, Francisco 1. *Diccionario Bio-Bibliográfico de la Compañía de Jesús en México.* 13 vols. México, D.F., 1961–1970.

Zambrano, Malleen 2. *Los Zambrana.* Multi-volume work. La Habana, 1952–1957.

Zañartu, Dario. *Cimería Roja*. Valparaiso, 1946. Genealogy of the families Aguila, Astaburuaga, Cuevas, Cruz, Errázuriz, Lecaros, Reyes, Rodríguez del Manzano, Ovalle, Tupper, Santa María, and Subercaseaux.

Zavala, Carlos 1. "Ascendencia de los Fernández de Córdova Radicados en el Sur del Perú," *IPI 1* (1946): 41–87.

Zavala, Carlos 2. "Un Sanjuanista del Siglo XIV," *IPI 7* (1954): 166–181.

Zavala, Joaquín 3. *Huellas de una Familia Vasco-Centroamericana en Cinco Siglos de Historia*. n.p., 1969.

Zavalia, Roberto. *Bazán: La Casa de Tucumán, Historia de la Casa de la Independencia*. Tucumán, 1971.

Zayas, Pablo 1. *Las Casas de Rincón Gallardo y Romero de Terreros*. México, D.F., n.d.

Zayas, Pablo 2. "Los Zayas en las Cuatro Ordenes Militares de España," *AMG 5–6* 1ª Series (1947): 109–111.

Zazo, Ramón. *Información de Nobleza de Don Fernando Miyares*. Madrid, 1778.

Zenarruza, Jorge G. 1. "Antecedentes para un Estudio del Marquesado del Valle de Tojo," *IAC 17* (1977): 505–517.

Zenarruza, Jorge G. 2. "Linaje de Irala," *IAC 18* (1979): 451–600.

Zenarruza, Jorge G. 3. "Líneas de las Dinastías Astur-Leoneas; Aragonesa y Navvara, en la Provincia de Jujuy," *IAC 16* (1976): 219–266.

Zenarruza, Jorge G. 4. "Los Bustamante de Quijas en España y América," *IAC 17* (1977): 411–503.

Zenarruza, Jorge G. 5. "Tercera Fundación de la Ciudad de San Salvador de Jujuy," *IEI 1* (1980): 241–356.

Zentner, Federico, Jr. *Nombres y Apellidos de Forjadores de la Patria*. Panamá, 1984.

Zevallos, Jorge 1. "Lambayeque en el Siglo XVIII," *IPI 1* (1946): 90–152; 2 (1947): 53–116.

Zevallos, Jorge 2. "Los Lisperguer en el Peru," *IPI 7* (1954): 98–118.

Zevallos, Jorge 3. "Mis Antepasados," *IPI 5* (1951): 5–15.

Zinny, Antonio. *Historia de los Gobernadores de las Provincias Argentinas.* Buenos Aires, 1920.

Zubillaga, Carlos A. *Los Gallegos en el Uruguay: Apuntes para una Historia de la Inmigración Gallega Hasta Fines del Siglo XIX.* Montevideo, 1966.

Zúñiga, Angel. *Morazán y su Familia.* n.p., n.d.

APPENDIX 1

SPANISH PERSONAL NAMES

Raymond L. Gorden's work *Spanish Personal Names as Barriers to Communication between Latin Americans and North Americans* (Antioch College, Yellow Springs, Ohio, 1968) is an extremely valuable study. Although limited in scope, it is unique. For purposes of this compilation, the rankings that Mr. Gorden used are a valuable comparison to the other studies included in this book. Listings from the text are included hereafter without explanation as to how they were derived. Generally speaking, only telephone directories in the principal capitals of Latin America were used. These lists are not strictly Hispanic in origin even though the individuals represented by these surnames have made their lives, sometimes over several generations, among Latin Americans.

On page fifteen of his study Mr. Gorden gives the following priority listing for the ten most prevalent surnames: Rodríguez 1, González 2, Fernández 3, Martínez 4, López 5, Pérez 6, Sánchez 7, Gómez 8, Díaz 9, and Alvarez 10.

On page seventy begins a "Priority List of Apellidos for Latin America." The main problem with this study is that the surnames are for the most part alphabetical within a grouping and cannot be accurately listed by their specific priority. A general similiarity to the IGHL surname study in the United States is apparent.

Surname 11: García.

Surnames 12–65: Acosta, Aguilar, Aguirre, Alonso, Blanco, Cabrera, Campos, Castillo, Castro, Cruz, Delgado, Espinosa, Flores, Franco, Fuentes, Guerrero, Gutiérrez, Hernández, Herrera, Jiménez, León, Márquez, Martín, Medina, Méndez, Mendoza, Miranda, Molina, Morales, Muñoz, Navarro, Núñez, Ortega, Ortiz, Otero, Peña, Ramírez, Ramos, Reyes, Ríos, Rivas, Rojas, Romero, Ruiz, Silva, Sosa, Soto, Suárez, Torres, Vargas, Vásquez, Vega, Velásquez.

pp. 71–72 Surnames 66–239: Acevedo, Acuña, Alarcón, Alfonso, Alvarado, Andrade, Arce, Arias, Avila, Ayala, Barreiro, Barrera, Barrios, Barros, Becerra,

Beltrán, Bello, Benítez, Bermúdez, Bernal, Bianchi, Bravo, Briceño, Bruno, Burgos, Bustamante, Bustos, Caballero, Cáceres, Calderón, Calvo, Camacho, Cano, Cárdenas, Carvajal, Carrasco, Carrera, Carrillo, Casas, Castañeda, Castellanos, Cohen, Colombo, Contreras, Córdoba, Cortés, Correa, Costa, Crespo, Cháves, Dávila, Díez, Domínguez, Duarte, Durán, Echeverría, Escobar, Estévez, Estrada, Ferrari, Ferreira, Ferrer, Ferro, Figueroa, Fuente, Gallardo, Gallo, Garrido, Gil, Giménez, Guerra, Guevara, Guzmán, Hidalgo, Hurtado, Ibáñez, Ibarra, Iglesias, Jaramillo, Juárez, Lara, Leiva, Levy, Linares, Lorenzo, Lozano, Luna, Maldonado, Marín, Mejía, Menéndez, Molinari, Montero, Montes, Mora, Muller, Nieto, Ochoa, Ojeda, Olivera, Ordóñez, Osorio, Pacheco, Padilla, Palacios, Palma, Pardo, Paredes, Parodi, Parra, Patiñó, Paz, Peralta, Pereira, Pinto, Ponce, Prado, Prieto, Quintana, Quintero, Quiroga, Restrepo, Rey, Rincón, Rivera, Rivero, Robles, Roca, Rocha, Román, Romano, Rosas, Rossi, Rozo, Rubio, Russo, Saavedra, Sáenz, Salas, Salazar, Salcedo, Salgado, Salinas, Sandoval, Sanguinetti, San Martín, Santos, Sarmiento, Segura, Sepúlveda, Serrano, Sierra, Solarí, Tapia, Toledo, Trujillo, Uribe, Valdés, Valencia, Valenzuela, Valera, Valle, Varela, Velasco, Vera, Vergara, Vidal, Vila, Villa, Villanueva, Villar, Villegas, Zapata.

pp. 72 – 74 Surnames 240 – 510: Agüero, Aguilera, Ahumada, Alba, Alberti, Albornoz, Alcántara, Alfaro, Altamirano, Allende, Amaya, Angulo, Aparicio, Arana, Aranda, Araujo, Arellano, Arenas, Arévalo, Arteaga, Arroyo, Avendaño, Avíez, Ballesteros, Baquero, Barbieri, Barragán, Barreto, Basso, Bautista, Benavides, Bernasconi, Betancourt, Bianco, Bonilla, Brito, Bueno, Cadena, Camargo, Campo, Canales, Cánepa, Capurro, Carballo, Carbone, Cardona, Cardozo, Carmona, Caro, Carranza, Carreño, Casal, Casanova, Castaño, Castelli, Ceballos, Cervantes, Cifuentes, Cisneros, Conti, Cordero, Cornejo, Coronel, Corral, Cosentino, Cuéllar, Cuevas, Chacón, Chiesa, De la Fuente, De la Torre, Delfino, Del Río, Devoto, Donoso, Duque, Elías, Enríquez, Escalante, Escudero, Espósito, Etcheverry, Fajardo, Falcón, Farías, Ferrando, Ferraro, Ferreiro, Ferrero, Fischer, Fonseca, Fontana, Fraga, Freire, Frías, Gaitán, Galán, Galindo, Gálvez, Gallegos, Galli, Gamboa, Garay, Garcés, Garibaldi, Garzón, Gatti, Giraldo, Godoy, Granados, Greco, Guillén, Heredia, Hermida, Herrero, Hoyos, Huerta, Iriarte, Izquierdo, Jara, Jáuregui, Katz, Lago, Lagos, Lamas, Lanza, Latorre, Leal, Ledesma, Lema, Lima, Lombardi, Losada, Lugo, Machado, Manrique, Mariño, Martino, Massa, Mayer, Mazza, Meléndez, Mena, Meneses, Mercado, Merino, Mesa, Meyer, Meza, Miguez, Millán, Moncada, Monroy, Montenegro, Montoya, Morán, Moreira, Mosquera, Moya, Moyano, Mujica, Muñiz, Murillo, Naranjo, Narváez, Navarrete, Navas, Neira, Niño, Noriega, Novoa, Ocampo, Oliva, Olivares, Oliver, Orellana, Orozco, Páez, Palacio, Parada, Pascual, Pastor, Pazos, Pena, Perdomo, Perrone, Pineda, Pino, Pintos, Piñeiro, Pizarro, Podestá, Porras, Posada, Puente, Puig, Pulido, Quesada, Quevedo, Quiroz, Raffo, Rangel, Repetto, Reynoso, Rial, Ricci, Rico, Rinaldi, Río, Risso, Riva, Roa, Rizzo, Rojo, Roldán, Romo, Rosa,

Rosales, Rueda, Sáez, Salamanca, Sanabria, Santa María, Santamaría, Santillán, Santoro, Sanz, Segovia, Seonane, Serra, Solano, Soler, Solís, Solórzano, Soria, Soriano, Sotomayor, Souto, Taboada, Tamayo, Téllez, Terán, Toro, Torre, Tovar, Traverso, Ugarte, Ulloa, Urbina, Urrutia, Valderrama, Valdivia, Valdivieso, Valero, Vallejo, Vélez, Venegas, Ventura, Vicente, Videla, Villalba, Villalobos, Villamil, Villarreal, Vitale, Yáñez, Zabala, Zambrano, Zamora, Zárate, Zavala, Zúñiga.

pp. 74–77 Surnames 511–1003: Abad, Abarca, Abella, Abreau, Acero, Aguayo, Aguiar, Aguila, Alayza (Alaiza), Albarracín, Alcalá, Alcalde, Alcázar, Aldana, Alegre, Alegría, Alemán, Alexander, Aliaga, Almada, Almaraz, Almeida, Alvear, Alzamora, Ampuero, Anaya, Anderson, Angarita, Angeles, Antelo, Antúnez, Anzola, Aponte, Aragón, Aramburú, Arancibia, Araóz, Araúz, Arciniegas, Arcos, Arguedas, Arispe, Armas, Armendariz, Artigas, Arredondo, Arregui, Arriaga, Arrieta, Arriola, Ascanio, Astudillo, Avalos, Avilés, Ayllón, Baca, Bacigalupi, Bahamonde, Balarezo, Balbi, Ballón, Banchero, Baptista, Barahona, Barba, Barbosa, Barón, Barra, Barraza, Barreda, Barrenchea, Barrero, Barrientos, Barriga, Barrón, Barroso, Bastidas, Basurto, Bayona, Bedoya, Bejarano, Benvenuto, Berger, Bernales, Berríos, Bilbao, Boada, Bobadilla, Bolaños, Bolívar, Borda, Borges, Borjas, Bosch, Botta, Braga, Brea, Briones, Brun, Buendía, Bustillos, Cabello, Cabezas, Cabral, Caicedo, Calcagno, Caldas, Calero, Calle, Campero, Campuzano, Candia, Canseco, Capriles, Carbajal, Carbonell, Carcelén, Carpio, Carrasquilla, Carrión, Casado, Casella, Castañón, Castellano, Castiglioni, Castilla, Cavero, Cedeño, Celis, Cepeda, Cerda, Cerón, Céspedes, Cevallos, Cid, Clavijo, Cobos, Coello, Colmenares, Coloma, Copello, Coppola, Corona, Coronado, Corrales, Cossío, Costas, Cuadra, Cuadros, Cuba, Cubillos, Cuello, Cuenca, Cuervo, Cuesta, Cueto, Cueva, Cúneo, Curiel, Chamorro, Chaparro, Checa, Chrinos, Dávalos, Daza, De Castro, Del Campo, Del Castillo, Delgadillo, Del Valle, De Sousa, Dueñas, Durand, Echevarría, Eguiguren, Elizalde, Endara, Escalona, España, Esparza, Espejo, Esquivel, Eyzaguirre, Falconi, Farfán, Fariña, Fernandini, Fierro, Firpo, Flor, Font, Forno, Galarraga, Galarza, Galván, Gallego, Gamarra, Gámez, Gandolfo, Garmendia, Gaviria, Gordillo, Granda, Graña, Guajardo, Guido, Haddad, Haro, Henríquez, Hinojosa, Hinostroza, Holguín, Huertas, Illanes, Infante, Iñiguez, Irigoyen, Iturralde, Iturriaga, Izaguirre, Jaimes, Jordán, Kaplan, Klein, Laguna, Lama, Landa, Landazuri, Lanz, Larco, Larenas, La Rosa, Larrañega, Larrea, Lastra, La Torre, Lavalle, Lavín, Lazarte, Lazcano, Lazo, Leguizamón, Lemos, Lemus, Lerner, Leyton, Lezama, Liendo, Lira, Loayza (Loaiza), Lobo, Lombardo, Lora, Loyola, Loza, Lucas, Lucero, Luque, Llanos, Llerena, Llona, Macedo, Macías, Madrid, Málaga, Mancera, Mancilla, Mantilla, Manzano, Marcos, Marrero, Marroquín, Mas, Mata, Matallana, Matos, Maya, Mayorga, Mazzini, Medrano, Melgar, Melo, Menacho, Mendieta, Mendiola, Mendizával, Merizalde, Michel, Mier, Mijares, Mogollón, Monasterios, Monge, Monsalve, Montáñes, Montaño, Montecinos,

Monteverde, Montiel, Moral, Moscoso, Mota, Musso, Nápoli, Nava, Negrete, Noboa, Nogueira, Noguera, Obando, Obregón, Olea, Olguín, Olivos, Olmedo, Olmos, Oneto, Orihuela, Oropeza, Orrego, Ossa, Otálora, Ovalle, Oviedo, Pabón, Pagani, Paladino, Palomino, Pantoja, Pareja, París, Patrón, Pavón, Pedraza, Pedroza, Peirano, Peláez, Penagos, Peñafiel Peñalosa, Peraza, Perea, Peredo, Perera, Pesce, Piedra, Pimentel, Pinedo, Pinilla, Piña, Piñero, Pizano, Plata, Plaza, Poggi, Pombo, Pons, Porta, Portela, Portilla, Portillo, Portocarrero, Portugal, Posse, Póstigo, Poveda, Pozo, Preciado, Proaño, Puga, Queirolo, Quijano, Quintanilla, Quinteros, Quiñones, Rada, Raggio, Real, Rebolledo, Recalde, Reina, Rendón, Renjifo, Revilla, Reyna, Ricaurte, Riquelme, Rivadeneira, Rivarola, Riveros, Robayo, Robledo, Rodas, Rodrigo, Ron, Rosenberg, Rossel, Rubin, Ruggiero, Saa, Sabogal, Sacco, Saldaña, Salmón, Salomón, Salvo, Samaniego, Santacruz, Santana, Santander, Santiago, Santibáñez, Sarabia, Saucedo, Schmidt, Seijas, Serna, Sevilla, Silberman, Simón, Smith, Solá, Solar, Sotelo, Sousa, Tagle, Talavera, Tavera, Tejada, Tello, Tenorio, Terrazas, Tinajero, Tinoco, Tirado, Tobar, Torrealba, Toscano, Trejo, Trijo, Triviño, Troncoso, Tudela, Unda, Urdaneta, Ureta, Uriarte, Useche, Vaca, Valverde, Valladares, Vallejos, Vegas, Vela, Velarde, Verástegui, Vértiz, Vigil, Vilches, Vilela, Villafuerte, Villagómez, Villagran, Villamarín, Villamizar, Villarroel, Villaveces, Villavicencio, Villazón, Villena, Viola, Vivanco, Vivas, Volpe, Yáñez, Yépez, Zabaleta, Zamorano, Zamudio, Zayas, Zeballos, Zegarra, Zelada, Zenteno, Zepeda, Zorrilla, Zuleta, Zuluaga, Zuniño, Zurita.

The following lists of unique surnames were divided by Mr. Gorden into five categories, which are unimportant for purposes of the listings here. However, because of the five categories, the lists were not strictly alphabetical in his study. This book has indexed them within the individual countries for ease in referencing what is available. These lists include Portuguese, Italian, and German names in addition to the Spanish names most common to these countries.

pp. 78–79 SURNAMES UNIQUE TO PARAGUAY: Coscia, Escauriza, Espínola, Estigarribia, Florentín, Frutos, Gorostiaga, Masi, Melgarejo, Morínigo, Saguier, Urbieta, Vierci, Yegros.

pp. 80–84 SURNAMES UNIQUE TO COLOMBIA: Abello, Abenoza, Abondano, Abril, Afanador, Agudelo, Almanza, Amado, Amézquita, Angel, Arango, Arbeláez, Ardila, Aristizábal, Ariza, Avella, Avellana, Ballén, Bohórquez, Borrero, Botero, Buenaventura, Buitrago, Cabra, Cala, Camelo, Canón, Cantor, Carrizosa, Castelblanco, Castiblanco, Caycedo, Cely, Charry, Chavarro, Correal, Corredor, Cristancho, Cubides, De Francisco, Echeberri,

Echeverry, Escallón, Esguerra, Eslava, Espinel, Espitia, Estefan, Fandiño, Forero, Gacharná, Galvis, Gamba, Henao, Herrán, Higuera, Iregui, Isaza, Galeano, Garavito, Guarín, Guerrero, Laserna, Laverde, Leaño, Lesmes, Lizarazo, Lizcano, Lleras, Lombana, Lobo, Londoño, Mahecha, Malagón, Mallarino, Mateus, Matiz, Merchán, Michelsen, Mojica, Molano, Montaña, Montealegre, Montejo, Munévar, Murcia, Mutis, Nariño, Narváez, Olano, Olarte, Olaya, Orduz, Orjuela, Ortegón, Ospina, Pachón, Pava, Peñuela, Perilla, Piedrahita, Pinzón, Plazas, Prada, Pradilla, Puentes, Puerta, Puerto, Riaño, Roncancio, Ronderos, Rubiano, Samper, Suescún, Talero, Tarazona, Tobón, Triana, Turriago, Ucrós, Umaña, Urrea, Urrego, Valbuena, Vanegas, Varón, Vejarano, Velandia, Vesga, Villarraga, Villate, Wiesner, Wilches, Wills.

pp. 85 – 89 SURNAMES UNIQUE TO ARGENTINA: Aiello, Amato, Andrés, Antonelli, Arcuri, Arena, Ares, Azar, Ballester, Barbieris, Barcia, Barone, Barral, Barrionuevo, Basile, Battaglia, Benito, Berman, Bernardez, Bevilacqua, Blasco, Botto, Caamaño, Calabrese, Calviño, Canosa, Caputo, Carnevale, Carreras, Carril, Carrizo, Carro, Carruso, Castello, Castiñeira, Catalano, Cattáneo, Cavalieri, Conde, Conte, Cortese, Corti, Croce, Chiappe, D'Agostino, D'Alessandro, D'Amato, D'Amico, Daneri, De Angelis, D'Angelo, De Gregorio, Della, Dellepiane, De Luca, Demarco, De María, De Rosa, De Simone, De Vita, Diéguez, Donadío, Donato, Durante, Estéban, Falcone, Fariña, Federico, Feijoo, Feldman, Ferrairo, Ferreyra, Fontan, Fontenla, Forte, Funes, Furman, Gagliardi, Gago, Galante, Gatto, Gentile, Giordano, Golderberg, Goldman, Goldstein, Goñi, Grande, Grassi, Grasso, Graziano, Grillo, Grinberg, Grosso, Insúa, Jorge, Juan, Kauffmann, Kohan, Lafuente, Larocia, Lauría, Lenín, Leone, Liberman, Loiacano, Longo, Lopardo, Lynch, Maggi, Mancini, Mancuso, Mansilla, Marchese, Marchetti, Mariani, Marinelli, Marini, Marino, Marti, Martinelli, Martini, Mauro, Mazzei, Mazzeo, Mazzitelli, Merlo, Messina, Miguel, Monaco, Monti, Morelli, Moretti, Moro, Moure, Negri, Nigro, Oliveira, Olivero, Olivieri, Orlando, Padín, Pagano, Palazzo, Palermo, Palmieri, Parisi, Pellegrino, Pellegrini, Pepe, Perazzo, Pereyra, Pérsico, Picasso, Porto, Pozzi, Pugliese, Pujol, Rabinovich, Raimondi, Ratto, Rimoldi, Rocco, Romeo, Rubinstein, Sala, Salerno, Santamarina, Schneider, Segal, Simonetti, Sívori, Somoza, Spinelli, Stella, Sturla, Tedesco, Tomás, Tripodi, Trotta, Vaccaro, Veiga, Vigo, Villafañe, Villaverde.

pp. 90 – 94 SURNAMES UNIQUE TO VENEZUELA: Acedo, Adrian, Aguerrevere, Alamo, Alture, Añez, Aranguren, Araque, Arismendi, Aristequieta, Arocha, Arnal, Arreaza, Arria, Arvelo, Atencio, Azpúrua, Azuaje, Baldó, Basalo, Behrens, Belisario, Belloso, Benaim, Benarioch, Benedetti, Bondayán, Bigott, Boscán, Bracho, Bruzual, Bufete, Calcaño, Calzadilla, Camejo, Camero, Canelón, Caraballo, Carías, Carrasque, Carrasquero, Carrero, Centeno, Chacín, Colimodio, Coll, De Armas, De la Rosa, Dubuc, Fuenmayor,

Gabaldón, Galavís, Goncalves, Graterol, Guédez, Hamann, Hermoza, Hernando, Heros, Herrada, Higa, Higueras, Horna, Huaamán, Huambachano, Huapaya, Hung, Irazábal, Iribarren, Istúriz, Itriago, Kassin, Landaeta, Lander, Lange, Lares, Larrazábal, Laya, Lemoine, Lilue, Limongi, Lovera, Lupi, Madriz, Maduro, Malavé, Manzo, Mariano, Marturet, Matas, Matheus, Matuto, Mejías, Mayorca, Michelana, Mirabal, Monagas, Montilla, Morillo, Moros, Nieves, Obadía, Olivo, Omaña, Orta, Osío, Osuna, Ovalles, Padrón, Pagés, Paul, Penso, Pernía, Pietri, Piñango, Pocaterra, Poleo, Ponte, Prato, Pulgar, Quijada, Quincalla, Rauseo, Ravelo, Reverón, Riera, Roche, Rondón, Russian, Sabala, Sanoja, Santaella, Senior, Sequera, Sierralta, Sifontes, Siso, Socorro, Sojo, Sotillo, Sucre, Troconis, Urbaneja, Urbano, Uzcátegui, Vaamonde, Valecillos, Valery, Vallenilla, Velutini, Verde, Viera, Viloria, Villasmil, Zerpa.

pp. 95 – 100 SURNAMES UNIQUE TO BOLIVIA: Abela, Acha, Adler, Agramot, Agudo, Alborta, Alcoreza, Aldazosa, Alipaz, Alvéstegui, Antezana, Antognelli, Anze, Aramayo, Aranibar, Archondo, Ardiles, Argote, Ariñes, Armaza, Arratia, Arraya, Arze, Asbún, Ascarrunz, Asturizaga, Auza, Ayoroa, Azcui, Azurduy, Bacarreza, Balboa, Baldivieso, Ballivian, Banzer, Barbato, Barja, Bartos, Basaure, Bascón, Bascopé, Batki, Bedregal, Belmonte, Biruet, Blacutt, Block, Bocangel, Botello, Bozo, Bretel, Burgoa, Bustillo, Caba, Cajías, Callisperis, Calvimontes, Camberos, Campanini, Canedo, Canelas, Careaga, Carretero, Casablanca, Casanovas, Castaños, Castrillo, Catacora, Centellas, Cernadas, Cerruto, Chaín, Chumaceros, Claros, Claure, Clavel, Coca, Collao, Condorí, Coritza, Criales, Crispieri, Cusicanqui, Dalenco, Daneley, Deheza, Doria, Duchón, Echalar, Echazú, Eduardo, Eguía, Eguino, Elio, Elman, Elsner, Encinas, Ergueta, Ernest, Escobari, Espada, Esprella, Estenssoro, Estívaris, Florilo, Follman, Fishzang, Forrufino, Fortún, Franck, Freudenthal, Gainsborg, Gallequillos, Garnica, Garvizu, Garrón, Gemio, Gironda, Gisbert, Gonzalves, Gorriti, Gotia, Gottschalck, Granier, Grissi, Grumucio, Guacha, Gurenberger, Guarachi, Guisbert, Gutman, Handal, Harb, Helguero, Henrich, Herbas, Huet, Humboldt, Ibargüen, Ichazo, Imaña, Inchauste, Irahola, Irusta, Iturri, Jahnsen, Jemio, Johnson, Justiniano, Kattan, Kawai, Keiffer, Knaudt, Komori, Krutzfeldt, Kusher, Landívar, Lavadez, Lijerón, Lizarazu, Lizárraga, Lozada, Luza, Machiavelli, Machicao, MacClean, Machicado, Mallea, Manríquez, Manzaneda, Marañón, Mariaca, Marzana, Mealla, Meave, Mediancelli, Meier, Meruvia, Mogro, Mollinedo, Monje, Monterrey, Morató, Mourraille, Mugía, Navajas, Navia, Nemer, Nemtala, Nielsen, Nistahuz, Nogales, Nothmann, Novillo, Oblitas, Olaguivel, Oporto, Orías, Ormahecha, Ossío, Osterman, Ostría, Palenque, Palza, Pando, Paniagua, Paravicini, Peinado, Peñaranda, Pierola, Pol, Prudencio, Quijarro, Quint, Quintela, Quisbert, Quispe, Ramallo, Renjel, Reque, Requena, Revollo, Reynolds, Rocabado, Romay, Romecin, Roncal, Rudón, Safar, Sagarnaga, Sahonero, Said, Saínz, Salguiero, Salvatierra, Sanjinés, Sara, Sardón,

Schwartzberg, Siles, Sluvis, Soruco, Steg, Strauss, Subieta, Taborga, Tardio, Tejerina, Terceros, Thaine, Tobia, Torrez, Torrico, Troche, Urdinidea, Uría, Urioste, Urquido, Urquieta, Urquiola, Urquizo, Vacaflor, Valda, Veintemillas, Viaña, Vidangos, Vidaurre, Vildoso, Virreira, Viscarra, Wasson, Weill, Werner, Wilde, Zalaquett, Zalles, Zambrana, Zbinden, Zegada, Zetzsche, Zuazo, Zubieta, Zumarán.

pp. 101 – 107 SURNAMES UNIQUE TO PERU: Abugattas, Abusada, Accinelli, Ackerman, Adrianzén, Agurto, Alarco, Alcedo, Almenara, Amat, Ames, Amezága, Amorós, Antola, Arata, Arbulú, Arca, Argüelles, Arizola, Arnillas, Arrarte, Arrese, Arróspide, Asín, Aspillaga, Aste, Astete, Ayulo, Bacigalupo, Balbuena, Bambarén, Barandiarán, Barco, Bardales, Barrantes, Bartra, Barúa, Basadre, Báscones, Basombrío, Basurco, Batievsky, Battifora, Battillana, Battistini, Baumann, Bazán, Bazar, Bazo, Belaúnde, Bellido, Belmont, Bell, Bendezú, Beraún, Bernizón, Berrocal, Bevavente, Bonifaz, Bontín, Boza, Burgo, Bustios, Busto, Cabada, Cabieses, Cabrejo, Cáceda, Cahuas, Callirgos, Calmet, Camino, Campodónico, Cantuarios, Carlín, Carrallo, Cavasa, Cebrián, Chavarri, Chocano, Chueca, Cillóniz, Colina, Collazos, Conroy, Corzo, Cox, Daniño, Dasso, Del Carpio, Denegri, Deza, Dianderos, Dibos, Dulanto, Echeandía, Echeapar, Echegaray, Ego, Eguren, Egúsquiza, Elejaldo, Eléspuro, Elguera, Elmore, Eskemazi, Espantoso, Ezeta, Farah, Ferradas, Ferrand, Ferreyros, Figari, Galdós, Gallese, Gamero, Gamio, Ganoza, Garaicochea, Garland, Gastañeta, Gastelumeldi, Grados, Guerinorri, Guimet, Icochea, Indacochea, Isola, Jeri, Labarthe, Lafranco, La Hoz, Lainez, Lam, Lanata, Landman, Laos, Larraluire, Lino, Lisárraga, Liza, Loli, Loredo, Lostaunau, Luján, Lury, Llamosas, Llosa, Machiavello, Madueño, Magnani, Maguiña, Majluf, Malesta, Malpartido, Mandel, Mariátegui, Marquina, Marticonera, Martín, Marzano, Matellini, Maximiliano, Menchaca, Mendívil, Merin, Mesones, Milla, Miró, Mispireta, Mogrovejo, Montore, Morante, Morjano, Morón, Mulanovich, Murguía, Muro, Odría, Olaechea, Olazábal, Olceso, Orbegozo, Oré, Orlandini, Ormeño, Osores, Ostaloza, Pachas, Pajares, Pásara, Penny, Periano, Peschiera, Piaggio, Pimental, Pinasco, Pinillos, Pinzás, Polo, Portal, Puccio, Puertas, Ravines, Raygada, Reátegui, Regal, Revoredo, Risco, Roda, Romaní, Roselló, Saba, Salanerry, Saldarriaga, Salem, Salvador, Samanamud, Samaní, Samonéz, San Ramón, Santa, Sarriá, Sayán, Sifuentes, Sin, Solimano, Suito, Tabja, Talledo, Taramona, Tealdo, Terán, Testino, Tidela, Tizón, Tola, Tori, Torrejón, Trelles, Ubilluz, Ugaz, Urmeneta, Urtuega, Vacari, Valdeavillano, Valderve, Valcárcel, Valdizán, Valega, Vallenas, Velaochaga, Velazco, Venturo, Verme, Viacara, Viale, Vidalón, Villacorta, Villarán, Vinotea, Vizcarra, Yábar, Yrigoyen, Zelaya.

pp. 108 – 113 SURNAMES UNIQUE TO MEXICO: Aburto, Aceves, Achar, Adame, Aguado, Ahedo, Aja, Alazez, Alatorre, Albarrán, Alcaráz, Alcócer, Amador, Amezcua, Amor, Ampudia, Ancona, Anda, Anguiano, Antón, Araiza,

Armenta, Arvizu, Arzate, Arreola, Badillo, Balderas, Baños, Bañuelos, Barajas, Barcena, Barcenas, Barranco, Becerril, Béjar, Beristain, Borballa, Borja, Bretón, Bribiesca, Buenrostro, Cacho, Calva, Calvillo, Calleja, Camarena, Camarillo, Cantú, Caraza, Carral, Carreón, Casillas, Casimires, Caso, Castelano, Castrejón, Cedillo, Cejudo, Celorio, Cervera, Chapa, Chavarría, Colin, Collado, Coria, Cortina, Covarrubias, Daniel, Diego, Dorantes, Elizondo, Enciso, Escamilla, Escobedo, Espíndola, Espino, Esponda, Esqueda, Félix, Fragoso, Galicia, Gama, Garduño, Garibay, Garza, Godínez, Grajales, Guadarrama, Gudiño, Guizar, Hararí, Hermosilla, Herrejón, Herrería, Herrerías, Hierro, Hoyo, Huesca, Huitrón, Ibarrola, Iglesia, Islas, Iturbe, Iturbide, Jaimes, José, Junco, Jurado, Kuri, Lagunes, Lamadrid, Larios, Laris, Lascuarín, Lebrija, Lechuga, Legarreta, Legorreta, Liceaga, Limón, Llano, Lomeli, Loyo, Llamas, Madero, Madrazo, Madrigal, Magallanes, Magaña, Malo, Manjarrez, Manzanilla, Margaín, María, Mariscal, Marrón, Mateos, Medellín, Mizrahi, Moctezuma, Moguel, Mondragón, Montemayor, Munguía, Murguia, Nájera, Novelo, Oliveros, Olvera, Ontoveros, Ordaz, Ornales, Orvañamos, Oseguerra, Paniagua, Pastrana, Peniche, Peón, Pereda, Pichardo, Pliego, Quintanar, Reballo, Rebollo, Riveroll, Rosado, Saad, Saldivar, Sámano, Santiestéban, Santoyo, San Vicente, Sentíes, Sernín, Sordo, Soverón, Solana, Támez, Tawil, Teja, Templo, Tena, Tlapalería, Trueba, Ugalde, Ultramarinos, Urquiza, Valadéz, Valles, Verdusco, Vidales, Villapando, Villasana, Villaseñor, Viveros, Zaga, Zaldívar, Zendejas, Zermeño, Zertuche, Zetina.

pp. 114 – 118 SURNAMES UNIQUE TO URUGUAY: Abal, Abellanda, Aguerre, Aicardy, Albano, Algorta, Alves, Amaro, Amestoy, Amores, Amoroso, Arigón, Arocena, Artola, Baccino, Badano, Bado, Baldomir, Barlocco, Barreira, Batista, Bazzano, Bellini, Berta, Berrutti, Betancor, Berro, Bocage, Bonifacio, Bonimi, Bonino, Borras, Borrazás, Britos, Brum, Bruzzone, Buela, Burgueño, Cal, Camaño, Canabal, Cancela, Caorsi, Carlebaro, Carnelli, Carvalho, Carrara, Carrau, Caviglia, Cereviño, Cibils, Collazo, Comas, Comesaña, Corbo, Cotelo, Couto, Crespo, Crosa, Curbelo, De León, De los Santos, Dodera, Doldán, Dutra, Etchegaray, Facal, Falco, Figueredo, Folle, Fossati, Franchi, Gadea, Gallinal, Gambetta, Garabarino, Genta, Gioraldo, Giorello, Hughes, Laborde, Lagomarsino, Lapido, Lerena, Levrero, Levy, Lista, Loureiro, Luzardo, Maeso, Magariños, Marenco, Mato, Mattos, Mautote, Misa, Mondiño, Montaldo, Montana, Moratorio, Mussio, Nin, Novo, Noya, Ottonello, País, Panizza, Pascale, Pastorino, Patrone, Pedemonte, Peluffo, Pera, Pereiro, Piñerúa, Pírez, Píriz, Pitamiglio, Pizzorno, Ponce de León, Porro, Puppo, Rama, Regueira, Regueiro, Revello, Ribeiro, Riet, Robaina, Roig, Rolando, Rovira, Salgueiro, Sapiro, Sassón, Savio, Scalone, Scarone, Scasso, Secco, Sena, Seré, Servetti, Sica, Sienra, Silveira, Silvera, Siri, Soca, Speranza, Tabárez, Techera, Tejera, Tellechea, Terra, Tomé, Torrano, Tosi, Trias, Umpiérrez, Vallarino, Vieira, Vignoli, Viña, Zaffaroni, Zas.

pp. 119–123 SURNAMES UNIQUE TO ECUADOR: Aguinaga, Albán, Albuya, Amorín, Arboleda, Argüello, Armijos, Arroba, Arteta, Autestia, Ayora, Baldeón, Balseca, Banderas, Barona, Basantes, Batallas, Bayas, Benalcázar, Bermeo, Bucheli, Buitrón, Burbano, Burneo, Cajiao, Calisto, Calveche, Campana, Campaña, Canelos, Cañadas, Cañizares, Cartagenova, Casares, Cazar, Chediak, Chiriboga, Coba, Cobo, Constante Cordovez, Costales, Custode, Darquea, Del Hierro, Del Paso, Egas, Eguez, Erazo, Espín, Estrella, Estupiñán, Fabara, Fiallos, Gabela, Galiano, Gándara, Gangoneta, Gavilanes, Gaybor, Gómezjurado, Gordón, Granja, Grijalba, Gross, Guamán, Guaña, Guarderas, Guayazamín, Guerrón, Guijarro, Herdoiza, Hervas, Hidrobo, Icaza, Idrobo, Iza, Izurrieta, Jácome, Jarrín, Játiva, Jervis, Jijón, Kohn, Landeta, Lizarzaburú, Lovato, Lupera, Luzurriaga, Mancero, Mancheno, Manosalba, Mera, Mesías, Miño, Moncayo, Montalvo, Montesdeoca, Montúfar, Moréano, Morejón, Moreta, Muerragui, Murgueytio, Murillo, Nicolalde, Nolivos, Norona, Oleas, Ona, Ontaneda, Oquendo, Orbe, Ormaza, Ortuño, Pallares, Pasquel, Pazmiño, Peñaherra, Pesantez, Pico, Polanco, Pólit, Posso, Punina, Racines, Raza, Ríofrío, Roa, Revelo, Ribaneneira, Ripalda, Robalino, Rosero, Ruales, Salguero, Sampedro, Santiana, Saona, Sarzoza, Suasnavas, Terneus, Tipán, Toapanca, Tufiño, Uquillos, Urresta, Utreras, Vacas, Valarezo, Vallas, Varea, Vasco, Váscónez, Veintinilla, Velástegui, Vélez, Verdesoto, Villacís, Villacres, Villacreses, Villamar, Villota, Vinueza, Vivar, Viteri, Vizcaíno, Vizueta, Yepes, Yeroni, Zambudine.

pp. 124–129 SURNAMES UNIQUE TO CHILE: Abarzúa, Abumohor, Abusleme, Aedo, Aguiló, Alamos, Alcayaga, Aldunate, Alemparte, Alessandrini, Alliende, Almarza, Amenábar, Amunátegui, Anguita, Aracena, Araneda, Aránguiz, Araos, Aravena, Araya, Argandoña, Aristía, Armijo, Arrau, Arriagada, Arriaza, Astaburruaga, Asenjo, Astorga, Avaria, Awad, Azócar, Badilla, Baeza, Bahamondes, Balbontín, Balmaceda, Baltra, Bañados, Baraona, Barría, Bascuñán, Bastías, Basulto, Beas, Becker, Belmar, Benavente, Besa, Bescaín, Bezanilla, Bórquez, Bruce, Bruna, Bulnes, Bunster, Busquets, Cádiz, Café, Callejas, Calzados, Camus, Cancino, Cañas, Canessa, Cárcamo, Carvaldo, Catalán, Celedón, Cisternas, Claro, Casanueva, Cavada, Caviedes, Cereceda, Concha, Contador, Covarrubias, Cristi, Cruzat, Davis, De la Barca, De la Cerda, De la Cruz, De la Cuadra, De la Maza, De la Vega, Del Canto, Del Pino, Del Pedregal, Del Solar, Del Villar, Doren, Droguett, Echavarría, Echenique, Elgueta, Encina, Errázuriz, Espina, Fabros, Faúndes, Feliú, Fontecilla, Fredes, Fuentealba, Fuenzalida, Gacitúa, Gaete, Gajardo, Galaz, Galleguillos, Gana, Gandarillas, Gárate, Garretón, Gasmuri, Gática, Giacamán, Goycoclea, Gracia, Grau, Greene, Grez, Gumuchio, Hermosilla, Herreros, Hevia, Homozábal, Honorato, Humeres, Ilabaca, Inostroza, Jadue, Jarpa, Jérez, Jofré, Jorquera, Konapp, Labarca, Labbé, Labra, Larraín, Larrondo, Lecaros, Letelier, Lillo, Lobos, Lorca, Lonzana, Luco, Lyon, Madariaga, Manríquez,

Manzur, Marambio, Marchant, Matte, Maturana, Mella, Mendiola, Menares, Mery, Moller, Monreal, Montalva, Moraga, Morandé, Morel, Morgado, Munita, Munizaga, Nagel, Nazal, Nazar, Neumann, Norambuena, Olabarría, Opazo, Ordenes, Ossadón, Osses, Ortúzar, Oyadanel, Oyarzún, Parraguez, Pastene, Pavez, Pinochet, Poblete, Portales, Prat, Puelma, Ravanal, Ravera, Recabarren, Retamal, Retamales, Reveco, Riesco, Risopatrón, Rosende, Rozas, Ruz, Sabat, Sagredo, Saldías, San Fuentes, Sanhueza, Santelices, Santís, Seguel, Soza, Tala, Telías, Tocornal, Ubilla, Undurraga, Urra, Urzúa, Valdebenito, Varas, Veliz, Veloso, Vial, Vicencio, Vicuña, Villablanca, Villalón, Villaseca, Yrarrazával, Vives, Yarur, Yavar, Zañartu, Zarala, Zaror, Zegeros.

APPENDIX 2

1980 CENSUS LIST OF SPANISH SURNAMES

The following list of Spanish surnames was compiled in 1979 by the Bureau of the Census with input from a number of Hispanic experts, including the author. There are 12,567 surnames represented in this census study. Many of these surnames have the same origin, however, and should not technically be considered as separate surnames. The surnames have been alphabetized following the English alphabet for easy access by the majority of readers.

There are several thousand surnames which are not represented here that have since come into the country, or that were not identified in the original study. Some of these are noted in the 1,000 and 1,500 name lists on pages 31 and 37 and, of course, in the Latin American study. Some of the surnames listed here are actually Portuguese surnames and should not be included in a Spanish list. However, IGHL uses the criteria in its studies that once a surname has existed for three generations in a Hispanic family, it is considered Hispanic. This list is a good reference point for the time in history it represents.

A Abad, Abadía, Abadiano, Abadías, Abadilla, Abadín, Abaigar, Abajo, Aballe, Abalo, Abalos, Abaonza, Abarca, Abarco, Abaroa, Abárquez, Abarta, Abarzúa, Abascal, Abasta, Abastas, Abasto, Abaunza, Abaurrea, Abay, Abaya, Abbadie, Abdala, Abea, Abeita, Abeja, Abelairas, Abelar, Abeldaño, Abeledo, Abella, Abellán, Abelleira, Abellera, Abendaño, Aberásturi, Aberasturia, Abergel, Abesada, Abete, Abeyta, Abeytia, Abiega, Abila, Abilés, Abilez, Abín, Abiña, Abio, Abiol, Abislaiman, Abitia, Abitu, Abitua, Ablanedo, Abogado, Aboite, Aboites, Abolila, Abonce, Aborlleile, Aboy, Aboytes, Abrahante, Abrahantes, Abraján, Abrante, Abrea, Abrego, Abreu, Abreus, Abreut, Abrev, Abrew, Abreyo, Abrica, Abrigo, Abril, Abriol, Abuín, Abundes, Abundez, Abundis, Abundiz, Abundo, Aburto, Abutin, Acaba, Acabeo, Acarón, Acasta, Accosta, Accuar, Acebal, Acebedo, Acebo, Aced, Acedo, Aceituno, Acencio, Acenedo, Acera, Aceredo, Acero, Acety, Aceuedo, Acevdo, Aceveda, Acevedo, Aceves, Acevez, Acevido, Acha, Achez, Achón, Acido, Acín, Acobe, Acosta, Acoya, Acuesta, Acuña, Acusta, Adame, Adames, Adamez, Adán, Adanza, Adargo, Adaros, Adauto, Adelo, Adona, Adorno, Adriasola, Adrover, Adrovet, Aduna, Advíncula, Aedo, Afán, Afanador, Afre, Agado, Agala,

Aganza, Agapito, Ageitos, Agirre, Agón, Agosto, Agra, Agrait, Agramonte, Agras, Agraz, Agreda, Agredano, Agregado, Agront, Aguabella, Aguado, Aguallo, Aguano, Aguaristi, Aguas, Aguasvivas, Aguaya, Aguayo, Agudelo, Agudo, Agueda, Aguelar, Agüera, Agüero, Agüeros, Aguerre, Aguerrebere, Aguerría, Aguet, Aguigui, Aguila, Aguilar, Aguiler, Aguilera, Aguiles, Aguillar, Aguillén, Aguillera, Aguillón, Aguilo, Aguilón, Aguilor, Aguilos, Aguilu, Aguiluz, Aguinaga, Aguiniga, Aguino, Aguins, Aguire, Aguirra, Aguirre, Aguirrechu, Aguirregaviria, Aguirres, Aguirrezábal, Agular, Aguliar, Agulles, Agullo, Agundes, Agundez, Agundis, Agundiz, Aguón, Agurries, Agurto, Agusti, Agvilar, Ahedo, Ahin, Ahuero, Ahumada, Aibar, Ainsa, Ainz Ainza, Aira, Aisa, Aiso, Aispuro, Aizpuru, Ajuntas, Ajuria, Alabado, Alacán, Alacar, Aladro, Alaez, Alafa, Alaffa, Alaga, Alago, Alamán, Alamano, Alamanza, Alamares, Alambar, Alameda, Alamia, Alamilla, Alamillo, Alamo, Alamos, Alanis, Alaniz, Alanso, Alanzo, Alaquines, Alaquinez, Alarco, Alarcón, Alard, Alarde, Alardín, Alarí, Alarico, Alarid, Alary, Alas, Alatorre, Alatriste, Alava, Alavarado, Alavardo, Alaya, Alayeto, Alayo, Alayón, Alba, Albacete, Albaladejo, Albalate, Albalos, Albaña, Albandoz, Albanez, Albareda, Albarenga, Albarez, Albarico, Albarracín, Albarrán, Albear, Albelo, Alberca, Alberío, Alberro, Albertorio, Alberu, Alvez, Albiar, Albídres, Albídrez, Aibillar, Albines, Albiol, Albisó, Albitre, Albizó, Albizú, Albo, Alboniga, Albor, Albornoz, Albors, Albuerne, Albujar, Albuquerque, Alcade, Alcaida, Alcaide, Alcalá, Alcalán, Alcalde, Alcaniz, Alcanta, Alcántar, Alcántara, Alcántaro, Alcántor, Alcarás, Alcaráz, Alcarez, Alcasás, Alcayde, Alcázar, Alce, Alcedo, Alcerreca, Alcibar, Alcivar, Alcober, Alcocer, Alcocés, Alcola, Alcolea, Alcón, Alcontar, Alcorta, Alcoser, Alcoset, Alcover, Alcozar, Alcozer, Alcudia, Aldaba, Aldabe, Aldaco, Aldahondo, Aldama, Aldana, Aldapa, Aldape, Aldarondo, Aldas, Aldasoro, Aldava, Aldave, Aldaya, Aldaz, Aldazábal, Aldebot, Aldecoa, Aldecocea, Aldeis, Aldereguia, Alderete, Alderette, Alderte, Aldrete, Alduén, Alduenda, Aleantar, Alebis, Aledo, Alegado, Alegre, Alegret, Alegría, Alejandre, Alejandres, Alejandrez, Alejandro, Alejo, Alejos, Alelunas, Alemán, Alemania, Alemany, Alemar, Alén, Alencastro, Alequin, Alers, Alerte, Alevedo, Alexandrino, Alfalla, Alfara, Alfard, Alfaro, Alfassa, Alfau, Alférez, Alfonseca, Alfonso, Alfonzo, Alfrido, Algara, Algarín, Algarra, Algava, Algea, Algeciras, Algora, Algoria, Algorri, Alguacil, Algueseva, Aliaga, Alicante, Alicca, Alicea, Alicia, Alija, Alinaya, Alipaz, Alire, Alires, Alirez, Alladice, Allado, Allala, Allande, Allarid, Allegranza, Allegue, Alleguez, Allende, Allenegui, Allesandro, Allongo, Alloza, Alma, Almada, Almado, Almadova, Almager, Almagher, Almagro, Almaguer, Almance, Almandoz, Almansa, Almanza, Almanzán, Almanzar, Almanzo, Almaquer, Almaras, Almaraz, Almares, Almarez, Almarza, Almazan, Almeda, Almedina, Almejo, Almena, Almenar, Almenara, Almenares, Almendares, Almendarez, Almendariz, Almendral, Almendras, Almenger, Almengor, Almera, Almeraz, Almería, Almestica, Almeyda, Almezquita, Almirall, Almirudis, Almodóbar, Almodóuar, Almodova, Almodóvar, Almogabar, Almoguera, Almoina,

Almonacid, Almondóvar, Almonte, Almontes, Almora, Almuina, Aloma, Alomar, Alona, Alonso, Alonzo, Aloy, Aloyo, Alpizar, Alpuche, Alpuín, Alquicira, Alsina, Altagracia, Altamira, Altamirano, Altarriba, Altenes, Altimirano, Altonaga, Altosino, Altruche, Altube, Altuna, Altur, Alturet, Altuzarra, Aluarez, Aluizo, Alustiza, Aluyón, Alva, Alvanado, Alvara, Alvarada, Alvarado, Alvarez, Alvardez, Alvardo, Alvaredo, Alvarenga, Alvares, Alvarez, Alvarido, Alvarino, Alvarodo, Alvarrán, Alvary, Alvear, Alvelais, Alveló, Alverado, Alveranga, Alveres, Alverez, Alverio, Alvero, Alvez, Alviar, Alvidres, Alvidrez, Alvillar, Alvira, Alvirde, Alvirez, Alvisó, Alvitre, Alvizar, Alvizó, Alvizú, Alvo, Alvorado, Alza, Alzaga, Alzalde, Alzate, Alzina, Alzola, Alzugaray, Alzuri, Amabisca, Amador, Amago, Amalbert, Amalla, Amargos, Amarilla, Amarillas, Amaro, Amavisca, Amavizca, Amaya, Ambe, Ambeguía, Ambert, Ambía, Ambris, Ambriz, Amejorado, Amely, Amenabar, Amenedo, Amengual, Amescua, Amesguita, Amesola, Amésqua, Amesquita, Amesti, Amestoy, Amézaga, Amézcua, Amezola, Amezquita, Amézua, Amial, Amieiro, Amieva, Amigo, Amill, Amira, Amires, Amor, Amores, Amoros, Amoroz, Amóstegui, Amozurrutia, Amparán, Amparano, Amparo, Ampudia, Ampuero, Anadón, Analco, Analla, Anamosa, Anaságasti, Anaya, Anazágasty, Anchando, Anchía, Anchieta, Anchondo, Anchundía, Ancira, Anciso, Anda, Andablo, Andalón, Andaluz, Andasola, Andavazo, Andaverde, Andazola, Anderez, Andiarena, Andina, Andino, Andolid, Andraca, Andrada, Andrade, Andrades, Andrado, Andreolas, Andreu, Andrez, Andrial, Andrino, Anduaga, Andueza, Anduiza, Anduja, Andújal, Andújar, Andujo, Anduyo, Anduze, Aneiro, Aneiros, Anel, Anero, Angeles, Anglada, Anglade, Anglero, Angoco, Angón, Angueira, Anguera, Anguiano, Anguino, Anguita, Angulo, Anias, Anibarro, Anillo, Aniz, Anorga, Anquiano, Ansaldua, Ansalno, Ansiso, Ansoátegui, Ansolabehere, Ansures, Anta, Antablín, Antelo, Antequera, Antigua, Antillón, Antino, Antolín, Antolínez, Antonarchy, Antonetty, Antopia, Antrillo, Antú, Antuna, Antuñano, Antúnez, Anzalda, Anzaldo, Anzaldúa, Anzar, Anzara, Anzardo, Anzelde, Anzorena, Anzúa, Anzualda, Anzueto, Anzules, Anzures, Apablasa, Apadaca, Apaez, Apalátegui, Apalátequi, Aparicio, Apellaniz, Apezteguia, Apodaca, Apocado, Apolinar, Aponte, Aportela, Aprato, Apricio, Apuán, Aquayo, Aquero, Aqueveque, Aquiar, Aquilar, Aquilera, Aquiles, Aquillar, Aquín, Aquinaga, Aquines, Aquirre, Ara, Arabala, Arabi, Arabitg, Aracena, Arache, Aradillas, Arago, Aragón, Aragones, Aragonez, Araguas, Aragundi, Aragus, Araguz, Araica, Arain, Araiz, Araiza, Aramayo, Arambel, Arambul, Arambula, Arambulo, Aramburo, Aramburu, Aramendia, Arán, Arana, Aranalde, Aranas, Aranaz, Arancibia, Aranda, Arandia, Arando, Arandules, Aranegui, Araneta, Arango, Arangua, Aranguiz, Arangure, Aranguren, Aranibar, Aranjón, Arajo, Aranza, Aranzazu, Aranzubia, Araoz, Araque, Arater, Araugo, Araus, Arausa, Araux, Arauz, Arauza, Aravena, Aravjo, Araya, Arayata, Arballo, Arbelaez, Arbelbide, Arbello, Arbelo, Arbesú, Arbide, Arbisó, Arbizó, Arbizú, Arbolaez, Arbolay, Arboleda, Arboleya, Arbona, Arbucias, Arburua, Arca, Arcacha, Arcadia, Arcarazo, Arcas, Arcaute,

Arcay, Arcaya, Arce, Arcega, Arcelay, Arceló, Arcelona, Arcentales, Arceo, Arche, Archibeque, Archila, Archilla, Archuleta, Archuleto, Archuletta, Archulta, Archunde, Archundía, Archuteta, Archvleta, Arcía, Arciaga, Arciba, Arcides, Arciga, Arcila, Arcinas, Arciniaga, Arciniega, Arcino, Arcizo, Arcos, Arcoverde, Arculeta, Ardaiz, Ardanaz, Ardans, Ardanz, Ardavin, Ardigo, Ardila, Ardilla, Ardois, Ardón, Area, Arean, Areas, Arébalo, Arébalos, Areces, Arechaga, Arechavaleta, Areche, Arechiga, Areco, Aredondo, Aregón, Aregullín, Areizaga, Arejula, Arelano, Arellana, Arellando, Arellanes, Arellanez, Arellano, Arellanos, Arellin, Arenal, Arenas, Arenaz, Arenaza, Arencibia, Arendaín, Arenibas, Arenivar, Arenivas, Ares, Aréstegui, Areu, Aréstegui, Areu, Arévalo, Arévalos, Areyán, Areyano, Arfe, Argaez, Argaín, Argais, Arganda, Argandona, Arganza, Argeanas, Argel, Argenal, Argentín, Arbigay, Argil, Argilagos, Argiz, Argomaniz, Argote, Argudín, Argudo, Argüelies, Argüell, Argüelles, Argüellez, Argüello, Arguera, Argueso, Argueta, Arguez, Arguijo, Arguilez, Arguilles, Arguillín, Arguindegui, Arguinzoni, Argula, Argullín, Argumaniz, Argumedo, Argumosa, Aria, Arias, Ariaz, Ariaza, Aribas, Aricheta, Ariey, Ariga, Arigullín, Ariles, Ariñez, Ariño, Arisméndez, Arismendi, Arisola, Arispe, Arisso, Arista, Ariste, Aristizábal, Aristo, Aristondo, Aristud, Aristy, Ariyasu, Ariz, Ariza, Arizábal, Arizabaleta, Arizaga, Arizala, Arizaleta, Arizméndez, Arizmendi, Arizméndis, Arizméndiz, Arizola, Arizón, Arizpe, Ariztia, Arizu, Arjón, Arjona, Armada, Armadillo, Armado, Armaiz, Armandariz, Armario, Armas, Armenda, Armendares, Armendarez, Armendaris, Armendariz, Arméndez, Armendia, Armengol, Armenta, Armentero, Armenteros, Armero, Armesto, Armienta, Armigo, Armijo, Armijos, Armiñán, Armiñána, Armito, Armo, Armola, Armora, Arnado, Arnaez, Arnaiz, Arnaldo, Arnavat, Arnedo, Arnero, Arniella, Arocena, Arocha, Aroche, Arochi, Arocho, Aroiza, Aros, Arosemena, Aróstegui, Aroya, Aroyo, Aroz, Arozena, Arpón, Arqüelles, Arqüello, Arquer, Arquero, Arques, Arqueta, Arquimbau, Arquiza, Arrabal, Arrache, Arraiga, Arraiza, Arrambide, Arranaga, Arrastia, Arratia, Arraya, Arrazcaeta, Arrazola, Arrea, Arreaga, Arreala, Arreazola, Arrebola, Arreche, Arrechea, Arredendo, Arredonda, Arredondo, Arregui, Arreguín, Arreguy, Arrellano, Arrellín, Arrendo, Arrendondo, Arrenquín, Arreola, Arrequibe, Arrequín, Arrestoy, Arretche, Arrey, Arreygue, Arrezola, Arriaga, Arriago, Arriarán, Arriasola, Arriba, Arribas, Arriera, Arriero, Arrieta, Arriete, Arrietta, Arriga, Arrillaga, Arriola, Arriquidez, Arrisola, Arritola, Arrivillaga, Arrizola, Arrizón, Arrocena, Arrojas, Arrojo, Arrollado, Arrollo, Arrona, Arrondo, Arronge, Arroniz, Arronte, Arroya, Arroyas, Arroyave, Arroyo, Arroyos, Arroz, Arrue, Arrufat, Arsate, Arsola, Arsuaga, Artache, Artalejo, Artau, Artaud, Artavia, Artaza, Artea, Arteaga, Arteago, Arteche, Artecona, Artega, Artego, Artellán, Artero, Artesona, Arteta, Artiaga, Artidiello, Artieda, Artiga, Artigas, Artigo, Artiles, Artime, Artiz, Artola, Artolozaga, Arturet, Artuz, Aruca, Arufe, Aruizu, Arujo, Arus, Aruz, Arvallo, Arvayo, Arvelo, Arvisú, Arvizá, Arvizó, Arvizú, Arza, Arzábal, Arzabala, Arzaga, Arzagoitia, Arzamendi, Arzapalo, Arzate, Arzave, Arzeno,

Arzola, Arzón, Arzu, Arzuaga, Asad, Ascano, Ascar, Ascarate, Ascarrunz, Ascencio, Ascención, Ascensio, Ascunce, Asebedo, Asencio, Asención, Asenjo, Asensio, Aseo, Asevedo, Aseves, Asis, Asomoza, Aspeitia, Asperín, Aspeytia, Aspiazu, Aspillaga, Aspiras, Aspra, Aspuria, Aspuro, Aspuru, Asseo, Assis, Astacio, Astencio, Astengo, Astiazarán, Astiz, Astol, Astorga, Astrán, Astudillo, Asturias, Asúa, Asuega, Asunsolo, Asurmendi, Asusta, Atala, Atanacio, Atancio, Atayde, Ateca, Atehortua, Atencio, Atienza, Atienzo, Atilano, Atiles, Atondo, Atra, Atrio, Attencio, Atucha, Auces, Audelo, Auffant, Augilar, Auila, Auiles, Aulet, Aumada, Aurioles, Aurrecoechea, Auza, Avala, Avalo, Avalos, Avoloz, Avarca, Avechuco, Avecillas, Avelar, Avellán, Avellanal, Avellaneda, Avellanet, Avendaño, Avigael, Avila, Avilas, Avilés, Avilez, Avillán, Avilucea, Aviña, Avita, Avitea, Avitia, Avitua, Ayabarreno, Ayala, Ayalla, Ayalo, Ayán, Ayarzagoitia, Aybar, Aycart, Ayende, Ayerbe, Ayerdi, Ayerza, Ayes, Ayestaran, Ayllón, Aymat, Aymerich, Ayola, Ayón, Ayora, Ayorda, Ayuso, Aza, Azares, Azcano, Azcarate, Azcarraga, Azcarreta, Azcoitia, Azcona, Azcue, Azcui, Azcuy, Azios, Aznar, Aznarez, Azoca, Azócar, Azofra, Azor, Azoy, Azpeitia, Azpiazu, Azpiri, Azpiroz, Azúa, Azuara, Azucena, Azuela, Azueta, Azurdia.

B Babarán, Babida, Babilonia, Babio, Baca, Bacallao, Bacardi, Bacca, Bacelis, Bacerra, Bachicha, Bacilio, Bacos, Bacosa, Bada, Badajos, Badajosa, Badella, Badello, Badía, Badial, Badías, Badilla, Badillo, Badío, Badiola, Baella, Baello, Baena, Baerga, Baesa, Baez, Baeza, Baezcruz, Bagu, Bague, Baguer, Baguero, Bágues, Báguez, Bahadue, Bahamón, Bahamonde, Bahamondes, Bahamundi, Bahena, Baida, Baigen, Bailez, Bailleres, Bailón, Baires, Baisa, Baisdón, Baiz, Baiza, Bajada, Bajana, Bajandas, Baje, Bajo, Baladés, Baladéz, Balado, Baladrón, Balaez, Balagia, Balagot, Balague, Balaguer, Balaguera, Balais, Balajadía, Balandra, Balandrán, Balandrano, Balanga, Balañón, Balanza, Balarezo, Balarín, Balart, Balasquide, Balbaneda, Balbas, Balbastro, Balbín, Balbina, Balboa, Balbona, Balbontín, Balbuena, Balcácer, Balcárcel, Balcazar, Balcells, Balcorta, Baldaramos, Baldarrama, Baldarramos, Baldazo, Baldelomar, Baldenegro, Baldeón, Baldera, Balderama, Balderamos, Balderas, Balderaz, Balderos, Balderrama, Balders, Baldevarona, Baldez, Baldillez, Baldit, Baldivia, Baldiviez, Baldizán, Baldizón, Baldomero, Baldonado, Baldoquín, Baldor, Baldovino, Baldivinos, Baldoz, Baldriche, Balene, Balencia, Balerio, Balero, Balesterri, Balgos, Balia, Balido, Balina, Balizán, Balladares, Balladarez, Ballagas, Ballardo, Ballate, Ballejo, Ballejos, Balleras, Ballesta, Ballestas, Balleste, Ballester, Ballesteras, Ballestero, Ballesteros, Ballestros, Ballez, Balleza, Balli, Ballina, Ballinas, Ballote, Balmaceda, Balmana, Balmaseda, Balmores, Balosso, Balsa, Balseca, Balseiro, Balsera, Balsinde, Baltar, Baltasar, Baltazar, Baltierra, Baltierrez, Baltodano, Baluja, Balveneda, Balverde, Balzola, Bamuelos, Bana, Banaga, Banagas, Bañales, Banando, Banarer, Banares, Bances, Banciella, Banda,

Banderas, Bandín, Bandurraga, Banegas, Báñez, Baniqued, Baños, Banrey, Bañuelas, Bañuelos, Banuet, Banvelos, Bao, Baptisto, Baquedano, Baquera, Baquerizo, Baquero, Baquirán, Baragán, Baragana, Baragas, Barahona, Barajas, Barajos, Baralt, Baranda, Barandiarán, Barasorda, Baray, Baraz, Barba, Barbachano, Barbarena, Barbasa, Barbeito, Barberán, Barberena, Barboa, Barbola, Barbontín, Barbosa, Barcala, Barceló, Barcelón, Barcena, Barcenas, Barcenes, Barcenez, Barcenilla, Barcía, Barcigalupia, Barcinas, Barcino, Barcón, Barcos, Bardales, Bardinas, Bardisa, Barea, Bared, Barela, Barelas, Barenco, Bareno, Baretto, Bárez, Bargara, Bargas, Bargos, Barguiarena, Barillas, Barín, Bariñas, Barloco, Barnachea, Baro, Barocio, Barojas, Baros, Barosela, Baroz, Barquera, Barquero, Barquet, Barquez, Barquín, Barrad, Barragán, Barragar, Barragón, Barrajas, Barral, Barrales, Barrameda, Barrandey, Barrano, Barrantes, Barrque, Barrara, Barrasa, Barratachea, Barraz, Barraza, Barreda, Barredo, Barrego, Barreiro, Barrena, Barreneche, Barrenechea, Barreno, Barrera, Barreragarcia, Barreras, Barreraz, Barrero, Barreta, Barreto, Barrezueta, Barria, Barriaga, Barrial, Barrias, Barrientes, Barrientez, Barriento, Barrientos, Barriera, Barriero, Barriga, Barrillas, Barrio, Barrionuevo, Barrios, Barro, Barrocas, Barrona, Barrosa, Barroso, Barroterán, Barroza, Barrozo, Barroterán, Barroza, Barrozo, Barrueco, Barrueta, Barsenas, Bartolomé, Bartolomey, Barturen, Barza, Barzaga, Barzana, Barzilla, Barziza, Barzola, Bas, Basabe, Basadre, Basites, Basaldo, Basaldu, Basaldúa, Basaldúe, Basallo, Basalo, Basalova, Basáñes, Basáñez, Basaño, Basantes, Bascón, Basconcillo, Bascoy, Bascuas, Basdeo, Basilla, Basoco, Basora, Básques, Básquez, Bastanchury, Bastardo, Basterrechea, Bástida, Bástidas, Bástidos, Basúa, Basualdo, Basulto, Basura, Basurco, Basurto, Batalla, Batallán, Batán, Batanides, Batilla, Batine, Batist, Batista, Batiz, Batiza, Batlle, Batllia, Batres, Batrez, Batriz, Batule, Bausa, Baustista, Bauta, Bautista, Bauza, Bauzo, Bayanilla, Bayardo, Bayarena, Bayas, Baycora, Baydes, Baylina, Baylón, Bayo, Bayón, Bayona, Bayrón, Bayuga, Baza, Bazain, Bazaldúa, Bazamán, Bazán, Bazaure, Bazúa, Bazurto, Beada, Beanes, Beas, Beaz, Becaria, Beccera, Beccerra, Beceiro, Becena, Becera, Becerra, Becerril, Becerro, Bechara, Becho, Becuar, Bedía, Bedolla, Bedoy, Bedoya, Bega, Begano, Begona, Beguiristain, Beiro, Beistegui, Beitia, Beitra, Béjar, Bejarán, Bejarano, Bejerano, Bejínes, Bejínez, Bela, Belancourt, Belandres, Belarde, Belardes, Belardo, Belásquez, Belásquida, Belaunde, Belaunzarán, Belaústegui, Belaval, Bélchez, Belderol, Belén, Beléndez, Belette, Belez, Belio, Bellaflores, Bellez, Belliard, Bellido, Bellmas, Belloso, Belmares, Belmarez, Belmontes, Belmontez, Belmúdes, Belmúdez, Belmas, Beloz, Beltra, Beltrán, Beltranena, Beltre, Belvado, Benabé, Benabides, Benado, Benalcázar, Benallo, Benauides, Benavediz, Benavent, Benavente, Benavidas, Benavides, Benavidez, Benavidos, Bencomo, Bencosme, Bendalín, Bendamio, Benegas, Beneján, Benero, Benestante, Benetez, Benevídez, Bengoa, Bengochea, Beníguez, Benine, Beníquez, Benítes, Benítez, Benito, Benitoa, Benovidez, Benta, Bentancour, Bentancourt, Bentancud, Bentancur,

Bentura, Benudiz, Benún, Benzaquen, Beovides, Bequer, Berain, Berasátegui, Beraza, Berbán, Berbena, Berber, Berberena, Bercedonis, Berdeal, Berdecia, Berdeja, Berdejo, Berdugo, Berdusco, Berea, Bereal, Berenguer, Bereny, Bergado, Bergara, Bergez, Bergolla, Bericochea, Berján, Berlanga, Berlango, Bermea, Bermejillo, Bermejo, Bermeo, Bermuda, Bermúdes, Bermúdez, Bermúndez, Bernabé, Bernal, Bernáldez, Bernall, Bernárdez, Berndes, Bernell, Bernez, Bernúdez, Beroiz, Beronda, Berrayarza, Berreles, Berrelez, Berrellez, Berrelleza, Berrera, Berreyesa, Berríos, Berriozábal, Berriz, Berroa, Berrocal, Berrocales, Berrones, Berros, Berrospe, Berroterán, Berru, Berruesco, Berruescos, Bersosa, Bersoza, Bertaina, Bertot, Bertrán, Berubén, Berumén, Beruvides, Berzoza, Besa, Besada, Besares, Bescos, Beserra, Besinaiz, Bestard, Besteiro, Besú, Betance, Betances, Betancis, Betancourt, Betancourth, Betancur, Betancurt, Beteta, Bethencourt, Betoncourt, Betrán, Béxar, Beza, Bezanilla, Bezares, Bezerra, Biane, Bianes, Biangel, Biar, Biascoechea, Bibian, Bibiano, Bibiloni, Bilbao, Bilbraut, Billafranco, Billalba, Billalobos, Billescas, Biñas, Binelo, Bingochea, Binimelis, Birba, Birondo, Birriel, Birrueta, Bisa, Bisbal, Biscailuz, Biscaino, Biscayart, Bistrain, Bisuano, Bitela, Bithorn, Bitolas, Bladuell, Blajos, Blancarte, Blancas, Blanco, Blancocerda, Blanes, Blanquet, Blánquez, Blánquiz, Blásquez, Blaya, Blázquez, Blea, Blondet, Boada, Boado, Bobadilla, Bobadillo, Bobe, Bobea, Bobeda, Bobele, Bobián, Bobillo, Bocachica, Bocanegra, Bocardo, Bochas, Bodero, Bodiroga, Boeras, Boez, Bofill, Bogarín, Bohórquez, Boiles, Boites, Bojórges, Bojórguez, Bojórques, Bojórquez, Boladeres, Bolado, Bolaño, Bolaños, Boleda, Bolet, Bolivar, Boloix, Boltares, Bolufe, Bombalier, Bonachea, Bonafont, Bonal, Bonales, Bonefont, Bonet, Boneta, Boniche, Bonilla, Bonillas, Bonillo, Bonuz, Borad, Borboa, Borbolla, Borbón, Bordagaray, Bordallo, Bordano, Bordayo, Bordegaray, Bordenave, Bordoy, Borego, Borela, Borepo, Bórguez, Borja, Borjas, Borjón, Bornia, Boronda, Borondo, Borovay, Bórquez, Borrajo, Borras, Borrayo, Borrego, Borrer, Borrero, Borrico, Borrios, Borroel, Borroto, Borruel, Borunda, Bosmenier, Bosque, Bósques, Bósquez, Botana, Botard, Botas, Botell, Botella, Botello, Botero, Botiller, Botillo, Boucourt, Boullón, Bouza, Bouzas, Bovadilla, Boveda, Boves, Bracamonte, Bracamontes, Bracamontez, Bracero, Braceros, Bracho, Brador, Bramasco, Brambila, Brambill, Bran, Brana, Brancacho, Brancacio, Brandariz, Brañuelas, Brasselero, Brasuel, Braulio, Bravo, Brea, Breceda, Breijo, Brema, Brenes, Brenlla, Bretado, Breto, Bretos, Briales, Briano, Brias, Bribiesca, Bribiescas, Briceño, Brieno, Brieva, Brignoni, Brijalba, Brijil, Brillantes, Bringas, Brínguez, Brío, Briones, Brionez, Briseño, Brisita, Briso, Brisuela, Brito, Briz, Brizal, Brizeño, Brizo, Brizuela, Brocas, Broche, Brondo, Brotons, Brucelas, Bruciaga, Brugera, Brugeras, Brusuelas, Bruzos, Buantello, Bubela, Buceta, Bucio, Buelna, Buenabad, Buenafé, Buenaventura, Buenconsejo, Buendel, Buendía, Buenfil, Bueno, Buenrostro, Buenrrostro, Buensuceso, Buentello, Buenteo, Buentiempo, Buentillo, Bueras, Bueres, Buergo, Bufanda, Bugallo, Bugarín, Buigas, Buigues, Builes, Builtrón, Buitrago, Buitrón, Buitureida, Buitureira, Buján,

Bujanda, Bujanos, Bujosa, Bulerín, Bullas, Bulnes, Bulos, Bultrón, Burbano, Burboa, Burcet, Burciaga, Burciago, Burcos, Burdeos, Burgado, Burgoa, Burgos, Burguán, Burgueño, Burguete, Buriel, Burillo, Buritica, Burneo, Burnias, Búrquez, Burra, Burriel, Burriola, Burrola, Burrón, Burruel, Bursiaga, Buruato, Busigo, Busquet, Busquets, Bustabad, Bustabade, Bustamante, Bustamantes, Bustamantez, Bustamarte, Bustamente, Bustamonte, Bustanante, Bustas, Busted, Bustelo, Bustemante, Bustillo, Bustillos, Bustinza, Bustio, Busto, Bustos, Bustoz, Busutil, Butanda, Butero, Butrón, Buttanda, Buxeda, Buxo, Buyon, Buzani, Buznego, Buzo.

C Caal, Caamal, Caamaño, Caampued, Caba, Cabada, Cabal, Cabaleiro, Caballa, Caballer, Caballero, Caballeros, Caballes, Caballo, Cabán, Cabañas, Cabanelas, Cabanero, Cabanillas, Cabanzón, Cabarcas, Cabarcos, Cabarga, Cabasa, Cabasier, Cabasos, Cabassa, Cabasso, Cabaza, Cabazos, Cabeiro, Cabeje, Cabellero, Cabello, Cabera, Caberera, Caberra, Cabesuela, Cabeza, Cabezadebaca, Cabezas, Cabezudo, Cabezuela, Cabias, Cabido, Cabeides, Cabigas, Cabillo, Cabla, Cabrales, Cabralez, Cabranes, Cabre, Cabreja, Cabrejas, Cabrejos, Cabrer, Cabrera, Cabreras, Cabrerizo, Cabrero, Cabrerra, Cabret, Cabreva, Cabriales, Cabrieles, Cabriles, Cabrillo, Cabrillos, Cabrisas, Cabrito, Cabrón, Cabuena, Cabuto, Caceras, Cáceres, Cácerez, Cacharrón, Cacho, Cachón, Cachora, Cachua, Cacicedo, Cadahia, Cadava, Cadaval, Cadavid, Cadavieco, Cadema, Cadena, Cadenas, Cadenaz, Cadengo, Cadierno, Cadilla, Cadillo, Cádis, Cádiz, Cadorniga, Cadriel, Cagiga, Cagigal, Cagigas, Caguias, Cahue, Caicedo, Caigoy, Caillau, Cainas, Cainzos, Cajar, Cajas, Cajen, Cajero, Cajiao, Cajide, Cajiga, Cajigal, Cajigas, Cajina, Cajo, Cajuste, Calabaza, Calafat, Calafell, Calama, Calamaco, Calamars, Calamón, Calana, Calanche, Calandres, Calas, Calaytayud, Calbillo, Calcado, Calcaneo, Calcano, Calcines, Calda, Caldarón, Caldas, Caldelas, Caldera, Calderas, Calderilla, Calderín, Caldero, Calderón, Caldevilla, Calejo, Calenzani, Calera, Calero, Calez, Calibo, Calienes, Calix, Calixto, Calixtro, Cáliz, Callado, Callanta, Callava, Callazo, Calle, Calleiro, Callejas, Callejo, Callejón, Callejos, Callella, Calleros, Calles, Calleyro, Callinicos, Callistro, Caloca, Calomarde, Calonga, Calonge, Calonje, Calsada, Calsadillas, Calveiro, Calvera, Calvero, Calves, Calvet, Calvillo, Calvo, Calzada, Calzadías, Calzadilla, Calzadillas, Calzado, Calzia, Calzoncín, Camach, Camache, Camacho, Camama, Camancho, Camanez, Camaño, Camaraza, Camarella, Camarena, Camareno, Camarero, Camargo, Camarillo, Camaro, Camarón, Camarrillo, Camaya, Camayd, Camba, Cambaliza, Cambero, Camberos, Cambianica, Cambis, Camblor, Cambo, Cambón, Camcho, Camejo, Camerena, Camero, Camez, Camilo, Camiña, Camiñas, Caminero, Camocho, Camoroda, Campa, Campacos, Campaneria, Campanioni, Campas, Campaz, Campero, Campillo, Campins, Campirano, Campista, Campiz, Campoamor, Campodonica, Campolla, Campomanes, Camporredondo, Campos, Campsagrado, Campoverde, Campoy, Campoz, Campozano, Campusano, Campuzano,

Camueiras, Camunas, Camunes, Camunez, Cana, Canaba, Canabal, Canabate, Canahuati, Canalda, Canalejo, Canales, Canalez, Canalita, Canals, Cañamar, Cañamero, Cañas, Cañava, Cañavati, Cañaveral, Cañaves, Cancel, Cancela, Cancelo, Canche, Canchola, Cancino, Cancinos, Cancio, Candales, Candanedo, Candano, Candanosa, Candanoza, Candelari, Candelaria, Candelarie, Candelario, Candelas, Candeleria, Candía, Candías, Caneda, Canedo, Canegata, Caneiro, Canela, Canellas, Canellis, Canelo, Canero, Canes, Canet, Cañete, Cáñez, Canga, Cangas, Canion, Canisales, Canizal, Canizales, Canizalez, Canizares, Canizarez, Canjura, Canlas, Cano, Canovas, Canseco, Cansino, Cantarero, Cantero, Cantillo, Cantorán, Cantos, Cantou, Cantoya, Canire, Canires, Cantú, Cantúa, Cantútijerina, Cañuelas, Canzona, Capablanca, Capacete, Caparra, Caparros, Capas, Capata, Capdevila, Capeles, Capellán, Capelo, Caperón, Capestany, Capetillo, Capifali, Capilla, Capín, Capiro, Capistrán, Caplano, Capmany, Capote, Capriles, Caprine, Capuchín, Capuchina, Capuchino, Caquias, Caraba, Carabajar, Carabal, Caraballo, Caraballopérez, Carabantes, Carabay, Carabaza, Carabella, Carabeo, Carabes, Carabez, Caracena, Caracheo, Caracosa, Caracoza, Carajal, Caralt, Carambot, Carameros, Carames, Caramillo, Caranta, Caranza, Carapia, Carara, Carasa, Carasco, Caratachea, Caratán, Carattini, Caravaca, Caravajal, Caravantes, Caravayo, Caraveo, Caraves, Caraza, Carazo, Carba, Carbajal, Carbajales, Carbajo, Carballar, Carballea, Carballeira, Carballido, Carballo, Carballosa, Carbellido, Carbia, Carbonel, Carbot, Carcache, Carcamo, Carcana, Carcanaques, Carcano, Carcas, Carcellero, Cardelle, Cardelles, Cardena, Cardenal, Cardenales, Cárdenas, Cárdenaz, Cárdenes, Cárdenez, Cardeno, Cardenos, Cardenosa, Cardentey, Cardet, Cardeza, Cardiel, Cardinas, Cardinez, Cardona, Cardonas, Cardosa, Cardova, Careaga, Carela, Careta, Carias, Caribe, Caride, Carides, Carielo, Cariga, Carillo, Caringal, Carinhas, Carire, Carisalez, Carla, Carletello, Carlos, Carmenate, Carmenates, Carmenaty, Carmoega, Carmona, Carnera, Carnero, Carnicer, Carnicero, Caro, Caronado, Caropino, Carpena, Carpintero, Carpinteyro, Carpio, Carpizo, Carraballo, Carracedo, Carrada, Carradero, Carral, Carralejo, Carralero, Carrales, Carralez, Carraman, Carranca, Carranco, Carrandi, Carransa, Carranza, Carrasco, Carrascosa, Carrasguillo, Carraso, Carrasquilla, Carrasquillo, Carratala, Carrau, Carrazana, Carrazco, Carreaga, Carredo, Carrejo, Carreno, Carreón, Carrera, Carreras, Carrero, Carrete, Carretero, Carreto, Carriaga, Carriazo, Carrica, Carricaburu, Carricarte, Carrido, Carriedo, Carrijo, Carril, Carriles, Carrilla, Carrille, Carrillo, Carrilo, Carrio, Carrión, Carrique, Carrisal, Carrisales, Carrisalez, Carrisosa, Carrisoza, Carrizal, Carrizales, Carrizalez, Carrizo, Carrizosa, Carrizoza, Carrodeguas, Carrola, Carrosquillo, Carrsco, Carruesco, Cartagen, Cartagena, Cartago, Cartana, Cartas, Cartaya, Caruajal, Carvajal, Carvajales, Carvajalino, Casablanca, Casabo, Casadas, Casades, Casado, Casados, Casais, Casal, Casales, Casals, Casamayor, Casanas, Casanora, Casanova, Casanovas, Casanueva, Casares, Casarez, Casariego, Casarrubias, Casas, Casasnovas,

Casasola, Casagus, Casaus, Casavantes, Cascante, Cascon, Cascos, Cascudo, Caselas, Casellas, Cáseras, Cáseres, Caserma, Casero, Caserza, Cases, Casia, Casián, Casiano, Casias, Casica, Casielles, Casilla, Casillán, Casillas, Casillos, Casines, Casique, Casiquito, Casis, Casmero, Casorla, Casparis, Caspillo, Cássares, Cassas, Cassias, Cassillas, Cassinerio, Casso, Castaigne, Castan, Castaña, Castañada, Castañares, Castañeada, Castañed, Castañeda, Castañedo, Castaner, Castanieto, Castaño, Castañola, Castañón, Castaños, Castañuela, Castany, Castejón, Castela, Castelán, Castelano, Castelao, Castelar, Castelazo, Castelblanco, Casteldeoro, Casteleiro, Castellanas, Castellanes, Castellanos, Castellanoz, Castellar, Castellón, Castelis, Castellvi, Castelnau, Casteló, Casteñada, Casteñeda, Castiblanco, Castiel, Castilio, Castill, Castilla, Castillanos, Castillas, Castilleja, Castillejo, Castillejos, Castillero, Castillio, Castillo, Castillón, Castineira, Castineiras, Castineyra, Castorena, Castoreno, Castra, Castrejón, Castrellón, Castresana, Castrillo, Castrillón, Castriz, Castro, Castrodad, Castroman, Castrón, Castroverde, Castruita, Casul, Casuso, Cata, Catacalos, Catache, Catala, Catalán, Catalena, Catanach, Cataño, Cataquet, Catasca, Catasus, Cateora, Catete, Católico, Catzeola, Cauazos, Cauce, Caudales, Caudillo, Caula, Caunder, Causo, Cavanas, Cavasas, Cavasos, Cavaz, Cavazas, Cavazos, Cavazoz, Caveda, Cavero, Caveza, Caviedes, Caviel, Cavla, Cavos, Cavozos, Cayado, Cayaman, Caycedo, Cayere, Cayeros, Cayias, Cayón, Cayuela, Cayuso, Cazamias, Cazanas, Cazares, Cazarez, Cazarin, Cazón, Cdebace, Cdevaca, Cebada, Ceballes, Ceballo, Ceballos, Cebey, Cebollero, Cebrero, Cebreros, Cebrián, Cecena, Cedaño, Cedeño, Cedillo, Cedillos, Cediño, Cedo, Cegarra, Cegueda, Ceide, Ceijas, Ceja, Cejas, Cejo, Cejudo, Cela, Celada, Celado, Celardo, Celaya, Celayeta, Celedón, Celeiro, Celiceo, Celis, Celiz, Celorio, Cena, Cendah, Cendejas, Cendoya, Ceniceros, Ceniseros, Ceniseroz, Cenoz, Ceniellas, Centeno, Centero, Centurión, Cepeda, Cépedes, Cepero, Cerabella, Ceralde, Cerbantes, Cerbantez, Cercado, Cerda, Cerdeira, Cerdeiras, Cereceda, Cerecedes, Cerecedo, Cereceres, Cerecerez, Cerecero, Cereijo, Cerezo, Cerín, Cermeño, Cerna, Cernas, Cerno, Cernuda, Cerón, Cerpa, Cerrillo, Cerrillos, Cerritos, Cerros, Certeza, Ceruantes, Cervanes, Cervante, Cervantes, Cervantez, Cerventes, Cervera, Cesani, Cesena, Cesín, Céspedes, Céspedez, Cestero, Cevallo, Cevallos, Cevilla, Ceyanes, Chabarría, Chabera, Chábez, Chabolla, Chaboya, Chabrier, Chaca, Chacanaca, Chacón, Chades, Chadez, Chaffino, Chafino, Chagas, Chagolla, Chagollán, Chagoy, Chagoya, Chagoyán, Chagoyen, Chagra, Chaguaceda, Chaides, Chaidez, Chaira, Chairez, Chala, Chalambaga, Chaldu, Chamartín, Chamizo, Chamoro, Chamorro, Chandarlis, Cháñes, Cháñez, Changala, Chano, Chanona, Chantaca, Chantala, Chantres, Chapa, Chaparro, Chapela, Chaparro, Chapela, Chapero, Chapoy, Chapparo, Chapralis, Chaprón, Charafa, Charanza, Charba, Charbula, Charca, Charcas, Chardón, Charfauros, Chaneco, Charo, Charres, Charría, Charriez, Charrín, Charris, Charro, Charvez, Chatón, Chauarría, Chavana, Chavanna, Chavarela, Chavaría, Chavarillo, Chavarín, Chavarra, Chavarri, Chavarría, Chavarriaga,

Chavarro, Chaveco, Chavera, Chavero, Chávez, Chaviano, Chavira, Chaviro, Chavolla, Chavoya, Chayra, Chayre, Chayrez, Chazaro, Chazarreta, Checa, Checo, Cheda, Chemali, Chente, Cherena, Cherene, Cherino, Cherta, Chessani, Chevannes, Chevarría, Chevas, Cheveres, Cheverez, Chevez, Chevres, Chiago, Chiapa, Chica, Chicas, Chico, Chicvara, Chide, Chifalo, Chihuahua, Chilimidos, Chimal, Chinana, Chinchilla, Chinea, Chino, Chiong, Chiono, Chiovare, Chipi, Chipres, Chiques, Chiquete, Chiquito, Chiriboga, Chirino, Chirinos, Choa, Cholico, Chomat, Chomori, Chono, Choperena, Chorna, Choto, Chouza, Choza, Chuca, Chudalla, Chumacero, Chumiso, Chupe, Churbe, Churruca, Ciberay, Cibrián, Cicerón, Cicilia, Cid, Ciddio, Ciego, Ciena, Ciénega, Ciénegas, Cienfuegos, Cierra, Cifré, Cifredo, Cifuentes, Cigar, Cigarroa, Cillero, Cimadevilla, Cimarrón, Cimental, Cindo, Cineus, Cinia, Cinias, Cintora, Cinira, Cintrón, Cionco, Cipres, Cirerol, Cires, Ciria, Cirilco, Cirilo, Ciriza, Cirlos, Ciruli, Cisner, Cisneras, Cisnernos, Cisnero, Cisneros, Cisneroz, Cisterna, Civerolo, Clara, Clarit, Claro, Claros, Clarot, Claudio, Claustro, Clavel, Clavell, Clavelo, Claverán, Clavería, Clavero, Clavijo, Clemena, Clero, Climent, Coba, Coballes, Cobar, Cobarrubia, Cobarrubias, Cobarrubio, Cobarruvias, Cobas, Cobelo, Cobeo, Cobián, Cobiella, Cobio, Cobo, Cobos, Cobreiro, Coca, Cocio, Codina, Codón, Codorniz, Coello, Cofino, Cofresi, Coira, Colación, Colaco, Colarte, Colas, Colato, Colca, Colchado, Colderón, Coldivar, Colegio, Colet, Colima, Colina, Colindres, Colio, Collada, Collado, Collantes, Collaso, Collazo, Colls, Colmenar, Colmenares, Colmenero, Colocho, Colocio, Colodro, Colóm, Coloma, Colomar, Colombana, Colombani, Colombero, Colome, Colomer, Colomes, Colominas, Colono, Colón, Colondres, Colonnetta, Colontorres, Colorado, Colorbio, Colore, Colores, Coloroso, Colsa, Coluoro, Columbie, Colunga, Comacho, Comadurán, Comas, Combarro, Comellas, Comesana, Comesanas, Común, Comorre, Companioni, Comparán, Compary, Compean, Compián, Compito, Compos, Comptis, Concepción, Conceptión, Concha, Conchado, Conchas, Concho, Conchola, Conchos, Chondado, Condarco, Conde, Condensa, Conejero, Conejo, Conesa, Conforme, Conrado, Conreras, Conríque, Conríquez, Cons, Consonero, Constancio, Constante, Consuegra, Consuelo, Contador, Contemprato, Conteras, Contereas, Contero, Contival, Contraras, Contreas, Contrera, Contreras, Contrerass, Contreraz, Contreres, Contreros, Contrerras, Contresas, Contrestano, Contrevas, Copado, Copetillo, Copriviza, Coquoz, Cora, Corales, Coranado, Corazón, Corbala, Corbea, Corbella, Corbera, Corces, Corchado, Corchero, Corchete, Corcho, Corcino, Corcoles, Corcovelos, Cordeniz, Cordero, Cordillo, Córdoba, Cordobés, Cordola, Cordona, Cordoso, Córdova, Cordover, Cordovés, Cordovéz, Cordovi, Cordoza, Coreano, Corella, Corenie, Coria, Coriano, Coriat, Coriz, Cormalis, Cornejo, Cornejos, Cornide, Corniell, Cornier, Corodova, Coroninas, Corona, Coronada, Coronado, Coronas, Coronel, Corpas, Corpión, Corporán, Corpus, Corrada, Corral, Corralejo, Corrales, Corralez, Corraliza, Corralls, Corrca, Correa, Corredera, Corredor, Correo, Corres, Corretjer,

Correu, Corrillo, Corripio, Corriz, Corros, Cortada, Cortaza, Cortazar, Cortes, Cortez, Cortijo, Cortina, Cortinas, Cortinaz, Cortines, Cortinez, Cortizo, Corusedo, Corujo, Corván, Corvera, Corvison, Corza, Corzo, Cos, Cosculluela, Cosillo, Cosillos, Cosío, Cosme, Cossío, Cosso, Costales, Costelón, Costilla, Costillo, Costoso, Costruba, Cota, Cotarelo, Cotayo, Cotelo, Cotera, Coterillo, Cotero, Cotilla, Cotinola, Cotitta, Coto, Cotrina, Cottes, Cotto, Cotulla, Couarrubias, Couce, Couceyro, Coumparoules, Couso, Coutin, Coutino, Couvertier, Covarrubia, Covarrubias, Covarrubiaz, Covarrubio, Covarruvias, Covarrybias, Covarubias, Covas, Covian, Covillo, Covio, Covo, Covos, Coya, Coyazo, Creitoff, Cremar, Cremata, Crespín, Crespo, Criado, Cribeiro, Criollo, Crioyos, Crisantes, Crisanto, Crisantos, Crisosto, Crisostomo, Cristales, Cristan, Cristancho, Cristerna, Cristia, Cristián, Cristín, Cristóbal, Cristófol, Crixell, Crosas, Croz, Cruanes, Cruanyas, Cruces, Cruceta, Cruz, Cruzado, Cruzat, Cruzata, Cruzcosa, Cruzcruz, Cruzón, Cruzrodríguez, Cuadra, Cuadrado, Cuadras, Cuadraz, Cuadro, Cuadros, Cuan, Cuara, Cuarenta, Cuarón, Cuartas, Cuascut, Cuate, Cubano, Cubas, Cubenas, Cubero, Cubias, Cubillas, Cubillo, Cubillos, Cubio, Cubriel, Cucalón, Cucuta, Cueba, Cuebas, Culiar, Cuella, Cuéllar, Cuéller, Cuello, Cuen, Cuenca, Cuenco, Cuentas, Cuento, Cuerdo, Cuero, Cuervo, Cuesta, Cuestas, Cueto, Cueva, Cuevas, Cuevaz, Cuevos, Cuilan, Cuin, Cuizón, Culebro, Cultreri, Cumba, Cumpián, Cumpiano, Cuñanán, Cúñes, Cúñez, Cuni, Cunill, Cunyus, Cupeles, Cuprill, Cura, Curbello, Curbelo, Curet, Curiel, Currais, Curras, Currea, Curz, Cusco, Custodia, Custodio, Cutie, Cuya, Cuyar, Cuza.

D Dábalos, Dábila, Dacumos, Dagnesses, Dago, Daguerre, Daguilar, Dalama, Dalbosco, Dalipe, Dalmau, Dalmida, Damache, Dantus, Dapeña, Dardanes, Dardiz, Dardón, Darias, Darnauo, Darquea, Darriba, Daruna, Dastas, Datil, Daubar, Dáuila, Dausa, Dauz, Dávalos, Dávila, Dávilas, Dávilla, Dávilo, Daza, Dcruz, Deagen, Deagüero, Deaguilar, Deaguirre, Dealba, Dealcalá, Dealejandro, Dealva, Deálvarez, Deamador, Deanda, Deande, Deandrés, Deaqüero Dearagón, Dearce, Dearco, Dearcos, Dearellano, Dearias, Dearmas, Dearo, Dearriba, Dearrillaga, Dearroyo, Dearteaga, Deases, Deávila, Deayala, Deazevedo, Debaca, Debare, Debarra, Debatista, Debato, Debayona, Debesa, Debonilla, Debras, Debravo, Debruyán, Debueno, Decabral, Decalderón, Decalle, Decamacho, Decantú, Decapriles, Decárdenas, Decasas, Decaso, Decastañeda, Decastillo, Decastro, Decena, Decerda, Decervantes, Decéspedes, Dechávez, Dechoudens, Deciga, Declet, Decollado, Decolón, Decontreras, Decórdoba, Decórdova, Decoro, Decorona, Decoronado, Decorse, Decortez, Decos, Decristino, Decruz, Decueva, Decuevas, Dedelgado, Dedías, Dediego, Dedios, Dedomínguez, Deduarte, Deesparza, Deesirado, Defalcón, Defalla, Deferia, Defernández, Defex, Defiesta, Defigueroa, Defillo, Deflores, Defrese, Defrisco, Defuentes, Degani, Degaray, Degarcía, Degarza, Degelia, Degoes, Degollado, Degómez,

Degonzáles, Degonzález, Degracia, Deguara, Deguardia, Deguerra, Deguerrero, Deguevara, Deguimera, Degutiérrez, Deguzmán, Deharo, Dehernández, Deherrera, Dehesa, Dehombre, Dehorta, Dehostos, Dehoyas, Dehoyos, Deibarra, Deida, Deimes, Deiro, Deisla, Deita, Deiturrondo, Dejara, Dejáuregui, Dejesu, Dejesús, Dejesúsgarcía, Dejesúsortiz, Dejímenez, Dejoria, Dejuan, Delaarena, Delabarca, Delabarcena, Delabarrera, Delabarza, Delabra, Delacabada, Delacal, Delacalle, Delacamara, Delacampa, Delacanal, Delacerda, Delachica, Delaconcepción, Delaconcha, Delacorte, Delacotera, Delacruz, Delacuadra, Delacuesta, Delacueva, Delacurz, Delaespriella, Delafe, Delafuente, Delafuentes, Delafunte, Delagadillo, Delagado, Delagarrigue, Delagarza, Delagdo, Delagrana, Delaguardia, Delaguerra, Delaguila, Delahera, Delaherrán, Delahoya, Delahoz, Delahuerta, Delaisla, Delajara, Delalastra, Delalcazar, Delallata, Delallave, Delallera, Delaloza, Delalto, Delaluz, Delamadrid, Delamancha, Delamata, Delamaza, Delamella, Delamerced, Delamo, Delamora, Delamorena, Delamota, Delanda, Delangel, Delanoval, Delanuez, Delao, Delaosa, Delaossa, Delaparra, Delapass, Delapaz, Delapeña, Delapeza, Delapiedra, Delaplata, Delaportilla, Delapoza, Delaprida, Delapuente, Delara, Delarea, Delareza, Delaríos, Delariva, Delaroca, Delarocha, Delarosa, Delaroza, Delarra, Delarroyo, Delarua, Delasantos, Delascasas, Delascuevas, Delaserna, Delasheras, Delasierra, Delateja, Delatejera, Delatoba, Delatorre, Delatorres, Delatorriente, Delatrinidad, Delauz, Delavara, Delavega, Delavellano, Delavictoria, Delaviña, Delaya, Delazerda, Delbarrio, Delblanco, Delbósque, Delbósquez, Delbózque, Delbrey, Delbusto, Delcado, Delcalvo, Delcampillo, Delcampo, Delcastillo, Delcastro, Delcerro, Delcid, Delcollado, Delcorral, Delcorro, Delcristo, Delcueto, Delcurto, Deldago, Deleganis, Deleija, Deleón, Delerío, Delerne, Delescaille, Deleza, Delfante, Delfierro, Delfín, Delfrancia, Delgada, Delgadill, Delgadillo, Delgado, Delgadodeoramas, Delgiorgio, Delgodo, Delharo, Delhierro, Delhoyo, Deliganis, Delira, Deliseo, Deliz, Deljunco, Dellano, Delllano, Delmargo, Delmendo, Delmercado, Delmoral, Delmundo, Delmuro, Delnodal, Deloa, Deloen, Deloera, Delolmo, Delópez, Delora, Deloro, Delosada, Delosángeles, Delosantos, Deloscobos, Delosmonteros, Delosprados, Delosreyes, Delosríos, Delossant, Delossantos, Deloya, Deloyola, Deloza, Delozada, Delpalacio, Delpardo, Delpilar, Delpín, Delpinal, Delpino, Delportillo, Delposo, Delpozo, Delprado, Delpuerto, Delrazo, Delreal, Delrey, Delrico, Delriego, Delrincón, Delrío, Delrisco, Delrivero, Delrosal, Delrosario, Delsalto, Delsol, Deltejo, Deltiempo, Deltoro, Delua, Deluao, Deluján, Deluna, Delval, Delvalle, Delvillar, Delvino, Demacias, Demalade, Demarchena, Demarín, Demarquez, Demarrero, Demartínez, Demata, Dematas, Demateo, Demedina, Demeire, Demena, Deméndez, Demendoza, Demercado, Demesa, Demiguel, Demiranda, Demolina, Demontebello, Demontes, Demonteverde, Demontoya, Demorales, Demoreno, Demoya, Demúñoz, Demurga, Dena, Denava, Denavarro, Denavas, Denavejar, Denecochea, Denieves, Deniña, Denogean, Denoriega, Denúñez, Deoca, Deocampo, Deochoa, Deoleo,

Deoliviera, Deolmo, Deoro, Deorta, Deortega, Deortiz, Deosdade, Deosorio, Deoteris, Deotero, Depablo, Depacheco, Depaco, Depadilla, Deparra, Depaz, Depedro, Depeña, Depérez, Deplata, Deponce, Deportillo, Deporto, Deportola, Depozo, Deprad, Deprado, Dequesada, Dequevedo, Dequintana, Dequiroz, Deramírez, Deramos, Deras, Derenia, Dereyes, Deríos, Derivas, Derivera, Derma, Derobles, Deroca, Derodríguez, Derodríquez, Derojas, Deromero, Derosario, Deroza, Derrera, Derubio, Derueda, Deruisa, Desabota, Desáenz, Desalas, Desalazar, Desalernos, Desales, Desalinas, Desánchez, Desantiago, Desantiasgo, Desantos, Desaracho, Descalzo, Desevilla, Desierra, Desiga, Desocarrás, Desocarráz, Desolo, Desosa, Desoto, Desotomayor, Despania, Desplantes, Después, Desraviñes, Dessero, Destrada, Desuacido, Detapia, Detejada, Detevis, Detoledo, Detorres, Detranaltes, Detrés, Detrinidad, Deulloa, Devaca, Devaldez, Devalencia, Devalle, Devalón, Devara, Devargas, Devarona, Devásquez, Devázquez, Devega, Develasco, Devélez, Devencenty, Devera, Devia, Devian, Devicente, Devictoria, Devila, Devilla, Devillar, Devillegas, Devolin, Deya, Deycaza, Deynes, Deza, Dezamora, Dezara, Dezarraga, Dezayas, Dezúñiga, Diacos, Diago, Diamos, Diasdeleón, Díaz, Díazacevedo, Díazcolón, Díazcruz, Díazdearce, Díazdelcampo, Díazdelcastillo, Díazdeleón, Díazdevillegas, Díazmedina, Díazpiedra, Díazrivera, Díazrodríguez, Diego, Dieguez, Dieppa, Diez, Dimas, Diodonet, Diodosio, Diones, Dios, Diosdado, Dioses, Directo, Disarufino, Disla, Distabile, Dobal, Dobao, Dobarganes, Doblado, Docal, Docampo, Doce, Dojáquez, Dolatre, Dolmo, Domena, Domenech, Doménguez, Domeno, Domenzain, Domíguez, Dominco, Domíngez, Domíngnez, Domínguez, Domínguiz, Domíníguez, Domínquez, Domio, Domondón, Donado, Donate, Doneis, Dones, Donestevez, Donez, Donias, Donjuan, Donlucas, Donoso, Dopazo, Dopico, Doporto, Dorado, Dorame, Dorantes, Dorrego, Doria, Dorticos, Dosal, Dosamantes, Dosela, Doval, Dovales, Dovalina, Dovo, Dozal, Dspain, Duardo, Duarte, Duartes, Dubón, Ducos, Duen, Dueñas, Dueñes, Dueñez, Dueño, Dueños, Duhagon, Duhalde, Dulzaides, Dumaguindín, Dumbigue, Dume, Dumeng, Dumenigo, Duque, Durán, Durango, Durahona, Duranza, Durate, Durazo, Durón.

E Echabarne, Echandi, Echandía, Echaniz, Echarren, Echarri, Echartea, Echauarria, Echauri, Echavaria, Echavarri, Echavarría, Echavarry, Echave, Echavería, Echaves, Echaveste, Echavez, Echazábal, Echazarreta, Echeagaray, Echeandía, Echebarría, Echegaray, Echegoyen, Echeguren, Echemendia, Echenique, Echerivel, Echerri, Echevaria, Echevarría, Echevarrieta, Echevarrío, Echeveria, Echeverri, Echeverría, Echeverry, Echeveste, Echezábal, Echezarreta, Echiribel, Echiverri, Echivester, Ederra, Edesa, Edeza, Edillo, Edquivel, Edreira, Edrosa, Edrosolán, Edrozo, Egana, Egas, Egea, Egipciaco, Eglesias, Egued, Egues, Eguez, Eguia, Eguiguren, Eguiluz, Eguino, Eguizábal, Egure, Egurrola, Egusquiza, Eiras, Eiriz, Elebario, Elegino, Elejalde, Elemen, Elena, Elenes, Elenez, Elevario, Elezondo,

Elgarresta, Elgo, Elguea, Elguera, Elgueseba, Elguezábal, Elicier, Elisalda, Elisalde, Elisaldez, Elisarraraz, Eliserio, Elisondo, Elixavide, Elizade, Elizaga, Elizalda, Elizalde, Elizaldi, Elizando, Elizandro, Elizarde, Elizardi, Elizardo, Elizarraras, Elizarraraz, Elizarras, Elizonda, Elizondo, Eljaua, Elorduy, Elorreaga, Elorriaga, Elorza, Elosegui, Elosua, Elugardo, Elvira, Elycio, Emmanuelli, Emmite, Empasis, Emperador, Empleo, Enamorado, Encalada, Encallado, Encarnación, Encerrado, Enchautegui, Enchinton, Encina, Encinas, Encinia, Encinias, Encinios, Encino, Encinosa, Encisco, Enciso, Encizo, Endara, Endaya, Endemano, Endoso, Engpacio, Enguidanos, Enjady, Enriguez, Enrique, Enriques, Enriquez, Enrriquez, Ensenat, Epidendio, Equia, Equihua, Eras, Eraso, Erausquin, Erazo, Erched, Ercilla, Ercillo, Erdozain, Erebia, Eredia, Eres, Erevia, Eribes, Erives, Erivez, Eroles, Erosa, Errea, Erreca, Errisuriz, Erro, Erroa, Escabar, Escabedo, Escabi, Escabia, Escajeda, Escala, Escalada, Escalante, Escalente, Escalera, Escalet, Escalle, Escallón, Escalón, Escalona, Escalonte, Escamilla, Escamillas, Escamillo, Escaname, Escandell, Escandón, Escanes, Escanio, Escano, Escanuela, Escanuelas, Escapa, Escapita, Escapule, Escar, Escárcega, Escarcida, Escarciga, Escarda, Escarenio, Escareno, Escariz, Escarpio, Escarra, Escarraman, Escarrega, Escarsega, Escarsiga, Escartin, Escarzaga, Escarzega, Escasena, Escatel, Escatell, Escatiola, Escauriza, Escobado, Escobal, Escobales, Escobar, Escobarete, Escobebo, Escobeda, Escobedo, Escober, Escobido, Escobio, Escobosa, Escoboza, Escochea, Escodedo, Escojido, Escolar, Escomilla, Escontrias, Escorcia, Escoriaza, Escoppiso, Escorza, Escota, Escoto, Escovado, Escovar, Escuvedo, Escover, Escriba, Escribano, Escriche, Escuadra, Escuder, Escudero, Escueta, Escujuri, Escutia, Esguerra, Espada, Espadas, Espaillat, Espalin, España, Españo, Español, Española, Esparaza, Esparra, Esparsa, Esparsen, Esparz, Esparza, Espejel, Espejo, Espeleta, Espendez, Espenosa, Espenoza, Espera, Esperanza, Esperas, Espericueta, Esperiqueta, Espero, Esperon, Espigul, Espina, Espinal, Espinales, Espinar, Espindola, Espindula, Espineira, Espinel, Espinell, Espinet, Espino, Espinor, Espinosa, Espinoz, Espinoza, Espiricueta, Espíriti, Espíritu, Espitaleta, Espitia, Esplana, Esponda, Espriu, Espronceda, Espudo, Espurvoa, Esquea, Esqueda, Esquedo, Esquell, Esquenazi, Esquer, Esquera, Esquerdo, Esquero, Esquerra, Esquerre, Esquevel, Esquibal, Esquibel, Esquibias, Esquierdo, Esquijarosa, Esquijarrosa, Esquiliano, Esquilín, Esquinca, Esquinel, Esquival, Esquivel, Esquivez, Esquivias, Estaba, Estabillo, Estada, Estades, Estala, Estampa, Estañol, Estape, Estavilla, Estavillo, Estéban, Estébane, Estébañez, Estébes, Estébez, Estéfan, Estefani, Estela, Estenoz, Estepa, Estépan, Estéras, Estero, Esteues, Esteva, Estévan, Estevane, Estevanes, Estevanez, Estéves, Estévez, Estévis, Estéviz, Estien, Estimbo, Estolano, Estolas, Estopellán, Estopiñán, Estoque, Estorga, Estraca, Estrad, Estrada, Estradas, Estrade, Estrado, Estralla, Estrany, Estrella, Estrellas, Estrello, Estremera, Estremo, Estringel, Estronza, Estudillo, Estupiñán, Etchebarren, Etchebenere, Etchechury, Etchegaray, Etchepare, Etcheverría, Etcheverry, Eudave, Eufracio, Eulate, Eureste, Euresti, Eurioste,

Eusebio, Eustaquio, Euzarraga, Evangel, Evangelatos, Evaro, Evia, Exiga, Exinia, Exparza, Expósito, Eylicio, Eyzaguirre, Ezcurra, Ezeta, Ezqueda, Ezquer, Ezquerra, Ezquerro, Ezratty, Ezrre.

F Fabal, Fabela, Fabelo, Fabila, Fabra, Fabregas, Fabregat, Fabros, Fabrygel, Facio, Facundo, Fadrique, Faget, Fagoaga, Fagundo, Faila, Failde, Fajardo, Falche, Falcón, Falero, Fallejo, Falomir, Falquez, Falto, Falu, Famania, Familia, Fandiño, Fanego, Fangon, Fangonilo, Fanjul, Farach, Faragoza, Farfán, Farga, Fargas, Farias, Farillas, Fariñas, Fariños, Farios, Farpella, Farrales, Farray, Farrera, Farrias, Farros, Farrulla, Fas, Faudoa, Fauela, Fauni, Faura, Fauria, Faustinos, Fausto, Favela, Favella, Favelo, Favila, Faya, Faz, Feal, Febles, Febre, Febres, Feiga, Feijoo, Feito, Felan, Felando, Feliberty, Felicano, Feliciano, Felicitas, Felico, Felipe, Feliscian, Feliu, Felix, Feliz, Felpeto, Felumero, Femat, Femath, Fematt, Fentanes, Fente, Feo, Feramisco, Ferdin, Ferez, Feria, Fermández, Fermín, Fernadez, Fernande, Fernández, Fernándezcueto, Fernándezdecastro, Fernándezdelara, Fernando, Fernéndez, Ferniz, Ferniza, Ferradas, Ferradaz, Ferraez, Ferraiz, Ferrales, Ferralez, Ferrandes, Ferrandiz, Ferras, Ferre, Ferregur, Ferreiras, Ferreiro, Ferrer, Ferreras, Ferreris, Ferreytra, Ferreyro, Ferrez, Ferrua, Ferrusca, Festejo, Feyjoo, Fiallo, Fiallos, Fidel, Fierova, Fierro, Fierros, Fierroz, Fiestal, Figal, Figaredo, Figarella, Figarola, Figeroa, Figirova, Figorda, Figueiras, Figuera, Figueras, Figuerda, Figueredo, Figuereo, Figueria, Figuero, Figueroa, Figuerola, Figuerón, Figuerora, Figuerosa, Figuerra, Figuroa, Figveroa, Filgueiras, Filizola, Fillas, Filoteo, Fimbres, Fimbrez, Finales, Fiol, Foqueroa, Fira, Firpi, Fiuza, Flaco, Flamenco, Flándes, Flández, Flaquer, Flecha, Fleches, Fleitas, Fleites, Flemate, Flete, Fletes, Flopes, Floratos, Florencia, Florencio, Flores, Floresdelgado, Florez, Florido, Florit, Florita, Fluxa, Fojo, Folgar, Folgueira, Folgueiras, Fonalledas, Foncerrada, Fonnegra, Fonseca, Font, Fontán, Fontañes, Fontañet, Fontaney, Fontañez, Fontanills, Fontanoza, Fonteboa, Fontecha, Fontela, Fonteño, Fonticiella, Fonticoba, Forcelledo, Forcen, Fordis, Forero, Formano, Forment, Formeza, Fornaris, Fornasero, Fornos, Forns, Fortanel, Fortez, Forteza, Fortiz, Fortuño, Foyo, Fracisco, Fradejas, Fradera, Fraga, Fraginals, Frago, Fragomeno, Fragosa, Fragoso, Fragozo, Fragua, Fraguada, Fraguas, Fraguela, Fraguio, Fraide, Fraijo, Fraire, Framil, Franca, Francisca, Franco, Francos, Frangui, Franjul, Franquero, Fránquez, Franqui, Fránquiz, Fransua, Franzoy, Fraqua, Frases, Frasquillo, Fraticelli, Frau, Frausto, Fraustro, Fraxedas, Frayo, Frayre, Fredeluces, Fregosa, Fregoso, Fregozo, Freijo, Freire, Freiria, Freixas, Frenes, Fres, Frescas, Frescaz, Fresneda, Fresnedo, Fresnillo, Fresno, Frésques, Frésquez, Freyre, Freyta, Freytes, Frías, Fríaz, Frietze, Frigola, Frisan, Frometa, Frondarina, Frontado, Frontella, Fronteras, Frosto, Frugia, Frutos, Frutoz, Fuenmayor, Fuentas, Fuente, Fuentecilla, Fuentefría, Fuentes, Fuentez, Fuenzalida, Fuero, Fuerte, Fuertes, Fuertez, Fueyo, Fulgencio, Fulgueira, Fumero, Funcia, Fundora, Funes, Funez, Funo, Fusano, Fuste, Fuster.

G Gabalden, Gabaldon, Gabancho, Gabasan, Gabela, Gabilondo, Gabina, Gabino, Gabriles, Gabrillo, Gacharna, Gachupin, Gadal, Gadea, Gadía, Gaetán, Gafare, Gago, Gahona, Gainza, Gaitán, Gaitero, Gaivan, Gajardo, Gajate, Galabeas, Galache, Galagarza, Galán, Galarce, Galarraga, Galarreta, Galarsa, Galarte, Galarza, Galarze, Galavez, Galavis, Galaviz, Galaz, Galbán, Galcerán, Galdames, Galdamez, Galdeano, Galdos, Galduroz, Galeana, Galeano, Galéndez, Galera, Galería, Galguera, Gali, Galiana, Galicia, Galinañes, Galino, Galinda, Galíndez, Galindo, Galindro, Galinzoga, Galiz, Gallaga, Gallagos, Gallanes, Gallard, Gallarde, Gallardo, Gallareto, Gallart, Gallarza, Gallarzo, Gallastegui, Galleg, Gallegas, Gallego, Gallegoes, Gallegos, Gallegoz, Gallegus, Galleno, Gallerán, Gallerito, Gallinal, Gallinar, Gallor, Gallosa, Galmes, Galofre, Galorza, Galván, Galve, Gálves, Gálvez, Gama, Gamallo, Gamarra, Gamaza, Gamazo, Gamboa, Gamero, Gameros, Gameroz, Gamey, Gámez, Gamiño, Gamio, Gamiz, Gamoneda, Ganadonegro, Ganan, Gancedo, Ganceres, Gandar, Gandara, Gandaria, Gandarilla, Gandarillas, Gandía, Gandón, Gandora, Ganivet, Gañuelas, Ganuza, Gánzalez, Gaona, Garabay, Garabito, Garacochea, Garaicoechea, Garalde, Garamendi, Garamillo, Garana, Garansuay, Garanzuay, Garat, Gárate, Garateix, Garavito, Garay, Garayalde, Garaygordobil, Garayua, Garayzar, Garaza, Garbani, Garbayo, Garbiso, Garbizo, Garca, Garced, Garcel, Garcell, Garceo, Garcera, Garcerán, Garcés, Garcéz, García, Garcíacárdenas, Garcíagonzález, Garcíaguerrero, Garcíaguzmán, Garcíalópez, Garcíamártinez, Garcíapeña, Garcíaríos, Garcías, Garciav, Garcidueñas, Garciga, Garcilaso, Garcilazo, Garcio, Gardea, Gardía, Gardunio, Garduño, Garduque, Gareia, Garfías, Garfío, Gargueña, Gari, Garia, Garib, Garibaldo, Garibay, Gariby, Garica, Garife, Garispe, Garita, Garite, Garivay, Garmendía, Garmendiz, Garmisa, Garnica, Garrandes, Garrastazu, Garrido, Garriga, Garrigas, Garrigo, Garrigos, Garrio, Garrobo, Garrocho, Garrote, Garsa, Garses, Gartica, Garviso, Garza, Garzacantú, Garzagarcía, Garzagóngora, Garzamartínez, Garzapeña, Garzaro, Garzes, Garzón, Garzona, Garzoria, Gasca, Gascot, Gasero, Gasio, Gaspardealba, Gasporra, Gastello, Gastellum, Gastelo, Gastelum, Gasu, Gatán, Gatell, Gatica, Gato, Gatseos, Gattorno, Gauba, Gauchas, Gaucín, Gaud, Gaudier, Gauna, Gauzens, Gavaldón, Gavales, Gavay, Gavia, Gavica, Gavidia, Gavila, Gavilán, Gavilanes, Gavilla, Gavillán, Gaviña, Gaviño, Gavira, Gaviria, Gavito, Gaxiola, Gaya, Gayarre, Gayo, Gayol, Gayoso, Gayosso, Gaytán, Gazca, Gazivoda, Gazolas, Gaztambide, Gaztelu, Gea, Geada, Geaga, Gebara, Geigel, Gelabert, Gelacio, Gelera, Geli, Gelista, Gely, Genao, Gendes, Genel, Gener, Genera, Genesta, Geniño, Geniz, Genoves, Geraldes, Geraldino, Geraldo, Gerardo, Gerena, Gérez, Germenis, Germes, Germono, Gerolaga, Gerones, Gerro, Gerusa, Ghigliotty, Gijón, Gil, Gilas, Gilbes, Gilbuena, Gildelamadrid, Giménez, Gimeño, Gimínez, Ginart, Ginarte, Ginoro, Giner, Ginet, Ginez, Ginori, Ginorio, Ginoris, Ginory, Girado, Girald, Giraldes, Giraldez, Giraldo, Giralt, Girau, Giraudo, Girela, Girion, Giro, Girón, Girona, Gironella, Gisbert, Gispert, Giz, Gloria, Gobea, Gochez, Gochicoa, Godina,

Godines, Godinet, Godinez, Godoy, Goena, Goenaga, Goicochea, Goicouria, Goicuria, Goiricelaya, Goitia, Golderos, Gomar, Gome, Gómez, Gómezdemolina, Gómeztorres, Gómeztrejo, Gomzález, Gonález, Gonazlez, Gondar, Gondrez, Gongáles, Gongález, Góngora, Goni, Gonsale, Gonsáles, Gonsález, Gonzaba, Gonzaes, Gonzague, Gonzal, Gonzálas, Gonzale, Gonzalea, Gonzáles, Gonzalex, González, Gonzálezdías, Gonzálezhernández, Gonzálezleón, Gonzálezsoto, Gonzalo, Gonzálvez, Gonzalvo, Gonzalz, Gonzáque, Gonzélez, Gonzell, Gonzlaes, Gonzlaez, Gonzles, Gonzlez, Gonzóles, Gonzólez, Gorbea, Gordiany, Gordillo, Gordils, Gordo, Gordoa, Gorena, Gorosave, Gorostieta, Gorostiza, Goroza, Gorraiz, Gorricho, Gorrindo, Gorrita, Gorritz, Gorriz, Gortápez, Gorzela, Gosálvez, Gotanda, Gotay, Gotera, Gotiérrez, Gotor, Govantes, Govea, Govella, Goyanes, Goyco, Goycochea, Goycoechea, Goycoolea, Goyeneche, Goyos, Goytia, Goyzueta, Gozman, Gracia, Gracian, Graciani, Graciano, Gracida, Gradias, Gradilla, Gradillas, Gradisar, Grado, Grafals, Grageda, Graibe, Grajales, Grajeda, Grajera, Grajiola, Gramajo, Granada, Granadas, Granadino, Granado, Granados, Granadoz, Granas, Granda, Grandez, Grandio, Grandos, Granela, Granero, Graniela, Granillo, Granis, Granizo, Granja, Gratacos, Graulau, Graupera, Graveran, Graza, Greigo, Gres, Griego, Grihalva, Grijalba, Grijalua, Grijalva, Grillasca, Grillias, Grimaldo, Grisales, Grolon, Grona, Groso, Grovas, Grueso, Grullon, Grusman, Guaba, Guada, Guadagnin, Guadalajara, Guadalupe, Guadamuz, Guadarama, Guadarrama, Guaderrama, Guadian, Guadiana, Guadiano, Guadrón, Guaida, Guajaca, Guajardo, Gual, Gualdarrama, Guamán, Guana, Guanajuato, Guanche, Guangorena, Guanill, Guante, Guantes, Guantez, Guapo, Guara, Guaracha, Guarch, Guardado, Guardamondo, Guardarrama, Guardarramos, Guarderas, Guardian, Guardias, Guardiola, Guareno, Guaris, Guarjardo, Guarmero, Guarneros, Guartuche, Guas, Guasch, Guash, Guasp, Guayante, Guaydacan, Gudiel, Gudino, Guebara, Guecho, Guede, Guedea, Guedes, Guedin, Gueimunde, Gueits, Guel, Guelbenzu, Guelmes, Güemes, Güemez, Guera, Guerara, Guereca, Guerena, Guereno, Guereque, Guerero, Guererro, Guernica, Guerra, Guerreo, Guerrer, Guerrero, Guerrido, Guerrios, Guerro, Guevara, Guevarez, Guevarra, Guevera, Gueverra, Guez, Guía, Guiboa, Guicho, Guidero, Guijarro, Guijosa, Guilarte, Guilbe, Guilez, Guillama, Guillemard, Guillén, Guillena, Guillermety, Guillermo, Guina, Guirado, Guirales, Guiremano, Guirola, Guisa, Guisado, Guisao, Guisar, Guitano, Guitérrez, Guitian, Guitiérrez, Guitron, Guittérrez, Guittérrez, Guity, Guiu, Guivas, Guiza, Guizado, Guizar, Gujardo, Gularte, Gulbas, Guldris, Guldriz, Guliérrez, Guma, Gundín, Guraro, Gurell, Gurides, Gurola, Gurrero, Gurria, Gurries, Gurrola, Gurruchaga, Gurulé, Gurvle, Gurzi, Gusmán, Gusme, Gustamante, Gustamente, Gusto, Gutérrez, Gutiéres, Gutiérez, Gutiériez, Gutierr, Gutierre, Gutierrea, Gutierrer, Gutiérres, Gutiérrez, Gutiérrezgarcía, Gutíerrezríos, Gutiérrz, Gutírrez, Gutérez, Guttérrez, Guttíerez, Guttiérrez, Guzmán, Guzmeli, Guzmón.

H Haces, Haedo, Hamond, Hargita, Harispuru, Haro, Haros, Harvier, Hayos, Hechanova, Hechavarria, Hechevarria, Heguy, Helguera, Helguero, Helgueros, Henandez, Henao, Henares, Henojosa, Henríguez, Henríquez, Heráldez, Herández, Heras, Heraz, Herbello, Herebia, Heredero, Heredia, Hereida, Herena, Herera, Hererra, Hereter, Heria, Heridia, Hermández, Hermida, Hermidas, Hermis, Hermocillo, Hermogeno, Hermosa, Hermosillo, Hermoso, Hernádez, Hernaez, Hernaiz, Hernand, Hernande, Hernándel, Hernánder, Hernándes, Hernández, Hernández-Cantú, Hernández-Ortiz, Hernando, Hernandorena, Hernándz, Hernáñez, Herndez, Hernéndez, Heronema, Herrada, Herrador, Herrán, Herranz, Herrara, Herrarte, Herrea, Herrejón, Herrena, Herrer, Herrera, Herreras, Herreria, Herrerias, Herrero, Herreros, Herrerra, Herroz, Hervas, Hervella, Hervis, Hevia, Heysquierdo, Hibarra, Hidalga, Hidalgo, Hidalgogato, Hidas, Hidrogo, Hierrezuelo, Hierro, Higadera, Higareda, Higares, Highojos, Highojoz, Higuera, Higueras, Higuero, Higueros, Híjas, Hilario, Hilerio, Hinajosa, Hinestrosa, Hinojas, Hinojo, Holguín, Homar, Homs, Honesto, Hongola, Honorio, Honrada, Horabuena, Horacio, Horcasitas, Horelica, Hormachea, Hormaza, Hormazábal, Hormilla, Hornedo, Horruitiner, Horta, Hostas, Hostos, Hoyo, Hoyos, Hoyuela, Huacuja, Hualde, Huamán, Huantes, Huape, Huaracha, Huarte, Hueda, Huereca, Huerena, Huereque, Huergas, Huergo, Huerta, Huertas, Huertaz, Huertero, Huerto, Huertos, Huesca, Hueso, Huete, Huezo, Huguez, Huici, Huicochea, Huidor, Huipe, Huísar, Huitrón, Huízar, Humada, Humildad, Hurado, Hurbina, Huriega, Hurón, Hurriega, Hurtada, Hurtado, Hurtarte, Hysquierdo.

I Iañez, Iaños, Ibáñes, Ibáñez, Ibar, Ibarbo, Ibarguengoitia, Ibarlucea, Ibarra, Ibarria, Ibarrondo, Ibave, Ibaven, Iberra, Iberri, Ibinarriaga, Ibos, Ibuado, Icamen, Icardo, Icasiano, Icaza, Icedo, Ichinaga, Idarraga, Idiáquez, Idigoras, Idoy, Idrogo, Idrovo, Igaravídez, Igartua, Iglecias, Iglesia, Iglesias, Ignacio, Igoa, Igualada, Iguina, Ilarraza, Ildefonso, Ilharreguy, Ilizaliturri, Illán, Illañes, Illas, Illera, Illescas, Imas, Imaz, Inchaurregui, Inchaustegui, Inchausti, Inclán, Indart, Iñesta, Inestroza, Iñez, Infante, Infantes, Infanzón, Infiesta, Ingelmo, Ingrande, Inguanzo, Inguito, Iñigo, Iñígues, Iñíguez, Iñíquez, Iñoa, Inocencio, Inostros, Inostrosa, Inostroza, Insausti, Inserni, Insignares, Insúa, Insular, Insunza, Insurriaga, Interian, Intriago, Inurrigarro, Inzunza, Iparraguirre, Ipiña, Iquiña, Iracheta, Iragui, Iraheta, Irala, Iraola, Irastorza, Irazábal, Irazoqui, Iriart, Iriarte, Iribarren, Iribe, Irigaray, Irigonegaray, Irigoyen, Irimia, Irineo, Iriondo, Iriqui, Irisarri, Iriye, Irizar, Irizarri, Irizarry, Irizary, Irizzary, Irlas, Iroz, Irribarren, Irrizarri, Irrizarry, Irrizary, Irrobali, Iruegas, Irungaray, Iruretagoyena, Irvegas, Isaguirre, Isais, Isaiz, Isales, Isarraras, Isas, Isassi, Isern, Isias, Isidrón, Isla, Islas, Islava, Isona, Isordia, Isquierdo, Isunza, Ithier, Ituarte, Itule, Iturbe, Iturbi, Iturbide, Iturmendi, Iturralde, Iturraspe, Iturregui, Iturri, Iturria, Iturriaga, Iturrino, Iturrioz, Iváñez, Ivarra, Ixta, Iza, Izabal, Izaguirre, Izaquirre, Izar, Iznaga, Izquierdo, Izurieta.

J Jacas, Jacinto, Jacobo, Jácome, Jacomino, Jacovo, Jácquez, Jacuinde, Jaidar, Jaile, Jaime, Jaimerena, Jaimes, Jaimez, Jairala, Jalamo, Jalleo, Jaloma, Jalomo, Jalteco, Janer, Janero, Jáquez, Jaquias, Jara, Jaraba, Jaramilio, Jaramilla, Jaramillo, Jardines, Jardinez, Jarero, Jarmillo, Jaromillo, Járquez, Jarquin, Jarrín, Jarro, Jaso, Jasso, Jativa, Jauma, Jaume, Jaunarena, Jaunes, Jaure, Jáuregui, Jáureguiberry, Jáureguy, Jaurena, Jáurequi, Jaurez, Jáurgui, Jáurigi, Jáurigue, Jáurigui, Jáurique, Jáuriqui, Jáurqui, Jaurrieta, Javier, Javierre, Jemente, Jerez, Jesús, Jimarez, Jimémez, Jimena, Jimene, Jiménes, Jiménez, Jimeno, Jimenz, Jimínez, Jinete, Jínez, Jinzo, Jirau, Jirón, Jofre, Jojola, Jomarrón, Joramillo, Jordana, Jorganes, Jorge, Jornación, Jorquera, Jórquez, Jorrín, Jove, Jovellanos, Jover, Jovet, Joya, Juachón, Juan, Juancho, Juanero, Juanes, Juanez, Juaneza, Juanico, Juanitas, Juano, Juara, Juarbe, Juardo, Juare, Juáregui, Juares, Juarez, Juaristi, Juarrero, Juarros, Jubela, Juelle, Juez, Jufiar, Julbe, Juliá, Juncadella, Juncal, Junco, Juncosa, Juñez, Junguera, Junquera, Jurado, Juraez, Jurahui, Jurdi, Jure, Juri, Jurrez, Jusiano, Jusino, Justiniani, Justiniano, Justiz, Juver, Juvera.

L Labador, Labady, Labandeira, Labarga, Labarta, Labastida, Labastilla, Labio, Labiosa, Labiste, Laboca, Laborda, Labori, Laborico, Laborín, Laboy, Labra, Labrada, Labrado, Labrador, Labuzán, Laca, Lacalle, Lacarra, Lacasa, Lacasella, Lacayo, Lacebal, Lacedonia, Lacera, Lachappa, Lachica, Lachico, Lacomba, Lacombe, Laconcha, Lacret Llacrue, Lacruz, Lacsamana, Ladaga, Lafarga, Lafebre, Laffont, Laforteza, Lafuente, Lafuentes, Lagar, Lagarda, Lagares, Lageyre, Lago, Lagoa, Lagomasino, Lagrana, Laguer, Lagueruela, Laguillo, Laguna, Lagunas, Lagunes, Lahoz, Laija, Laijas, Lailes, Lainez, Laiseca, Laiz, Lajara, Lajes, Lallave, Laloma, Lalueza, Laluz, Lamadrid, Lamadriz, Lamas, Lamasa, Lamata, Lamazares, Lambardia, Lambaren, Lambarena, Lambaria, Lambarri, Lamboy, Lameira, Lamela, Lamelas, Lamigueiro, Lamorena, Lamosa, Lamoso, Lamourt, Lamoutte, Lamparello, Lampedusa, Lampón, Lanas, Lancara, Lancha, Landa, Landavaso, Landavazo, Landaverde, Landazuri, Landeira, Landero, Landeros, Landestoy, Landeta, Landez, Landín, Landívar, Landol, Landrau, Landrian, Landrón, Lanet, Lanfranco, Langara, Langarcía, Langarica, Lantigua, Lanuez, Lanuza, Lanzisero, Lanzot, Lao, Laos, Laosa, Lapadura, Laparra, Lapaz, Lapeña, Lapica, Lápiz, Lapuerta, Lapuz, Lara, Laracuenta, Laracuente, Laralde, Laran, Laras, Lardizábal, Laredo, Larena, Larenas, Lares, Larez, Larios, Lariva, Lariz, Larra, Larrache, Larraga, Larragoite, Larragoity, Larrainzar, Larralde, Larramendi, Larrán, Larranaga, Larranga, Larrasquito, Larrasquitu, Larrauri, Larraya, Larraz, Larrazábal, Larrazola, Larrazolo, Larrea, Larregui, Larreta, Larreynaga, Larriba, Larribas, Larrinaga, Larrinua, Larriva, Larronde, Larrondo, Larrosa, Larroy, Larrua, Larrubia, Lartundo, Larzábal, Lasa, Lasaga, Lasalde, Lasanta, Lasas, Lasavio, Lascano, Lascor, Lascurain, Laserna, Lases, Lasheras, Laso, Lasos, Lassós, Lastra, Lastre, Lastres, Latasa, Latigo, Latoni, Latorres, Laugier, Laurean, Laureano, Lauredo, Laureiro, Laurel, Laureles,

Lauriano, Laurias, Laurido, Lausell, Lauterio, Lauzardo, Lauzuríque, Lavandeira, Lavandera, Lavandero, Lavars, Lavastida, Lavayen, Lavea, Laveaga, Lavega, Lavendera, Lavergata, Lavernia, Laviada, Lavilla, Lavios, Lavorico, Lavorín, Layana, Layna, Laza, Lazaga, Lazala, Lazalde, Lazano, Lazarín, Lazarine, Lázaro, Lazarte, Lazcano, Lazcos, Lazes, Lazo, Lazodelavega, Lazos, Lazrine, Lazu, Lazurtegui, Leal, Leanos, Lebario, Lebrija, Lebrón, Lecaro, Lecaros, Lecea, Lechón, Lechuga, Lectora, Lecumberri, Lecusay, Ledesma, Ledezma, Ledo, Ledón, Legarda, Legarra, Legarreta, Legarretta, Legaspe, Legaspi, Legorreta, Legoza, Legra, Leguina, Leiba, Leibas, Leigón, Leija, Leimon, Leira, Leiro, Leisa, Leiseca, Leita, Leites, Leiva, Leivas, Leizán, Lejarza, Lejarzar, Lelevier, Lemes, Lemus, Lemuz, Lenero, Lente, Leodoro, León, Leones, León-Guerrero, Leonis, Leonor, Leos, Leoz, Lepe, Lera, Lerdo, Lerena, Leret, Lerma, Lermo, Lerno, Lero, Lesa, Lescano, Lesmes, Lespier, Lesprón, Letamendi, Letona, Letriz, Leura, Levaldo, Levario, Leyba, Leybas, Leyja, Leyra, Leyro, Leyúa, Leyva, Leyvas, Leza, Lezaja, Lezama, Lezana, Lezcano, Liano, Lianoz, Lianza, Liboy, Librán, Libreros, Licano, Licea, Liceaga, Licerio, Licon, Licona, Licor, Licudine, Liendo, Liera, Lieras, Lierra, Lievano, Lievanos, Ligues, Liguez, Limardo, Limas, Limia, Limón, Limones, Limonez, Limonta, Limón-Torres, Limosnero, Limuel, Linaje, Liñán, Linares, Linarez, Lineiro, Linera, Linero, Lineros, Liquet, Liquez, Lira, Lira-Alvarado, Liranzo, Lires, Liriano, Lirio, Lisalda, Lisalde, Lisama, Lisardo, Lisboa, Liscano, Lisea, Lisera, Liserio, Lisojo, Liza, Lizalda, Lizalde, Lizama, Lizan, Lizano, Lizaola, Lizáraga, Lizarde, Lizardi, Lizardo, Lizárraga, Lizárrago, Lizarralde, Lizarraras, Lizarzaburu, Lizaso, Lizasuain, Lizcano, Llabres, Llaca, Llacer, Llado, Llagostera, Llaguno, Llama, Llamas, Llamazares, Llambes, Llamosa, Llana, Llanas, Llanera, Llaneras, Llanes, Llanez, Llanio, Llano, Llanos, Llantada, Llantín, Llanusa, Llapur, Llarena, Llata, Llauger, Llaurado, Llaurador, Llausas, Llave, Llaverías, Llavet, Llavona, Llenín, Llenza, Lleo, Lleonart, Llera, Llerandi, Lleras, Llerena, Llerenas, Lleverino, Llibre, Llinas, Lliteras, Llizo, Llobera, Llobet, Llompart, Llona, Llopis, Llopiz, Llorca, Lloreda, Llorens, Llorente, Lloret, Llorín, Llosa, Llovera, Lloveras, Llovet, Llovio, Lluberes, Lluch, Lluis, Lluria, Lluveras, Loa, Loaiza, Loarte, Loayza, Lobaina, Lobato, Lobatos, Lobatoz, Lobera, Lodeiro, Lodevico, Lodos, Lodoza, Loera, Loeza, Logoluso, Logroño Loinaz, Loira, Loja, Lojero, Lojo, Lomana, Lomayesva, Lombana, Lombardia, Lombera, Lombrana, Lombpano, Lomelí, Lomelín, Lomellín, Lomely, Lona, Londoño, Longoria, Longorio, Longovia, Longuevan, Lonvelín, Lopátegui, Lope, Lopena, Lopera, Loperena, Lopétegui, López, López-Castro, López-Mendoza, López-Rodríguez, López-Sánchez, López-Vega, Lópoz, Loquet, Lora, Loranca, Lorca, Loredo, Lorences, Lorente, Lorenzana, Lorera, Loret-de-mola, Lorez, Lorido, Loriega, Loriga, Lorigo, Lorona, Lorono, Lorta, Lorza, Losa, Losada, Losado, Losana, Losoya, Lostaunau, Louato, Loubriel, Lourido, Loustaunau, Lovato, Lovaton, Loveira, Lovera, Loveras, Loville, Lovio, Loya, Loynaz, Loyo, Loyola, Loza, Lozada,

Lozado, Lozana, Lozano, Lozez, Lozolla, Lozoya, Lua, Luaces, Luan, Luas, Lube, Luberta, Lubian, Lucario, Lucatero, Lucatorta, Lucena, Lucer, Lucero, Lucio, Luco, Lucos, Lucret, Luebano, Luengas, Luengo, Luera, Lueras, Luevano, Luevanos, Lueza, Lugardo, Lugaro, Lugo, Lugón, Lugones, Luina, Luis, Luitin, Luján, Lujano, Lujardo, Lujo, Lujón, Lumbrera, Lumbreras, Luna, Lunares, Lupercio, Lúpez, Lupian, Lupianez, Lupiba, Lupio, Luque, Luquez, Luquin, Luquis, Luras, Luviano, Luyanda, Luyando, Luza, Luzania, Luzanilla, Luzano, Luzardo, Luzarraga, Luzbet, Luzunaris, Luzuriaga.

M Macaraig, Macardican, Macareno, Macarón, Macavinta, Macaya, Macayan, Macdonado, Maceda, Maceira, Macen, Macena, Maceo, Maceyra, Machiche, Machín, Machorro, Machuca, Macia, Macial, Macías, Macíaz, Maciel, Macotela, Mada, Madala, Madariaga, Madera, Maderis, Madero, Madiedo, Madoz, Madrazo, Madria, Madrid, Madrigal, Madrigales, Madrigual, Madril, Madriles, Madrill, Madriz, Madrona, Madrueño, Madruga, Maduano, Maduell, Madueña, Madueño, Maduro, Maelia, Maes, Maese, Maeso, Maestas, Maestaz, Maestes, Maestos, Maestre, Maestrey, Maestu, Maeva, Maez, Magalde, Magallán, Magallanes, Magallanez, Magallón, Magalona, Magana, Magante, Magariño, Magaz, Magdael, Magdalano, Magdalena, Magdaleno, Magdirila, Mageno, Maglica, Magluta, Magpayo, Magpuri, Magrina, Magsombol, Maguregui, Maimes, Maimo, Mainegra, Mainero, Mainez, Maiquez, Mairena, Maisonave, Maisonet, Maisterra, Maitia, Maito, Maiz, Majalca, Majano, Majarucón, Majeno, Majia, Majul, Majuta, Malabanan, Malabe, Malabéhar, Malacara, Malagón, Malana, Malanche, Malandris, Malarin, Malaue, Malave, Malaves, Malavet, Malavez, Maibaez, Malbas, Maldanado, Maldenado, Maldonado, Maldona, Maldonada, Maldonado, Maldonaldo, Maldondo, Maldonodo, Maléndez, Malfavón, Maliaros, Malibran, Malicay, Mallano, Mallea, Malloque, Mallorca, Malonado, Maloncón, Malove, Malpica, Maltes, Maltos, Maluia, Malvaez, Malvarez, Malvido, Mamaradlo, Mancebo, Mancera, Mancero, Mancha, Manchaca, Manchan, Manchego, Mancías, Mancilla, Mancillas, Mancinas, Mancito, Mandado, Mandonado, Mandugaro, Manduján, Mandujano, Mangome, Mangual, Manguía, Manicom, Maniquis, Manito, Manjares, Manjarez, Manjarres, Manjarrez, Manosa, Manquero, Manqueros, Manresa, Manríguez, Manríque, Manríques, Manríquez, Manrríque, Manrríquez, Mansanales, Mansanalez, Mansanares, Mansanarez, Mansilla, Mansillas, Mansito, Manso, Manteca, Mantecón, Manterola, Mantilla, Mantínez, Manuz, Manzana, Manzanal, Manzanares, Manzanarez, Manzanedo, Manzanera, Manzaneres, Manzanero, Manzanet, Manzanilla, Manzano, Manzur, Mapalo, Mapula, Maqueda, Maqueira, Maquinalez, Maquivar, Marabotto, Maradiaga, Marales, Marañán, Marañón, Marante, Marantos, Marascola, Maratas, Maravez, Maravilla, Maravillas, Maravillo, Marban, Marcadis, Marcano, Marceleno, Marcelín, Marcha, Marchan, Marchante, Marchany, Marcheco, Marchena, Marchiondo, Marcial, Marcilla, Marcillo, Marcor, Marcos, Mardomingo,

Mardueño, Mareina, Marenco, Marentes, Marentez, Mareque, Marero, Mares, Maresma, Marez, Marfil, Marfileño, Margaillán, Margarito, Marguez, Marianes, Marians, Marichal, Marichalar, Maridueña, Marín, Marinas, Marinelarena, Marinero, Marines, Marinez, Mariona, Mariscal, Maristany, Marisy, Maritnez, Marlano, Marmol, Marmolejo, Marmolejos, Marones, Márquez, Marquina, Márquiz, Marrasquin, Marreno, Marrero, Marriaga, Marrietta, Marrodan, Marroguin, Marroquin, Marroro, Marrozos, Marruffo, Marrufo, Marrugo, Marrujo, Marsach, Marsalia, Marsellos, Marte, Martelón, Marténez, Martes, Martez, Martiarena, Marticorena, Martín-del-Campo, Martínes, Martinets, Martínex, Martínez, Martínez-de-Castro, Martínez-García, Martínez-González, Martínez-Ortiz, Martínez-Rodríguez, Martíniz, Mártir, Martirena, Mártiz, Martlaro, Martnez, Martorrell, Martos, Maruffo, Marufo, Marulanda, Maruno, Maruri, Marvez, Marxuach, Marzan, Marzoa, Marzol, Marzovilla, Mas, Mascardo, Mascarena, Mascarenas, Mascarenaz, Mascareno, Mascarinas, Mascarro, Mascorro, Masdeo, Masdeu, Maseda, Masero, Masferrer, Masías, Masiel, Masjuan, Maspero, Maspons, Masquida, Massana, Massanet, Massas, Massiatte, Mastache, Mastrapa, Masvidal, Mata, Mataiya, Matallana, Matalobos, Matamoros, Matanzo, Mateas, Mateo, Mateos, Mateu, Matías, Matienzo, Matilla, Matos, Matoso, Matoza, Mattillo, Maturana, Maturino, Matute, Mauleón, Mauna, Maupome, Mauras, Maurel, Mauricio, Mauries, Mauriz, Maurosa, Mauroza, Maya, Mayagoitia, Mayans, Mayas, Mayate, Maydon, Mayen, Maymi, Maynez, Mayol, Mayora, Mayoral, Mayorca, Mayordomo, Mayorga, Mayorquín, Maysonet, Maytin, Maytorena, Maza, Mazara, Mazariego, Mazariegos, Mazón, Mazorra, Mazpule, Mazquiaran, Mazuca, Mazuelos, Meastas, Meave, Mecado, Mecartea, Mecenas, Mechoso, Medel, Medeles, Medelez, Medellín, Medero, Mederos, Mediano, Mediavilla, Medina, Medinas, Medinilla, Medio, Mediz, Medola, Medrán, Medrano, Megariz, Megui, Meija, Meireles, Meizoso, Meja, Mejía, Mejías, Méjico, Mejido, Mejilla, Mejillas, Mejorada, Mejorado, Melández, Melano, Melchor, Melcón, Melecio, Melena, Melenciano, Melende, Meléndes, Meléndez, Meléndres, Meléndrez, Meléndedez, Melénez, Melenudo, Melero, Melgar, Melgarejo, Melgares, Melgosa, Melgoza, Melián, Melías, Melíndez, Meliota, Mellado, Melocotón, Membreno, Membrila, Mena, Menache, Menacho, Menchaca, Menchaea, Menchávez, Menchego, Mencia, Mencio, Mencos, Mendana, Mendaros, Mendeola, Méndez, Mendia, Mendias, Mendiaz, Mendibles, Mendiburo, Mendiburu, Mendieta, Mendietta, Mendigutia, Mendine, Mendiola, Mendiolea, Mendiondo, Mendita, Mendivel, Mendivil, Mendiz, Mendizábal, Mendosa, Mendoz, Mendoza, Mendozo, Mendre, Mendrín, Menédez, Menéndez, Menes, Meneses, Menez, Menjares, Menjívar, Menjuga, Menocal, Menoscal, Menoud, Menoyo, Mera, Merancio, Meras, Meraz, Mercad, Mercada, Mercadal, Mercade, Mercader, Mercado, Mercardo, Merced, Mercedes, Merchain, Merchan, Mercodo, Mercola, Merconchini, Mereles, Merendón, Merez, Mergil, Merino, Merizalde, Merjil, Merla, Merlos, Mermea, Mermejo, Mermella, Merodio, Merono, Meru,

Meruelo, Mesa, Meseguer, Mesia, Mesías, Mesillas, Mesinas, Mesonero, Mesorana, Mesquías, Mesquit, Mesquita, Mesquite, Mesquiti, Messarra, Messeguer, Mesta, Mestas, Mestaz, Mestre, Mestres, Mestril, Mexía, Mexicano, Meza, Mezquita, Micán, Michaca, Michelena, Micheltorena, Miedes, Mieles, Mielgo, Miera, Mieres, Mierez, Mieses, Mignardot, Migoya, Miguel, Migueles, Miguelez, Migueliz, Migura, Mijangos, Mijares, Mijarez, Mijenes, Mila, Milanes, Milanez, Milara, Milera, Milián, Milina, Millán, Milland, Millanes, Millanez, Millan-ponce, Millares, Millayes, Mimiaga, Minabe, Minaga, Minagorri, Minamide, Minatre, Minaya, Minchaca, Mindieta, Mindiola, Minera, Minero, Minguela, Mingura, Miniarez, Minica, Minítrez, Minjares, Minjarez, Minobe, Minondo, Minoso, Minsal, Miqueo, Mir, Mirabal, Mirabel, Mirabent, Mirada, Miraflores, Mirales, Miralla, Miralles, Miramón, Miramontes, Miramontez, Mirana, Miranda, Mirano, Mirasol, Miraval, Miraya, Miraz, Mirazo, Mirdita, Mireles, Mirelez, Miret, Miriles, Miro, Mirolla, Misas, Misla, Mísquez, Miyar, Miyares, Mocega, Mocete, Mocho, Moctezuma, Modero, Modia, Modroño, Mogas, Mogollón, Mogro, Moguel, Mohedano, Moiza, Mojado, Mojarro, Mojeda, Mojena, Mójica, Molano, Moldes, Moldonado, Moledo, Molena, Moléndez, Molera, Moleres, Molerio, Molgado, Molina, Molinar, Molinares, Molinary, Molinas, Moliner, Molineros, Molinet, Molleda, Molles, Mollindo, Mollinedo, Monagas, Monarco, Monares, Monarez, Monarque, Monarres, Monarrez, Moncada, Moncado, Moncayo, Moncevais, Moncevaiz, Moncevias, Moncibais, Moncibaiz, Moncivais, Moncivaiz, Moncivalles, Monclova, Mondaca, Mondejar, Mondelo, Mondoña, Mondoza, Mondragón, Moneda, Monedero, Monegro, Moneo, Monge, Monges, Monguía, Monita, Monjaras, Monjaraz, Monjardín, Monje, Monjes, Monleón, Monllor, Monnar, Monoz, Monraz, Monreal, Monrial, Monroig, Monroy, Monrreal, Monrrial, Monsalve, Monsalvo, Monsebais, Monsegur, Monserrat, Monserrate, Monsevais, Monsevalles, Monsibais, Monsibaiz, Monsisvais, Monsivais, Monsivaiz, Montaivo, Montalban, Montalbo, Montaluo, Montalvan, Montalvo, Montán, Montañe, Montañer, Montañes, Montañez, Montanio, Montaño, Montantes, Montaya, Montaz, Monteagudo, Montealegre, Monteavaro, Montecelo, Montecino, Monte-de-Oca, Montefalcón, Montejano, Montejo, Montellano, Montelongo, Montemajor, Montemayor, Montenegro, Monteon, Montera, Monterde, Monterey, Montero, Monterola, Monteros, Monterrey, Monterrosa, Monterroso, Monterroza, Monterrubio, Montes, Montes-de-Oca, Montesino, Montesinos, Monteverde, Montez, Montezuma, Montiel, Montijo, Montilla, Montion, Montmayor, Montolla, Montoño Montoto, Montova, Montoy, Montoya, Montoyo, Montúfar, Montuya, Monzón, Monquete, Moquino, Mora, Morado, Moraga, Morago, Moraguez, Moraida, Moraila, Moral, Morale, Moralejo, Morales, Morales-González, Morales-López, Morales-Ramos, Morales-Torres, Moralez, Moranda, Morantes, Morata, Moratalla, Morataya, Morato, Moraza, Morcate, Morciego, Morciglio, Morcos, Moreda, Moredo, Moreida, Moreiras, Morejón, Moreles, Morelion, Morellón, Morelo, Morelos,

Moreno, Morentin, Morera, Morero, Moreia, Moreyra, Morfa, Morffi, Morfi, Morfín, Morga, Morgalo, Morgas, Morhar, Moriel, Morilla, Morillas, Morillo, Morillón, Morillos, Moriones, Moriyón, Morla, Morles, Morlet, Morlote, Morocho, Morodo, Moroles, Morolez, Morón, Morones, Moronez, Moroyoqui, Morquecho, Morquez, Morras, Morraz, Morrero, Morrina, Morteo, Mortera, Morua, Morva, Moscoso, Mosino, Mosquea, Mosqueda, Mosquedo, Mosquera, Mota, Motal, Motilla, Moure, Mouren, Mourino, Mouriz, Moya, Moyado, Moyano, Moyeda, Moyeno, Moyet, Moyron, Mozas, Mozqueda, Mucala, Mucino, Mudafort, Muela, Muelas, Muentes, Muga, Mugartegui, Mugerza, Mugica, Muguercia, Muguerza, Muguiro, Muil, Muina, Muinas, Muino, Muinos, Muirragui, Muis, Mujica, Mulero, Mulet, Mulgado, Muna, Muñana, Munarriz, Mundo, Munecas, Munera, Munero, Munet, Munetón, Muñez, Mungaray, Mungarro, Mungía, Munguía, Munilla, Munive, Munivez, Múñiz, Munne, Muñoa, Múños, Múñoz, Múñoz-Cano, Munquia, Muntaner, Muradas, Muradaz, Murado, Muraida, Muraira, Muralles, Murane, Muratalla, Muravez, Murcia, Murciano, Murcio, Murga, Murgado, Murguia, Murias, Muriedas, Muriel, Muriente, Murietta, Murillo, Muro, Murolas, Muros, Muroya, Murrieta, Murrietta, Murrillo, Mursuli, Murua, Muruaga, Muruato, Músquez, Músquiz, Mustelier, Mutio, Muxart, Muxo, Muzaurieta, Múzquiz.

N Naba, Nabarrete, Nabarrette, Nabayan, Nabeta, Nacer, Nachón, Nacianceno, Nadal, Nafarrate, Nafarrete, Nagore, Najar, Najara, Najares, Najarro, Najera, Nalda, Nandin, Nandino, Náñez, Nápoles, Naranjo, Naravez, Narbaiz, Narcho, Narcía, Naredo, Nares, Narez, Narezo, Nariño, Nario, Naronjo, Narranjo, Narro, Narvaes, Narvaez, Narvais, Narvaiz, Narvarez, Narvarte, Natal, Natera, Nateras, Natividad, Nava, Navaira, Navajar, Naval, Navales, Navallo, Navanjo, Navar, Navarete, Navarette, Navarez, Navaria, Navarijo, Navarr, Navarrete, Navarrette, Navarro, Navas, Naveda, Navedo, Naveira, Naveiras, Naveja, Navejar, Navejas, Naverán, Navia, Navidad, Navo, Navoda, Naya, Nayares, Nazabal, Nazario, Nazco, Nazur, Neblina, Nebreda, Nebrida, Neco, Necochea, Necoechea, Necuze, Negre, Negreira, Negret, Negrete, Negrette, Negrín, Negrón, Negrón-Colón, Negroni, Negueruela, Neira, Neito, Neives, Néjar, Nerada, Nerey, Neria, Nerio, Nerios, Neris, Nervais, Nevares, Nevarez, Nevarrez, Neyra, Nials, Niave, Niaves, Niavez, Nicacio, Nicasio, Nicot, Nidez, Nido, Niebla, Nieblas, Niego, Nieles, Nieto, Nieva, Nieve, Nieves, Nievez, Niez, Nigaglioni, Nigos, Nila, Nin, Niña, Niño, Nira, Nisperos, Nistal, Nival, Nivar, Nives, Niz, Noa, Nobara, Nobida, Noboa, Nobregas, Nocas, Noceda, Nocedal, Noche, Nochera, Nodal, Nodar, Nodarse, Nogales, Nogare, Nogue, Nogueda, Nogueiras, Noguelles, Noguer, Noguera, Nogueras, Nogues, Noguez, Nolasco, Noline, Nolla, Nombrana, Nombrano, Noperi, Norales, Noralez, Norat, Norda, Nordella, Nordelo, Noreiga, Norena, Norero, Noria, Noriega, Noriego, Noriz, Normandia, Norona, Norte, Norzagaray, Novales, Novas, Novela, Novelo, Novembre, Novian,

Novillo, Novo, Novoa, Noya, Noyas, Noyola, Nuañes, Nuañez, Nuche, Nuevo, Nuez, Nuin, Númez, Nuncio, Núñez, Nungaray, Nuño, Nuntez.

O Oaxaca, Oballe, Oballes, Obando, Obarrio, Obas, Obaya, Obera, Obeso, Obezo, Obiedo, Obispo, Oblea, Obledo, Obligación, Obrador, Obregón, Oca, Ocacio, Ocadiz, Ocampo, Ocampos, Ocaña, Ocañas, Ocaño, Ocanio, Ocaranza, Ocariz, Ocariza, Ocasio, Ocegueda, Oceguera, Ocejo, Ocequeda, Ochea, Ochinero, Ochipa, Ochoa, Ochos, Ochoterena, Ochotorena, Ocón, Odama, Odio, Odriozola, Ofarrill, Oferral, Ogaldez, Ogando, Ogarrio, Ogarro, Ogas, Ogaz, Oguendo, Oguete, Ohiggins, Ojeda, Ojinaga, Ojito, Olabarria, Olabarrieta, Olachea, Olaechea, Olaeta, Olaez, Olage, Olague, Olagues, Olaguez, Olaguibel, Olais, Olaiz, Olalde, Olalla, Olaque, Olaquez, Olarte, Olascoaga, Olascuaga, Olavarri, Olavarria, Olavarrieta, Olave, Olaya, Olayo, Olazaba, Olazábal, Olazágasti, Olazarán, Olba, Olbera, Olbes, Oldrate, Olea, Oleas, Oleta, Olgín, Olguín, Olibares, Olibarez, Olibarria, Olide, Oliu, Oliva, Olivan, Olivar, Olivare, Olivares, Olivarez, Olivaros, Olivarri, Olivarria, Olivas, Olivencia, Olivera, Oliveras, Oliveraz, Oliveres, Oliverez, Olivero, Oliveros, Olives, Olivias, Olivis, Olivo, Olivos, Ollaca, Ollerbidez, Ollervides, Ollervidez, Ollivares, Olloque, Olloqui, Olme, Olmeda, Olmedo, Olmo, Olmos, Olmoz, Olona, Olonia, Olono, Olortegui, Olquín, Oltivero, Olveda, Olvedo, Olveira, Olvera, Olvez, Omaechevarria, Omana, Oms, Oñate, Ondaro, Ondarza, Ondoy, Ondreas, Ondrías, Ongania, Ongay, Onofre, Onoz, Onsurez, Ontañeda, Ontiberoz, Ontiveras, Ontivero, Ontiveros, Ontiveroz, Opio, Oporto, Oquendo, Oquita, Orabuena, Oración, Orama, Oramas, Orana, Oranday, Orante, Orantes, Orantez, Orate, Orbay, Orbea, Orbegozo, Orca, Orcasitas, Ordaz, Ordenana, Ordener, Ordenes, Ordenez, Ordiales, Ordinario, Ordoñes, Ordoñez, Ordoño, Ordoqui, Ordorica, Ordover, Orduña, Orduñez, Orduño, Oregel, Orejel, Orellana, Orellano, Orendain, Orengo, Orense, Oretega, Oretga, Orfila, Organista, Orge, Oria, Oriba, Oribe, Origel, Originales, Orihuela, Orijel, Orique, Orisio, Oritiz, Oritz, Orive, Orizaga, Orjales, Orjuela, Ornelas, Ornelaz, Orneles, Orobio, Orol, Oroña, Oroñoz, Oropesa, Oropeza, Orosa, Orosco, Oroz, Orozco, Orozeo, Orpilla, Orpinel, Orquiz, Orraca, Orradre, Orrante, Orrantia, Orrego, Orriola, Orriols, Orsaba, Orsúa, Orta, Ortal, Ortas, Orteg, Ortega, Ortegas, Ortegon, Ortes, Ortez, Ortigas, Ortigosa, Ortigoza, Ortivez, Ortiviz, Ortiz, Ortiz-Ypiño, Ortolaza, Ortunio, Ortuño, Ortúzar, Orue, Oruna, Orvananos, Orza, Orzábal, Orzo, Osa, Osano, Oscos, Oscoy, Oseda, Osegueda, Oseguera, Osejo, Oselio, Osequera, Oses, Osete, Osio, Osle, Osnaya, Oso, Osollo, Osona, Osoria, Osorio, Osornia, Osornio, Osorno, Ospina, Ospino, Ospital, Ossa, Ossorgin, Ossorio, Osteguín, Ostiguín, Ostiquín, Ostolaza, Ostos, Osuna, Otañez, Otano, Otazo, Otegui, Oteiza, Oteo, Otera, Otero, Othon, Oti, Otondo, Ovadia, Ovalle, Ovalles, Ovallez, Ovando, Ovares, Ovieda, Oviedo, Oxios, Oyaca, Oyague, Oyanguren, Oyarbide, Oyarzabal, Oyarzún, Oyas, Oyerbides, Oyervides, Oyervidez, Oyola, Oyoque, Oyuela, Ozaeta, Ozeta, Ozores, Ozoria, Ozornia, Ozuña, Ozuñiga.

P Pabey, Pablico, Pablo, Pablos, Pabón, Pabros, Pacharzina, Pachec, Pachecano, Pacheco, Pachelo, Pacheo, Pachero, Pachicano, Pacho, Pachón, Pachuca, Pacías, Pacificar, Pacillas, Pacín, Pacina, Paco, Paddilla, Pader, Padía, Padial, Padías, Padierna, Padill, Padilla, Padillia, Padillo, Padín, Pador, Padrés, Padrino, Padro, Padrón, Padua, Paez, Pagán, Pagán-Rivera, Pages, Pagola, Pagón, Paguaga, Paguio, Pahissa, Paiacios, Pairada, Pairis, Paíz, Pajarito, Pájaro, Pajuelo, Palacies, Palacio, Palacios, Paladines, Palafos, Palafox, Palaganas, Palamo, Palasota, Palato, Palau, Palazón, Palazuelos, Palencia, Palenzuela, Paleo, Palgón, Palicio, Palitos, Palizo, Pallais, Pallán, Pallanes, Pallanez, Pallares, Pallarez, Palleja, Pallens, Pallot, Palmares, Palmarez, Palmarín, Palmas, Palmeiro, Palmerin, Palmeros, Paloma, Palomar, Palomares, Palomarez, Palomeque, Palomera, Palomín, Palomino, Palominos, Palomo, Palop, Palos, Palou, Pamanes, Pamarán, Pamblanco, Pamias, Pamintuan, Pampin, Pamplona, Panales, Pañalez, Panamá, Panameño, Panariso, Pancegran, Panchana, Pancho, Pancorbo, Pandal, Pandas, Pandes, Pando, Panduro, Panelo, Paneno, Paneque, Panero, Paneto, Paniagua, Paniaqua, Paniz, Panopio, Panta, Pantaja, Pantaleón, Pantiga, Pantín, Pantleo, Pantoja, Pantojas, Pantoya, Pantusa, Pánuco, Panzardi, Panziera, Parache, Parada, Paradeda, Paradela, Paradelo, Parades, Paradez, Paramo, Parapar, Parayno, Parayuelos, Parazo, Parces, Pardave, Pardillo, Pardinas, Pardo, Pardos, Parducho, Paredes, Paredez, Pareira, Pareja, Parellada, Parera, Pares, Parets, Pareya, Parez, Parga, Pargas, Pariz, Parocua, Parque, Parra, Parrado, Parraga, Parral, Parrales, Parras, Parraz, Parreño, Parriera, Parrilla, Parrondo, Partagas, Partida, Partido, Pasada, Pasamonte, Pasantes, Pasarell, Pasaret, Pasarín, Pascacio, Pascual, Pascuali, Pasena, Pasillas, Pasols, Pasos, Passapera, Pastora, Pastoriza, Pastran, Pastrana, Pastrano, Patiña, Patiño, Patlan, Patranella, Patrón, Pauda, Paula, Paullada, Pavedes, Pavila, Pavón, Payan, Payano, Payares, Payas, Payen, Payero, Paz, Pazmiño, Pazos, Pecaro, Pecelunas, Pecero, Pechero, Pecina, Pecos, Pedevilla, Pedraja, Pedras, Pedrayes, Pedraz, Pedraza, Pedre, Pedregal, Pedrego, Pedregón, Pedreguera, Pedreira, Pedreiro, Pedrera, Pedrero, Pedrianes, Pedrino, Pedroche, Pedrogo, Pedrola, Pedrosa, Pedroso, Pedroza, Pego, Pegoda, Peguero, Pegueros, Peinado, Peiro, Pelache, Pelaez, Pelaiz, Pelallo, Pelata, Pelayo, Pelegrina, Pellecer, Pellerano, Pellicier, Pellot, Peluffo, Peña, Peñabad, Penado, Peñafiel, Peñaflor, Peñaflorida, Peña-Garza, Peña-Herrera, Peñalba, Peñales, Peñalo, Peñalosa, Peñaloza, Peñalver, Peñalvert, Penaño, Peñaranda, Peñate, Pendas, Peñez, Peniche, Penichet, Penilla, Peñón, Pensado, Peñuela, Peñuelas, Peñuelaz, Penunuri, Peón, Peperas, Pepito, Pequeño, Pequero, Peral, Perales, Peralez, Peralta, Peralto, Peratis, Peraza, Perches, Perchez, Perdices, Perdido, Perdigón, Perdomo, Perea, Pereda, Peredia, Peredo, Peregrina, Peregrino, Pereida, Pereiro, Pereles, Perera, Péres, Pereyda, Pereyo, Pereyra, Pérez, Pereza, Pérez-Cano, Pérez-Chica, Pérez-colón, Pérez-de-Alejo, Pérez-del-Río, Pérez-Díaz, Pérez-González, Pérez-Jiménez, Pérez-López, Pérez-Mendez, Pérez-Montes, Pérez-Ramos, Perfecto, Perfino, Pericas, Perlas, Permuy,

Pernas, Peroldo, Perozo, Perres, Perriraz, Pertierra, Perú, Perumean, Perusina, Perusquia, Peruyera, Peruyero, Pervez, Peryatel, Pesante, Pesantes, Pesantez, Pescado, Pescador, Pesina, Pesqueda, Pesqueira, Pesquera, Pesquiera, Peydro, Peynado, Peyro, Peza, Pezez, Pezina, Piard, Picallo, Picar, Picart, Picascia, Picaso, Picazo, Piceño, Pichardo, Pico, Picón, Picos, Piedad, Piedra, Piedrahita, Piedras, Piélago, Pieras, Pijuan, Pila, Pilar, Pilarte, Pillado, Piloto, Pimienta, Pimiento, Pimintel, Piña, Piña-de-Arcos, Piñal, Piñales, Piñalez, Piñares, Pincay, Piñeda, Piñedo, Piñeira, Piñeiro, Piñela, Piñelo, Piñera, Piñero, Piñeros, Piney, Pineyro, Pingarrón, Piniella, Pinilla, Pinillo, Pinillos, Piño, Piñol, Piñon, Piñones, Pintado, Pintor, Pintos, Piñuela, Piñuelas, Pinzón, Pioquinto, Piquero, Pirez, Pirinea, Piris, Piriz, Pis, Pisana, Piseño, Pisonero, Pita, Pitaluga, Pitarch, Pitones, Pitrones, Pizana, Pizano, Pizaro, Pizarra, Pizarro, Pizula, Pla, Placencia, Placencio, Placensia, Placentia, Placeres, Plaja, Plana, Planas, Plancarte, Plancencia, Planell, Planellas, Planes, Planos, Plantillas, Planto, Plascencia, Plasencia, Plasencio, Plata, Platamone, Platas, Platero, Plaza, Plazas, Plazola, Pliego, Pluma, Plumas, Plumeda, Plumey, Pobar, Poblano, Poblete, Pobre, Podilla, Poey, Pogan, Pola, Polaco, Polanco, Polendo, Polidura, Polina, Politrón, Pollerana, Polloreno, Polvado, Pomale, Pomales, Pomares, Pomarez, Pombrol, Pomeleo, Pompa, Poncabare, Ponce, Ponce-de-León, Poncho, Ponciano, Poncio, Ponsdomenech, Ponzoa, Porata, Porcayo, Porchas, Porcho, Pordia, Porfil, Porlas, Porras, Porrata, Porraz, Porrero, Porres, Porros, Portal, Portalatin, Portales, Portalez, Portela, Portelles, Portes, Portieles, Portilla, Portillo, Portillos, Portocarrero, Portolán, Portorreal, Portugal, Portugués, Portuguéz, Portuondo, Posada, Posadas, Posas, Poso, Posos, Postigo, Postil, Potestad, Pouges, Pousa, Poveda, Poventud, Poviones, Poyorena, Poza, Pozas, Pozero, Pozo, Pozos, Pozuelos, Pradas, Pradere, Pradia, Prado, Prat, Prats, Pratts, Preciado, Prellezo, Prendes, Prendez, Prendiz, Presa, Presas, Presiado, Presno, Préstamo, Prezas, Prida, Priede, Priego, Prieguez, Prieto, Primelles, Primera, Primero, Prio, Proa, Proaño, Procel, Procela, Procsal, Proenza, Pronias, Proo, Provencio, Proveyer, Prudencio, Pruna, Pruneda, Prunes, Pubill, Pubillones, Puchades, Puebla, Puella, Puello, Puente, Puentes, Puentez, Puerta, Puertas, Puerto, Puertos, Pueyo, Puga, Pugeda, Puig, Pujadas, Pujal, Pujals, Pujol, Pujols, Pulgar, Pulgarín, Pulida, Pulido, Pulomena, Pumar, Pumarada, Pumarejo, Pumares, Pumariega, Pumarol, Puñales, Puññara, Puño, Punta, Puntiel, Pupo, Pura, Purcella, Purísima, Puyada, Puyol.

Q Quadreny, Qualia, Quasada, Queclas, Queipo, Queiro, Queiruga, Quéllar, Quemada, Queralt, Querdo, Querido, Quero, Quert, Quesada, Quesado, Quetel, Quetglas, Quevedo, Quezada, Quiala, Quian, Quibuyen, Quiceño, Quichocho, Quidera, Quihuis, Quihuiz, Quijada, Quijalvo, Quijano, Quijas, Quilala, Quilantán, Quilenderino, Quiles, Quilez, Quilimaco, Quimbar, Quimiro, Quinal, Quincoces, Quinde, Quindnez, Quinenes, Quines, Quini,

Quiñiones, Quinoa, Quinone, Quiñones, Quiñonez, Quiñonos, Quiñores, Quintama, Quintana, Quintanal, Quintanar, Quintanilla, Quintans, Quintaro, Quintas, Quinteiro, Quintela, Quintenilla, Quintera, Quintero, Quinteros, Quintino, Quintona, Quintones, Quintonez, Quintos, Quiones, Quirarte, Quirch, Quireno, Quirindongo, Quirino, Quiro, Quiroa, Quiroba, Quiroga, Quirol, Quirola, Quirós, Quiróz, Quita, Quitania, Quitos, Quitugua, Quiz.

R Rabade, Rabago, Rabaja, Rabano, Rabasa, Rabassa, Rabaza, Rabeiro, Rabell, Rabelo, Rabia, Rabiela, Rabina, Rabino, Rabos, Radavero, Radilla, Radillo, Radríguez, Rael, Raez, Rafael, Rafalín, Rafuls, Raíces, Raigosa, Raigoza, Raimúndez, Raimundi, Raisola, Rajoy, Raldiris, Ramallo, Ramariz, Ramas, Rambes, Ramblas, Rambonga, Ramentol, Ramérez, Ramériz, Ramero, Ramery, Ramiérez, Ramiérz, Ramiez, Ramil, Ramínez, Ramir, Ramire, Ramíres, Ramírez, Ramiro, Ramis, Ramon, Ramoneda, Ramones, Ramos, Ramos-González, Ramos-Medina, Ramos-Rivera, Ramos-Rodríguez, Ramoz, Ramudo, Ramuz, Rancano, Randez, Ranero, Raneses, Rangel, Rangell, Rangell-López, Ranjel, Ransola, Raquenio, Raqueno, Raquepo, Rasales, Rascón, Raspaldo, Rasura, Ratón, Rauda, Ravago, Ravaro, Ravelo, Raventos, Raxach, Raya, Rayas, Raygosa, Raygoza, Raymos, Raymundo, Rayna, Rayonez, Rayor, Rayos, Razatos, Razo, Reales, Realivásquez, Realme, Realyvásquez, Reaño, Reátegui, Reaza, Reazola, Rebeles, Rebelez, Rebellón, Rebeterano, Rebollar, Rebolledo, Rebollo, Rebolloso, Reboredo, Reboso, Reboyras, Rebozo, Rebustillo, Recalde, Recarey, Recarte, Recendes, Recendez, Rechani, Rechany, Rechy, Recillas, Recinos, Recio, Reclusado, Recovo, Recuset, Rede, Redero, Redoña, Redondo, Redruello, Refuerzo, Regalado, Regaldo, Regales, Regalo, Regalos, Regato, Regino, Regojo, Regos, Regrutto, Regua, Regueira, Regueiro, Reguera, Reguero, Regules, Regusa, Reicen, Reíces, Reigosa, Reina, Reinaga, Reinaldo, Reinat, Reinero, Reinosa, Reinoso, Reinus, Rejas, Rejino, Rejo, Rejón, Rel, Relles, Rellez, Relucio, Remache, Remedios, Remigio, Remos, Renderos, Rendón, Renedo, Renge, Renobato, Renova, Renovales, Renovato, Renta, Rentas, Rentería, Renterías, Reorda, Reoyo, Repollet, Repreza, Requejo, Requena, Requenes, Requenez, Requeno, Requiro, Reschman, Resendez, Resendis, Resendiz, Reserva, Resina, Resma, Resún, Respeto, Ressy, Resto, Restoy, Restredo, Restrepo, Resurez, Reta, Retamal, Retamales, Retamar, Retamosa, Retamoza, Retana, Retano, Retes, Retez, Retiz, Retta, Retureta, Revada, Revado, Reveles, Revelez, Revelles, Reverón, Revilla, Revillas, Revollar, Revolledo, Revoredo, Revuelta, Revueltas, Rexach, Rey, Reyeros, Reyers, Reyes, Reyes-Pérez, Reyes-Rodríguez, Reyez, Reygadas, Reyna, Reynado, Reynaga, Reynaldo, Reynaldos, Reynero, Reyneros, Reynos, Reynosa, Reynoso, Reynoza, Reynozo, Reyo, Reyos, Reza, Rezéndez, Riali, Riancho, Rianda, Riave, Riaza, Ribadeneira, Ribal, Ribalta, Ribas, Ribera, Riberal, Riberas, Ribot, Ribota, Ricabal, Ricalde, Ricano, Ricardez, Ricardo,

Ricart, Ricarte, Richarte, Richiez, Richina, Rico, Ricondo, Ridríguez, Riedo, Riega, Riego, Riegos, Riera, Rieras, Riesco, Riesgo, Riestra, Rigal, Rigales, Rigau, Rigual, Riguera, Riguero, Rijo, Rijos, Rimblas, Rinauro, Rinche, Rincón, Rinconeno, Rincones, Ringlero, Riobo, Riocabo, Riofrío, Rioja, Riojas, Riojaz, Riojos, Riollano, Rionda, Riopedre, Ríos, Rioseco, Ríos-Espinoza, Ríos-Flores, Ríos-Martínez, Ríos-Pérez, Ríoz, Ripalda, Ripes, Ripol, Ripoll, Ripolles, Riquelme, Riquero, Risquet, Risueño, Rius, Riusech, Rivada, Rivadeneira, Rivadeneyra, Rivadulla, Rivale, Rivali, Rivares, Rivarola, Rivas, Rivaz, Riveira, Riveiro, Rivera, Rivera-Colón, Rivera-Cruz, Rivera-Díaz, Rivera-Lugo, Rivera-Pérez, Rivera-Rivera, Riveras, Rivería, Rivero, Riverol, Riveroll, Riverón, Riveros, Riverra, Riviero, Rizo, Roa, Roacho, Roaño, Robaina, Robali, Robalín, Robalino, Robau, Robayna, Robayo, Robeda, Robeldo, Robelo, Roblas, Robleda, Robledo, Roblejo, Roblero, Robles, Robleto, Roblez, Robredo, Roca, Rocafort, Rocafuerte, Rocamontes, Rocamontez, Rocero, Roces, Rocha, Rochas, Roches, Rochín, Rochoa, Rocio, Rodado, Rodallegas, Rodarte, Rodas, Rodea, Rodela, Rodelas, Rodelo, Rodena, Rodenas, Rodero, Rodez, Rodgríguez, Rodicio, Rodíguez, Rodil, Rodiles, Rodíquez, Rodírguez, Rodréguez, Rodrguez, Rodríg, Rodrígeuz, Rodrígez, Rodrígiez, Rodrígnez, Rodrígoez, Rodrígs, Rodrígu, Rodriguea, Rodriguera, Rodríguez, Rodríguez-Martínez, Rodríguezs, Rodríguiez, Rodríguiz, Rodríguz, Rodríquez, Rodríquiz, Rodríuez, Rodríugez, Rodrízuez, Rodróguez, Rodrúguez, Rodrúquez, Rodúguez, Rodulfo, Rodz, Roel, Rogans, Rogerío, Roges, Rogríguez, Rogue, Rohena, Roibal, Roide, Roig, Rois, Roiz, Roja, Rojano, Rojas, Rojel, Rojero, Rojes, Rojo, Rojos, Roldán, Roldón, Roldos, Rolón, Romagosa, Romaguera, Romandía, Romanes, Romanez, Romanillos, Romay, Romayor, Romera, Romero, Romeros, Romeu, Romez, Romirez, Romiro, Romo, Romos, Rompal, Ron, Ronces, Ronda, Rondán, Rondero, Rondez, Rondón, Rongavilla, Ronje, Ronquillo, Roque, Roqueni, Roquero, Roqueta, Ros, Rosa, Rosabal, Rosada, Rosado, Rosal, Rosales, Rosales-del-Río, Rosalez, Rosaly, Rosaria, Rosario, Rosario-Díaz, Rosaro, Rosas, Roseli, Rosello, Rosellón, Rosendo, Roseney, Rosero, Roses, Rosete, Rosiles, Rosilez, Rosillo, Rositas, Rosquete, Rostro, Rotea, Rotela, Rotger, Rouco, Roura, Roure, Rovayo, Rovera, Rovira, Rovirosa, Roxas, Roybal, Royball, Roybol, Royero, Royo, Royos, Royval, Rozada, Rozales, Rozo, Ruacho, Ruales, Rualo, Ruan, Ruaño, Ruas, Rubalaca, Rubalcaba, Rubalcada, Rubalcado, Rubalcaua, Rubalcava, Rubero, Ruberte, Rubí, Rubia, Rubiales, Rubianes, Rubiano, Rubido, Rubiella, Rubiera, Rubildo, Rubinos, Rubio, Rubiola, Rucio, Rucobo, Rueda, Rueda-Flores, Ruedas, Ruelas, Ruelaz, Ruelos, Ruempel, Ruenes, Ruesga, Ruezga, Rufat, Ruffeno, Rufín, Regama, Rugarcia, Rugerio, Ruibal, Ruidas, Ruidiaz, Ruiloba, Ruisánchez, Ruiseco, Ruíz, Ruíz-Calderón, Ruíz-Castañeda, Ruíz-de-Esparza, Ruíz-del-Vizo, Ruize, Ruíz-Esparza, Ruizz, Rul, Rullán, Rumayor, Rumbaut, Rutiaga, Rutiz, Ruvalcaba, Ruvira, Ruybal, Ruybalid, Ruybol, Ruz.

S Saa, Saabedra, Saauedra, Saavedra, Sabala, Saballos, Sabalza, Sabando, Sabater, Sabates, Sabedra, Sabi, Sabicer, Sabido, Sabines, Sablatura, Sabogal, Sabori, Saborido, Saborio, Saborit, Saboya, Sabres, Sabroso, Sabugo, Saca, Sacarello, Sacasas, Sacerio, Sacos, Sacristán, Sada, Sades, Sadule, Saeda, Sáens, Sáenz, Saeta, Sáez, Safady, Safille, Safont, Sagara, Sagardía, Sagardoy, Sagaribay, Sagarnaga, Sagaro, Sagarra, Sagas, Sagasta, Sagástegui, Sagástume, Sagrado, Sagredo, Sagrero, Sagún, Sahagún, Saijo, Sailas, Saina, Sáinez, Sáinz, Sáis, Sáiz, Saiza, Sala-Barria, Sala-Berrios, Salacán, Salado, Salaets, Salaices, Salais, Salaises, Salaiz, Salamanca, Salanas, Salano, Salars, Salas, Salasar, Salavaria, Salavarria, Salavarrieta, Salaverria, Salaya, Sala-y-Andía, Salaz, Salaza, Salazan, Salazar, Salbato, Salceda, Salcedo, Salcida, Salcido, Salcines, Saldama, Saldamando, Saldaña, Saldaño, Saldarriaga, Saldate, Saldez, Saldierna, Saldívar, Saldona, Saldua, Salegui, Salgado, Salgado-Luna, Salgueiro, Salguera, Salguero, Salhuana, Salias, Salido, Salinas, Salinas-García, Salinas-Ramírez, Salinaz, Salinos, Saliva, Salivas, Saliz, Salizar, Salles, Salmerón, Salmina, Salmones, Salort, Salos, Salsa, Salsameda, Salsedo, Salsido, Saltares, Saltero, Saltos, Saludes, Salumbides, Salvación, Salvaria, Salvarrey, Salvat, Salvatierra, Salvide, Samada, Samala, Samalot, Samanego, Samaniego, Samano, Samario, Samaripa, Samaro, Samarripa, Samarripas, Samarrón, Samayoa, Sambado, Sambolín, Sambrano, Sambueso, Sambula, Samilpa, Samoniego, Samora, Samorano, Samot, Sampayán, Sampayo, Sampedro, Sampera, Samperio, Samtos, Samudia, Samudio, Sanabia, Sanbria, San-Agustín, Saname, Sanandrés, Sanbartolome, Sanbrano, Sancedo, Sancen, Sancha, Sanche, Sanchen, Sánches, Sánchez, Sánchez-de-Tagle, Sánchez-Pérez, Sanchidrian, Sánchiz, Sancho, Sanchoyerto, Sánchz, Sanciprian, Sandate, Sandaval, Sandavol, Sandez, Sandía, Sandiego, Sandigo, Sandobal, Sandomingo, Sandoual, Sandova, Sandoval, Sandoz, Sanemeterio, Saneto, Sánez, Sanfelipe, Sanfélix, Sanféliz, Sanfiel, Sanfiorenzo, Sangabriel, Sangre, Sanguesa, Sanguily, Sanguino, Sanin, Saninocencio, Sanjenis, Sanjorge, Sajjorjo, Sanjosé, Sanjuan, Sanjurjo, Sanlucas, Sanmartín, Sanmiguel, Sanmillán, Sannicolás, Sanoguet, Sanora, Sanpedro, Sanquiche, Sanromán, Sanserino, Sansores, Santa-Ana, Santa-Anna, Santacoloma, Santacruz, Santaella, Santago, Santaliz, Santalla, Santalo, Santamarina, Santamato, Santana, Santander, Santandreu, Santano, Santapau, Santarosa, Santarriaga, Santeiro, Santelices, Santelises, Santellán, Santellana, Santellanes, Santellano, Santestéban, Santeyan, Santiag, Santiago, Santiana, Santibáñes, Santibáñez, Santiestéban, Santiestévan, Santillán, Santillana, Santillanes, Santillanez, Santillano, Santillián, Santistéban, Santistévan, Santistéven, Santiváñez, Santizo, Santodomingo, Santorinios, Santos, Santoscoy, Santovena, Santovenia, Santoy, Santoya, Santoyo, Santurio, Sanudo, Sanvicente, Sanz, Sapata, Sapeda, Sapena, Sapien, Sapiens, Sapinoso, Sarabia, Sarachaga, Saracho, Saragosa, Saragoza, Saragueta, Saralegui, Sarante, Sarate, Saravia, Sarceda, Sardaneta, Sardinas, Sarduy, Sarellano, Sarenana, Sariá, Sariego, Sariña, Sariñana, Sariñas, Sariol, Sarmentero, Sarmienta, Sarmiento,

Sarmiento-Flores, Sarmientos, Saroza, Sarquis, Sarquiz, Sarracino, Sarraga, Sarraraz, Sarratea, Sarreal, Sarriá, Sarriera, Sartuche, Sarzo, Sarzoza, Saspe, Sastre, Sasturain, Satarain, Sataray, Saturnino, Sauceda, Saucedo, Saucido, Saucillo, Saudia, Sauedra, Sauleda, Sauma, Saumell, Saura, Saurez, Sauri, Sausameda, Sauseda, Sausedo, Sauza, Savala, Savalza, Savedra, Savellano, Saviñón, Savorillo, Sayago, Sayavedra, Saygidia, Seanez, Seara, Seavello, Seballos, Sebeo, Seca, Secada, Secades, Secatero, Seco, Seda, Sedano, Sedeno, Sedilla, Sedillio, Sedillo, Sedillos, Segana, Segarra, Segobia, Segonia, Segoria, Segovia, Segoviano, Segrera, Seguera, Segui, Segundo, Segura, Segure, Segurola, Seguy, Seijas, Seijo, Sein, Seisdedos, Seja, Sejas, Selaya, Selayandia, Selem, Selestino, Selgado, Selgas, Selles, Selvera, Semaya, Sembera, Sembrano, Semexant, Semey, Semiday, Semidei, Semidey, Seminario, Sempertegui, Sempre, Sena, Sención, Sendejar, Sendejas, Sendejo, Sendis, Sendón, Senoral, Seneriz, Senjudo, Senosiain, Senquiz, Sentena, Senteno, Sentmanat, Seoane, Seoanes, Sepeda, Sepián, Septién, Sepúlbeda, Sepúlueda, Sepúlveda, Sepúlvedo, Sepúlvida, Sequeida, Sequeiro, Sequera, Sequerra, Sequra, Seraballs, Serabia, Seralena, Serantes, Serasio, Seraydar, Serbantes, Serbantez, Serda, Serdas, Serenil, Sermeño, Sermiño, Serna, Sernas, Serracino, Serradell, Serrado, Serralles, Serralta, Serrano, Serranía, Serrano, Serrantes, Serrat, Serrata, Serrate, Serrato, Serratos, Serravillo, Serravo, Serret, Serritos, Serrono, Serros, Sertuche, Servantes, Servantez, Servera, Servilla, Servillo, Servín, Sesanto, Sesate, Sese, Sesma, Sesmas, Sesteaga, Sestiaga, Seva, Sevallos, Sevilla, Sevillano, Sevillo, Sexto, Sezate, Sezumaga, Siaca, Siador, Siañez, Síaz, Sibaja, Siberío, Siberón, Sibrián, Sicairos, Sicardo, Sicre, Sida, Siedo, Sierra, Sierras, Sierro, Sierze, Sifonte, Sifontes, Sifre, Sifuentes, Sifuentez, Sifventes, Sigala, Sigales, Sigarán, Sigarroa, Sigua, Sigueiros, Sigüenza, Silbas, Silerio, Silgero, Silguero, Siliezar, Sillano, Sillart, Sillas, Sillen, Siller, Sillero, Silos, Silot, Silquero, Silvarrey, Silvas, Silverio, Silvestre, Silvestry, Silveyra, Simental, Simentel, Simiano, Sintas, Siordía, Siprián, Sipula, Siqueido, Siqueiro, Siqueiros, Siqueros, Siquieros, Sira, Siret, Sirias, Sirio, Siros, Sisnero, Sisneros, Sisneroz, Sisniegas, Sistos, Sital, Sitjar, Siurano, Siva, Siverio, Sixto, Sixtos, Soba, Sobalvarro, Soberal, Soberanes, Soberanez, Soberanis, Soberón, Sobrado, Sobremonte, Sobrero, Sobrevilla, Sobrín, Sobrino, Soca, Socarras, Socas, Socias, Socorro, Sodoy, Soegaard, Sojo, Sol, Solache, Solanilla, Solano, Solares, Solarez, Solario, Solarzano, Solaun, Soldevila, Soldevilla, Soled, Soledad, Soleno, Soler, Solera, Solero, Solis, Solisgarza, Soliva, Soliván, Soliz, Solono, Solorio, Solórsano, Solorza, Solórzano, Solozábal, Solsona, Soltero, Somano, Somarriba, Somavia, Sombra, Somoano, Somodevilla, Somohano, Somonte, Somoza, Sonabria, Sonchar, Sónchez, Sonera, Sonico, Sonoqui, Sonora, Sopena, Soqui, Sor, Soratos, Sorba, Sordia, Sordo, Soria, Soriano, Sorieno, Sorio, Sornoso, Sorda, Sorola, Sorondo, Sorrano, Sorroche, Sortillón, Sorzano, Sosa, Sosapavón, Sosaya, Sosías, Sostre, Sota, Sotello, Sotelo, Soteras, Sotero, Sotillo, Soto, Sotolongo, Sotomayer, Sotomayor, Sotorrío, Sotro, Sotto, Sottosanto, Sotura,

Sotuyo, Souchet, Souffront, Sourina, Soveranez, Soza, Spindola, Suare, Suáres, Suárez, Suaste, Suástegui, Suávez, Suazo, Subealdea, Subedar, Subega, Subeldía, Subes, Subia, Subias, Subido, Subirana, Subirias, Suco, Sudaria, Seuiras, Sueiro, Suela, Suelto, Suengas, Suera, Suérez, Suero, Suescún, Sueyras, Sugranes, Suina, Sulaica, Suliveres, Sullano, Sulpacio, Sulsona, Sumalla, Sumaya, Sumbera, Sumberaz, Sune, Suner, Súnica, Súñiga, Suquet, Sureda, Suria, Surillo, Surinach, Suris, Surita, Suro, Suros, Susana, Sustache, Sustaeta, Sustaita, Sustayta, Susuras, Swazo.

T Tabada, Tabaldo, Tabales, Tabana, Tabanico, Tabares, Tabarez, Tabbada, Tabera, Taberas, Tabernero, Tabio, Tabizón, Tablada, Tablado, Taboada, Taboas, Tabora, Taborda, Tabraue, Tabuena, Tabuenca, Tabullo, Tachias, Tachiquin, Tacorda, Tacoronte, Tadeo, Taffolla, Tafola, Tafolla, Taford, Tafoya, Tagaban, Taganas, Tagle, Tagudar, Tajes, Talabera, Talache, Talamante, Talamantes, Talamantez, Talamas, Talamente, Talamentes, Talamentez, Talana, Talancón, Talavera, Tallabas, Tallavas, Talleda, Talledo, Tallerino, Tamame, Tamares, Tamarez, Tamargo, Tamarit, Tamariz, Tamaya, Tamayo, Tambara, Tambunga, Tamerón, Támez, Tamguma, Tánchez, Tanco, Tanda, Tanforán, Tanguma, Tañón, Tanori, Tantao, Tanuz, Tapanes, Tapetillo, Tapia, Tapias, Tapiceria, Tapiz, Taporco, Tarabino, Taracena, Tarafa, Taragón, Tarailo, Tarajano, Taramasco, Taranco, Tarango, Tarazón, Tarazona, Tarbes, Targa, Tarín, Tarnava, Tarrago, Tarrango, Tarrats, Tarrau, Tarraza, Tarride, Tarula, Tasabia, Tatis, Tavales, Tavar, Tavarez, Tavera, Taveras, Tavira, Tavisón, Tavitas, Tavizón, Tavora, Tayabas, Teba, Tebaqui, Tebar, Tehas, Teijeiro, Teijiz, Teijo, Teissonniere, Teixidor, Tejada, Téjas, Tejeda, Tejedas, Tejedo, Tejedor, Tejeiro, Tejera, Tejeras, Tejerina, Tejero, Tejidor, Tejo, Telas, Telavera, Tellado, Tellaeche, Tellechea, Tellería, Telles, Tellez, Tello, Tellos, Telón, Temblador, Tembras, Temer, Temores, Tempo, Temprana, Tena, Tenario, Tenas, Tenerías, Tenerío, Tenes, Teneyuca, Teneyuque, Teniente, Tenoría, Tenorío, Tepera, Tepezano, Teposte, Tequida, Terán, Tercero, Terceros, Tercilla, Terminel, Terón, Terrado, Terrasa, Terrasas, Terrasaz, Terraza, Terrazas, Terrero, Terreros, Terríguez, Terríquez, Terroba, Terrón, Terrones, Tersero, Teruel, Terusa, Terviño, Terzado, Tesillo, Tevere, Texcahua, Texidor, Teyechea, Tezcucano, Tezino, Thillet, Tía, Tibaldeo, Tibljas, Tibón, Tiburcio, Tico, Tienda, Tijerina, Tijerino, Tijero, Tinajero, Tinaza, Tineo, Tinerella, Tinoco, Tío, Tirado, Tirador, Tirán, Tirre, Tirres, Tirrez, Tirse, Tiscareno, Tisino, Tisnado, Tixier, Tiznado, Tizol, Tobal, Tobar, Tobares, Tobas, Tobilla, Tobon, Toca, Tofoya, Togar, Togores, Toimil, Tojeira, Tojeiro, Tolano, Toledano, Toledo, Tolentino, Tollardo, Tolosa, Toloza, Tolsa, Tomada, Tomayo, Tomelloso, Tomeu, Tomines, Topete, Topia, Toquero, Toral, Toralba, Torales, Torano, Torans, Toranzo, Tordesillas, Toreno, Toribio, Torices, Torijano, Toriz, Tormes, Tormos, Tornel, Tornero, Toro, Torquemada, Torrado, Torralba, Torralbas, Torrales, Torralva, Torrano, Torreblanca, Torrech, Torrecilla, Torrecillas,

Toreegrosa, Torrellas, Torrentera, Torres, Torrescano, Torresdíaz, Torres-Martínez, Torresola, Torres-Rodríguez, Torress, Torrez, Torricella, Torriente, Torrijos, Torrio, Torroella, Torrón, Torros, Torruella, Torruellas, Tortalita, Tortes, Tortilla, Toruga, Turuno, Tosa, Tosado, Tosar, Tossas, Tosta, Tostado, Tova, Tovalín, Tovanche, Tovar, Tovares, Tovarez, Tovías, Toya, Toyens, Toymil, Toyos, Traba, Trabal, Trabanco, Trabazo, Traconis, Trancosa, Tranquada, Trapaga, Traslaviña, Trasobares, Traspeña, Trasviña, Traval, Travaso, Traverzo, Travieso, Trebizo, Trefilio, Tregaro, Trejo, Trejos, Trelles, Tremillo, Trenzado, Tres, Trespalacios, Treto, Trevilla, Treviña, Treviño, Treviño, Tresiso, Trevizo, Trevizu, Triana, Trias, Triay, Tricoche, Trigo, Trigos, Trigoura, Triguero, Trigueros, Trijillo, Trilla, Trillanes, Trillas, Trillayes, Trilles, Trillo, Trillos, Trimiño, Trincado, Trinchet, Trinidad, Tripis, Tristán, Triste, Triunfo, Triviso, Triviz, Trivizo, Troche, Trochez, Trojillo, Troncosa, Troncoso, Troncoza, Troncozo, Troya, Trozera, Trucios, Trueba, Truijillo, Truillo, Trujano, Trujeque, Trujilla, Trujillio, Trujillo, Truyol, Tualla, Tuando, Tuasón, Tuazón, Tubens, Tubón, Tudela, Tudón, Tueme, Tuero, Tufares, Tulier, Túnches, Túnchez, Tuñididor, Tuñón, Tur, Turbay, Turbe, Turcios, Turiace, Turincio, Turizo, Turrey, Turrieta, Turrietta, Turrubiartes, Turrubiate, Turrubiates, Turull, Tuya.

U Ubalde, Uballe, Uballez, Ubals, Ubando, Ubarri, Ubay, Ubeda, Ubias, Ubides, Ubiera, Ubieta, Ubiles, Ubilla, Ubiña, Ubiñas, Uceda, Uceta, Ucha, Uchita, Uchizono, Udabe, Udaeta, Udave, Udero, Ufracio, Ufret, Ugalde, Ugarriza, Ugarte, Ugartechea, Ugues, Ujueta, Ulacia, Ulate, Ulibari, Ulibarri, Ulivarri, Ullivarri, Ulloa, Ultreras, Umana, Umanzor, Umarán, Umpierre, Unale, Unamuño, Unanue, Unate, Uneda, Ungo, Unzalu, Unzueta, Uraga, Uraine, Uranday, Uranga, Urango, Urbaez, Urbalejo, Urbay, Urbieta, Urbina, Urbino, Urbistondo, Urbizu, Urcadez, Urcelay, Urciel, Urdaneta, Urdanivia, Urdaz, Urdiales, Urdialez, Urena, Urenda, Urenia, Ureno, Ureste, Uresti, Ureta, Urgell, Urgelles, Urgiles, Urguidi, Uria, Uriarte, Urías, Uríaz, Uribarri, Uribe, Uribes, Uriburu, Uriega, Uriegas, Uriel, Urieta, Uriola, Urionaguena, Urioste, Urióstegui, Urista, Urita, Urive, Uriz, Uriza, Urizar, Uroza, Urquia, Urquiaga, Urquides, Urquidez, Urquidi, Urquieta, Urquijo, Urquilla, Urquiola, Urquiza, Urquizo, Urquizu, Urra, Urrabas, Urrabaz, Urrabazo, Urraca, Urrea, Urrechaga, Urrego, Urreta, Urrieta, Urriza, Urroz, Urruchua, Urrutia, Ursua, Ursulo, Urtado, Urtasún, Urteaga, Urtez, Urtiaga, Urtusuástegui, Urtuzuástegui, Uruburu, Uruchurtu, Uruena, Urueta, Urvanejo, Urvina, Urzo, Urzúa, Usallán, Usatorres, Uscanga, Useda, Usón, Utria, Utrilla, Utset, Uvalle, Uvalles, Uviedo, Uzeta, Uzueta

V Vaca, Vacío, Vadell, Vadi, Vadía, Vadillo, Vadiz, Vaell, Vaello, Váez, Vaeza, Vaio, Vaisa, Vaiz, Vaiza, Val, Valadez, Valadón, Valague, Valarde, Valarezo, Valásquez, Valázquez, Valbuena, Valcarce, Valcárcel, Valcazar,

Valdaso, Valdemar, Valdenegro, Valdepeña, Valderama, Valderas, Valderaz, Valderez, Valderrain, Valderrama, Valdés, Valdespino, Valdés-Rodríguez, Valdesuso, Valdez, Valdezate, Valdilles, Valdillez, Valdiva, Valdivia, Valdivieso, Valdiviez, Valdiviezo, Valdo, Valdonando, Valdovín, Valdovino, Valdovinos, Valdriz, Valea, Valedón, Valencia, Valenciana, Valenciano, Valeneuela, Valenquela, Valensuela, Valentín, Valenzuela, Valenzula, Valenzvela, Valera, Valerios, Valero, Valésquez, Valez, Valgas, Valhuerdi, Valido, Valiente, Valigura, Valina, Valinas, Valino, Valladares, Valladarez, Vallado, Valladolid, Vallarta, Valldeperas, Valle, Vallecilla, Vallecillo, Vallecillos, Valledor, Vallegos, Valleja, Vallejo, Vallejos, Vallellanes, Vallens, Vallerino, Valles, Vallez, Vallin, Valls, Valmana, Valmores, Valquez, Valterza, Valtier, Valtierra, Valtierrez, Valverde, Vando, Vanegas, Vanga, Vañuelos, Vanzura, Vaque, Vaquer, Vaquera, Vaquero, Vaquilar, Vara, Varada, Varajas, Varas, Varcarcel, Varcos, Varela, Varelas, Vargas, Vargaz, Varguez, Varia, Varona, Varonín, Varos, Varoz, Várquez, Vasaldúa, Vasallo, Vascones, Vasconez, Vascos, Vásguez, Vásque, Vásques, Vásquez, Vássquez, Vasti, Vázguez, Vázque, Vázquel, Vázques, Vázquetelles, Vázquez, Vázquez-Rivera, Veálsquez, Veas, Vecin, Vecino, Vedarte, Vedía, Vega, Vegara, Vega-Torres, Vegazo, Vegerano, Veges, Vego, Vegos, Vegue, Véguez, Veguilla, Veiguela, Veintidos, Veitia, Véjar, Vejara, Vejarano, Vejil, Vejo, Vela, Vela-Arce, Vela-Cuéllar, Velado, Velador, Veláquez, Velar, Velarde, Velardes, Velardez, Velasco, Velásguez, Velásques, Velásquez, Velástegui, Velazco, Velázguez, Velázques, Velázquez, Velderrain, Velenzuela, Veles, Velésquez, Vélez, Vélez-Pérez, Vélez-Román, Velilla, Velis, Veliz, Vellas, Villido, Vellón, Velo, Velos, Veloso, Veloz, Velózquez, Velunza, Veluz, Vences, Vendrell, Venecia, Venegas, Veneración, Venereo, Venezuela, Vensor, Venta, Ventoso, Venzal, Venzor, Venzuela, Vera, Veracruz, Veramendi, Verandas, Veras, Verástegui, Verástequi, Verástigui, Verástique, Verástiqui, Veray, Veraz, Veraza, Verbera, Verceles, Verdaguer, Verdecanna, Verdecia, Verdeguez, Verdeja, Verdejo, Verdera, Verdesca, Verdese, Verde-Soto, Verdia, Verdoza, Verduga, Verdugo, Verdusco, Verduzco, Verduzeo, Verea, Verela, Verez, Vergara, Vergaro, Vergel, Verguizas, Verino, Verjil, Vernengo, Veronin, Verquer, Vertiz, Verver, Veta, Veve, Veyna, Veytia, Viacava, Viacobo, Viada, Viadas, Viade, Viadero, Viades, Viado, Viagran, Viales, Vializ, Vialpando, Viamonte, Viana, Vianes, Viapando, Viarreal, Viarrial, Viayra, Vicaria, Vicedo, Vicencio, Vicens, Vicent, Vicente, Vicenty, Vichot, Viciedo, Vicinaiz, Vicioso, Victorero, Victores, Vicuña, Vidaca, Vidal, Vidales, Vidalez, Vidana, Vidano, Vidaure, Vidauri, Vidaurrazaga, Vidaurre, Vidaurreta, Vidaurri, Vidaurry, Videna, Vides, Vidot, Vidriales, Vidrio, Vidrios, Viduya, Viego, Vieites, Viejo, Vielma, Vielman, Vielmas, Vientos, Viera, Vieras, Viesca, Viescas, Vieta, Vietty, Vieyra, Viezcas, Vigil, Vigilia, Vignau, Vigo, Vigoa, Vigon, Viguera, Vigueras, Vigueria, Vigues, Vijarro, Vijil, Vila, Vilaboy, Viladrosa, Vilano, Vilanova, Vilar, Vilarchao, Vilardell, Vilarino, Vilaro, Vilas, Vilásquez, Vilato, Vilaubi, Vilches, Vilchez, Vilchis, Vildósola, Villa, Villablanca, Villacampa, Villanana, Villacarlos,

Villacis, Villacorta, Villacorte, Villacres, Villacreses, Villada, Villado, Villadoniga, Villaerreal, Villaescusa, Villafan, Villafana, Villafañe, Villaflores, Villafranca, Villafrancio, Villafuerte, Villagas, Villagómes, Villagómez, Villagrama, Villagran, Villagrana, Villahermosa, Villalabos, Villalba, Villalbazo, Villalbos, Villalobas, Villalobo, Villalobos, Villaloboz, Villalomos, Villalón, Villalona, Villalonga, Villalongin, Villalongo, Villalovas, Villalovos, Villalovoz, Villalpando, Villalta, Villalua, Villaluna, Villaluz, Villalva, Villalvaso, Villalvazo, Villaman, Villamar, Villamarín, Villamayor, Villamia, Villamil, Villamor, Villán, Villaneda, Villanes, Villaneuva, Villaneva, Villanez, Villanueva, Villanueba, Villanuera, Villanueva, Villanuevo, Villanveva, Villao, Villapadierna, Villapando, Villaplana, Villapol, Villapondo, Villapudua, Villaquiran, Villar, Villarán, Villaraos, Villaraus, Villareal, Villarejo, Villares, Villarico, Villarino, Villariny, Villariza, Villaroel, Villaronga, Villaros, Villarre, Villarreal, Villarrial, Villarroel, Villarrubia, Villarruel, Villarruz, Villarta, Villarubia, Villaruz, Villas, Villasaiz, Villasana, Villasano, Villasante, Villaseca, Villaseñor, Villasis, Villastrigo, Villasuso, Villate, Villatoro, Villava, Villaverde, Villavicencio, Villavisencio, Villazana, Villazón, Villeda, Villega, Villegas, Villeges, Villegos, Villejo, Villela, Villena, Villereal, Villerreal, Villesca, Villescas, Villescaz, Villete, Villezcas, Villicana, Villicano, Villiegas, Villis, Villoch, Villodas, Villoldo, Villoria, Villorín, Villoro, Villot, Villota, Vilorio, Viltre, Viña, Vinageras, Viñaixa, Viñaja, Viñajeras, Viñales, Viñals, Viñas, Viñat, Vincenty, Vincioni, Vindiola, Vinegra, Vinent, Vinfrido, Vingochea, Viniegra, Viñuela, Viñuelas, Vinzón, Violeta, Viorato, Viota, Víquez, Viradia, Viramonte, Viramontes, Viramontez, Virata, Viray, Virchis, Virella, Virgen, Virjan, Virola, Virrey, Virrueta, Viruegas, Viruet, Viruete, Viruzo, Visarraga, Visarriagas, Viscaina, Viscaino, Viscarra, Viscasillas, Viscaya, Viserto, Visoso, Visperas, Vissepo, Vistro, Vital, Vitar, Vitela, Vitier, Vivanco, Vivancos, Vivar, Vivas, Vivero, Viveros, Vives, Vivo, Vizcaino, Vizcarra, Vizcarro, Vizcarrondo, Vizcaya, Vizcón, Vizoso, Vizuet, Vizueta, Volbeda, Vósquez, Vózquez, Vuelta.

X Ximénes, Ximénez, Ximínez, Xiques, Xochicale, Xuárez.

Y Yabut, Yáñas, Yáñes, Yáñez, Yaneza, Yáñiz, Yanoso, Yáques, Yara, Yarrito, Yarritu, Yarte, Ybaben, Ybáñez, Yabara, Ybarbo, Ybarra, Ybarrola, Ybarrondo, Ybera, Yberra, Ycaza, Ycedo, Yciano, Ydrogo, Yebara, Yebra, Yedo, Yedor, Yedra, Yepa, Yepes, Yepez, Yepis, Yepiz, Yera, Yeras, Yerena, Yero, Yescas, Yeseta, Yeste, Yeverino, Yglecias, Yglesias, Ygnacio, Yguado, Yguerabide, Ylarregui, Ylizaliturri, Ylla, Yllada, Yllanes, Yllescas, Yncera, Ynclan, Ynda, Ynegas, Yneges, Ynfante, Yñigo, Yñíguez, Yñíquez, Ynoa, Ynocencio, Ynosencio, Ynostrosa, Ynostroza, Ynzunza, Yóguez, Yorba, Yordán, Yparraguirre, Yparrea, Ypiña, Yraceburu, Yracheta, Yrastorza, Yriarte, Yribarren, Yribe, Yrigolla, Yrigollen, Yrigoyen, Yrineo, Yrique, Yriqui, Yrisarri, Yrizarry, Yroz, Yruegas, Yrungaray, Yruretagoyena, Ysaguirre, Ysaís,

Ysaquirre, Ysasaga, Ysasi, Ysassi, Yser, Ysern, Yset, Ysla, Yslas, Yslava, Ysquierdo, Ytuarte, Yturbe, Yturralde, Yturri, Yturria, Yturriaga, Yubeta, Yucupicio, Yudesis, Yudice, Yidico, Ylan, Yulfo, Yuriar, Yuste, Yváñez, Yvarra, Yzabal, Yzaguirre, Yznaga, Yzquierdo.

Z Zabal, Zabala, Zabaleta, Zaballa, Zabalo, Zabalza, Zacarías, Zacuto, Zadrima, Zaera, Zafereo, Zafra, Zagala, Zagales, Zagona, Zalacain, Zalace, Zalmea, Zalapa, Zalazar, Zaldaña, Zaldívar, Zaldúa, Zaldumbide, Zalduondo, Zalvidea, Zamacona, Zamago, Zamaniego, Zamanillo, Zamano, Zamar, Zamaripa, Zamarippa, Zamaro, Zamarri, Zamarripa, Zamarripas, Zamarrón, Zamayoa, Zamazal, Zambada, Zambrana, Zambrano, Zamilpa, Zamora, Zamorano, Zamores, Zamorez, Zamoi, Zamudio, Zanabria, Zandate, Zandona, Zangroniz, Zanudo, Zapara, Zapata, Zapater, Zapatero, Zapeda, Zapiain, Zapien, Zarabozo, Zaragosa, Zaragoz, Zaragoza, Zaragozi, Zarate, Zarazua, Zarco, Zarcos, Zardeneta, Zardenetta, Zardo, Zardón, Zardoya, Zarogiza, Zarraga, Zarragoitia, Zarragoza, Zarriá, Zarrubica, Zarzana, Zarzosa, Zarzoza, Zarzuela, Zasueta, Zatarain, Zataray, Zatarian, Zatoren, Zauala, Zaul, Zauza, Zavala, Zavaleta, Zavaletta, Zavalla, Zavalza, Zavat, Zayas, Zayas-Bazán, Zayaz, Zazueta, Zazuetta, Zeas, Zeballos, Zedeño, Zedillo, Zegarra, Zelada, Zelaya, Zeledón, Zemen, Zendejas, Zengotita, Zenizo, Zenoz, Zentella, Zenteño, Zepada, Zepeda, Zequeira, Zerda, Zerin, Zermeño, Zerpa, Zerquera, Zertuche, Zervigón, Zetiña, Zetiño, Zevallos, Zilbar, Zillas, Zoleta, Zomora, Zorola, Zorrilla, Zozaya, Zuaznabar, Zuazo, Zuazua, Zubeldía, Zubia, Zubiate, Zubieta, Zubillaga, Zubiran, Zubiri, Zubiria, Zubizarreta, Zugasti, Zulaica, Zuleta, Zuloaga, Zuluaga, Zulueta, Zumarraga, Zumaya, Zúñiga, Zúñiza, Zuño, Zunzúnegui, Zurbano, Zurbarán, Zurita, Zurrica, Zuvia, Zuvieta, Zuzuarregui.

APPENDIX 3

GARCIA CARRAFFA

Enciclopedia Heráldica y Genealógica

The *Enciclopedia Heráldica y Genealógica* [EHG] by Arturo García Carraffa, which deals principally with Spanish surnames in Spain, includes some histories with information about families in Latin America. All of the histories discuss the Spanish, or in some cases other European, origins of the surnames in question. Garcia Carraffa's book includes some information on the following surnames. They are not strictly alphabetical in order to maintain the integrity of where they are found within the volumes in question. Surnames that were added later in the development of the collection have been referenced at the end of each letter, with the volume in which they are found and the page numbers given for ease of access.

A EHG Volume 1: Aanda, Abad, Abadal, Abades, Abadía, Abaeto, Abaigar, Abaínza, Abairza, Abaito, Abajo, Abalcisqueta, Abalia, Abalillos, Abalón, Abalos, Aballe, Abanades, Abande, Abandero, Abando, Abango, Abanto, Abanzón, Abaña, Abar, Abarca, Abarca de Bolea, Abare, Abargues, Abaria, Abarino, Abarzuza, Abarrategui, Abarrisqueta, Abas, Abascal, Abásolo, Abasons, Abasto, Abastras, Abat, Abate, Abaunza, Abaurza, Abaurre, Abaurrea, Abaygar, Abbad, Abbate, Abceta, Abea, Abecia, Abecilla, Abechuco, Abedillo, Abeeta, Abel, Abela, Abelal, Abelas, Abelastrui, Abelda, Abeldone, Abelos, Abelt, Abella, Abellán, Abellanada, Abellanas, Abellaneda, Abellas, Abello, Abelló, Abenand, Abenandi, Abendaño, Abendíbar, Abendívar, Abengoza, Abenia, Abeo, Aber, Aberancioa, Aberasturi, Aberín, Abersín, Aberso, Abete, Abeu, Abeyro, Abia, Abián, Abidabe, Abidave, Abiega, Abiego, Abieta, Abila, Abilés, Abilla, Abillas, Abinia, Abinin, Abinio, Abinó, Abinón, Abinou, Abio, Ablanedo, Ablanque, Ableu, Ablitas, Aboa, Abogadro, Abogaro, Aboin, Abona, Abor, Aborín, Abós, Abraldes, Ablanchez, Abrantes, Abreo, Abrego, Abregos, Abreu, Abrí, Abrichi, Abrichio, Abril, Abrill, Abrines, Absons, Abul, Abulia, Aburto, Aburruza, Abuta, Acanares, Acaño, Acaraso, Acciaboli, Acciapacia, Acciapacio, Acebal, Acebe, Acebedo, Acebes, Acebo, Acedo, Acega, Aceija, Aceijas, Aceituno, Aceja, Acelain, Acelegui, Acella, Acellana, Acenar, Aceña, Acera, Acero, Acerola, Acevedo,

Acevillo, Aciapacio, Aciapi, Acijas, Acillona, Acín, Acinellas, Aciprés, Acireci, Acitain, Acitores, Acivoli, Aco, Acoda, Acorella, Acosta, Acre, Acuavera, Acua-viva, Acuña, Acurio, Acutain, Acha, Achaboli, Achaburu, Acharán, Acharpasa, Ache, Acheeta, Achega, Achegua, Acheros, Acheta, Achey, Achezaeta, Achipacio, Achioli, Achisaeta, Achivite, Achoarán, Achurdi, Achurriaga, Adabane, Adaíz, Adalid, Adamanden, Adame, Adán, Adán de Yarza. End of EHG Volume 1.

EHG Volume 2: Adana, Adano, Adanza, Adaola, Adarbe, Adarno, Adaro, Adarró, Adarzo, Adaves, Adebas, Adeliño, Adelmón, Adell, Ademar, Adena, Aderigui, Adeva, Adiño, Adoaín, Adorno, Adrada, Adrián, Adrián de Torres, Adsor, Aduanas, Aduanes, Aduca, Aduna, Adurriaga, Adurza, Adurzai, Aduza, Ae, Aechaga, Aedo, Aegea, Aellos, Aendardo, Aerrementería, Aesain, Aeza, Aezcoa, Afaitaro, Afán, Afán de Rivera, Afitis, Afituyes, Aflita, Aflito, Aflitto, Agrape, Africa, Afrontes, Afuera, Agadeburu, Agaiz, Aganduro, Aganduro-Iturriaga, Agar, Agarriga, Agazones, Agea, Ager, Ageris, Agofrin, Agoitiz, Agoiz, Agomia, Agón, Agondaro, Agorero, Agorraeta, Agorreta, Agorría, Agós, Agosta, Agostín, Agostines, Agote, Agralhos, Agramont, Agramonte, Agramontena, Agramunt, Agraz, Agreda, Agreda-Tejada, Agremunt, Agro, Aguada, Aguado, Aguanevados, Aguas, Aguasca, Aguayo, Agudelo, Agudo, Agueri, Agüero, Aguerre, Agurreta, Aguerri, Agüeso, Aguiar, Aguila, Aguilar, Aguilar (a second), Aguileo, Aguileor, Aguiler, Aguilera, Aguileta, Aguilio, Aguiló, Aguilón, Aguilue, Aguinaga, Aguinares, Aguiniga, Aguiñaga, Aguiñares, Aguiñiga, Aguión de Ponte, Aguiriano, Aguirre, Aguirre-Azpe, Aguirre-Basaldúa, Aguirre-Basagoitia, Aguirebengoa, Aguirrebeña, Aguirregabiria, Aguirre-Goienaz, Aguirregoikoa, Aguirreplazocoa, Aguirre-Recalde, Aguirre-Sarasúa, Aguirresarobe, Aguirrezábal, Aguirrezabala, Aguirre-Zaldúa, Aguirrezazona, Aguirri, Aguisardo, Aguisgrán, Agujares, Agullana, Agulló, Agundez, Agurreta, Agurri, Agurrio, Agurto, Agustí, Agustín, Agustina, Agusto, Agut, Ahajadas, Ahe, Ahedo, Aheja, Aheya, Ahín, Ahonen, Ahón, Ahones, Ahotares, Ahumada, Aibar, Aibelles, Aibri, Aicaroz, Aiceburu, Aich. End of EHG Volume 2.

EHG Volume 3: Aichiavoli, Aicoz, Aicute, Aiguaviva, Aignanariz, Aileme, Ailome, Aillón, Aillones, Ailly, Aimar, Aimaric, Aimerich, Aincio, Ainciondo, Aindorfer, Aines, Aineto, Ainsa, Ainza, Aiñón, Aisa, Aisca, Aisea, Aitamarren, Aitera, Aiturguy, Aiz, Aizaga, Aizaldebarrena, Aizarna, Aizarnatea, Aizarnazábal, Aizarte, Aizate, Aizbay, Aizcorbe, Aizoaín, Aizpegoena, Aizpiri, Aizpuru, Aizpurúa, Aizquibel, Aiztondo, Aiztuz, Aja, Ajanguiz, Ajesa, Ajober, Ajofrín, Ajos, Ajuria, Alabaña, Alabasos, Alabayna, Alabio, Aladro, Alagno, Alagón, Alaín de Beaumont, Alaíz, Alaiza, Alaja, Alajín, Aláma, Alamán, Alambarranta, Alameda, Alamín, Alamo, Alandí, Alango, Alanguer, Alanís, Alanquer, Alansón, Alanzón, Alaó, Alañón, Alapont, Alarán, Alaraz, Alarcón, Alardos, Alaregus, Alaris, Alarys, Alas, Alascón, Alastra, Alastrué, Alastruey,

Alastuey, Alatrista, Alaurna, Alava, Alaviano, Alaxa, Alaxín, Alaya, Alazán, Alba, Albacete, Albalat, Albalate, Albalibus, Albamonte, Albán, Albana, Albandois, Albanel, Albarado, Albaredo, Albarenga, Albarez, Albarfáñez, Albaroto, Albarracín, Albe, Albear, Albeeta, Albelda, Albelos, Albénil, Albéniz, Albentoja, Albentosa, Alberca, Alberche, Albergaria, Alberín, Alberite, Albero, Alberó, Alberola, Alberro, Albert, Albertí, Albertín, Albertino, Alberto, Albertos, Alberuelas, Albesa, Albez, Albia, Albiano, Albide, Albín, Albinagorda, Albinagorta, Albines, Albiñana, Albión, Albircio, Albisco, Albisto, Albistrio, Albistro, Albistur, Albito, Albiz, Albizu, Albizua, Albizubaso, Albizuri, Albo, Albó, Albocar, Alborñoz, Albricio, Albristio, Albrizu, Albuerne, Albun, Alborquerque, Albuquerque, Alburquerque, Albuxech, Alcaforado, Alcahones, Alcaín, Alcaizaga, Alcayzaga, Alcalá, Alcalde, Alcanabe, Alcanadre, Alcanave, Alcantade, Alcántara, Alcañiz, Alcaones, Alcarán, Alcaraz, Alcariz, Alcarsa, Alcasa, Alcasaba, Alcaseba, Alcasoba, Alcate, Alcaudete, Alcavarilla, Alcayada, Alcayaga, Alcazaba, Alcázar, Alcedo, Alcega, Alcegui, Alcelegui, Alcelus, Alcepes, Alcereca, Alcerieca, Alcerreca, Alchacoa, Alchirria, Alcíbar, Alcibias, Alciga, Alcina, Alzina, Alckemoer, Alcober, Alcoberro, Alcocer. End of EHG Volume 3.

EHG Volume 4: Alcocés, Alcochola, Alcolea, Alconada, Alconer, Alcoroche, Alcoz, Alcuberri, Alcubierre, Alcubillo, Alcuide, Alcuza, Aldá, Aldaba, Aldabalde, Aldavalde, Aldabe, Aldave, Aldaco, Aldacoro, Aldai, Aldalur, Aldama, Aldamar, Aldana, Aldaola, Aldaolaechea, Alda-Olea, Aldape, Aldapebeitia, Aldaret, Aldarete, Aldasa, Aldasoro, Alday, Aldaza, Aldazábal, Aldazábal-Murguía, Aldazazábal, Aldazo, Aldea, Aldecoa, Aldehuela, Aldeire, Aldemoresco, Alderec, Alderete, Aldoba, Aldobea, Aldobera, Aldobrandini, Aldobrandino, Aldonalde, Aldovera, Aldrete, Aldrolea, Alduacin, Aldunate, Alducín, Alduncín, Aleda, Aledo, Alegre, Alegret, Alegría, Aleiza, Aleja, Alejandre, Alejandro, Alejos, Alemán, Alemañ, Alemani, Alemany, Alemparde, Alemparte, Alén, Alencastre, Alencastro, Alensón, Alentón, Alentorn, Alenyá, Alenzón, Aleo, Alepus, Aler, Aleristio, Alesanco, Alesano, Alesón, Alebio, Alevio, Alexandre, Alexandro, Alfambra, Alfaro, Alfay, Alfeirán, Alférez, Alférez de Xódar, Alfocea, Alfoceres, Alfonseca, [EHG Volume 5: Alfonsín, Alfonso Rosicas, Alfonso de Sousa, Alfonso de Teruel, Alfonso Villagómez], Alfonsia, Alfonsín, Alfonso, Alfos, Algaba, Algara, Algarbe, Algarín, Algarines, Algarra, Algarui, Algarve, Algecira, Algeo, Algeta, Algola, Algora, Algorta, Alguacil, Alguea, Alguerdo, Algueta, Alguíbar, Alguín, Alguiso, Alhaja, Alhama, Alí, Aliaga, Aliaxa, Alicante, Alien, Aliende, Aliendi, Alier, Aliers, Alifante, Alife, Alija, Alinez, Alió, Alipasolo, Aliprandi, Aliprando, Aliri, Alirias, Alirubia, Alis, Alisón, Alix, Alixa, Almada, Almagro, Almaicoz, Almandoz, Almansa, Almanza, Almao, Almaraz, Almarcha, Almarza, Almas, Almau, Almaycoz, Almazán, Almeida, Almela, Almelda, Almena, Almenar, Almenara, Almendáriz, Almendral, Almendras, Almendros, Almendurúa, Almenuez, Almeri, Almería, Almirano, Almirón, Almodóvar, Almogábar,

Almogávar, Almoguera, Almoina, Almonaster, Almonacid, Almonte, Almoragas, Almorant, Almoravid, Almorca, Almoyna, Almudévar, Almugáver, Almunia, Almuzara. End of EHG Volume 4.

EHG Volume 5: Aloi, Alomar, Alona, Alondris, Alonso, Alonso (Fernández), Alonso de Andrade, Alonso de Arce, Alonso Benavides, Alonso Bracho, Alonso Calderón, Alonso de Caso, Alonso Castañeda, Alonso Huidobro, Alonso de la Jarrota, Alonso de Liébana, Alonso Magadán, Alonso Maluenda, Alonso Pimentel, Alonso del Pino, Alonso de Quiñones, Alonso Rufranco, Alonso Salinas, Alonso de Sande, Alonso de Septién, Alonso Trevejo, Alonso de Villasante, Alonso de Vivero, Alonsotegui, Aloristio, Alóriz, Alórriz, Alós, Alosa, Alost, Aloy, Aloyto, Alpedrete, Alpedrín, Alpicat, Alpizcueta, Alpoem, Alpoens, Alpoim, Alpont, Alponte, Alprano, Alquézar, Alquíjar, Alquiza, Alquizalete, Alsaín, Alsava, Alsedo, Alsín, Alsina, Alsos, Alstón, Altamira, Altamirano, Altares, Altarriba, Altecha, Altemir, Altemiz, Altera, Altero, Altet, Alteza, Altier, Altieri, Altiga, Altigo, Altiro, Altiurre, Alto, Alto de Salinas, Altolaguirre, Altra, Altrigo, Altube, Altuna, Altuya, Altuza, Aluces, Alustiza, Alvarado, Alvarenga, Alvarez, Alvarez (another), Alvarez de Acevedo, Alvarez de Aguiar, Alvarez de Alarias, Alvarez Alfonso, Alvarez de Alvarez, Alvarez de Arcaya, Alvarez Arintero, Alvarez Armesto, Alvarez Arroyo, Alvarez de las Asturias, Alvarez de Bandujo, Alvarez Baragaña, Alvarez Barahona, Alvarez Barba, Alvarez de la Barreda, Alvarez Barreiro, Alvarez Barrero, Alvarez Barriada, Alvarez Becerra, Alvarez Benavides, Alvarez Bobadilla, Alvarez Bohórques, Alvarez de la Bolada, Alvarez de la Braña, Alvarez Cabañas, Alvarez Cabril, Alvarez de Cabuérniga, Alvarez de Calatañazor, Alvarez Caldero, Alvarez Campana, Alvarez Campillo, Alvarez Campomanes, Alvarez Carballo, Alvarez de Cardemuela, Alvarez de la Carrozal, Alvarez Castellano, Alvarez de Castro, Alvarez Cedrón, Alvarez Cereijido, Alvarez de Cienfuegos, Alvarez Cimbrón, Alvarez Coque, Alvarez Cornas y Caballero, Alvarez de Cuenllas, Alvarez Dopacio, Alvarez Escaja, Alvarez de Escalante, Alvarez de Escandón, Alvarez Espearpizo, Alvarez de Espejo, Alvarez de Estrada, Alvarez de Eulate, Alvarez de Faes, Alvarez Faria, Alvarez Feito, Alvarez de la Fuente, Alvarez García, Alvarez Gato, Alvarez González de Castro, Alvarez Guarida, Alvarez de los Hitos, Alvarez Jiménez, Alvarez de Lasarte, Alvarez Lorenzana, Alvarez Losada, Alvarez Maldonado, Alvarez Marrón, Alvarez de Meda, Alvarez de Mendieta, Alvarez Menéndez, Alvarez de Meneses, Alvarez Monjardín, Alvarez Monteserín, Alvarez Moreno, Alvarez de Nava, Alvarez Ojea, Alvarez Olmedo, Alvarez Ordoño, Alvarez Osorio, Alvarez de la Pandilla, Alvarez Panizo, Alvarez de la Pedrosa, Alvarez Peinado, Alvarez de Peralta, Alvarez Pozueco, Alvarez Prada, Alvarez de la Puente, Alvarez del Puerto, Alvarez de Puga, Alvarez de Quiris, Alvarez de Quiroga, Alvarez Rabanal, Alvarez Ramos, Alvarez Requejo, Alvarez Reyero, Alvarez Reymondes, Alvarez del Río, Alvarez de la Rivera, Alvarez de

Robledo, Alvarez de Rollán, Alvarez de Ron, Alvarez de Saavedra, Alvarez Salazar, Alvarez Salgado, Alvarez San Martín, Alvarez San Martino, Alvarez de Santisteban, Alvarez Serrano, Alvarez de Sierra, Alvarez Sotomayor, Alvarez de Toledo, Alvarez Trincado, Alvarez de la Torre, Alvarez de Villacorta, Alvarez del Valle, Alvarez de Villabol, Alvarez de la Villeta, Alvaro, Alvea, Alvear, Alveruela, Alvira, Alvircio, Alvirto, Alviz, Alza, Alzáa-Echea, Alzaga, Alzáibar, Alzamora, Alzarán, Alzarbe, Alzarte, Alzas, Alzate, Alzátegui, Alzava, Alzayaga, Alzíbar, Alziturri, Alzola, Alzolaras, Alzolaras-Guevara, Alzórriz, Alzu, Alzúa, Alzuaín, Alzualde, Alzuarán, Alzubide, Alzueta, Alzugaray, Alzumbarrant, Alzuru. End of EHG Volume 5.

EHG Volume 6: Allado, Allafor, Allamonte, Allande, Allarcelli, Allarcigui, Allastigui, Alláriz, Allata, Allén, Allén del Agua, Allén de Salazar, Allendesalazar, Allende, Aller, Allí, Allín, Alliri, Allisi, Allo, Alló, Alloc, Alloz, Alloza, Allué, Amaciano, Amachesco, Amada, Amadei, Amadín, Amado, Amador, Amaeiro, Amagano, Amaguno, Amaín, Amairra, Amalrich, Amallo, Amollobieta, Amandi, Amanis, Amantegui, Amar, Amaral, Amarelle, Amarelli, Amargos, Amarilla, Amarit, Amarita, Amariz, Amás, Amasa, Amasada, Amasorraín, Amat, Amate, Amatescho, Amatiano, Amato, Amatria, Amatriaín, Amaya, Amayrra, Amaza, Amazada, Ambe, Ambel, Ambesi, Ambia, Amblard, Amboage, Ambós, Ambram, Ambruc, Ambulodi, Ambulodibu, Amburz, Amejir, Ameler, Amelis, Amell, Ameller, Amelli, Amenabar, Amendíbar, Amer, Amés, Amescoa, Amescua, Amesti, Ametller, Ameyugo, Amez, Amézaga, Amezcueta, Amézola, Amezqueta, Amezquita, Amezua, Amiano, Amibiscar, Amigant, Amigo, Amigó, Amigot, Amilano, Amileta, Amilibia, Amilidia, Amira, Amirola, Amis, Amises, Amix, Amo, Amoeiro, Amolaz, Amor, Amora, Amoragas, Amorebieta, Amores, Amoreto, Amorillo, Amorín, Amorlaz, Amorós, Amorós de Satelo, Amoroso, Amoroto, Amoroz, Amoscotegui, Ampara, Amparán, Ampiedes, Ampiés, Ampudia, Ampuero, Ampurias, Amuerio, Amunabarro, Amurrio, Amusco, Amuscotegui, Amustegui, Amuzcotegui, Ana, Anachuri, Anaduri, Anae, Analso, Anasco, Anasto, Anastro, Anaut, Anaya, Anceo, Ancieta, Ancilla, Anciola, Anciondo, Anciso, Ancisto, Ancitia, Ancizaraimburu, Ancollana, Anconja, Ancora, Ancoronat, Anchea, Ancheos, Anchés, Ancheta, Anchía, Anchías, Anchieta, Anchieva, Anchoca, Anchóniz, Anchorena, Anchóriz, Anchotegui, Anchura, Anda, Andaburu, Andagoya, Andalucía, Andaluz, Andallón, Andanza, Andaraz, Andaya, Andeca, Andeiro, Andelos, Andelot, Anderal, Anderaz, Anderica, Andériz, Andeyro, Andía, Andiano, Andicano, Andicona, Andiconagoitia, Andina, Andino, Andión, Andirengoechea, Andoín, Andonaegui, Andonegui, Andosilla, Andraca, Andrada, Andrada Vanderwilde, Andrade, Andradegui, Andraituni, Andramendi, Andraza, Andrea, Andrequaín, Andrés, Andreu, Andrey, Andriani, Andrino, Anduaga, Anduce, Andueza, Anduga, Anduizu, Andújar, Anduzu, Anero, Anés. End of EHG Volume 6.

EHG Volume 7: Anescar, Anesta, Anfriano, Angel, Angelats, Angelo, Angeloa, Anglada, Anglasell, Anglería, Anglés, Anglesola, Angola, Angoncillo, Angos, Angostina, Angosto, Angrisol, Angueira, Anguelao, Anguelado, Anguelo, Anguera, Anguiano, Anguiles, Anguiozar, Anguis, Angulo, Angulosa, Angumedo, Ania, Aniaya, Aniés, Aniesa, Anieto, Anievas, Aniguino, Anil, Anillo, Animio, Aniñón, Anitúa, Aniz, Anizqueta, Anjada, Anjiano, Anleo, Anna, Annecour, Annés, Anoegui, Anoés, Anoz, Anríquez, Anrubia, Ansa, Ansaldo, Ansello, Ansellón, Ansill, Ansilla, Ansillo, Ansó, Ansoaín, Ansoátegui, Ansodi, Ansorena, Ansorregui, Ansotegui, Ansoti, Ansoyán, Ansu, Ansuaga, Ansuaín, Ansúrez, Antayo, Antecha, Antenor, Antenorio, Antenza, Antequera, Antezana, Antia, Antich, Antígono, Antiguo, Antillo, Antillón, Antín, Antist, Antoine, Antolí, Antolínez, Antón, Antón del Olmet de Lanuza, Antona, Antoniano, Antonio, Antoñana, Antoñano, Antrago, Antúnez, Antuñano, Anucibay, Anués, Anuncibay, Anxiano, Anzano, Anzati, Anzeta, Anziola, Anzola, Anzuán, Anzuane, Anzué, Anzules, Anzuola, Añana, Añas, Añasco, Añel, Añes, Añez, Añón, Añorbe, Añorga, Añover, Añoz, Añués, Aoiz, Aostre, Aozaraga, Apalategui, Apaolaga, Apaolaza, Apara, Aparabasco, Aparici, Aparicio, Aparisi, Apate, Apategui, Apazaola, Apellániz, Apenza, Aperain, Aperregui, Aperribay, Apeta, Apeztegui, Apezteguía, Apioca, Apioza, Apocoa, Apodaca, Aponte, Apráiz, Aprano, Aquareta, Aquese, Aquilué, Aquino, Aquiriano, Aquiso, Ara, Arabaolaza, Arabigui, Arabio, Arabués, Aracama, Araceli, Araciel, Aracil, Aracu, Aracubia, Arachea, Arada, Arados, Araeces, Araeta, Araeza, Araiza, Aragall, Argallo, Aragón. End of EGH Volume 7.

EGH Volume 8: Aragonés, Aragorri, Araguás, Aragüés, Arahuete, Araíco, Araín, Arainguibel, Aráiz, Araiztegui, Araldes, Aramayona, Arámbarri, Arámberri, Arambiaga, Arambide, Arambone, Aramburo, Aramburu, Aramendi, Aramendía, Arana, Aranada, Aranaga, Aranaiba, Aranalde, Aranarache, Aranariche, Aranaz, Arancava, Arance, Aranceaga, Arances, Aranceta, Aranze, Arancibia, Aranco, Aranda, Arandia, Arándiga, Arando, Arandojo, Arandujo, Arandoña, Araneta, Arango, Arangoiti, Arangoitia, Arangozqui, Aranguesqui, Aranguis, Aranguiti, Aranguiz, Aranguren, Aranguti, Aranguyti, Aranibar, Arano, Aransay, Aransolo, Aransu, Aranza, Aranzábal, Aranzadi, Aranzate, Aranzeaga, Aránzazu, Aranzu, Aranzubia, Araña, Araoz, Araque, Araquil, Arardo, Ararte, Arasanz, Arascot, Arasia, Arasnabarreta, Araso, Arata, Araube, Arauco, Arauna, Araus, Arauz, Aravide, Araya, Arazama, Arazuri, Arbaiza, Arbe, Arbea, Arbee, Arbeiza, Arbeláez, Arbeláiz, Arberas, Arberoa, Arbestain, Arbia, Arbicio, Arbide, Arbidea, Arbieto, Arbilaga, Arbilde, Arbildi, Arbillaga, Arbizu, Arbolancha, Arbolanche, Arbolea, Arboleda, Arboleya, Arbón de Bellón, Arbona, Arbonies, Arbonis, Arborea, Arborser, Arbués, Arbuet, Arbueta, Arbuixech, Arbulo, Arbulu, Arburúa, Arbusech, Arc, Arca, Arcacha, Arcachaga, Arcagas, Arcaine, Arcales,

Arcaraso, Arcarasu, Arcas (or Arqués), Arcauri, Arcaute, Arcaya, Arcayna, Arce, Arcella, Arceo, Arci, Arcila, Arcilla, Arcillero, Arcillo, Arciniega, Arcocha, Arco, Arcos, Archega, Archiguinolasa, Archimbaud, Ardaiz, Ardanaz, Ardanza, Arde, Ardena, Arderise, Ardid, Ardila, Ardiles, Ardingello, Arduino, Area, Areaga, Areano, Arecha. End of EHG Volume 8.

EHG Volume 9: Arechaga, Arechavala, Arechavaleta, Areche, Arechea, Arechederra, Arechederreta, Arecia, Areco, Aregita, Areiceta, Areilza, Areitio, Areizaga, Aréjola, Arellano, Arena, Arenal, Arenas, Arenaza, Arendigoyen, Arenillas, Arenio, Arenós, Areny, Arenzana, Arenzano, Arequita, Arés, Arescurrenaga, Areses, Aresorena, Arespacochaga, Arespagundegui, Areste, Aresti, Areta, Arévalo, Aréxola, Arezo, Arfe, Argáez, Argain, Argáiz, Argandoña, Arganza, Arganzón, Arganzúa, Arganzura, Argaña, Argañaras, Argarate, Argemir, Argensola, Argenet, Argentona, Argerich, Argibay, Argizaín, Argoaín, Argoarín, Argoín, Argomániz, Argomeda, Argomedo, Argos, Argote, Arguas, Argudo, Argüelles, Argüello [see also Argüello, Volume 23, p. 217], Argueta, Arguiano, Arguibarri, Arguillur, Arguinao, Arguindegui, Arguiñáriz, Arguis, Arguijo, Arguiso, Arguiz, Arguizan, Argumosa, Aria, Ariapi, Arias, Ariazábal, Ariceta, Aricio, Aricheta, Arichz, Ariese, Arieta, Arigoren, Arigoy, Ariguel, Ariguela, Arilza, Arimasagasti, Arimendi, Arin, Arindez, Arindiz, Arinio, Arintero, Arinzano, Ariño, Ariola, Ariortua, Arismendi, Arispe, Arista de Zúñiga, Aristaraín, Aristerrazu, Arístegui, Aristeguieta, Aristarrazu, Aristi, Aristigaya, Aristizábal, Aristo, Aristondo, Arisuso, Ariszubiaga, Ariz, Ariza, Arizabalaga, Arizabaleta, Arizabalo, Arizaga, Arizaleta, Arizavaleta, Arizcorreta, Arizcun, Arizluzo, Arizmendi, Ariznabarreta, Ariznoa, Arizola, Arizón, Arizteguieta, Ariztigaya, Ariztoy, Arizu, Arjona, Arlas, Arlegui, Arlés, Arleta, Armada, Armadans, Armal, Armala, Armañanzas, Armaolea, Armañas, Armaynanza, Armendáriz, Armendia, Armendurua, Armengol, Armengot, Armenta, Armenteros, Armentia, Armer, Armero, Armesto, Armiaga, Armida, Armijo, Armíldez, Armilodea, Arminios, Armiñán, Armiñanque, Armiño, Armona, Armóniz, Armuña, Arnado, Arnaiz, Arnal, Arnaldi, Arnalte, Arnaños, Arnao, Arnaobidao, Arnardeler, Arnau, Arnaud, Arnaut de Ozta, Arnaza, Arne, Arnedo, Arnero, Arnés, Arnez, Arnu, Arnuero, Arnus de Ferrer, Arnuve, Aro, Aroca, Aroiz, Arolas, Aroldo, Aronal. End of EHG Volume 9.

EHG Volume 10: Aronsena, Arosemena, Arosena, Aróstegui, Arozarena, Arozqueta, Arpajón, Arpajou, Arper, Arpide, Arquellada, Arquer, Arquero, Arqués, Arquillada, Arrabal, Arracas, Arracate, Arracietaia, Arráes, Arráez, Arrafán, Arragoaga, Arráiz, Arrain, Arral, Arrambide, Arramendi, Arramendia, Arrameru, Arranales, Arrandolaza, Arránguez, Arránguiz, Arranomendi, Arranzubia, Arraña, Arraño, Arrarás, Arrasa, Arrasal, Arrasate, Arrastia, Arrastra, Arrasúa, Arratabe, Arrate, Arratea, Arrateguibel, Arratia, Arratibel,

Araya, Arrayez, Arrayoz, Arrazaín, Arrazola, Arrazubi, Arrazubia, Arrechea, Arredondo, Arregui, Arreguia, Arreguibar, Arreguibarrena, Arréjola, Arreluz, Arrepiso, Arrese, Arrézola, Arria, Arriaga, Arriarán, Arriati, Arriaza, Arribas, Arribillaga, Arrichaz, Arriesta, Arrieta, Arrillaga, Arriola, Arrigorriaga, Arriorriaga, Arripa, Arripe, Arrisubiaga, Arris, Arriuz, Arrizábal, Arrizabalaga, Arrizubiaga, Arroaga, Arrobi, Arroce, Arroitia, Arrojo, Arrola, Arrom, Arrona, Arrondo, Arróniz, Arrónez, Arróñez, Arroquia, Arróyabe, Arroyo, Arrozubi, Arrubla, Arrue, Arrueira, Arrueta, Arrufat, Arruti, Arrutia, Arruza, Arscia, Arseche, Arsoriz, Arsu, Arsua, Arsuaga, Arsueta, Artacona, Artacoz, Artacho, Artadi, Artadia, Artajo, Artajona, Artal, Artalezu, Artan, Artanga, Artano, Artapea, Artaraín, Artariaín, Artascoz, Artaso, Artasona, Artavia, Artaza, Artazcoz, Artazona, Artazubiaga, Arteaga, Arteasuaincar, Arteche, Arteis, Arteiz, Arteita, Arteri, Artés, Arteta, Arteya, Arti, Artia, Artiaga, Artidiello, Artieda, Artiga, Artigosa, Artigues, Artiles, Artiz, Arto, Artola, Artoleta, Artosilla, Artucha, Artuda, Artundiaga, Artunduaga, Artusella, Artusia, Arturo, Artus, Artune, Aruec, Aruza, Arxella, Arza, Arzábal, Arzabe, Arzac, Arzadun, Arzaga, Arzalaya, Arzamendi, Arzola, Arzoz, Arzu, Arzúa, Arzubia, Arzueta, Asaburu, Asalido, Asarta, Asas, Ascaín, Ascanio, Ascargoitia, Ascargorta, Ascarza, Ascasibar, Ascaso, Ascasua, Asco, Ascoeta, Ascón, Asconiga, Asconiza, Ascuénaga, Ascho, Asencio, Asenjo, Asensio, Asiaín, Asiapi, Asien, Asín, Asio, Asión, Asiresi, Asiulines, Asla, Asnara, Aso, Asola, Asolo, Asorín, Asoza, Aspa, Asparray, Aspergota, Asperen, Aspegorta, Asperilla, Aspiroz, Aspre, Asprer, Assante, Assin, Asso, Assu, Asta, Astaburuaga, Asteasuaín, Asteguieta, Asteiza, Astete, Astiasarán, Astigar, Astigarraga, Astigarribia, Astina, Astiria, Astirias, Astiz, Astón, Astor, Astordúa, Astorga, Astoriza, Astoviza, Astravantes, Astruantes, Astrus, Astudillo, Astuni, Astuniazaga, Asu, Asúa, Asuaga, Asuara, Asula, Asura, Asurcia, Asurdui, Asurduy, Asuria, Asurmendi, Ata, Ataide, Atalaya, Ataldo, Atarés, Ataún, Atazo, Ateca, Ategui, Ateguren, Atehortúa, Atibar, Atienza, Atilano, Atiza, Atocha, Atodo, Atondo, Atorella, Atorilla, Atorrasagasti, Atorrella, Atorzgui, Atristaín, Atrocillo, Atrojillo, Atrosillo, Attard, Atucha, Atue, Atuelles, Auber, Aubert, Aubray, Aud, Audivert, Audor, Auguenez, Aulestia, Aulet, Auli, Aulia, Aumátegui, Aumendia, Aumentia, Auñón, Aurgaste, Auriol, Aurioles, Ausa, Auses, Ausina, Austoa, Aux, Auxes, Avalos, Avanto, Avanzago, Avanzón, Avecilla, Avellaneda, Avendaño, Avero, Avila, Avilés, Avinyó, Aviñón, Axa, Axaló, Axartell, Axella, Axpe, Axtera, Ayala, Ayalde, Ayaldeburu, Ayandegoller, Ayanz, Ayar, Ayardi, Ayardia, Ayardiga, Ayarza, Ayensa, Ayenza, Ayerbe, Ayerde, Ayerdi, Ayerdipea, Ayergis, Ayerguir, Ayerola, Ayesa, Ayestá, Ayestarán, Ayet, Ayete, Ayora, Ayordamúñoz, Ayoerín, Ayorín, Ayosa, Ayosi, Ayuela, Ayues, Ayuno, Ayuso, Az, Aza, Azaceta, Azadón, Azagra, Azaldegui, Azanza, Azaña, Azara, Azaro, Azarola, Azanfo, Azca, Azcain, Azcaraldea, Azcaraldia, Azcárate, Azcaray, Azcargota, Azcárraga, Azcarratezábal, Azcoa, Azcón, Azcona, Azconegui, Azconobieta, Azcue, Azcune, Azelm, Azlor, Azme, Aznar, Aznárez, Aznáriz, Azo, Azoca, Azofra, Azonero, Azopardo, Azor,

Azorero, Azorín, Azpa, Azparren, Azpeitia, Azperen, Azpiazu, Azpilcueta, Azpilicueta, Azpillaga, Azpilleta, Azpiriz, Azpiroz, Azpitarte, Azpitia, Azqueta, Azquez, Azqui, Azterani, Azterrica, Azúa, Azuela, Azuelo, Azugar, Azzia. End of EHG Volume 10.

EHG Volume 23: Argüello, p. 217; EHG Volume 28: Aceña de Butrón, p. 199; Alberola, p. 201; Amesti, p. 202; Andonaegui, p. 206; Anguita, p. 208; Azarola, p. 209; EHG Volume 29: Azcárraga, p. 237; EHG Volume 31: Alverico, p. 211; EHG Volume 32: Azara, de Barbuñales, p. 203; EHG Volume 33: Albuerne, p. 281; EHG Volume 44: Argüelles, p. 227; EHG Volume 50: Alfaro, p. 246; EHG Volume 58: Aicinena, p. 222; Aycinena, p. 222; Arsu, p. 225; Arzu, p. 225; Alvarez de las Asturias, p. 226; Albear, p. 238; EHG Volume 59: Acedo, p. 255; Antillón, p. 256; EHG Volume 67: Azcón, p. 227; EHG Volume 68: Avila or Dávila, p. 239; EHG Volume 73: Agüera, p. 199; Aguirre de Aizpegoena, p. 200. End of Letter A.

B EHG Volume 11: Baana, Baamonde, Babelón, Babét, Babia, Babiano, Babit, Babot, Baca, Bacara, Bacaro, Bacazábal, Bacelar, Bacelares, Bacerola, Bacie, Bacinas, Bacó, Back, Bach, Bachicao, Bachod, Bada, Badajoz, Badajoz (Sánchez de), Badarán, Badia, Badino, Badiola, Bado, Badoera, Badoero, Badolato, Badostaín, Baeda, Baelo, Baena, Baene, Baenst, Baeza, Bafeo, Bagá, Bagache, Bagalde, Bagán, Bagaroto, Bager, Bages, Baget, Bago, Bagos, Báguena, Bagueña, Baguer, Bagues, Bagur, Bahamonde, Bahi, Baiden, Baides, Baidiola, Baigorri, Baiguela, Bailén, Bailo, Baillo, Bailly, Baio, Baizábal, Bajano, Bajoles, Bajuelo, Bal, Balabil, Balacloy, Balades, Baladoy, Balaguer, Balán, Balandre, Balandrek, Balandro, Balanyá, Balanza, Balanzó, Balariaín Balás, Balbás, Balbi, Balbín, Balboa, Balbuena, Balcárcel, Balcázar, Balda, Baldabacayta, Baldabazayta, Baldaura, Baldelomar, Baldespino, Baldivia, Baldocinas, Baldocinos, Baldoví, Baldovín, Baldovinos, Baldrich, Balduz, Balearra, Balech, Balencegui, Balencianos, Balenchana, Balentín, Baleras, Balerdi, Bales, Baley, Balez, Balguarnera, Balicó, Balman, Balmaseda, Balmau, Balmazán, Balonga, Balparda, Balpuesta, Bals, Balsa, Balsells, Balsera, Balsorga, Baltanas, Balterra, Baltodano, Balú, Balza, Balzola, Balla, Ballabriga, Balladares, Ballariaín, Ballaró, Ballartilla, Ballastros, Balle, Ballecillos, Ballenilla, Ballera, Ballero, Ballester, Ballesteros, Ballet, Balleta, Ballín, Ballina, Ballines, Ballo, Ballu, Balluguera, Balluibar, Bam, Ban, Bances, Banchs, Banda, Banda (La), Bandera, Bandera (La), Bandiola, Bandos, Bandrés, Bandujo, Bandurraga, Banessón, Bango, Banfi, Banioles, Banyeres, Banyoles, Banys, Banyuls, Banzo, Bañales, Bañares, Báñez, Báñez de Artazubiaga, Bañolas, Baños, Bañuelos, Bañules, Bañuls [see also Bañuls EHG Volume 23, p.217], Bao, Baptista, Baquedano, Baquer, Baquería, Baquerie, Baquerín, Baquerizo, Baquero, Baquijano, Baquillas, Baquillo, Bara, Baracaldo, Baraez, Barahona, Baraibar, Baraiz, Barajas,

Barajón, Barajoen, Baramba, Barambio, Baranda, Barande, Barandel, Barandet, Barandiano, Barandiarán, Barandica, Barañano, Baraona, Barasiartu, Barata, Baratel, Barau, Barazábal, Barazate, Barba, Barbadillo, Barbado, Barbaez, Barbáchano, Barbanzón, Barbarigo, Barbarín, Barbará, Bárbaro, Barbasco, Barbaza, Barbazán, Barbeito, Barbena. End of EHG Volume 11.

EHG Volume 12: Barbens, Barber, Barberá, Barberán, Barberena, Barbería, Barbier, Barbín, Barbo, Barbón, Barbosa, Barbudo, Barca, Barcáiztegui, Barcalis, Barcana, Barceló, Barcelona, Bárcena, Barcenilla, Barcia, Barcinilla, Barcheta, Barchete, Barco, Bardales, Bardají, Bardas, Bardaverrín, Bardaxí, Barderi, Bardón, Bardoy, Bareta, Bargas, Bargayo, Bariaín, Barieta, Barín, Barinaga, Barluenga, Barnigal, Barnola, Barnués, Barnuevo, Baró, Baro, Baroja, Barón, Barostaín, Barquer, Barquero, Barquín, Barquinero, Barra, Barracha, Barrachina, Barradas, Barrafón, Barragán, Barraicoa, Barraicua, Barraincua, Barral, Barranco, Barrantes, Barraondo, Barras, Barrasa, Barrasgui, Barraya, Barreda, Barredón, Barreira, Barreiro, Barracate, Barrat, Barrena, Barreneche, Barrenechea, Barrera, Barrero, Barrés, Barreto, Barreyarza, Barri, Barria, Barriach, Barriaín, Barriano, Barriceta, Barrientos, Barrieta, Barriga, Barrigón, Barrilaro, Barrile, Barrillas, Barrilos, Barrio, Barrioceta, Barriodajo, Barrionuevo, Barrios, Barriza, Barroeta, Barrón, Barrondo, Barros, Barroso, Barroz, Barruca, Barruchi, Barrueco, Barruelo, Barruezo, Barrundi, Barrutia, Barsola, Bartlett, Bartomeu, Bartrola, Barturen, Barutell, Barzosla, Bas [see also Bas EHG Volume 23, p.219], Basabe, Basabil, Basabilbaso, Basabrú, Basaburu, Basagoiti, Basagoitia, Basaguchia, Basagutia, Basaldua-Aguirre, Basani. End of EHG Volume 12.

EHG Volume 13: Basanta, Basante, Basáñez, Basarate, Basarola, Basart, Basarte, Basayaz-Goyena, Bascanó, Bascaróns, Basco, Basconcillos, Bascones, Bascourt, Bascuñán, Bascuñana, Basedas, Baserola, Baset, Basguas, Basiá, Basilio, Basoco, Basora, Basos, Basozábal, Basquier, Bassa, Bassecourt, Basset, Bassoco, Bassols, Basta, Bastard, Bastart de la Nota, Baster, Bastero, Basterolaza, Basterra, Basterrechea, Basterrica, Baptista, Bastida, Basualdo, Basurto, Bastó, Bastóns, Basturs, Batalla, Bataller, Batet, Batista, Batlle, Batres, Bau, Baucells, Baudet, Baudín, Bauer, Bautista, Baux, Bauzá, Bave, Baxter, Baxter de Kilmarón, Bayalardo, Bayán, Bayarde, Bayarte, Bayer, Bayetola, Bayle, Baylla, Baynanos, Bayo, Bayola, Bayón, Bayona, Bayos, Bazán, Bazcardo, Bazo, Bea, Bealmede, Beaqui, Bearín, Bearn, Bearne, Bearte, Beas, Beascán, Beasoaín, Beasquen, Beasqui, Beato, Beauchamp, Beaufort, Beaumont, Beazquen, Bec, Becerra, Becerril, Bech, Bechi, Becoechea, Becos, Béker, Bécquer, Beda, Bedia, Bediola, Bedmar, Bedorra, Bedoya, Bedua, Begoña, Beguinarru, Beguiristain, Begur, Beibacar, Beina, Beingo, Beinza, Beinzola, Beistegui, Beitia, Beizama, Beiztegui, Beja, Béjar, Bejarano, Bejel, Belandía, Belaochaga, Belart, Belarriaga, Belarro, Belarroa,

Bellascoaín, Belastegui, Belaunza, Belaunzarán, Belaustegui, Belda, Belderraín, Belendiz, Belenguer, Beleret, Belesar, Belestegui, Belmar, Belmonte, Belney, Belniur, Beloque, Beloqui, Belprato, Beltraenea, Beltrán, Beltranilla, Beluaño, Belveder, Belver, Belvis, Belzunce, Belzunegui, Bella, Bellaet, Bellafilla, Bellarido, Bellcastell, Bellera, Bellet, Belletmalgar, Bellfort, Bellido, Bellina, Bellisca, Bello, Belloch, Bellogín, Bellón, Bellosillo, Belloso, Bellosta, Bellot, Belloto, Bellprat, Bellpuig, Belluis, Bellvehí, Bellver, Bellvey, Vellvis, Benaján, Benajas, Benajiger, Benasar, Benar, Benavent, Benavente, Benavides. End of EHG Volume 13.

EHG Volume 14: Bencarza, Bencome, Benda, Bendaña, Beneche, Benedet, Benedete, Benedit, Benegorri, Beneito, Benesa, Benet, Beneyto, Bengoa, Bengoechea, Bengolea, Benítez, Benito, Benosa, Benso Bentades, Bentibolla, Bentrilla, Benvengut, Beorlegui, Beortegui, Beotix, Beraiz, Beraliga, Berama, Beramendi, Berancegui, Berandón, Beranga, Beránger, Berard, Berardo, Berart, Berasaluce, Berasiartu, Berasibia, Berástegui, Berastibia, Beratarrechea, Beratúa, Beraud, Beraun, Beray, Beraza, Berbegal, Berbejal, Berberán, Berbis, Berbizana, Berciano, Berda, Bereceibar, Berecibar, Beregaña, Bereiti de Armendáriz, Berema (or Bortamea Berema), Berenguel, Berenguer, Beresiartu, Bereterbide, Beretereche, Berga, Bergadá, Bergadans, Berganzo, Bergara, Bergé, Berges, Berghes, Bergonces, Bergoños, Bergosa, Bergua, Beriña, Beristain, Berlanga, Bermeo, Berminghan, Bermúdez, Berna, Bernabé, Bernabeu, Bernabeitia, Bernad, Bernal, Bernaldez, Bernales, Bernard, Bernart, Bernat, Bernaldo de Quirós, Bernaola, Bernau, Bernedo, Bernet, Berni, Bernins, Bernis, Berniz, Bernués, Bernuy, Beroiz, Berra, Berraburo, Berrahondo, Berraondo, Berrasoeta, Berraut, Berregarza, Berrearza, Berri, Berria, Berridi, Berrio, Berriozábal, Berris, Bérriz, Berroa, Berroburu, Berroeta, Berrosonaga, Berrospe, Berrotarán, Berroy, Berrueta, Berruezo, Bert, Bertegui, Bertendona, Bertereche, Bertier, Bertiz, Bertodano [see also Bertodano EHG Volume 22, p. 315], Bertrola, Beruete, Bervises, Berzallarta, Berzosa, Besalú, Besant, Besante, Besanche, Bescós, Besga, Besora, Bespeón, Bespes, Bestix, Betana, Betancourt, Betanzos, Betelu, Beterio, Beteta, Betete, Béthencourt [see also Béthencourt EHG Volume 23, p.220], Betolaza, Betoño, Beunza, Beunzalarrea, Beuso, Beutas, Beya, Beyán, Beyas, Beydazar, Beytia, Bezado, Bezanilla, Bezón, Bezzina, Biados, Biamonde, Biamonte, Bianchi, Bianes, Biaés, Bibiloni, Bictorián, Bicuña, Bidania, Bidasola, Bidarte, Bidaur, Bidaurre, Bidaurreta, Bidea, Biedma, Bieige, Bielaray, Bielsa, Bienes, Bienvengut, Bierama, Bieto, Bigot, Bigüezal, Bilbao, Bilbatue, Bicuña, Bildósola, Billón, Bimbre, Bimón, Binal, Binales, Binelo, Binimelis, Binós, Binuesa, Biota, Biquendi, Birués, Birruejas, Bisbal, Bisorna, Bisquerra, Bisallach, Bistué, Biteri, Bitezio, Bitoria, Bitrián, Biu, Biuna, Biura, Biuro, Bivas, Biya, Bizcaíno, Bizcarra, Bizcarret, Bizuete, Blake, Blan, Blanc, Blancafort, Blancas, Blancazo, Blanch, Blanchs. End of EHG Volume 14.

EHG Volume 15: Blanco, Blanes, Blasco, Blay, Blázquez, Blau, Blecua, Boado, Boan, Boares, Boatella, Bobadilla, Bobea, Bobes, Boca, Bocacho, Bocal, Bocalan, Bocanegra, Boci, Bocos, Bocull, Bodega, Bodet, Bodí, Boelegue, Boera, Bofarull, Bofill, Boguet, Bohorques, Boiga, Boigues, Boil, Boillar, Bois-Abrán, Boisol, Boix, Boixols, Boiza, Boja, Bojados, Bojedo, Bolante, Bolaño, Bolas, Bolde, Bolea, Boleo, Boles, Bolet. End of EHG Volume 15.

EHG Volume 16: Boliaga, Bolimburu, Bolinaga, Bolívar, Bolo, Bolós, Bolterra, Bolturra, Bolumbízca, Bolumburu, Bolle, Bollegui, Bollo, Bollullo, Bomaytin, Bomaza, Bona, Bonactu, Bonafós, Bonafous, Bonal, Bonald, Bonany, Bonapart, Bonaparte, Bonart, Bonaselva, Bonastre, Bonavia, Boncompaño, Bonel, Bonell, Boneo, Bonera, Bones, Bonet, Boneta, Bonete, Boniete, Bonifaci, Bonifacio, Bonifaz, Bonig, Bonigués, Boniguet, Boníguez, Bonilla, Bonivel, Boniver, Bonivern, Bononat, Bonnici, Bóo, Boot, Boquel, Boquet, Borau, Borbolla, Borbón, Borca, Borcano, Borda, Bordas, Bordabere, Bordaberri, Bordaberry, Bordachipia, Bordalba, Bordallo, Borde, Bordeix, Bordell, Bordiles, Bordils, Bordons, Bordoy, Borea, Borella, Borgés, Borges, Borgoñón, Borgoñós, Borguño, Bori, Boria, Borilla, Borinaga, Borja, Borjen, Bornas, Bornechea, Borolla, Borodad, Borondate, Bort, Borralla, Borrás, Borrasá, Borrego, Borrell, Borrer, Borruel, [Borrull EHG Volume 23, p.220], Bos, Boscá, Boscados, Bosco, Boscot, Bosch, Boscho, Bosello, Boser, Bosna, Bosnia, Bosque, Bosquet, Bost, Bostia Botaya, Bote, Botebasit, Botella, Boteller, Botello, Botero, Botija, Botiller, Botinés, Boto, Botor, Botoro, Bou, Bouchet, Bouffart, Boulet, Bouligni, Bourguet, Bouvier, Bóveda, Bover, Bovera, Box, Boxadós, Boxadors, Boxeda, Boxés, Boxó, Boyca, Boza, Bracamonte, Bracerolas, Bracho, Bramasachs, Braganza, Brandón, Brañas. End of EHG Volume 16.

EHG Volume 17: Braramuño, Brasa, Brasco, Brasenge, Brasense, Brasonga, Brasonte, Brat, Bravo, Braza, Brazago, Breciano, Breda, Brederote, Bregantín, Brel, Breña, Breserola, Bret, Bretón, Bretona, Bretoña, Breuch, Briceño, Bricianos, Brieba, Briele, Briffa, Brignoné, Brihuega, Brillones, Bringas, Briñas, Brioles, Briones, Bris, Brisal, Brito, Briz, Brizuela, Brochado, Brochero, Brondo, Brossa, Broto, Brotolo, Brú, Brualla, Brugada, Bruguera, Brulato, Brull, Brun, Brunet, Bruno, Bruñón, Brusca, Bruquer, Brutel, Bucareli, Bucarelli, Bucarocoa, Bucot, Bucheli, Buedano, Buedo, Buenafé, Buendía, Bueno, Buenrostro, Buentalante, Bueras, Buerba, Buerdo, Buergo, Buerón, Buerva, Buesa, Bueso, Bufalá, Bugarin, Buges, Bugino, Builla, Buira, Buirón, Buitrago, Buitrón, Buiza, Bujanda, Bujedo, Bujo, Bulacia, Bulano, Bulnes, Bulocoa, Bulucua, Bulla, Bullón, Burbano, Burces, Burdapal, Burdils, Burgés, Burghesio, Burgo, Burgoa, Burgos, Burgucahar, Burgueño, Burguera, Burgues, Burguet, Burguete, Burguillos, Burguiño, Burgunio, Burgunyo,

Burguzahar, Burló, Burón, Burós, Burunda, Burutain, Burrial, Burriel, Burruda, Busambert, Busel, Buseña, Buserola, Buslenza, Busot, Busquets, Bustamante, Bustenza, Bustares, Bustillo, Bustindui, Bustinduy, Bustinza, Bustinzoro, Bustinzuria, Busto, Bustos, Busturia, Busutil, Butrón, Buzón. End of EHG Volume 17.

EHG Volume 22: Bertodano, p. 315; EHG Volume 23: Bañuls, p. 217; Bas, p. 219; Béthencourt, p. 220; Borrull, p. 221; EHG Volume 26: Blanca, p. 213; EHG Volume 28: Botello, p. 211; EHG Volume 44: Bassave, p.221; Bances, p.229; Beyens, p. 222; EHG Volume 47: Bereterrechea, p. 225; EHG Volume 50: Benito, p. 247; Blázquez, p. 249; EHG Volume 58: Barón de Berrieza, p. 228; Barrera, p. 235; EHG Volume 59: Basarte, p. 259; EHG Volume 62: Brizuela, p. 237; EHG Volume 67: Barril, p. 227; EHG Volume 73: Bueno, p. 207. End of Letter B.

C EHG Volume 18: Caamaño, Cabale, Caba, Cabada, Cabalicurre, Cavalicuve, Cabalza, Cabases, Caballa, Caballera, Caballería, Caballer, Caballero, Caballo, Caballón, Cabana, Cabanellas, Cabanelles, Cabanes, Cabanias, Cabaniellas, Cabanillas, Cabanilles, Cabanyelles, Cabanyes, Cabañas, Cabañuelas, Cabarcos, Cabarchos, Cabarrús, Cabaspre, Cabedo, Cabelo, Cabellat, Cabello, Cabero, Cabestany, Cabex, Cabeza, Cabeza de Vaca, Cabezas, Cabezón, Cabichudo, Cabiedes, Cabirol, Cabitán, Cabitchudo, Cabo, Caborrado, Cabot, Cabra, Cabral, Cabrales, Cabranes, Cabrejas, Cabren, Cabrene, Cabrens, Cabrer, Cabrera, Cabrerizo, Cabrero, Cabreta, Cabrío, Cabrito, Cabueñas, Cabués, Cacena, Cacera, Cáceres, Caciara, Cacos, Cachero, Cachiprieto, Cachapín, Cacho, Cachola, Cachopín, Cachorro, Cachurpín, Cadalso, Cadalla, Cadavid, Cadell, Cadelo. End of EHG Volume 18.

EHG Volume 19: Cadena, Cadenas, Cadernosa, Cadiñanos, Cadórniga, Cadorra, Cadreita, Cadret, Caes, Caesco, Caetano, Cafont, Cafranga, Cagarriga, Cagide, Cagiga, Cagígal, Cagigas, Cagiguera, Cagromiz, Cahors, Cahorts, Cahicedo, Caicedo, Caicoegui, Caifero, Caiguegui, Caimo, Caín, Cainiser, Cairada, Caixal, Caixás, Caja, Cajal, Cajígal, Cal, Cála, Calabaza, Calac, Cálad, Calado, Calafat, Calahorra, Calán, Calancha, Calnadro, Calanova, Calante, Calanzaro, Calasanz, Calatañazor, Calatayud, Calatazaro, Calatrava, Calaza, Calba, Calberi, Calbetón, Calbijo, Calcena, Calcina, Calchetas, Caldas, Caldeira, Caldentey, Caldera, Calderer, Calderín, Calderina, Calderón, Calders, Caldés, Caldevilla, Caldirán, Caldueño, Calella, Calella, Calera, Calero, Calha, Calheiros, Calienes, Caliens, Calimano, Calis, Calo, Calomarde, Calomardo, Calsa, Calser, Calva, Calvache, Calvente, Calveras, Calvet, Calvete, Calvillo, Calvís, Calvó, Calvo, Calvón, Calzada, Calzadilla, Calzador, Calzas, Calzón, Call, Callar, Calle, Calleiros, Calleja, Callejas, Callejo, Callejón, Calles, Callet, Callus, Cam, Camacho, Camalva, Calmavide, Camanes, Camango, Camañes, Camar, Cámara, Camargo, Camaró, Camasa,

Camasobras, Camazón, Camba, Cambas, Cambrils, Cambrón, Cambronero, Camero, Camet, Camfullós, Camilleri, Caminha, Camino, Camiña, Camio, Camisón, Camoens, Camón, Camor, Camós, Campa, Campamar, Campán, Campana, Campanario, Campaner, Campani. End of EHG Volume 19.

EHG Volume 20: Campano, Campanón, Campaña, Camparraga, Campegio, Campenan, Campero, Campezo, Campi, Campillo, Campino, Campins, Campión, Campitello, Campllonch, Campmany, Campo, Campoa, Campoamor, Campofrío, Campograjo, Campomanes, Campoó, Campora, Camporell, Camporells, Camporredondo, Comporrell, Camporrells, Camporroso, Campos, Campoy, Campra, Camprodón, Camps, Campsor, Camptor, Campuzano, Camus, Camuso, Cana, Canal, Canales, Canalizas, Canals, Cananea, Canares, Canat, Cánaves, Cáncer, Canciller, Cancino, Candal, Candamo, Candano, Candau, Cándenas, Canedo, Canel, Canela, Canelas, Canell, Canellas, Canelles, Canencia, Canet, Canga, Cangas, Canicia, Caniego, Caniellas, Canielles, Canillas, Canisar, Cano, Canonoche, Canou, Canoura, Cánovas, Cánoves, Canseco, Cansor, Canta, Cantabrana, Cantalapiedra, Cantarini, Cantelmo, Canter, Cantera, Cantére, Canterelles, Cantero, Cantillo, Cantín, Canto, Cantolla, Cantón, Cantonal, Cantoni, Cantoral, Cantos, Canuno, Canyellas, Canyelles, Cañas, Cañavate, Cañaveral, Cañedo, Cañellas. End of EHG Volume 20.

EHG Volume 21: Cañete, Cañizares, Cañizo, Caño, Cañoles, Cao, Capa, Capaguindegui, Capagundegui, Capacho, Capalvo, Caparriaga, Caprrós, Caparroso, Capdeviella, Capdevila, Capdevilla, Capecce, Capeccelatro, Capeche, Capeleti, Capelo, Capello, Capero, Capetillo, Capí, Capiaín, Capilla, Capisagasti, Caplá, Caplana, Capmani, Capó, Capobianco, Capoche, Caponi, Capons, Capranica, Caprara, Capreti, Capriata, Cápua, Capuchines, Capús, Capuz, Cara, Caraá, Carabeo, Carabes, Carac, Caracciolo, Carafa, Caraffa, Caralt, Carama, Caraman, Caramanos, Caramany, Carandil, Carasa, Caravantes, Caraveo, Caraves, Carávias, Carbajo, Carballido, Carballo, Carbí, Carbín, Carbó, Carbolay, Carbón, Carbone, Carbonell, Carcabuey, Cárcamo, Carcasona, Carcedo, Cárcel, Carcelén, Cárcer, Cárcova, Cardaberaiz, Cardaveras, Cardell, Cardenal, Cárdenas, Cardeña, Cardi, Cardiel, Cardil, Cardischo, Cardo, Cardona, Cardoso, Careaga, Cari, Cariaco, Cariaga, Carier, Cariniar, Cariojos, Caritat, Caritates, Carlán, Carles, Carlino, Carlos, Carlot, Carmena, Carmenate, Carmenati, Carmenatis, Carmona, Carnero, Carneval, Carnicer, Carnicero, Caro, Carol, Carola, Caroli, Carra, Carrach, Caudevilla, Carvallo. End of EHG Volume 21.

EHG Volume 22: Carafa, Caraffa, Carondelet, Caroto, Carpio, Carquizano, Carra, Carrabal, Carracedo, Carrafa, Carraffa, Carral, Carralón, Carralval, Carramain, Carrandi, Carranes, Carranza, Carrasco, Carrascón, Carrasquedo,

Carrasquilla, Carratalá, Carreño, Carrera, Carreras, Carrere de Abense, Carriazo, Carriedo, Carrigas, Carrillo, Carrio, Carrió, Carrión, Carrizo, Carrizosa, Carro, Cárroz, Carrunio, Carserán, Carse, Carta, Cartagena, Carte, Cartellá, Caruana, Carui, Carvajal, Casa, Casabases, Casabuena, Casademunt, Casadevall, Casadevante, Casador, Casajús, Casal, Casaldaguilla, Casalón, Casals, Casamayor, Casamijana, Casa-mitjana, Casante, Casani, Casanova, Casanueva, Casaprima, Casaprín, Casar, Casares, Casariego, Casas, Casasana, Casasano, Casasayes, Casasola, Casaus, Casaviella, Cascajares, Cascales, Cascall, Cascant, Cascante, Cascasona, Cascos, Cáseda, Cases, Casita, Caso, Casón, Caspe, Casquen, Casquero, Cassador. End of EHG Volume 22.

EHG Volume 23: Castant, Castañares, Castañeda, Castañedo, Castañer, Castañera, Castañiza, Castaño, Castañón, Castaños, Castejón (or González de Castejón), Castel, Castell, Castellá, Castellanos, Castellar, Castellarnau, Castell-Arnau, Castellauli, Castellbell, Castellbisbal, Castell-Blanch, Castellblanco, Castellbó, Castellcir, Castelldaséns, Castelle, Castellfollit, Castellgalí, Castellizuelo, Castellmir, Castellmoltó, Castellnou, Castello, Castelló, Castellón, Castellot, Castellroig, Castellrós, Castells, Castellsir, Castellsis, Castelltersol, Castelltort, Castellvell, Castellví, Castellvisval, Castilblanque, Castilla, Castillejo, Castillo, Castillón, Castobella, Castolba, Castorada, Castorena, Castresana, Castrillo, Castrillón, Castro, Castropol, Castroverde, Castrovid, Castrovido, Casuso, Catá, Catalá, Catalán, Catandil, Catanea, Cataneo, Cataño, Catañy, Catarecha, Catategui, Cathelin, Cático, Catllar, Catón, Cattá, Cattaá, Caulers, Caulellas, Caunedo, Caurín, Caus, Cava, Cavada, Cavalcante, Cavalcanti, Cavaleta, Cavia, Caviedes, Cayacegui, Cayas, Cayón, Cayrasco, Cayuela, Cazalín, Cazalla, Cazos, Cea, Cearreta, Cebada, Cebadero, Cebadilla, Ceballos, Cebericha, Ceberio, Cebollero, Cebrián, Ceceil, Cedrón, Cegama, Cegastía, Cegri, Cehegín, Ceitán, Cejudo, Cela, Celada, Celaeta. Cabrera, p. 222. End of EHG Volume 23.

EHG Volume 24: Celain, Celaya, Celayanda, Celayandia, Celayandra, Celayarán, Celayeta, Celdrán, Celis, Celma, Celoca, Celsi, Celso, Cella, Cellers, Celles, Cellorigo, Cemborain, Cembrano, Cembranos, Cenarbe, Cenarruza, Cendoya, Cendrera, Cenitagoya, Cenoz, Centellas, Centelles, Centeno, Centurión, Cepeda, Ceprián, Cerain, Cerbatos, Cerborain, Cerca, Cercito, Cerda, Cerdá, Cerdán, Cerdanya, Cerdeño, Cereceda, Cerecedo, Cererols, Ceret, Cerezo, Cerezuela, Cerf, Cergaya, Cerijuso, Cerio, Cernadas, Cernadilla, Cernesio, Cerón, Cerra, Cerrada, Cerradas, Cerraeta, Cerrajería, Cerrato, Cerratón, Cerro, Cerroa, Cervantes, Cerrudo, Cervato, Cervató, Cervatón, Cervatos, Cervelló, Cervellón, Cervera, Cerveró, Cervetto, Cerviá, Cervino, Cerviño, César, Céspedes, Cetian, Cetina, Cetrillas, Cia, Cianca, Ciantar, Ciaño, Ciaurriz, Cibar, Cibiz, Cibo, Cicero, Cid, Cidón, Cienfuegos, Ciervo, Cieza, Cifré, Cifontes, Cifuentes, Ciga, Cigala, Ciganda, Cigarra,

Cigarán, Cigarroa, Cigordi, Ciguerondo, Ciguri, Cilaurren, Ciloiz, Cillanco, Cillario, Cima, Cimbor, Cimborain, Cimbrón, Cincunegui, Cinejo, Cini, Cinos, Cintas, Cintora, Cintruénigo, Ciordia, Ciprés, Cirarrueta, Cirarruista, Ciraurrieta, Cirera, Ciria, Cirieño, Ciriza, Cirna, Ciruelo, Cirueña, Cirva, Cirvent, Ciscar, Cisneros, Cisternas, Cisternes, Cistué, Citjó, Ciudadano, Ciudad-Real, Ciurana, Ciutadella, Ciutadilla, Civerio, Ciya, Cladera, Clapes, Clar, Clarac, Claraco, Claramonte, Claramunt, Claravalls, Clarebout, Claresvalls, Claret, Clariana, Claris, Clascá, Clascar, Clascari, Clasqueri, Clauses, Claver. End of EHG Volume 24.

EHG Volume 25: Clavería, Clavero, Claverol, Clavijo, Clemente, Clericat, Cleriguet, Climent, Climente, Clos, Clus, Clusa, Coaco, Coalla, Coaña, Coazo, Coba, Cobaleda, Cobanillas, Cobarrubias, Cobera, Cobián, Cobillas, Cobo, Cobos, Cobrinas, Coca, Cocar, Coch, Coche, Cocho, Coco, Cocón, Cocote, Cocquiel, Codevila, Codevilla, Codill, Codina, Codinats, Codol, Codomino, Coello, Coeto, Cogolls, Cogombrellas, Cola, Colarte, Colas, Coldranes, Colina, Colindres, Colip, Colmenares, Colmenero, Cólogan, Colom, Coloma, Colombres, Colomer, Colomina, Colominas, Colomines, Colomo, Colón, Colonna, Colunga, Coll, Collado, Collandra, Collantes, Collar, Collazo, Collell, Collferrer, Colltort, Comabella, Comalada, Comallonga, Comas, Comes, Combeller, Comber, Combes, Combis, Comellas, Comelles, Comenge, Comor, Comores, Compains, Compañy, Compta, Comyn, Conadall, Conalos, Conangles, Concabellas, Concejo, Concha, Conchares, Conchillos, Conde, Coneja, Conejo, Conesa, Conill, Conlledo, Conrado, Constantí, Contador, Contamina, Contestei, Contreras, Copeiro, Copete, Copóns, Coque, Coquero, Coquiel, Corao, Corau, Corbache, Corbacho, Corbalán, Corbarán, Corbatón, Corbellas, Corbenosa, Corbera, Corbet, Corbí, Corbies, Corbinos, Corbis, Corces, Corco, Córcoles, Corcos, Corcuera, Cordellas, Corder, Cordera, Cordero, Corders, Cordido, Córdova, Cordovil, Corella, Corera, Corita, Corn, Cornado, Cornago, Cornara, Cornaro, Cornás, Cornejo, Cornel, Cornellá, Cornellana, Corner, Cornet, Cornus, Corona, Coronado, Coronas, Coronel, Corono, Coroño, Corostola, Corraiz, Corral, Corral-Llansa, Correa, Corrent, Corres, Correza, Corriera, Corro, Corroza, Cors, Corsavi, Corta, Cortabarri, Cortabarria, Cortada, Cortalandaburu, Cortalló, Cortázar, Corte, Cortecedo, Cortejana, Cortejarena, Cortejo, Corte-Real, Corterreal, Cortés, Cortesero, Cortey, Cortiada, Cortiguera, Cortijera, Cortils, Cortiles, Cortina, Cortit, Cortito, Cortizos, Corts, Corvara, Corvari, Corvera, Corvinos, Corzos, Cos, Cosca, Coscó, Coscoll, Coscón, Cosculluela, Cosgalla, Cos-Gayón, Cosida, Cosin, Cosío, Cossío, Costa, Costabella, Costalacg, Costales, Costana, Costanti, Costelecg, Costeyos, Costilla, Costurer, Cota, Cotel, Cotera, Cotes, Cotilla, Cotillo, Cotoner, Cotorro, Cotrinas, Cots, Cousiño, Coutiño, Covarrubias, Covián, Cózar, Credenza, Crespanes, Crespi, Crespi de Valdaura, Crespin, Crespo, Creus, Crexel, Criades, Criado, Criales, Cribel, Critana,

Critania, Crispani, Cristantes, Crooke, Croses, Croy, Cruillas, Cruilles, Cruchaga, Cruz, Cruzado, Cruzat, Cuadra, Cuadrado, Cuadros, Cuaiz, Cuartas, Cuartero, Cuaznavar, Cubas, Cubells, Cubero, Cubides, Cubiesca, Cubillas, Cubillos, Cubiri, Cucala, Cucaller, Cucaló, Cucalón, Cudillero, Cueli, Cuéllar, Cuello, Cuenca, Cuerla, Cuerno, Cuero, Cuervo, Cuesta, Cueto, Cueva, Cuevas, Cueznava, Cufristiaga, Cugui, Cugull, Cular, Culeta, Culhar, Cumbis, Cumplido, Cunilleras, Cunvas, Cunyat, Cunzuta, Cuquejo, Curco, Curiaciviart, Curiel, Curmi, Curucheta, Cusagages, Custurer, Cutanda, Cutuneguieta. End of EHG Volume 25.

EHG Volume 31: Cárdiff, p. 205; Cabiedes, p. 212; EHG Volume 32: Cárdiff, p. 209; EHG Volume 35: Cotapos, p.283; EHG Volume 41: Cossío, p. 267; EHG Volume 42: Cortadellas, p. 275; EHG Volume 44: Cepeda, p. 201; Coalla, p. 230; Craene (de), p. 226; EHG Volume 50: Cortey, p. 251; Cuervo Arango, p. 252; EHG Volume 58: Chamorro, p. 230; Casanova, p. 244; EHG Volume 59: Ciordia, p. 261; EHG Volume 62: Castilla-Portugal, p. 240; EHG Volume 64: Cabrera, p. 242; EHG Volume 71: Caamaño, p. 199; EHG Volume 73: Chueca, p. 212. End of Letter C.

CH EHG Volume 26: Chabelas, Chacim, Chacin, Chacón, Chalecu, Chalez, Chambarin, Chamar, Chamizo, Chamorro, Chanciller, Chapar, Chapari, Chaparreta, Chaparris, Chaparro, Chaperón, Chapin, Chapretua, Charta, Charrania, Charreta, Charrio, Charroalde, Charrualde, Chasado, Chasarri, Chassarri, Chaucel, Chauzel, Chávarri, Chavarría, Chavarriaga, Chaves, Chazarreta, Checón, Cheparre, Chica, Chicano, Chicategui, Chico, Chico de Guzmán, Chicote, Chicharra, Chilla, Chimino, Chinchilla, Chindurza, Chipre, Chiprés, Chiriboga, Chirino, Chirinos, Choquihuanca, Chorem, Choribit, Chuecos, Chumacero, Churón, Churruca. End of Letter Ch.

D EHG Volume 26: Dábalos, Dabán, Dabancasa, Dacahuete, Dach, Dagama, Daguerre, Dalana, Dalbi, Dalfín, Dalmases, Dalmao, Dalmau, Dalos, Dalpas, Dalza, Dalzell, Dalzu, Damassio, Dambel, Dameto, Danguso, Danna, Dansa, Danús, Daoiz, Da-Pelo, Dapifer, Daragües, Darazuri, Dardalla, Darder, Darieta, Darnius, Darnos, Daroz, Dasso, Dat, Dato, Datue, Dauder, Daudedor, Daudor, Daulo, Davi, David, Dávila, Daxeisas, Dayún, Daza, Dazar, Dazne, Debener, Deblore, Decia, De-Combes, Dédalos, De Gregorio, Dehesa, De la Caballería, Delalana, De la Lana, Delanda, Delantorne, De Lantorne, Delas, Delaporetella, Delaunet, Deles, Delfín, Delgadillo, Delgado, Delicado, Delmas, Delpás, Del Pas, Della, Dello, Dellor, Dellore, Denia, Denti, Dentici, Dermins, Derrech, Desbach, Desbalps, Desbanchs, Desboch, Desbrull, Descalabrado, Descall, Descallar, Descamps, Descatllar, Desclápez,

Desclergues, Desclópez, Descoll, Descós, Descuain, Desfar, Desfran, Desgastell, Desguai, Desgual, Desguanechs, Desguarets, Desgüel, Desgurb, Desgurra, Desjuny, Desllor, Deslluc, Desmás, Desmont, Desmur, Despalau, Despapiol, Despasey, Despens, Despéon, Desperes, Despés, Despí, Despinal, Desplá, Despontell. End of EHG Volume 26.

EHG Volume 27: Despou, Desprat, Desprats, Despuig, Despújol, Destano, Destany, Destorrent, Desvalls, Desvern, Desvilar, Desvilaró, Desvivers, Desvola, Deu, Deuceln, Dewitte, Deyá, Deyna, Deza, Diácono, Diago, Diamante, Diáguez, Díaz, Díaz de Aguilar, Díaz de Aguilera, Díaz de Arce, Díaz de Argandoña, Díaz de Cadórniga, Díaz de la Calle, Díaz de Campomanes, Díaz de la Caneja, Díaz de Cedrón, Díaz de Cerio, Díaz de Collantes, Díaz de Corcuera, Díaz de Cossío, Díaz de Garfías, Díaz de Garayo, Díaz de Lavandero, Díaz de León, Díaz de Liaño, Díaz de Lorenzana, Díaz del Mazo, Díaz de Mendivil, Díaz de Mendoza, Díaz Montero, Díaz Ortega, Díaz Pimienta, Díaz de Quijano, Díaz de la Quintana, Díaz del Quintanal, Díaz de Rábago, Díaz de Reguero, Díaz de Riguero, Díaz de Rojas, Díaz Román, Díaz Romero, Díaz de Solmayor, Díaz de Terán, Díaz Trechuelo, Díaz de Vivar, Díaz de Zumento, Díaz de Burbano, Díaz, Dicastillo, Diedo, Diego, Dientes, Dieris, Diest, Dieste, Díez, Díez de Arellano, Díez de Artazcoz, Díez de Aux, Díez de Bonilla, Díez de Escorón, Díez de Espinosa, Díez Gallardo, Díez de Jáuregui, Díez de Ledesma, Díez de Medina, Díez Navarro, Dñiez de Portillo, Díez de Quijada, Díez Quijano, Díez de Quiñones, Díez de Recalde, Díez de Sepúlveda, Díez de Tablares, Díez de Tejada, Díez de Ulzurrun, Díez de Valdeón, Díez de Zorrilla, Díez, Diezma, Dijar, Dillanes, Dios (de), Diosayuda, Diosdado, Diosdat, Disorua, Diustegui, D'Ixar, Diz, Dobarán, Doblado, Doblas, Dobomi, Do-cal, Docio, Dódena, Dolaguitiz, Dolara, Dolcinellas, Doliva, Dolius, Dolms, Doloraga, Dolorde, Dolorraga, Doluye, Dolz, Domee, Domeco de Girauta, Domedel, Doménech, Domezain, Domica, Domingo, Domingoegui, Domingón, Domingorena, Domingotegui, Domínguez, Domonte, Doms, Donado, Donaire, Donat, Donato, Don Blasco, Doncel, Doncinellas, Doncostal, Condo, Donelfa, Donella, Donez, Dongo, Donguillén, Don Guillén, Doni, Donís, Don Lope, Dono, Donoso, Don Pablo, Donvela, Doñamaría, Doña María, Doña Mayor, Doña Palla, Dora, Dorado, Dorante, Dorcas, Corcau, Dordá, Dordás, Dórdena, Dórdenas, Dorenga, Dorfila, Doria, Doriga, Dorils, Dornellas, Dornutegui, Doró, Dorramas, Dorriols, Dortal, Dosal, Dosma, Dosrius, Dostals, Dot, Dotxe, Dou, Doz, Drago, Draper, Dronda, Duacosla, Duany, Duart, Duarte, Dueñas, Duero, Duerta, Duget, Dujardín, Dulonci, Dumpiérrez, Duodo, Duque, Duque de Estrada, Du-Quesnay, Du-Quesne, Durá, Durall, Durán, Durandio, Durango, Durbán, Durc, Durch, Dure, Duren, Dureta, Durfort, Duris, Duriz, Duro, Durpas, Durru, Dusay, Duse, Dustegui, Dutari, Duzay. End of EHG Volume 27.

EHG Volume 28: Despujol, p. 199; EHG Volume 29: Díez de Medina, p. 234; EHG Volume 44: De Craene, p. 226; EHG Volume 57: Delgado de Antequera, p. 249; EHG Volume 68: Dávila or Avila, p. 239; Dorronsoro or Dorronzoro, p. 241; End of Letter D.

E EHG Volume 28: Ebazquin, Ecala, Ecay, Eceiza, Ecenarro, Ecija, Echábarri, Echabarría, Echabarrieta, Echabarrio, Echabe, Echaburu, Echagüe, Echáide, Echalar, Echalaz, Echalecu, Echande, Echandi, Echániz, Echavove, Echapare, Echaray, Echart, Echarte, Echartea, Echarri, Echasarri, Echauri, Echaurren, Echauz, Echávarri, Echavarría, Echavarrieta, Echave, Echaverri, Echazarreta, Echea, Echeandia, Echebarne, Echébarri, Echebarría, Echebarrieta, Echebarrio, Echebaltz, Echebelz, Echebercea, Echeberri, Echeberría, Echebers, Echebert, Echeberz, Echebeste, Echebezte, Echegaray, Echegoyán, Echegoyano, Echegoyen, Echenagusa, Echenique, Echepare, Eche-Erreaga, Echerreaga, Echevarne, Echévarri, Echevarría, Echevarrieta, Echeverca, Echeverri, Echeverría, Echevers, Echevert, Echeverz, Echeveste, Echevezte, Echezarreta, Echezuría, Echoza, Ederra, Edigorraz, Edo, Eduegui, Edueguin, Egaña, Egea, Egoabil, Egocheaga, Egozcue, Eguaras, Egües, Eguía, Eguiaga, Eguiara, Eguiarte, Eguiarreta, Eguiguren, Eguilaz, Eguiluz, Eguina, Eguiniz, Eguino, Eguiña, Eguioiz, Eguizábal, Egúrbide, Eguren, Egurza, Egurrola, Egusquiza, Eguzquiza, Eibar, Eibas, Eibiti, Eical, Eidocain, Eireguy, Eito, Eixarc, Eizaga, Eizaguirre, Eizarrara, Eizmendi, Ejarque, Ejérica, Elar, Elazarriaga, Elcano, Elcaraeta, Elcareta, Elcoro, Elcorobarrutia, Elduayen, Elegraveicia, Eleicigui, Eleizalde, Eleizamendi, Elejabeitia, Elejaga, Elejalde, Elejarriaga, Elena, Elespuru, Eleta, Elexalde, Elexpuru, Eleyjalde, Elezalde, Elezarriaga, Elezgaray, Elezgueta, Elgorriaga, Elgucena, Elguea, Elguera, Elguero, Elgueta, Elguezábal, Elguezua, Elía, Eliceche, Elicegui, Eliceiri, Elío, Eliza, Elizabelar, Elizaga, Elizagarate, Elizagaray, Elzaicine, Elizalde, Elizgaray, Elizondo, Elmir, Elnos, Elo, Elola, Elordi, Elordui, Eloregui, Elorio, Elormendi, Elorregui, Elorriaga, Elorga, Elorrieta, Elorz, Elorza, Elósegui, Elosidieta, Elosta, Elosu, Elso, Elusa, Ellaurri. End of EHG Volume 28.

EHG Volume 29: Ellul, Emaldi, Emaldia, Emanuel, Emasábal, Embeytia, Embil, Embún, Emerando, Emmo, Emparán, Ena, Enasteasu, Enatorriaga, Encalada, Encarnado, Encas, Encina, Encío, Enciso, Enclapes, Endara, Endemaño, Endélica, Endérica, Endonaguiz, Endueñas, Enebro, Enecotegui, Enériz, Engarán, Engómez, Engraba, Enguera, Enjastia, Enrich, Enrile, Enrile (p.229), Enríquez, Enseña, Ensuyo, Entenza, Enterrias, Entralgo, Entrambasaguas, Entrena, Entriago, Enveig, Enveja, Enyego, Equioy, Era, Eransus, Erarrizaga, Eras, Eraso, Eraustieta, Erbás, Erbeta, Erbetegui, Erbiti, Ercazti, Ercilla, Erdará, Erdoñana, Erdozain, Eredia, Eregui, Ereguyen, Ereinozaga, Ereinuzqueta, Erenuzqueta, Ereño, Eres, Ereux, Erice, Eril, Erill, Erinazu, Erinozu, Eristain, Eriz, Erlés, Erloeta, Ernaiz, Eroles, Erquiñigo,

Erralde, Errarán, Errasti, Errazquin, Errazu, Errázuriz, Errea, Errerica, Erro, Errotaeche, Ervillas, Esain, Esaube, Esais, Escajadillo, Escala, Escalada, Escalante, Escalera, Escales, Escalona, Escalzo, Escalloso, Escama, Escamendi, Escamilla, Escandón, Escanona, Escanilla, Escaño, Escapa, Escaraga, Escarajayo, Escaramo, Escaray, Escardó, Escargue, Escario, Escarit, Escarramad, Escarrer, Escartín, Escatrón, Escavias, Escayola, Escobal, Escobar, Escobedo, Escobillas, Escoces, Escofet, Escoiquiz, Escolano, Escolar, Escolonea. End of EHG Volume 29.

EHG, Volume 30: Escorcia, Escoriaza, Escorna, Escornallón, Escorón, Escorrata, Escorz, Escorza, Escós, Escosura, Escoto, Escribá, Escribán, Escribano, Escrivá, Escudero, Escuer, Escurrechea, Esfar, Esfardas, Esguezábal, Esgrecho, Eslava, Esles, Esmir, Esnaola, Espada, Espadero, Espalter, Espantoso, Espalza, Espanyol, España, Español, Espar, Esparraguera, Espartero, Esparza, Espasa, Espasens, Espejo, Espel, Esperún, Espés, Espiau, Espicia, Espiga, Espigol, Espiguel, Espilla, Espilles, Espín, Espina, Espinal, Espinar, Espinel, Espino, Espinosa, Espital, Esplán, Espleda, Espluga, Esplugas, Esplugues, Espolla, Esporrín, Esprals, Esprats, Espriella, Espronceda, Espuche, Espuny, Esqueda, Esquerdo, Esquerit, Esquerra, Esquerrer, Esquier, Esquinas, Esquivel, Esquivias, Estacasola, Estacasolo, Estacazola, Estada, Estadé, Estadilla, Estage, Estalrich, Estampa, Estanartos, Estanga, Estanibó, Estanybó, Estanyol, Estaña, Estañol, Estaper, Estasart, Estaun, Estéban, Estébanez, Estefanía, Esteíbar, Estela, Estella, Estelrich, Estenaga, Estenoz, Estens, Estensoro, Estepa, Esterlié, Esteva, Esteve, Estévez, Estizar, Estolaza, Estoles, Estonal, Estopa, Estopiñán, Estor, Estorch, Estra, Estrada, Estrader, Estramiana, Estramigas, Estrella, Estremera, Estremoz, Estrimiana, Estruch, Estrús, Estupa, Estupiñán, Esturs, Euguí, Eulate, Eusa, Euza, Eva, Eván, Everardo, Evigui, Exalto, Exérica, Exerrat, Eyt, Eyundiano, Eza, Ezaval, Ezcaray, Ezcarte, Ezcay, Eztanga, Ezcurra, Ezgal, Ezmir, Eznaurriza, Eznaola, Eznarizaga, Ezpeleta, Ezquerra, Ezquieta, Ezquioga, Ezteibar, Ezterripa. End EHG Volume 30.

EHG Volume 32: Echeverz, p.211; EHG Volume 42: Egea or Gea, p. 278; EHG Volume 47: Echarri, p. 226; EHG Volume 58: Echeverría, p. 241; EHG Volume 62: Echeverz, p. 238; EHG Volume 64: Esnaola or Esnaola-Goicoa, p. 227; EHG Volume 85: Eleta, p.225. End of Letter E.

F EHG Volume 31: Fabalis, Fabera, Fabián, Fabra, Fábregas, Fábregues, Fabrer, Fabri, Fabro, Facio, Facos, Facha, Fachs, Fada, Fadrique, Faelle, Faena, Faes or Faez, Fagoaga, Fagoñoles, Faguez, Fagundes, Fagúndez, Faigni, Faing, Faini, Faix, Fajardo, Falaguado, Falas, Falces, Falceto, Falcó, Falcón, Falconi, Falcos, Faleba, Falero, Faletro, Faleva, Falguera, Falguira, Falí, Falier, Faliero, Falnes, Falla, Fallón or O'Fallón, Falzzacappa, Fandino,

Faneltgmont, Fanés, Fanín, Fanlo, Fano, Fantoni, Fañanás, Fáñez, Faquel, Farainello, Farán, Fardela, Farfán, Faria, Farina (de la), Fariña, Fariñas, Farnés, Farnesio, Faro, Farraz or Ferraz, Farrera, Farreras, Fasigni, Faulo, Faura, Faxs, Fay, Fayas, Fazano, Fazio, Febrer, Federigui, Fegundo, Feijó, Feijóo, Felapane or Fregapane, Felices, Felipes, Felipez de Guzmán, Feliú, Feloaga, Fenares, Fenech, Fenestrosa, Fenollar, Fenollet, Feio, Feo, Férez, Fermat, Fernán-Gil, Fernández, Fernández Ahumada, Fernández Alejo, Fernández Alonso, Fernández del Alto, Fernández Alvarado, Fernández Angulo, Fernández Anleo, Fernández de Apodaca, Fernández del Arca, Fernández de Argote, Fernández de Arlóndiga, Fernández de Astiz, Fernández de Atenzana, Fernández de Baena, Fernández Barba, Fernández de las Bárcenas, Fernández Barrera, Fernández de la Barrera, Fernández Bautista, Fernández de Biedma, Fernández Blanco, Fernández de Boán, Fernández de Bobadilla, Fernández Briñas, Fernández Brizuela, Fernández Buenache, Fernández Campero, Fernández Campino, Fernández del Campo, Fernández de Campos, Fernández Camuño, Fernández Carabeo, Fernández Carracea, Fernández de la Carrera, Fernández Casas, Fernández Casamayor, Fernández Casanova, Fernández de Castrillón, Fernández de Castro, Fernández de Córdova, Fernández de la Cuadra, Fernández Cueto, Fernández Daza, Fernández Durán, Fernández de Espinosa. End of EHG Volume 31.

EHG Volume 32: Fernández de Córdova, Fernández de Estenoz, Fernández de Floranes, Fernández Folgueras, Fernández Franco, Fernández de Fuenmayor, Fernández Galindo, Fernández de Gandarillas, Fernández de Garayalde, Fernández Golfín, Fernández de Gorostiza, Fernández de Granados, Fernández Grandoso, Fernández de Grijota, Fernández Guerra, Fernández de Guiso, Fernández de Heredia, Fernández de Heres, Fernández de Híjar, Fernández de Hinestrosa, Fernández de Huidobro, Fernández Iglesias, Fernández de Isla, Fernández de Larrea, Fernández de Larrinos, Fernández de las Eras, Fernández de Leganés, Fernández de León, Fernández de Linares, Fernández de Lorca, Fernández de Luarca, Fernández de Lloreda, Fernández de Madrid, Fernández de Madrigal, Fernández de Magallón, Fernández Maqueira, Fernández Manrique, Fernández Mansilla, Fernández Manzanos, Fernández Marmolejo, Fernández Medrano, Fernández Mendivil, Fernández Mercado, Fernández de Mesa, Fernández Mier, Fernández Miñano, Fernández de Molina, Fernández Molinillo, Fernández Monjardín, Fernández Montenegro, Fernández Montiel, Fernández de Moreda, Fernández Muras, Fernández de Murugarren, Fernández de Navarrete, Fernández de Nuncibay, Fernández de Ojeca, Fernández de la Oliva, Fernández de Olivar, Fernández de Padilla, Fernández Pacheco, Fernández de Paredes, Fernández de la Peña, Fernández de Peñaranda, Fernández Perdones, Fernández de Perlines, Fernández de Piédrola, Fernández del Pino, Fernández de Porto de Pedre, Fernández de la Pradilla, Fernández de la Puente, Fernández Quevedo de Heres, Fernández de la Reguera, Fernández del Río, Fernández de Rioja,

Fernández de Rivero, Fernández de Romaelle, Fernández Romo, Fernández de Santa Cruz, Fernández de Santillán, Fernández de Santo Domingo, Fernández Sarmiento, Fernández de Somonte, Fernández de Soto, Fernández de Sotomayor, Fernández Tejeiro, Fernández de Tejerina, Fernández Toribio, Fernández de Treviño, Fernández Vallejo, Fernández de la Vega, Fernández Velarde, Fernández de Velasco, Fernández de Vergonde, Fernández de Vicuña, Fernández de Villalobos, Fernández de Villanueva, Fernández de Villarreal, Fernández Villaverde, Fero, Ferollet, Ferrá, Ferragud, Ferragut, Ferrán, Ferrandell, Ferrández, Ferrándiz, Ferrándiz de Mesa, Ferrando, Ferrant, Ferrara, Ferrari, Ferrater, Ferraz, Ferreira, Ferrer, Ferrera, Ferrero, Ferreró, Ferreros, Ferri, Ferrices, Ferrigo, Ferriol, Ferris, Ferrón, Ferroso, Ferruces, Ferrueros, Ferrus, Fiallo, Fidalgo, Fiella, Fienes, Fierláns, Fierro, Fierros, Fiesco, Figueira, Figueiredo. End of EHG Volume 32.

EHG Volume 33: Figuera, Figueras, Figueres, Figueroa, Figuerola, Figueruela, Filera, Filingier, Filingiero, Filomarino, Fillol, Fina, Fines, Finestres, Fiol, Fiscolo, Fivaller, Fitero, Flabanico, Flaquer, Fleming, Flicagaray, Fliseos, Flons, Flor, Floreaga, Florencia, Flores, Florez, Florián, Floriategui, Florín, Florios, Floris, Florit, Flos, Fluviá, Foces, Focinos, Fogas, Fogassot, Fogaza, Foguet, Foica, Foix, Foja, Fojón, Folcrás, Folch, Folchs, Folgons, Folguer, Folguera, Folgueras, Follaman, Foncalada, Foncerrada, Foncillas, Foncueva, Fondesviela, Fondevila, Fonnegra, Fonfría, Fonoll, Fonollar, Fonollet, Fons, Fonsaro, Fonseca, Font, Fontalquer, Fontana, Fontaneda, Fontanel, Fontanella, Fontanellas, Fontanet, Fontanets, Fontanillas, Fontarnau, Fontauret, Fonteuberta, Fonte, Fontecilla, Fontecha, Fontes, Fonticheli, Fontejuncosa, Fontoba, Fontrubia, Font-Rubia, Fonz, Foquet, Foradada, Foraster, Forcadell, Forcades, Forcallo, Forcas, Forcén, Forciá, Forero, Forés, Forestier, Forma, Forment, Formento, Formiredo, Forn, Fornara, Fornari, Forner, Fornelos, Fornos, Fornoz, Foronda, Forrado, Fort, Fortes, Fortesa, Fortón, Fortunel, Fortuny, Fortuño, Fortuñy, Foscari, Foscarini, Fossani, Founa, Fox, Foxá, Foxe, Fradello, Fraga, Frago, Fragoso, Fraguas, Franc, Franca, Francés, Francia, Franco. End of EHG Volume 33.

EHG Volume 34: Francolí, Franqueza, Franchi, Franquis, Frasquet, Frasán, Frasso, Frau, Fraxanet, Frazo, Frechel, Frechilla, Frederich, Fregoso, Freijanes, Freire, Freitas, Freixomil, Freja, Frejomil, Frella, Frera, Fresneda, Fresnedo, Frexa, Frexanet y Avinyó, Frey Jomiles, Freyre, Frías, Frigola, Frisa, Frisón, Frómista, Frontín, Fruliene, Frullo, Fruniz, Fruta, Fuembuena, Fuencirio, Fuenlabrada, Fuenleal, Fuenllana, Fuenmayor, Fuensalida, Fuente, Fuentecilla, Fuentes, Fuentesclaras, Fuenzalida, Fuertes, Fuica, Fullana, Fuller, Funes, Funoll, Furundarena, Fuster, Fuser. End of EHG Volume 34, surnames F.

EHG Volume 35: Fernández de Peñaranda, p.283; EHG Volume 36: Fernández de Cañete, p.300; EHG Volume 47: Ferreros, p. 233; EHG Volume 50: Fallón, p. 254; Fernández de Castro, p. 255; Fernández de Madrid, p. 257. End of Letter F.

G EHG Volume 35: Gambacorta, Gamecho, Gamero Cívico, Gámez, Gamio, Gamioa, Gamir, Gamiz, Gamón, Gamoneda, Gana, Ganaberro, Ganca, Ganchaegui, Ganchegui, Gandaberro, Gandala, Gándara, Gandarey, Gandarias, Gandarillas, Gandaris, Gandásegui, Gandía, Gandolfo, Gandulfo, Ganer, Ganogald, Ganosa, Ganoya, Gante, Ganuza, Ganzo, Gaña, Gañena, Gaona, Garagarza, Garagorri, Garaiburu, Garaicoa, Garaicoechea, Garaondo, Garardi, Garascorena, Garástegui or Garrástegui, Garat, Gárate, Garategui, Garau, Garaunaga or Laurnaga, Garavito, Garay, Garayalde, Garayburu, Garayena, Garayo, Garayoa, Garayzábal, Garayzar, Garaz, Garazatua, Garbalda, Garbijo, Garbuna, Garbuno, Garburu, Garcés, García, García Abello, García Abellón, García de Albizu, García de Alcaraz, García Alesón, García de Aplicanos, García de Arazuri, García Arenas, García-Arista, García Arrafán, García de Asarta, García de Assian, García de Axpe, García de Azañón, García Barbón, García de la Barrera, García de de la Barros or García Barrosa, García Bermejo, García Bermúdez, García de Bustamante, García Caballero, García de Cáceres, García Calderón, García de Camargo, García Camba, García de la Cárcova, García de Cárdenas or García Blanco de la Cárcova, García de Cardo, García de Carpintero, García de Carrasco, García de Casiellas, García del Castillo, García de Castro, García de Ceballos, García Cid, García de Coaña, García de la Cruz, García de la Cuesta, García de Cueto, García de la Espina, García de Eulate, García Excajadillo, García de Falces, García Ferreros, García de la Fuente, García Gamarra, García González, García de Guadiana, García Guerra, García Guerrero, García Herreros, García Hidalgo, García Huidobro, García Hurtado, García Ibáñez, García Labarces, García de Labartes, García Labreda, García de la Lama, García de Laporta, García de Laspra, García Lavín, García Lázaro Dávila, García de Lizasoaín, García Lozano, García de Luera, García de Luna, García de Llanilla, García de Llovera, García de Manzaneda, García de Matías, García Mesa, García de Muzábal, García de Múzqui, García de Navascués, García de Ocáriz, García de Olloqui, García de Orovio, García de Ovalle, García Palacio, García Pando, García de Paredes, García Peñalosa, García Peñuela, García de la Plata. End of EHG Volume 35.

EHG Volume 36: García y Portilla, García de Pronga, García Puerta, García Pumariño, García Quesada, García de Quintana, García Rabanal, García del Racillo, García de la Rasilla, García Reyes, García-Rigueira, García Robés, García Rodríguez, García Sala, García de Samaniego, García Sancho, García Sañudo, García de Segovia, García de Sobrecasa, García Solís del Caterón,

García de Toledo, García de Trasmiera, García de Ucar, García de Urieta, García Valdés, García Valladolid, García del Valle, García de la Vega, García de Velasco, García de Villa, García de Villalba, García de Villazian, García de Zárate, García de Zúñiga, Garcifuentes, Garcini, Garcipérez, Garci-Sánchez, Gardoqui, Gardosa, Gareca, Gareza, Garezaybar, Gargallo, Gargano, Gargollo, Gari, Gribay, Garicaza, Garidell, Garín, Garinoaín, Garisas, Garisoaín, Garita-Bergara, Garitano, Garivell, Garlén, Garlón, Garma or de la Garma, Garmendía, Garnica or Guernica, Garófalo, Garosa, Garóstegui, Garóstidi, Garramuño, Garre, Garret, Garretón, Garriador, Garridell, Garrido, Garriga, Garriz, Garro, Garrucho, Garrunaga, Garsoni, Garulo, Garunaga, Garví, Garza, Garzo, Garzón, Garzoni, Gasca, Gascó, Garcón, Gascué, Gasparis, Gasque, Gastañaduy, Gastañaza, Gastañiza, Gastea, Gastealzategui, Gastero, Gastesi, Gastey, Gastía, Gastiain, Gastón, Gassía, Gassius, Gassol, Gassola, Gat, Gata, Gatell, Gática, Gatinara, Gato, Gau, Gauca, Gaucen, Gauci, Gauna, Gausi, Gavari, Gavarret, Gaver, Gavilán, Gavilanes, Gavin, Gaviola, Gaviria, Gay, Gaya, Gayán, Gayangos, Gayo, Gayolá, Gayón, Gayones, Gayoso, Gaytán, Gazo, Gazón, Gazpio, Gaztambide, Gaztañaduy, Gaztañaga, Gaztañeta, Gaztealzátegui, Gaztelu or Velázquez-Gaztelu, Gazzola, Gebalí, Gebelí, Gecio, Gelabert or Gilabert, Gelcem, Gélida, Gelpi, Geltrú, Gemaldo, Genaro, Gener, Generés, Genovard, Gentil, Gerardina, Germá, Germán, Gerona, Gerino, Geronella, Gerradell, Gesquier, Geta, Getino, Geultrú, Ghiseli, Ghisi, Gibaja, Gibert, Giblé, Gicón, Giginta, Gijón, Gil, Gil de Aponte, Gil de Atienza, Gil de Borja, Gil Cano, Gil de la Cuesta, Gil Delgado, Gil de Gibaja, Gil Guerrero, Gil Negrete, Gil de Palacio, Gil Ramírez, Gil de la Redonda, Gil de Vivero, Gil de Zúñiga, García-Moreno. End of EHG Volume 36.

EHG Volume 37: Gilabert, Gilbarrasa, Gilbert, Gilberte de Soberrón, Giles, Gilete, Gili, Gilimón, Gilioli, Gilus, Gillis, Gimez, Gina, Ginard, Ginea, Giner, Ginés, Ginestá, Ginovés, Gioenio, Giorgio, Giraldes, Giráldez, Giraldo, Giralt, Girao, Girardi, Girardo, Girart, Girau, Girgós, Girolami, Giromena, Girón, Girona, Gironda, Gironella, Girota, Gisbert, Gispert, Giumil, Giunano, Giunazzio, Giuri, Givert, Gleu, Glimes, Goacola, Goacona, Goayeneche, Goba, Gobantes, Gobeo, Gochicoa, Godina de Olacao, Godínez, Godoy, Goenaga, Goenechea, Goes, Goetegui, Goez, Gogeascoa, Gogeazcoa, Gogenola, Gogorza, Goiburu, Goicoa, Goicoechea, Goicolea, Goicolejea, Goiri, Goiria, Goiriz, Goite, Goitia, Goitisolo, Golaez, Golar, Golaz, Golfín, Gollart, Gomar, Gomara, Gombal, Gombau, Gomedio, Gomendradi, Gomensoro, Gómez, Gómez de Aguilar, Gómez de Alba, Gómez de Arce, Gómez de Arteche, Gómez de Ayala, Gómez de Barreda, Gómez de Barreiro, Gómez de la Blanca, Gómez de Bonilla, Gómez Bores, Gómez de Bustamante, Gómez de Calzerrada, Gómez Castrillo, Gómez de Castro, Gómez Collado, Gómez de la Cortina, Gómez de Don Benito, Gómez de Enterrías, Gómez de Espinosa, Gómez de Gorraiz, Gómez Herrador, Gómez Jara, Gómez Lamadrid,

Gómez de Lasprilla, Gómez de Lastra, Gómez de Liaño, Gómez de Llamosa, Gómez de Monzolo, Gómez de Mercado, Gómez de Merodio, Gómez de Mier, Gómez de Ontiveros, Gómez Pardo, Gómez de Porras, Gómez de la Presa, Gómez de Revenga, Gómez del Río, Gómez del Rivero, Gómez de Rozas, Gómez de Salazar, Gómez de Sandoval, Gómez de Santa Cruz, Gómez de la Serna. End of EHG Volume 37.

EHG Volume 38: Gómez de Silva, Gómez de Terán, Gómez de la Torre, Gómez de Torres, Gómez de Ureña, Gómez de la Vega, Gómez de Villafufre, Gómez de Villamayor, Gomeza, Gomezain, Gomicio, Gomucio, Gomide, Gomiecourt, Gomila, Gomis, Gondar, Gondi, Góngora, Gonzaga, González, González de Agüero, González de Aguilar, González de Albelda, González de Almunia, González de Andía, González Arango, González de Arce, González de Argumanes, González de Arrieta, González de Artiaga, González de Asarta, González de Avilés, González de la Bárcena, González de Barreda, González-Berbeo, González de Berdasquera, González-Bravo, González de Bustamante, González Caballo, González Cadrana, González de Caldas, González Calderón, González de la Cámara, González del Campillo, González del Campo, González Campuzano, González Cañaveral, González Carbonera, González Carvajal, González de Castañeda, González de Castejón, González de Cavada, González de Celosía, González de Cienfuegos-Jovellanos, González-Colloto, González Cordero, González Cortina, González Cosío, González Cossío, González de Cuenca, González de Cuenia, González de Chacín, González de Echábarri, González de Echávarri, González de Estéfani, González de Ferrero, González de Foronda, González de las Fráguas, González de Galeano, González de Garaño, González de Grado, González-Grano de Oro, González de Guerreño, González de Guerzno, González de Heredia, González de Herrera, González Ibarra, González de Jate, González de Lanzas, González de Legarda, González de Legaria, González de León, González López, González de Lucena, González Llanos, González de Madrid, González Maldonado, González de Mata, González Mateo, González de Matos, González Melgarejo, González de de Mena, González Merchante, González de Mesa, González Montero, González Montoya, González Negrete, González de Ocón, González de Orbón, González de Orduña, González de Otazu, González de Párraga, González de la Pasapuente, González Peñuecos, González Pimentel, González Pondal, González de la Pontonilla, González de Prado, González de Prío, González de Proaño, González de la Pumariega, González Quijano, González del Real, González de la Reguera, González Rejón, González Remírez de Arellano, González Remusgo, González de los Ríos, González Rivas, González del Rivero, González de Robés, González de la Rúa, González Salmón, González de Santa Cruz, González de Sepúlveda, González de Socasa, González de Socueva, González Tamón, González Torres de Navarra, González de Uzqueta, González del Vado, González del Valle,

González Vallejo, González de Vega, González de Villa, González de Villalva, González de Villoslada, González Zorrilla, Gonzalo, Gonzálves, Goñi, Goñiz, Gondar, Goosens, Gorbea, Gordejuela, Gordillo, Gordo Gordoa, Gordón, Gordoncillo, Gorduaz, Gordún, Gorena, Goriezo, Gorgoa, Gorjoji, Gorgot, Gormaz, Gorocín or Gorozín, Goroneta or Goronaeta, Gorosábel, Gorospizcar, Gorostegui, Gorostiaga, Gorostidi, Gorostigui, Gorostiola or Goroztiola, or Gorostioca, Gorostola, Gorostiza, Gorostizaga, Gorostizu, Gorostorzu, Goroziga, Gorráiz or Gorráez, Gorráunz, Gorriarán, Gorrichátegui, Gorriola, Gorritepe, Gorrite, Gorriti. End of EHG Volume 38.

EHG Volume 39: Górriz, Gorrizarri, Goroochategui, Gort, Gortabarrí, Gortaire, Gortairia, Gortari, Gortázar, Gossa, Gotiortua, Gotor, Gotrano, Goxenechea, Goya, Goyara, Goyaz, Goyena, Goyeneche, Goyenechea, Goyeneta, Goiri, Gozón, Grabalosa, Gracia, Gracián, Gradilla, Grado, Gradolí, Graell, Grafull, Graffeo, Gragera, Graham, Grajal, Grajeda, Grajera, Grajo, Gralla, Gram, Gramacho, Gramajo, Gramón, Granada, Granado, Granalosa, Granda, Grandallana, Grandenero, Grandesnero, Granell, Graner, Granero, Grani, Granollachs, Granollés, Granuela, Granullás, Granullés, Granyena, Grañón, Gras, Grasa, Grases, Grasins, Grasís, Grassa, Grasull, Grau, Grava, Gravalosa, Gravalossa, Gravé (de), Gravilosa, Gravina, Gray, Grecio, Grech, Gregorio, Grest, Gretis, Grez, Griegos, Grifé, Griffo, Grijalba, Grijalva, Grilla, Grillet, Grillo, Grillón, Grima, Grimalda, Grimaldi, Grimaldo, Grimau, Grimón, Grimosachs, Griñó, Grior, Grisón, Grisone, Griver, Grizaña, Groni, Grony, Gros, Groso, Grua (La), Grub, Gruilles, Gruny, Brustán, Guacarapaucara, Guadalajara, Guadalix, Guadiana, Guaita, Guajardo, Gual, Gualba, Gualbes, Gualda, Gualsoro, Gualterio, Gualutxo, Guallar, Guallart, Guallarto, Guamis, Guanes, Guanter, Guara, Guarda, Guardamino, Guardato, Guardia, Guardiola, Guarnizo, Guaro, Guart, Guarrat, Guasco, Guaso, Guasp, Guasso, Guayango, Guazo, Guazola, Gubert, Gúdal, Gudiel, Gudiellas, Gudín, Gueba, Guevara, Guebide, Güeco, Guecho, Guedeja, Guedes, Guelasoro, Guelbas, Güel, Guells, Güemes, Guendica, Guendulain, Guerán, Guerau, Guerbillano, Guercolata, Guereca, Guerendiaín, Guereño, Guereñu, Guerequiz, Guereta, Guerforat, Guergo, Guergué, Guerguetiaín, Guernica, Guerra, Guerradell, Guerreiro, Guerrero, Guerrico, Guésquier, Guesala, Guetador, Guetaria, Guevara, Guexar, Guezala, Guesala, Guezuraga, Gui, Guiana, Guil. Eng of EHG Volume 39.

EHG Volume 40: Guilisagasti, Guilisasti, Guiliz, Guilo, Guiluz, Guill, Guilla, Guillamas, Guillarte, Guillemés, Guillemota, Guillén, Guilles, Guilleuma, Guilleztegui, Guim, Guimaraes, Guimaraus, Guimerá, Guimerans, Guinart, Guindazo, Guinea, Guani, Guinoiseau, Guiñazú, Guio, Guiral, Guirall, Guirao, Guirarte, Guirior, Guirola, Guisasa, Guisasola, Guisla, Guital, Guitart, Guitian, Guitio, Guiu, Guixart, Guixós, Guizaburuaga, Guizamonde, Gulina, Gumiel, Gumucio, Gutin, Gunuz, Guraya, Gurb, Gurendes, Guridi, Guriezo, Gurmendi,

Gurp, Gurpegui, Gurpide, Guruceta, Gurrea, Gurría, Gurrola, Gurruchaga, Gurruchategui, Gusseme, Gutarrate, Gutiérrez, Gutiérrez de Arce, Gutiérrez de Bárcena, Gutiérrez de Barona, Gutiérrez de la Barreda, Gutiérrez de Bustamante, Gutiérrez de Cabiedes, Gutiérrez de la Calzadilla, Gutiérrez de Carriazo, Gutiérrez de Caviedes, Gutiérrez de Celis, Gutiérrez de la Concha, Gutiérrez de Cosío, Gutiérrez de Cossío, Gutiérrez de Ferrera, Gutiérrez de Gandarilla, Gutiérrez de Hernán Pérez, Gutiérrez de Herrera, Gutiérrez de la Huerta, Gutiérrez de León, Gutiérrez del Mazo, Gutiérrez de Montalvo, Gutiérrez de Moya, Gutiérrez de Otero, Gutiérrez de Palacio, Gutiérrez de la Peña, Gutiérrez de Piñeres, Gutiérrez de Puertas, Gutiérrez de Quevedo, Gutiérrez de los Ríos, Gutiérrez de Rozas, Gutiérrez de Ruvalcava, Gutiérrez de Santibáñez, Gutiérrez de Solana, Gutiérrez del Solar, Gutiérrez de Solórzano, Gutiérrez Tello, Gutiérrez de la Torre, Guzmán. End of EHG Volume 40.

EHG Volume 41: Gramunt, p. 271; EHG Volume 42: Gea or Egea, p.278; EHG Volume 44: Gastón, p. 209; EHG Volume 50: Galvez, p. 259; EHG Volume 58: Gaztelu, p. 254; EHG Volume 62: Gutiérrez-Marroquín, p. 241; EHG Volume 68: Garde, p. 243; EHG Volume 71: Garaicoa, p. 205; Garaycoa, p. 206; García de Olalla, p. 210; EHG Volume 73: Garibi, p. 223; EHG Volume 74: González, p. 189. End of Letter G.

H EHG Volume 41: Hartos, Hastas, Haya, Hayas, Hayos, Hazaños, Hecho, Hechosa, Hederra, Hedilla, Hegaro, Hegual, Helausa, Heles, Helguera, Helguero, Hemerando, Henales, Henao, Hera, Heras, Herada, Herados, Heraña, Herboso, Henestrosa, Herdara, Herdoñana, Heredia, Herencia, Hereñozu, Herloeta, Hermida, Hedmigas, Hermildes, Hermosa, Hermosilla, Hermoso, Hermúa, Henáez, Hernáiz, Hernández, Hernández de Alba, Hernández de Alba, Hernánez de la Iruela, Hernández del Campo, Hernández de Gincio, Hernández Pizarro, Herández de Soto, Hernando, Hernando de Soto, Hernani, Herniti, Heros, Herrada, Herraiz, Herrainz, Herrán, Herránz, Herrementería, Herrera, Herrerías, Herrero, Herreros, Herreruelo, Herrezuela, Hervás, Hervías, Héspital, Hevia, Hidalgo, Hidrón, Hielz, Hiermo, Hierro, Hierais, Higuera, Hijero, Híjar, Hilera. End EHG Volume 41.

EHG Volume 42: Hilgueros, Himadas, Hiniesta, Hinojosa, Hipato, Hipenza, Hipólito, Hiribago, Hirizar, Hispano, Hita, Hizurún, Hoa, Hoceja, Hocera, Hocés, Hoef, Hogażón, Holgado, Holguín, Hojacastro, Holviá, Homar, Homas, Hombau, Homdedeu, Home, Homedes, Homen, Homodeus, Homs, Honesto, Honorato, Hontaneda, Hontañón, Hontiveros, Honze, Horachita, Horaicoechea, Horazachea, Horazqueta, Horbeña, Horcasitas, Hore,

Horesinón, Hordeñana, Horguibel, Hormaeche, Hormaechea, Hormaza, Horna, Hornillos, Horólogo, Horue, Horta, Horteu, Hortezuelo, Hortí, Hortolá, Hortuño, Horra, Horrioldegui, Horroalde, Horroitinel, Hospital, Hostales, Hostalrich, Hoyo, Hoyos, Hoyuela, Hoz, Hozcariz, Hoznayo, Hozta, Hualde, Huarte, Huelgues, Huérgo, Huerta, Huertas, Huete, Huguet, Huici, Huidobro, Huinaguenta or Huinagonta, Huirravoso, Hulibarri, Humada, Humaña, Humara, Humeres, Hunecus, Hungría, Hurmeneta, Hurmenta, Huró, Hurone, Hurosa, Hurtado, Hurtado de Amézaga, Hurtado de Corcuera, Hurtado de Mendoza, Hurtado de Zaldívar, Huyarramendi. End of EHG Volume 42.

EHG Volume 45: Humada, p. 247. End of Letter H.

I EHG Volume 42: Ibacax, Ibaeta or Ibaceta, Ibaigane, Ibaizábal or Ibaizázal, Ibalbuen, Ibáñez, Ibáñez de Arteaga, Ibáñez de Arriola, Ibáñez de Camús, Ibáñez de Corvera, Ibáñez de Ibero, Ibáñez de Irarrázabal, Ibáñez de Lamadrid, Ibáñez de Leiba, Ibáñez de Monreal, Ibáñez de Muruzábal, Ibáñez Ocerin, Ibáñez de Pacheco, Ibáñez de la Rentería, Ibáñez de Segovia, Ibáñez de Zabala, Ibao, Ibar, Ibarbaiz, Ibarbia, Ibarbeste or Ibarbeitio, Ibarburu, Ibares, Ibargoen or Ibargüen, Ibarguren, Ibarluce, Ibarlucea, Ibarra, Ibarreta, Ibarrieta, Ibarrola, Ibarrondo, Ibarraundia, Ibarrundia. End of EHG Volume 42.

EHG Volume 43: Ibars de Povil, Ibartola, Ibarzábal, Ibero, Ibia, Ibiaga, Ibilosqueta, Ibinarri, Ibio, Ibiricu, Ibasate, Iborra, Ibrea, Ibros, Icabalceta, Icara, Icart, Icaza, Icazate, Iceta, Ichaso, Ichazarreta, Iciar, Iciesta, Icio, Icis, Icoaga, Idiacáiz, Idiacón, Idiáquez, Idiazábal, Idigoras, Idiolo, Idirín, Idoate, Iduate, Idhuate, Idoyaga, Idoyeta, Iduarte, Iduya, Igal, Igala, Igaralde, Igartúa, Igarza, Igarzábal, Igay, Igea, Iglesia, Iglesias, Igoa, Igola, Igor, Igoraín, Iguacel, Iguala, Igualdo, Iguarán, Igueldo, Iguerabide, Iguereta, Igueribar, Iguinaga, Iguiñiz, Iguña, Iguzquiza, Ijurieta, Ilárraza, Ilarregui, Ilasa, Ilasaga, Ilazábal, Iliberri, Ilorobeitia, Ilumbe, Ilumberri, Iluna, Ilundaín, Ilurdoz, Iluz, Ilzarbe, Ilzauspea, Illa, Illán, Illanes, Illano, Illarradi, Illarramendi, Illarrasu, Illarregui, Illera, Illescas, Illoces, Illorobeitia, Illumbe, Illuz, Illuzuel, Imaz, Imbaurraga, Imberto, Imbonati, Imbrea, Imbrechts, Imbuluzqueta, Imizcoz, Imirizaldu, Imperátor, Imperial, Imorcoaín, Inarra, Inarrea, Inca, Inchaurandieta, Incháustegui, Inchausti, Incinillas, Inclán, Inda, Indaburu, Indaneta, Indart, Indo, Infantas, Infante, Infanzón, Inga, Inglés, Ingolati, Inguanzo, Ingunza, Inistarte, Inoldi, Inoriza, Inoso, Inquiforte, Insaurandiaga, Insaurbe, Insaurraga, Insausti, Insiodo, Interián, Interiana, Interiano, Inturia, Inurea, Inurrieta, Inurritegui, Inurrigarro, Inurriza, Intriago, Inviciati, Inza, Inzas Ermenteros, Inzaurdiaga, Iñarra, Iñigo, Iñigo Ruiz, Iñiguez, Iñiguez Abarca, Iñiguez Beortegui, Iñiguez de Endérica, Iñiguez de la Fuente, Iñiguez de Guereña

Colodro, Iñiguez de Heredia, Iñiguez de Ulibarri-Gamboa, Iñiguiz, Ipatalegui, Iparraguirre, Ipas, Ipenarrieta, Ipeñarrieta, Ipenza, Ipinza, Ipiña, Ipirieta, Ipróxita, Irabien, Irabigui, Iracusta, Iracheta, Iraeta, Iragorri, Iragorria, Irala, Iramaín, Iranzo, Iraola, Irarraga, Irarraín, Irarramendi, Irarrázabal, Irategui, Irauqui, Iráuregui, Iraurgui, Iravedra de Paz, Irazábal, Irazagorria, Irazazábal, Irazoqui, Irazusta. End of EHG Volume 43.

EHG Volume 44: Irgas, Iriarte, Iriartea, Iribago, Iribar, Iribarne, Iribarren, Iribarrena, Iribas, Iribe, Iriberri, Iribi, Irigaray, Irigoras, Irigoyen, Irigoyenzar, Irimo, Irisarri, Irisco, Iriso, Irizar, Iriztaín, Irles, Irogazte, Iros, Iruegas, Iruela, Irueta, Iruín, Irutegui, Iruleta, Irulogos, Irumberri, Irún, Irunciaga, Irujo, Irunzqui, Iruña, Irunela, Irure, Irureta, Irurozqui, Irurreta, Irurtia, Irurzun, Irusta, Iruxta, Iruzubieta, Irrabaza, Irradreta, Irrebago, Isaba, Isachar, Isais, Isarbiribil, Isarvirivil, Isarraga, Isarre, Isasa, Isásaga, Isasbiribil, Isasbirivil, Isasi, Isasola, Isasprivil, Isasti, Isastia, Isaundariaga, Isaza, Isázaga, Ischiros, Isequilla, Isern, Iserna, Isidro, Isimbardi, Isla, Islaba, Isoba, Isola, Isona, Isorna, Isorno, Istillartea, Istueta, Isturiz, Isturizaga, Isuerre, Isundegui, Isunza, Isurieta, Isurrieta, Isusi, Isusorbe, Isusquiza, Ituarte, Ituño, Iturbe, Iturberoaga, Iturbide, Iturburu, Iturbusti, Itúren, Iturgoyen, Iturmendi, Iturralde, Iturrao, Iturrarán, Iturraspe, Iturrate, Iturrebaso, Iturregui, Iturren, Iturri, Iturriaga, Iturribalzaga, Iturricha, Iturrieta, Iturrigaray, Iturriospe, Iturrioz, Iturrista, Iturriza, Iturrizaga, Iturrizarra, Iurrebago, Iza, Izaga, Izaguirre, Izarra, Izarraga, Izal, Izarraín, Izasa, Izasa, Izcaray, Izcariz, Izco, Izcue, Izgüe, Izis, Iziz, Izeta, Izmendi, Iznardi, Izoaga, Izquierdo, Iztegui, Iztueta, Izu, Izunza, Izurieta, Izurrategui, Izurraín, Izurzu. End of Volume 44.

EHG Volume 47: Inchaurrandieta, p. 229; Iturrarán, p. 235; EHG Volume 62: Icaza, p. 244; EHG Volume 68: Ibars de Povil, p. 244. End of Letter I.

J EHG Volume 45: Jabaloyas, Jabare, Jabariz, Jabarra, Jabat, Jaca, Jaces de Sos, Jacob, Jacobs, Jacoisti, Jácome, Jacot, Jado, Jaén, Jaime, Jalón, Jalpí, Janariz, Janaro, Janche, Jandategui, Janer, Janiz, Januas, Jaolaza, Jaques, Jara, Jaraba, Jarabeitia, Jaramillo, Jaraquemada, Jarica, Jardín, Jarl, Jarrán, Jasa, Jaso, Jaspe, Jasso, Jaúdenes, Jaume, Jaunes, Jaureaga, Jaureda, Jáuregui, Jaureguibarria, Jaureguiondo, Jaureguizar, Jaureguizarra, Jaurgain, Jaurizar, Jaurola, Jaurrieta, Jausolo, Jausoro, Javier, Jedler, Jelpí, Jerez, Jérica, Jibaja, Jijante, Jilet, Jiménez, Jiménez de Allo, Jiménez de Andosilla, Jiménez de Aragüés, Jiménez de Arroniz, Jiménez de Ayerbe, Jiménez de Bagüés, Jiménez de Bohorques, Jiménez Bretón, Jiménez de Cascante, Jiménez de Cisneros, Jiménez de los Cobos, Jiménez de Embúm, Jiménez de Enciso, Jiménez de la Fontaza, Jiménez de Frontin, Jiménez de Lierta, Jiménez Lobatón, Jiménez del Moral, Jiménez de Murillo, Jiménez Navarro, Jiménez Sandoval, Jiménez de San Juan, Jimeno, Jiorge, Jiráldez, Jironda, Joaistena, Joalla, Joan, Joanin, Joara, Jódar, Jodra, Jofrá, Jofré, Jolit, Jomacelo, Jorada, Jorba, Jordá, Jordán, Jordi, Jorganes, Jornada, Jorondorena, Jorrano, Josá, Joso, Jossá, Jou, Joval, Jovani, Jove, Jovel, Jovellanos, Jover, Juan, Uanes, Juanicotena, Juaniz, Juanmartitena, Juansansoro, Juara, Juarbe, Juárez, Juarte, Jubare, Jubarte, Jubero, Jubindo, Júdez, Júdice, Juez, Jugo, Juhun, Juitra, Juliá, Julián, Jultrú, Jullá, Jument, Jumilla, Juncar, Junco, Junqueira, Junquito, Junta, Junterón, Juny, Junyent, Jurado, Jurdanarena, Juseu, Juste, Jutge, Justicia, Justiniani, Justiniano, Justiz, Justo, Jusué, Juyá. End of EHG Volume 45.

EHG Volume 59: Jiménez de Antillón, p. 257; EHG Volume 68: Jiménez de Cascante, p. 245. End of Letter J.

L EHG Volume 46: Labaca, Labadía, Labanda, La Bandera, Labandero, Labania, Labárcena, La Barreda, La Barrera, Labarrua, Labasay, Labastida, Labata, Labayen, Labayru, Labazui, Labeaga, Labeaza, Labetz, Labia, Labiá, Labiaga, Labiano, Labora, Laborda, Laborde, Labra, Labraña, Labrit, Labroche, Labueche, Laca, Lacaballería, Lacadena, Lacambra, Lácar, Lacarbuera, Lacarra, Lacaruza, Lacenty, Lacera, La Cerda, Lacerna, Laciana, Lacoma, Lacoizqueta, Lacruz, Lacuaga, Lacunza, Lacy, Lacha, La Chica, Lada, Ladornosa, Ladosa, Ladró, Ladrón, Lafarga, Lafetat, Lafiguera, Lafita, Laffitte, Lafuente, Lagarto, Lago, Laguanaz, Laguarta, Laguaya, Laguna, Lagunilla, Laguras, Laharria, La Haya, La Hera, Lahora, Laiglesia, Lain, Lainez, Laiseca, Laita, Lajust, Laka, La Laguna, Lalaing, La Lama, La Lana, La Loy, La Llana, Lallave, Lama, Lamadrid, Lamariano, Lamarque de Novoa, La Marra, Lamas, Lamata, Lambarca, Lamblea, Lamblene, Lamego, Lamela, Lamo, Lampazo, Lamus, Lana, Lanaberri, Lanaja, Lanana, Lanareja, Lanario, Lanaz, Lanciego, Landa, Landaberea, Landaberro, Landaburu, Landacaranda, Landacur, Landaeta, Landagorrieta, Landajuela, Landaluce, Landamela Veascoa, Landas, Landaverde, Landazuri, Lande, Landeche, Landecho, Landelles, Landeras, Landeribar, Landeta, Lando, Landolina, Landriano, Landro, Landrope, Laneiras, Lángara, Langarica, Langarza, Langlés, Langosco, Langurel, Lanio, Lannoy, Lanoguera, Lantabat, Lantadilla, Lantaro, Lanterio, Lantoria, Lanuza, Lanz, Lanza, Lanzabuena, Lanzaeta, Lanzagorta, Lanzarot, Lanzarote, Lanzol, Lanzón, Lanzós, Laortiga, Lapacharán, Laparada, Lapaza, Lapazaga, Lapazarán, Lapedriza, Lapeña, Lapezuela, Lapiceta, La Piedra, Lapieza, Lapila, Lapiratua, Laplana, La Plaza, La Porta, La Porte, Lapresa, Lapuerta, Lapurdi, Laquedano, Laquidiola, Laquistegui, Lara, Larachao, Larán, Larande, Laranizal, Lararguren, Larburu. End of EHG Volume 46.

EHG Volume 47: Lardíes, Lardizábal, Laredo, Larena or La Arena, Largacha, Largos (Pérez de), Lario, Larios, Laris, Lariz, Larozqui, Lartaun, Lartando,

Lartitegui, Lartundo, Larués, Larumbe, Larzábal, Larzanguren, Larra, Larrabide, Larraca, Larracea, Larracoechea, Larrachao, Larrache, Larrachea, Larracho, Larrad, Larraga, Larragán, Larragoiti, Larragoyen, Larragueta, Larraguibel, Larrain, Larraingoa, Larrainzar, Larraisoaña, Larraíz or La Raíz, Larralde, Larrambebere, Larramendi, Larramendía, Larrán, Larranda, Larrandi, Larrangoz, Larrano, Larrañaga, Larrañeta, Larraón, Larrar, Larrarte, Larrasa or La Rasa, Larrasoaña, Larrasoro, Larraspuru, Larrategui, Larratiz, [Laita, p. 234], Larraul, Larrauri; Larrauz, Larraya, Larrayoz, Larraz, Larraza, Larrazábal, Larrazuri, Larrea, Larreandi, Larreategui, Larreburu, Larreche, Larrechi, Larrequiandía, Larrerdi, Larrerdia, Larrestegui, Larreta, Larria, Larriaga, Larriasoro, Larriategui, Larriba, Larrieta, Larrimpe, Larrina, Larrinaga, Larrino, Larrinoa, Larrión, Larriva or La Riva, Larrondo, Larrondobuno, Larrondomuno, Larrosa, Larrua, Larrumbe, Larrumbide, Larrume, Larzábal, Larzacea, Larzanguren, Lasa, Lasaeta, Lasaga, Lasagabaster, Lasague, Lasala, Lasalde, Lasao, Lasarte, Lascamburu, Lascoaín, Lascort, Lascortegui, Lascortes, Lascorz, La Serna, Laserra, Lasiaín, Lasierra, Lasio, Laso de la Vega, La Sota, Lasquetty, Lasquibar, Lastanosa, Lastarria, Lastaun, Lasterra, Lasteros, Lastiarro, Lastiri, Lastra or de la Lastra, Lastres, Lastur, Lasuin, Lasurrutegui, Lasurtegui, Latadia, Latado, Latalu, Lataoiz, Latarza or Lataraza, Latasa or Latassa, Latejera, Latenda, Latodi, Latorre or La Torre, Latrás, Laudans, Laudati, Lauquiniz, Laurán, Laurencin, Laurgain, Lauria, Laurnaga, Laurreguiondo, Lausagarreta, Lanzurica, Lavaggi, Lavandeira, Lavalle, Lavaqui, Lavecilla or La Vecilla, Laviesca, Lavín or García de Lavín, Laxaga, Laxet, Laya, Layana, Layeto, Layosa, Laza, Lazaga, Lazán, Lázaro, Lazarra, Lazartuzábal, Lazárraga, Lazcaibar, Lazcamburu. End of EHG Volume 47.

EHG Volume 48: Lazcano, Lazcanotegui, Lazoaín, Lazón, Lazquibar, Laztorria, Leaburu, Leaeche, Leaegui, Leal, Leaniz, Learreta, Learrigartu, Leazarraga, Leazgue, Leazgui, Leazogue, Lebanto, Le Boffa, Lebrón, Lebrun, Leca, Lecanda, Lecanduri, Lecaros, Lecaroz, Lecca, Lecea, Lécera, Leceta, Lecica, Lecina, Lecoandiz, Lecumberri, Lecuona, Lechuga, Lecundis, Ledesma, Ledos, Leet, Legarbarrena, Legarda, Legaria, Legarra, Legarbarrena, Legarda, Legaria, Legarra, Legarrasua, Legarreta, Legarria, Legarza, Legazpi, Legazpia, Legasa, Legasso, Legorburu, Legorreta-Zarra, Legoyaga, Legrós, Leguía, Leguina, Leguizamón, Leibar, Leici, Leicigoena, Leijalde, Leira, Leis, Leitago, Leite, Leiva, Leiza, Leizalde, Leizaola, Leizargárate, Leizaur, Leizola, Lejarasua, Lejarazu, Lejardi, Lejarza, Lejo, Lemizón, Lemona, Lemonia, Lemos, Lemus, Lena, Lendines, Lendinez, Lengarán, Lenguazo, Lenguela, Leni, Lenis, Leniz, Lentisclá, Lentisco, Lentorn, Lenzarán, Lenzol, Leofrin, León, Leonardo, Leonarte, Leonés, Leonikiz, Leoniquez, Leorenten, Leorraga, Leoz, Lepizamo, Lepuzain, Lequedano, Lequeitio, Lequerica, Lequido, Lera, Leraza, Lercara, Lercaro, Lerchundi, Lereche, Lerés, Lerga, Lerin, Lerinda,

Lerinena, Lerito, Lerma, Lermita, Lersundi, Leruela, Lerun, Lerruz, Lesaca, Lesguitcero, Lesparza, Lesquina, Lesol, Leste, Lete, Letemendia, Letona, Leturia, Leturiondo, Leunda, Lexalde, Leyaristi, Leyarzu, Leyun, Leys, Lez, Lezabaleta, Lezaeta, Lezalde, Lezama, Lezana, Lezaun, Lezo, Lian, Liana, Liaño, Liarza, Libano, Libero, Liberri, Libiá, Liceaga, Licer, Licergárate, Licona, Licordi, Licher, Lidueña, Liébana, Liédena, Liegui, Lienda, Liermo, Ligomano, Liger, Liguaro, Ligués, Lila, Lili, Licardi, Lilet, Lillo, Lima, Limbeu, Limes, Limós, Limpias, Limpos, Linares, Lincolne, Linde, Linden, Lines, Lingan, Liñalea, Liñán, Liñas, Liñieta, Lio, Lión, Liorca, Liori, Liponti, Liquicio, Lira, Lirón, Lisa, Lisafo, Lisasoaín, Lisón, Lisperguer, Litago, Litola, Lizana, Lizaraco, Lirazaza, Lizarazu, Lizaransu, Lizardi, Lizardo, Lizargárate, Lizárraga. End of EHG Volume 48.

EHG Volume 49: Lizarralde, Lizarraraz, Lizarriturri, Lizarza, Lizarzaburu, Lizarrondo, Lizaso, Lizasoaín, Lizatu, Lizaur or Leizaur, Lizaurzábal, Lizcaga, Lizoaín, Lizola, Lizundia, Loaisa, Loarte, Lobato, Lobatón, Lobera or Llobera, Lobet or Llobet, Lobiano, Lobo, Locaña, Loci, Loctri, Locy, Lodeña, Lodi, Lodosa, Loges, Logran, Loidi, Loigorri, Loina, Loinaz, Lois, Loiteguy, Loiti, Loiztarraín, Loizaga, Lolin, Loma, Lomba, Lombana, Lombardo, Lombera, Lombero, Lomelín, Lomelina, Lonarte, Londaiz, Londinez, Londoño, Longa, Longo, Longoria, Longrat, Lope, Lopeola, Loperena, Lopetedi, Lopetegui, López, López de Aberásturi, López de Acevedo, López de Adán, López de Aguilera, López de Albizu, López-Almonacid, López Alonso, López de Amaya, López de Ansó, López de Ansorena, López de Arcos, López de los Arcos, López de Arellano, López de la Arena, López de Arrieta, López Atuesta, López de Ayala, López de Ayllón, López de Bailo, López-Ballesteros, López de Baños, López de Baquedano, López de Barajas, López-Barthe, López-Bravo, López de Briñas, López de Burgos, López de Cabués, López de Cangas, López del Cano, López de Carrizosa, López-Carvajal, López de Casal, López de Casbas, López del Castillo, López del Corral, López de Cotilla, López de Dicastillo, López de Doypa, López de Ecala, López de Espinosa, López de Estaún, López de Fanlo, López de Echaburu, López-Ferro, López de la Flor, López Flores de Molina, López de Galarza, López de Gallegos, López de Gamarra, López de Ganuza, López de Gárate, López de Garayo or Garayoa, López de Goicoechea, López de Goveo, López Guerrero, López Guijarro, López de Gurrea, López de Haro, López de Hernani, López de la Huerta, López de Humara, López de Inarra, López de Irusta, López de Lamadrid, López de Lerena, López de Letona, López de Luna, López de Maella, López Maldonado, López de Manzanedo, López Medrano, López de Mendizábal, López de Mendoza, López de Menoyo, López de Mesa, López Mesas, López de Mirafuentes, López de Miranda, López Montenegro, López de Morla, López Mosquera, López Olavarri, López Padilla, López de Páez, López Pedruel, López Pelegrín, López Peña, López Peñaranda, López Pinilla, López de la Plata, López Portillo, López de Porras, López de Poveda, López de Prado, López de Puga, López Quintana, López de Restrepo, López de Reta, López de Río, López de Rivaforada, López de Rivero, López de Robredo, López de Sabando, López Sagredo, López de Salcedo, López de Sanilorente, López de San Martín, López de San Román, López de Santillana, López Sedano, López de la Serna, López de Spínola, López de Sobás, López de Sotomayor, López Tello, López Teruel, López Toñanejos, López de Torinde, López de la Torre, López de Vinuesa, López de Vitoria, López de Ugarte, López de Ulloa, López de Uralde, López de Uría, López de Zárate, López de Zúñiga, Lorca, Lordat, Lorde, Lordoro, Lorea, Loredo, Lorencio, Lorente, Lorenz, Lorenzana, Lorenzo, Lores, Loret, Lorfelin, Loria, Loriega, Lorieri, Loriga, Loris or Lloris, Lorit, Lorite, Loro, Loroño, Lorza, Losa, Losada, Loscertales, Losilla, Loscós or Lloscós, Lotero, Lowenfeld, Loxau, Loya, Loyo, Loyola, Lozana, Lozano, Luaces, Luango, Luarca, Lubet, Lubelza, Lubián, Lubiano, Lucas, Lucena, Lucerga, Luciá, Lucio or Lucero, Luco, Luchana, Luchas, Ludeña, Lué, Luebana, Luengas, Luera, Luertos, Luga, Lugariz or Lugaritz, Lugo, Lugones, Luis, Luján, Lumbier, Lumbreras, Lull, Lupiá, Luna, Lunell, Luno, Luque, Luqui, Luquin, Lusagasti, Luscando or Lusgando, Lusia, Luso or Luxo, Lustiz, Lutago, Luxa, Luyando, Luzán or Luzar, Luzón, Luzuriaga. End of EHG Volume 49.

EHG Volume 50: Llordat or Lordat, Lloreda, Llorens, Llorente, Lloret, Llosa, Lloscós, Llosellas, Lloselles, Llucas, Lluch, Lluis, Llull, Llunas, Llunell, Llupiá, Lluria, Llusa. End of EHG Volume 50, Letter L.

EHG Volume 50: López de Alava, p. 237; López de Ayala, p. 239; López de San Román, p. 240; López de Haro R. de Baeza, p. 242; EHG Volume 56: Lisa, p. 251; EHG Volume 62: Lasa, p. 260; EHG Volume 64: López-Barajas, p. 245; EHG Volume 67: López Marcote, p. 231; EHG Volume 68: Luz, p. 249. End of Letters L and LL.

M EHG Volume 50: Mabaja, Macaiziola, Macaya, Macazaga, MacClure, MacCrohom, Macé, Maceda, Macedo, Maceira, Maceta, Macías, Maciel, Macip, Mach, MacKean, MacKenna, MacMahón, Macuso, Machado, Machain, Machín, Machinena, Machón, Machuca, Madaleno, Madán, Madariaga, Madera, Madero, Madeira, Madeiro, Maderazo, Madina, Madinabeitia, Madinagoicoa, Madinagoitia, Madrazo, Madriaza, Madrid, Madrigal, Madroño, Madueño, Madureira, Maduxer, Maeda, Maella, Maestre, Maestu, Maeztu, Maffet, Magallanes, Magallón, Magán, Magaña, Magara, Magarola, Magarzo, Magastre, Magdaleno, Magrizo, Magro, Maguna, Maguña, Maguregui, Mahiques, Mahull, Maía, Maillar, Maimo, Maimón, Maina, Maioz, Maiquez, Maíz, Maiztegui, Malaca, Malacara, Malany, Malars, Malatesta, Malaver, Malcampo, Malcuarto, Maldá. End of EHG Volume 50.

EHG Volume 51: Maldonado, Malendrich, Maleo, Maler, Malet, Malferit, Malgar, Maliá, Maliaño, Malo, Malón, Malonda, Malpica, Malrich, Maluecio, Maluenda, Malzán, Malla, Mallano, Mallavia, Mallea, Mallén, Mallendrueda, Malleza, Mallia, Mallo, Mallol, Mallón, Mallorca, Manca, Mancebo, Manceta, Mancicidor, Mancisidor, Mancha, Mancheño, Mancho, Mancilla, Manchola, Mandabil, Mandaca, Mandiá, Mandieses, Mandiola, Mandolena, Manegat, Manent, Manente, Manero, Mangas, Manglano, Mangino, Manjarrés, Manjón, Manobella, Manlleu, Mannat, Mannig, Manola, Manolla, Manresa, Manrique, Manrique de Arana, Manrique de Luna, Mansa, Mansilla, Manso, Manso de Andrade, Manso de Velasco, Manso de Zúñiga, Mantecón, Manterola, Mantilla, Manuel, Manuflo, Manurga, Manyalich, Manzanal, Manzanares, Manzaneda, Manzanedo, Manzano, Mañara, Mañaria, Mañarigua, Mañariturriaga, Mañeras, Mañeru, Mañozca, Mañueco, Maomones, Maortúa, Mapfey, Maqueda, Maquibar, Maquieira, Maquilón, Marán, Marano, Maranyosa, Marañón, Marañosa, Marabel, Maracote, Marata, Maraver, Marbán, Marca (de la), March, Marchán, Marchao, Marcé, Marcel, Marcelo, Marcello, Marcén, Marcer, Marcilla, Marco, Marcó, Marcoleta, Marcos, Marcote, Marcuat, Marcuello, Marcús, Mandaratz, Mardones, Marentes, Marfil, Marfúl, Margalés, Margarit, Margens, Mariaca, Marialva, Mariana, Marí, Mariarto, Maribona, Marica, Marichalar, Marielus, Marieri, Marigni, Marimón, Marín. End of EHG Volume 51.

EHG Volume 52: Marina, Marinas, Marinoy, Mariñas, Mariño, Mariqueta, Maris, Mariscal, Marizo, Mariztegui, Marlés, Marlet, Marmo, Mármol, Marmolejo, Marola, Maroja, Maroto, Marpí, Marqués, Marquesa, Marquet, Márquez, Márquez de Avellaneda, Márquez de la Plata, Márquez de Prado, Marquiegui, Marquillos, Marquina, Mars, Marsá, Marsal, Marsano, Marsell, Marser, Marta, Martal, Martel, Marteli, Martell, Martí, Martiarena, Martiarto, Martiartu, Martibaso, Marticorena, Martierto, Martín, Martín-Crespo, Martín de la Parra, Martín-Ponce, Martinengo, Martinet, Martínez, Martínez Agulló, Martínez de Aibar, Martínez de Alegría, Martínez de Almonacid, Martínez de Alzueta, Martínez de Amileta, Martínez de Andosilla, Martínez de Angelo, Martínez de Araciel, Martínez de Arellano, Martínez de Arenaza, Martínez de Areria, Martínez de Arizala, Martínez de Armeñanzas, Martínez de Aspuz, Martínez de las Balsas, Martínez Balza, Martínez Baños, Martínez-Arenal, Martínez de Bárcena, Martínez-Beltrán, Martínez de Berástegui, Martínez de Béthencourt, Martínez de Bujanda, Martínez de Bustos, Martínez de Cabredo, Martínez del Campo, Martínez Campos, Martínez-Carlón, Martínez Carrasco, Martínez del Castillo, Martínez Cerralón, Martínez de Cestafe, Martínez Corcán, Martínez Concha, Martínez de Checa, Martínez de Doña Palla,

Martínez de Durana, Martínez de Espinosa, Martínez de Espronceda, Martínez de Fresneda, Martínez-Fortún, Martínez de Galdiano, Martínez de Galinsoga, Martínez de Galtero, Martínez-García, Martínez-Gil, Martínez de Goyenechea, Martínez de Grimaldo, Martínez Hermosa, Martínez Hervás, Martínez de Irujo, Martínez de Jarabeitia, Martínez de la Junta, Martínez de Leiva, Martínez de Marcilla, Martínez de la Mata, Martínez de Mendívil, Martínez de Morentin, Martínez de Murguía, Martínez de Maturana, Martínez de la Pera, Martínez de Peralta, Martínez de Pinillos, Martínez de Pisón, Martínez de la Quintana, Martínez de Ralas, Martínez de Recalde, Martínez de Rituerto, Martínez de la Riva, Martínez-Salazar, Martínez de Salcedo, Martínez de Sel, Martínez de Tejada, Martínez de Tineo, Martínez Toledano, Martínez de la Torre, Martínez-Valera, Martínez de Vera, Martínez de San Vicente, Martínez-Viergol, Martínez del Villar, Martínez de Villarreal, Martínez de Vicuña, Martínez de Zalduendo, Martiniano, Martino, Martinocis, Martiz, [Maroto, see Volume 55, p. 268], Martón, Martorell, Martos, Marulanda, Marullo, Marure, Maruri, Marza, Marzán, Marzana, Marzoa, Marra, Marraco, Marradas, Marrades, Marrón, Marroquín. End of EHG Volume 52.

EHG Volume 53: Marrubiza, Marrufo, Mas, Masa, Masaguer, Masana, Masanellas, Masanet, Masarnau, Mascaba, Mascarell, Mascareñas, Mascaró, Mascarua, Mascayano, Mascó, Mascón, Masdovellas, Masferrer, Masó, Masons, Masparranta, Maspe, Masquesa, Massana, Massanellas, Massanet, Massenlli, Masserati, Massieu, Massó, Mastrillo, Mata, Matalobos, Matallana, Matamala, Matami, Matamoros, Matanza, Mataplana, Mataredona, Mataró, Matarón, Matas, Matauco, Matayans, Mate, Matei, Mateo, Materiaín, Matienzo, Matilla, Matines, Mato, Matos, Matoses, Maturana, Matute, Maubía, Mauleón, Maull, Maullen, Maurica, Maurich, Maxans, Maxella, May, Maya, Mayá, Mayans, Mayaya, Mayén, Maymó, Maymón, Maynar, Mayo, Mayol, Mayona, Mayone, Mayora, Mayoral, Mayoralgo, Mayordomo, Mayorga, Maza, Maza de Lizana, Mazal, Mazariegos, Mazarisqueta, Mazarrasa, Mazarredo, Mazas, Mazatorcosa, Mazcayano, Mazmela, Mazo, Mazolagain, Mazón, Mazorra, Mazparrat, Mazparauta, Mazquiarán, Mazuca, Mazueco, Mazuela, Mazuelo, Mea, Meabe, Meacaur, Meacher, Meade, Meana, Meaza, Meca, Meceta, Mecina, Mecolalde, Medel, Mediana, Medianila, Mediano, Mediaras, Mediavilla, Medidas, Medina, Medinilla, Medinyá, Mediona, Medrano, Megino, Megue, Meira, Meirelles, Meiztegui, Mejía, Melada, Melani, Melchor, Melcón, Meléndez, Melero, Melgar, Melgarejo, Meliante, Melicua, Melo, Mella, Mellado, Mello, Melludi, Mena, Menaguerra, Menaut, Menaute, Mencauz, Mencía, Mencos, Menchaca, Mendalde, Mendaña, Mendarichaga, Mendarozqueta, Mendeja, Méndez, Méndez de Cavia, Méndez de Gigunde, Méndez de San Julián, Méndez de Sotomayor, Méndez Testa, Méndez de Vigo, Mendezona, Mendi, Mendia, Mendiaras, Mendiarechaga, Mendibe, Mendibelzua, Mendibil, Mendibure. End of EHG Volume 53.

EHG Volume 54: Mendicoa, Mendicruzaga, Mendichueta, Mendieta, Mendigaña, Mendigoitia, Mendigorría, Mendíguchia, Mendiguren, Mendigutia, Mendijur, Mendiluce, Mendinueta, Mendiola, Mendiolagoitia, Mendiondo, Mendiroz, Menditivar, Mendívil, Mendizábal, Mendocino, Mendoza, Mendracabeitia, Menéndez, Menéndez de Bango, Menéndez de la Torre, Meneses, Mengot, Mengual, Menocal, Menoyo, Mensa, Menso, Meñaca, Meoz, Merás, Merayo, Mercader, Mercadillo, Mercado, Mercaida, Mercer, Merchant, Mere Reis, Merelo, Mereztegui, Mergelina, Merica, Mérida, Merino, Meriorena, Mérita, Merlano, Merodio, Merola, Merquelin, Meruelo, Merrua-Artadi, Merry, Mesa, Mesares. End of EHG Volume 54.

EHG Volume 55: Mescua, Mescuas, Mesía, Mesonero, Mesones, Mesquida, Mesquita, Messía, Metauten, Metelin, Metella, Metello, Metje, Mexía, Meyá, Meyreles, Meza, Mezquía, Mezquita, Micallef, Micó, Michelena, Micheo, Miedes, Mier, Miera, Mieres, Mifsud, Migueis, Miguel, Miguel-Romero, Miguelena, Migueletorena, Miguez, Mijares, Milá, Milagro, Milagros, Milán, Milanés, Miláns, Miláns del Bosch, Milany, Milara, Milazo, Milicua, Militano, Milla, Millán, Millars, Millás, Millia, Milludi, Milsocós, Millsocós, Mimena, Mimendi, Mimendía, Mimenza, Mimpinty-Facende, Mina, Minayo, Minceta, Mindeguía, Miner, Mingot, Mongrano, Minguela, Minguell, Monondo, Mintegui, Minteguiaga, Mintezar, Minuart, Minuarte, Minutillo, Miñana, Miñano, Miñaur, Miñer, Miño, Mioño, Miota, Miquel, Miquelena, Miquelestegui, Mir, Mira or Amira, Mirabel, Miracastell, Miracle, Miracles, Mirafuentes, Miralcamp, Miralles, Miramiña, Miramón, Miramonte, Miranda, Mirandola, Miraval, Miravalles, Miravalo, Miravel, Miravete, Mirez, Miró, Mirón, Mirones, Mirubia, Misas, Mitarte, Mitarra, Mitre, Miura, Mixavilla, Miyares, Mizquia, Mizzi, Mocenea, Mocozuaín, Mocorrea, Moctezuma, Modaguer, Modet, Moge, Mogrovejo, Moix, Mojategui or Monxategui, Mojón, Mola, Molera, Molero, Moles, Moli, Molina, Molinar, Molinas, Molinedo, Moliner, Molines, Molinet, Molinillo, Molino, Molins, Molinuevo, Moll, Molla, Molleda, Molledo, Mollet, Mollinedo, Molner, Molón, Molviedro, Mompalau, Mompaón, Monabe, Monach, Monasterio or Monesterio, Monasteriobide, Moncada, Moncayo. End of EHG Volume 55.

EHG Volume 56: Monclares, Moncorp, Monclús, Monchoe, Mondaca, Mondales, Mondó, Mondona, Mondragón, Moneba, Moneda (La), Moneguerra, Monella, Monells, Moner, Monesma, Moneva, Monferrato, Monforte, Moní, Monistrol, Moniz, Monjaraz, Monjardín, Monjategui, Monje, Monjo, Monjuic, Monlleó, Monller, Monllor, Monmacip, Monmani, Monoay, Monoy, Monreal, Monredó, Monrodón, Monroy, Monsagrati, Monsalve, Monseo, Monserrat, Monsó Monsoliu, Monsonis, Monsoriu, Monsuar, Montagud, Montagudo, Montagut, Montalbán, Montalivet, Montalt, Montalva, Montalván, Montalvo, Montaner, Montanies, Montano, Montanyana,

Montanyans, Montanyón, Montaña, Montañá, Montañana, Montañans, Montañés, Montañez, Montaño, Montaot, Montargull, Montblanch, Montbrió, Montbrú, Montbuy, Montclar, Monte, Monteagudo, Montealegre, Montealto, Montecillo, Montehano, Montehermoso, Montejo, Montellano, Montells, Montemayor, Montenegro, Monter, Monterde, Monternes, Montero, Montero de Espinosa, Monterois, Monterroso, Monterroyo, Montes, Montes de Oca, Montesa, Montescot, Monteser, Montesinos, Monteverde, Montfá, Montfalcó, Montgay, Montgri, Montrríu, Monti, Montiano, Montiel, Montijo, Montilla, Montis, Montjuich, Montlleó, Montmacip, Montmany, Montmorency, Montnegre, Montoliu, Montoris, Montornés, Montoro, Montoto, Montoya, Montpalat, Montpalau, Montpaller, Montreal, Montrodón, Montrós, Montsá, Montsó, Montsoliu, Montsonis, Montsoriu, Montsuaderino, Montsuar, Montt, Montúfar, Montull, Monzón, Moñino, Mora, Moraces, Moradell. End of EHG Volume 56.

EHG Volume 57: Moraga, Moragas, Moragrega, Moragues, Moral, Moraleda, Morales, Morán, Morana, Morandais, Morandé, Morant, Moranta, Morante, Morata Manuel, Moratalla, Morate, Morato, Morató, Moratona, Morays, Moraza, Morcillo, Moreda, Moredo, Moreira, Morejón, Morel, Morell, Morenes, Moreno, Morentín, Morer, Morera, Moreta, Moreu, Morey, Moreyra, Morga, Morgadell, Morgado, Morgan, Morgota, Mori, Moriana, Morillas, Morillo, Moriones, Morlá, Morla, Morlán, Morlanes, Morlans, Mormile, Moro, Morocea, Morodo, Morón, Morote, Morovede, Morovelli, Morozúa, Morquecho, Morra, Morrano or Morano, Morrás, Morro, Morso, Mortara, Mortera, Moscoso, Moset or Mosset, Mosinos, Mosiños, Mosquera, Mota (de la), Motila, Motilla, Motrico, Moura, Mourelle, Mouse, Mouta, Moutas, Movellán, Mox, Moxa, Moxiga, Moxó, Moya, Moyá, Moyano, Moyua, Mozo. End of EHG Volume 57.

EHG Volume 58: Mozo de la Torre, Mua, Muccioli, Mucíbar, Mulcio, Mucientes, Mudarra, Muduate, Muela or La Muela, Muerza, Mueses, Muez, Muga, Mugabrú, Mugarrieta, Mugártegui, Muguértegui, Mugarza, Mugeto, Múgica, Mújica, Múxica, Móxica, Muguera, Muguerza, Mugueta, Muguiro, Muguruza, Muiños, Mujetola, Mula, Mulegui, Mulet, Mulner, Munabe, Munarizqueta, Munar, Munárriz, Muncharaz, Munduate, Munguía, Munguilán, Muniaín, Munibe, Munichaga, Munio, Munita, Munive, Munizaga, Munsaras, Munuera, Munyós, Muñatones, Muñecas, Muñescán, Muñiz, Muñiz-Barreto, Muñoa, Muño Fierro, Muñofierro, Muñoz, Muñoz Alarcón, Muñoz de Baena, Muñoz Bezanilla, Muñoz Bocos, Muñoz de Guzmán, Muñoz Palacios, Muñoz de Pamplona, Muñoz de Pando, Muñoz de Rojas, Muñoz de Roxas, Muñoz de Salazar, Muñoz de San Pedro, Muñoz Serrano, Muñoz del Tejo, Muñoz de Torres, Muñoz Treviño, Muñoz de Umbría, Muñoz de Velasco, Mupán, Mur,

Muro, Murba, Murcia, Murega, Murell, Muret, Murga, Murgaola, Murguía, Murguialday, Murguiondo, Murgunti, Murgutio, Murias, Muriedas, Muriel, Murillas, Murillo, Muriones, Muro, Muru, Murrieta, Murúa, Murube, Murueta, Murugarren, Muruzábal, Musaurieta, Muscetola, Muscot, Musques, Muslera, Muso, Mut, Mutiloa, Mutino, Mucio, Mutio, Mutiozábal, Muzo, Múzquiz, Muzúa. End of EHG Volume 58.

EGH Volume 55: Maroto, p. 268; EHG Volume 56: Mon, p. 252; Monsoriu, p. 252; Montoliu, p. 254; EHG Volume 58: Mora, p. 231; Miranda, p. 236; EHG Volume 64: Maluenda, p. 248; EHG Volume 67: Málaga, p. 229; Marcote or López Marcote, p. 231; Miralles, p. 232; Montorio, p. 233; EHG Volume 71: Maldonado, p. 213; EHG Volume 73: Meneses, p. 228; EHG Volume 74: Maluenda, p. 193; Malvar, p. 193. End of Letter M.

N EHG Volume 59: Naarruza, Nabanos, Nabarlaz, Nabagochea, Nabaz, Naberos, Nabio, Nablerua, Naclario, Nadal, Naeza, Nafarrasagasti, Nafarrua, Nafarrondo, Nafría, Nagori, Nagrell, Nagriz, Naguel, Naguiola, Naguisa, Naharria, Naharriondo, Naia, Naja, Nájara, Nájera, Namur, Nalón, Nanclares, Nani, Nano, Naparra, Napier, Nápoles, Napolitano, Naranjo, Narbaiza, Narbaja, Narbanes, Narbarte, Narbat, Narbona, Norciates, Nardillero, Nardiz, Nardo or de Leonardo, Narejos, Narel, Nari, Narrego, Narriá, Narriondo, Narro, Narváez, Narvaiza, Narvarte, Narvaja, Narvego, Nasao, Nasarre, Nasau, Naselis, Naselo, Nasello, Natera, Nateira, Nateiro, Natero, Nates, Natteri, Nava, Navacerrada, Navaces, Navaez, Navagier, Navajas, Naval, Navalarpe, Navalas, Navales, Navamuel, Navardún, Navarejo, Navares, Navarijo, Navarlaz, Navarra, Navarrete, Navarro, Navarrolas, Navas, Navascués, Navaz, Naveda, Navel, Naverán, Navero, Navés, Navez, Navia, Navio, Naya, Nazabal, Nebel, Nebot, Nebreda, Necochea, Necolalde, Nedin, Negorta, Negra, Negrales, Negreiros, Negrell, Negrete, Negri, Negrilla, Negrita, Negro, Negrón, Negrona, Negroni, Negroto, Negueitía, Nequesa, Neila, Neyla. End of EHG Volume 59.

EHG Volume 60: Neira, Nemba, Neraso, Nerin, Nernay, Nero, Nestares, Net, Neta, Neurba, Nevares, Neve, Nicolalde, Nicolás, Nicolau, Nicoleta, Nicolete, Nicolini, Nicuesa, Nidrist, Niebla, Niedos, Nieto, Nieva, Nievesa, Nifarmendia, Nigui, Nin, Ninot, Niño, Nipiser, Niscoas, Niseno, Noaín, Noballes, Nobar, Nobia, Noble de Entenza, Noblecia, Nobleza, Noboa, Nobrega, Noceda, Nocedal, Noceda, Nocedo, Noceta, Noel de Izarra, Nofre, Nofrecomells, Nofuentes, Nogales, Nograro, Noguer, Nogueira, Noguera, Noguerido, Noguerol, Nogués, Nojas, Nola, Nolivos, Nomas, Nonguel, Nonzón, Noreña, Noreviella, Noriega, Normant, Normile, Noroña, Norta, Norte, Norueba, Noruega, Norueña, Norzagaray, Notales, Notario, Nouta,

Novaes, Novailles, Novales, Novallas, Novar, Novaz, Novell, Novella, Novés, Novia, Novoal, Noyán, Noyers, Nuberga, Nueco, Nuébalos, Nueros, Nuevas, Nuevo, Nuez, Nuncibay, Nuix, Núñez, Núñez del Arco, Núñez de Cabrera, Núñez del Castillo, Núñez de Chaves, Núñez de Guzmán, Núñez de Lara, Núñez de Prado, Núñez de Robles, Núñez Varona, Núñez Velázquez, Núñez de Villavicencio, Nurueña, Nuverga, Nuza. End of EHG Volume 60.

EHG Volume 67: Noriega, p. 234. End of Letter N.

O EHG Volume 60: Oa, Oarriz, Oairrichena, Obaldia, Obalin, Obando, Obana, Obanos, Obañez, Obarrio, Obásolo, Obecola, Obejero, Obineta, Obelerico, Obeso, Obicho, Obierna, Oblitas, Obneda, Obra, Obrador, Obregón, O'Brien, O'Bruin, Oca, Ocalas, Ocaliz, Ocamina, Ocampo, Ocán, Ocana, Ocandi, Ocanela, Ocaña, Ocara, Ocarandi, Ocaranza. End of EHG Volume 60.

EHG Volume 61: Ocariz, Oceja, Ocejo, Ocels, Ocelló, Ocerea, Ocerin, Ocespos, Ocete, Ocilis, Ocina, Ocio, Ocloriz, Oco, Ocollo, Ocón, Ochagavia, Ochaita, Ochandátegui, Ochandiano, Ochando, Ocharán, Ocharcoaga, Ochayeta, Ochoa, Ochoa de Alda, Ochoa Aperregui, Ochoa de Arin, Ochoa de Berrio, Ochoa de Chinchetrú, Ochoa de Eguiara, Ochoa de Lecea, Ochoa de Lexalde, Ochoa de Noaín, Ochoa de Olza, Ochoa de Oro, Ochoa de Orobio, Ochoa de Rivera, Ochoa de Sagües, Ochoa de Zuasti, Ochoarena, Ochoarín, Ochob, Ochovi, Ochoiti, Ochotorena, Oddi, Odena, Odériz, Odiaga, Odón, Odoardo, O'Donnell, Odoronza, Odria, Odriozola, Odriscol, Oechabera, Oestor, O'Farrill, Ogara, Ogarrio, Ogate, Ogayar, Ogazón, Ogier, Ogonue, Oguia, O'Higgins, Ohuella, Ohuet, Oclabert, Oineder, Oinquina, Oiquina, Ojacastro, Ojalvo, Ojancuderra, Ojanguren, Ojascun, Ojea, Ojeda, Ojinaga, Ojirondo, Ojo, Ojuz, Ola, Olabarri, Olabarria, Olabarriaga, Olabarrieta, Olabarriyerroa, Olabe, Olaberria, Olaberriaga, Olaberrieta, Olabezar, Olabide, Olabuénaga, Olaciregui, Olacueta, Olaechea, Olaegui, Olaerrega, Olaerreta, Olaerrota, Olaeta, Olagorta, Olagüe, Olaguer, Olaiz, Olaizola, Olalde, Olalla, Olalquiaga, Olamendi, Olanas, Olanda, Olano, Olano Ochoa, Olanotegui, Olañeta, Olaño, Olaondo, Olaraga, Olarán, Olariaga, Olariena, Olariene, Olarieta, Olarte, Olarra, Olarraga, Olarreta, Olarria, Olarriaga, Olasa, Olasagasti, Olasarri, Olascoaga, Olaso, Olásolo, Olasoro, Olastre, Olaun, O'Lawlor, Olaza, Olazábal, Olazagoitia, Olazagutia, Olazan, Olazarán, Olazarra, Olazarraga, Olbera, Olcina. End of EHG Volume 61.

EHG Volume 62: Olcinellas or Olcinelles, Olcoz, Olea, Oleaga, Olejo or Olexo, Olerde, Oleza or Olesa, Olgarines, Olginat, Olguin, Olias, Oliban, Olibera, Olibito, Olid or Olit or Olite, Oliden, Oliet, Olins Muscot, Olit, Olite,

Oliva, Oliván or Olibán, Olivar, Olivares, Olivart, Olivella, Oliver, Olivera, Oliveras, Oliverio, Olives, Olivó, Olivo, Olivos (de los), Olmeda, Olmedo, Olmera, Olmo or del Olmo or Olmos, Olms or Dolms, Oloa, Oloalde, Olochea, Olodio, Olofredo, Olondriz, Oloño, Olorda or Olerde, Olóriz, Oloroz, Oloso, Olózaga, Oluja or Olujas or Oluya, Olvera, Olvia, Olza, Olzamendi, Olzo, Ollabehesa, Ollacarizqueta, Ollarra, Ollauri, Oller or Ollers, Olleta, Olli, Ollimiri, Ollo, Olloqui, Oma, O'Mallun, Omaña, Omara, Ombau, Omeda or Omedes, Omelina, Omioño or Omoño, Omonte, Oms, Omul-Rian, Ona, Onaindia, Oncina, Onchoca, Onchocarte, Ondalde, Ondalgorri, Ondarra, Ondarza, Ondátegui, Ondeano, Ondegardo, Ondona, Ondiz, Ondramuño, O'Neale, Onel, Onés, Onesto, Onesti, O'Neylle, Onez, Ongastigue, Ongay, Ongoz, Onis or Donis, O'Kelly, O'Kindelan, Onofre, Onofrene or Oñofrene, Onorato, Onrado, Onsoño, Onsuani, Ontaneda or Hontaneda, Ontañón or Hontañón, Ontiveros, Onzavina, Onzoño, Oña, Oñaederra, Oñate, Oñatibia, Oñaz, Oñez, Oñiz, Oñofrene, Opacua, Opata, Opazo, Oquendo, Oquiza, Oraá or Horaá, Oramuño, Oranella, Orante, Orbaiceta, Orbaiz, Orbaneja, Orbara, Orbe, Orbea, Orbegoso or Orbegozo, Orbejón, Orbelaun, Orbezu, Orbezúa, Orbilla, Orbin or Orvin, Orbistelu, Orbori, Orcau, Orcáiztegui, Orcasitas, Orcaza, Orcazaguirre, Orcolaga, Orcoyen, Orchaita, Orda or Orde, Ordás, Orderica, Ordenes, Ordeñana or Ordoána, Ordi, Ordiales, Ordines. End of EHG Volume 62.

EHG Volume 63: Ordonias, Ordóñez, Ordoño, Ordorica, Ordovás, Orduña, Orduñana, Orea, Oregar, O'Reilly, Oreitia, Orejo, Orejón, Orejudo, Orell, Orella, Orellana, Orendaín, Orense, Oreña, Oresbetelu, Orez, Orfila, Orgaste or Orgaeste, Orgaz, Orguibel, Orguilen or Orguillen, Oria, Oriar, Oribar, Oribe or Orive, Orifice or Orefice, Orig, Origan, Origuen, Orihuela, Orila, Orilla, Orio, Oriol, Oriola, Orioles or Oriolis, Oriols, Oris, Orisoaín or Orisuaín or Orisonaín, Orita, Oriz, Orizín or Oricín, Orlandis, Orlando, Orlé, Orloeta, Orma, Ormaeche or Hormaeche, Ormaechea or Hormaechea, Ormáiztegui, Ormat, Ormaza, Ormazábal or Hormazábal, Orna or Horna, Ornat, Ornoa, Ornós, Oro, Orobio or Orovio, Orobirrutia, Oroles, Oromi, Orones, Oronoz, Oronzúa, Oroño, Oroquieta, Ororbia, Orós, Oroz, Orozbetelú, Orouz, Orozco, Orozqueta, Orquecio or Orquezio, Orrandi, Orrantia, Orregar, Orriola, Orriols, Orrius, Orrizmendi, Orruño, Orsi, Orta, Ortafá or Ortaffá, Ortal or Ortales, Ortals, Ortedia, Ortega, Ortegón, Ortegui, Ortells, Ortés, Orteu, Orti or Ortis, Ortiga (La), Ortigas or Ortigues, Ortigó or Ortigós, Ortigosa, Ortiguaín, Ortiguera, Ortin, Ortis, Ortiz, Ortiz de Aedo, Ortiz de Amézaga, Ortiz de Artaza, Ortiz de Bedoya, Ortiz de Bidasolo or Bidasola, Ortiz de la Cagiguera, Ortiz de Carranza, Ortiz Cortés, Ortiz de Elguea, Ortiz de Escobar, Ortiz de Foronda, Ortiz de Guinea, Ortiz de Igoroín, Ortiz de Jaume, Ortiz de Landazuri, Ortiz de Lanzagorta, Ortiz de Largacha, Ortiz de Matienzo, Ortiz de Otálora, Ortiz de Padilla, Ortiz Ponce de León, Ortiz de la Riva, Ortiz de

Rojano, Ortiz de Rozas, Ortiz de Sandoval, Ortiz de Santecilla, Ortiz de la Sierra, Ortiz de Sologuren, Ortiz de Taranco, Ortiz de la Torre, Ortiz de Urbina, Ortiz de Uriarte, Ortiz de Velasco, Ortiz de Vitoriano, Ortiz de Zárate, Ortiz de Zarauz, Ortiz de Zugasti, Ortiz de Zúñiga, Ortizá, Orto, Ortolá, Ortosol, Ortubia, Ortúburu, Ortueta, Ortuñez, Ortuño or Hortuño, Ortuoste, Ortusausgesti, Ortúzar, Orúe, Orueta, Oruezábala, Oruezabaleta, Oruín, Orumbela, Oruna. End of EHG Volume 63.

EHG Volume 64: Oruña, Orús, Orutia, O'Ryan, Orzales, Os, Osa or Ossa, Osado, Osango, Osansola or Osandola or Ossandola, Osategui, Osborne, Oscariz, Oscorta, Osello, Oses or Osses, Oset or Osete or Ossete, Osiesnare, Osinaga or Ojinaga or Oxinaga, Osinalde or Osinalde-Barrera, Osios or Ossios, Osma, Oso, Osoarín, Osollo, Osona or Ossona, Osonilla, Osopasau, Osorio or Ossorio, Osorno, Osoro, Ospaz, Ospina or Ospin, Osqueras, Osquiguelea, Ossa, Ossandola, Osses, Ossete, Ossó, Ossona, Ossorio, Ostabat, Ostalaza or Ostolaza, Ostalrich, Ostavares Aransus, Ostoles, Ostos, Ostudaín, Osuelgaray, Osúa, Osuna, Osunivez, Otadizábal, Otadui or Otaduy, Otaegui, Otal, Otálora, Otamendi, Otano, Otañez or Otañes, Otaño, Otaola or Otaolea, Otaolaurruchi or Otaola Urruchi, Otazábal, Otazo, Otazu, Otazúa, Oteiza or Oteyza, Otegui, Oteo or Otheo, Otermin, Otero, Otin or Ottin, Oto or Ott or Ottho, Otodio, Otondo, Ouñoz, Ovada, Ovalle, Ovando or Obando, Ovejas, Ovejero, Ovieco, Oviedo, Oxangoiti or Oxangoti, Oxiñaga, Oxirando or Oxirondo, Oxobi, Oya, Oyaga, Oyague, Oyancas, Oyanederra, Oyangüe, Oyanguren or Ojanguren, Oyanune or Oyanume or Oyayume or Oyambe, Oyarate or Oyararte, Oyarbide, Oyardo, Oyarzábal, Oyarzo, Oyarzun, Oyauren, Oyeregui, Oyo, Oyolo, Oyones, Oyos, Oyuz, Ozaeta, Ozio, Ozcariz, Ozcocena, Ozcoidi, Ozcorta or Azcorta, Ozerea, Oznayo or Hoznayo, Ozores, Ozta, Ozticaín. End of EHG Volume 64. End of Letter O.

P EHG Volume 65: Pablo or de Pablo, Pablos, Pabolleta, Pabón or Pavón, Pabulino, Pace, Paco, Pache, Pacheco, Pacho, Pachón, Padellás, Padierna, Padilla, Padró, Padrón, Padura, Páez, Pagadi, Pagaduygorria, Pagaldamacaceta, Pagalday, Pagán, Pagana, Paganeras, Pagano, Pagave, Pagazartundúa, Pagazaurtundúa, Page, Pagés, Pagoaga, Pagola, Pagolleta, Paguera, Pairo, Paisa, Paiva or Paiba, Paiveta or Paibeta, Paix, Paizueta, Pajada, Pajari, Pajarín or Pajarines, Pajarón, Pajaza, Paje or Page, Pajón, Palacián, Palacio, Palacios, Palacines, Palafox, Palandarias, Palandegui or Palantegui. End of EHG Volume 65.

EHG Volume 66: Palafurgell, Palaganas, Palancos, Palao, Palau, Palavicino, Palaya, Palazol, Palazuelos, Paleci, Palencia, Palenque, Palentegui, Paenzuela, Palicer, Paliza (de la), Palma, Palmela, Palmer, Palmerola, Palol (or Paloll),

Palomar or Palomares, Palomeque, Palomera or Palomero, Palomino, Palomo, Palón, Palos, Palou, Palladas, Pallarés, Pallás or Pallars, Pallasol, Pallejá, Pallicer, Pambley, Pamo, Pamones or Pamón, Pamos, Pamplona, Pancirolo, Pancorbo, Pando, Pandor, Panduro or Panduros, Paneque, Panés, Panfilo or Pamfilo, Paniagua or Pan y Agua, Panicer, Panizo or Panico, Pano or Panno, Pantaleón, Pantearrojos, Pantigosa, Pantigoso, Pantoja, Pan y Vino, Panzano, Pañelles, Papacoda, Papado, Papafaba, Papaletere, Pape, Papillas, Papiol, Para, Parobia, Paracuellos, Parada or Paradas, Paradevere, Paradis, Paradiso, Parado or Parados, Parafán, Paraíso, Paralejas, Páramo, Paraquieres, Paratge, Parayos, Parbayón, Parcel, Parcero, Pardavé or Pardabé, Pardebe, Pardelana, Pardina, Pardinas, Pardiñas, Pardiñaur, Pardo, Paredes, Paredeve, Paredinas, Pareja, Parejo, Parente, Pareña, Parestrellos, Parets, Parga, Pariente, París, Pariza, Parladé, Parma, Parnis, Parr, Parra, Párraga, Parral or Parrales, Parraya, Parrella, Parreño, Parrilla, Parro. End of EHG Volume 66.

EHG Volume 67: Parrondo, Parte (de la), Partidares, Partiella, Pasalacqua or Pasalaigua, Pasamonte, Pasarello, Pasarón, Pascual or Pasqual, Pascualigo or Pasqualigo, Pasillas, Pasos, Pasquel, Pasquier, Pastene, Pastor, Pastrana, Pastranas, Pastrio, Patas, Patau, Patelin, Patelines or Patalines, Paternaín, Paternia, Paternina, Patrnoy or Patrnoi, Patia, Patinales or Patineles, Patiño, Pato, Patón, Patos, Patus, Pau, Paul, Paulazas, Paules, Paulet, Paulin, Paupux, Pavaes, Pavia, Pavó, Pax, Payá, Payades, Payán, Payno, Payo, Payró or Peyró, Payueta, Paz, Paza, Pazañas or Pezañas, Pazarpo, Pazos, Pecellín or Villapecellín, Peceros or Pezeros, Peco or Pezo, Pecha, Pedave, Pedraja, Pedrajas, Pedrajo, Pedrarias, Pedraza, Pedredo, Pedredo de las Agüeras, Pedregal, Pedreguera, Pedriñán, Pedriza, Pedro (de), Pedrol, Pedrola, Pedrolo, Pedrós, Pedrosa, Pedroso, Pedruel, Pedrueza, Pedruja or Pedrujo, Pedruzo, Pegado, Pegas, Pegura or Peguero, Peijo or Peixo or Pejo, Peinado, Peiro, Peirona, Pejaza, Pejo, Peis, Peláez, Pelatero or Platero, Pelayo, Pelegero, Pelegri or Pelegrin, Pelilla, Peludo, Pellicer, Pellón. End of EHG Volume 67.

EHG Volume 68: Pemán, Pemartín, Pena, Penagos, Penalba, Penavera, Pences, Pendes, Peneirua, Penela, Penella, Penia, Penilla, Penlos, Penyafort or Peniafort, Peña or la Peña or de la Peña, Peñacastil or Peñacastillo, Peñafiel, Peñalacia, Peñalosa, Peñalver, Peñalvo, Peñamacor, Peñamil, Peñaranda, Peñarredonda, Peñarrieta, Peñarroja, Peñas, Peñate, Peñuela, Peñuelas, Peón, Pera, Peraesteve, Perafeta, Peral, Peralada, Peraleda, Peraleja, Perales, Peralta, Perálvarez, Peramán, Peramatos, Peramola, Peranensa, Peranriquez, Perapertusa, Perarnau, Peras, Perastorlas, Peratallada or Piedratallada, Peray, Peraza, Percástegui, Percatxo, Perdigaón, Perdigoes, Perdigón, Perdomó, Perea, Pereceira, Perecellines, Pereces, Pereda, Peredo, Pereira or Pereyra, Pereiro, Perejón, Perelacia, Perelada, Perelló, Perellones, Perellós or Perelló, Perellones, Pere Miqueu, Pereña, Perera, Peretó, Pereyda, Pérez, Pérez Abad,

Pérez de Adana, Pérez de Albéniz, Pérez de Alderete, Pérez de Almazán, Pérez de Abreu, Pérez de Andión, Pérez de Anuncita de la Torre, Pérez de Araciel, Pérez de Arandia, Pérez de Aránsolo, Pérez Arenas, Pérez de Aristizábal, Pérez de Ariza, Pérez de Arramendia. End of EHG Volume 68.

EHG Volume 69: Perestorte, Pérez de Arroyo, Pérez de Artacoz, Pérez de Azcona, Pérez de Azarola, Pérez de Bañatos, Pérez de Baños, Pérez de Baraez, Pérez de Barradas, Pérez Bejarano, Pérez Beltrán, Pérez Bobadilla, Pérez Borroto, Pérez Bou, Pérez de Brea, Pérez de Bustamante, Pérez Calvillo, Pérez del Camino, Pérez Cano, Pérez Cantarero, Pérez Cañas de Aro, Pérez Castejón, Pérez de Castro, Pérez Cavellos, Pérez Ciria, Pérez de los Cobos, Pérez de Cuende, Pérez Donza, Pérez Dardón, Pérez Echeverría, Pérez de Escó, Pérez de la Espada, Pérez de Espiñeira, Pérez de Eubia, Pérez de Elizalde, Pérez Falla, Pérez de la Figuera, Pérez del Frago, Pérez de la Fuente, Pérez Gallego, Pérez de Gamaneda, Pérez de Garayo, Pérez Guerrero, Pérez de Guzmán, Pérez de Herrasti, Pérez de Hita, Pérez de las Higueras, Pérez de Huesca, Pérez Inclán, Pérez de Inoriza, Pérez de Inurreta, Pérez de Laborda, Pérez de Lanciego, Pérez de Largos, Pérez de Larrieta, Pérez de Larraya, Pérez de Lazcano, Pérez de Lezcano, Pérez Maldonado, Pérez Manrique, Pérez Manuel, Pérez de Meca, Pérez de Mendívil, Pérez Minayo, Pérez Monte, Pérez Moreno, Pérez de Muñoz, Pérez Navarrete, Pérez Navarro, Pérez Navaz, Pérez de Nueros, Pérez de Obanos, Pérez de Ocampo, Pérez de Ocáriz, Pérez de Onraita, Pérez Orejón, Pérez Oteiro, Pérez de Palazuelos, Pérez Pastor, Pérez del Palomar, Pérez Pando, Pérez de Panticosa, Pérez de Pariza, Pérez de Parsifal, Pérez de Perceval, Pérez-Petinto, Pérez Piquero, Pérez de la Puente, Pérez del Pulgar, Pérez de Rada, Pérez de Regúlez, Pérez Rellan, Pérez de Roa, Pérez Romeo, Pérez Ruiz de Corella, Pérez de Saavedra, Pérez de San Román, Pérez de Santa Cruz, Pérez de Santoyo, Pérez de Sarrio, Pérez de Sarrión, Pérez Serrano, Pérez de Sigler, Pérez de Siles, Pérez de Soñanes, Pérez de Soria, Pérez de Sotopalacios, Pérez de Suelves, Pérez de Tafalla, Pérez de Tiermas, Pérez de la Torre, Pérez de Trigueros, Pérez de Tris, Pérez de Tudela, Pérez de Ubeda, Pérez de Umendía, Pérez de Urria, Pérez de Urzainqui, Pérez de Urzanqui, Pérez Valdés, Pérez de Valenzuela, Pérez Valiente, Pérez de Vargas, Pérez de la Vega, Pérez Venegas, Pérez Verdugo, Pérez de Viana, Pérez de Villaloz, Pérez de Villamar, Pérez de Villarroel, Pérez de Vivero, Pérez de Yanguas, Pérez de las Yeguas, Pérez de Zabalza, Pérez de Zalduendo, Pérez Zamora, Pérez Zapata, Pérez Zayas, Pérez de Zarayde, Pérez de Zubieta, Pérez de Zubiete, Periche, Pericorena, Perillán Barba, Perillos, Peris, Perisanz, Periz de Perey, Periz de Viana, Perler, Perlines, Pernia, Perobayón, Perochena, Perola, Peromato, Perón, Perona, Perones, Peropadre, Perosancena, Perostena, Perota, Peroto, Perovayón, Perreria, Perpinián, Perpinyá, Perpiñá, Perpiñán, Perpiyá, Perqueres, Perquetes, Pertica, Pertika, Pertiella, Pertierra, Pertiesa, Peruchena, Perucho, Perujo, Perurena, Peruzabala, Peruzo, Perverán, Perves,

Pes, Pesadilla, Pesaro, Pescuezo, Peso, Pesoa, Perola (again), Pesquera, Pessac, Pesso, Pessoa, Pestaña, Petra, Petrirena, Petriz, Pettriz, Petruche, Peus, Peusoda, Pevedilla, Peverán, Pexan, Pexó, Peyrestortes, Peyrí, Peyró, Pez, Pezuela (de la), Pi, Piau, Piazuelo, Pica, Picabea, Picabo, Picado, Picalqués, Picamendi, Picano, Picanzo, Picaondo, Picardo, Picasarri, Picavea, Picavo, Picaza, Picazarri, Picazo, Pich, Pichardo, Pichón, Picina, Pickman, Picó, Picón, Picornell, Pidal, Piedra, Piedrabuena, Piedrafita, Piedralzada, Piedrahita, Piedramillera, Piédrola, Piedrula, Pieragullano, Piérola, Pierredonda, Piferrer, Pignateli, Pignatilli, Pignatelo, Piguert, Pila, Pilares, Pildaín, Piles, Pileta, Pileto, Pilo, Piloña, Pillado, Piñateli, Piñatelo. End of EHG Volume 69.

EHG Volume 70: Pimentel, Pimienta or Díaz Pimienta, Pina, Pinachos, Pinan, Pinar, Pinazo, Pineda, Pinedes, Pinedo, Pinel, Pinela, Pineles, Pineli, Pinelo, Pinell, Pinelli, Pinells, Pinero, Piniaragut, Piniés, Pinilla, Pinillos or Martínez de Pinillos, Pino, Pinós, Pinoser, Pintero, Pinto, Pintó, Pintor, Pinuaga, Pinyá, Pinyana, Pinyó, Pinza, Piña, Piñal, Piñán, Piñango, Piñera, Piñeira, Piñeiro, Piñeros, Piñó, Piñola, Piñón, Pío, Pío de Saboya, Pipiol, Pipiola, Piquer, Pires, Pirez, Pis, Pisa, Pisalgues, Piscina or Peciña or Picina, Pisuerga, Piscopo, Pisón or Martínez de Pisón, Pita, Pita da Vega, Pitarque, Pitillas, Pizá, Pizano, Pizaño, Pizarque, Pizarro, Pizón, Pizueta, Pla, Plana, Placencia, Placeres, Plandalit, Planella, Planes, Planiello, Plano or del Plano, Plansón, Plasencia, Plata (de la), Platzaert, Plaza, Plazaola, Plazuela, Plegamana, Pliego or Pliego Valdés, Plugues, Po, Poado, Poal, Poaras, Pobeña, Pobla, Poblaciones, Poblet, Poblete, Podazas, Podi, Podio, Pol, Pola, Poladura, Polanco, Polestres, Polinas, Polit. End of EHG Volume 70.

EHG Volume 71: Polo, Poloni, Poll, Pollafols, Pollanen, Pollart, Pollastre, Pollino, Pollón, Pomar, Pomareda, Pombo, Pomposo, Pon, Ponce, Ponce de León, Pongen, Pons, Ponset, Ponsgen, Ponsich, Pont, Pontanilla, Ponte, Pontejos, Pontés, Ponti, Póntica, Pontón, Pontones, Pontons, Pontos, Popado, Poquet, Porcallo, Porcejana, Porcel, Porcell, Porlier, Porquera, Porqueras, Porqueres, Porquero, Porqués, Porquet, Porquete, Porras, Porres, Porrúa, Porsefanas, Porsefanes, Porta, Portadora, Portal, Portalá, Portalecoa, Portales, Portas, Portel, Portela, Portell, Portella, Porter, Portero. End of EHG Volume 71.

EHG Volume 72: Portes, Portilla, Portillo, Portocarrero, Portolá, Portolés, Portu, Portugal, Portugalete, Portugués, Portuondo, Portura, Portusagasti, Posada, Posadas, Posadero, Posadilla, Posadillo, Posa, Possa, Postigo, Potan, Potes, Potestad, Pou, Poumola, Pous, Poveda, Povedilla, Poves, Power, Poyanos, Poyo, Poza, Pozaños, Pozo, Pozuelo, Pozueta, Prad-Narbones, Prada, Pradeda, Pradela, Pradilla, Prado, Prases, Prat, Prats, Pravia, Precedo, Prego,

Prejo, Prelo, Prellezo, Premontoria, Premuntegui, Prendergast, Prendes, Presa, Presilla, Presillas, Presno, Pretel, Prexeana, Prexeanes, Priego, Prieto, Primo, Primo de Rivera, Prior, Privado, Proaña, Proaño, Probais, Proenza, Proleón, Provanza, Proxita, Pruneda, Pruner, Pruneres, Pruners, Puch, Puche, Pucheta, Puebla, Puellas, Puelles, Puente, Puerta, Puertas, Puertanueva, Puerto, Puertolas, Pueyo, Puga, Pugari, Puig, Puig-Gat. End of EHG Volume 72.

EHG Volume 73: Puigbacó, Puigcerver, Puigdasens, Puigdesalit, Puigdespi, Puigdollers, Puigdorfila or Orfila, Puigesteva, Puigesteve, Puigfaragut, Puigfarnés, Puiggali, Puiggener, Puigjaner, Puigmari, Puigmidó, Puigmitjá, Puigmoltó, Puignau, Puigpardinas, Puigperdiguer, Puigperdines, Puigperdius, Puigserver, Puigventós, Puigvert, Puigsuriguer, Puivecino, Pujadas, Pujades, Pujals, Pujalt, Pujana, Pujarán, Pujasol, Pujazons, Pujol, Pulgar or Pérez del Pulgar, Pulgaren, Pulgarín, Pulido, Puliga, Pulmar, Pullares, Pumaz, Pumarejo, Pumariño, Pumaripo, Puncet, Punter, Puñana, Puranos, Purroy, Puyol, Puyvecino, Puxmarín. End of EHG Volume 73, Letter P.

EHG Volume 73 (out of order in volume): Peraza de Ayala, p. 70; Pinzón, p. 72; Poy or Poy del Bose, p. 76; Prado, p. 77; Prim, p.84; Puig p. 93. End of Letter P.

Q EHG Volume 73: Quadernigas, Quadra, Quadrado, Quadrech, Quadreny, Quadrillero or Cuadrillero, Quadro, Quaga, Quart, Quartango or Cuartango, Quarteroni or Cuarteroni, Queipo or Queipo de Llano, Queire, Queirón, Quejaba, Quejada, Quejar, Queralt, Queraltó, Querblanch, Querforadat, Querejazu, Querijazu, Quero or Cuero, Querol, Quesada, Quevedo, Quexar, Quijada, Quijano, Quilchano, Quilez, Quilimodi, Quina, Quinacos, Quinas, Quincoces, Quintalina, Quixada, Quixano. End of EHG Volume 73.

EHG Volume 74: Quinquer, Quint, Quintana, Quintanadueñas, Quintanal, Quintananos, Quintanilla, Quintano, Quintero, Quinto, Quiñones, Quiranes, Quirant, Quirino, Quiroba, Quiroga, Quirós, Quiza. End of EHG Volume 74. End of Letter Q.

R EHG Volume 74: Raa, Rábago, Rabanal, Rábano, Rabasa, Rabaschiero, Rabayo, Rabaza, Rabelo, Rabia, Rabiellas, Rabollet, Rabós, Racta, Rada, Radillo, Radin, Rado, Raeta, Rafart, Rafel, Ragasol, Raguanato, Raguer, Raigada, Raimo, Raimondes, Rainoso, Raizábal, Rajadell, Raja, Rajo de Argeriz, Ralas, Ralentegui, Ralte, Rallo, Rallón, Ram, Rama, Ramalo, Ramazote, Rambla, Ramera, Ramery, Rami, Ravelo, Raxa, Raxadell, Raynoso, Reigada, Relas, Rigada. End of EHG Volume 74.

EHG Volume 75: Ramírez, Ramírez de Aguilera, Ramírez de Amatriaín, Ramírez de Arellano, Ramírez de Baquedano, Ramírez de Esparza, Ramírez or Remírez de Estenoz, Ramírez Fariña, Ramírez de Ganuza, Ramírez de Guzmán, Ramírez de Haro, Ramírez de Labastida, Ramírez de Laredo, Ramírez de Montalvo, Ramírez de Ordás, Ramírez de Piscina, Ramírez de Prado, Ramírez de Ripa, Ramírez de la Rosa, Ramírez de Saavedra, Ramírez de la Trapera, Ramírez de Undiano, Ramírez de Villaescusa, Ramírez de Zabal, Ramiro, Ramis, Ramón, Ramóndemur, Ramos, Ramos Izquierdo, Rancaño, Randa, Ranedo, Raner, Ranero, Ranés, Rangel, Ranjel, Rano, Rañada, Rañaga, Rañeta, Rañón, Raón, Rapado, Raposo, Rapún, Raro, Rasa, Rasal or Arrasal, Rascó, Rascón, Raset, Rasilla, Rasines, Rasquín, Rasset, Ratera, Ratés, Raudón, Raurer, Raxach, Raxadell, Raxaiz, Raya, Rayado, Raymondes, Rayón, Real, Real de Asúa, Real Híjar, Reales, Reart, Rebatta, Rebelles, Rebilles, Rebollar, Rebolleda, Rebolledo, Rebollo, Recabarren or Erecabarren, Recain, Recalde, Recamán, Recart, Recarte, Recas, Recasens, Recio, Recondo, Recul, Rechs, Redín, Redonda, Redondo, Redonet, Refojo, Regales, Regaliz, Regato, Régil, Reguart, Regüe, Regueira, Regueiro, Reguer, Reguera, Regueras or Escuderos de las Regueras, Reguero, Reguilón, Reguillaga, Regules, Regúlez, Reín, Reina, Reinalt, Reinalte, Reinosa, Reinoso, Reiza, Reizábal, Reizaldo, Reizu, Rejón, Relas, Relat, Relosillas, Reluz, Relló, Rellón, Rementaritegui or Errementaritegui, Remetería or Errementería, Rementero, Remesal, Remírez, Remolins, Remón, Renart, Rencaño, Rendón, Rengel, Rengifo, Renier, Renobau, Renovales, Rentea, Rentería, Reñizal, Reolid, Reolies, Reoyo, Reparaz, Repiso, Represa, Reguena, Reguer, Reguesens, Resa, Rescall, Resende, Respaldiza, Restrepo or López de Restrepo, Resusta or Erresusta, Reta, Retamal, Retana, Retegui, Retes, Rétola, Retortillo, Retuerto, Reuell, Reure, Reus, Revenga or Gómez de Revenga, Reverter, Revilla, Revuelta or Rebuelta del Pedredo, Rexach, Rey, Reyero, Reyes, Reyllo, Reyna, Reynosa, Reyó, Reyzábal, Rezábal, Rezola, Rezul, Rezusta, Rivilla. End of EHG Volume 75.

EHG Volume 76: Riabeyo, Rialp, Rimbau, Riaño, Riaría, Riaz, Riaza, Riazo, Riba, Ribadeneira, Ribaforada, Ribalta, Ribas, Ribella, Ribelles, Ribera, Ribero, Ribes, Ribón or Germán Ribón, Ribot, Ric, Ricafort, Ricardo, Ricardos, Ricart, Ricarte, Ricaurte, Richards, Rico, Ricote, Ridado, Ridao, Riego, Riera, Riesco, Riesgo, Riestra or García de la Riestra, Riet or Eriete, Riezu, Rigada, Rigadell, Riglos, Rilla, Rincón, Río, Riobo, Riobón, Ríofrío, Rioja, Riomol, Rionda, Riopar, Ríos or Gutiérrez de los Ríos, Ríoseco, Ríotord, Ríosa, Ripa, Ripalda, Ripodas, Ripol, Ripoll, Ripollés, Ripperdá, Riquelme, Riquer, Riscos, Risel, Rítola, Riu, Riudecols, Riudeperas, Riudepers, Rius, Riusech, Riutord, Riva, Rivacoba, Rivadeneira, Rivadeneyra, Rivaforada, Rivaguda, Rivamontán, Rivares, Rivas, Rivellas, Rivelles, Rivera, Rivero, Rives, Riviella, Rix, Rizo. End of EHG Volume 76.

EHG Volume 77: Roa, Roalera, Roales, Roballa, Robert or Roberto, Robina, Robí, Robió, Robledano, Robledo, Robles, Robollet, Robray, Robrado, Robres, Robuster, Roca or Roca de Togores, Rocaberti, Rocabranca or Rocablanca, Rocabruna, Rocacrespa, Rocafort or Ricafort or Rocafuerte, Rocafull or Rocaful, Rocalay, Rocamayor, Rocamora, Rocaño, Rocarrossa, Roco, Rocosano, Roch, Rocha, Roche, Roda, Rodarte, Rodeiro, Rodellar, Rodera, Rodero, Rodés, Rodesbo, Rodezno, Rodillos, Rodrigo, Rodríguez, Rodríguez de Albuerne, Rodríguez de Alburquerque, Rodríguez de Almeida, Rodríguez de Arciniega, Rodríguez Baltodano, Rodríguez de Biedma, Rodríguez del Campal, Rodríguez Campomanes, Rodríguez Carasa, Rodríguez Castañón, Rodríguez de Cossío or Cosío, Rodríguez Chacón, Rodríguez Chaviano, Rodríguez de Ebán, Rodríguez de la Encina, Rodríguez de Ledesma, Rodríguez de León, Rodríguez del Manzano, Rodríguez de Medina, Rodríguez de Mena, Rodríguez de Mendarozqueta, Rodríguez de Mercado, Rodríguez de Millia, Rodríguez de Mira, Rodríguez de Miranda, Rodríguez de Monroy, Rodríguez de Morales, Rodríguez Moreno, Rodríguez Navarro, Rodríguez Ortiz, Rodríguez de la Piedra, Rodríguez Requejo, Rodríguez de los Ríos, Rodríguez de Rivas, Rodríguez de Rivera, Rodríguez de Rozas, Rodríguez de Salamanca, Rodríguez de Santisteban, Rodríguez Solano, Rodríguez de Taboada, Rodríguez del Toro, Rodríguez Valcárcel, Rodríguez de Vargas, Rodríguez de las Varillas, Rodríguez de Vivar, Rodríguez Zambrano, Rodríguez Zorrilla, Roelas or de las Roelas, Roger, Rogero, Roies, Roig, Roiguez, Rois, Roiz or Roiz de la Parra, Rojano, Rojas or Roxas, Rojo, Rol or Roll, Roldán, Rollán, Romagosa, Romaguera, Roma, Roma Galarza, Román, Romana, Romano, Romanos, Romarate, Romay, Romañá, Romaza. End of EHG Volume 77.

EHG Volume 78: Romero or Romeo or Romeu, Romillo, Romo, Ron, Ronante, Roncal, Roncali, Roncesvalles, Rondino, Roneta, Ronquillo, Roñeta, Ropiana, Ros, Rosa (de la), Rosado, Rosal, Rosales, Rosanes or Rosant, Rosar, Rosell or Rossell, Roselló or Rosselló, Roser or Rosser, Roset, Rosillo, Rosinos, Rosiñol, Rosique, Roso or Rosso, Rosón, Rota, Rotaeche or Errotaeche, Rotaesa, Rotaetagogeascoa, Rotalde, Roteta or Erroteta, Rotger, Rogtlá or Rotlá, Rotten Roura or Roure, Rovina, Rovira, Rovirola, Royo, Roza, Rozadilla, Rozas, Rua (de la), Ruano, Rubalcaba or Rubalcava, Rubayo, Rubi, Rubiano, Rubiera, Rubiero, Rubin, Rubinat, Rubino, Rubio, Rubió, Rucabado, Rucandio, Ruebas, Ruecos, Rueda, Rueiro, Ruenes, Ruescas or Ruesques, Ruesga, Ruesta, Ruete, Rufas, Rufo, Rugama, Rugido, Ruiloba, Ruiz, Ruiz de Aguayo, Ruiz de Alarcón, Ruiz de Apodaca, Ruiz del Arco, Ruiz de Asin, Ruiz de Azcona, Ruiz de Bujanda, Ruiz de Camargo, Ruiz de Carabantes, Ruiz de Cascante, Ruiz de Erenchun, Ruiz de Esparza, Ruiz de Galarreta, Ruiz de Galdeano, Ruiz de Gámiz or Ruiz-Soldado, Ruiz de Gaona, Ruiz de Giménez, Ruiz de Lopegui, Ruiz de Gordejuela, Ruiz de Landa, Ruiz de León,

Ruiz Mateos, Ruiz de Milagro, Ruiz de Murillo, Ruiz de Ocerin, Ruiz de Rabé, Rújula, Rul or Rull, Rullán, Rumayor, Rupiá, Rupit, Rus, Rusa or Russa, Rusca, Rusiñol or Rusiñol or Rossinyol, Ruso, Ruberte, Ruy de Peras. End of EHG Volume 78. End of Letter R.

S EHG Volume 79: Sáa, Saalegui, Saavedra, Sabadell, Sabadia, Sabando, Sabastida, Sabata, Sabater, Saburgada, Sacabechs, Sacalm, Sacalsada, Sacana, Sacarrera, Sacirera, Saclam, Saclosa, Saco, Sacoma, Sacorra, Sacoromina, Sacosta, Saba, Sadava, Sadurní, Saeirel or Salirel, Sáenz, Sáenz de Tejada, Sáenz Valiente, Saera or Zaera, Sacrín, Sáez, Safont or Zafont or Sasfonts, Saforteza, Saga or Sagua, Saganta, Sagaraicar, Sagaraigar, Sagarbinaga, Sagardí or Sagardía, Sagardiburu, Sagardizar, Sagariola, Sagarminaga, Sagarna, Sagarnaga, Sagarra or Segarra, Sagarraga, Sagarribay, Sagarriga or Zagarriga, Sagarró, Sagartegui or Sagarteguieta, Sagarza, Sagarzazu, Sagarzurieta, Sagaseta, Sagasta, Sagasti or Sagastiya, Sagastibelza, Sagastiberria, Sagastiberridi, Sagastigoitia, Sagastiguchia, Sagastizábal, Sagastizar, Sagastume, Sagobia, Sagranada, Sagranadella, Sagrau, Sagredo, Sagreda, Saguardia or Zaguardia, Saguaro, Sagueró, Sagües, Saguardia, Saigós, Sáinz, Sáinz or Sáinz-Delgado, Sáinz Pierre, Sáinz de Santayana, Sáinz de los Terreros, Saizar, Saja, Sala, Salaberri or Salaberry or Salaverri, Salaberria or Salaverria, Salabert or Salavert, Salad or Salar, Saladrigas, Salafranca, Salamanca, Salamó, Salanova, Salanueva, Salas, Salaverdenya, Salayusan, Salazar, Salbo, Salboch, Salceda, Salcedo, Salces, Salcines, Saldamando, Sadaña, Saldías, Saldosa, Salelles or Salellas, Sales, Saleta, Salete, Salett, Salezán, Salgado, Salgueda or Salguida, Salgueiros, Salido, Salinas. End of EHG Volume 79.

EHG Volume 80: Sall, Sallana, Sallent, Sallet, Salmantón, Salmellá, Salmerón, Salmón, Salmurri, Saló, Saloguen or Saloguene, Salom, Salort, Salrá, Salsamendi, Salsfores, Salsoro, Salt, Saltells, Salteraín, Salto, Salturri, Salugárate, Salvá or Salbá or Zalba, Salvador or Salvadores, Salvago, Salvaje, Salvat, Salvati, Salvatierra, Salzat, Samá, Samaniego, Sámano, Samar, Samasó or Samassó, Samasoir, Sambafart, Samitier, Samora, Samorera, Samper or Semper or Samperes or Samperes, Samperio, Sampol, Sampsó, Samuntada, Sanabria, Sanahuja or Sanauja, San Andrés, Sanceloní or Sant Celoní, Sancena, Sancetenea, San Clemente, San Clodio or San Cloyo or San Claudio, San Cristóbal, Sánchez, Sánchez de Aranda, Sánchez Arjona, Sánchez de Badajoz, Sánchez Chaparro, Sánchez de la Bárcena, Sánchez del Campo, Sánchez de Cutanda, Sánchez Griñán, Sánchez Herrador, Sánchez Herrero, Sánchez Hidalgo, Sánchez de Landaeta, Sánchez de la Lastra, Sánchez de Lerín, Sánchez de Loria, Sánchez Melgar, Sánchez de Muniaín, Sánchez Muñoz, Sánchez-Pereira, Sánchez del Pozo, Sánchez de la Sierra, Sánchez de Toca, Sánchez de Torres, Sánchez Toscano, Sánchez de Tuesta, Sánchez Yáñez,

Sanchiz or Sanchís, Sancho, Sanchorena, Sandallo, Sande, Sandias, Sandoval, Sandracelain, San Esteban, San Feliú, Sanfelici, Sanfert, Sanfrechoso, Sanfuentes, Sangariz, Sangenis, Sangil or San Gil, San Ginés, Sangorrín, Sangro, Sangróniz or Zangroniz or Cangrones, Sangüesa, Sangutia, Saniera, San Jaime, San Juan, Sanjuanena or San Juan Ena, San Julián, Sanjurjo, San Llorente or Sanllorente, San Martín, San Miguel, San Millán, Sanoguera, Sanou or Zanou, San Pedro, San Pelayo or Sampelayo, San Prudencio, San Ramón, San Román, Sans, San Severino, San Simón, Sansinenea, Sansomaín, Sansuts, Santacilia or Santa Cilia, Santa Clara, Santa Coloma, Santa Creus, Santa Cruz, Santa Eugenia, Santa Fe or Santafé, Santaló, Santallana or Santayana, Santa Mans, Santa María, Santa Marina, Santander, Santandreu, Santángel or Sant Angel. End of EHG Volume 80.

EHG Volume 81: Santaolaria or Santolaria, Santa Oliva, Santa Pau, Santarén, Santa-Román, Sant Climent, Sant Dionis, Santecilla, Santelices, Santevás, Santesteban or Santisteban, Sant Esteve, Sant Geroní, Sant Guim, Sant Hilari, Santiago, Santibáñez, Santillán, Santillana, Santisbun, Santiscle or Sant Iscle, Santiso, Santiuste or Santiusde, Santiyán, Sant Jordí, Sant Just, Sant Llay or Sant Llayr, Sant Llimor, Sant Martí or Santmarti, Sant Miquel, Santocildes, Sant Sadorni, Sant Serni, Santo or Santu, Santo Domingo, Santos, Santos Guzmán, Santoyo, Santu, Santurce, Santuro, Sanveyt, San Vicente or Sant Vicents, Sanz, Sanz de Aguirre, Sanz de Aramburu, Sanz de Asarta, Sanza de Asiaín, Sanz de Azcona, Sanz de Cebollero, Sanz de Cortés, Sanz de Eguilaz, Sanz de Elciego, Sanz de Elgueta, Sanz de Eulate, Sanz de Ezcurra, Sanz de Guirguillano, Sanz de Lanciego, Sanz de Larramendi, Sanz de Latrás, Sanz de Lezaún, Sanz Normant, Sanz de Ochagavia, Sanz del Redal, Sanz de Urrizola, Sañudo, Saola, Saorra, Sapararte, Saparra, Sapera, Sapila, Sapiña or Sapina, Saplana, Saporta, Saportella or Zaportella, Saquan, Sarabia or Saravia, Saracelas, Saracibar, Saráchaga, Saracho, Saraechea, Saragosa, Saralegui, Sarasa, Sarasaga, Sarasate, Sarasola, Saraspe, Sarasqueta, Sarasti, Sarastume, Sarasúa, Saravases, Sardá, Sardalla, Sardaneta or Sardeneta, Saren, Sarmiento, Saro, Sarde, Saroe, Saroviza, Sartelo, Sarrá, Sarracoa, Sarralde, Sarraoa or Zarraoa, Sarrat, Sarratea, Sarray, Sarria or Sarría, Sarri-Almaza, Sarribera, Sarricolea, Sarriegui, Sarriera, Sarriguren, Sarrión, Sarró, Sarroca, Sarrovira, Sas, Sasa or Sarsa, Sasaeta-Chancoenea, Sasagudas, Sasala, Saseasas, Saseras, Saserra, Sasguardia, Sasgunyola, Sasúa, Sasiaín, Sariete, Sasiola, Sasoaín, Sasoeta, Sasso, Sastre, Sasturain, Sasuátegui, Satariz, Saterain, Satorres or Satorra, Satrilla, Satrilles, Satrústegui, Sanguis, Saula, Sault, Saura, Saurin, Sauto or Sautu, Savall, Savanell, Savasona, Savila, Saviñón, Savola, Sayas, Sayes, Sayfores or Sayforas. End of EHG Volume 81.

EHG Volume 82: Sebastián, Sebil, Secada or Secadas, Secades, Secadura, Secanilla, Seco, Secorún, Sedano, Sedeño, Segarra, Segovia, Segrelles, Seguí,

Seguino, Segura, Segurola, Seijas or Seixas, Sein, Selaya, Selgas, Selva, Sella, Sellán, Sellés, Semir, Semontete, Semper, Sempertegui, Sena, Senall, Senar, Sendagorta, Sendegui or Cendegui, Sendoa, Sendoquiz, Senespleda or Serrispleda, Senillosa, Senisterra or Sinesterra, Senosiaín, Sentis, Sentjust, Sentmenat or Sentmanat, Seoane, Septién or Setién or Septiem, Sepúlveda, Sequellar, Sequeiros or Sequeira or Sequera, Seral, Serantes, Serchs, Serdá, Seregut, Serna or La Serna or de la Serna or Laserna, Serdio, Serón, Serpa, Serra, Serralta, Serrallonga, Serrán, Serrano, Serras, Serrat, Serrateix, Serrauguet or Serra-Uguet, Sertucha, Servando, Servent, Serviá, Sescala or Sesescalas or Escalas, Sesclergues, Sescomes, Sesé, Sesguardia, Ses Iglesias, Sesma, Sespujades, Sestrada, Setanti, Sevá, Severiche, Sevil, Sevilla, Sevillano, Sexá, Seyerona, Sicart, Sidrac, Siero, Sierra, Sierralta, Siggas, Sigler, Siles, Silió, Silos, Silva, Silvano, Silvela or Santa María de Silvela, or da Lamea de Silvela, Silvestre, Sillero, Sillos, Simitur, Simó, Simonet, Sinisterra, Sintas, Sipán, Siquier or Siqués, Sirerols, Sirtema. End of EHG Volume 82.

EHG Volume 83: Sirvent or Sirvente, Siscar or Siscart, Siscones, Sisniega, Sisternes, Sitgo, Sitjar, Sitjes, Sitorras, Siurana, So, Soaje or Soage or Soaxe, Soba, Sobarzo, Soberón or Soberrón or Soverón, Sobies or Sovies, Sobirats, Soblechero, Sobrado, Sobrecasa, Sobremazas, Sobrepeña, Sobresoto, Sobrino, Sobrón, Socies, Socobio, Socueva, Sodres, Sodupe, Sojo, Sol or del Sol, Sola, Solá, Solache, Solachi, Solaeta, Solana, Solanas, Solance, Solanell, Solanes, Solanilla, Solano, Solapeña, Solar, Solarana, Solares, Solarte, Solaún, Solaurren, Solchaga, Soldevila or Soldevilla, Soler, Solier, Solís, Solius, Solivella, Soll, Soloaga, Sologaistoa or Sologaxtoa or Sorogaxtoa, Sologoiti, Sologuren, Solora, Solórzano, Solsona, Sonvi, Somado, Somarriba, Somocurcio, Somodevilla, Somonte, Somoza, Soñanes, Sopelana, Sopena or Sopeña, Sopoyo, Sopranis or Cibo de Sopranis, Soquia, Soquín, Sora, Soraburu, Sorain, Soraindo, Soraiz, Soraluce, Során, Soravilla, Sorazábal or Sorozábal, Sorchaga, Sordo, Sorell, Soret, Soria, Soriano, Sorita, Sorlada, Soroa, Soroeta, Sorogoxtoa, Soromendi, Sorondo, Sorozábal, Sorreguieta, Sorribas, Sorróiz, Sorrombegui, Sors, Sorts, Sorviá, Sos, Sosa, Sosoaga, Sostoa, Sota or de la Sota, Sotelo, Soter, Soteras, Sotés, Sotillo, Soto, Sotolongo, Sotomayor, Sousa or Sosa, Souviron, Soverón, Sovies, Suárez, Suárez de Deza, Suárez de Lezo, Suárez de Tangil, Suasola, Suan, Subías, Subirá, Subirana, Subiza, Subizar, Sucre, Sucunza, Suelves, Suesa, Suescun, Sugasti, Suinaga, Suldain, Sullá, Sumendiaga or Sumendiaca, Sumiano, Sunien, Sunyol, Sunza, Sunaga, Suñez or Sunyer, Suñol, Suolieta, Suquiza, Sureda, Suriol, Surís, Susaeta, Sustacha, Sustaeta, Sustinaga, Susunaga. End of EHG Volume 83. End of Letter S.

T EHG Volume 84: Tabar or Tavar, Tabares or Tavares, Taberner or Taverner or Tavertet or Tabernero, Tablada, Tablas, Tabernero, Tabernilla, Teboada, Tabora or Tavora or Tavara, Taborda, Tacón, Tafalla, Tafur, Tafurer, Tagamanet, Tagle, Tagoras, Taguí, Taibo, Tajada, Tajonar, Talamanca, Talarn, Talaverano, Talayero, Taliate, Talón, Tallada or Talladas, Tallander, Tallarán, Talledo, Tama or Gómez de Tama, Tamarit or Tamariz, Tamargo, Tamayo, Tapia, Tapiolas, Taqui, Taradell, Tarafa, Taranco, Tarascó, Tarazona, Tarbá, Tarcua, Tardet, Tarés, Tarín, Tárraga, Tarragó, Tarragona, Tarragua, Tarrasa, Tarré, Tárrega, Tarza, Tartas, Tasis, Tauste, Tavira or Tavera, Tavar, Tavara, Tavares, Tavera, Taverner, Tavisón de Recalde, Taxaquet, Tayadella, Teijeiro, Tejada, Tejedor, Tejeiro, Tejera, Tejeria, Tejerina, Tejerizo, Tejero, Tejo, Teleña, Tell or Téllez or Tello, Tellaeche, Tellaechea or Tellechea, Tellería, Tellitu, Temiño, Tena, Tendilla, Tenorio, Tenza, Terán, Terazas, Tercilla, Terés or Tarés, Teresa, Teresano, Termens, Terrades or Terradas, Terré, Terreros, Terrollada, Terroso, Tersa, Terto, Teruel, Tesillo, Teula, Teza, Tezanos, Thomás, Tiebas, Tierranueva, Tijera, Tijero, Timor, Tinajas, Tineo, Tinoco, Tinto, Tío, Tirado, Tirapu, Tizón, Tobalina, Tobia or Tovia, Toca, Tocho, Todoneras, Todonyans, Togores, Toledano, Toledo or Alvarez de Toledo, Tolosa, Tolosana, Tolosano, Tolosans. End of EHG Volume 84.

EHG Volume 85: Tolrá, Tolsá, Tomás, Tomasena, Tompes, Tona, Tonda, Toñarejos, Topalda, Topete, Torá, Toral, Toralla or Torralla, Toralló, Torán, Toranzo, Toraya, Torcida, Tord or Tort, Tordosa, Torell, Torella, Torelló, Toresano, Toribio, Torices, Torma, Tormaleo, Tormé, Tormo, Tormoye, Tornamira, Tornel, Torner, Tornera, Tornero, Tornet, Tornos, Toro, Toroño, Torquemada, Torra, Torrafeta, Torralba, Torralla, Torrano, Torrarroja, Torre, Torrealde, Torrebidarte, Torreblanca, Torrecilla, Torrecoa, Torre-Ibarbia, Torrejón, Torrejosa, Torre-Landaberro, Torre-Lucea, Torrell, Torrella or Torroella or turricella, Torrellas or Torrelles, Torrellena, Torrendell, Torrent, Torrentaller, Torrentó or Torrente, Torrero, Torrerroja, Torres, Torreta, Torrezábal, Torrezar, Torrezarra, Torrezurri, Torriente (de la), Torrijos, Torró, Torroja, Torrón, Torróntegui, Torsá, Tort, Tortellá, Tosantos, Tosca, Toscano, Tost, Tostado, Totorica, Totorica-Geona or Totoricagoena, Tous, Tovia, Tovar or Tobar, Trabuezo, Traginer, Tragó, Tragosa, Trallero, Trasmiera, Tramacet, Tramassat, Traña-Jáuregui, Trápaga, Traper, Trapera, Trasierra or Trassierra, Traslaviña, Traspuesto, Traver, Travi or Travy, Trebolazabala, Trebuesto, Treceño, Trecu, Trejo, Trelles, Trempo, Trenor, Trespalacios, Tresserres, Trevailla, Trevalls, Trevilla, Treviño or Triviño, Trías, Tricio, Trigón, Trigorá, Trigueros, Trihergua, Trilla, Trilles, Trillo, Trimen, Trincado, Trinchería, Tristany, Triz, Tro or Tron or Trons, Trobat, Trobica, Trocóniz, Troncones, Troncoso, Troya, Trucios, Trueba, Trujillo, Trullench, Trullés, Truyols, Tudela, Tudó, Tueros, Tuesta, Tufino, Tuhun, Turcal, Turell, Turiel, Turona, Turrillas, Turpino, Tutor. End of EHG Volume 85. End of Letter T.

U EHG Volume 86: Uacué, Ualde, Ubach, Ubago, Ubalde, Ubao, Ubarri, Ubayar, Uberta, Ubierog, Ubieta, Ubilla, Ubillos or Urbillos, Ubillotz, Ubiria, Ubirichaga, Ubitarte, Ucar, Uceda or Ucedo, Ucelay or Urcelay, Uciola or Uiciola or Viciola, Ucharain, Udabe or Udave, Udaeta, Udala, Udi, Ugalde, Ugalpegolea, Ugao, Ugarra, Ugarrechea or Ugarrechena, Ugarriza, Ugarte, Ugarteburu, Ugartondo, Uguet, Uguiricha or Uguirichaga, Uhagón, Uhalde, Uhart, Uhuartiuson, Ulacia, Ulibarri or Ullibarri or Uribarri, Ulin, Ulzurrun, Ulldemolins, Ullestres, Ullibarri, Ulloa, Umbarambe, Umarán, Umansoro, Umbert, Umendía, Umérez, Unamuno, Unamúnzaga, Unano, Unanue, Uncella, Unceta, Uncote, Unda, Undiano, Undués, Undúrraga, Ungo, Ungría, Unis, Unsain, Unza, Unzaga, Unzalu, Unzola, Unzué, Unzueta, Upategui, Upelategui, Urabain, Uraga, Urain, Uralde, Urandurraga, Uranga, Uranzu, Urasandi de Meñaca, Urazandi, Urbasos, Urbieta, Urbillos, Urbina or Ortiz de Urbina, Urbiola, Urbiota, Urbiguiain, Urbizu or Urbuzu, Urcelay, Urcola, Urcullu, Urch, Urdaibay, Urdalleta, Urdambeluz, Urdambidelus or Urdan-Videlus, Urdampilleta, Urdanegui, Urdaneta, Urdangarin, Urdanibia, Urdanitivar, Urdaniz, Urdanoz, Urdapilleta or Urdampilleta, Urdaspal, Urdax, Urdayaga, Urdiaín, Urdiales, Urdinarana, Urdinola, Urdinzu, Urdízibar or Urdídinar or Urdanítibar, Urdoz, Ureder, Ureta, Urgell, Urgoiti or Urgoitia, Uria, Uriarte, Uribarren, Uribarrena, Uribarri, Uribarria, Uribe, Uribelarra or Uribe-Larrea, Uriberri, Uribia, Uribitarte, Uriburu or Uruburu or Urraburu, Uricoechea, Urien, Urieta, Urietagoico, Urigoitia, Urigüen, Uriona, Urionagoena, Uriondo, Urioste, Urizarri, Uriz, Urizar, Urmeneta or Urmenta, Urnieta, Urniza, Uroz, Urozberoeta or Urrezberoeta, Urquía, Urquiaga, Urquide, Urquidi, Urquijo, Urquiola, Urquista, Urquiza, Urquizo, Urquizu, Urra, Urraca, Urraga, Urrapain or Urrupain, Urraría, Urraza, Urrea, Urreaga or Urriaga, Urrecazulo, Urrecha, Urrechaga, Urrechu, Urreiztieta, Urréjola, Urrelo or Pérez de Urrelo, Urrengoechea, Urrestarazu, Urresti, Urreta, Urretavizcaya, Urriaga, Urribarrena, Urrichi, Urríes or Jordán de Urríes, Urrijote, Urrimendi or Urrizmendi, Urriola, Urriolanzacoa, Urrispuro or Urrispuru, Urrista, Urriza. End of EHG Volume 86. End of Letter U. End of EHG: Letters V, W, X, Y, and Z were never printed.

APPENDIX 4

JULIO DE ATIENZA

Nobiliario Español: Diccionario Heráldico de Apellidos Españoles y de Títulos Nobiliarios

I n *Nobiliario Español: Diccionario Heráldico de Apellidos Españoles y de Títulos Nobiliarios* (DHA) by Julio de Atienza, which deals principally with heraldic titles and Spanish surnames in Spain, there are brief references containing information about families in Latin America. Most of the entries treat the Spanish, or sometimes other European, origins of the surnames in question. The work includes some information on the following surnames:

A Aa, Abaceta, Abad, Abadal, Abades, Abadía, Abaeto, Abaigar, Abainza, Abajo, Abalcisqueta, Abalia, Abalón, Abalos, Aballe, Abánades, Abande or Abando, Abandero, Abango, Abanto, Abaña, Abar or Abare, Abarca, Abarca de Bolea, Abare, Abargues, Abaria, Abaroa, Abarrátegui, Abarzuza, Abas, Abascal, Abasóns, Abastras, Abat, Abaunza, Abaurrea, Abaurza, Abbad, Abceta, Abea, Abecia, Abecilla, Abedillo, Abeeta, Abel, Abela or Abelas, Abelal, Abelásturi, Abelda, Abelt, Abella, Abellán, Abellanas, Abello, Abelló, Abendívar, Abengoza, Abeo, Aber, Aberancioa, Aberásturi, Aberín, Abersín, Aberso, Abete, Abia, Abián, Abidabe, Abiega, Abiego, Abilla, Abinia, Abinín, Abio, Ablanedo, Ablanque, Abléu, Ablitas, Abril, Abrines, Abulia, Aburruza, Aburto, Acanares, Acaño, Acciaboli, Acebal, Acebedo, Acebes, Acebo, Acedo, Acega, Aceija, Aceituno, Acelaín, Acelegui, Acella, Acenar, Aceña, Aceña de Butrón, Acera, Acero, Acerola, Acevedo, Acevillo, Aciapi, Acillona, Acín, Acinellas, Aciprés, Acireci, Acitaín, Aco, Acoda, Acorella, Acosta, Acre, Acuavera, Acuaviva, Acuña, Acurio, Acutaín, Acha, Achaburu, Acharán, Acharpasa, Ache, Achega, Achegua, Acheros, Acheta, Achey, Achisaeta, Achistegui, Achivite, Achorán, Achurdi, Achurriaga, Adabane, Adaíz, Adalid, Adam, Adame, Adán, Adán de Yarza, Adana or Adano, Adanza, Adaola, Adarbe, Adaro, Adarró, Adarzo, Adaves, Adebas, Adeliño, Adelmón, Adell, Ademar, Adena, Aderigui, Adión, Adoaín, Adorno, Adrada, Adrián, Adrián de Torres, Aduanes, Aduna, Adurriaga, Adurza, Aduza, Aechaga, Aedo, Aellos, Aendardo, Aerrementería, Aesaín, Aeza, Aezcoa, Afaitaro, Afán de Ribera, Afrontes, Agadeburi, Agaíz, Aganduro, Agar, Agarriga, Agazones, Agea, Ager,

Ageris, Agóitiz, Agondaro, Agorero, Agorraeta or Agorreta, Agós, Agosti, Agozti, Agramont, Agramunt, Agraz, Agreda, Agreda de Tejada, Agremunt, Aguado Aguanevados, Aguas, Aguayo, Agudo, Agueri, Agüero, Aguerre, Aguerreta, Aguerri, Agüeso, Aguiar, Aguila, Aguilar, Aguileor, Aguiler, Aguilera, Aguileta, Aguiló or Aguilón, Aguilué, Aguinaga, Aguinares, Aguiniga, Aguión de Ponte, Aguiriano, Aguirre, Aguirrea, Aguirreacotegui, Aguirrearanzamendi, Aguirreaspiroz, Aguirrebasabe, Aguirre-Basagoitia, Aguirre-Basaldúa, Aguirrebeco, Aguirrebéiztegui, Aguirrebengoa, Aguirrebeña, Aguirregoicoa, Aguirregoitia, Aguirrelorezuri, Aguirremota, Aguirre-Sarasúa, Aguirrezábal or Aguirre-Zabala, Aguirre-Zaldúa, Aguirrezazona, Aguirri, Aguisardo, Agujares, Agulla, Agullana, Agulló, Agúndez, Agurto, Agustí, Agustín, Agustina, Agusto, Agut, Ahajadas, Ahé, ·Ahedo, Aheja, Ahón or Ahones, Ahonen, Ahotares, Ahumada, Aibar, Aibri, Aicaroz, Aiceburu, Aicicute, Aicinena, Aicoz, Aich, Aignanariz, Aiguaviva, Aillón or Aillones, Aimar, Aimerich, Aincildegui, Aincio, Ainciondo, Aineto, Ainsa, Ainza, Aiñón, Aisa, Aisea, Aitamarren, Aitera, Aiturguy, Aíz, Aizaga, Aizaldebarrena, Aizarnatea, Aizate, Aizbay, Aizcorbe, Aizoaín, Aizpegoena, Aizpiri, Aizpuru, Aizpurúa, Aizquibel, Aiztondo, Aiztuz, Ajanguiz, Ajesta, Ajober, Ajofrín, Ajúbita, Ajuria, Alabaina, Aladro, Alagón, Aláin de Beaumont, Alaiz, Alajín, Alamán, Alambarranta, Alambra, Alameda, Alamo, Alandí, Alanís, Alanquer, Alanzón, Alapont, Alarán, Alaraz, Alarcón, Alaregus, Alas, Alastra, Alastrué, Alastruey, Alatrista, Alava, Alaviano, Alazán, Alba, Albacete, Albalat, Albalate, Albalibus, Albamonte, Albán, Albana, Albandóis, Albanell, Albaredo, Albarenga, Albarracín, Albe, Albear, Albelas, Albelda, Albéniz, Albentosa, Alberca, Alberche, Alberdi, Albergaria, Alberín, Alberite, Alberó, Alberola, Alberro, Albert, Albertí, Albertín, Albertino, Alberto, Alberuela, Albia, Albiano, Albín, Albinagorda, Albines, Albiñaña, Albión, Albircio, Albisco, Albisto, Albistur, Albisúa, Albiz, Albizu, Albizúa, Albizubaso, Albizuri, Albo, Albocar, Albornoz, Albret, Albrizu, Albuerne, Albún, Alburquerque, Alcachoa, Alcaín, Alcaizaga, Alcalá, Alcalá-Galiano, Alcalde, Alcanabe, Alcanadre, Alcantade, Alcántara, Alcañiz, Alcaones, Alcarán, Alcaraz, Alcariz, A arsa, Alcasoba, Alcate, Alcaterena de Garayoa, Alcatezarena, Alcaudete, Alcavarilla, Alcayada or Alcayaga, Alcazaba, Alcázar, Alcazoba, Alcedo, Alcega, Alcegui, Alcelegui, Alcelus, Alcepes, Alcerreca, Alcíbar, Alcíbar-Azpicoa, Alcíbar-Jáuregui, Alcibias, Alciga, Alcina, Alcine, Alcober, Alcocer, Alcocés, Alcochola, Alcolea, Alcón, Alconada, Alconer, Alcoz, Alcuberri, Alcubierre, Alcubillo, Alcuide, Alcuza, Aldá, Aldaba, Aldabalde, Aldabe, Aldaco, Aldama, Aldamar, Aldán, Aldana, Aldanza, Aldao, Aldaola, Aldaolea, Aldape, Aldapebeitia, Aldasoro, Aldava, Aldave, Alday, Aldaz, Aldaza, Aldazábal, Aldazazábal, Aldazo, Aldea, Aldecoa, Aldehuela, Aldemoresco, Alderete, Aldoba, Aldobrandini, Aldonalde, Aldovera, Aldrete, Aldrolea, Aldui, Aldunate, Alduncin, Aleda, Aledo, Alegre, Alegret, Alegría, Aleiza, Alejandre, Alejandro, Alemán, Alemany, Alemparte, Alén, Alencastre, Alencastro, Alensón, Alentón or Alentorn, Alenyá, Alenzón, Aleo, Alepus, Aler, Aleristio, Alesano, Alesón, Alexandre, Alfaro, Alfay, Alfeirán, Alférez,

Alférez de Xódar, Alfocea, Alfoceres, Alfonseca, Alfonsia, Alfonsín, Alfonso, Aliaxa, Alicante, Alier or Aliers, Alifante, Alife, Alija, Alínez, Alió, Alipasolo, Aliprandi, Aliri, Alís, Alix, Almada, Almagro, Almaicoz, Almandoz, Almansa or Almanza, Almao, Almaraz, Almarza, Almas, Almáu, Almazán, Almeida, Almela, Almelda, Almena, Almenar, Almenara, Almendáriz, Almendral, Almerá, Almeri, Almería, Almirano, Almodóvar, Almogábar, Almoguera, Almoina, Almonte, Almoragas, Almorant, Almoravid, Almudévar, Almugáver, Almunia, Alói, Alomar, Alona, Alondris, Alonso, Alonso-Calderón, Alonso de Caso, Alonso de Hoyos, Alonso-Pimentel, Alonso del Pino, Alonso-Reguero, Alonso-Rosicas, Alonsotegui, Aloristio, Alóriz, Alórriz, Alós, Alost, Aloy, Aloyto, Alpedrete, Alpedrín, Alpicat, Alpizcueta, Alpoem, Alpont, Alponte, Alprano, Alquíjar, Alquiza, Alquizalete, Alsaín, Alsava, Alsedo, Alsín, Alsina, Alsos, Altamira, Altamirano, Altares, Altarriba, Altecha, Altemir or Altemiz, Altero, Altet, Alteza, Altier or Altieri, Altiga or Altigo, Altiro, Altiurre, Alto, Alto de Salinas, Altolaguirre, Altra, Altrigo, Altube, Altuna, Altuza or Altuya, Alustiza, Alvarado, Alvarez, Alvarez-Baragaña, Alvarez-Barriada, Alvarez-Cardamuela, Alvarez de Coca, Alvarez de Espejo, Alvarez de Eulate, Alvarez de Faria, Alvarez de Lorenzana, Alvarez de Meda, Alvarez de Pedrosa, Alvarez-Rabanal, Alvarez-Salazar, Alvarez de Toledo, Alvarez de la Torre, Alvarez del Vayo, Alvarez de la Villeta, Alvaro, Alvaro de los Ríos, Alvear, Alvira, Alvitro, Alviturría, Alza, Alzaa-echea, Alzaga, Alzáibar, Alzamora, Alzarán, Alzarbe, Alzarte, Alzas, Alzate, Alzátegui, Alzava, Alzayaga, Alzíbar, Alzola, Alzolaras, Alzórriz, Alzu, Alzúa, Alzuaín, Alzualde, Alzuarán, Alzubarrant, Alzubide, Alzueta, Alzugaray, Alzuru, Allado, Allafor, Allande, Allarcegui, Allarcigui, Allastigui, Allata, Allén, Allén del Agua, Allende, Allendesalazar, Aller, Alli, Allín, Allo, Alló, Alloc, Alloz, Allué, Amaciano, Amada, Amadéi, Amado or Amador, Amagano, Amaín, Amalrich, Amallo, Amallobieta, Amanis, Amantegui, Amar, Amaral, Amarante, Amarelle, Amargós, Amarilla, Amarit or Amarita, Amáriz, Amás, Amasa, Amasada, Amasorraín, Amat, Amate, Amatiano, Amatria, Amatriaín, Amaya, Amayrra, Amaza, Amazada, Ambe, Ambía, Amblard, Amboage, Ambós, Ambram, Ambulodi, Ambulodibu, Amburz, Ameller, Amelli, Amer, Amés, Amescoa or Amescua, Amesti, Ametiller, Ameyugo, Amez, Amézaga, Amézola, Amezqueta, Amezquita, Amezúa, Amiano, Amigant, Amigo or Amigó, Amigot, Amilano, Amileta, Amilibia, Amilidia, Amira, Amix, Amoeiro, Amolaz, Amor, Amora, Amoragas, Amores, Amoreto, Amorillo, Amorín, Amoriurtu, Amorlaz, Amorós, Amoroso, Aroroz, Amorrortu, Amoscotegui, Ampara, Ampiedes, Ampiés, Ampudia, Ampuero, Ampurias, Amueiro, Amunabarro, Amunátegui, Amusco, Amustegui, Amuzcotegui, Ana, Anachuri, Anae, Anasco, Anastro, Anaya, Anceo, Ancieta, Ancilla, Anciola, Anciondo, Anciso, Ancisto, Ancitia, Ancollana, Anconja, Ancora, Ancoronat, Ancheos, Anchés, Ancheta, Anchía, Anchieta, Anchieva, Anchoca, Anchóniz, Anchorena, Anchóriz, Anda, Andaburu, Andagoya, Andalucía, Andaluz, Andallón, Andanza, Andaraz, Andaya, Andéchaga, Andeiro, Andelos, Anderal or Anderaz, Andériz, Andía, Andiano, Andicano, Andicona, Andina, Andino,

Andión, Andirengoechea, Andoín, Andonaegui, Andosilla, Andraca, Andrada, Andrada-Vanderwilde, Andrade, Andrade-Moreyra, Andramendi, Andrea, Andrequiaín, Andrés, Andréu, Andriani, Andrino, Anduaga, Anduce, Andueza, Anduga, Anduiza, Andújar, Anduzu, Anero, Anescar, Anesta, Angel, Angelats, Angelo, Angeloa, Angioletti, Anglada, Anglasell, Anglería, Anglés, Anglesola, Angola, Angoncillo, Angos, Angueira, Anguelao, Anguelo, Anguera, Anguiano, Anguiles, Anguiozar, Anguita, Angulo, Angulosa, Angumedo, Ania, Aniés, Anieto, Animio, Aniñón, Aniz, Anizqueta, Anjada, Anjiano, Anleo, Annés, Anoegui, Anoz, Anrich, Anrubia, Ansa, Ansaldo, Ansello, Ansilla, Ansó, Ansoaín, Ansoátegui, Ansodi, Ansoregui, Ansorena, Ansótegui, Ansoti, Ansu, Ansuaga, Ansuaín, Ansúrez, Antayo, Antecha, Antenza, Antequera, Antezana, Antía, Antich, Antígono, Antiguo, Antillón, Antín, Antist, Antolí, Antolínez, Antón, Antón del Olmet, Antona, Antoniano, Antoñana, Antroido, Antúnez, Antuñano, Anués, Anuncibay, Anzano, Anzati, Anzeta, Anzuán, Anzuane, Anzué, Anzules, Añas, Añasco, Añes, Añón, Añorbe, Añorga, Añués, Aoíz, Apalategui, Apaolaza, Apara, Aparici, Aparicio, Apate, Apategui, Apellániz, Aperregui, Aperribay, Apeztegui or Apezteguía, Apioza, Apocoa, Apodaca, Aponte or Ponte, Apraiz, Aquareta, Aquino, Ara, Arabaolaza, Arabigui, Arabio, Araca, Aracama, Araceli, Aracil or Araciel, Aracubia, Arachea, Arados, Araeta, Araeza, Aragall, Aragón, Aragonés, Aragorri, Araguás, Aragüés, Arahuete, Araín, Arainguibel, Araiz, Araiztegui, Aramayona, Arámbarri, Arambiaga, Aramburu, Aramendi, Aramendía, Arana, Aranada, Aranaga, Aranaiba, Aranalde, Aranarache, Aranaz, Arancava, Arance, Aranceta, Arancibia, Aranda, Arandia, Arando, Arandojo, Araneta, Arango, Arangoiti, Arangozqui, Aránguiz, Aranguren, Aranibar, Arano, Aransolo, Aransu, Aranza, Aranzadi, Aranzate, Aránzazu, Aranzu, Aranzubia, Araoz, Araque, Araquil, Araquistáin, Arardo, Ararte, Aras, Arascot, Arasia, Arasnabarreta, Araso, Araube, Arauco or Araucoa, Arauina, Araújo, Arauna, Aráus, Arauz, Aravide, Arazama, Arazu, Arazuri, Arbaiza, Arbe, Arbea, Arbee, Arbeiza, Arbeláez or Arbelaiz, Arberas, Arberoa, Arbestáin, Arbia, Arbicio, Arbide, Arbieto, Arbilaga, Arbilde, Arbizu, Arbolancha, Arboleda or Arbolea or Arboleya, Arbón de Bellón, Arbona, Arboniés, Arborser, Arbués, Arbuet, Arbulo, Arburúa, Arcachaga, Arcagas, Arcaine, Arcales, Arcaraso, Arcas, Arcauri, Arcaute, Arcaya, Arcayna, Arce, Arceo, Arci, Arcilla, Arcillero, Arcillo, Arciniega, Arco, Arcocha, Arcos, Archega, Archiguinolasa, Archimbaud, Ardaiz, Ardanaz, Ardanza, Arde, Ardena, Ardid, Ardiles, Area, Areaga, Areano, Arecia, Areco, Arecha, Aréchaga, Arechaundieta, Arechavala, Arechavaleta, Arechea, Aregita, Areiceta, Areilza, Areitio, Aréizaga, Aréjola, Arellano, Arenal, Arenas, Arenaza, Arendigoyen, Arenillas, Arenós, Areny, Arenzana, Arequita, Arés, Arescurenaga, Arespacochaga, Arespagundegui, Areste or Aresti, Areta, Arévalo, Arézaga, Arezo, Arfe, Argáin, Argaiz, Argamasillade la Cerda, Argandoña, Arganza, Arganzón, Arganzúa, Argañaras, Argarate, Argemir, Argensola, Argent, Argentona, Argerich, Argibay, Argizáin, Argoaín, Argomániz, Argomedo, Argos, Argote, Argudo, Arguedas, Argüelles,

Argüello, Argueta, Arguiano, Arguibarri, Arguijo, Arguindegui, Arguiñáriz, Arguis, Arguiso, Arguiz, Arguizán, Argumosa, Ariapi, Arias, Ariazábal, Ariceta, Aricio, Aricheta, Ariese, Arigoy, Ariguel, Arilza, Arimasagasti, Arimendi, Arín, Aríndez, Arines, Arinzano, Ariño, Ariola, Ariortúa, Arispe, Aristaráin, Arístegui, Aristerrazu, Aristi, Aristigaya, Aristiguieta, Aristimuño, Aristizábal, Aristo, Aristondo, Ariszubiaga, Ariz, Ariza, Arizabalaga, Arizabaleta, Arizaga, Arizaleta, Arizcorreta, Arizcún, Arizmendi, Ariznabarreta, Ariznoa, Arizola, Arizón, Arjona, Arlas, Arlegui, Arlés, Arleta, Armada, Armadáns, Armañanzas, Armendáriz, Armendia, Armendurúa, Armengol, Armengot, Armenta, Armenteros, Armentia, Armero, Armesto, Armijo, Armíldez, Armiño, Armóniz, Armuñá, Arnado, Arnaiz, Arnal, Arnalte, Arnaños, Arnao or Arnaobidao, Arnau, Arnedo, Arnero, Arnés, Arnesbaita, Arnez, Arnu, Arnuero, Arnús de Ferrer, Aroca, Aroiz, Arolas, Aroldo, Arosena, Aróstegui, Arozarena, Arozqueta, Arper, Arpide, Arquellada, Arquer or Arquero, Arqués, Arrabal, Arrabate, Arracietaia, Arraiz, Arrameru, Arranales, Arrandolaza, Arranomendi, Arraño, Arrarás, Arrasa, Arrasate, Arrastia, Arrasúa, Arrate, Arrateguibel, Arratia, Arratibel, Araya, Arrayoz, Arrazola, Arrazubi, Arrechandieta, Arrecheandieta, Arredondo, Arregui, Arreguía, Arreguibarrena, Arréjola, Arreluz, Arrese, Arria, Arriaga, Arriarán, Arriati, Arriaza, Arribas, Arribillaga, Arriesta, Arrieta, Arrigorriaga, Arrillaga, Arriola, Arripe, Arrisubiaga, Arris, Arriuz, Arrizábal, Arroaga, Arrobi, Arroce, Arrojo, Arrola, Arrom, Arrona, Arrondo, Arrónez, Arróniz, Arroquia, Arróyabe, Arroyo, Arrozubi, Arrúe, Arrueira, Arrueta, Arrufat, Arruti, Arruza, Arscia, Arsóriz, Arsu, Arsúa, Arsuaga, Arsueta, Artacho, Artadi, Artajo, Artajona, Artal, Artalezu, Artán, Artanga, Artano, Artariaín, Artasona, Artavia, Artaza, Artazcoz, Artazubiaga, Arteaga, Arteasuaincar, Artecona, Arteche, Arteita, Arteiz, Arteri, Artés, Arteta, Arteya, Artí, Artiaga, Artidiello, Artieda, Artigas, Artigosa, Artigues, Artiñano, Artiz, Arto, Artola, Artoleta, Artosilla, Artucha, Artuda, Artundiaga, Artunduaga, Arturo, Artusia, Aruec, Arza, Arzábal, Arzabe, Arzac, Arzadun, Arzaga, Arzalaya, Arzamendi, Arzola, Arzoz, Arzubia, Asaburu, Asalido, Asarta, Asas, Ascanio, Ascargoitia, Ascarza, Ascarzaga, Ascasíbar, Ascaso, Ascasúa, Asco, Ascoeta, Asconiza, Ascho, Asenjo, Asensio, Asiaín, Asién, Asín, Asio, Asiresi, Asiulines, Asnara, Asola, Aspergorta, Asperilla, Asprer, Assante, Assó, Asta, Astaburuaga, Asteguieta, Asteiza, Astiasarán, Astigar, Astigarraga, Astigarribia, Astina, Astiria, Astiz, Astor, Astoraica, Astoreca, Astordúa, Astorga, Astoriza, Astoviza, Astruantes, Astudillo, Astuni, Asturias, Asturiazaga, Asu, Asúa, Asuaga, Asuara, Asula, Asura, Asurcia, Asurdi, Asurmendi, Ata, Ataide, Atalaya, Atarés, Ataún, Atazo, Ateca, Ategui, Ateguren, Atehortúa, Atibar, Atienza, Atilano, Atiza, Atocha, Atodo, Atondo, Atorella, Atorrasagasti, Atorzgui, Atristaín, Atrosillo, Atue, Aubert, Aúd, Audivert, Audor, Auguenez, Aulestia, Aulet, Auli, Aulia, Aumátegui, Aumendia, Auñón, Aurgaste, Auriol or Aurioles, Aurre, Ausa, Ausina, Austoa, Avalos, Avecilla, Avellanal, Avellaneda, Avendaño, Avero, Aveyro, Avila, Avilés, Avinyó, Aviñón, Axa, Axaló, Axartell, Axpe, Axtera,

Axúbita, Ayala, Ayaldabarrena, Ayalde, Ayaldeburu, Ayandegoller, Ayanz, Ayara, Ayardía, Ayardiga, Ayechu, Ayensa, Ayerbe, Ayerdi, Ayrguir, Ayesa, Ayesta, Ayestarán, Ayet, Ayete, Aymerich, Ayora, Ayordamúñoz, Ayorín, Ayosa, Aysa, Ayuela, Ayuso, Aza, Azaceta, Azadón, Azagra, Azamar or Azamor, Azanza, Azara, Azaro, Azarola, Azca, Azcaín, Azcaraldea, Azcárate, Azcaray, Azcagorta, Azcárraga, Azcarretazábal, Azcoa, Azcón, Azcona, Azconegui, Azconobieta, Azcue, Azcuénaga or Azcúnaga, Azcune, Azelm, Azlor, Azme, Aznar, Aznáriz, Azo, Azocaechea, Azofra, Azopardo, Azor, Azorero, Azorín, Azpa, Azparren, Azpeitia, Azpiazu, Azpilcueta, Azpilicueta, Azpillaga, Azpiriz, Azpíroz, Azpitarte, Azpitia, Azqueta, Azterani, Azterrica, Azúa, Azuela, Azuelo, Azugar. End of DHA, Letter A.

B Babia, Babiano, Baca, Bacara, Bacazábal, Bacerola, Bacó, Bach, Bada, Badajoz, Badino, Badiola, Bado, Baena, Baeza, Bagá, Bagache, Bagalde, Bages or Baget, Bago, Bagos, Bágueña, Baguer, Bagur, Bahamonde, Bahana, Baiden, Baides, Baigorri, Baiguela, Bailén, Bailo, Baillo, Baío, Baizábal, Bajano, Bajoles, Bajuelo, Balades, Balandre, Balaguer, Balán, Balanyá, Balanza, Balanzátegui, Balanzo, Balariaín, Balbín, Balboa, Balbuena, Balda, Baldaura, Baldenaches, Baldocinos, Baldoví, Baldovinos, Baldrich, Balduz, Balearra, Balencegui, Balenchana, Balentín, Balez, Bálgoma, Balicó, Balonga, Balparda, Bals, Balsa, Balsera, Balsorga, Baltanás, Baltodano, Balza, Balzola, Ballano, Ballariaín, Ballaró, Ballartilla, Ballastros, Ballenilla, Ballero, Ballester, Ballestero or Ballesteros, Ballet, Ballín or Ballina, Bam, Bances, Banchs, Banda, Bandama, Bandera (La), Bandiola, Bandos, Bandrés, Bandujo, Bandurraga, Bango, Banyeres, Banyoles, Banys, Banyuls, Banzo, Bañales, Bañares, Báñez, Baños, Bañuelos, Bañueta, Bañuls, Bao, Baón, Baquedano, Baquería, Baqueríe, Baquerín, Baquerizo, Baquero, Baquijano, Baquillo, Bara, Baracaldo, Barahona, Baráibar, Baraiz, Barajón, Baramba, Barambio, Barandiarán, Barañano, Baraona, Baráu, Barazate, Barba, Barbadillo, Barbado, Bárbara, Barbarán, Barbarín, Barbaza, Barbazán, Barbeito, Barbena, Barbéns, Barber or Barberá, Barberena, Barbería, Barbín, Barbo, Barbón, Barbosa, Barcáiztegui, Barceló, Barcelona, Bárcena, Barcenilla, Barcia, Barco, Barcheta, Bardají, Bardales, Bardas, Bardaverrín, Barderí, Bardoy, Bares, Bareta, Bargundía, Bariaín, Barillas, Barinaga, Barluenga, Barnola, Barnuevo or Barrionuevo, Baro, Baró, Baroja, Barón, Barona, Barostaín, Barquer, Barquero, Barquinero, Barra, Barracate, Barracha, Barrachina, Barradas, Barragán, Barraicoa, Barral, Barranco, Barrantes, Barraondo, Barrasa, Barrasgui, Barrat, Barraya, Barrecheguren, Barreda, Barredón, Barreira, Barrena, Barreneche, Barrenechea, Barrera, Barrero, Barreto, Barreyarza, Barri, Barria, Barriach, Barriano, Barricarte, Barrientos, Barriga, Barrillas, Barrio, Barrionuevo, Barrios, Barriza, Barroeta, Barrón, Barrondo, Barros, Barroso, Barroz, Barruca, Barruchi, Barruelo, Barruezo, Barrundi, Barrutia, Barruza, Barsola, Bartoméu, Bartrola, Barturen, Barúa, Barutell, Barzosla, Bas, Basabe, Basabil, Basaburu, Basacha, Basagoiti, Basagoitia, Basaguchia,

Basaldúa, Basanta or Basante, Basarate, Basart, Basauri, Basazar, Bascanó, Bascaróns, Basco, Bascones, Bascuñán, Bascuñana, Basedas, Baserola, Baset, Basiá, Basigo, Basoco, Basos, Basozábal, Bassá, Bassecourt, Basset, Bassols, Bastard, Bastardo, Baster, Basterolaza, Basterra, Basterrechea, Basterrica, Bastida (La), Bastidas, Bastó, Bastoncillo, Bastóns, Basturs, Basualdo, Basurto, Batalla, Batet, Batista, Bátiz, Batlle, Batres, Baucells, Báuer, Bautista, Bauzá, Bayano, Bayarde or Bayarte, Bayer or Boyer, Bayetola, Bayle, Baylla, Bayo, Bayón, Bayona, Bayos, Bazán, Bazo, Bea, Bearín, Bearne, Beas, Beascan, Beasoaín, Beato, Beauchamp, Beaufort, Beaumont, Beazquen, Becerra, Becerril, Bécquer, Bech, Beda, Bedia, Bedmar, Bedoya, Bedua, Begoña, Begur, Beibacar, Beinza, Beinzola, Beitia, Beizama, Béiztegui, Bejarano, Belaochaga, Belart, Belarrinaga, Belascoaín, Belástegui, Belaunza, Belaunzarán, Belda, Beléndiz, Beleret, Belesar, Belestegui, Belmar, Belmonte, Beloque, Beltraena, Beltrán, Beltrán de Caicedo, Beltranilla, Beluaño, Belveder, Belvís, Belzunce, Belzunegui, Bella, Bellaet, Bellafilla, Bellcastell, Bellera, Bellet, Bellfort, Bellido, Bellisca, Bello, Belloch, Bellón, Bellosillo, Belloso, Bellosta, Bellpuig, Belluís, Bellvehí, Bellver, Bellvey, Bellvís, Benaján, Benajas, Benajiger, Benar, Benasar, Benavent, Benavente, Benavides, Bencarza, Benda, Bendaña, Beneche, Benedet, Benegorri, Benet, Beneyto, Bengoa, Bengochea, Bengoechea, Bengolea, Benítez, Benítez de Lugo, Benito, Benosa, Benso, Benvengut, Beorlegui, Beortegui, Beraiz, Beraliga, Berama, Beramendi, Berancegui, Berandón, Beranga, Beránger, Berard, Berardo, Berart, Berasiartu, Berástegui, Beratarrechea, Beratúa, Beraún, Beraza, Berbegal, Berberán, Berbis, Berbizana, Bercianos, Berda, Berecéibar, Berenguer, Bereterreche, Berga, Bergadá, Bergadáns, Berganza, Berganzo, Bergé, Berges, Bergua, Beristáin, Bermejo, Bermeo, Bermúdez, Bermúdez de Castro, Berna, Bernabé, Bernabéu, Bernad, Bernal, Bernáldez, Bernaldo de Quirós, Bernales, Bernaola, Bernat, Bernáu, Berni, Berniz, Bernués, Bernuy, Beroiz, Berra, Berraondo, Berrasoeta, Berraut, Berregarza, Berri, Berridi, Berrio or Berriozábal, Bérriz, Berroa, Berroeta, Berrosonaga, Berrotarán, Berroy, Berrozpe, Berrueta, Bertegui, Bertendona, Bertereche, Bertier, Bertiz, Bertodano, Beruete, Bervises, Berzosa, Besanche, Bescós, Besga, Besora, Betanzos, Betelu, Beterio, Beteta, Betete, Bethencourt, Betolaza, Betoño, Beunza, Beunzalarrea, Beuso, Beyán, Beyas, Beyens, Bezado, Bezanilla, Bezón, Biamonte, Bianes, Bidángoz, Bidasola, Bidaur, Bidaurre, Bidaurreta, Biedma, Bielaray, Bielsa, Bierama, Bieto, Bilbao, Bilbatúa, Bildósola, Bimón, Binal, Binelo, Biota, Biquendi, Birués, Bisbal, Bisorna, Bistué, Bitezio, Bitrián, Biuna, Biuro, Bivas, Biya, Bizcarra, Bizcarret, Bizuete, Blake, Blan, Blanc, Blanca, Blancafort, Blancas, Blanco, Blanch, Blanchs, Blandianes, Blandón, Blanes, Blasco, Blay, Blázquez, Blecua, Boada, Boado, Boán, Boares, Boatella, Bobadilla, Bobea, Bocacho, Bocal, Bocanegra, Bocos, Bodega, Bodet, Bodí, Boera, Bofarull, Bofill, Boga, Boguet, Bohorques, Boigues, Boíl, Boillar, Boisol, Boix, Boixols, Boja, Bojados, Bojedo, Bolante, Bolaños, Bolas, Bolde, Bolea, Boleo, Bolet, Bolia, Boliaga, Bolinaga, Bolívar,

Bolo, Bolóis, Bolós, Bolterra, Bolomburu, Bollegui, Bollullo, Bomaitín, Bomaza, Bonactu, Bonafós, Bonal, Bonany, Bonapart, Bonart, Bonaselva, Bonastre, Bondeno, Bonel or Bonell, Boneo, Bonet, Boneta, Bonifacio, Bonifaz, Bonig, Boníguez, Bonilla, Bonivern, Bonmatí, Bonnefoy, Bóo, Boquel, Boquet, Boráu, Borbolla, Borbón, Borda or Bordas, Bordabere, Bordalva, Bordallo, Bordanaba, Bordeix, Bordils, Bordóns, Bordoy, Borella, Borges, Borgia, Borguño, Bori, Boria, Borillas, Borinaga, Borja, Borjén, Bornás, Borolla, Borondad, Borragueiro, Borrajo, Borralla, Borrás, Borrasá, Borrego, Borrell, Borrer, Borriol, Borruel, Borrull, Bort, Boscá, Boscados, Boscot, Bosch, Bosello, Boser, Bosque, Botaya, Bote, Botella, Boteller, Botello, Botinés, Bou, Bouffart, Boulet, Bóveda, Bover, Boves, Box, Boyer, Boza, Bracamonte, Bracerolas, Bracho, Bramasachs, Branciforte, Brandón, Brañas, Braramuño, Brasa, Brasco, Bravo, Bravo de Lagunas, Bravo de Rivero, Bravo de Sarabia, Brea, Breganziano, Breña, Breserola, Bretón, Briceño, Bricianos, Brieba, Brihuega, Bringas, Briñas, Briones, Brisal, Brito, Briz, Brizuela, Brochero, Brondo, Brossa, Broto, Brú, Brugada, Bruguera, Brull, Brun, Brunet, Brusca, Bucareli, Bucarocoa, Buédano, Buendía, Bueno, Bueras, Buerba, Buerdo, Buergo, Buesa, Bueso, Bufalá, Bugarín, Buges, Buil, Buira, Buitrago, Buján, Bujedo, Bulacia, Bulnes, Bulocoa, Bullón, Burbano, Burces, Burdaspal, Burdaya, Bureba, Burel, Burgés, Burgo, Burgoa, Burgos, Burgucahar, Burgueño, Burguera, Burgués, Burguet, Burguete, Burguillos, Burguiño, Burón, Burós, Burreta, Burrial, Burriel, Burutáin, Busambert, Busel, Buserola, Busot, Busquets, Bustamante, Bustares, Bustenza, Bustillo, Bustindui, Bustinza, Bustinzoro, Bustinzuría, Busto or Bustos, Busturia, Butler, Butrón, Buzón. End of DHA, Letter B.

C Caamaño, Caba, Cabale, Caballa, Caballer, Caballera, Caballería, Caballero, Caballón, Cabana, Cabanellas, Cabanes, Cabanillas, Cabañas, Cabañuelas, Cabarcos, Cabarrús, Cabaspre, Cabedo, Cabelo, Cabello, Cabero, Cabestany, Cabex, Cabeza, Cabeza de Vaca, Cabezas, Cabezón, Cabias, Cabiedes, Cabirol, Cabitán, Cabo, Cabot, Cabra, Cabral, Cabrales, Cabranes, Cabrejas, Cabrera, Cabrerizo, Cabrero, Cabreta, Cabrío, Cabueñas, Cabués, Cacera, Cáceres, Caciara, Cacique, Cacos, Cachero, Cacho, Cachola, Cachupín, Cadalso, Cadalla, Cadaval, Cadell, Cadena or Cadenas, Cadórniga, Cadorra, Cadreita, Cadret, Caetano, Cafont, Cafranga, Cagide, Cagígal, Cagigas, Cagrómiz, Cahorts, Caicedo, Caifero, Caín, Cairada, Caixas, Caja, Cajal, Cal. Calabaza, Calafat, Calahorra, Calán, Calancha, Calante, Calasanz, Calatañazor, Calatayud, Calatrava, Calberi, Calbetón, Calbijo, Calcena, Calcina, Caldas, Caldeira, Caldelas, Caldentey, Caldera, Calderer, Calderón, Calders, Caldés, Caldevilla, Caldirán, Calella, Calera or Calero, Caliéns, Calimano, Calis, Calo, Caloca, Calomarde, Calsa, Calser, Calva, Calvache, . Calveras, Calvet, Calvillo, Calvino, Calvis, Calvo, Calvó, Calzada, Calzadilla, Calzador, Calzón, Call, Callar, Calle, Calleja, Callejo, Callejón, Callero, Calles,

Callus, Camacho, Camalva, Camango, Cámara, Camargo, Camariñas, Camaró, Carasobras, Camazón, Camba, Cambero, Cambra, Cambrón, Cambronero, Camero, Camfullós, Camino, Camio, Camisón, Camoens, Camón, Camor, Camós, Campa, Campamar, Campana, Campanario, Campaner, Campani, Campano, Camparraga, Campero, Campezo, Campi, Campillo, Campino, Campins, Campllonch, Campmany, Campo, Campoamor, Campofrío, Campomanes, Campoo, Camporrells, Campos, Campoy, Campra, Camprodón, Camps, Campsor, Camptor, Campuzano, Camus, Camuso, Cana, Canabal, Canal, Canales, Canals, Canares, Canat Cánaves, Cáncer, Canciller, Cancino, Candal, Candamo, Candamo de Tablas, Candas, Candenas, Candía, Canedo, Canel, Canela, Canell, Canellas, Canencia, Canet, Canga or Cangas, Canga-Argüelles, Caniego, Caniélles, Canillas, Canisar, Cano, Canóu, Canoura, Cánovas, Cánoves, Canseco, Cansino, Cansor, Cantabrana, Cantalapiedra, Canter, Cantera, Canterelles, Cantillo, Cantín, Canto, Cantolla, Cantón, Cantonal, Cantoni, Cantoral, Cantos, Cañas, Cañavate, Cañaveral, Cañedo, Cañellas, Cañete, Cañizares, Cao de Benós, Capaguindegui, Capalvo, Caparriaga, Caparrós, Caparroso, Capdevila, Capeche, Capero, Capetillo, Capí, Capiaín, Capilla, Capisagasti, Caplá, Capmany, Capó, Capóns, Capua, Capuchines, Caraa, Caralt, Caramallo, Caramaní, Caramaño, Caramillo, Carandil, Carantoña, Carapio, Carasa, Caravantes, Caraveo, Caraves, Caravia, Carbajo, Carballido, Carballo, Carbó, Carbón, Carbonell, Carcabuey, Cárcamo, Carcasona, Carcedo, Carcelén, Cárcer, Cárcova, Cardaveras, Cardell, Cárdena, Cardenal, Cárdenas, Cardeo, Cardiel, Cardil, Cardo, Cardona, Cardoso, Careaga, Cariaco, Cariño, Caritat, Carlán, Carles, Carlos, Carlot, Carmena, Carmona, Carnero, Carnicer, Carnicero, Caro, Carol, Carondelet, Carpinteiro, Carpio, Carquizano, Carra, Carrabal, Carracedo, Carrafa, Carral, Carralón, Carrandi, Carranes, Carranza, Carrasco, Carrasquedo, Carrasquilla, Carratalá, Carreño, Carrera, Carreras, Carrere de Abense, Carriazo, Carrillo, Carrio, Carrió, Carrión, Carrizo, Carrizosa, Carro, Cárroz, Cartagena, Cartellá, Caruana, Carui, Carvajal, Casa, Casabases, Casabuena, Casademunt, Casadevall, Casadevante, Casador, Casajús, Casal, Casaldaguilla, Casalón, Casals, Casamayor, Casamijana, Casanate, Casani, Casanova, Casanueva, Casaprín, Casar, Casares, Casariego, Casas, Casasana, Casasayes, Casasola, Casáus, Cascajares, Cascales, Cascall, Cascante, Cascasona, Cascos, Cáseda, Cases, Caso, Casón, Caspe, Casquero, Castañares, Castañeda, Castañedo, Castañer, Castañera, Castañón, Castaños, Castejón, Castel, Castellá, Castellanos, Castellar, Castellarnáu, Castellauli, Castellbell, Castellbisbal, Castellblanch, Castellbó, Castellcir, Castelldaséns, Castellet, Castellfollit, Castellgalí, Castellmir, Castellmoltó, Castellnóu, Castelló, Castellón, Castellot, Castellroig, Castellrós, Castells, Castellsir, Castellsis, Castelltersol, Castelltort, Castellví, Castilla, Castillejo, Castillo, Castillón, Castolba, Castrelo, Castresana, Castrillo, Castrillón, Castro, Castro-Pinós, Castropol, Castroverde, Castrovido, Casuso, Cata, Catalá, Catalán de Ocón, Catandil, Cataneo, Catañy, Catarecha, Catategui, Cático, Catón, Catoyra, Caulellas, Caulers, Caunedo,

Caus, Cava, Cavada, Cavalcanti, Cavaleta, Cavia, Cayacegui, Cayas, Cayón, Cayuela, Cazorla, Cazos, Cea, Cebada, Cebadilla, Ceballos, Ceballos-Zúñiga, Cebeiro, Cebollero, Cebrián, Cegama, Cegastía, Cejudo, Cela, Celada, Celaeta, Celaín, Celanova, Celaya, Celayanda, Celayanda, Celayarán, Celayeta, Celdrán, Celis, Celma, Celoca, Cella, Cellorigo, Cemboraín, Cenarbe, Cenarruza, Cendegui, Cendoya, Cendrera, Cenoz, Centellas, Centeno, Centurión, Cepeda, Cequeira, Ceraín, Cerda, Cerda or Cerdán, Cerdeño, Cereceda, Cerecedo, Cererols, Ceret, Cerezo, Cerezuela, Cerio, Cermeño, Cernadas, Cernesio, Cerón, Cerra, Cerrada, Cerraeta, Cerragería, Cerrato, Cerro, Cerroa, Cervantes, Cervatos, Cervelló or Cervellón, Cervera, Cerveró, Cerviá, César, Céspedes, Ceta, Cetina, Cevallos, Cía, Cianca, Ciaño, Ciaurriz, Cicero, Cid, Cidrón, Cienfuegos, Ciervo, Cieza, Cifré, Cifontes or Cifuentes, Ciga, Cigala, Cigarán, Cigarra, Cigordi, Ciguerondo, Ciguri, Cilaurren, Ciloiz, Cillanco, Cillario, Cima, Cimbor, Cimbrón, Cincunegui, Cintora, Ciprés, Cirarrueta, Cirarruista, Cirera, Ciria, Cirieño, Cirna, Ciruelo, Cirueña, Císcar, Cisneros, Cisternas, Cistué, Citjó, Ciudadano, Ciurana, Ciutadella, Civerio, Civo de Sopranis, Ciya, Cladera, Clairac, Clar, Claramunt, Claravalls, Claret, Clariana, Claris, Clascá, Clauses, Claver, Clavería, Clavero, Claverol, Clavijo, Clemente, Clericat, Cleriguet, Climent, Clos, Clus, Clusa, Coalla, Coaña, Coazo, Coba, Cobanillas, Cobián, Cobo or Cobos, Coca, Cocón, Cocote, Coche, Cocho, Codina, Codinats, Codol, Coello, Coenza, Cogolls, Cogombrellas, Cola, Colarte, Colina, Colindres, Colip, Colmelo, Colmenares, Colmenero, Cólogan, Colom, Coloma, Colomer, Colomina or Colominas, Colomo, Colón, Colunga, Coll, Collado, Collandra, Collantes, Collar, Collell, Collferrer, Colltort, Coma, Comalada, Comallonga, Comas, Combeller, Comber, Combis, Comellas, Comenge, Comes, Comor, Compáins, Compañy, Compta, Comyn, Conadall, Conalos, Conangles, Concabella, Concejo, Concha, Conchares, Conchillos, Conde, Conejo, Conesa, Conill, Conlledo, Conrado, Contador, Contamina, Contesti, Contreras, Copeiro, Copóns, Coque, Coquero, Cora, Corao, Corbacho, Corbalán, Corbarán, Corbatón, Corbet, Corbí, Corvinos, Córcoles, Corcuera, Cordellas, Corder, Cordera, Cordero, Corders, Cordido, Córdoba, Corella, Corera, Coria, Corn, Cornado, Cornago, Cornejo, Cornel, Cornellá, Cornellana, Cornet, Cornus, Corona, Coronado, Coronas, Coronel, Corono, Coroño, Coros, Corraiz, Corral, Correa, Corres, Corro, Corsavi, Corsia, Corta, Cortabarría, Cortada, Cortalló, Cortázar, Corte, Cortecedo, Cortejana, Cortejo, Cortés, Cortesero, Cortey, Cortiada, Cortiguera, Cortina, Cortit, Corts, Corvera, Cos, Cosca, Coscó, Cosculluela, Cosida, Cosín, Cossío, Costa, Costabella, Costales, Costana, Costanti, Cota, Cotapos, Cotarelo, Cotera, Cotes, Cotoner, Cotorro, Cotrina, Cots, Cousiño or Coutiño, Covarrubias, Cózar, Credenza, Crespanes, Crespí, Crespo, Creus, Crexel, Criades, Criado, Criales, Cristantes, Crooke, Cros, Croses, Croy, Cruilles, Cruz, Cruzado or Cruzat, Cuadérnigas, Cuadra, Cuadrado, Cuadrillero, Cuadros, Cuaga, Cuaiz, Cuarrachino, Cuartango, Cuartas, Cubas, Cubells, Cubero, Cubides, Cubillas, Cubillos, Cucalá or Cucaló, Cucales, Cucaller,

Cueli, Cuéllar, Cuello, Cuenca, Cuerla, Cuerno, Cuero, Cuervo, Cuesta, Cueto, Cueva, Cuevas, Cugull, Culeta, Cumbis, Cumplido, Cunilleras, Cunvas, Cunyat, Cunzuta, Cuñada, Curco, Curiaciviart, Curiel, Curucheta, Cusagages, Custurer, Cutanda, Cutuneguieta. End of DHA, Letter C.

CH Chaca, Chacín, Chacón, Chamizo, Chamorro, Chanciller, Chanteiro, Chapar, Chapari, Chaparo, Chaparris, Chaparro, Chapartegui, Chapat, Chaperón, Charino, Charrania, Charrio, Charta, Chasarri, Chávarri, Chaves, Chell, Chelli, Chica, Chicarro, Chico, Chico de Guzmán, Chicote, Chilla, Chipre, Chiriboga, Chirinos, Chumacero, Churruca, Churruchano. End of DHA, Letter CH.

D Dábalos, Dach, Daguerre, Dalana, Dalbi, Dalmases, Dalmáu, Dalpas, Dalza, Dameto, Danguso, Dansa, Dantás, Danús, Daoíz, Dapifer, Dardalla, Darder, Darias, Darnius, Daso, Dat, Dato, Davalillos, Dávalos, Davi, Dávila, Daza, Dazar, Dazne, Deblore, Decia, Dehesa, Delaportella, Delás, Deles, Delfín, Delgadillo, Delgado, Delicado, Delpás, Dello, Denia, Derrech, Desbach, Desbalps, Desbanchs, Desboch, Desbrull, Descall, Descallar, Descamps, Desclapez, Desclergues, Desclópez, Descoll, Descós, Desfar, Desfrán, Desgastell, Desguái, Desgual, Desguanechs, Desguarets, Desguell, Desburb, Desgurra, Desjuny, Deslobes, Desllor, Deslluc, Desmás, Desmont, Desperes, Despí, Despinal, Desplá, Desportell, Despóu, Desprat, Despuig, Despújol, Destañy, Desvalls, Desvivers, Desvola, Deu, Dueceln, Deyá, Deyna, Deza, Diago, Díaguez, Díaz, Díaz de Arcaya, Díaz de Cadórniga, Díaz de Campomanes, Díaz de Casariego, Díaz de Casariego, Díaz de Cedrón, Díaz de Garayo, Díaz de Lavandero, Díaz de Ledesma, Díaz-Pimienta, Díaz de Reguero, Díaz de la Serna, Díaz de Trechuelo, Díaz de Vargas, Dicastillo, Diego, Dieste, Díez, Díez de Arellano, Díez de Aux, Díez de Escorón, Díez de la Losa, Díez de Medina, Díez de Quijano, Díez de Segura, Díez de Ulzurrun, Diezma, Dillanes, Diosayuda, Diosdado, Diosdat, Disorna, Diustegui, Doblas, Docal, Dolara, Dolarraga, Dolcinellas, Doliva, Dolius, Dolorde, Dolz, Doménech, Domezaín, Domingo, Domingotegui, Domingorena, Domínguez, Doms, Donaire, Donat, Doncel, Donella, Donez, Doni, Donis, Donlebrún, Donoso, Donvela, Doñamaría, Doñapalla, Dora, Dorante, Dorcas, Dorda, Dordás, Dorenga, Doria, Dóriga, Dornutegui, Dorregaray, Dorriols, Dosma, Dosríus, Dostals, Dot, Dou, Doz, Draper, Duany, Duart, Duarte, Dueñas, Duero, Duque, Duque de Estrada, Du-Quesne, Dura, Durall, Durán, Durand, Durandio, Durango, Durban, Duriz, Dusay, Dutari. End of DHA, Letter D.

E Eban, Ebazquin, Ecay, Eceiza, Ecenarro, Ecija, Echaburu, Echagüe, Echaide, Echalar, Echalaz, Echalecu, Echandi, Echániz, Echanove, Echaray, Echarri, Echarte, Echauri, Echauz, Echávarri, Echavarría,

Echavarríabengoa, Echavarrieta, Echave, Echaverrialzueta, Echazarreta, Echazuria, Echea, Echeandía, Echebarri, Echebarría, Echebarrieta, Echebelz, Echeberri, Echeberría, Echeberz, Echebeste, Echegaray, Echegoyen, Echenagusia, Echenique, Echepare, Echerreaga, Echezarreta, Echezuria, Ederra, Edigoraz, Eduegui, Egaña, Egea, Egoabil, Egocheaga, Egozcue, Egües, Eguía, Eguiaga, Eguiarte, Eguílaz, Eguina, Eguiniz, Eguino, Eguioíz, Eguiruren, Eguizábal, Eguras, Egurbide, Eguren, Egurrola, Egurza, Egusquiza, Eibitt, Eidocaín, Eiriz, Eito, Eizaga, Eizaguirre, Eizarrara, Eizmendi, Ejarque, Elcano, Elcareta, Elcoro, Elduayen, Eleicigui, Eleizalde, Eleizamendi, Elejabeitia, Elejalde, Elespuru, Eleta, Elezarriaga, Elezgueta, Elgorriaga, Elguea, Elguera, Elguero, Elgueta, Elguezábal, Elguezúa, Elía, Eliceche, Elicegui, Elío, Eliot, Elizabelar, Elizaga, Elizagaray, Elizalde, Elizondo, Elo, Elola, Elordi, Elordui, Eloregui, Elorio, Elormendi, Elorregui, Elorriaga, Elorrieta, Elorza, Elósegui, Elosidieta, Elosu, Elso, Elusa, Ellaurri, Emaldi, Emanuel, Emasábel, Embil, Embún, Emparán, Ena, Enasteasu, Enatorriaga, Encalada, Encina or Encinas, Enciso, Endara, Endemaño, Endérica, Endueñas, Engarán, Engómez, Enrile, Enríquez, Enseña, Ensuyo, Entenza, Entralgo, Entrambasaguas, Entriago, Enveig, Enveja, Enyego, Epalza, Epelde, Eransus, Erarrizaga, Eraso, Eraustieta, Erbeta, Erbiti, Ercilla, Erdara, Erdoñana, Erdozaín, Eregui, Ereinozaga, Ereinuzqueta, Ereño, Eres, Erice, Eril, Erinazu, Eristín, Eriz, Erlés, Erloeta, Eroles, Erosa, Errazquin, Errazu, Errázuriz, Errea, Erro, Esaín, Esaís, Esaube, Escajadillo, Escalada, Escalante, Escalera, Escales, Escalona, Escalzo, Escama, Escamilla, Escandón, Escanilla, Escaray, Escardó, Escario, Escarit, Escarramad, Escarrer, Escartín, Escauriaza, Escavias, Escayola, Escobal or Escobar, Escobedo, Escofet, Escóiquiz, Escolano, Escoriaza, Escorna, Escornallón, Escorón, Escorza, Escós, Escribano, Escrivá, Escrivá de Romaní, Escudero, Escuer, Escurra, Esguezábal, Eslava, Esles, Esmir, Espada, Espadañedo, Espalter, Espalza, Espantoso, Espanyol, España, Español, Espar, Esparraguera, Espartero, Esparza, Espasa, Espaséns, Espejo, Espel, Esperún, Espés, Espiáu, Espicia, Espiga, Espilla, Espín, Espina, Espinal, Espinel, Espino, Espinosa, Espital, Espleda, Espluga, Esplugas, Espolla, Espronceda, Espuñy, Esqueda, Esquerdo, Esquerrer, Esquier, Esquinas, Esquivel, Esquivias, Estacasolo, Estadé, Estalrich, Estanga, Estanyol, Estaña, Estañol, Estáun, Estéban, Estébanez, Estéibar, Estela, Estelrich, Estella, Esteller, Estenaga, Estenoz, Estensoro, Esteva, Esteve, Estévez, Estoles, Estor, Estorch, Estrada, Estrader, Estramiana, Estramigas, Estruch, Estua, Estúñiga, Estupiñán, Eguí, Eulate, Eume, Eusa, Euza, Eva, Evigui, Exérica, Exerrat, Eyundiano, Eza, Ezabal, Ezcaray, Ezcarte, Ezcay, Ezcurra, Ezgal, Ezmir, Eznariaga, Eznaurriza, Ezpeleta, Ezquerra, Ezquieta, Ezquioga, Eztéibar. End of DHA, Letter E.

F Fabera, Fabián, Fabra, Fábregas, Fábregues, Fabrer, Fabro, Facio, Fachs, Faena, Faes, Fagoaga, Faguez, Fagúndez, Faix, Fajardo, Falas, Falces, Falceto, Falcó, Falcón, Faleba, Falguera, Fallón, Fanlo, Fano, Fantoni,

Fañanás, Fañez, Faquel, Farfán de los Godos, Faria, Fariñas, Farnés, Faura, Fayas, Febrer, Federigui, Feijóo, Felgoso, Felices, Feliu, Feloaga, Fenares, Fenech, Fenollar, Fenollet, Feo, Férez, Fermat, Fernán-Gil, Fernández, Fernández Anleo, Fernández de Astiz, Fernández Bautista, Fernández de Bea, Fernández de Bobadilla, Fernández de Cañete, Fernández Casal, Fernández Casariego, Fernández Castrillón, Fernández de Córdoba, Fernández de Cossío, Fernández del Cueto, Fernández Chicharro, Fernández Daza, Fernández Espartero, Fernández Folguera, Fernández de Granados, Fernández de Granda, Fernández Grandoso, Fernández de Henestrosa, Fernández de Híjar, Fernández de Landa, Fernández de Larrinoa, Fernández de Linares, Fernández de Lorca, Fernández de Luarca, Fernández de Madrigal, Fernández de Magallón, Fernández de Mediavilla, Fernández de Mesa, Fernández de Miranda, Fernández de Mugartegui, Fernández de Muras, Fernández de Navarrete, Fernández Pacheco, Fernández de Peñaranda, Fernández Perdones, Fernández de la Puente, Fernández de la Reguera, Fernández del Río, Rernández Roces, Fernández de Santo Domingo, Fernández del Solar, Fernández Somonte, Fero, Ferollet, Ferra, Ferráez, Ferragut, Ferrán, Ferrandell, Ferrández, Ferrándiz, Ferrando, Ferrant, Ferrara, Ferrari, Ferrater, Ferraz, Ferreira, Ferrer, Ferrera, Ferrero, Ferreró, Ferreros, Ferriol, Férriz, Ferro, Ferrón, Ferroso, Ferruces, Ferrueros, Ferrús, Fidalgo, Fierro, Figueira, Figueras, Figueredo, Figueroa, Figuerola, Figueruela, Filera, Fillol, Fines, Finestre, Fiol, Fitado, Fitero, Fivaller, Flaquer, Flons, Flor, Floreaga, Florencio, Flores or Flórez, Floriategui, Florín, Florit, Flos, Fluviá, Foces, Fogas, Fogassot, Fogaza, Foguet, Foica, Foix, Folcrás, Folch de Cardona, Folchs, Folgóns, Folguer, Foncalada, Foncillas, Foncueva, Fonfría, Fonoll, Fonollar, Fons, Fonseca, Font, Fontalquer, Fontana, Fontaneda, Fontanellas, Fontanet, Fontanets, Fontanillas, Fontarnáu, Fontauret, Fontcuberta, Fonte, Fontecilla, Fontecha, Fontes, Fontrubia, Fonz, Foquet, Foraster, Forcadell, Forcades, Forcas, Forciá, Forés, Forment, Formidero, Forn, Fornari, Fornelos, Forner or Fornels, Fornos, Fornoz, Foronda, Forrado, Fort, Fortón, Fortuny, Fortuño, Foxá, Frago, Fragoso, Fraguas, Franca, Francés, Francia, Franco, Francolí, Franchi, Franqueza, Frasquet, Frau, Fraxanet, Frechel, Frechilla, Frederich, Freijomil, Freire, Freixa, Frella, Frera, Fresneda, Frexa, Frexanet, Frías, Frígola, Frisa, Frólaz, Fromesta, Frómista, Frontín, Frutos, Fuembuena, Fuencirio, Fuenlabrada, Fuenleal, Fuenllana, Fuenmayor, Fuensalida, Fuente, Fuentearmejil, Fuentecilla, Fuentes, Fuentidueña, Fuertes, Fullana, Funes, Furundarena, Fúster. End of DHA, Letter F.

G Gabalí, Gabat, Gabea, Gabert, Gabiño, Gabiola, Gabirondo, Gabriel, Gáceta, Gacias, Gacitúa, Gadeas, Gaínza, Gainzar, Gaitán, Gaizaraín, Gaiztarro, Gajano, Galaín, Galainena, Galán, Galaón or Galalón, Galaquio, Galar, Galardi, Galarie, Galarmendi, Galarraga, Galarreta, Galarza, Galaz, Galbarriatu, Galbarro, Galbarrulí, Galbete, Galcerán, Galdames, Galdeano,

Galdo, Galdocha, Galdona, Galdós, Galeano, Galeote or Galeoto, Galián, Galiana, Galiano, Galicia, Galíndez, Galindo, Galinsola, Galo, Galtero, Galván, Galve, Galves, Gálvez, Gallach, Gallaga, Gallard, Gallardo, Gallart, Gallarza, Gállego, Gallego or Gallegos, Gallifa, Galligo, Gallinato, Galliners, Gallo, Gallón, Galloz, Gama, Gamacho, Gamarra, Gamboa, Gamecho, Gámez or Gámiz, Gamón, Gamoneda, Gana, Ganaberro, Ganca, Ganchaegui, Gand, Gandaberro, Gandala, Gandara, Gandarias, Gandarilla, Gandía, Ganer, Ganesoro, Ganogald, Ganoya, Gante, Ganuza, Gaña, Gaona, Garagarza, Garagorri, Garaiburu, Garaicoa, Garaicoechea, Garaigorta, Garaita, Garardi, Garástegui, Garat, Gárate, Garategui, Garáu, Garavito, Garay, Garayalde, Garayo, Garayzábal, Garaz, Garazatúa, Garbalda, Garbijo, Garbuna, Garburu, Garcés, Garcés de los Fayos, Garcés de Garro, Barcés de Marcilla, Garcés de la Mota, García, García de Alcaraz, García-Arista, García Arrafán, García de Axpe, García Barbón, García de la Barrosa, García de Blanes, García de Burunda, García de Cáceres, García de Camargo, García-Camba, García de Cárdenas, García Carpintero, García de Carranque, García Casielles, García del Castillo, García-Castrís, García de Coaña, García de la Cuesta, García de Cueto, García de Eulate, García Ferreros, García de la Fuente, García-García, García-González, García-Herreros, García Huidobro, García Labarces, García de Lavín, García de Lizasoaín, García de Luera, García de la Llanilla, García-Mesa, García Moreno, García de Ocáriz, García Orovio, García Palacio, García de Paredes, García Peñuela, García de Piedra, García de la Plata, García Puerta, García del Racillo, García-Rigueira, García-Sala, García de Samaniego, García-Sancho, García-Sañudo, García de Segovia, García-Soberón, García de Sobrecasa, García de Toledo, García de Veas, García de la Vega, García de Zúñiga, Garcifuentes, Garcini, Gardoqui, Gardosa, Gareca, Gareza, Garezaybar, Gargallo, Gargollo, Garibay, Garicaza, Garín, Garinoaín, Garisas, Garita, Garitano, Garivell, Garma, Garmendía, Garnica, Garosa, Garóstegui, Garóstidi, Garre, Garret, Garriador, Garrido, Garriga, Garriz, Garro, Garrote, Garrunaga, Garví, Garza or Garzo, Garzón, Gascón, Gasque, Gassia, Gassius, Gassol, Gastañadúy, Gastañiza, Gastea, Gastealzátegui, Gastey, Gastía, Gastón, Gatell, Gática, Gatinara de Legnano, Gato, Gau, Gauca, Gauna, Gavarret, Gaver, Gavilán, Gavilanes, Gavín, Gaviria, Gay, Gaya, Gayán, Gayangos, Gaynna, Gayolá, Gayón, Gayones, Gayoso, Gaytán, Gazo, Gazón, Gazpio, Gaztañaga, Gaztañeta, Gaztelu, Gebalí, Gebelí, Gelabert, Gelcem, Gélida, Gelmírez, Gelpi, Geltrú, Gener, Generés, Genovard, Gentil-Lloch, Gerardina, Germán, Gerona, Geronella, Gerradell, Gesquier, Getino, Giance de Caamaño, Gibert, Giblé, Giginta, Gijón, Gil, Gil de Aponte, Gil de Atienza, Gil de Borja, Gil Cano, Gil de la Cuesta, Gil de Gibaja, Gil Negrete, Gil de Palacio, Gil de la Redonda, Gil de Vivero, Gil de Zúñiga, Gilabert, Gilbarrasa, Gilbert, Gilete, Gili, Gilimón, Giménez, Ginard, Giner, Ginés, Ginestá, Ginovés, Giraldeli, Giráldez, Giraldo, Giralt, Girart, Giráu, Grigós, Girón, Girona, Gironda, Gironella, Gispert, Gleu, Glimes, Goacola, Gobantes, Godínez, Godoy, Goenaga, Goenechea, Goetegui, Goiburu, Goicoa, Goicoechea, Goicoerroeta,

Coicolea, Goicolejea, Goiri, Góiriz, Goitia, Goitisolo, Gojenechea, Gojenola, Goláez, Golar, Golfín, Golpillanes, Gomar, Gombáu, Gomendio, Gomendradi, Gomensoro, Gómez, Gómez de Alba, Gómez de Avellaneda, Gómez de Barreda, Gómez de la Blanca, Gómez de Bonilla, Gómez de la Cortina, Gómez Dávila, Gómez de Espinosa, Gómez LaMadrid, Gómez de Mercado, Gómez de Merodio, Gómez de Ontiveros, Gómez de Pedroso, Gómez del Rivero, Gómez de la Serna, Gómez de Terán, Gómez de la Torre, Gómez de la Vega, Gómez de Villamayor, Gomicio, Gomide, Gomila, Gomis, Gomucio, Góngora, Gonzaga, González, González-Alegre, González de Almunia, González de Andía, González de Argumanes, González de Asarta, González de Avilés, González de la Bárcena, González-Calderón, González del Campillo, González Carbonera, González de Carvajal, González de Castejón, González-Cavada, González-Colloto, González de Cuenia, González de Chacín, González de Echávarri, González de Estéfani, González de las Fraguas, González de Grado, González-Grano de Oro, González de Guezno, González de Jate, González-Llanos, González de Orbón, González de los Palacios, González de la Pezuela, González Pondal, González de Prado, González-Priorio, González-Remusgo, González de los Ríos, González de Santa Cruz, González de Sepúlveda, González de Socueva, González Uzqueta, González del Vado, González del Valle, González de Villa, González Zorrilla, Gonzalo, Gonzalves, Gondar, Goñi, Goosens, Gorbea, Gordejuela, Gordo, Gordoa, Gordón, Gordoncillo, Gorduaz, Gorena, Gorgoa, Gorgojí, Gormaz, Gorocín, Goroneta, Gorosabel, Gorospizcar, Gorostazu, Gorostegui, Gorostiaga, Gorostidi, Gorostiola, Gorostola, Gorostiza, Gorostizu, Gorostorzu, Goroziga, Gorráez, Gorrirán, Gorrite, Gorriti, Gorriz, Gorrizarri, Gorrochátegui, Gort, Gortabarri, Gortaire, Gortairia, Gortari, Gortázar, Gossa, Gotiortúa, Gotor, Gotrano, Govantes, Govea, Goya, Goyanes, Goyara, Goyaz, Goyena, Goyeneche, Goyenechea, Goyeneta, Gozón, Graaf, Gracia, Gradilla, Grado, Gradolí, Graell, Graful, Gragera, Grajal, Grajo, Gralla, Gramajo, Gramunt, Granada, Granado or Granados, Granalosa, Granda, Granell, Graner, Granero, Granollachs, Granollés, Granullás, Granullés, Granyena, Grañón, Gras, Grasa, Grau, Grava, Gravalosa, Gravina, Gray, Gregorio (de), Grest, Grifé, Grijalva, Grilla, Grillet, Grillo, Grima, Grimaldi or Grimaldo, Grimáu, Grimón, Grimosachs, Griño, Griver, Groni, Gros, Groso, Grub, Gruilles, Gruny, Grustan, Guadalajara or Guadalfajara, Guadalix, Guadiana, Guaita, Gual, Gualba, Gualbes, Gualda, Gualsoro, Guallart, Guamis, Guanes, Guanter, Guara, Guardamino, Guardia, Guara, Guardiola, Guarnizo, Guaro, Guarrat, Guart, Guaso, Guasp, Guazo, Guazola, Gubert, Gúdal, Gudiel, Gueba, Guebide, Gueco, Guecho, Guedeja, Guelbas, Güell, Güells, Güemes, Guendica, Guendulaín, Gueráu, Guerbillano, Guercolata, Guereca, Guerendiaín, Guereta, Guerforat, Guergué, Guerguetiaín, Guernica, Guerra, Guerradell, Guerrero, Guerrico, Guetadar, Guetaria, Guevara, Guexar, Guezala, Guezuruaga, Gui, Guiana, Guignard, Guijo, Guil, Guilisasti, Tuiliz, Guiluz, Guilla, Guillamas, Guillemota, Guillen, Guilleuma, Guim, Guimera, Guinart, Guinea, Guini, Guiñazu, Guio, Guiral, Guirao or

Guirarte, Guirior, Guirola, Guisasola, Guisla, Guitarra, Guitart, Guitián, Guitio, Guixart, Guixós, Gulina, Gumiel, Gumucio, Guntín, Gunuz, Guraya, Gurendes, Guridi, Guriezo, Gurmendi, Gurp, Gurpegui, Gurrea, Gurría, Gurrola, Gurruchaga, Gurruchátegui, Guruceta, Gutarrate, Gutiérrez, Gutiérrez de Arce, Gutiérrez de la Barreda, Gutiérrez-Calderón, Gutiérrez de Caviedes, Gutiérrez de Celis, Gutiérrez de la Concha, Gutiérrez de Cossío, Gutiérrez de Gandarilla, Gutiérrez de la Huerta, Gutiérrez de León, Gutiérrez de los Ríos, Gutiérrez del Solar, Guzmán. End of DHA, Letter G.

H Habani, Habantos, Haedo, Hago, Halcón, Hano, Haretche, Haro, Hartos, Haya, Hayos, Héctor del Busto, Hedilla, Helasua, Heles, Helguero, Hemerando, Henales, Henao, Henche, Henestrosa, Henin, Henríquez, Hera or Heras, Herada, Herados, Herboso, Heredia, Herencia, Hereñozu, Hermigas, Hermosa or Hermoso, Hermosilla, Hernández, Hernández de Alba, Hernández del Campo, Hernández de la Iruela, Hernández de Luna, Hernández de Mérida, Hernando, Hernando de Soro, Hernani, Herrada, Herraiz, Herrán, Herrasti, Herrementería, Herrera, Herrerías, Herrero or Herreros, Herreros de Tejada, Herreruelo, Herreta, Herrezuela, Herrezuelo, Hervás, Hervías, Hespital, Hevia, Hidalgo, Hierro, Hiesáis, Higuera or Higueras, Híjar, Hijero, Hilera, Himadas, Hiniesta, Hinojosa, Hipenza, Hipólito, Hita, Hizurún, Hocera, Hoces, Holgado, Holguín, Holviá, Hombau, Homdedéu, Homedes, Homs, Honesto, Honorato, Hontiveros, Honze, Horachita, Horaicoechea, Horazqueta, Horbeña, Horcasitas, Horion, Hormaza, Horna, Hornillos, Horrioldegui, Horroalde, Horta, Hortéu, Hortezuelo, Hortola, Hospital, Hostales, Hostalrich, Hoya, Hoyo, Hoyos, Hoyuela, Hoz, Hozta, Hualde, Huarte, Huelgues, Huelves, Huergo, Huerta, Huete, Huguet, Huici, Huidobro, Huinaguenta, Huirravoso, Humaña, Humara, Humarán, Humeres, Hungría, Hurmenta, Hurtado, Hurtado de Amézaga, Hurtado de Mendoza, Hurtado de Zaldívar, Huyarramendi. End of DHA, Letter H.

I Ibaceta or Ibaeta, Ibaigane, Ibaizábal, Ibaizázal, Ibáñez, Ibáñez de Aedo, Ibáñez de Corvera, Ibáñez de Ibero, Ibáñez de Irrarrázabal, Ibáñez de Lamadrid, Ibáñez de Monreal, Ibáñez de Ocerín, Ibáñez Pacheco, Ibar, Ibarbia, Ibarburen, Ibárburu, Ibares, Ibargüen, Ibarluce, Ibarra, Ibarreta or Ibarrieta, Ibarrola, Ibars de Povil, Ibartola, Ibero, Ibia, Ibiaga, Ibinarri, Ibiricu, Iborra, Ibros, Icart, Icaza, Iceta, Iciar, Icis, Icoaga, Ichaso, Idiáquez, Idiazábal, Ibigoras, Idiolo, Idirín, Idoyaga, Idoyeta, Iduarte, Iduya, Igala, Igaralde, Igartúa, Igarza, Igarzábal, Iglesia or Iglesias, Igoa, Igola, Igor, Iguacel, Iguarán, Igueldo, Iguerabide, Iguereta, Iguríbar, Iguinaga, Iguiñiz, Igusquiza, Ijurieta, Ilarduya, Ilárraza, Ilasa, Ilásaga, Iliberri, Ilorobeitia, Ilúmbe, Ilumberri, Ilurdoz, Iluz, Ilzarbe, Ilzauspea, Illa, Illán or Illanes, Illarradi, Illarramendi, Illarrasu, Illarregui, Illera, Illescas, Imaz, Imbuluzqueta, Imizcoz, Imperial, Inarra, Inclán, Inchaurandieta, Inchausti or Incháustegui, Inda, Indacoechea, Indaneta,

Infantas, Infante, Infanzón, Inglés, Infuanzo, Ingunza, Inistarte, Inoriza, Inoso, Insaurandiaga, Insaurbe, Insaurraga, Insausti, Insiodo, Interiana, Intriago, Inturia, Inurrieta, Inurrigarro, Inurriza, Inza, Inzaurdiaga, Iñarra, Iñigo or Iñiguez, Iñiguez-Abarca, Iñiguez de la Fuente, Iñigo-Ruiz, Ipalategui, Iparraguirre, Ipas, Ipenarrieta, Ipenza or Ipinza, Ipiña, Irabien, Irabigui, Iracusta, Iracheta, Iraeta, Iragorri, Iragorría, Irala, Iramaín, Iranzo, Iraola, Irarraga, Irarraín, Irarramendi, Irarrazábal, Irategui, Irauqui, Iráuregui, Iraurgui or Iraurqui, Irazábal, Irazagorría, Irazazábal, Irazoqui, Irgas, Iriarte, Iribago, Iribar, Iribarne, Iribarren, Iribarrena, Iribe, Iriberri, Iribi, Iribias, Irigay, Irigoyen, Irimo, Irisarri, Irisco or Iriso, Irizar, Iriztaín, Irles, Irogazte, Iros, Iruegas, Iruela, Irueta, Iruín, Irulegui, Iruleta, Irumberri, Irún, Irujo, Iruña, Iruñela, Irureta, Irurozqui, Irurtia, Irusta, Iruzbieta, Isarbiribil, Isárraga, Isarre, Isasa, Isásaga, Isasbiril, Isasi, Isasola, Isasti, Isaundariaga, Isaza, Isequilla, Isern, Iserna, Isla, Islaba, Istillartea, Istueta, Istúriz, Isturizaga, Isundegui, Isunza, Isurieta, Isusi, Isusorbe, Isusquiza, Ituño, Iturbe, Iturberoaga, Itúrbide, Itúrburu, Ituren, Iturmendi, Iturralde, Iturrao, Iturrarán, Iturraspe, Iturrate, Iturrebaso, Iturregui, Iturren, Iturri, Iturriaga, Iturrieta, Iturrigaray, Iturriospe, Iturrioz, Iturrista, Iturriza, Iza, Izaga, Izaguirre, Izal, Izarraín, Izaza, Izcáriz, Izco, Izis, Izmendi, Izoaga, Izquierdo, Iztueta, Izu, Izutarregui. End of DHA, Letter I.

J Jabaloyas, Jabare, Jabariz, Jabat, Jaca, Jaces, Jacob, Jacoisti, Jácome, Jado, Jaén, Jaime, Jafer, Jalón, Jalpí, Jamar, Janariz, Jandátegui, Janer, Janiz, Januas, Jaolaza, Jaques, Jara, Jaraba, Jarabeitia, Jaramillo, Jaraquemada, Jardín, Jasa, Jaso, Jaspe, Jasu, Jáudenes, Jaumar, Jaume, Jaunes, Jaureaga, Jáuregui, Jaureguibarría, Jaureguiondo, Jaureguízar, Jaureguizarra, Jaureguizuría, Jaurizar, Jaurola, Jaurrieta, Javat, Javier, Jelpí, Jenis, Jerez, Jérica, Jibaja, Jijón, Jiménez, Jiménez de Almodóvar, Jiménez de Allo, Jiménez de Andosilla, Jiménez de Bagüés, Jiménez de Bohorques, Jiménez de Cascante, Jiménez de los Cobos, Jiménez de Embrún, Jiménez de Enciso, Jiménez de la Fontaza, Jiménez de Fontoba, Jiménez de Góngora, Jiménez de Lierta, Jiménez del Moral, Jiménez de Murillo, Jiménez-Navarro, Jiménez de San Juan, Jimeno, Jironda, Joanín, Joara, Joaristi, Jober, Jódar, Jodra, Jofré, Jofré de Loaisa, Jolit, Jones, Jorada, Jorba, Jordá, Jordán, Jordán de Urríes, Jordi, Jorondorena, Jorrano, Josá, Joso, Jou, Joval, Jove, Jovel, Jovellanos, Jover, Juan, Juanes, Juániz, Juanmartinena, Juansoro, Juara, Juarbe, Juárez, Juaristi, Jubarte, Jubero, Júdez, Juhún, Juliá, Jultrú, Jullá, Jumilla, Junco, Junquera, Junquito, Junta, Junterón, Junyet, Jurado, Jurdanarena, Juséu, Juste, Justicia, Justiniani, Justiz, Jusué, Jutge, Juyá. End of DHA, Letter J.

L AND **LL** Labadía, Labanda, Labandera, Labandero, Labania, La Barreda, La Barrera, Labastida, Labata, Labayru, Labeaza, Labetz, Labiá, Labiaga, Labiano, Labora, Laborda, Labra, Labraña,

Labrit, Labueche, Laca, La-Cadena, Lacambra, Lácar, Lacarra, Lacaruza, Lacenty, Lacera, La Cerda, Laciana, Lacoizqueta, Lacoma, Lacunza, Ladornosa, Ladra, Ladró, Ladrón, Ladrón de Guevara, Laffite, Lafita, La Fuente, Lago, Lagos, Lagraba, Laguanaz, Laguarta, Laguaya, Laguna, Laharra, Laínez, Laiseca, Laisequilla, Lalaing, La-Lastra, Lama, Lamadrid, Lamamié de Clairac, Lamariano, Lamarque de Novoa, Lamas, Lamata, Lamela, Lamo, Lana, Lanaberri, Lanaja, Lanareja, Lanciego, Landa, Landaberea, Landaberro, Landaburu, Landacur, Landaeta, Landagorrieta, Landaluce, Landamela, Landaverde, Landázuri, Landecho, Landellés, Landeras, Landeta, Lando, Langarica, Langarza, Langlés, Lanoguera, Lantadilla, Lantoira, Lanuza, Lanz, Lanza, Lanzaeta, Lanzol de Romaní, Lanzón, Lanzós, Lapaza, Lapeña, Lapezuela, Lapicea, Lapido, Lapieza, Laplana, LaPorta, Lapurdi, Lara, Laracho, Larán, Lararguren, Larburu, Lardizábal, Laredo, Larena, Largacha, Lariz, Larozqui, Larra, Larrabía, Larrabide, Larraca, Larracea, Larracoechea, Larrachea, Larrad, Larraga, Larragoiti, Larragoyen, Larraguibel, Larraín, Larraingoa, Larrainzar, Larraisoaña, Larraiz, Larrambere, Larramendi, Larramendía, Larrandi, Larrangoz, Larrañaga, Larraón, Larraondo, Larrar, Larrasa, Larraspuru, Larrátegui, Larrauri, Larrauz, Larraya, Larrayoz, Larrazábal, Larrazuri, Larrea, Larreandi, Larreátegui, Larreche, Larreguiandía, Larrerdi, Larreta, Larriba, Larrimpe, Larrina, Larrínaga, Larrinoa, Larrión, Larrondo, Larrondobuno, Larrosa, Larrúa, Larrumbe, Larrúmbide, Lartitegui, Lartundo, Larumbe or Larrumbe, Larzábal, Larzacea, Larzanguren, Lasa, Lasaeta, Lasaga, Lasala, Lasalde, Lasao, Lasarte, Lascamburu, Lascoaín, Lascoiti, Lascortes, Lascorz, Laserna, Lasiaín, Lasierra, Laso de la Vega, Lasquetti, Lasquíbar, Lastanosa, Lastarría, Lasteros, Lastiarro, Lastra, Lastres, Lastur, Lasuén, Lasuín, Latado, Latalu, Lataoíz, Latarza, Latasa, Latejera, Latenda, Latorre, Lauquiniz, Laurán, Laurencín, Laurgaín, Lauria, Laurnaga, Laurreguiuondo, Lausagarreta, Lavandeira, Lavandera, Lavalle, Lavecilla, Laviesca, Lavín, Laya, Layosa, Lázaro, Lazarra, Lazárraga, Lazcaiba, Lazcano, Lazoaín, Lazón, Lazquibar, Leaeche, Leaegui, Leal, Learreta, Leazgui, Lebrón, Lecanduri, Lecaros, Lecca, Lecea, Lécera, Leceta, Lecina, Lecoándiz, Lecumberri, Lecundis, Lecuona, Lechuga, Ledesma, Ledínez, Ledos, Legarda, Legaria, Legarra, Legarrasúa or Legarreta, Legarza, Legasa, Legazpi, Legorburu, Legorreta, Legoyaga, Leguía, Leguina, Leguizamón, Leici, Leiguarda, Leis, Leiva, Leiza, Leizaola, Lejarazu, Lejarza, Lejo, Lema, Lemaur, Lemona, Lemonia, Lemos, Lena, Léniz, Lentisclá, Lentisco, Lentón, Lentorn, Lenzol, León, Leonarte, Leoníquez, Leorentén, Leoz, Lepizamo, Lepuzaín, Lequedano, Lequeitio, Lequerica, Leraza, Lercara, Lerchundi, Lereche, Lerés, Lerín, Lerinena, Lerma, Lerruz, Lersundi, Leruela, Lesaca, Leste, Lete, Letona, Leturia, Leturiondo, Leyún, Lezabaleta, Lezaeta, Lezalde, Lezama, Lezana, Lezaún, Lezcano, Lezica, Lezo, Liana, Liarza, Líbano, Libarona, Liceaga, Licergárate, Licona, Licordi, Licht, Lidueña, Liébana, Liédena, Liegui, Lienda, Liermo, Lilet, Lili, Lillo, Lima, Limbéu, Limes, Limós, Limpias, Linares, Lincolne, Linde, Lingán, Liniers, Liñán, Liñas,

Liñieta, Lío, Liorca, Liori, Liquicio, Lira, Lisa, Lisalde, Lisasoaín, Lisón, Litago, Lizana, Lizarago, Lizarazu, Lizardi, Lizardo, Lizargárate, Lizárraga, Lizarralde, Lizarraraz, Lizarriturri, Lizarzaburu, Lizaso, Lizasoaín, Lizatu, Lizaur, Lizcaga, Lizoaín, Lizola, Loaces, Loaisa, Loarte, Lobato, Lobatón, Lobello, Lobera, Lobet, Lobiano, Lobo, Locaña, Loci, Lodeña, Lodosa, Lográn, Loidi, Loigorri, Loina, Loinaz, Loiti, Loizaga, Lombana, Lombardía, Lombera, Lomelín, Lonarte, Londaiz, Londoño, Longa, Longoria, Loperana, Lopetedi, Lopegegui, López, Lopéz de Aberásturi, López de Alcántara, López de Ansó, López de los Arcos, López de la Arena, López de Ayala, López-Ballesteros, López-Barthe, López de Baylo, López de Camarena, López de Cancela, López de Cangas, López de Carracedo, López de Carrizosa, López de Casal, López de Casbas, López del Castillo, López de Ecala, López de Estaún, López de Fanlo, López de la Flor, López-Fernández de Heredia, López de Gomarra, López Guerrero, López de Haro, López de Letona, López-Marcote, López de Mendizábal, López de Montemayor, López de Morales, López de Morla, López-Mostacero, López-Negreros, López-Paredes, López-Pedruel, López de la Peña, López de Recalde, López de Reta, López de Rivero, López de Salcedo, López de Sobás, López de Soria, López de Valdelvira, López de Vinuesa, López de Viñas, López de Zárate, Lora, Lorca, Lordat, Lorde, Lordoro, Loredo, Lorencio, Lorenz, Lorenzana, Lorenzo, Lorero, Lorés, Loret, Loria, Loriega, Loriga, Loris, Lorit, Lorite, Loroño, Losa, Losada, Loscertales, Loscós, Losilla, Loureiro, Loya, Loyo, Loyola, Lozano, Luaces, Luango, Luarca, Lubet, Lubiano, Lucas, Lucena, Lucerga, Lucero, Lucia Lucio, Luco, Luchas, Ludeña, Lué, Luébana, Luengas, Luera, Luertos, Lugariz, Lugo, Lugón, Lugones, Luis, Luján, Lumbier, Lumbreras, Luna, Lunell, Luno, Lupiá, Luque, Luqui, Luquín, Lusagasti, Luscando, Lusia, Luso, Lustiz, Lutago, Luyando, Luzán, Luzardo, Luzón, Luzurriaga. End of DHA, Letter L.

Llabiá, Llabrés, Llácer, Llach, Lladernosa, Llado, Llagostera, Llaguno, Llama, Llamas, Llamazares, Llambias, Llamós, Llamosas, Llana, Llanarreal, Llanas, Llandera, Llanderal, Llaneras, Llanes, Llano, Llanol, Llanos, Llanosos, Llantada, Llanza, Llapada, Llapisera, Llar, Llares, Llasera, Llauder, Llaudes, Llave, Llenes, Llentes, Llera, Llerana, Llers, Lleu, Llicarza, Llinares, Llinás, Lliori, Llivia, Llobató, Llobera, Llobes, Llobet, Llobregat, Llombart, Llompard, Llona, Llop, Llopis, Llor, Llorach, Llordá, Llordat, Lloreda, Lloréns, Llorente, Lloret, Lloris, Lloselles, Llucas, Lluch, Lluis, Llull, Llunas, Llupiá, Llusa. End of DHA, Letter LL.

M Macaiziola, Macaya, MacCrohom, Maceda, Macedo, Maceira, Maceta, Macías, Maciel, Macip, Mackenna, MacMahón, Macquenna, Macuso, Mach, Machado, Machaín, Machín, Machinena, Machón, Machuca, Madaleno, Madán, Madariaga, Madera, Maderazo, Madero, Maderuelo,

Madina, Madinabeitia, Madinagoicoa, Madinagoitia, Madrazo, Madriaza, Madrid, Madrigal, Madroño, Madueño, Maeda, Maestre, Maeztu, Magadán, Magallanes, Magallón, Magán, Magaña, Magara, Magariños, Magarola, Magarzo, Magastre, Magdaleno, Maguña, Mahiques, Mahull, Maigadán, Maillar, Maimo, Maimón, Maiquez, Maíz, Maiztegui, Malacara, Malany, Malars, Malatesta, Malaver, Malcuarto, Malda, Maldonado, Malendrich, Maleo, Maler, Malet, Malferit, Maliá, Maliaño, Malo, Malón, Malonda, Malpica, Malrich, Maluenda, Malzán, Malla, Mallavia, Mallea, Mallén, Mallendrueda, Malleza, Mallo, Mallol, Mancebo, Mancisidor, Mancha, Mancho, Manchola, Mandabil, Mandaca, Mandia, Mandieses, Mandiola, Manegat, Manent, Manera, Manero, Manero de Seoane, Manglano, Manjón, Manlléu, Mannig, Manolla, Manosalbas, Manresa, Manríque and Manríque de Lara, Mansa, Mansilla, Manso, Manso de Andrade, Manso de Velasco, Manso de Zúñiga, Mantecón, Manterola, Mantilla, Mantua, Manuel, Manurga, Manyalich, Manzanares, Manzanedo, Manzano, Mañara, Mañariturriaga, Mañeru, Mañozca, Mañueco, Mao, Maortua, Maquibar, Marabel, Marabí, Marañón, Marañosa, Marata, Marbán, Marcé or Marcel, Marcén, Marcer, Marcilla, Marco, Marcó or Marcos, Marcote, Marcuello, Marcus, March, Marchán, Marchao, Mardaras, Marentes, Margalés, Margarit, Margéns, Marí, Mariaca, Mariana, Mariátegui, Maribona, Marica, Marichalar, Marielus, Marimón, Marín, Marinas or Mariñas, Mariño or Mariños, Mariqueta, Marís, Mariscal, Marizo, Mariztegui, Marlés, Marmol, Marmolejo, Maroja, Marola, Maroto, Marpí, Marqués, Marquesa, Marquet, Marquez, Marquez de la Plata, Marquez de Prado, Marquiegui, Marquillos, Marquina, Marra, Marraco, Marrades, Marrón, Marroquín, Mars, Marsá, Marsal, Marsell, Marser, Marta, Martel, Martell, Martí, Martiánez, Martiarena, Martiarto, Martibaso, Marticorena, Martín, Martín-Albarrán, Martín de Cezalia, Martín-Crespo, Martín de Don Benito, Martín-Montanero, Martín de la Parra, Martín-Ponce, Martinet, Martínez, Martínez de Arellano, Martínez de Arízala, Martínez de Armeñanzas, Martínez de Aspurz, Martínez de las Balsas, Martínez Baños, Martínez de Cabredo, Martínez-Campos, Martínez-Carlón, Martínez de Cortabarría, Martínez de Checa, Martínez de Elizalde, Martínez-Fortún, Martínez de Galinsoga, Martínez-García, Martínez de Goñativia, Martínez de Gorriti, Martínez de Ilarduya, Martínez de Marcilla, Martínez de Maturana, Martínez de Medinilla, Martínez de Pinillos, Martínez de Pisón, Martínez de la Quintana, Martínez de Rozas, Martínez-Salazar, Martínez de Soto, Martínez de Vera, Martínez del Villar, Martínez de Zalduendo, Martino, Martón, Martorell, Martos, Marulli, Maruri, Marza, Marzana, Marzo, Marzoa, Mas, Masa, Masaguer, Masana, Masanellas, Masanet, Mascaba, Mascarell, Mascareñas, Mascaró, Mascarúa, Mascó, Masdovellas, Masegosa, Masferrer, Masó, Maspe, Masquefa, Masquiarán, Massenlli, Massiéu, Massó or Massot, Masucariola, Mata, Matalobos, Matallana, Matamala, Matamí, Matamoros, Matanza, Mataplana, Mataredona, Mataró, Matarrón, Matas, Matauco, Mate, Mateo, Mateos, Matéu, or Mathéu, Materiaín, Matienzo, Matilla, Matines,

Mato, Matos, Matoses, Maturana, Matute, Maubía, Mauleón, Maull, Maurich, Maxáns, Maxella, May, Maya, Mayá, Mayáns, Mayén, Maymó, Maynar, Mayo, Mayol, Mayone, Mayor, Mayora, Mayoralgo, Mayorga, Maza, Maza de Lizana, Mazal, Mazariegos, Mazarizqueta, Mazarrasa, Masarredo, Mazas, Mazatorcosa, Mazcayano, Mazmela, Mazo, Mazón, Mazorra, Mazparauta, Mazparrat, Mazquiarán, Mazueco, Mazuelas, Mazuelo, Mea, Meabe, Meacaup, Meacher, Meade, Meana, Meaza, Meca, Meceta, Mecina, Mecolalde, Medel, Mediana, Medianilla, Mediano, Mediaras, Mediavilla, Medina, Medinilla, Medinyá, Mediona, Medranda, Medrano, Meinteneyen, Meira, Méiztegui, Mejía, Melada, Melaní, Melchor, Meléndez, Melero, Melgar, Melgarejo, Meliá, Melianta, Melicua, Melida, Melio, Melo or Mello, Mella, Mellado, Melludi, Mena, Menacho, Menárguez, Menaure, Menaute, Mencauz, Mencia, Mencos, Menchaca, Mendalde, Mendaña, Mendarichaga, Mendarozqueta, Mendeja, Méndez, Méndez de Sotomayor, Méndez de Vigo, Mendezona, Mendi, Mendía, Mendiarechaga, Mendibe, Mendibelzúa, Mendiburo, Mendicoa, Mendichueta, Mendieta, Mendigoitia, Mendigorría, Mendiguchía, Mendiguren, Mendinueta, Mendiola, Mendiondo, Mendiroz, Menditivar, Mendívil, Mendizábal, Mendo, Mendocino, Mendoza, Mendracabeitia, Menéndez, Meneses, Mengot, Menocal, Menoyo, Mensa, Menso, Meñaca, Meoz, Mera, Meras, Mercader, Mercadillo, Mercado, Mercaida, Mercer, Merchante, Merdaroz, Merelo, Mergelina, Merica, Merino, Meriorena, Mérita, Merlo, Merodio, Merola, Merquelín, Merrua-Artadi, Merry, Meruelo, Mesa, Mesares, Mescua, Mesía, Mesonero, Mesones, Mesperuza, Mesquida, Mesquita, Messía, Metauten, Metelín, Metella, Metje, Meyá, Meyreles, Mezquia, Mezquita, Michelena, Micheo, Miedes, Mier, Miera, Mieres, Miertral, Miguel, Miguel-Romero, Miguelena, Míguez, Mijares, Milá or Milán, Milagro, Milán de Aragón, Milanés, Miláns, Milany, Milara, Milazo, Milicua, Militano, Milsocós, Milla, Millán, Millars, Millia, Milludi, Mimena, Mina, Minayo, Minceta, Mingrano, Minguela, Minguell, Mínguez, Minondo, Mintezar, Minuarte, Minzo, Miñano, Miñer, Miño, Mioño, Miota, Miquell, Miquelena, Miquelestegui, Mir, Mira, Mirabal, Miraballo, Miracastell, Miracle, Miradán, Mirafuentes, Miralcamp, Miralles, Miramiña, Miramón, Miramonte, Miranda, Mirandola, Mirasierra, Miravall, Miravalles, Miravete, Mirez, Miró, Mirón, Mironés, Mirubia, Misa, Mitarte, Mizquia, Mocorrea, Mocozuaín, Moctezuma, Mochedano, Modaguer, Moge, Mogollón, Mogrovejo, Moix, Moja, Mojategui, Mójica, Mojón, Mola, Moldes, Molera, Molero, Moles, Molí, Molina, Molinar, Molinas, Molinedo, Moliner, Molinero, Molines, Molinet, Molino, Molíns, Molinuevo, Molner, Molón, Moll, Molla, Molleda, Molledo, Mollet, Mollinedo, Mompaláu, Mompaón, Mon, Monabe, Monach, Monasterio, Monasteriobide, Moncada, Moncayo, Monclares, Monclús, Moncorp, Mondó, Mondona, Mondoñedo, Mondragón, Moneba, Moneguerra, Monella, Monells, Moner, Monesma, Monforte, Mongado, Moní, Monistrol, Moniz, Monje, Monjo, Monlleo, Monller, Monmacip, Monoay, Monreal, Monredó, Monrodón, Monroy, Monsalve, Monseo, Monserrat,

Monsó, Monsolíu, Monsonis, Monsoríu, Monsuar, Montados, Montagud, Montagut or Monteagudo, Montalbán, Montalt, Montalvo, Montaner, Montaniés, Montano, Montanyana, Montanyas, Montanyón, Montaña, Montañá, Montañana, Montañáns, Montañés, Montañez, Montaño, Montaot, Montargull, Montblanch, Montbrió, Montbrú, Montbúy, Montclar, Monte, Monteagudo, Montealegre, Montealto, Montecillo, Montehano, Montehermoso, Montejo, Montells, Montemayor, Montenegro, Monter, Monterde, Monternes, Montero, Montero de Espinosa, Monterroso, Montes, Montes de Oca, Montesa, Montescot, Montesinos, Monteverde, Montfá, Montfalcó, Montgay, Montgrí, Montgríu, Monti, Montiano, Montijo, Montilla, Montis, Montjuich, Montlleó, Montmacip, Montmany, Montmorency, Montnegre, Montojo, Montolíu, Montoris, Montornés, Montoro, Montoto, Montoya, Montpalat, Montpaller, Montreal, Montrodón, Montrós, Montsuaderino, Montúfar, Montull, Monzón, Moñino, Moore, Mora, Moradell, Moragas, Moragues, Moral, Maraleda, Morales, Morán, Morana, Morandáis, Morano, Moranta, Morante, Morata, Moratalla, Morato, Morató, Moraza, Morcillo, Moreda, Moredo, Moreira, Morejón, Morel, Morell, Moreno, Moreno de Guerra, Morentín, Morer, Morera, Moreta, Morey, Morga, Morgadell, Morgán, Mori or Moris, Moriana, Moriano, Morillas, Morillo, Moriones, Moris, Morla, Morlá, Morlán, Moro, Morocea, Morodo, Morote, Morozúa, Morquecho, Morrás, Morro, Morso, Mortera, Moscoso, Moset, Mosiños, Mosquera, Mostacero, Mota (de la), Motila or Motilla, Motrico, Moura, Mourelle, Mouse, Mouta, Movellán, Mox, Moxa, Moxiga, Moxó, Moya, Moyá, Moyúa, Mozo, Múa, Muazo, Mucharaces, Mudarra, Mudate, Muela, Muelas, Muez, Muga, Mugabru, Mugaburu, Mugarrieta, Mugártegui, Mugarza, Múgica, Mugraza, Muguera, Muguerza, Muguiro, Muguruza, Muher, Muigutia, Mújica, Mula, Mulegui, Mulet, Mulner, Mun, Munar, Munarizqueta, Munárriz, Muncharaz, Mundate, Munguía, Munguilán, Muniáin, Munibe, Muniós, Munir, Munita, Munuera, Muñatones, Muñíz, Muñón, Muñoz, Muñoz de Loaysa, Muñoz-Serrano, Mur, Murba, Murbiedro, Murcia, Murell, Murena, Muret, Murga, Murguerio, Murguía, Murguialday, Murgutio, Murieda, Muriel, Murillas, Murillo, Muriones, Muro, Muros, Murphi, Murua, Murueta, Murugarren, Muruzábal, Musaurrieta, Muscot, Mut, Mutiola, Muza, Muzábal, Muzol, Múzquiz. End of DHA, Letter M.

N Nabagochea, Nabardun, Nabares, Nabarlaz, Nablerua, Nadal, Naera or Naeza, Nafarrasagasti, Nafarrondo, Nagrell, Naja, Nalón, Nanclares, Nanclares de Alba, Napier, Naranco, Narbaiza, Narbaja, Narbat, Narbona, Nardillero, Nardiz, Narejo, Narriondo, Narváez, Narvaiza, Narvaja, Narvate, Nasarre, Naspleda, Nateira or Nateiro, Natera, Nates, Nava, Navailles, Navajas, Navajas de Barrenengoa, Naval, Navaldún, Navarlanz, Navarra, Navarrete, Navarro, Navarro-Balboa, Navarro de Vereterra, Navarrolas, Navas, Navascués, Navat, Navata, Navaz, Naveda, Navel, Naverán, Navés, Navia,

Naya, Nebedra, Nebel, Nebot, Nebreda, Necochea, Necolalde, Nedín, Negorta, Negra, Negrales, Negreiros, Negrell, Negreta, Negrete, Negri, Negrilla, Negrillo, Negrón or Negrona, Negroto, Neira, Nembra, Nepoto, Net, Neta, Neurba, Nevado, Nevares, Neve, Neyra, Nibeiro, Nicolás, Nicoláu, Nicuesa, Niedos, Nieto, Nieva, Nieves-Ravelo, Nin, Ninot, Niño, Niño de Castro, Nipiser, Noaín, Nobas, Noblecia, Nobleza, Nocaleda, Noceda, Noceta, Nochebuena, Nodal, Noé, Noel de Izarra, Nofre, Nofuentes, Nogales, Nograro, Nogueira, Noguer, Noguera, Noguerol, Noguerola, Nogués, Nola, Nomas, Noreña, Noriega, Normante, Normile, Noroña, Norueba, Norzagaray, Noseta, Notario, Novaes, Novajas del Valle, Novar, Novell, Novés, Novia, Novoa, Noya, Noyán, Noyers, Nuébalos, Nuevas, Nuez, Nuezo, Nuncibay, Nunques, Núñez, Núñez de Avila, Núñez de Bobadilla, Núñez de Prado. End of DHA, Letter N.

O Oa, Oar, Oárriz, Obada, Obaldía, Obalín, Obando, Obanes, Obanos, Obeso, Obiano, Obicho, Obierna, Obineta, Oblites, Obrador, Obregón, O'Brian, Oca, Ocadiz, Ocaeta, Ocalcís, Ocampo, Ocan, Ocaña, Ocarandi, Ocaranza, Ocariz, Ocariz-Gorostitegui, O'Caroll, Ocáus, Ocejo, Ocello, Ocerea, Ocerín, Oceta, Ocio, Oclóriz, O'Collo, Ocón, O'Connor, Ochadiz, Ochandátegui, Ocandiano, Ochando, Ochaniz, Ocaran, Ocharcoaga, Ocharcoasa, Ochayeta, Ochoa, Ochoa de Aedo, Ochoa de Alda, Ochoa de Lejalde, Ochoa de Noaín, Ochoarena, Ochoarín, Ochobi, Ochoteco, Ochotorena, O'Daly, Odena, Odériz, Odiaga, Odón, O'Donnell, O'Donojú, Odriozola, Oechabera, O'Farrill, Ogate, Ogáyar, Ogazón, Ogier, Oido, Oig, Oiquina, Ojabí, Ojacastro, Ojea, Ojeda, Ojinaga, Ojirondo, Ojocasto, Ojuelos, Ola, Olábarri, Olabarría, Olabarriaga, Olabarrieta, Olabarriyerro, Olabe, Olabelarrinaga, Olabuénaga, Olaciregui, Olacueta, Olaechea, Olaegui, Olaerreta, Olaeta, Olagorta, Olagüe, Olaiz, Olaizola, Olalde, Olalquiaga, Olalla, Olamendi, Olanda, Olano, Olanotegui, Olañeta, Olaondo, Olaraga, Olaran, Olariaga, Olariena, Olariene, Olarieta, Olarra, Olarría, Olarriaga, Olarte, Olasa, Olasagasti, Olasarri, Olascoaga, Olaso, Olastre, Olavide, O'Lawlor, Olaza, Olazábal, Olazarán, Olazarra, Olazarraga, Olcina, Olcinellas, Olcoz, Olea, Oleaga, Olejo, Oleta, Oleza, Olguín, Olías, Olibarri, Olid, Oliden, Oliet, Olit, Olite, Olius, Oliva, Oliván, Olivar, Olivares, Olivart, Olivas, Oliveira, Olivella, Oliver, Olivera, Olives, Olivito, Olivó, Oliz, Olmedilla, Olmedo, Olmella, Olmera, Olmo, Olms, Oloa, Olodio, Olondris, Olorda, Olóriz, Oloroz, Olózaga, Olset, Olucor, Oluja, Olvera, Olvías, Olzamendi, Olzo, Ollacarisqueta, Ollarra, Ollauri, Ollavesa, Oller, Olleta, Ollo, Olloqui, Omaña, Omar, Omazur, Ombáu, Omeda, Omedes, Ompes, Oms, Oncejo, Oncina, Oncinellas, Onchoca, Ondalde, Ondarra, Ondarza, Ondegardo, Ondiz, Ondovilla, O'Neill, Ones, Ongastigue, Ongay, Onís, Onofre, Onsoño, Ontañón, Onzono, Oña, Oñate, Oñativia, Oñaz, Oñederra, Oñez, Oñiz, Oñoro, Opácoa, Oquendo, Oquina, Oquiza, Oráa, Orantes, Orbaneja, Orbata, Orbe, Orbea,

Orbegozo, Orbejón, Orbezu, Orbilla, Orbolancha, Orbutelu, Orcarís, Orcasitas, Orcáu, Orcazaguirre, Orcoyen, Orda, Ordanes, Ordás, Orden or Ordenes, Ordeñana, Orderica, Ordes, Ordi, Ordiales, Ordines, Ordis, Ordoñana, Ordóñez, Ordorica, Orduña, Orea, Oredaín, Oregar, Oreiro, Orejón, Orell, Orellana, Orendaín, Orense, Oreña, Ores, O'Reylli, Orfila, Orgaste, Orguibel, Oria, Oríbar, Oribe, Origán, Origlia, Origó, Origuen, Orihuela, Orila, Oriol or Oriola, Orion, Oris, Orisoáin, Orita, Oriz, Orizmendi, Orlandis, Ormachea, Ormaechea, Ormáiztegui, Ormat, Ormaza, Ormazas, Orna, Ornelas, Ornós, Oro, Orobeztulu, Orobio, Orolles, Orón, Oronoz, Oronzúa, Oroño, Oroquieta, Ororbia, Oros or Orosa, Oroz, Orozbetelu, Orozco, Orozqueta, Orquecio or Orquizo, Orrigar, Orriola, Orriols, Orrius, Orruño, Ors, Orta, Ortafa, Ortal, Ortaza, Ortedia, Ortega, Orteiza, Ortells, Ortés, Ortéu, Ortigas, Ortigó, Ortigosa, Ortigues, Ortín, Ortis, Ortíz, Ortiz de Cueto, Ortiz de Igoróin, Ortiz de Largacha, Ortiz de Taranco, Ortiz de Villa, Ortiz de Zúñiga, Ortiza, Ortolá, Ortolano, Ortosa, Ortubia, Ortuñez, Ortúñez, Ortuño, Ortuzar, Ortuzausgesti, Ortuzaustegui, Orúe, Orueta, Oruna or Oruña, Orus, Orutia, Orveta, O'Ryan, Osa, Osado, Osandola, Osares, Osay, Oscáriz, Osera, Osés, Oset or Osete, Osinaga, Osma, Oso, Osoarín, Osorio, Osorno, Ospina, Osset, Ossó, Ostabat, Ostalaza, Ostavaers, Ostolaza, Ostoles, Osuelgaray, Osuna, Otadui, Otaegui, Otago, Otal, Otálora, Otamendi, Otáñez, Otarola, Otazábal, Otazo, Oteiza, Otero, Oto, Ovalle, Ovando, Ovejas, Ovejero, Ovellar, Oviedo, Owens, Oya, Oyabren, Oyanederra, Oyanguren, Oyanune, Oyarate, Oyarbide, Oyarzábal, Oyarzo, Oyarzun, Oyascun, Ozaeta, Ozcorta, Ozerea, Ozores, Ozticaín, Oztúburu. End of DHA, Letter O.

P Pacho, Pachón, Padellas, Padilla, Padró, Padrón, Padura, Páez, Pagadi, Pagán, Paganeras, Pagazartundúa, Pagazaurtundúa, Pagés, Pagoaga, Pagola, Paguera, Pahissa, Pairó, Paisal, Pajaza, Paje, Palacals, Palacio, Palacios, Palacios de Moro, Palafox, Palafrugell, Palandarias, Palao, Paláu, Paláu-Sabardera, Paláu-Sarroca, Palavicini or Palavicino, Palaya, Palazol, Palazuelos, Paleci, Palencia, Palenzuela, Palicer, Paliza, Palma or Palmas, Palmeiro, Palmela, Palmer, Palmerola, Palol, Palomar or Palomares, Palomeque, Palomero, Palomino, Palomo, Palón, Palóu, Pall, Palladas, Pallars or Pallarés, Pallas, Pallás, Palleja, Palles, Pambley, Pamones, Pamos, Pancirdo, Pancorbo, Pando, Pandone, Panés, Paniagua, Panicer, Pano, Panone, Pantaleón, Pantoja, Pañelles, Papilla, Papiol, Para, Parada, Paradinas, Paraíso, Páramo, Páramo de la Focella, Paraquieres, Paratge, Paravia, Parcel, Parcero, Pardabes, Pardebe, Pardelana, Pardiñas, Pardo, Pardo de la Casta, Pardo de Cela, Pardo de las Marinas, Paredes, Pareja or Parejo, Parets, Parga, Paris, Pariza, Parma, Parra (de la), Párraga, Párragues, Parrales, Parrará, Parrella, Parreño, Parrilla, Partearroyo, Partidores, Partiella, Pasamonte, Pasarón, Pascual, Pasillas, Pasquier, Pastor, Pastors, Pastrana, Pastrío, Patalines, Patáu, Patelín, Paternoy, Patia, Patiño, Pato, Patón, Patulino, Patus, Pau, Paul, Paulazas, Paules, Paulín,

Pavía, Pavó, Pavón, Pax, Payá, Payán, Payo, Payró, Payua, Payueta, Paz, Pazos, Pebernat, Pech or Pecha, Pedrajas, Pedrarias, Pedraza, Pedredo, Pedregal, Pedreguera, Pedriñán, Pedro, Pedrola, Pedrolo, Pedrosa, Pedroso, Pedruja, Pegado, Peguera, Peijo, Peijoto, Peinado, Peiró, Peirón, Peirona, Peláez, Pelat, Pelayo, Pelegrí, Pelegrín or Pelegriz, Peludo, Pellicer, Pelliser, Penagos, Pences, Pendes, Penela, Penella, Penia, Penilla, Penlos, Penyafort, Penyaroja, Peña, Peña-Aguilera, Peñacastil, Peñafiel, Peñalosa, Peñalver, Peñaranda, Peñarroja, Peñate, Peñuela, Peón, Pequera, Pera, Peraesteve, Perafeta, Perafita, Peral, Peralada, Peraleda, Peraleja, Perales, Peralta, Peramán, Peramás, Peramatos, Peramola, Peranensa, Peranríquez, Perapertusa, Perapertuya, Perarnáu, Peras, Perastortas, Peratallada, Peraza, Percástegui, Perdigón, Perdones, Perea, Pereceira, Pereces, Pereda or Peredo, Perelada, Perelli, Perelló, Perellón, Perellós, Perepertusa, Perera, Péres, Perestrelo, Peretó, Pereyra, Pérez, Pérez de Adana, Pérez de Albéniz, Pérez de Almazán, Pérez de Andián, Pérez-Antolínez, Pérez de Ariz, Pérez de Ariza, Pérez de Arrién, Pérez de Baraiz, Pérez de Berberigo, Pérez-Calvillo, Pérez de la Calzada, Pérez de Coaña, Pérez del Cuende, Pérez de Escó, Pérez de Garayo, Pérez de Goñativia, Pérez de Herrasti, Pérez de Illarza, Pérez de Meca, Pérez de Mendía, Pérez-Monte, Pérez de Nueros, Pérez de Ocampo, Pérez de Ocariz, Pérez de Oteyro, Pérez-Pando, Pérez de Panticosa, Pérez-Pertusa, Pérez de la Puente, Pérez del Pulgar, Pérez de Siles, Pérez de Soria, Pérez de Soto, Pérez de Tiermas, Pérez de Tudela, Pérez de Uriondo, Pérez de Vargas, Pérez de Villaescusa, Pérez de Vivero, Pérez de Zabalza, Pérez de Zamora, Periáñez, Peribán, Peribañez, Pericinea, Pericozena, Periche, Peris, Perisáus, Périz, Pernia, Perón, Peropadre, Perpinyá, Perpiñán, Perqueres, Perramón, Pertierra, Pertusa, Peruechena, Perujo, Perurena, Perves, Pesadilla, Pescuezo, Pesquera, Pestaña, Petel, Petra, Petrafisa, Petrirena, Petriz de Cruzat, Peus, Peusada, Pevedán, Pexáu, Pexo, Peyri, Peyró, Pezo, Pezuela, Phillips, Pi, Picabo, Picalquet, Picanzo, Picaño, Picavea, Picaza, Piccolomini, Pickman, Picó, Picó de Coaña, Picón, Picornell, Pich, Pichardo, Pichones, Pidal, Piedra, Piedrabuena, Piedrahita, Piedramillera, Piedratallada, Piedras, Piédrola, Piferrer, Pignatelli, Piguer, Pila, Pilares, Pildáin, Pileta, Pileto, Pilo, Pilulla, Pimentel, Pimienta, Pina, Pinar, Pinazo, Pineda or Pinedo, Pinel, Pinela or Pinelo, Pinell, Pinells, Pinesta, Pinets, Piniés, Pinilla, Pino, Pinós, Pinto, Pintor, Pinuaga, Pinyana, Pinza, Pinzón, Piña, Piñal, Piñango, Piñaragut, Piñera, Piñeira, Piñeiro, Piñeiro de Andrade, Piñero, Piño, Piñol, Piñón, Pío, Piquer, Pirez, Pis, Pisa, Piscina, Pisón, Pisuerga, Pita da Veiga, Pitarque, Pitillas, Piz, Pizá, Pizaño, Pizarro, Pizón, Pizueta, Pla, Placencia, Placeres, Plana (de la), Plandolit, Planella, Planes, Plano, Plansón, Plantáin, Plata, Plaza (de la), Plazaola, Plegamáns, Plegamayas, Pliego, Pliego-Valdés, Poal, Pobla, Poblaciones, Poblet, Poblete, Podazas, Podi or Podio, Poeti, Pol, Pola, Polanco, Polano, Polestres, Polit, Polo, Poll, Pollart, Pollastre, Pollino, Pomar or Pomares, Pombo, Pon, Ponce, Ponce de León, Pongem, Pons, Ponsez, Ponsich, Pont, Ponte, Pontejos, Pontés, Pontón, Pontos, Ponts, Poquet, Porcalles, Porcel or Porcell, Porquera or Porquero, Porquet, Porras or Porres, Porrer, Porsefanas, Porta, Portal, Portalecoa, Portales, Portela, Portell, Portella, Porter or Portero, Portés, Portilla (de la), Portillo, Portocarrero, Portu or Portua, Portugal, Portugalete, Portusagasti, Posada or Posadas, Posadero, Posadilla, Postigo, Potáu, Potestad, Pou, Poumola, Poveda, Power de Strickland, Poyo, Poza, Pozanos, Pozo, Pozos, Pozuelo, Pozueta, Pozzi, Prabes, Prada, Pradeda, Pradell, Prado, Prat, Prats, Pravia, Prego, Prementoria, Prendes, Presa, Presillas, Presno, Pretel, Prexana, Prexanes, Priego, Prieto, Prim, Primo, Primo de Rivera, Prioli, Prior or Priorio, Privado, Proaño, Probáis, Prous, Próxita, Pruna, Pruner or Pruners, Puch or Puche, Puebla, Puelles, Puente, Puente-Hurtado, Puerta, Puerto, Puertolas, Pueyo, Puga, Pugarí, Puig, Puigalt, Puigbacó, Puigcerver, Puigdesalit, Puigdespí, Puigdorfila, Puigesteva, Puigfaragut, Puiggalí, Puigjaner, Puigmarí, Puigmidó, Puigmitjá, Puigmoltó, Puignáu, Puigperdines, Puigperdiguer, Puigvecino, Puigvert, Pujadas or Pujades, Pujals, Pujol, Pulgar, Pulgarén, Pulgarín, Pulido, Pullarés, Pumariño, Pumaripo, Punter, Puñana, Purroy, Purroy de la Montanera, Puxmarín, Puyol. End of DHA, Letter P.

Q Quadra, Quadrado, Quadrillero, Quadros, Quart, Queipo, Queipo de Llano, Queirón, Quejada, Quejar, Quejo, Queralt, Queralto, Querejazu, Querforadat, Queríe, Quero, Querol, Quesada, Quevedo, Quijada, Quijano, Quílez, Quinacos, Quina, Quincoces, Quindós, Quint, Quintal, Quintana, Quintanilla, Quintano, Quintero, Quinto, Quiñones, Quiranes, Quiroga, Quirós, Quitañano, Quituera, Quiza. End of DHA, Letter Q.

R Raa, Rábago, Rabal, Rabanal, Rábano, Rabante, Rabasa, Rabelo, Rabía, Rabollet, Rabós, Rada, Rades, Radillo, Rafart, Rafel, Ragal, Ragasol, Raguanato, Raimondo or Raimóndez, Raizábal, Rajadell, Rajoy, Ram, Ram de Víu, Ramales, Ramazote, Rambla, Ramery, Ramírez, Ramírez de Arellano, Ramírez de Aristarán, Ramírez de Cardemuño, Ramírez de Jove, Ramírez de Labastida, Ramírez de Peñaranda, Ramírez de la Piscina, Ramírez de Villaescusa, Ramírez de Villafranca, Ramiro, Ramis, Ramoíno, Ramón, Ramos, Ramos del Manzano, Rampito, Rams, Ran, Rana or Rano, Rancaño, Rangeis, Rangel, Randa, Raneta, Rapado, Rapiana, Raposo, Raro, Rasal, Rascón, Rascurri, Raset, Rasín, Rasines, Rasta, Rastells del Mas, Rastia, Rastilliano, Ratera, Ratés, Ratia, Rávago, Ravé, Raxa, Raxach, Raxadell, Raxel, Raya, Rayadell, Rayado, Rayón, Rayones, Razábal, Rea, Real, Reales, Reart, Rebelo, Rebilla, Rebollar, Rebolledo, [Rebollet, see p. 1139], Rebollo, Rebujo, Recabarren, Recaín, Recalde, Recamán, Recaño, Recari, Recart, Recarte, Recaute, Recio, Recondo, Rechs, Redín, Redondo, Refojo, Regás, Regi, Régil, Regina, Regodón, Reguale, Reguart, Regué, Reguera, Reguero, Reguilón, Reichico, Reig, Reimúndez, Reina, Reinalte, Reino, Reinoso, Reíu, Rejón, Relat, Relosilla, Rellos, Rementaritegui, Rementería, Remesil,

Remesal, Remírez, Remiro, Remón, Remóndez, Renart, Rencaño, Rencuejo, Rendón, Renero, Rengel, Rengifo, Renier, Renobáu, Renosa, Renovales, Rentea, Rentería, Reñizal, Reolar, Reolí, Repados, Repala, Reparaz, Requejo, Requelme, Requena, Requeséns, Resa, Rescall, Resende, Resi, Respaldiza, Resusta, Reta, Retana, Retegui, Retes, Retola, Retuerto, Returbio, Reúl, Reure, Reus, Revaldo, Revena, Revenga, Reverter, Revilla, Rexach, Rey, Reyero, Reyes, Reynoso, Rézola, Rialp, Riancho, Riambáu, Rianjo, Riaño, Riarán, Riaria, Riaza, Riazo, Riba, Riba (La), Riba de Uceda, Ribadell, Ribadeneira, Ribafría, Ribalta, Ribas, Ribellas, Ribelles, Ribera, Riberol, Ribes, Ribilla, Ribot, Ric, Rica, Ricardo, Ricart or Ricarte, Ricio, Rico, Ricote, Ricuejo, Riego, Riello, Riera, Riero, Riestra, Riet, Rigal, Riguer, Rijón, Rilla, Rimors, Rincón, Rins, Río, Ríoboo, Ríofrío, Rioja, Ríos, Ripa, Ripalda, Rípoda, Ripol or Ripoll, Ripollés, Riquelme, Riquer, Risco, Ríu, Ríudecols, Ríudeperas, Ríus, Ríusech, Ríutord, Riva, Riva-Herrera, Rivacoba, Rivada, Rivadeneira, Rivadeo, Rivas, Rivas del Sil, Rivera, Rivero, Riverones, Rizo, Roa, Robalos, Roballa, Robert, Roberts, Robí, Robió, Robladillo or Robledillo, Robledano, Robledo, Robles, Rebollet, Robredo, Robres, Robuster, Roca, Roca de Togores, Rocabado, Rocaberti, Rocabruna, Rocacrespa, Rocadilla, Rocafort, Rocafull, Rocamora, Rocarrosa, Rocásito, Roco, Roco de Campofrío, Rocoíz, Rocón, Roch, Rocha (de la), Roche, Rochefoucauld (La), Rochel, Roda or Rodas, Rodales, Rodayega, Rodelas, Rodelo, Ródenas, Rodera, Rodero, Rodezno, Rodino, Rodolfo, Rodovallo, Rodrigo, Rodríguez, Rodríguez-Bejarano, Rodríguez de Figueroa, Rodríguez de León, Rodríguez de Llano, Rodríguez-Mafra, Rodríguez-Magariños, Rodríguez de Mora, Rodríguez de Rivadeneyra, Rodríguez de Sanabria, Rodríguez-Solano, Rodríguez de las Varillas, Rodríguez de Vivar, Rodríguez-Zorrilla, Roelas, Roger, Roger de Lluria, Rogero, Roig, Roíz, Roíz de Salazar, Rojas, Rojo, Rol, Roldán, Rolf, Rolins, Rolón, Rollán, Rollizo, Roma, Romagosa, Romaguera, Román, Romana, Romandiola, Romaní, Romano, Romaña, Romarate, Romay, Romen, Romeo, Romero, Roméu, Romo, Romree, Ron, Ronante, Roncal, Roncali, Roncesvalles, Ronda, Rondino, Rondón, Ronquillo, Ropiana, Roquefort, Ros, Rosa or Rosas, Rosado, Rosal, Rosales, Rosanes, Rosar, Rosel, Rosell or Roselló, Roset, Rosicas, Rosillo, Rosilloy, Rosique, Rosón, Rossi or Rosso, Rossiñol, Rotaeche, Rotaeta, Rotalde, Roteta, Rotger, Rotigoite, Rotlá, Rottel, Roura, Rovira, Rovirola, Roya, Royo, Roza or Rozas, Rozas de Ezquerra, Rúa (de la), Ruano, Rubalcava, Rubayo, Rubens, Rubert, Ruberte, Rubí, Rubiales, Rubián, Rubiero, Rubín, Rubín de Celis, Rebinat, Rubio, Rubió, Rubión, Rubira, Rueba, Rueda, Rueiro, Ruel, Ruenes, Ruesta, Rufo, Rugama, Ruiloba, Ruimayor, Ruiz, Ruiz de Alarcón, Ruiz de Allende, Ruiz de Apodaca, Ruiz de Borja, Ruiz de Burgo, Ruiz del Burgo, Ruiz de Castilla, Ruiz-Colorado, Ruiz-Jiménez, Ruiz de Liori, Ruiz-Lobillo, Ruiz de Morales, Ruiz de Velorado, Ruiz de Vergara, Ruiz de Zuazu, Rujido, Rújula, Rull, Rullán, Rulle, Ruperto, Rupiá, Rupit, Rus, Ruso, Rutia, Rutinel, Ruy de Peras, Ryan. End of DHA, Letter R.

S Sáa, Saavedra, Sabadía, Sabadino, Sabalza, Sabando, Sabanza, Sabarico, Sabariego, Sabasquida, Sabastida, Sabata, Sabatelli, Sabater, Sabiñano, Sabogal, Sacabechs, Sacabres, Sacana, Sacedo, Sacedón, Saceler, Saciola, Sacirera, Saclam, Saclosa, Saco, Sacoromina, Sacosta, Sacota, Sacristán, Sacuam, Sada, Sádava, Sadurní, Sáenz, Sáenz de Adana, Saera, Saerín, Sáez, Sáez de Uribarri, Safont Saforteza, Saga, Sagante, Sagaraicar, Sagardi, Sagardiburu, Sagariola, Sagarminaga, Sagarra, Sagarraga, Sagarriaga, Sagarribay, Sagarrida, Sagarriga, Sagarró, Sagartegui or Sagarteguieta or Sagarteguyeta, Sagarzazu, Sagaseta, Sagasta, Sagasti, Sagastibelza, Sagastiberría, Sagastigoitia, Sagastizábal, Sagnes, Sagoriola, Sagramena, Sagredo, Sagrera, Saguardia, Sagueró, Sagües, Saguino, Sagurdía, Sahera, Saigós, Saint-Pierre, Sainz, Sainz de la Maza, Sala, Sala de San Pelay, Salaberri, Salabert, Salad, Salado, Salamanca, Salanova, Salar, Salas, Salaya, Salayusán, Salazar, Salba, Salbaro, Salboch, Salce, Salceda, Salcedo, Salces, Salcete, Saldaña, Saldías, Salecungerte, Salelles, Salende, Sales, Saleta, Salete, Salgado, Salgueda, Salicán, Salido, Saligo, Salinas, Salmantón, Salmerón, Salmón, Salm-Salm, Saló, Saloaga, Saloguén, Salra, Salsfores, Salsidúa, Salt, Saltador, Saltells, Salto, Salvá, Salvador, Salvago, Salvany, Salvare, Salvat or Salvate, Salvatierra, Salzat, Sallana, Sallar, Sallent, Sallet, Sallmella, Sallmurri, Sallot, Samá, Samames, Samaniego, Samano, Samarán, Samaso, Samboyo, Samorera, Sampayo, Samper, Sampis, Sampso, Samuntada, San Andrés, San Antón, San Bonifacio, San Claudio, San Clemente or San Climente, San Clodio, San Cloyo, San Cristóbal, San Dionís, San Felíu, San Germán, San Isidro, San Jaime, San Jorge or San Jordí, San Juan, San Juanena, San Julián, San Junces, San Justo, San Llorente, San Marcelo, San Martín, San Miguel, San Millán, San Pedro, San Pelayo, San Pis, San Prudencio, San Román, San Severino, San Simón, San Suárez, San Vicente, San Vítores, Sanabria, Sanaspleda, Sancibrián, Sánchez, Sánchez de la Cuerda, Sánchez-Durán, Sánchez de Madrid, Sánchez-Muñoz, Sánchez-Navarro, Sánchez-Ossorio, Sánchez de Oviedo, Sánchez-Pleites, Sánchez de Santa Cruz, Sánchez de Teruel, Sánchez de Urízar, Sánchez de Villanueva, Sanchíez, Sanchiz, Sancho, Sande, Sandianes, Sandín, Sandoval, Sanfo, Sanfrechoso, Sangariz, Sangenís, Sangorrín, Sangro, Sangróniz, Sangüeza, Sanguino, Sangutia, Sanjurjo, Sanle, Sanoguera, Sanosiaín, Sanóu, Sanllayr, Sans, Sanso or Sansón, Sansoaín, Sansoles, Sansores, Sant Celoní, Sant Climent, Sant Dionís, Sant Esteva, Sant Felíu, Sant Guim, Sant Hilari, Sant Iscle, Sant Llay, Santa Ana, Santa Coloma, Santa Colomba or Santa Columba, Santa Creus, Santa Cruz, Santa Cruz de Olábarri, Santa Engracia, Santa Eugenia, Santa Fe, Santa María, Santa Marina, Santa Olalla, Santa Oliba, Santa Pau or Santa Paz, Santa Sofía, Santacilla, Santafinia, Santalla, Santander, Santángel, Santarén, Santarena, Santas Creus, Santayana, Santecilla, Santelices, Santerbás, Santesteban, Santiago, Santibáñez, Santico, Santillán or Santillana, Santiso, Santisteban, Santo or Santu, Santo Domingo, Santoina, Santos, Santoyo, Sants, Santu, Santurce, Santuro, Sanz, Sanz del Castillo, Sanz de Cortés, Sanz de la Llosa, Sanzina,

Sánzoles, Sañudo, Saona, Saorra, Sapano, Sapera, Sapila, Sapina, Saplana, Saporta, Saportella, Sara, Sarabia, Saracelas, Saracha or Saracho, Sarachaga, Saradén, Saragosa, Saralegui, Sarasa, Sarasola, Saraspe, Sarasqueta, Sarasúa, Sardá, Sardalla, Sardaneta, Sardina, Sardón, Sarela, Sariego, Sarmiento, Sarmiento de Valladares, Sarnes, Sarobe, Saroya, Sarra, Sarracina, Sarracine, Sarrachaga, Sarralde, Sarraoa, Sarrasa, Sarrat, Sarria, Sarriá, Sarriá-Gardel, Sarribera, Sarrible, Sarricolea, Sarriera, Sarriguren, Sarroca, Sarrosales, Sarrovira, Sarsá, Sarsola, Sartolo, Sarzábal, Sarzosa, Sasaeta, Sasclosa, Sasía, Sasiaín, Sasieta, Sasiola, Saso, Sasoaín, Sasoeta, Sasona, Sassa, Sastrada, Sastre, Sasuátegui, Satanti, Satariz, Saterán, Satorra or Satorre, Satrilla, Satrústegui, Saucelles, Sauguís, Saula, Sauli, Sault, Saurín, Sauriste, Sauto, Savalls, Savanell, Savasona, Savila, Savirata, Sayavedra, Sayas, Sayes, Sayol, Saz, Scanaldo, Schell, Sebastián, Sebil, Secades, Secanellas or Secanillas, Seco, Sech, Sedano, Sedeño, Sedillo, Sediño, Segador, Segarra, Segovia, Seguí, Seguino, Segundera, Segura, Segurola, Segurre, Seijas, Sein, Sejas, Selgas, Selma, Selmo, Selva, Sella, Sellán, Sellent, Sellés, Sem, Semir, Semper, Sempertegui, Sempey, Sena, Senall, Sendagorta, Sendín, Senespleda, Senillosa, Senisterra, Senoguera, Senra, Sentís, Sentimenat, Seña, Señorino, Seoane, Sepertegui, Sepúlveda, Sequeira, Sequeiro or Sequeiros, Sequilla, Seraceda, Serantes, Serdá, Seregut, Serena, Serna, Serón, Serona, Serqueira, Serra, Serraburu, Serrada, Serrador, Serralta, Serrallonga, Serram, Serrano, Serras, Serrasín, Serri or Serria, Sert, Sertucha, Servent, Servía, Sesclergues, Sescomes, Sesguardia, Sesma, Sesmonde, Sessé, Sestadón, Sestrada, Sesúmaga, Setantí, Setién, Seva, Sevil, Sevilla, Sevillano, Sexalbo, Seyerona, Sicart, Sicero, Sidrac, Sierra, Sierralta, Sietiel, Sifra, Sigardo, Sigler, Siguero, Sil, Siblo, Silos, Silva, Silvano, Silveira, Silvela, Silvera, Silvestre, Silvio, Siller, Sillero, Simal, Simancas, Simiente, Simó, Simonet, Sinfuegos, Sipán, Sirerols, Sirgad or Sirgado, Siria, Sirvente, Sisalde, Siscar, Síscara, Síscome, Sitante, Sitgo, Sitién, Sitjar, Siurana, So, Soane, Soárez, Sober, Soberón, Sobías, Sobies, Sobirat, Soblechero, Sobradillo, Sobrado, Sobrino, Sobroano, Sobroso, Socarrats, Socasa, Socías, Sodre, Soga, Sogordí, Soinera, Sojo, Sol, Solá, Solablanca, Solana, Solanas, Solane, Solanell, Solano, Solanot, Solar or Solares, Solarana, Solares, Solaun, Solaurren, Solchaga, Soldevilla, Soler, Soler de las Galeras, Solera, Solier, Solís, Solíus, Solivella, Sologoiti, Sologuren, Solora, Solorana, Solórzano, Solozábal, Solsona, Soltero, Solví, Soll, Sollozo, Soma, Sombrero, Somero, Somocarrera, Somocurcio, Somodevilla, Somonte, Somorriba, Somoza, Soneime, Soneira or Sonora, Sopando, Sopelana, Sopeña, Sopranis, Sopuerta, Soquín, Sora, Soráburu, Soraindo, Soraiz, Soraluce, Sorarte, Soravilla, Sorazábal, Sorba, Sorell, Soret, Soria, Soriano, Sorlada, Sormendi, Sorna, Sornoza, Soro, Soroa, Soroeta, Sorolla, Soromendi, Sorozábal, Sorreguieta, Sorrentino, Sorriba, Sorribas, Sorribes, Sorroiz, Sorrombegui, Sort, Soru or Soruet, Sos, Sosa, Sosoaga, Sota, Sota (de la), Sotelo, Sotés, Sotillo, Soto, Soto-Gayoso, Sotolongo, Sotomayor, Soto-Santos, Sousa, Soutelo, Sovies, Spernáu, Spilles, Spinello, Spinola,

Stader, Staña, Statugenia, Stens, Stúñiga, Suarbán, Suárez, Suárez de Albergaria, Suárez de Albuerne, Suárez de Deza, Suárez de Lugo, Suárez-Pardo de la Casta, Suaso, Suasola, Suau, Subías, Subilleta, Subirá, Subiri, Subisca, Subiza, Suchet, Suelves, Suero, Suesa, Suescun or Suescura, Suevo, Sugaduy, Suilly, Suínaga, Suis, Sujerigu, Sujuz, Suldáin, Sulzabar, Sulla, Sumay, Sumendiaga, Sumiano, Sunier, Sunza, Suñaga, Suñer, Suobieta, Suquía, Suquiza, Sureda, Surell, Suriol, Suris, Surrasua, Susá, Suso, Susteren, Sustinaga, Susunaga, Suzola, Sweerts. End of DHA, Letter S.

T Tabar, Tábara, Tabares, Tabarra, Tabera, Taberner, Tabira, Tablada, Tablas de Candamo, Tablares, Taboada, Tabuyo, Tacón, Tafalla, Tafoya, Tafur, Tafurer, Tagamanent, Tagle, Tagoras, Taguí, Tahuste, Tajonar, Talamanca, Talarn, Talavera, Talaya, Talayero, Taliata, Talomandia, Talón, Talora, Tallada, Tallado, Tallamillo, Tallander, Tallarn, Talledo, Tamara, Tamargo, Tamaría, Tamarit or Tamariz, Tamariza, Tamarón, Tamayo, Tanagona, Tangil, Tape, Tapia, Taqui, Taracena, Tarafa, Taranco, Tarasco, Tarazona, Tarba, Tarcua, Tarde, Tardillán, Tardío, Tarés, Tarín, Tárraga, Tarragó, Tarragona, Tarragua, Tarrapela, Tarrasa, Tarraza, Tarrazona, Tárrega, Tarrique, Tarrius, Tarroya, Tarsa, Tasís, Taura, Tauste, Tavara, Tavares, Tavira, Tavora, Taxonera, Tayadella, Tazo, Teballina, Tebernia, Tebes, Techo, Tegaliano, Teibes, Teixeira, Tejada, Tejadillo, Tejeiro, Tejera or Tejería, Tejerina, Tejero, Tejo, Teleña, Tellaeche, Tellería, Téllez, Téllez-Girón, Téllez de Meneses, Tellitu, Tello, Tello de Eslava, Temes or Témez, Temple, Tena, Tener, Tenilla, Tenorio, Tenza, Terán, Tercero, Terciado, Tercilla, Terés, Teresano, Terlegui, Termens, Ternera, Terra, Terrades, Terraza, Terrazas, Terrazo, Terré, Terreros, Terrers, Terrín, Terrón, Tersa, Tersón, Teruel, Testa, Testales, Teverga, Texeira, Texiero, Texindo, Texiña, Teza, Tibir or Tibur, Tiburcio, Ticón, Tidoga, Tiebas, Tierín, Tilly, Timino or Timón, Timor, Tinaja, Tineira, Tineo, Tinoco, Tinto, Tión, Tirado, Tiuz, Tizón, Toar, Toba, Tobalina, Tobar, Tobía, Tocho, Tofino, Tofiño, Togores, Toledo, Tolosa, Tolosano, Tolrá, Tomás, Tomasena, Tomillo, Tompes, Tonent, Tonera, Tonillo, Topete, Topinán, Torá, Toral, Toralla, Toralló, Torán, Toranzo, Torcazo, Tord, Tordesillas, Tordoisa, Tordosa, Torell, Torella, Torelló, Torero, Toriz, Torma, Tormé, Tormo, Tornamira, Tornegoitia, Tornel or Tornes, Torner, Tornet, Tornogres, Tornuntegui, Toro, Toroya, Torquemada, Torquillo, Torra, Torrado, Torralba, Torralla, Torrano, Torre or de la Torre, Torrealde, Torrebidarte, Torreblanca, Torrecilla, Torregrosa, Torrejón, Torre-Landaberro, Torrell or Torrella, Torrelles, Torremoroso, Torrent, Torrendell, Torrero, Torre-Roja, Torres, Torres de Carazo, Torreta, Torrezar, Torrezarra, Torrijos, Torrizo, Torro, Torroella, Torroja, Torrón, Torróntegui, Tort, Tortellá, Tórtoles, Tosantos, Tosca, Toscano, Toso, Tost, Tostado, Tortorica, Touriño, Tourlón, Tous de Monsalve, Tovada, Tovar, Tovía, Tovilla, Toyos, Tozubando, Traba, Trabeco or Trabepo, Trabezo, Trabudo or Trabudua, Traginer, Trago, Tragosa, Traina, Tramacat or Tramacet,

Tramassat, Transalgado, Trápaga, Traper, Trapera, Trapiella, Trasanco, Trasganda, Trauco, Travada, Traver, Trebejo, Trebolazabala, Trecu, Trechuelo, Trejo, Trelles, Trempo, Trepiana, Trespalacios, Tresserres, Trevalls, Trevilla, Treviño, Trevisán or Trevisano, Trezuelo, Trías, Trigo, Trigona, Trigorá, Tirgueiro, Trigueros, Trihergua, Trilles, Trillo, Trillón, Trincado, Trinchería, Tristán, Tristrany, Triz, Trobat, Trobeza, Trobica, Trocóniz, Troche, Trón, Troncón, Troncoso, Trono, Trosantos, Troya, Trubarje, Trucios, Trujillo, Trulles, Trullo, Truyols, T'Serclaes, Tubián, Tudela, Tudó, Tuero or Tueros, Tuesta, Tufo (del), Tunco, Tuñón, Turán, Turcal, Turcios, Turell, Turiel, Turill, Turista, Turmo, Turpín, Turpita, Turrido, Turrillas, Turrina, Turrutelo, Tutor, Túy. End of DHA, Letter T.

U Ubach, Ubago, Ubaldía, Ubarte, Ubao, Ubarri, Ubaya, Ubierna, Ubieta, Ubilla, Ubillos, Ubillotz, Ubina, Ubiría, Ucar, Uceda or Ucedo, Ucelay, Ucero, Uceta, Udabe, Udaeta, Udi, Udía, Ugalde, Ugaldebarrera, Ugarra, Ugarrechea, Ugarriza, Ugarte, Ugarteburu, Ugene, Uguet, Uguí, Uguiricha or Uguirichaga, Uhalde, Ulacia, Ulibarri, Ulzurrun, Ullauri, Ulldemolíns, Ullestret, Ulloa, Ullueta, Umansoro, Umarán, Umbarambe, Umbert, Umendia, Umérez, Unamunsaga, Unano, Unanúe, Unate, Unceta, Uncibay, Unda, Undarza, Undiano, Ungría, Unibaso, Unis, Unzá, Unzaga, Unzalu, Unzola, Unzué, Unzueta, Uraga, Uralde, Urandurraga, Uranga, Uranzadi, Uranzu, Urban, Urbea, Urbieta, Urbillos, Urbina, Urbizu, Urcelay, Urcullo, Urch, Urdaibái, Urdanbideluz, Urdanegui, Urdaneta, Urdangarín, Urdanibia, Urdaniz, Urdanoz, Urdaspal, Urdayaga, Urdiaín, Urdinola, Urdinzu, Urdizibar, Urdoz, Urecha, Ureder, Ureña, Ureta, Urezberoeta, Urgel, Uría, Uriarte, Uribarren, Uribarri, Uribe, Uribeapalla, Uribe de Salazar, Uriberri, Uribia, Uriburu, Urien, Urieta, Urigoitia, Uriguen, Uriondo, Urioste, Urisarri, Uriz, Uriza, Urízar, Urjaraz, Urmeneta or Urmenta, Urnaude, Urnieta, Urniza, Urosa, Uroz, Urquía, Urquijo, Urquiola, Urquista, Urquizo or Urquizu, Urra, Urraca, Urraga, Urrana, Urrapaín, Urraria, Urraza, Urrazandi, Urrea, Urrecazuolo, Urrecha, Urreiztieta, Urréjola, Urrestarazu, Urresti, Urrestieta, Urreta, Urriaga, Urribarrena, Urríes, Urrijate, Urrimendi, Urriola, Urrispuru, Urriza, Urrizola, Urroz, Urruela, Urrueta, Urrumbella, Urrupaín, Urruti, Urrutia, Urrutiabergui, Urrutiajáuregui, Urrutigoiti, Urruzuno, Urs, Ursúa, Ursularre, Urtasun, Urtate, Urtaza, Urteaga, Urtrigo, Urtubia, Urtusáutegui, Uruena, Uruñuela, Urzaiz, Usandivaras, Usánsolo, Usaola, Usarralde, Usátegui, Uscátegui, Usodemar, Ustés, Usua, Uterga, Uzcariz, Uzés, Uztáriz, Uztarroz. End of DHA, Letter U. End of (DHA): Letters V, W, X, Y, & Z were not published.

APPENDIX 5

LUIS VILAR Y PASCUAL

Diccionario Histórico, Genealógico y Heráldico de las Familias Ilustres de la Monarquía Española

There are brief references containing information about families in Latin America in the eight-volume *Diccionario Histórico, Genealógico y Heráldico de las Familias Ilustres de la Monarquía Española* (DME) by Luis Vilar y Pascual, which deals with the origins of the families of Spain; their ancestral family seats; illustrious representatives of each surname; branches and genealogies of the various families spread throughout the peninsula and adjacent islands; and their titles, estates, inheritances, legacies, coats of arms, etc. Most of the entries treat the Spanish, or sometimes other European, origins of the surnames in question. These volumes are found on microfilm at the Family History Library in Salt Lake City as follows: volumes 1–3 (283584), volumes 4–7 (283585), and volume 8 (283586). They include some information on the following surnames, which are not strictly alphabetical in order to maintain the integrity of where they are found within the volumes in question:

A Volume 1: Abad, Abalos, Abella, Abellaneda, Abello, Abendaño, Abreu, Acebedo, Acevedo, Alcalde, Aldaret, Aldarete, Alderete, Aldrete, Avalos, Avelia, Avellaneda, Avello, Avendaño, Avreu; Volume 2: Aedo, Aguayo, Ahedo, Alfonsin, Alfonso, Alonso, Aloyto, Analso; Volume 3: Alarcón, Andia, Arias, Avila; Volume 4: Abello Castrillón, Abruzo, Acevedo, Acosta, Afán de Rivera, Aguayo, Aguilar, Alava, Alagón, Albornoz, Alburquerque, Alcalde, Aldama, Alegría, Alencastre, Alvarez de Toledo, Alvarez de Villacorta, Andraca, Angulo, Antillón, Aragón, Arenas, Arenillas, Argote, Armentia, Arroyta, Avellaneda, Averna, Ayala, Azagra; Volume 5: Aguilar, Aguirre Jiménez, Alarcón, Albornoz, Alvarez, Angulo, Aragón, Arce, Arse or Arze, Arellano, Argote Godoy, Arias, Arias Dávila, Asturias y Naya, Ayala, Ayala Ceballos, Aza or Daza, Azagra; Volume 6: Aguiar, Aguilar, Alonso de Caso, Alvarez Benavides, Amat, Artidiello; Volume 7: Acuña, Alamán, Alvarez de Toledo, Argote; Volume 8: Alamo, Arbizu, Arce, Arse, or Arze, Arias, Armentia, Avellaneda, Autrán, Azorin. A combined index that includes some surnames not found above, therefore indicating they are of a subnature within the text, is found at the end of Volume 7 as follows: Abad, Abalos, Abella, Abellaneda, Abello, Abello Castrillón, Abendaño, Abreu, Abruzo, Acebedo, Acosta, Acuña, Aedo, Afán de Rivera, Aguayo, Aguiar, Aguilar, Aguirre Jiménez, Ahedo, Alagón, Alamán, Alamo, Alarcón, Alava, Albornoz, Alburquerque, Aldalde, Aldama, Aldarete, Alderete, Aldrete, Alegría, Alencastre, Alfonsin, Alfonso, Alonso, Alonso de Caso, Aloyto, Alvarez de Toledo, Alvarez de Villacorta, Alvarez, Alvarez Benavides, Amat, Analso, Andia, Andraca, Angulo, Antillón, Aragón, Arbizu, Arce, Arse or Arze, Arellano, Arenas, Arenillas, Argote, Argote Godoy, Arias, Arias Dávila, Armentia, Arroyta, Artidiello, Asturias y Nava, Avalos, Avella, Avellaneda, Avello, Averna, Avendaño, Avila, Avreu y Abreu, Autrán, Ayala, Ayala Ceballos, Aza or Daza, Azagra, and Azorín. End of DME, Letter A.

B Volume 1: Borbón; Volume 2: Baca, Barca, Bernardo or Bernaldo de Quirós; Volume 3: Bardagi, Bardaji, Bardax, Bardaxi, Barnier, Beaumont, Berlanga, Bermúdez de Castro, Bignoni, Bracamonte, Bretón; Volume 4: Baena, Baquena, Baquerizo, Bañuelos, Barba, Barchino, Bázquez de Rivera, Beaumont, Bello, Beltrán Cerrato, Bermúdez, Berna, Bizarrón, Bobadilla, Bocanegra, Borbón, Butrón, Busto; Volume 5: Baeza, Barba, Barich, Barona, Barrientos, Barrionuevo, Bazán, Benavides, Bique, Bofarrull, Bonifós, Borgón, Braganza, Bravo de Lagunas, Brocá; Volume 6: Barreda, Benavides, Boulet or Bohulet, Borja, Bover; Volume 7: Barberan, Beaumont; Volume 8: Nothing. A combined index that includes some surnames not found above, therefore indicating they are of a subnature within the text, is found at the end of Volume 7 as follows: Baca, Baeza, Baena, Baquera, Baquerizo, Bañuelos, Barba, Barchino, Bardagi, Bardaji, Bardax, Barich, Barnier, Barona, Barreda, Barrientos, Barrionuevo, Bazán, Bázquez de Rivera, Beaumont, Bello, Beltrán Cerrato, Benavides, Berlanga, Bermúdez, Bermúdez de Castro, Berna, Bignoni, Bique, Bizarrón, Bobadilla, Bocanegra, Bofaruell, Bonifós, Borbón, Borja, Bover, Boulet or Bohulet, Bracamonte, Braganza, Bravo de Lagunas, Bretón, Broca, Busto, Butrón. End of DME, Letter B.

C Volume 1: Nothing; Volume 2: Caamaño, Caballer or Caballero, Cabeza de Vaca, Camaña, Camaño, Camano, Caramaño, Caramañy, Camoes, Camuña, Cavaller or Cavallero, Calderó, Calderón, Calderón de la Barca, Chavarría, Chavarríes, Chavarrieta, Chaverri, Chiner; Volume 3: Calderón, Calzadilla, Campo, Campo Amor, Campo de Arve, Campo Fregoso, Campo Frío, Campo Maldonado, Campo Marino, Campo Nuevo, Campo Redondo, Campo Santos, Campos, Campos Crusbek, Camps, Cárdenas, Castilla, Cominges, Contreras; Volume 4: Cabrera, Calella, Campoy, Cancio, Cantero, Carvajal, Cárcamo, Cárdenas, Cardeña, Cardeñes, Caro, Carrillo, Carrillo de Albornoz, Carrillo de Ortega, Castellá, Castelví, Càstillo, Cayaba, Caicedo,

Celis, Centelles, Cerda, Cerezo, Cervico, Concha, Córdoba, Cruillas, Cueva; Volume 5: Caballro, Cabeza de Vaca, Cabrera, Caicedo Mesa, Calella, Campo, Carasa, Cárdenas, Carnicero, Carrafa Carrillo, Caso Nava, Castro Portugal, Ceballos, Cebos, Cerda, Céspedes, [Chávez, p. 206], [Chumacero Eraso, p. 247], Cisneros, Claherhont, Cobos, Coello, Córdoba or Fernández de Córdoba, Cortés, Crespi Brondo, Cuello, Cueva, Cuinghien; Volume 6: Carranza, Caso, Casteloblanco, Cendrera, Cervantes, Cintora, Cobos, Contreras, Correa, Cueva, Curado; Volume 7: Cañas, Catllar, Celis, Cervellón; Volume 8: Cabrera, Cáceres, Cárdenas, Castro, Cruz, Chenard. A combined index that includes some surnames not found above, therefore indicating they are of a subnature within the text, is found at the end of Volume 7 as follows: Caamaño, Caballer or Caballero, Caballero, Cabeza de Vaca, Cabrera, Cáceres, Caicedo, Caicedo Mesa, Calderó, Calderón, Calderón de la Barca, Calella, Calzadillo, Camaña, Camano, Camaño, Camoes, Campo, Campo Amor, Campo de Arce, Campo Fregoso, Campo Frío, Campo Maldonado, Campo Marino, Campo Nuevo, Campo Redondo, Campo Santos, Campos Crusbek, Campos, Campoy, Camps, Camuña, Cancio, Cañas, Cantero, Caramañy, Carasa, Carbajal, Carcamo, Cárdenas, Cardeña, Cardeñes, Carnicero, Caro, Carrafa, Carranza, Carrillo, Carrillo de Albornoz, Carrillo de Ortega, Caso, Caso Nava, Castella, Casteloblanco, Castelví, Castilla, Castillo, Castro Portugal, Castro, Catllar, Cavaller or Caballero, Cayaba, Ceballos, Cebos, Celis, Cendrera, Centelles, Cerda, Cerda, Cerezo, Céspedes, Cervantes, Cervellón, Cevizo, Cintora, Cisneros, Claheront, Cobos, Coello, Cominges, Concha, Contreras, Córdoba, Córdoba or Fernández de Córdoba, Correa, Cortés, Crespo Brondo, Cruillas, Cruz, Cuello, Cueva, Cuinghien, Curado, Chavarría, Chavarríes, Chavarrieta, Chaverri, Chaves. Chenard, Chiner, Chumacero Eraso. End of DME, Letter C.

D Volume 1: Dábalos, Dávalos; Volume 2: Daoiz; Volume 3: Darias, Dávila, Del Campo, Del Campo Ordóñez, Descamps; Volume 4: Descals, Denti, Despuig, Díaz de Sandoval, Díez Madroñero, Diez Navarro, Domínguez, Dueñas; Volume 5: Díaz de Velasco, Dormez, Duque de Estrada; Volume 6: Díaz, Díaz de Haro, Diez, Diez de Tejada; Volume 7: Du-Bois; Volume 8: Díaz, Durango. A combined index that includes some surnames not found above, therefore indicating they are of a subnature within the text, is found at the end of Volume 7 as follows: Dábalos, Daoiz, Daria, Dávalos, Dávila, Del Campo, Del Campo Ordóñez, Denti, Descals, Descamps, Despuig, Díaz, Díaz de Sandoval, Díaz de Velasco, Diez, Diez de Haro, Diez Madroñero, Diez Navarro, Diez de Tejada, Domínguez, Dormez, Du-Bois, Dueñas, Duque de Estrada, Durango. End of DME, Letter D.

E Volume 1: Ebreu, Evreu, Evreux; Volume 2: Eañez, Echabarri, Echavarria, Echaberri, Echavari, Echevarria, Echeverri, Echeverria,

Edo; Volume 3: Eduardo, Eguez, España, Eza or Deza; Volume 4: Enderica, Enríquez, Escala, Escrivá, Espeleta, Espian, Espinosa, Esquivel, Estrada; Volume 5: Equino, Enríquez, Enríquez de Noroña, Enríquez de las Casas, Escalante, Espinola, Espinosa; Volume 6: Echevarria, Elorza; Volume 7: Enríquez; Volume 8: Escobar. A combined index that includes some surnames not found above, therefore indicating they are of a subnature within the text, is found at the end of Volume 7 as follows: Eañez, Ebreu, Echabarri, Echaberri, Echavarri, Echevarría, Echeberri, Echeverria, Edo, Eduardo, Elorza, Eguez, Enderica, Enríquez, Enríquez de Noroña, Enríquez de las Casas, Entralgo, Equino, Escala, Escalante, Escobar, Escriva, España, Espeleta, Espian, Espinola, Espinos, Esquivel, Estrada, Evreu, Evreux, Eza or Deza. End of DME, Letter E.

F Volume 1: Nothing; Volume 2: Faedo, Fagiardo, Fajardo, Faxardo; Volume 3: Faria, Flórez, Foix, Fuenmayor; Volume 4: Federiqui, Feloaga, Fernández de Argote, Fernández de Córdoba, Fernández de Figueroa, Fernández de Velasco, Ferrer de Lis, Frías; Volume 5: Fernández, Fernández de Córdoba, Ferrández, Ferrera, Figueroa, Figueroa Gallinato, Folch de Cardona, Fonseca, Francia, Franqueza; Volume 6: Ferraz, Fogaza de Eza, Fernández de Cendrera, Fernández Cintora, Fernández de Córdoba, Fernández de Padilla; Volume 7: Nothing; Volume 8: Fernández Castrillón, Fernández de Córdoba, Fuentes. A combined index that includes some surnames not found above, therefore indicating they are of a subnature within the text, is found at the end of Volume 7 even as follows: Faedo, Fagiardo, Fajardo, Fanés, Faxardo, Faria, Federiqui, Feloaga, Fernández, Fernández de Argote, Fernández Castrillón, Fernández de Cendrera, Fernández de Cintora, Fernández de Córdoba, Fernández de Figueroa, Fernández de Padilla, Fernández de Velasco, Ferrández, Ferraz, Ferrera, Ferrer de Lis, Figueroa Gallinato, Figueroa, Flórez, Fogaza de Eza, Foix, Folch de Cardona, Fonseca, Francis, Franqueza, Frías, Fuenmayor, Fuentes. End of DME, Letter F.

G Volume 1: Gaviria; Volume 2: Gallego Fajardo, Gallegos, Gamano, Gener, Giner, Guevara, Gumuno; Volume 3: Garcés, Golfín, Guesala or Guezala; Volume 4: Gaete, Galindo, Gallarza, Gálvez, Gaviria, Giménez de Urrea, Godoy, Gómez de Córdoba, Góngora, González de Estrada, Guajardo, Gutiérrez, Gutiérrez de la Barreda, Gutiérrez de Caviedes, Gutiérrez de Gandarillas, Gutiérrez de León, Gutiérrez de Monasterio, Gutiérrez de los Ríos, Gutiérrez de la Torre, Guzmán; Volume 5: Galindo, Gamboa, Gante, Garcés, García del Postigo, García de Rellón, Garci Laso de la Vega, Gavaldá, Girón, Glimes de Brabante, Godoy, Gordó, Gómez, Guevara, Gutiérrez, Gutiérrez de Ferrera, Gutiérrez de los Ríos, Guzmán; Volume 6: Galindo, Gómes de Barreda, González de Barreda, González de Cámara; Volume 7: García, García de la Vega, García de la Laspra, García de Arévalo, García de

Arenas, García de Cáceres, Guzmán; Volume 8: Galvez, Garcés or Garcés de los Fayos, Godoy, Góngora, Guevara. A combined index that includes some surnames not found above, therefore indicating they are of a subnature within the text, is found at the end of Volume 7 as follows: Gaete, Galindo, Gallarza, Gallego Fajardo, Gallegos, Gálvez, Gamaño, Gamboa, Gante, Garcés, Garcés or Garcés de los Fayos, García, García del Postigo, García de Rellón, García de la Vega, García de la Laspra, García de Arévalo, García de Arenas, García de Cáceres, Garcilaso de la Vega, Gaviria, Gavaldá, Gener, Giménez de Urrea, Giner, Girón, Glimes de Brabante, Godoy, Golfín, Gómez, Gómez de Córdoba, Gómez de Barreda, Góngora, González de Estrada, González de Barreda, González de Camara, Gordó, Guajardo, Guesala or Gaezala, Guevara, Gumuno, Gutiérrez, Gutiérrez de la Barreda, Gutiérrez de Caviedes, Gutiérrez de Ferrera, Gutiérrez de Gandarillas, Gutiérrez de León, Gutiérrez de Monasterio, Gutiérrez de los Ríos, Gutiérrez de la Torre, Guzmán. End of DME, Letter G.

H Volume 1: Nothing; Volume 2: Haedo; Volume 3: Hanty; Volume 4: Haro, Heredia, Hernández de Velasco, Herrera, Híjar, Hoces; Volume 5: Haro, Henestrosa, Heredia, Herrera, Herreros de la Peña, Híjar, Hoces, Hurtado de Mendoza; Volume 6: Henestrosa; Volume 7: Nothing; Volume 8: Heredia. A combined index that includes some surnames not found above, therefore indicating they are of a subnature within the text, is found at the end of Volume 7 as follows: Haedo, Hanty, Haro, Henestrosa, Heredia, Hernández de Velasco, Herrera, Herreros de la Peña, Híjar, Hoces, Hurtado de Mendoza. End of DME, Letter H.

I Volume 1: Nothing; Volume 2: Yáñez; Volume 3: Idiaquez or Idiaguez, Irarrazábal, Isasi. Volume 4: Ibáñez, Illescas, Idiaquez; Volume 5: Nothing; Volume 6: Nothing; Volume 7: Nothing; Volume 8: Nothing. A combined index that includes some surnames not found above, therefore indicating they are of a subnature within the text, is found at the end of Volume 7 as follows: Ibáñez, Idiaquez or Idiaguez, Illescas, Infantas, Irarrazábal, Isasi. End of DME, Letter I.

J Volume 1: Nothing; Volume 2: Janer; Volume 3: Nothing; Volume 4: Jacob, Jacobs, Jácome, Jiménez de Góngora, Joya, Juárez; Volume 5: Justiniani; Volume 6: Nothing; Volume 7: Nothing; Volume 8: Nothing. A combined index that includes some surnames not found above, therefore indicating they are of a subnature within the text, is found at the end of Volume 7 as follows: Jacob, Jacobs, Jácome, Janer, Jiménez de Góngora, Joya, Juárez, Justiniani. End of DME, Letter J.

L Volume 1: Nothing: Volume 2: Ladrón, Ladrón de Cegama, Ladrón de Guevara, Ladrón de Lizana; Volume 3: Leal, Lizarazu, Logman; Volume 4: Lama, Laso de la Vega, Lauria, Leguizamón, Linden, Lizarazu, Lollano, Lorenzo, Luna, Luzón; Volume 5: Lamoral, Lannoy, Lara, Laso de la Vega, Laspra, Lemus Valladares, Leiva or Leiba, Llano Parreño, López de Zúñiga, Loredo, Loza, Lozada; Volume 6: Lallave; Volume 7: Labrit; Volume 8: León, Lorenzana, Luna. A combined index that includes some surnames not found above, therefore indicating they are of a subnature within the text, is found at the end of Volume 7 as follows: Labrit, Ladrón, Ladrón de Cegama, Ladrón de Guevara, Ladrón de Lizana, LaValle, Lama, Lamoral, Lannoy, Lara, Laso de la Vega, Laspra, Lauria, Leal, Leguizamón, Leiba or Leiva, Lemus Valladares, León, Linden, Lizarazu, Llano Parreño, Logman, Lollano, López de Zúñiga, Loredo, Lorenzana, Lorenzo, Loza, Lozada, Luna, Luzón. End of DME, Letter L.

M Volume 1: Nothing; Volume 2: MacCrohon; Volume 3: Macarti, Machado, Madan, Manuel, Menchaca, Monroy, Montezuma; Volume 4: Maldonado, Manrique, Manuel de Lando, Martel, Martínez de Guereñú, Melchor, Melcior or Mailior, Méndez de Sotomayor, Mendoza, Mesía, Mesía de la Cerda, Miera, Monsoriu, Montemayor, Morales, Moreno; Volume 5: Manzanedo, Manrique, Manuel, Marañón, Marín, Marmolejo, Mascaró Salas, Masinines, Maza, Melgarejo de las Roelas, Mendoza, Meneses, Merás, Mesa, Mesía Carrillo, Miranda, Moncayo Palafox, Monroy, Montagut Pedret, Montalvo, Monterroso, Muñoz, Musaurrieta; Volume 6: Mahit, Molina, Mora; Volume 7: Maldonado, Meana; Volume 8: Maldonado, Meana, Muñiz. A combined index that includes some surnames not found above, therefore indicating they are of a subnature within the text, is found at the end of Volume 7 as follows: Macarti, MacCrohon, Machado, Madan, Maíz, Maldonado, Manrique, Manuel, Manuel de Lando, Manzanedo, Marañón, Marín, Marmolejo, Martel, Martínez de Guereñú, Mascaró Salas, Masimines, Maza, Meana, Melchor, Melcior or Maillor, Melgarejo de las Roelas, Menchca, Méndez de Sotomayor, Mendoza, Meneses, Merás, Mesa, Mesía, Mesía Carrillo, Mesía de la Cerda, Miera, Miranda, Molina, Moncayo Palafox, Monroy, Monsoriu, Montagut Pedret, Montalvo, Montemayor, Monterroso, Montezuma, Mora, Morales, Moreno, Muñiz, Muñoz, Mussurrieta. End of DME, Letter M.

N Volume 1: Nothing; Volume 2: Narbaiz, Narvaez, Narvarez, Narvarte; Volume 3: Navarra, Noroña; Volume 4: Narvaez, Navarro, Neira, Noroña, Nuncibay; Volume 5: Nevares or Navares, Niño, Novoa; Volume 6: Nothing; Volume 7: Niño, Noroña; Volume 8: Nothing. A combined index that includes some surnames not found above, therefore indicating they are of a subnature within the text, is found at the end of Volume 7 as follows:

Narbaez, Narvaez, Narvarez, Narvarte, Navarra, Navarro, Neira, Nevares or Navares, Niño, Noroña, Novoa, Nuncibay, Núñez de Guzmán. End of DME, Letter N.

O Volume 1: Nothing; Volume 2: Obregón; Volume 3: Oca, Ocampo, Ocariz or Ozcariz, Occorrolls, Ochoa, Olariaga, Orellana; Volume 4: Ordóñez, Ortega, Ortiz de Zárate, Ortizá, Orueta, Osorio; Volume 5: Oca, Ocio, Olarte, Ordóñez, Orozco Sierra, Ortiz Calderón, Osorio; Volume 6: Nothing; Volume 7: Orozco, Ossorio; Volume 8: Olea. A combined index that includes some surnames not found above, therefore indicating they are of a subnature within the text, is found at the end of Volume 7 as follows: Obregón, Oca, Ocampo, Ocariz or Ozcariz, Occorrolls, Ocio, Ochoa, Olariaga, Olarte, Olea, Ordóñez, Orellana, Orozco, Orozco Sierra, Ortega, Ortiz de Zárate, Ortiz Calderón, Ortizá, Orueta, Osorio, Ossorio. End of DME, Letter O.

P Volume 1: Nothing; Volume 2: Pacheco; Volume 3: Pagola, Palma, Peralta, Picaza, Planell, Porres; Volume 4: Pacheco, Padilla, Padura, Páez de Castillejo, Palanca, Pardo, Pardo Montenegro, Pecha, Peralta, Piquer, Pita, Ponce, Ponce de León, Portocarrero, Presno; Volume 5: Pacheco, Pando, Pantoja de Cuenca, Paredes, Pérez, Pimentel, Pinazo, Plandolit, Ponce de León, Porres, Portocarrero, Portocarrero de Guzmán, Pujadas; Volume 6: Padilla, Puerta; Volume 7: Pacheco, Paredes, Portocarrero; Volume 8: Peraza, Pérez, Pintado, Ponce de León, Prendes. A combined Index that includes some surnames not found above, therefore indicating they are of a subnature within the text, is found at the end of Volume 7 as follows: Pacheco, Padilla, Padura, Páez de Castillejos, Pagola, Palanca, Palma, Pando, Pantoja de Cuenca, Pardo, Pardo Montenegro, Paredes, Pecha, Peralta, Peraza, Pérez, Picaza, Pimentel, Pinazo, Pintado, Piquer, Pita, Plandolit, Planell, Ponce, Ponce de León, Porres, Portocarrero, Portocarrero de Guzmán, Prendes, Presno, Puerta, Pujadas. End of DME, Letter P.

Q Volume 1: Nothing; Volume 2: Quirós; Volume 3: Nothing; Volume 4: Quero, Quesada, Quevedo, Queipo; Volume 5: Queipo or Queypo, Quesada, Quijada, Quiñones, Quirós; Volume 6: Nothing; Volume 7: Nothing; Volume 8: Quiñones. A combined index that includes some surnames not found above, therefore indicating they are of a subnature within the text, is found at the end of Volume 7 as follows: Queipo or Queypo, Quero, Quesada, Quevedo, Quijada, Quiñones, Quirós. End of DME, Letter Q.

R Volume 1: Nothing; Volume 2: Ramírez, Ramiro, Remírez; Volume 3: Rebolledo, Recalde, Redin, Robres, Román; Volume 4: Rada, Ramírez de Arellano, Rico, Rodríguez de Farisco, Rohan, Rojas, Romero, Romeu, Ron,

Roquelaure, Ros de Ursino, Rua, Rubín de Bracamonte, Ruiz de Corella; Volume 5: Rellón, Reinoso, Ribera, Ribera Aguilar, Ribera Alarcón, Rojas or Roxas, Romay, Ruiz de Vergara; Volume 6: Rivas; Volume 7: Nothing; Volume 8: Rengifo, Ribera, Ribera Aguilar, Rodríguez, Rojas or Rosas, Romagosa. A combined index that includes some surnames not found above, therefore indicating they are of a subnature within the text, is found at the end of Volume 7 as follows: Rada, Ramírez, Ramírez de Arellano, Ramiro, Rebolledo, Recalde, Redín, Reinoso, Rellón, Remírez, Rengifo, Ribera, Ribera Aguilar, Ribera Alarcón, Rico, Rivas, Robres, Rodríguez, Rodríguez de Farico, Rohan, Rojas, Rojas or Rosas, Romagosa, Román, Romay, Romero, Romeu, Ron, Roquelaure, Ros de Ursino, Rua, Rubín de Brancamonte, Ruiz de Corella, Ruiz de Vergara. End of DME, Letter R.

S Volume 1: Nothing; Volume 2: Saavedra; Volume 3: Sarasa, Sousa; Volume 4: Saavedra, Sáenz, Sánchez de Tobar, Sánchez de Velasco, Sandoval, Sanjurjo, Santirso, Sanz, Scala, Scals, Segovia, Silva, Solís, Soria, Sotomayor, Suárez de Góngora; Volume 5: Saavedra, Salamanca, Saldaña, Salcedo, Salvadores, Sánchez de Baraona, Sandoval Rojas, Santiesteban, Sanfrechoso, Sarmiento, Sartorio, Silva y Ribera, Solier, Soria, Sotomayor, Suárez; Volume 6: Saavedra, Saurin, Seelyn; Volume 7: Nothing; Volume 8: Salazar, Salcedo, Sánchez, Sánchez Ossorio, Sepúlveda, Silva, Sotolongo. A combined index that includes some surnames not found above, therefore indicating they are of a subnature within the text, is found at the end of Volume 7 as follows: Saavedra, Sáenz, Salamanca, Salazar, Salcedo, Saldaña, Salvadores, Sánchez, Sánchez de Baraona, Sánchez Ossorio, Sánchez de Tovar, Sánchez de Velasco, Sandoval, Sandoval Rojas, Sanjurjo, Santirso, Sanz, Sanfrechoso, Santistevan, Sarasa, Sarmiento, Sartorio, Saurin, Scala, Scals, Seelyn, Segovia, Sepúlveda, Silva, Silva y Rivera, Solier, Solís, Soria, Sotolongo, Sotomayor, Sousa, Suárez, Suárez de Góngora. End of DME, Letter S.

T Volume 1: Nothing; Volume 2: Trelles; Volume 3: Thuirney, Tolosa, Tovar; Volume 4: Tamayo, Tamariz, Temez, Tenrero, Toledo, Torquemada, Torres, Tous or Thous, Trejo, Trell; Volume 5: Tamayo, Tasis, Temez, Tenorio, Teruel, Tineo, Toledo, Torre, Traba, Trelles, Trelles Agliata; Volume 6: Terol, Torres de Navarra; Volume 7: Taverner, Tellez Girón; Volume 8: Talón, Tamayo, Toledo, Toledo or Alvarez de Toledo, Torreblanca. A combined index that includes some surnames not found above, therefore indicating they are of a subnature within the text, is found at the end of Volume 7 as follows: Talón, Tamayo, Tamariz, Tasis, Taverner, Tellez Girón, Temez, Tenorio, Tenrero, Terol, Teruel, Thuirney, Tineo, Toledo, Toledo or Alvarez de Toledo, Tolosa, Torquemada, Toro, Torre, Torreblanca, Torres, Torres de

Navarra, Tovar, Tous or Thous, Traba, Trejo, Trell, Trelles, Trelles Agliata. End of DME, Letter T.

U Volume 1: Nothing; Volume 2: Nothing; Volume 3: Ulloa; Volume 4: Uclés, Ustariz; Volume 5: Nothing; Volume 6: Nothing; Volume 7: Nothing; Volume 8: Nothing. End of DME, Letter U.

V Volume 1: Nothing; Volume 2: Vaca, Valloguera, Valluguera, Velez de Guevara; Volume 3: Valcárcel, Vargas, Vega, Velasco, Villacis, Villela, Vivero; Volume 4: Valdecañas, Valderrama, Valdés, Valledor, Vargas, Vázquez, Velasco, Venegas, Venegas de la Cueva, Vera, Veraza, Verdugo, Vereterra, Vergara, Villamayor, Villamil, Villacis, Villademoros, Villandrando; Volume 5: Valdés, Valdés de Llano, Valdivia, Vargas, Vega de Cisneros, Velasco, Velascori, Velázquez, Venegas, Verástegui, Villaín, Villamayor, Villarragut, Villareal, Villela; Volume 6: Velasco; Volume 7: Villamil, Villanueva; Volume 8: Valdivia, Valenzuela, Vázquez, Venegas. A combined index that includes some surnames not found above, therefore indicating they are of a subnature within the text, is found at the end of Volume 7 as follows: Vaca, Valcárcel, Valdecañas, Valderrama, Valdés, Valdés de Llano, Valdivia, Valenzuela, Valledor, Valloguera, Valluguera, Vargas, Vázquez, Vega, Vega de Cisneros, Velasco, Velascori, Velázquez, Velez de Guevara, Venegas, Venegas de la Cueva, Vera, Verástegui, Veraza, Verdugo, Vereterra, Vergara, Villacis, Villademoros, Villain, Villamayor, Villamil, Villandrando, Villanueva, Villarragut, Villareal, Villela, Vivero. There is also a non-Spanish surname: Wading in Volume 3, p. 382. End of DME, Letter V.

Y Volume 1: Nothing; Volume 2: Yáñez; Volume 3: Yturbe; Volume 4: Nothing; Volume 5: Nothing; Volume 6: Nothing; Volume 7: Yáñez; Volume 8: Nothing. End of DME, Letter Y.

Z Volume 1: Nothing; Volume 2: Zapata; Volume 3: Zárate, Zúñiga; Volume 4: Zuleta, Zuloeta, Zulueta, Zúñiga; Volume 5: Zapata, Zayas, Zorrilla, Zúñiga; Volume 6: Zendrera; Volume 7: Zúñiga; Volume 8: Zuricaray. A combined index that includes some surnames not found above, therefore indicating they are of a subnature within the text, is found at the end of Volume 7 as follows: Zapata, Zárate, Zayas, Zendrera, Zorrilla, Zuleta, Zuloeta, Zulueta, Zúñiga, Zuricaray. End of DME, Letter Z. End of DME.

BIBLIOGRAPHY

Ashley, Leonard R.N. *What's in a Name? Everything You Wanted to Know.* Baltimore: Genealogical Publishing Co., 1989.

Fernández-Pradel, Pedro Xavier. *Linajes Vascos y Montañeses en Chile.* Santiago, Chile: Talleres Gráficos "San Rafael," 1930.

Gonzalbo Aizpuru, Pilar. *Familias Novohispanas, Siglos XVI al XIX.* Mexico City: Centro de Estudios Históricos, El Colegio de México, 1991.

Gorden, Raymond L. *Spanish Personal Names as Barriers to Communication between Latin Americans and North Americans.* Yellow Springs, Oh.: Antioch College, 1968.

Gosnell, Charles F. *Spanish Personal Names: Principles Governing Their Formation and Use Which May Be Presented as a Help for Catalogers and Bibliographers.* New York: H. W. Wilson Co., 1938; Detroit: Blaine Ethridge Books, 1971.

Hook, Julius Nicholas. *Family Names: How Our Surnames Came to America, the Origins, Meanings, Mutations, and History of more than 2,800 American Names.* New York: Macmillan Publishing Co., 1982.

Jones, George F. *German-American Names.* 2nd ed. Baltimore: Genealogical Publishing Co., 1995.

Maduell, Charles R., Jr. *The Romance of Spanish Surnames.* New Orleans, Louisiana, priv. pub., 1967.

Platt, Lyman D. *Genealogical Historical Guide to Latin America.* Detroit: Gale Research Company, 1978.

Ragucci, Rodolfo M. *El Habla de mi Tierra.* 24th ed. Buenos Aires, Argentina: Instituto Salesiano de Artes Gráficas, 1960.

Shoumatoff, Alex. *Mountain of Names, a History of the Human Family.* New York: Simon and Schuster, Inc., 1985; New York: Vintage Books, 1990.